Annotated Instructor's Edition

Writing Paragraphs and Essays
Integrating Reading, Writing, and Grammar Skills

Fifth Edition

Joy Wingersky
Glendale Community College

Jan Boerner
Emerita, Glendale Community College

Diana Holguin-Balogh
Front Range Community College

THOMSON
WADSWORTH

Australia • Canada • Mexico • Singapore • Spain • United Kingdom • United States

THOMSON

WADSWORTH

Annotated Instructor's Edition
Writing Paragraphs and Essays:
Integrating Reading, Writing, and Grammar Skills, Fifth Edition
Joy Wingersky, Jan Boerner, Diana Holguin-Balogh

Publisher: Michael Rosenberg
Acquisitions Editor: Stephen Dalphin
Development Editor: Cathy Richard Dodson
Technology Project Manager: Joe Gallagher
Marketing Manager: Mary Jo Southern
Editorial/Marketing Assistant: Dawn Giovanniello
Advertising Project Manager: Brian Chaffee
Senior Project Manager, Editorial Production: Samantha Ross

Senior Print Buyer: Mary Beth Hennebury
Permissions Editor: Chelsea Junget
Compositor/Production Service: Lachina Publishing Services
Cover Designer: Diana Coe
Cover Art: © Matheisl/Getty Images
Cover Printer: Coral Graphic Services
Printer: Quebecor World-Taunton

Printed in the United States of America
1 2 3 4 5 6 7   09 08 07 06 05

For more information about our products, contact us at:
Thomson Learning Academic Resource Center
1-800-423-0563
For permission to use material from this text or product, submit a request online at
http://www.thomsonrights.com.
Any additional questions about permissions can be submitted by email to **thomsonrights@thomson.com**.

Library of Congress Control Number: 2004116843

Student Edition: ISBN 1-4130-1038-5

Annotated Instructor's Edition and Instructor's Manual:
ISBN 1-4130-1039-3

Thomson Higher Education
25 Thomson Place
Boston, MA 02210-1202
USA

Asia (including India)
Thomson Learning
5 Shenton Way
#01-01 UIC Building
Singapore 068808

Australia/New Zealand
Thomson Learning Australia
102 Dodds Street
Southbank, Victoria 3006
Australia

Canada
Thomson Nelson
1120 Birchmount Road
Toronto, Ontario M1K 5G4
Canada

UK/Europe/Middle East/Africa
Thomson Learning
High Holborn House
50–51 Bedford Road
London WC1R 4LR
United Kingdom

Latin America
Thomson Learning
Seneca, 53
Colonia Polanco
11560 Mexico
D.F. Mexico

Spain (including Portugal)
Thomson Paraninfo
Calle Magallanes, 25
28015 Madrid, Spain

Contents

Contents

Unit 3: Organizing Ideas and Writing Them Clearly   151

Part 2   Something to Think About, Something to Write About   388

Part 3   Essays for Discussion and Analysis   394

Part 4   Mechanics for Effective Writing: Capitalization   409

List of Readings Organized by Writing Skill

Coherence

Patterns of Development

Preface

The Integrated Approach

In this fifth edition of *Writing Paragraphs and Essays,* we continue to integrate writing instruction, readings, and grammar skills to teach students to write well. To ensure that your students develop as writers and thinkers, you will find these elements integrated throughout:

- **Writing Instruction and Writing Assignments**   Extensive writing instruction combined with many suggested assignments, some of which are based on the readings, others on Internet activities, engage student interest and help students immediately apply what they have learned.

- **Readings**   Both student and professional examples help students generate ideas and serve as strong models for their writing.

- **Grammar Skills**   Grammar skills that students need to write effective paragraphs and essays are integrated with the writing instruction, providing an opportunity for students to apply these skills in the context of their own writing.

- **Writings by Professionals**   Writings by professionals, followed by related quotations, help students think through issues before writing about them.

Integrating these processes accomplishes these key goals:

1. Gets students thinking and writing immediately

2. Engages students in the writing process, building their confidence in simple yet challenging steps

3. Enables students to succeed as they move toward more complex writing assignments.

Our approach also creates these advantages:

Simple, Challenging, and Comprehensive

We have written a simple, challenging, and comprehensive text that students can understand and assimilate with the guidance of their instructors. The text is thorough because it is important to bridge the gap for developmental students between the material covered in a lower-level text and the material covered in a freshman-level composition book. Thus, we present all of the skills necessary for mastering both paragraphs and short essays, complete with effective introductions, support paragraphs, and strong conclusions. We help students organize their ideas by stressing purpose in writing. We then show students how they can apply these skills to more advanced essays.

Encouraging and Motivating

We use explanations that encourage and motivate.

Accessible to a Diverse Student Body

We have kept the diction simple so that students coming from diverse backgrounds can understand the concepts presented in the text. We have also included job-related topics in the text and in the writing assignments so that the material will appeal to a variety of student populations.

Extensively Class-Tested

The text has been extensively class-tested and revised to facilitate instruction as much as possible.

Easy to Navigate

The textbook is easy for instructors and students to use:

- Icons are used to identify writing assignments, collaborative activities, quotations, Internet activities, and cumulative unit exercises.
- Grammar sections are marked with vertically colored page edges for easy identification.
- A final checklist is located at the end of each unit.

Major Changes in the Fifth Edition

- Added a section on ESL: Gaining Confidence in Using English (Appendix E)
- Added job-related professional readings
- Updated and revised Internet activities
- Added a section in Unit 2 that includes types of organization based on purpose:

    (1) how something is true (illustration with examples)

    (2) how two things are alike or different; how something has changed (compare/contrast)

    (3) why someone should do something (persuasion)

    (4) what happened (narrative)

    (5) what happened afterward (the effects or results of an event)

    (6) why something happened (cause/s)

    (7) what something means (definition)

    (8) how things can be sorted into groups (classification)

    (9) how to do something (process/give directions)

    (10) how something is done (process/describe the procedure)

- Updated and strengthened section on documentation by adding MLA and APA information
- Updated and changed thirty percent of the exercises and examples

Organization and Key Content

The text includes an introduction to writing and seven integrated units. Each of the units is clearly organized into separate numbered parts to help students find the material they need.

Introduction

This section introduces students to what it means to be a good writer, the writing process, and a writer's use of computers and the Internet.

Units

Each unit is broken into five key content sections. For example, Unit 1, "Writing Sentences and Paragraphs," is broken into (Part 1) Writing Skills: Sentences and Paragraphs, (Part 2) Something to Think About, Something to Write About, (Part 3) Paragraphs for Discussion and Analysis, (Part 4) Grammar for Effective Writing: Basic Sentence Skills, and (Part 5) Putting It All Together. These recurring subsections integrate the content of each unit by modeling the thinking processes that students must practice to accomplish particular tasks.

(Part 1)   Writing Skills This is the key writing instruction section. The first part of every unit focuses on one step of the writing process. The objectives identify the skills to be covered. After these skills are explained and modeled, the students apply them by working through exercises that reflect the kind of thinking that student writers have to do in composing, revising, and editing. They are also given collaborative exercises that encourage interactive learning.

(Part 2)   Something to Think About, Something to Write About This section includes a high-interest reading selection by a professional. The readings in this section cover a range of topics and are used to generate ideas that students can use for their writing assignments. Each reading is followed by vocabulary exercises and writing assignments based on the reading. Also included in this section is a list of quotations linked to each reading to give students additional help in generating ideas for writing. This is followed by a writing assignment and a collaborative group activity.

(Part 3)   Paragraphs for Discussion and Analysis This section includes many shorter readings by students and professionals for discussion and analysis. These readings illustrate the concepts taught in each unit. Because the authors of these selections have a range of writing experience and come from diverse backgrounds, their writing appeals to students of different ages, gender, and ethnic backgrounds. Each reading is followed by exercises that ask the students to analyze these readings for content, form, and vocabulary.

(Part 4)   Grammar for Effective Writing This section is devoted to grammar and mechanics instruction. Here students learn and practice grammatical concepts aimed at improving writing skills. Because students have already started writing by the time they get to this section, they have the chance to address their surface-level errors in context, thus reinforcing how essential grammar and mechanics are in written communication.

(Part 5)   Putting It All Together This section is dedicated to bringing together practical application of the material covered in each unit. It begins with a cumulative unit exercise that draws from the writing and grammar instruction. This section also includes collaborative writing activities, a writing assignment, group and individual work, a final checklist, and Internet activities.

Exercises

Each unit ends with a series of exercises that require students to think through and master the concepts taught in that unit. These exercises include the following:

- **Cumulative Unit Exercises** A cumulative exercise at the end of each unit helps students reinforce what they have just learned as well as what they have learned in previous units. As students progress through the text, they complete each unit by synthesizing writing skills and grammar concepts by revising paragraphs and essays. These exercises are suitable as individual, group, or class activities.

- **Collaborative Writing Projects**   Collaborative activities are a substantial part of each unit and often lead to writing assignments. Many of the collaborative activities include small-group discussion in the prewriting stages. They prepare students to work individually on their paragraphs or essays and then to return to groups for peer review. The activities are more detailed in the earlier units, but in later units allow students to work together without such detailed directions.

- **Internet Activities**   Internet activities have been updated. These resources are focused on helping students find useful, reliable information. Students are also encouraged to evaluate Internet sources as part of the thinking process. These activities are integrated into the text concepts to give students additional writing resources and exercises. The Internet activities will lead students to the links that correlate with the activities in each unit. Students are given the opportunity to obtain additional information as they move through their writing assignments.

Major Features of the Text

Integrated Text

Students use only one textbook, yet they still have access to the writing, reading, and grammar concepts normally found in a combination of texts. Instructors have access to a full range of teaching materials and may choose to use those they consider most important for their own course needs.

The logical progression of the text facilitates an integrated approach to instruction. Starting with simple writing, reading, and grammar, the text progresses to more sophisticated methods of writing.

Step-by-Step Approach to Writing Skills

Information on the writing process is presented in a clear step-by-step approach that builds student confidence as students see how the individual writing steps fit together to create a coherent paragraph or essay. This text reduces instructor and student frustration by setting up realistic goals for developing writers.

The text focuses on the development of the paragraph and short essay by helping students generate and support one main idea. Students concentrate on topic sentences with support and on thesis sentences with support so that they can transfer these skills to more sophisticated strategies, either in this course or in college-level composition courses.

Grammar and Mechanics Exercises Aimed at Improving Writing

The exercises in the grammar and mechanics section of each unit (Grammar for Effective Writing) go beyond drill and practice to include thinking exercises such as sentence combining and paragraph editing. Many exercises for in-class and out-of-class work are provided. Half of the answers are provided in "Answers to Odd-Numbered Items in Exercises," located after the appendixes, and all of the answers are in the Annotated Instructor's Edition. As a result, teachers can have the students check their own exercises, or they can have the students do the exercises as homework to be graded by the instructor.

Unit on Alternate Patterns of Development

This unit is self-contained, including essays illustrating how one topic can be developed into many different types of essays by using different patterns. The text begins with illustration, a strategy with which students are familiar, and progresses through comparison/contrast, classification, definition, cause/effect analysis, process analysis, and argumentation.

Content Prepares Students for Proficiency Testing

Writing Paragraphs and Essays provides instruction that will prepare students to perform well on proficiency tests. For example, it covers basic grammar and usage: subject-verb agreement; consistent verb tense; fragments, run-on sentences, and comma splices; consistent point of view; a thorough review of punctuation; and a review of capitalization.

The text encourages development of revision skills needed by students to pass proficiency tests. Appendix A includes commonly confused words, such as "their," "there," and "they're." Appendix D includes a section on spelling.

Writing Paragraphs and Essays provides practice in the skills students need in varied writing situations, including drafting, revising, and editing both paragraphs and essays. Because variety in sentence structure is one of the major criteria used to evaluate student essays, *Writing Paragraphs and Essays* also includes instruction in sentence combining to achieve sentence variety. Furthermore, the book includes a section on using purpose to help students organize their paragraphs. It also includes an entire unit on alternate patterns of development that provides the skills students need when they are asked to write an essay using a specific method of organization.

Appendixes

Appendix A: Confusing Words

Appendix B: Keeping a Journal

Appendix C: Irregular Verbs

Appendix D: Spelling

Appendix E: ESL: Gaining Confidence in Using English

Appendix F: Using Documented Support

Answers to Odd-Numbered Items in Exercises

Teaching Aids

Print Supplements

- **Annotated Instructor's Edition** (1-4130-1039-3). This edition includes answers to all of the exercises, teaching tips, and a complete Instructor's Manual.

- **Instructor's Manual** (Included in the Annotated Instructor's Edition). The Instructor's Manual includes our philosophy about teaching, unit notes, writing assignments, a sample syllabus, suggestions for a final exam essay, sample journal entry and journal log, and transparency masters.

- **Test Bank** (1-4130-1040-7). Sentence and paragraph editing, multiple-choice, and fill-in-the-blank questions test the skills and concepts taught in the book. Four versions of ten tests and answers are included.

Electronic Supplements

- **Website** http://developmentalenglish.wadsworth.com/wingersky   This free online resource offers resources for the student, including chapter objectives from the book, links to online writing centers and research resources, and extra quizzes to practice grammar.

- **Writer's Resources CD-ROM, Version 2.0** (0-8384-0674-2) is an interactive multimedia program that teaches all aspects of grammar and writing.

  - **A Complete Writing Course:** The four sections on the CD-ROM cover all the skills necessary for students to become effective writers—from grammar and mechanics to the steps of the writing process.

  - **Varied Types of Interactive Exercises:** Over 3,500 exercises, activities, and tests provide ample opportunity for students to practice the concepts presented. The CD-ROM includes a broad range of auto-graded exercises with explanatory feedback as well as guided writing activities.

  - **Audio and Animation:** Audio clips throughout reinforce and expand upon concepts presented. Animation clips demonstrate certain procedures, such as how to carry out various steps in the writing process or how to complete activities.

  - **Course Management:** A course management tie-in with the CD-ROM now enables instructors to grade students on their performance.

  - **More Types of Exercises:** Twelve new types of exercises have been added, including proofreading practice, capitalization, identifying parts of a paragraph, and writing assignments.

  - **Glossary and Searchable Index:** A glossary and a searchable index enhance the CD-ROM as a reference tool, improving its ease of use.

Writer's Resources CD-ROM, Version 2.0, may be bundled with *Writing Paragraphs and Essays*. Please contact your local Thomson representative for bundling options and pricing.

Please do not hesitate to email us with your comments about the book.

joy.wingersky@gcmail.maricopa.edu
dianahb@frontrange.edu
jkayb@cox.net

Acknowledgments

We wish to thank our colleagues at Glendale Community College and Front Range Community College for their suggestions, which arose out of several semesters of in-class testing. Other people we specifically wish to thank include Susan Bailor, Conrad Bayley, Tonya Bassett, Dave Grant, Patrick Haas, Phil Moloso, Marti Moraga, and Nancy Seifer, all of whom gave us continuing support.

We sincerely thank Linda Coble, Shyrl Emhoff, Patrick Haas, Bob Hartman, Susan Husemoller-Bailor, Betty Hufford, Eva Montoya, Jim Reed, and Dean Terasaki, the professionals whose thought-provoking and varied articles strengthened our text. We also thank Lorena Acosta, Kimberly Adair, Kathy Bagby, Eric Beach, Steve Bostrom, Nancy Chandler, Jeff Collins, Tim Darcy, Young Mi Dauer, Samuel David, Bill Devere, Terry M. Donaldson, Andrea Gonzalez, Muriel Gray, Mauro Guzman, Alberto Montaño Hernandez, Phyllis Hilding, Gudrun Waltraud Lorke, Charles Marchbanks, Lonnie B. Noah III, Jerry Palmer, Joan Papke, Jenefer Radas, Marlene Reed, Renee Robbe, Jan-Georg Roesch, Augustin Rojas, Peggy Scarborough, John Schulz, Cynthia Vinzant, and Kristi Von Aspen, our students whose fine models provide enrichment for *Writing Paragraphs and Essays*. We also thank Lucy Tribble McDonald, who contributed Internet Activities, and Marla DeSoto, for help with the revised Internet Activities.

We thank the outstanding Thomson Wadsworth team whose positive attitude and efficiency made completing the fifth edition of this textbook pleasant as they worked with us to make the process flow smoothly. We especially appreciate Steve Dalphin, Senior Acquisitions Editor, English, whose knowledge, experience, and leadership could always be trusted. His commitment to our book was encouraging and motivating, especially providing the opportunity to have Joe Gallagher, Technology Project Manager, develop the electronic test bank for the textbook. We also thank Samantha Ross, Senior Production Project Manager, who was upbeat, optimistic, and, best of all, always accessible. Equally helpful was Cathy Richard Dodson, who consistently tried to make it easier for us to solve problems as they came up. Chelsea Junget, Associate Permissions Editor, went out of her way to complete the permissions requirements, and we thank her for that. We thank Sheila McGill, Project Manager, who, once again, with the help of Diane Kimmel, Felicia Krawczynski, Carol Kurila, and Nancy Tenney, smoothly handled the production process.

We also thank the reviewers, all of whom suggested valuable revisions of our text:

Fifth Edition Reviewers:
Phyllis Gowdy, *Tidewater Community College*
Nadine Keene, *Indiana University*
Dennis Keen, *Spokane Community College*
Melissa Linkous, *National College of Business and Technology*
Luana Hoke Rarey, *Community College of Baltimore, County Essex Campus*

Fourth Edition Reviewers:
Jonathan Alexander, *Burlington County College*
Karen Craig, *Petit Jean College*
Sheryl Scholer, *Rochester Community and Technical College*
Karla Farmer Stouse, *Indiana University, Kokomo*
Dianne Waldron, *South Georgia College*
Paige Wilson, *Pasadena City College*

Third Edition Reviewers:
Christine M. Getz, *Pikes Peak Community College*
Roberta Rubin, *Loyola Marymount University*
Linnae Clinton, *Edison Community College*
Patricia Malinowski, *Finger Lakes Community College*
Linda Whisnant, *Guilford Technical Community College*

Second Edition Reviewers:
Mary Earp, *University of Alaska, Fairbanks*
Michael Erickson, *Monroe Community College*
Joan Mathis, *Paris Junior College*
Dee Ann Ward, *Weatherford College*
Paul Wardzinski, *Western Piedmont Community College*

First Edition Reviewers:
Nancy G. Allen, *Angelo State University*
Rebecca Argall, *Memphis State University*
Michael Baehr, *El Paso Community College*
Barbara Baxter, *State Technical Institute, Memphis*
Paula Beck, *Nassau Community College*
Judith Boschult, *Phoenix College*
Jeanne Campanelli, *American River College*
Linda Daigle, *Houston Community College*
Roger Horn, *Charles County Community College*
Anne Jackets, *Everett Community College*
Laura Knight, *Mercer County Community College*
Beatrice Mendez-Egle, *University of Texas, Pan American*
Vivian Thomlinson, *Cameron University*

Most importantly of all, we wish to thank our families who were willing to discuss ideas, answer questions, and tolerate many long working hours: George, Mike, Sam, Shirley, Anne, Nick, Bianca, Reyna, and Andrea. We will always appreciate their thoughtfulness and encouragement.

Joy Wingersky
Jan Boerner
Diana Holguin-Balogh

Introduction to Writing

About Writing

Pretest covering Intro. to Writing is on page 2 of the Test Bank.

Writing is a way to gain control over your ideas and get them down on paper. There is nothing mysterious about this process, and you can learn to write effectively and feel confident about your writing if you are willing to put in time and effort.

Many people find it necessary to write at one particular place or with a certain color of ink or a special type of keyboard. Having these things may help you write, but more important than these is developing the ability to concentrate. Sometimes it will be necessary to tune out everyone and everything in order to reflect inwardly and re-create incidents you have read or heard about, experienced, or observed. With total concentration, you can "replay" these incidents and share them with your reader. For instance, if you want to remember that first day of school long ago when you were six years of age, all you have to do is close your eyes until a mental picture enters your mind. That room, that teacher, that moment of fear, happiness, or excitement can be a video playing in your mind, and from your "mind's video," you can begin to write your thoughts on paper.

Ways to Help Yourself Become a Better Writer

What experiences have you had with writing? Have you had good experiences or bad experiences? How do you feel about yourself as a writer? How important is writing to you? If your feelings and experiences about writing have been negative, the best thing you can do for yourself is to try to put those impressions behind you. You need to be willing to take a risk, to be receptive, and to be yourself.

Being Willing to Take a Risk

Taking a risk may be the most difficult task you have ever had to do. Even though writing is often a personal experience, you can improve your writing if you relax and concentrate on what you have to say, rather than worrying about what your instructor or classmates will think.

Being Receptive

Along with taking risks, try to be receptive to your instructor's suggestions for improving your writing. As your instructor works with you on your paper or as you work in peer editing groups, keep an open mind about their comments. These comments are not intended to offend you; rather, they are directed toward helping you achieve your writing goals.

Being Yourself

When you write, it is not necessary to try to impress anyone with an artificial vocabulary. On the other hand, you do want to write on a level that is appropriate for the particular purpose the writing situation requires. The goal of writing should be to communicate with the reader simply and sincerely.

Benefits of Becoming a Better Writer

Maybe you are asking yourself questions like these: "Why is becoming a better writer so important?" "How can writing help me?" "Will improving my writing skills bring me money, self-worth, opportunities, or friends?" If you spend time on this valuable skill, your writing can improve. Writing well brings many rewards your way.

You can become more successful in school whether you write essays, do research papers, or take essay exams.

You can become more competent in your job.

You can help your children with their schoolwork.

You can bring satisfaction to yourself in personal journal writing or letters to friends.

You can defend yourself if you have been treated unjustly and have no recourse other than a letter to someone who has the power to correct the situation.

You can make writing a professional career.

The Writing Process

Writing is a process through which you discover, organize, and communicate your thoughts to a reader. When you speak, your tone of voice and facial expressions help you get your point across. You also have the chance to clarify miscommunications quickly. When you write, you have only words and punctuation to form your message, but you do have the opportunity to organize your thoughts and words until you are happy with the finished product. The writing process gives you a chance to compose, draft, rethink, and redraft to control the outcome of your writing.

The general steps in the writing process include prewriting, organizing ideas, drafting, revising, editing, and making a final draft. If you go through these steps when you have a writing assignment, you will make the most of your time and get your best ideas on paper. At times, you may repeat a particular step. When you become more comfortable with the writing process and become a more experienced writer, you may be able to do some steps in your mind, but skipping important steps is not advisable when you are learning the writing process.

Each step has different activities that will help you get your ideas down on paper in an organized fashion. **Prewriting** is a way to generate ideas, narrow a topic, or find a direction. **Organizing** involves sorting ideas in a logical manner to prepare to write a draft. **Drafting** is the part of the writing process in which you compose sentences in paragraph form to produce the first copy of your essay. **Revising**, one of the most important steps in writing a paper, involves smoothing out your writing, adding more detail, and making other changes that will help you say what you want to say in the best way. Checking for mechanical problems and correcting them is **editing**. **Making a final draft** and deciding it's ready for your intended audience is a step that takes patience and judgment. Being patient gives you a chance to take an honest look at your paper and decide whether the essay is in its best form. If not, more revision needs to take place.

Each of the steps of the writing process will be illustrated, beginning with prewriting.

Prewriting

The prewriting chart lists six useful activities to help you begin a writing project. Because taking the first step can seem difficult at times, all the prewriting activities are designed to help you get started. You may find some more useful than others. Though each offers a different approach, the objectives are the same for each activity. You may want to try all six of them to find out which ones work best for you.

Talking

One simple way to relieve anxiety and start the writing process is to talk about a subject with fellow students, instructors, family members, and other knowledgeable people who can provide the inspiration you need to begin writing. Talking helps you express ideas that can later be put onto paper. You may want to begin jotting down ideas that occur to you as you talk to others.

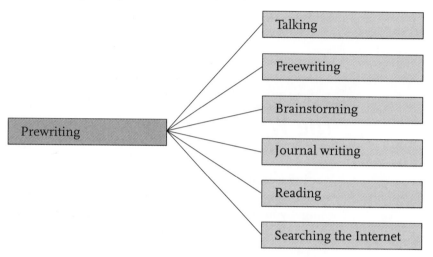

Talking to Find a Topic

The following conversation could very well be an actual dialogue between two students who are using talking to begin an assignment.

"What are you writing about?"

"I'm not sure. The teacher wants a pet peeve or a pleasure. I'm not sure what a pet peeve is, so I guess I'll do pleasure."

"A pet peeve is something that constantly irritates you, like not being able to do something you would like to do."

"If that's what it is, I have lots of those, like never having any free time."

"Well, why don't you dump your girlfriend, then?"

"It's more than just my girlfriend. I have to rush to work right after class. And then I work so many hours that I don't have much time to do my homework or see my girlfriend."

"Well, why don't you write about that problem—not having enough time to get everything done?"

"Maybe I will. That's it! That's what I'm going to write about—too many things to do and not enough time to get them done. At least this gives me a start on something to write about."

Keep in mind that it is not advisable to do only talking as a prewriting activity. Talking, unlike freewriting or brainstorming, is not on paper, and ideas can be lost unless you take notes as you go along. However, talking is a good starting point, and this student decided that he could write about the impact of his heavy workload on college and his personal life. Now that a subject for his writing assignment has begun to take shape, he could talk to someone else to gather even more ideas.

Talking with Direction: The Informal Interview

The student wanted to talk to someone who had graduated from college and who, he thought, had had a similar experience. After deciding to interview one of his instructors, he wrote out questions he felt would give him some ideas for his paper. Here are some of the questions he prepared. Other questions that came to mind during the interview are also included.

"You have graduated from college. Did you work while you were going to college?"

1. "No, I didn't have to work."

"Did you have plenty of time to get your homework done?"

2. "Yes, I did. I rode the bus, so I was able to get my homework done on the bus."

"Did you have to ride the bus because you didn't have a car?"

3. "You're right. I had to do without some things, and a car was one of those luxuries."

"Even though you had to do without things, why do you think it's better not to work?"

4. "I wouldn't have gotten through in four years. My sister did, though. She worked for two years before she started college so she could have enough money to get through college."

"Did she make more money after she graduated than she did before she went to college?"

5. "Oh yes, and she loved her job after she graduated."

"Would you do it differently?"

6. "No, because I wanted to make good grades. I appreciated the time I had to do my schoolwork."

This informal interview gave the student a different point of view, one that he had not considered before. After the informal interview, the student analyzed the information to see what could be used for his paper. Here is his analysis of the interview.

Ideas Gathered from Talking	Possible Use of Ideas
1. "No, I didn't have to work."	gives a new perspective of not working while going to school
2. "Yes, I did. I rode the bus, so I was able to get my homework done on the bus."	provides an advantage for new perspective of not working
3. "You're right. I had to do without some things, and a car was one of those luxuries."	offers support for a new slant

4. "I wouldn't have gotten through in four years. My sister did, though. She worked for two years before she started college so she could have enough money to get through college."

shows a different view; could be another paragraph

5. "Oh yes, and she loved her job after she graduated."

offers additional support for the new idea

6. "No, because I wanted to make good grades. I appreciated the time I had to do my schoolwork."

shows a good reason for not working

Once you have enough information after interviewing one or more people, you might go on to the next step: organizing. If you do not have enough information to write a paper, you will need to interview more people or go on to freewriting, brainstorming, journal writing, reading, or searching the Internet to generate information that can be used for writing. Next, examine freewriting.

Freewriting

Like other prewriting strategies, freewriting is intended to help you generate ideas. **Freewriting** is writing anything that comes to mind about your topic. It is writing without stopping to correct spelling or other mechanical errors. If you can't think of anything to write, just start with anything on your mind at that moment, even if it's just repeating the assignment. One idea usually leads to another, and you may soon find your page filled with many different ideas. You are not expected to stay with any one idea; as a matter of fact, freewriting should bring out many different thoughts. This prewriting technique can be used when you are trying to find something to write about or are trying to get more ideas about a chosen topic.

Freewriting involves writing ideas in sentence form. Freewriting has three basic steps:

1. freewriting for a topic and direction
2. deciding on a topic
3. freewriting with direction

Examine these steps more closely.

Freewriting for a Topic and Direction

Look at the following example of freewriting by a student who did not have a topic for a paper and who did not use talking as a prewriting aid. His freewriting was done without regard to correct mechanics and spelling.

> Well, I have to write for ten minutes on anything that I can think about. I'm not sure what I am interested in. I wish the other people in this room weren't writing so much. I wonder what they are writing about. I need to get my work done so I can get to work. I didn't get all of my work finished last night. I left the place in a mess. I hope my boss didn't notice. He is pretty nice most of the time. (1) <u>Sometimes that place gets to me.</u> I don't have enough time to get my school work done. Maybe Dad was right. (2) <u>I should try to cut down on my work hours so I can spend more time on school.</u> (3) <u>At this rate I won't ever get through.</u> Rob is almost ready to graduate and I only have one year behind me. If I could just take more courses I could get through and get the job I really want. But then I

wouldn't have money to take my girlfriend out. (4) <u>She is a pretty nice girl.</u> Maybe she would understand if I quit my job. If she broke up with me over that I guess she wouldn't be a very good girlfriend anyhow. (5) <u>There are lots of things we could do that don't cost a lot of money.</u> There is always something going on at school. (6) <u>Her brother is a lot of fun.</u> We enjoy playing racquetball with them. I bet we could find lots of things to do. (7) <u>I could get through school faster.</u> Let's see, what should I write about. I wonder if anyone will think that what I wrote is dumb. I hope we don't have to read this in class. I guess if I have to I will. Cheee, that guy next to me has a whole page filled up. I wonder if he is going to stop pretty soon. Oh well, I guess I will just have to keep writing.

Much of the content in this freewriting probably will not be used, but it has served the purpose of warming up. After you finish freewriting, go back and see if there is anything that looks interesting enough to write about. With close reading, you may find ideas that can be turned into possible topics for further development. Here is one way to analyze this freewriting to find a topic and direction.

Freewriting Idea	Possible Topic and Direction
1. "Sometimes that place gets to me."	negative aspects of my job
2. "I should try to cut down on my work hours. . . ."	educational benefits of cutting back on work hours
3. "At this rate I won't ever get through."	obstacles I face in finishing college
4. "She is a pretty nice girl."	neat traits of my girlfriend
5. "There are lots of things we could do that don't cost a lot of money."	enjoyable, low-cost recreational activities my girlfriend and I could do
6. "Her brother is a lot of fun."	her brother's personality
7. "I could get through school faster."	benefits of completing college as soon as possible

Deciding on a Topic

After you have finished freewriting, sort through your ideas. Decide which idea seems the most interesting, which one you know the most about, and which one you could write about most easily. The idea you choose may also suggest the direction for you to take.

Freewriting with Direction

After you have decided on the topic and direction, you need to freewrite again, this time with direction. This writing is generally easier because it concentrates on one topic. Usually most of the information that comes out in this freewriting is usable because a focus has been established, and this information can become support for a main idea. In the example, the student has chosen to freewrite with direction on "What would happen if I cut down on my work hours?" His next step was to do the freewriting with direction on that idea. Here is what he wrote:

What would happen if I cut down on my work hours? I would have (1) more time to go see my girlfriend, but I would have to do without money. That means I (2) would have to give up some things that are important to me like my car. That would be rough. I wonder if my girl would find a new boyfriend. If she did, I guess she wouldn't care about our future. I (3) could study in the afternoons without having to worry about getting to work on time. (4) At night I wouldn't be too tired to go out, but then I wouldn't have any money to go out. Of course, (5) if I graduated from college, I could get a good job that I like and that pays well. (6) Dad would like that. He would be unhappy now because he is tired of supporting me. (7) My boss is going to be unhappy because he is counting on me to work forty hours a week and he is going to have to hire another employee. Of course he only pays me $5.50 an hour. He might even fire me, but I have to decide what is most important for me. If I just cut down on my work hours, Dad would be happy because I was still making some money and I would be happy because I could take more courses.

Once you have completed your freewriting with direction, reread it and find any information that can be used in writing your paper. Here is how the student analyzed this freewriting:

Results of Cutting Work Hours	Interpretation of Results
1. "More time to see my girlfriend . . ."	helps my social life
2. "Would have to give up some things . . ."	may mean a sacrifice
3. "Could study in the afternoons . . ."	allows time to study
4. "At night I wouldn't be too tired to go out. . . ."	increases energy but not money
5. "If I graduated from college . . ."	could get better job later
6. "Dad would like that."	pleases Dad
7. "My boss is going to be unhappy. . . ."	not too important

This list shows many writing options for the student writer. The student may choose to write on the advantages of cutting work hours, the disadvantages of cutting work hours, or just the results of cutting work hours.

If you feel you have enough information to write a paper, go on to the part of the writing process called organizing. If not, you might need to freewrite further or try brainstorming. If you were to write a longer paper, your next step would be to group together the ideas that would make separate paragraphs. (This is covered in detail in Unit 3, "Organizing Ideas and Writing Them Clearly.")

Brainstorming

Brainstorming is writing words or phrases that occur to you spontaneously. This free association can be done individually or in a group. Brainstorming and freewriting are similar in that they both produce ideas. If your teacher gives you a topic, you can begin by brainstorming to get some direction. If not, you will need to brainstorm to find a topic. You may find it easier to brainstorm for a topic than to freewrite. When you are brainstorming for a topic, you will probably create a list of very general words that interest you.

Brainstorming to Find a Topic

When a student who did not have a topic was asked to brainstorm to find a topic, he responded with this list:

music	school	politics
fears	cities	homes
sports	family	vacation

As this list illustrates, the topics generated can be very broad. Because of this, it is necessary to brainstorm again, this time for direction.

Brainstorming for Direction

The student decided on "school" as a topic and brainstormed again. Here is what he wrote this time:

Topic: School

1. fun—social activities
2. not enough time to get work done
3. hate English and writing
4. tired and confused
5. enjoy school when there
6. money—where to get it
7. want to spend time with friends
8. still a freshman
9. why working hours should be cut
10. finish in four years or two years

This list shows some alternative topics for writing a paragraph. These topics are still general, so you need to decide which one seems the most interesting, and then brainstorm again. When you brainstorm again on the chosen topic, a new list of more focused topics will result.

Brainstorming with Direction

The student looked at the list of topics and decided that "why working hours should be cut" would be a good topic because it was important to him. He decided to find out what all the results would be if he cut his work hours. Here is the list he produced while brainstorming on this more focused topic:

more time to read assignments

making decisions is frustrating

boss will be unhappy

more time to study

more time to get help

less spending money to have on weekends

less money to spend on my girlfriend

can spend time with friends without worrying about studying

would miss the feel of money in my pocket

hate bad grades

could take more classes and graduate from college sooner

Dad will be unhappy

At this point, if you have enough information to write a paragraph, move on to the section on organizing. If not, try talking, freewriting, or brainstorming again—or you could begin keeping a journal for ideas.

Journal Writing

Journal writing is recording your daily inner thoughts, inspirations, and emotions in a notebook. This is usually done consistently and in a relaxed atmosphere. Writing in this manner gives you an opportunity to connect with important thoughts, analyze your life environment, relieve writing anxiety, and practice spontaneous writing. Journal writing can provide ideas that you may use in later writing assignments, and it can help you find a starting place for a writing assignment.

The following excerpt is taken from two pages of a journal in which the student wrote about the frustrations he was feeling. This segment shows his frustration at working and going to school at the same time. He found this part when he was skimming through material he remembered writing about his job. (Journal entries are written for content, so they often contain spelling and grammar errors. This is acceptable.)

> I am tired. I don't think I can ever keep this up. There is so much to worry about. Sometimes I wish I didn't have to grow up. Maybe I could just quit school for a little while and get a job. I don't want to work at a hamburger dump. Pa thinks I should work as a plumber, but I'm sick of working in the ditch. Last year I could tell the time of day by the flow of the sewer. I always knew it was noon because everyone was flushing toilets and the stuff began to flow fast and furious. No way—I want to get through with school. Maybe Pa wouldn't bitch too much if I could just hurry up and get through school. One semester I took twelve hours and got through OK. *If I quit work I could take even more hours and then get a good job.* [emphasis added]

Sometimes you will want to look through your journal to find a topic and a direction; other times you will already have your topic and direction and will simply be looking for ideas already expressed about your topic.

Much of this excerpt is not appropriate for a paragraph, but the student found one sentence that would support his idea. He also realized that because he had spent so much time writing about this subject, it must be important enough to write about.

Reading

Reading magazines or newspapers can also help you get started with your writing. For instance, browsing through a magazine like *Time* or *Newsweek,* whether you are in the library, at home, or at the doctor's office, can spark an idea for a topic. More thorough reading will help you become more informed about your topic so that you can write intelligently about important issues.

Reading can also help you get ideas to support your paragraph or essay. This might be necessary if you do not have enough firsthand information about your topic. Some papers, especially those concerning political issues or social problems, require reading for factual information that can be used in your writing. Unit 7, "Composing with Effective Alternate Patterns," illustrates how additional reading can give you the information you need.

Searching the Internet

Another practical and accessible resource you can use to find written information is the Internet. The Internet is a vast network of computers linked throughout the world so that users like you can share information. Through the Internet, you can access many places, including the Library of Congress, the Museum of Modern Art in New York City, the Louvre, the U.S. Senate, the U.S. House of Representatives, the libraries at most universities, and the websites of many corporations and businesses. You can use the Internet to send email, order from catalogs, join chat rooms, or do research on any subject. If you have access to a computer and an Internet connection, you can take advantage of this wonderful opportunity. However, because of the large variety of sources on the Internet, you cannot be sure all the material you find is reliable. Enjoy using the Internet, but remember that anyone can write whatever he or she wants on the Net. You need to document and validate sources carefully before using them. You will have help in doing so when you visit the writing sites on evaluating and documenting websites.

Summary of Ways to Get Started Writing

Talking:	informal conversation about a subject or topic
Freewriting:	writing (in sentences) anything that comes to mind without stopping
Brainstorming:	listing words or phrases as they come to mind
Journal writing:	recording your own thoughts in a notebook
Reading:	browsing through materials that might be used for writing
Searching the Internet:	looking through information for ideas

Organizing

Organizing is the second major step in the writing process. After you have completed one or more of the prewriting activities, it's time to think about organizing these ideas into a rough outline that includes a main idea and supporting ideas.

Before you use the ideas from your prewriting to compose your paragraph or essay, you need to decide which details support the main idea and in what order these ideas need to be presented. As you sort these details into groups, you are organizing your information. Logic and a sense for putting together similar ideas can help you perform this step quickly and easily. This step in the writing process, which involves putting similar ideas into groups, is called **clustering.** It is one of the most important steps in the writing process and is covered again in detail in Unit 1, "Writing Sentences and Paragraphs," and in Unit 3, "Organizing Ideas and Writing Them Clearly." Here is how clustering helps you organize ideas for writing.

Clustering

Here is the list generated by the student who brainstormed his topic "school" with respect to "cutting work hours":

more time to read assignments

making decisions is frustrating

boss will be unhappy

more time to study

more time to get help

less spending money to have on weekends

less money to spend on my girlfriend

can spend time with friends without worrying about studying

would miss the feel of money in my pocket

hate bad grades

could take more classes and graduate from college sooner

Dad will be unhappy

The task now is to organize the list into meaningful clusters of related ideas, which will eventually become paragraphs. Clustering related ideas is easy if you stop and ask yourself the following questions. These questions are intended to help you see how certain material can be put together to form one paragraph.

1. What phrases are similar or seem to be about the same idea?

    Cluster 1

      more time to read assignments

      more time to study

      more time to get help

      could take more classes and graduate from college sooner

    Cluster 2

      boss will be unhappy

      less spending money to have on weekends

      less money to spend on my girlfriend

      Dad will be unhappy

      would miss the feel of money in my pocket

2. In what way is each cluster alike?

    The first grouping shows the *advantages* of cutting work hours.

    The second grouping shows the *disadvantages* of cutting work hours.

3. What ideas don't seem to fit anywhere?

    making decisions is frustrating

    hate bad grades

    can spend time with friends without worrying about studying

4. What general word or phrase could be used to represent each cluster?

    The general phrase for Cluster 1 could be "educational advantages."

    The general word for Cluster 2 could be "disadvantages."

5. Are there other general words or phrases that would group the items differently?

    Financial matters

      less spending money to have on weekends

      less money to spend on my girlfriend

      would miss the feel of money in my pocket

    Social aspects

      less spending money to have on weekends

      can spend time with friends without worrying about studying

    Personal considerations

      making decisions is frustrating

      boss will be unhappy

      hate bad grades

      Dad will be unhappy

Remember, each cluster represents one paragraph. If a cluster has only two ideas, you may want to brainstorm again for additional ideas.

Outlining

Outlining involves identifying a word or phrase that represents a group of related ideas and then arranging these words or phrases in the order in which you want to discuss them. Notice that in answering questions 4 and 5 earlier, you have already grouped related ideas and found a general word or phrase that represents all of the ideas in the cluster, so you have made a rough outline that could be followed in writing your paragraph.

The student chose the cluster on "educational advantages." Here is one outline he could make:

Educational advantages

    more time to read assignments

    more time to study

    more time to get help

    could take more classes and graduate from college sooner

    bring up my grade point average*

    more time to use the library*

The general word or phrase will be made into a topic sentence, and each idea listed under them will become a support sentence.

Drafting

After you have organized your ideas in the form of an outline, you are prepared to write a first draft. **Drafting** involves taking the information that you have generated and organized and patiently writing a paragraph or an essay in which you consciously start with the main ideas and add supporting ideas that flow smoothly. You can feel confident about starting your draft because you have laid the foundation through prewriting and organizing your information. Try to write the ideas without worrying about spelling or other mechanical errors. In the first draft, you are simply interested in communicating content or meaning to the reader.

If you are writing a paragraph, look at the general word or phrase that represents the ideas in that group. Begin your draft with a sentence that includes this general word or phrase or a variation of it. Using the clustering shown above, "educational advantages," the student wrote the following first draft of a paragraph. (Note that this and future "topic sentences" have been highlighted for you by using bold type.)

> **If I cut down at work I could have more time to spend on my education.** By having more time to spend on school I could bring up my grade point average. Plus, I could probably have more time to do my work. I could spend as much time as I needed to get my assignments done and still have time to spend with my girlfriend. I could go to class and study in the afternoons without haveing to worry about getting to work on time. At night I wouldn't be too tired to go out. Tutoring is offered free of charge at school and I would have time to get a tutor. I

---

*These are new ideas that occurred to him as he studied the group.

could take more classes and still do well in all of them. I often have to go to the library but really don't have the extra time. It takes even more time to go to work and then have to drive back to campus on Saterdays to do my research. My car is not running right and this adds to my problems. Just as I am getting the material that I need it is time for the library to close or I begin to get tired.

After you finish your first draft, put it away for a while, if possible, so that when you come back to it, you will be able to see it from a fresh point of view. This new perspective will help you revise the draft.

Revising

Revising means making changes to clarify wording and organization. The revision of a paragraph should be done several times, until you are satisfied that it is the best you can do. It is all right, even recommended, that you let other people read your paper and make suggestions for change. It is not all right, however, to have other people actually make the changes for you. Your major objective is not to produce just one excellent paper but to be able to write many excellent papers, even when you have no one to help you. Here are some possible questions to ask yourself when you are revising:

1. Does the general word or phrase (or a similar one) from the cluster appear in the first sentence?
2. In the rest of the sentences, are there words, phrases, or sentences that are not related to the main idea in the first sentence?
3. Does the paragraph make sense to you and to someone else?
4. Have you covered all ideas in the cluster?
5. Can some words be changed for clarity?
6. Are any words repeated excessively?
7. Does the last sentence give a sense of closure to the paragraph?

As you learn how to revise, it is easier to read for one or two kinds of changes at a time. Notice in the following examples that only two or three questions are asked and that only those revisions are made in the next draft.

First Revision

The first revision is based on questions 1 and 2:

1. Does the general word or phrase (or a similar one) from the cluster appear in the first sentence?
2. In the rest of the sentences, are there words, phrases, or sentences that are not related to the main idea in the first sentence?

If I cut down at work I could have more time to spend on my **education.** By haveing more time to spend on school I could bring up my grade point average. Plus, I could probably have more time to do my work. I could spend as much time as I needed to get my assignments done ~~and still have time to spend with my girlfriend~~. I could go to class and study in the afternoons without having to worry about getting to work on time. ~~At night I wouldn't be too tired to go out.~~

Tutering is offered free of charge at school and I would have time to get a tutor. I could take more classes and still do well in all of them. I often have to go to the library ~~but really don't have the extra time~~. It takes even more time to go to work and then have to drive back to campus on Saterdays to do my research. ~~My car is not running right, and this adds to my problems. Just as I am getting the material that I need it is time for the library to close or I begin to get tired~~.

Note that points unrelated to the topic sentence have been crossed out.

Second Revision

The second revision is based on questions 3 and 4:

3. Does the paragraph make sense to you and to someone else?
4. Have you covered all ideas in the cluster?

If I cut down at work I could have more time to spend on my education. By

having more time to spend on school I could bring up my grade point average.
I would have more time to do my homework because
Plus, ~~I could probably have more time to do my work.~~ I could spend as much

time as I needed to get my assignments done. I could go to class and study in
every day
the afternoons without haveing to worry about getting to work ~~on time~~. Tutering

is offered free of charge at school and I would have time to get a tutor. I could

take more classes and still do well in all of them. I often have to go to the library.

It takes even more time to go to work and then have to drive back to campus on

Saterdays to do my research. *If I could take five courses instead of three I could finish college almost twice as fast. I bet I would be more interested in it because that is all I would have on my mind.*

Notice that script type has been used to indicate new ideas added to the draft.

Third Revision

The third revision is based on questions 5, 6, and 7:

5. Can some words be changed for clarity?
6. Are any words repeated excessively?
7. Does the last sentence give a sense of closure to the paragraph?

If I cut down at work I could have more time to spend on my education. By

haveing more time spend on school I could bring up my grade point average.

Also,
~~Plus,~~ I would have more time to do my homework because I could spend as
                          After class I could concentrate on studying
much time as I needed to get my assignments done. ~~I could go to class and~~

~~study~~ in the afternoons without having to worry about getting to work every day.
                                     work with someone.
Tutering is offered free of charge at school and I would have time to ~~get a tutor.~~

~~I could take more classes and still do well in all of them.~~ I often have to go to the
but really don't have enough time. If I cut down at work, I would have time to go
library. ~~It takes even more time to go to work and then have to drive back to~~
to the library after class as well as on   Also if
~~campus on~~ Saterdays ~~to do my research.~~ If I could take five courses instead of
                         Cutting my working hours would give me
three I could finish college almost twice as fast. ~~I bet I would be more interested~~
more time to concentrate on my studies.
~~in it because that is all I would have on my mind.~~

So, here is how the revised draft looked before editing:

> **If I cut down at work I could have more time to spend on my education.** By haveing more time to spend on school I could bring up my grade point average. Also, I would have more time to do my homework because I could spend as much time as I needed to get my assignments done. After class I could concentrate on studying in the afternoons without having to worry about getting to work every day. Tutering is offered free of charge at school and I would have time to work with someone. I often have to go to the library but really don't have enough time. If I cut down at work, I would have time to go to the library after class as well as on Saterdays. Also, if I could take five courses instead of three I could finish college almost twice as fast. Cutting my working hours would give me more time to concentrate on my studies.

Editing

Before you consider your paper finished, check for any problems in mechanics. When you are learning the writing process, content comes before mechanics and grammar, but correct mechanics and grammar will be expected as you master the writing process. The following list contains some of the items you want to find and check.

spelling	errors in sentence structure
punctuation	consistency in verb tense
capitalization	consistent point of view
grammar usage	abbreviations and numbers

You will not be expected to have all of these editing skills at first. But you will acquire these skills through writing your paragraphs and essays. To make this mechanical review easier, you might want to learn to use a good word processor that includes a spell checker and other writing aids. This is also a good time for revising and editing in small groups. (See the following section on "Working in Small Groups.")

The student took the time to make one final check before turning in his paper. Here is how the latest draft looked after editing:

work, I
If I cut down at ~~work I~~ could have more time to spend on my education. By
school, I
having more time to spend on ~~school I~~ could bring up my grade point average.

Also, I would have more time to do my homework because I could spend as
class, I
much time as I needed to get my assignments done. After ~~class I~~ could

concentrate on studying in the afternoons without having to worry about getting
Tutoring   *school, and I would*
to work every day. ~~Tutering~~ is offered free of charge at ~~school and I would~~ have time

to work with someone. I often have to go to the library but really don't have

enough time. If I cut down at work, I would have time to go to the library after
Saturdays   *three, I*
class as well as on ~~Saterdays~~. Also, if I could take five courses instead of ~~three I~~

could finish college almost twice as fast. Cutting my working hours would give

me more time to concentrate on my studies.

Note that commas have been added and spelling errors have been corrected. Here is an edited draft that could be used for small group work.

> **If I cut down at work, I could have more time to spend on my education.** By having more time to spend on school, I could bring up my grade point average. Also, I would have more time to do my homework because I could spend as much time as I needed to get my assignments done. After class, I could concentrate on studying in the afternoons without having to worry about getting to work every day. Tutoring is offered free of charge at school, and I would have time to work with someone. I often have to go to the library but really don't have enough time. If I cut down at work, I would have time to go to the library after class as well as on Saturdays. Also, if I could take five courses instead of three, I could finish college almost twice as fast. Cutting my working hours would give me more time to concentrate on my studies.

Working in Small Groups

Working in small groups is an important tool in the writing process. In a small student work group, you can talk about writing assignments, exchange ideas, and read and discuss each other's writing. Reading and discussing each other's writing, called peer review, gives you a new perspective on your writing and helps you revise your work. Ideas and information that come from this kind of work group are called collaborative learning.

Collaborative Learning

As part of your experience in this class, you will probably participate in collaborative projects. When working with others, you will become more accomplished if the members of your group are responsible. As a group member, you will need to be sensitive to the needs of others, listen to other members' comments, and generally contribute positively to the overall task. If you wish to be productive, all members of your group must be willing to follow a plan for the work session. Though you may prefer to work on your own, working with others helps you practice skills that will help you in college and that many employers expect their employees to have. On the job, you might be expected to explore problems, find solutions, or make recommendations based on an exchange of ideas with coworkers. Making collaborative learning a part of this writing class will give you a chance to improve your ability to work with others now as well as in the future.

Many of the writing assignments in this textbook are designed to help you work with a partner or in a small group. First, you will be able to talk about writing assignments and exchange ideas in an informal and yet productive way. After this prewriting phase, you will be ready to draft your assignment. Then you can do a peer review with a classmate. The peer review is an informal yet organized activity that gives you practice in evaluating writing and making revisions.

These collaborative activities will not slow you down. On the contrary, they will help you gain confidence in your own writing and in your thinking about writing. At first, your instructor will probably organize these partnerships and small group discussions for you. Eventually, your instructor might expect you to make collaborative activities a natural part of your class work.

Peer Review

Peer review is part of the writing process that gives you and your partner the chance to receive feedback on your paragraph or essay from someone who is doing the same assignment. The process works well if you have a genuine desire to help each other. You will be asked to critique each other's papers by responding to a set of prepared questions and directions. These will guide your responses so that your partner can make further revisions that will strengthen the paper. Your partner will make similar responses to your paper. Both of you will want to consider all comments and suggestions. You do not have to accept all the suggestions, but you need to think about them. Remember that you should not take the criticism personally; the comments are meant to be constructive and will help you improve your paper.

Revising with a New Perspective

After completing the peer review, you will be ready to revise your paper with a new perspective. If possible, set your paragraph or essay aside and come back to it later that day. Then carefully read all the comments your partner made and think through the revisions you might make. As you reread your paper, the comments may become clearer. After reading the comments and rereading your paper, decide if making the changes will result in better writing. Then make the changes you think are necessary, paying attention to the flow of the ideas. Reread your paper one more time to see if it is stronger. Mentally note what types of changes strengthened the paper the most. This knowledge will help you become a better writer in future assignments. Reading your own paper critically is one of the most valuable skills you can possess. You have become a critical listener and a critical reader of your own work as well as the work of others. You have also learned how to communicate your ideas to others and have learned which suggestions to implement and which to ignore.

Review the major steps in the writing process.

Steps in the Writing Process

Prewriting: gathering ideas

Organizing: grouping and ordering details

Drafting: writing the first copy of a paragraph or essay

Revising: changing wording and organization

Editing: making mechanical changes

Working in small groups: exchanging papers and responding

Learning to write is a challenging but fulfilling venture. Remember when you learned to ride a bike? The first time you tried, you had to take a risk that you would look silly as you wobbled down the street, or that you would fall and get hurt, or that you would get upset because others were moving faster than you were. However, you had more to lose by not trying, and if you had never taken that risk, you would never have been able to ride a bike.

Learning to write is similar to that experience. Writing is a skill that requires many thinking activities, and you must use them all to write well. Just as you didn't give up on your bike riding, don't give up on the writing process. The payoff will be your ability to turn out an effective piece of writing.

Using Computers

Computers are becoming so important that knowing how to use them is quickly becoming a basic skill for employees and for students. Becoming familiar with the world of computers or expanding your use of them may be necessary if you want to get a job or be promoted. You may also need computer skills if you want to use the resources your college has. When you register for classes, use the library, or perhaps communicate with other students and instructors worldwide, you will need to use a computer. You probably will even have to earn credits in a computer class before you can graduate from college. However, the most pressing need for you right now might be just to complete an assignment for your English class.

If you have access to computers in your English class, you have a wonderful tool to help you with your writing assignments. This technology can make all parts of the writing process easier and more effective whether you are working on a first draft or polishing a final draft. Working on a computer may allow you to progress at your own pace and revise your papers thoroughly until you are happy with the results. You can move, add, and delete text easily. In addition, you will have access to special features like a spell checker, a thesaurus, or a grammar checker. If spelling is a challenge for you, the spell checker becomes an excellent aid for finding and correcting misspelled words or just simple typos. A printer will turn out a finished copy, saving you the work of retyping a polished draft. At times, you will be working in a group and can end the session by making a hard copy for all group members to study and work on individually before coming back together as a group. A further bonus is that during the writing process, you may also have more chances to have one-on-one coaching from your instructor.

Whatever your current writing skills are, if you have access to word processing software on a computer, the process of planning, drafting, and completing writing assignments will be much easier and more positive for you.

Putting It All Together

Collaborative Activity

Bring in a sample of your writing that you would like to share with a small group. It may be a letter, a poem, a grocery list, a journal entry, a job résumé, or a school assignment. Based on what you know about the writing process, discuss your sample writing. Answer the following questions as a group.

1. How did you get started?
2. What steps did you take to do the writing?
3. What kinds of things slowed you down?
4. How did you get started again?
5. Were there periods of time when writing was easy? Why did it seem easy?
6. What did you accomplish as a result of this writing?

Be prepared to share your ideas with the rest of the class.

Internet Activities

Introduction

The Internet Activities section in each unit offers you online supplements for the writing and grammar focus of each unit. You will find that each website is relevant to the information presented in each unit. The assignments will direct you to general searches as well as established home pages. Keep in mind that thousands of sites exist and may be changed or updated; however, these activities are designed so that you can visit valuable sites that are well established.

Since almost anyone can post websites, you must use critical judgment in determining the value of each site when you are doing a general search. If the page is attempting to "sell" a product, recruit people, or advertise an unpopular belief, be skeptical. If a page has the backing of a well-known and respected professional organization, college, university, or government agency, or if it is an authoritative educational journal, it is most likely a good source. Remember that your paper is as legitimate and valuable as your resources, so make your selections critically.

Activity 1   Accessing the Web

This exercise provides an opportunity to explore the web to find information on the main topics in this textbook's "Introduction to Writing."

   a. Use Netscape Navigator or Internet Explorer. To find a website, you may open a location in one of two ways:

      • Under "File" select "Open." A box will appear where you can type the address.

or

- Type directly in the box labeled "Location" under the buttons on your browser toolbar.

b. Type in the following address. (Type all Internet addresses exactly as they appear.)

http://owl.english.purdue.edu

- You will find the home page for Purdue University's Online Writing Lab (OWL).

c. Bookmark this location by selecting "Bookmark" on the menu bar in Netscape. If you are using Explorer, save this site as a "Favorite." If you are not sure how to do this with your browser, click on "Tutorial" (or "Help") and take a tour of the features of your browser. The bookmark for this site will remain until you delete it. Any time you find a website you might use later, just bookmark it.

Activity 2   Finding Articles on the Writing Process

The OWL website that you just bookmarked is maintained by Purdue University and includes many excellent sites for grammar and writing activities. While you are at this site, notice the "Search for" box at the bottom right of the page. This gives you an opportunity to do a general or specific search on many topics. Try the following exercise.

a. Type in "brainstorming" or "planning," and click on "search," or just hit return.

b. Select any of the articles, and double-click.

c. Print the article by clicking on "Print" on your browser toolbar, and briefly summarize two or three main points made in the article.

d. Now click on "Back" on your toolbar to return to the original OWL page. Notice the many links you have within the OWL. You can also do a "Fast-track Navigation" by clicking on the various other Quick Links on the right. Try out the different links.

Unit 1 *Writing Sentences and Paragraphs*

Part 1

Writing Skills: Topic Sentences and Paragraphs

Pretest over Unit I, Parts 1 and 4, is on page 3 of the Test Bank.

Tests covering topic sentences are on pages 10–17 of the Test Bank.

Objectives

The Topic Sentence

- Recognize the parts of a topic sentence.
- Expand topics into topic sentence ideas.
- Recognize suitable topic sentences.
- Recognize the topic sentence within a group of related sentences.

The Paragraph

- Identify the parts of a paragraph: topic sentence, support sentences, and concluding sentence.
- Practice the steps in the process of writing a paragraph:

  Prewrite to generate ideas.

  Group ideas to find a direction and a focus for developing a topic sentence.

  Provide a general word that describes the group.

  Outline (list from the group) the topic sentence and the support sentences that will go into the paragraph.

  Add to the list a concluding sentence to put the main idea in final form.

- Recognize the four elements of a good paragraph: completeness, logical order, unity, and coherence.
- Write a paragraph that demonstrates completeness, logical order, unity, and coherence.

When you can write clear sentences, you can make yourself understood by others. You can express any idea, feeling, opinion, or belief that you desire. No matter how long, short, simple, or complicated your subject may be, you must write your ideas in sentences. The sentence, then, is the basis for almost all writing.

Most of your college writing, of course, involves not just one sentence, but several, because you probably will have to explain or discuss many details to make your meaning clear. The person reading your ideas, however, will not be able to understand the overall meaning of your sentences unless you group them in a logical way. This group of related sentences is called a **paragraph.**

Following specific steps is necessary for writing good paragraphs. Before you study this step-by-step process in depth, however, it is important for you to recognize and understand the parts of a well-written paragraph.

The Topic Sentence

Parts of a Topic Sentence

A good paragraph contains several related sentences that support *one main idea* which is limited to and focused in one sentence. This sentence helps guide your reader through the related sentences in the paragraph. This vital sentence commits the writer to explain or illustrate the main idea. The term used to identify this main idea is **topic sentence.**

A topic sentence has two parts:

a topic (key word or phrase)

a direction or general word, which may be a conclusion, an opinion, or a statement *about* the topic

For example, the following sentences could be topic sentences:

Doing housework can be very boring.

Browsing in a library is a rewarding experience.

My trip to the botanical garden taught me a lot.

You could use each of these sentences as a topic sentence because each main idea is limited to and focused on two essential parts: **a topic** (key word or phrase) and a **general direction** (conclusion or opinion) about the topic.

Topic	General Direction
Doing housework	is very boring.
Browsing in a library	is a rewarding experience.
My trip to the botanical garden	taught me a lot.

The following exercise will give you practice in recognizing the parts of topic sentences.

Exercise 1

In each sentence, identify the *topic* (key word or phrase) and the *general direction* (the conclusion or opinion) about the topic.

Example:

Weekends often leave college students exhausted.

Topic: _Weekends_

Direction: _often leave college students exhausted_

1. City traffic can be dangerous for pedestrians.

    Topic: _City traffic_

    Direction: _can be dangerous for pedestrians_

2. Playing chess helps people develop thinking skills.

    Topic: _Playing chess_

    Direction: _helps people develop thinking skills_

3. Staying physically fit demands self-discipline.

    Topic: _Staying physically fit_

    Direction: _demands self-discipline_

4. Providing nutritious snacks for children can be a challenge.

Topic: *Providing nutritious snacks for children*

Direction: *can be a challenge*

5. Good students often receive encouragement from family members.

Topic: *Good students*

Direction: *often receive encouragement from family members*

6. Living on a ranch can be relaxing.

Topic: *Living on a ranch*

Direction: *can be relaxing*

7. Doing well in college can be a challenge for many students.

Topic: *Doing well in college*

Direction: *can be a challenge for many students*

8. Large city zoos provide many different activities for children.

Topic: *Large city zoos*

Direction: *provide many different activities for children*

9. Soccer is becoming a popular sport in the United States.

Topic: *Soccer*

Direction: *is becoming a popular sport in the United States*

10. The children enjoy taking part in their field day.

Topic: *The children*

Direction: *enjoy taking part in their field day*

11. Going out to eat can be a cultural experience.

Topic: *Going out to eat*

Direction: *can be a cultural experience*

12. Volunteering in the community can benefit everyone involved.

Topic: *Volunteering in the community*

Direction: *can benefit everyone involved*

13. Owning more than one car can be expensive.

Topic: *Owning more than one car*

Direction: *can be expensive*

14. Listening to the news each day keeps people informed about current events.

Topic: *Listening to the news each day*

Direction: *keeps people informed about current events*

15. Working during a holiday creates stress for families.

Topic: _____ *Working during a holiday* _____

Direction: _____ *creates stress for families* _____

To help you become more familiar with the parts of topic sentences, the following exercise gives you practice in expanding simple topics into full topic sentences.

Exercise 2

Complete each topic by writing a *statement* (conclusion or opinion) *about it*. You will be focusing the topic by adding a **direction** (your opinion or conclusion).

Example:

San Diego _____ *is a good place for windjamming.* _____

1. Buying prescription drugs _____ *can be very expensive. / creates hardships for some senior citizens.* _____

2. Basketball players _____ *have glamorous lives. / have stressful lives.* _____

3. Crossword puzzles _____ *provide mental stimulation. / can be difficult for children.* _____

4. Working at a fast-food restaurant _____ *develops responsibility.* _____

5. Working on my car _____ *requires patience. / is expensive.* _____

6. Rebuilding an engine _____ *is time-consuming. / is a challenge.* _____

7. Country music _____ *often deals with relationships.* _____

8. A family reunion _____ *can be boring. / can be enriching.* _____

9. My sister _____ *gives me good advice. / can be a brat.* _____

10. Rainy days _____ *relax me. / make the children hyperactive.* _____

11. Swimming _____ *keeps people physically fit. / makes people very hungry.* _____

12. Riding a motorcycle _____ *can be dangerous. / can be exhilarating.* _____

13. Camping in a tent _____ *can be lots of fun. / can be frustrating.* _____

14. Feeding stray cats _____ *can lead to problems. / is a humane act.* _____

15. Losing weight fast _____ *can be dangerous. / may be medically necessary.* _____

As you can see, a topic sentence is limited to or focused on one main idea. At the same time, a topic sentence is *general* in nature because it sums up the information or details that you will present to make your writing believable for your reader. Thus, even though a topic sentence is limited, it is the most general statement in the paragraph.

Distinguishing Topic Sentences from Simple Facts

Because the topic sentence is general, it cannot be just a simple fact. The following would not be suitable topic sentences:

Susan paid $3.95 for her new blouse.

The living room contains an Early American desk.

Two of my friends went on Star Tours four times.

Study the following pairs of sentences. The first sentence in each pair is a simple fact that cannot be developed into a paragraph. The second sentence in each pair shows how the simple fact has been changed into a more general idea that can be used as a topic sentence for a paragraph.

Fact: Susan paid $3.95 for her new blouse.

Topic sentence: Susan loves to shop for bargains.

Fact: The living room contains an Early American desk.

Topic sentence: The living room is furnished in authentic Early American style.

Fact: Two of my friends went on Star Tours four times.

Topic sentence: My friends and I had an exciting day at Disneyland.

The second sentence in each pair is a suitable topic sentence because each contains a **general** word or phrase—the **direction** for the topic:

loves to shop for bargains

is furnished in authentic Early American style

had an exciting day at Disneyland

Each of these broader statements suggests details that you could provide—examples of bargains, examples of Early American furniture, and examples of activities and events at Disneyland. It is important to understand that the topic sentence in a paragraph is a general idea that is also focused in one direction or on one opinion. However, it is just as important to keep the topic sentence from being so general that it cannot be developed in one paragraph. For example, it would take much more than one paragraph to fully develop the idea in a sentence like this: "The causes of war are many."

Just remember that a topic sentence must be more than a simple fact because a simple fact cannot be expanded into a fully developed paragraph.

The following exercise will help you identify sentences that can be used as topic sentences.

Exercise 3

Study each sentence, and decide if it is a simple fact (F), too broad to be developed in one paragraph (B), or a more general but focused statement that could be used for a topic sentence (TS).

Examples:

___*F*___ **The birds ate all of the figs on the tree.**

___*TS*___ **The birds are enjoyable to watch.**

___*B*___ **The evolution of birds is complex.**

_F_ 1. The Britney Spears concert lasted over two hours.

_TS_ 2. The two preteen sisters were unhappy at home.

_TS_ 3. The background music in the grocery store was annoying.

_B_ 4. Politics affect the lives of many people.

_TS_ 5. Stephanie's room is a disaster.

_F_ 6. The employees at Fred's Forum are paid $8.95 an hour.

_F_ 7. The 911 call came into the police department at 12:00 noon.

_TS_ 8. The Internet has changed Tina's social life.

_F_ 9. The Iraqi War officially began in March of 2003.

_TS_ 10. The children's play area in the doctor's office included fun activities.

_B_ 11. Cultures in America are varied.

_B_ 12. The Iraqi War created controversy throughout the world.

_B_ 13. The history of evolution spans many years.

_TS_ 14. Cross-country skiing provides great exercise.

_F_ 15. Tampa Bay won the Super Bowl in 2003.

_B_ 16. Unemployment is a problem in many countries.

_TS_ 17. Keeping a diary helped me understand my divorce.

_B_ 18. Many varieties of aquatic life can be found in the ocean.

_F_ 19. Fifty-one percent of entering college freshmen choose to attend a community college.

_TS_ 20. The manager had a difficult time after he lost his job.

Additional practice in thinking about how sentences relate to each other will help you write better topic sentences.

The following exercise will help you distinguish general topic sentences from more specific, factual statements.

Study each group of related sentences. Underline the most general statement that could be a topic sentence. (Remember that all the other sentences will support that topic idea.)

Example:

The red oleanders have finally started to bloom.

The daisies have filled the side yard with white.

The peach trees are covered with pink blossoms.

Many beautiful flowers have begun to bloom this spring.

The path to the back door is edged with blue alyssum.

1. They can easily work out during their lunch hours.

   Employees can work out without driving anywhere.

   Employees benefit from on-site fitness centers.

   Usually, employers charge their employees low fees.

   Many fitness centers offer extra benefits such as aerobics or yoga classes.

2. Part of their effectiveness is being good listeners so that they can respond appropriately.

   They feel comfortable discussing personal issues.

   They can discuss current topics like politics and sports.

   Many successful people have effective communication styles.

   They can be intuitive when necessary, or they can be direct and straightforward on other occasions.

3. Tamales are made with delicious red chili, pork, and masa.

   Biscochitos are wedding-type cookies with anise that will delight any sweet tooth.

   Posole is a pork soup with hominy and spices, served generally on New Year's Eve.

   Christmas in a Mexican home offers many unique foods.

4. Small cars are easy to park.

   Many advantages result from owning and operating small cars.

   Small cars usually run on fewer gallons of gas per week, depending on the miles driven.

   Cleaning small cars does not take much time.

   Small cars are easier to drive in traffic.

5. Traffic congestion in the city creates breathing problems for children.

   The scarcity of parks and play areas leaves children nowhere to play.

   Evidence of gangs can be found in many neighborhoods.

   <u>Inner-city children have many obstacles to overcome.</u>

   Violence keeps the children from feeling safe outside.

6. Cleaning up after themselves is important.

   All parties must treat one another with respect, especially when using the phone.

   Informing one another of schedules helps relationships.

   Keeping noise levels down creates harmony instead of resentment.

   <u>Roommates need to be considerate of one another.</u>

7. <u>Spending the day at the beach is often enticing.</u>

   Playing volleyball on the beach adds excitement and fun.

   Grilling on an open pit brings closure to the day.

   Picking up seashells on the beach provides treasures.

   Surfing in the ocean can be exciting.

8. Eighteen out of twenty free throws were good.

   The team stole the ball three times in the second quarter.

   Three-point shots kept the opposing team behind.

   <u>The basketball game was exciting for the home team.</u>

   The players made several dunks.

9. Canoes can be rented at the lagoons.

   Many miles of quiet paths are reserved for walking or jogging.

   Tennis players can use the lighted courts for a few coins in the meter.

   In one corner of the park is an Olympic-sized swimming and diving pool.

   <u>The beautiful public park offers many inexpensive outdoor activities for city residents.</u>

10. Checking for a fresh bowl of water is essential.

    <u>Babysitting cats can be a lot of work.</u>

    The litter box needs to be cleaned every day.

    Playing with the cats keeps them from missing their owners.

    Most cats need to be fed twice a day.

The Paragraph

Parts of a Paragraph

Now that you have learned about topic sentences, you are ready to study the full paragraph. Becoming familiar with the parts of strong paragraphs will help you when you begin to write your own paragraphs.

A paragraph has three parts:

1. **a topic sentence**
2. **support sentences**
3. **a conclusion**

Read the following example of a paragraph that has these three parts.

> **Over the past few years, my responsibilities as an administrative assistant have increased greatly.** When I was hired, I took shorthand, typed letters, and answered the telephone. Today I am involved in managing many projects and recruiting and overseeing other staff members at the office. Throughout the year, I coordinate many activities in my office, including social events as well as my boss's schedule. I must communicate with many different types of people, not only in the office but outside the office. Now, I do much of my work on a computer. As a matter of fact, I am often the one to learn new computer programs so I can train other people in my department, including my supervisor. Many times, my boss discusses important situations and asks for my feedback before making major decisions. **I find my job challenging with additional responsibilities that I did not have when I was first hired.**

The topic sentence (main idea) and the conclusion are in bold type so that you can easily identify them. All the other sentences, which contain details that explain how the responsibilities of an administrative assistant have increased, are support sentences. The parts of the paragraph work together to express the main idea clearly so that the reader can understand in what way an administrative assistant's job has changed.

The Paragraph Writing Process

Now that you can identify and develop topic sentences, it's time for you to practice writing so that you can improve your ability to express your ideas in an organized way. There is no one right way to write a paragraph, but learning the process one step at a time makes writing go more smoothly. In this part you will see the writing process illustrated again so you can practice prewriting, organizing, and drafting. An example of the step-by-step process as done by a student is given so that you can see how it works. Getting enough ideas and information to put into a paragraph is not something that just happens, so be patient with yourself during each step of the process. Begin by choosing a topic.

Choose a Topic   Select a simple topic. (Choose from your instructor's list, or follow the directions your instructor gives you. You might choose a topic listed in Exercises 1 or 2 in this unit.) In the following example, the student selected "recreation."

Prewrite   Use one or more of the prewriting activities explained in Introduction to Writing: talking, freewriting, or brainstorming. Don't worry about spelling or grammar or having complete ideas. Just let your mind produce ideas that have some connection with your topic.

A sample brainstormed list for the topic "recreation" might look something like this:

Recreation

jet skiing on weekends	fishing
reading mysteries	needlepoint
making quilts	good fishing spots
fishing equipment	cooking light meals
aerobics for fitness	stamp collecting

The student now has more specific topics from which to find direction for one main idea. The student chose "fishing" for the topic.

Brainstorm for Direction Brainstorm to generate more ideas that can be clustered into details that seem to have something in common. As you might recall, this group of related ideas will suggest your focus or direction for the paragraph. You probably will have more than one group from which to choose your focus or direction. Here is what the student's brainstorming produced:

Fishing

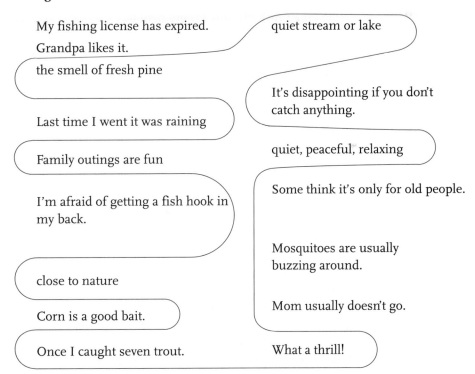

My fishing license has expired.
Grandpa likes it.
the smell of fresh pine

quiet stream or lake

It's disappointing if you don't catch anything.

Last time I went it was raining

quiet, peaceful, relaxing

Family outings are fun

Some think it's only for old people.

I'm afraid of getting a fish hook in my back.

Mosquitoes are usually buzzing around.

close to nature

Mom usually doesn't go.

Corn is a good bait.

Once I caught seven trout.

What a thrill!

Use General Words to Describe the Cluster of Ideas Notice that some ideas in the brainstorming about "fishing" are positive aspects of fishing. A **general word** that represents the ideas in this group might be "enjoyment." This grouping of details that have something in common has been marked in the above example. It is helpful to list them separately (and possibly add more).

quiet stream or lake
the smell of fresh pine

Family outings are fun.

close to nature

Once I caught seven trout.

quiet, peaceful, relaxing

What a thrill!

Some of the ideas have something negative in common. These could form another group that might be described by other general words: the "hazards" or "frustrations" of fishing.

I'm afraid of getting a fish hook in my back.

Last time I went it was raining.

It's disappointing if you don't catch anything.

Mosquitoes are usually buzzing around.

This group could be developed into a separate paragraph.

Finally, some of the items in the list introduce different ideas that might not fit anywhere.

Grandpa likes it.

My license is expired.

Mom usually doesn't go.

Some think it's only for old people.

Corn is a good bait.

Choose a Direction for the Topic Sentence   To find your focus and write your topic sentence, select the general word you want to use to represent your group: "enjoyment" or "frustration."

The student decided to focus on the "enjoyment of fishing."

Think About the Topic Sentence   Your next step is to develop your topic sentence. Remember that it must have two parts: a topic and a statement about the topic that includes a general word to represent your group. The topic sentence should also be broad enough to include all of the items in the group that you have selected for your direction.

Here are some *unacceptable* topic sentences for this group:

It is fun to tie flies.

Fishing is peaceful.

These two topic sentences do not contain the general word "enjoyment," and "It is fun to tie flies" is not broad enough to include all of the details in the group. "Fishing is peaceful" would make a good topic sentence, but not for this group of ideas.

Write the Topic Sentence   The next step is to write the topic sentence. You might say, "Fishing is enjoyable," "Fishing is an enjoyable activity," or "Fishing is an enjoyable leisure-time activity." Choose the version of the topic sentence that works best for you.

Outline the Paragraph   After you have written your topic sentence, it is time to list the supporting details and include a concluding (or summary) thought for the end of the paragraph. Put the sentences into an outline form, just as the student did in the following example. (If more support details occur to you as you make the outline, include them.)

Topic sentence	Fishing is an enjoyable leisure-time activity.
Support idea	quiet stream or lake
Support idea	I love the smell of fresh pine.
Support idea	Family outings are fun.
Support idea	close to nature
Support idea	Once I caught seven trout. What a thrill!
Support idea	quiet, peaceful, relaxing
Concluding idea	Fishing will always be a positive experience for me.

The supporting ideas are the "proof" given to the reader for the topic sentence. You will be able to write a strong paragraph if you develop a rough outline similar to this one.

Draft the Paragraph   The next step is to write the first version or draft of your paragraph. If new, *related* details occur to you, include them because they may help you clarify your main idea. You may want to put the ideas into a different order when you draft your paragraph. As you write, add whatever is needed to make the sentences flow smoothly and help the reader understand the experience.

Here is the student's draft. The topic sentence and concluding sentence are in bold type:

> **Although I have several hobbies, fishing is my most enjoyable leisure-time activity.** When I am fishing, this is the time I feel closest to the natural elements. The sunrise, the quiet stream or lake, the green pine scent, and the one-on-one experience with nature relax me more than any other activity. In this peaceful scene, there is also the thrill of conquering a bit of the wilderness. For years, I will remember the seven big trout I caught on a fishing trip several years ago. It was one of the greatest experiences I have ever had. **I am convinced that fishing will always be a positive experience for me.**

Notice that the supporting ideas have been expanded in the drafting process and give a clear and convincing picture of the main idea suggested by the topic sentence. They also clarify the idea of being "close to nature." The sunrise, the stream or lake, and the green pine scent all help complete the "picture."

The following exercises will help you practice the steps in prewriting, organizing, and drafting. Even though you have practiced these three skills in this unit, they are not the only important parts of the writing process. Revising and editing, which were introduced in "Introduction to Writing," are also important parts of the writing process.

Exercise 5

Brainstorm either the topic "children," the topic "rainstorms," or the topic you will use for your next writing assignment. Find your direction.

Topic: _____

Brainstorm for direction:

_____	_____
_____	_____
_____	_____

_____ _____

_____ _____

State the direction you have chosen:

_____

_____

Brainstorm with direction:

_____

_____

_____

_____

_____

_____

Make a new list of all the ideas that support the direction you have chosen:

_____

_____

_____

_____

_____

Write a general word that represents the group you have chosen: _____

_____

Write a possible topic sentence: _____

_____

_____

Write another possible topic sentence: _____

_____

_____

Select one of the topic sentences. Using your new list of ideas that support the direction of this topic sentence, list each idea in a rough outline. Add a concluding thought.

Topic sentence: _____

_____

Support idea: _____

Support idea: _____

Support idea: _____

Support idea: _____

Support idea: _____

Concluding idea: _____

_____

You now have ideas that can be used in a first version of a paragraph about your chosen topic.

Exercise 6

Using the information you have generated about your chosen topic, write a paragraph for practice.

_____

_____

_____

_____

_____

_____

_____

_____

_____

Elements of a Strong Paragraph

You have learned to recognize the topic sentence, the support sentences, and the conclusion in a paragraph. You have also learned to generate the ideas that you need to write a paragraph. Now you are ready to study the four elements of strong paragraphs:

completeness

logical or sensible order

unity

coherence

All these elements work together to make the paragraph clear and effective. Study each of these, and learn how to master them in your writing.

Completeness   A paragraph must include enough information to give the reader a clear picture or a full discussion of its main idea (the topic sentence). A paragraph without details or examples is vague and unconvincing. A paragraph that does not have enough information is called **incomplete** or **undeveloped.**

The following first version of a paragraph about dancing has a main idea but very little specific information. This draft is an incomplete or undeveloped paragraph. It needs more specific details that can be generated through talking, freewriting, brainstorming, looking through your journal, or reading. Then you will be ready to compose another draft.

> **Dancing can be good exercise.** It can be entertaining. It can be lots of fun as well. **Dancing can be very beneficial for everyone.**

This paragraph has a topic sentence and a conclusion, but it has only two very general statements about dancing. In fact, the "support" statements are neither details nor examples. The sentence "It can be lots of fun as well" could even be another main idea. What does "good exercise" really mean? Specific answers to this question are not in the paragraph. You can see, then, that this paragraph needs more information to explain what "good exercise" means. The reader can only guess at the meaning suggested by the topic sentence.

Here is a revised draft of this paragraph about dancing that contains more information:

> **Dancing can be good exercise.** The constant arm and leg movements are like aerobics. They can be a really good workout if the dance lasts long enough. If the dance requires lots of quick movements, many calories can be used up, and more fat will be burned. Some dances require movements that are like stretching, so flexibility and muscle tone will be increased. **Dancing can help maintain weight and can be beneficial exercise for everyone.**

There is no "correct" length for an effective paragraph, but four to eight support sentences make a strong paragraph if they contain supporting details. When you are judging the completeness of a paragraph, look for details and examples that make the topic sentence clear.

Exercise 7

Revise the following paragraphs for completeness. Underline the topic sentence and the conclusion in each paragraph. Then add two or more sentences that support the topic sentence.

Example:

Hawaii is fun to visit on a vacation. I can sample fresh pineapples served by friendly Hawaiians. I can scuba dive in the ocean. Having the chance to enjoy different activities in Hawaii could mean a great vacation.

Each island offers different sights and activities. I can attend luaus where I can sample wonderful ethnic foods and sip fresh fruit drinks.

<u>**Hawaii is fun to visit on a vacation.**</u> **I can sample fresh pineapples served by friendly**
                                    ∧

Close by, I can browse in a variety of interesting shops.   *I can join in native Hawaiian dances.*

Hawaiians. I can scuba dive in the ocean. <u>**Having the chance to enjoy different activities**</u>
                          ∧   ∧

<u>**in Hawaii could mean a great vacation.**</u>

Paragraph 1

Supporting sentences will vary.

<u>Playing Little League soccer can help teach eight-year olds many valuable lessons.</u> Working together as a team means passing the ball when another player has a better shot at the goal. Believing that winning is possible even if the team is behind teaches determination. Learning that everyone has something to offer helps the team avoid cliques. <u>The end of the season will reveal a group of kids with a positive team attitude.</u>

Paragraph 2

Customer service is very important in building a successful business. Customers who are treated well often return to the store. When making returns, customers know that defective merchandise will be replaced or their money will be refunded. Customers like to know that apparel that does not fit can be returned. All in all, satisfied customers spread the word about consumer-friendly stores.

Paragraph 3

After an automobile accident, drivers of the vehicles face many problems. Calling for help is crucial. They have to notify insurance companies. Drivers and passengers may need extended medical treatment. Cars have to be repaired. Sometimes the stress seems to go on forever.

Paragraph 4

Visiting a dentist can be an uncomfortable experience. X-ray tooth frames cut into gums. Lights in a person's eyes are annoying. Most people would rather do anything than go to the dentist.

Paragraph 5

Whether or not a person is hired for a job often depends on the interview. All the applicants must answer the same standardized questions. Many of the questions are intentionally open-ended so that the applicant can answer with personal responses. Near the end of the interview, the applicants usually have the opportunity to ask questions. Applicants should always take an interview seriously.

Logical Order   You have learned that all the sentences in a strong paragraph relate to one main idea and that there should be enough supporting details to make the main idea clear. A second element of strong paragraphs is **logical** or **sensible order.** All the support sentences should be in clear, logical order.

To start thinking about how to put sentences together in logical order, read the following sentences. Notice how they relate to each other but are *out* of logical order.

I opened the front door of my house and went inside.

I walked up the front steps to my front door.

These sentences are out of logical order because the person would have to walk to the door before it could be opened. This example shows what "logical" or "sensible" order is. The sentences should be in this order:

I walked up the steps to my front door.

I opened the front door of my house and went inside.

Here is another example of illogical order:

Henry washed the mud off his dog.

Henry made sure he put warm water in the big tub.

He dried the dog with a towel.

These sentences are not in logical or sensible order because they are not *in the order in which the actions would be done*. Here is the logical order:

Henry made sure he put warm water in the big tub.

Henry washed the mud off his dog.

He dried the dog with a towel.

Here is another example of logical order:

At noon today, the engineers met at a special luncheon.

The luncheon ended at two o'clock.

These sentences are in logical order because of the *time signal* in each sentence. "Noon" comes before "two o'clock."

Another kind of order exists in describing a place, such as a room in a house. The details are described or "seen" in the order in which they really exist in the room.

When I enter the living room, I see a couch on the left and a chair and table next to that. Walking straight ahead into the room, I see at the end of the dining room a fairly large table and four chairs. As I look to the right of this large table, I notice the door into the kitchen.

When several details flow together in a paragraph, it is important for the reader to be able to follow the ideas in a clear order. Sometimes—as in the previous example—the natural physical movement from one place to another will determine the order of the sentences.

One final example may help clarify this idea of order in a strong paragraph. In the following paragraph about sea turtles, the support sentences are in a clear, logical order. The ideas in bold type should not be rearranged because they show the logical order of what the scientists did.

American scientists are working hard to gather facts about sea turtles called leatherbacks. **The observers work,** no matter what the weather is like—on clear days or in pouring rain. **They count the turtles** as they come ashore. When the turtles lay their eggs, **the scientists walk up and down** the beaches for many hours at a time. **They count the eggs** in the sand. Then, later, **they count the eggs that hatch.** These biologists know that they are collecting information that will someday be important to other scientists.

The actions are described in the normal, natural order in which they occur.

Note Other ways of clarifying the logical order in a paragraph concern *coherence*, which will be explained later.

The following exercise will help you practice arranging sentences in logical order.

Exercise 8

Study the following sets of sentences and decide what their logical order would be in a paragraph. Number the sentences in the order in which they should logically appear.

Example:

___2___ She made plane reservations.

___1___ Sara decided to go to Atlanta, Georgia.

1. ___2___ Isaac called his buddy Mario to see if he wanted to go to the car auction.

   ___1___ Isaac wanted to go to the car auction with a friend.

2. ___1___ The hot water tank in Leslie's basement began to leak.

   ___2___ She called a plumber to have the tank replaced.

3. ___3___ Kenita turned in her essay at the beginning of class.

   ___1___ Kenita typed her assignment on the computer.

   ___2___ Kenita produced a hard copy on her printer.

4. ___3___ Rachel attended classes.

   ___2___ Rachel paid her registration fees for two classes in the fall.

   ___1___ Rachel took five hundred dollars from her savings account for her fees.

5. ___2___ Sammy and his uncle bought a fruit tree to plant in the backyard.

   ___1___ Sammy and his uncle went to the local plant nursery to look at trees.

   ___3___ They took the tree home and planted it immediately.

6. ___3___ The student must then decide how to solve the problem.

   ___1___ To solve a word math problem, students must read the problem.

   ___4___ The student must do the math to solve the problem.

   ___2___ The student must determine what is being asked.

7. ___4___ Justin finally bought a new truck.

   ___2___ He decided not to have his old car fixed.

   ___1___ Justin's old car needed a new transmission.

   ___3___ Justin spent two weeks looking for a new vehicle.

8. __1__ When the weather turns cold, rattlesnakes hibernate.

__5__ After eating the pack rats, the newly emerged rattlers may find their way to someone's warm patio.

__3__ They soon move through the desert for food.

__2__ After winter hibernation, snakes gradually resume their normal activities.

__4__ Any small desert animal like a pack rat could be the hungry snake's first meal of the spring.

9. __4__ Glen came in fourth.

__2__ Glen prepared by spending hours swimming, biking, and running.

__3__ Glen arrived early the day of the race.

__5__ Glen reflected on ways to make his next event even better.

__1__ Glen decided to participate in a triathlon.

10. __7__ Benton took the medicine as prescribed.

__2__ Benton bought some cough drops.

__4__ Benton went to the doctor.

__1__ Benton woke up with a sore throat.

__6__ Benton picked up the medicine from the pharmacy.

__3__ Even with the cough drops, his throat just kept getting worse.

__5__ The doctor prescribed some antibiotics.

__8__ Benton's throat started getting better.

Unity   All sentences in a good paragraph relate to the topic sentence (main idea). When any idea doesn't relate specifically to the topic sentence, then that paragraph lacks unity or is not unified. Look again at the paragraph about giant sea turtles. This draft has one main idea and several support sentences that help to explain the general word(s) expressed in the topic sentence.

> **American scientists are working hard to gather facts about sea turtles called leatherbacks.** The observers work, no matter what the weather is like—on clear days or in pouring rain. They count the turtles as they come ashore. When the turtles lay their eggs, the scientists walk up and down the beaches for many hours at a time. They count the eggs in the sand. Then, later, they count the eggs that hatch. **These biologists know that they are collecting information that will someday be important to other scientists.**

This paragraph shows the three parts of a good paragraph—topic sentence, support sentences, and concluding sentence (or conclusion). Now check to see if the paragraph has the important element of **unity.**

To check for unity, first separate the topic sentence into its two parts:

Topic: American scientists

Direction or general word(s): are working hard to gather facts about sea turtles called leatherbacks.

Second, check each support sentence against the topic sentence. Each supporting idea is a specific fact or detail that explains what the scientists actually do to gather information. In this case, all the sentences after the topic sentence must explain how the scientists are working hard to gather facts about sea turtles. So that you can judge the supporting sentences better, they are listed below.

Topic Sentence

American scientists are working hard to gather facts about sea turtles called leatherbacks.

Support Sentences

The **observers work, no matter what the weather is like**—on clear days or in pouring rain.

They count the turtles as they come ashore.

. . . the **scientists walk up and down the beaches for many hours** at a time.

They count the eggs in the sand.

Then, later, **they count the eggs that hatch.**

Notice that the bold words in each support sentence make reference to the main idea in the topic sentence.

This paragraph has unity because the information in it clearly and directly relates to the general idea in the topic sentence. All you have to do to check a paragraph's unity is to see if each sentence gives details that explain the main idea in the topic sentence. All the sentences between your topic sentence and your conclusion should explain your main idea.

Now read the following draft of the preceding paragraph. Look for the sentence that does not explain the topic sentence. This sentence breaks the unity of the paragraph.

American scientists are working hard to gather facts about sea turtles called leatherbacks. The observers work, no matter what the weather is like—on clear days or in pouring rain. The leatherback is the only kind of turtle that can live in the cold North Atlantic Ocean. They count the turtles as they come ashore. When the turtles lay their eggs, the scientists walk up and down the beaches for many hours at a time. They count the eggs in the sand. Then, later, they count the eggs that hatch. These biologists know that they are collecting information that will someday be important to other scientists.

The sentence that breaks the unity is "The leatherback is the only kind of turtle that can live in the cold North Atlantic Ocean." This sentence does not directly relate to how the observers work to get their information. Consequently, this sentence spoils the paragraph's unity.

The following exercise will help you identify sentences that do not support a topic sentence. Being able to identify such unrelated sentences will help you preserve the unity in the paragraphs you are writing.

Study each group of sentences. Identify the sentences as follows:

TS = a possible topic sentence

S = a support sentence

U = an unrelated sentence

___TS___ **Many elderly people enjoy outdoor activities.**

___U___ **Children swim in the pool next to the shuffleboard court.**

___S___ **Elderly people may play shuffleboard.**

1. ___TS___ At half-time, the hip-hop dancers entertained the audience.

___S___ Each member showed off fast-paced jumping movements.

___U___ My brother still enjoys break dancing.

2. ___S___ Employees can be fired for taking drugs during work hours.

___TS___ Most companies strive for a drug-free environment.

___U___ Smoking marijuana is legal in Amsterdam.

3. ___S___ This fashion trend is reflected in increasing sales of Asian clothes.

___TS___ Ethnic clothing is becoming increasingly popular in the United States.

___U___ People enjoy shopping.

4. ___S___ Thousands of people died in the earthquake.

___U___ Earthquakes have occurred in many other places.

___TS___ The earthquake in Iran was devastating.

5. ___S___ Sam wrote a research paper for his pharmacy class.

___TS___ Sam's pharmacy class required several writing assignments.

___U___ Sam never missed any of his pharmacy classes.

6. ___U___ My guinea pig has not learned when to stop eating.

___S___ The chimps have been taught to associate the picture of a ball with a real ball.

___TS___ Animals are very intelligent beings.

7. ___TS___ In the springtime in Georgia, the vegetation is beautiful.

___S___ The peach trees are filled with fragrant pink blossoms.

___U___ The peaches are sweet and juicy.

8. ___U___ Some people were afraid of the bears.

___TS___ The drought affected wildlife near the city.

___S___ Several young bears wandered into the suburbs looking for food and water.

9. __TS__ Learning to ride a jet ski can be challenging.

   __U__ The neon-blue-striped jet ski goes the fastest.

   __S__ Standing up and making a turn requires excellent balance.

10. __S__ Fifteen new American novels were added to the collection.

    __TS__ The library has an extensive collection of American literature.

    __U__ The library's art collection is outstanding.

11. __TS__ Swimming is good physical therapy.

    __U__ Many of my neighbors wonder why I swim at 6:00 a.m. every day.

    __S__ Paraplegics increase muscle tone in the swimming pool at Saint Luke's Hospital.

12. __TS__ Teenagers can often afford to restore Volkswagen bugs.

    __S__ Often they can find an old Volkswagen bug for a few hundred dollars.

    __U__ Teenagers like to drive Volkswagen bugs to school.

13. __S__ Injured birds are nurtured back to health.

    __TS__ Wildlife centers are dedicated to helping sick and injured animals.

    __U__ Wildlife centers are often privately funded.

14. __TS__ Robert Patton has been actively involved in the environmental movement in the United States.

    __S__ He donated $150,000 to preserve the Gila National Reserve.

    __U__ He plays golf every Sunday morning.

15. __U__ Alicia received financial aid while attending college.

    __S__ Alicia, a community-college graduate, earned an A average during her first year at the university.

    __TS__ Community-college graduates perform well at universities.

Exercise 10

Check each draft for **unity**. Underline any sentences that do not support or explain the main idea in the topic sentence.

Paragraph 1

People from other countries have different reasons for wanting to come to live in the United States. For example, some might want higher-paying jobs than they can get in their own countries. Some want the freedom to change jobs or professions. Some might want the chance to get more education for themselves and their families. Church groups often sponsor people coming to America. Perhaps one of the most important reasons would be the desire to own and operate a business. Many people wait a long time for the chance to live in the United States. Every year, regardless of the reasons, many more people come to live in America.

Paragraph 2

Adult reentry students often have special needs. They may have time constraints caused by family needs and jobs as well as by school. <u>Reentry students are willing to put in the extra time to be successful.</u> Since they sometimes work more slowly than younger students, they may require more time to complete tasks. As adults grow older, their vision is not as keen, so classrooms need excellent lighting with little glare. <u>They have had more experiences than younger students.</u> Also, reentry students may experience hearing problems, making it hard for them to hear everything that is said in the classroom. These problems, though serious, do not need to be a barrier to education.

Paragraph 3

Teachers who are student-centered create an environment that the students will never forget. <u>Some teachers seem to be rushed and not willing to show their personal sides.</u> Teachers who allow students to introduce themselves and meet others in the class establish an environment where everyone feels worthwhile and respected. Considerate teachers make class expectations clear on assignments and procedures. <u>Teachers take attendance at the beginning of the class period.</u> Instructors who want their students to have the best chance for success call them when the students are ill or absent for several class periods. Teachers who go out of their way to show their concern provide a true learning experience.

Coherence   One of the most important considerations in writing a paragraph is **coherence**—the way all the sentences should be clearly connected to each other. Without connecting words or phrases, supporting ideas may be hard to follow and may even seem unrelated to the topic sentence and to each other. A paragraph that lacks connecting words and phrases sounds like a list.

The following paragraph has the coherence it needs:

When Sue was a child, she learned from her dad how to be a hard worker. For example, she always helped in the yard. Many times they mowed the lawn together. Sue emptied the grass catcher (which her dad did not overfill), and he did the heavy part by lifting the barrels full of grass. Working together, they did not quit until the job was done. She and her dad worked even after the sun was gone, making sure that the edges of the lawn were neat. In this way, Sue learned to stay with a job until she had done it well and could feel proud of her effort.

This paragraph shows coherence because *at least one* of the key words or phrases—or variations of them—is repeated either directly or indirectly *in each sentence.*

Key Words and Phrases	Variations
Sue	she
learned	learned
her dad	he
Sue and her dad	they, together
hard worker	job, helped in the yard, did the heavy part, lifting, work, working, didn't quit until the job was done, making sure, stay with a job, effort

Each sentence in the paragraph is obviously connected to the one before it by a clear pronoun or a clear example of a key word.

Other words and phrases also help set the scene or provide time signals that clarify the experience for the reader:

Other Words and Phrases That Provide Coherence

always   many times   even after

A very important signal to the reader—"For example"—occurs near the beginning of the paragraph. This phrase tells the readers to watch for specific details that will clarify the topic sentence.

At the end of the paragraph, the most important connecting words, "In this way," introduce the concluding sentence. This phrase points back to all the examples that help make the main point clear.

Making clear connections between two consecutive sentences is very important. Do not assume that your readers know what you are talking about. Try to emphasize the relationship between sentences. The extra effort is well worth it. (You will learn more about coherence in Unit 7.)

The following exercise will help you understand and practice giving paragraphs coherence.

Exercise 11

Read each paragraph below. Underline the topic sentence. Circle the key words or phrases in the topic sentence that could be used to add coherence. Revise the paragraphs, and put in connecting words and phrases to show clearly how sentences relate to each other and to the topic sentence. Use the key words or variations of them. Put in "time signal" words like "then" or "next" or "later." Use "for example" to introduce specific examples. You may combine ideas if necessary to make each paragraph flow more smoothly. Finally, make sure that the concluding sentence clearly refers to the main idea in the topic sentence.

Example:

~~Carol and Bev~~ had a ~~good time~~ at the ~~movie~~. *When they went in, they* ~~Carol and Bev~~ decided to sit in the

back ~~where~~ *so* they could relax and have lots of room. ~~The music was~~ *They liked the movie because the*

exciting and the ~~exciting. The~~ story was suspenseful. *During the show, they* ~~They~~ ate popcorn and drank a soft

The best part of all was watching the drink. ~~There were lots of~~ good-looking guys ~~there. They enjoyed~~ *in front of them. All of these*

things added up to an enjoyable ~~their~~ afternoon at the movies.

Paragraph 1

Going to my daughter's soccer game turned out to be a disappointing experience. Someone broke into my vehicle and stole my purse and cell phone. I spent a lot of time remembering what was in my purse and what I had to do to replace missing items. I also had to change the locks for my house and car. The thieves ruined my day.

Paragraph 2

Renting videos has many advantages over going to the movies. Videos are approximately one-third the price of a theater movie ticket. Convenience is a factor. Videos can be rented from many different stores at convenient times, and selection is good. Control over the explicit nature of the movie is something many people do not realize they have. Inappropriate scenes can be avoided by using the fast-forward button. More and more people are watching movies at home rather than going to movie theaters.

Paragraph 3

My favorite birthday present was a trip through the zoo. I was ten years old. My mom took me and three of my friends. My sister went, too. We made a lot of noise when we saw the snakes. I learned that my mom liked tigers. We saw birds and monkeys at the zoo. I took pictures of everybody with a new camera. We had a picnic lunch. They gave me presents. We had a great time at the zoo.

Paragraph 4

In an attempt to stay healthy, more and more people in America are altering their lifestyles. They start the day with a healthful breakfast. They pass up junk food at lunch time. That evening, they eat a nutritious dinner. They often exercise. These people usually feel better and look forward to each new day.

Collaborative Activity

Option 1

Break into groups of three or four. Using Exercise 2 on page 27, discuss and write topic sentences for three of the topics. Each group will work on three different topics. Decide which topic sentence your group thinks is the best, and write it on the board for the class to see. Be prepared to discuss the topic sentences with your class.

Option 2

Read the student examples by Hilding, Scarbrough, Roesch, Donaldson, and Schulz in Part 3, pages 52–55. In groups of three or four, evaluate these paragraphs according to the statements given in the following chart. Rate each element on a scale of 1 (low) to 5 (high). Then share the results with the rest of the class, and be prepared to defend your scores.

The topic sentence focuses the paragraph.	The paragraph has a logical order of ideas.	The paragraph has sufficient support.	The paragraph links ideas together.
Hilding _____	_____	_____	_____
Scarbrough _____	_____	_____	_____
Roesch _____	_____	_____	_____
Donaldson _____	_____	_____	_____
Schulz _____	_____	_____	_____

Part 2

Something to Think About, Something to Write About

Professional Essay to Generate Ideas for Writing

Sometimes reading a scholarly article makes you stop and think about the world in which you live. Articles of this type can be about political or social issues that directly affect you. They can also make you think about your past or future. By reading these articles, you get information about the world as well as ideas to use in your writing. They may trigger something in your memory that you can put into your writing.

Read the following article, and reflect on events that happened early in your life or that are going on right now as a result of your past. These events can be a valuable resource for your writing.

After you have read the article, work through one or more of the suggested writing assignments that require remembering past events. If you cannot remember your past, then perhaps you can focus on something you have experienced recently.

Childhood

Dr. Linda Coble, *therapist and psychologist*

1   Do you remember what you were doing and how you were feeling in the first grade? Who was your teacher in kindergarten? Can you remember what you were doing before starting school? How far back can you reach into your past? Can you recollect your first experience of emotional awareness? What was it? fear? security? warmth? The answers to these questions can be extremely valuable to therapists working with their clients. Some people may think pulling out long-past, ancient detail is impossible, but Adlerian therapists and clients are doing it every day. In fact, a very important aspect of many psychotherapy approaches is to gather details from clients about their early history, for these early experiences may have an important impact on the clients' personality development.

2   Adlerian theory, a popular counseling approach, calls these events "early recollections." Clients are asked to recall incidents from as far back as they are able. Experiences can be both positive and negative. Therapists gather these memories. As they sort the information, they pay attention to the age of the person at the time of the recollection, the specific details of the occurrence, and the feelings the client experienced. The therapist, upon gathering several of these recollections, will use them in analyzing the client's goals and attitudes.

3   Birth order is also considered by Adlerian therapists to be an important influence on personality development. First interactions with people are within the family structure, and the position in the family may have set up certain expectations from significant family members. Children, in their effort to achieve a sense of belonging, will take on roles in the family. Commonly, the oldest children adopt the role of being responsible, serious, and dependable. The middle child is in the uncomfortable position of following the firstborn and will often experience pressure in her/his attempt to catch up with the older sibling(s). If the second-born feels a struggle, she or he may develop opposite traits from those of the older brother or sister. The youngest child is often a charmer who struggles with being taken seriously. Of

course, these are generalizations, and many combinations of the family structure can be more accurately analyzed by a qualified therapist. No doubt, however, this position in the family, as well as an understanding of how the child interpreted early family situations, provides valuable insight for the therapist.

4 In some extreme cases, a therapist may find that a client has had an unusually traumatic experience. Perhaps a serious fire, a prolonged illness of a family member, a death of a parent, or an early encounter with alcoholism may have affected a child's perception of family life, consequently affecting the child's view of the world. In this case, the therapist tries to help the client to explore the event. A therapist may use simulated drama, dialogue, simulated confrontation with conflicting family members, or writing to shed the negative feelings and "clean the slate" for the client. By reexposing the details of negative occurrences and accepting the help of a therapist to put the events to rest, so to speak, the client experiences a cathartic relief and can have a healthier, more positive outlook.

5 Early recollections and birth order are effective beginning places for therapists; however, what is done with the information once it is obtained is equally important. Even though such beginnings provide an insight into what may be the cause of the problem, the strategies for new directions or solutions provided by therapists are what make the total therapeutic process worthwhile for the client.

Understanding Words

Briefly define the following words as they are used in the above essay.

1. psychotherapy *using psychoanalysis to treat mental disorders*

2. sibling *brother or sister*

3. simulated *imitated, pretended to be like*

4. cathartic *related to alleviation or release of fears*

 ### Quotations: Additional Ideas on Childhood

The following quotations are also related to childhood memories and experiences. During the writing process for this assignment, you might want to read and think about them. They may help you focus on your topic by triggering memories and thoughts that will add strong information to your paragraph.

> "One of my favorite early memories is of my father taking me to school. I would ride on the handlebars of his bicycle, in a special little seat he made for me, and we would practice multiplication tables." *Dr. Ruth Westheimer*

> "In most human kinship systems over the course of history, grandparents have played an important role. They are the living link with the past, the repositories of wisdom." *Dr. Ruth Westheimer*

> "The next thought that crossed my mind was, 'I wish my father would hug me.'" *Robert Subby*

> "She is my daughter, and I am proud of her, and I am her mother, but she is not proud of me." *Amy Tan*

 ### Writing Assignment

Now that you have read the article and quotations about childhood, write a paragraph about one of the following topics.

1. How did it feel to be the oldest child? Middle child? Youngest child? Only child?

2. Describe a place that gave you a feeling of warmth or security as a child.

3. Describe the most negative or ugly place you remember as a child.

4. Describe the most beautiful object you remember seeing as a child.

5. What responsibilities did you have growing up?

6. What qualities should a good parent possess?

7. Which person influenced you the most?

8. What do you remember looking forward to as a child?

9. What do you remember worrying about or dreading as a child?

10. What was different about your childhood?

After reading through the topics, begin working on your writing assignment by following these steps.

1. Brainstorm or freewrite, using one of the above topics.

2. Develop a topic sentence that includes a topic and a direction.

3. Following the model shown on pages 34–35 in this unit under "Outline the Paragraph," make a rough outline of the ideas that will go into your paragraph.

4. Draft a paragraph, using your outline. As you are working, use any other related thoughts or details that occur to you. Be sure to include a closing sentence that will bring your reader back to the main idea in your topic sentence.

5. Make sure you have two copies of your draft—one for yourself and one for your partner for peer review.

 ## Collaborative Writing Project: Working and Learning Together

Choose a partner, and exchange paragraphs. Carefully read one of these paragraphs out loud. Then answer the following questions. Write directly on the paper so the author can consider the responses later. Then read the other paragraph, following the same procedure.

1. What is the topic sentence? Identify both the topic and the direction.

2. Underline all the details you can find. Discuss any information that could be added.

3. Circle all the words that link to the **topic idea** and to the **direction.** If an entire sentence does not have any variations of these **key words,** mark it so the author can think about revising it.

4. Check to see if the ideas are in clear, logical order. If a sentence seems out of place, suggest a change.

5. Does the last sentence bring the paragraph to a sense of closure? Does it seem to sum up the main idea?

6. If you are not sure about any of your partner's comments, include your instructor in the discussion.

7. Revise your paragraph, including any of the suggestions you feel will strengthen your paper.

Working together during this revision will help you learn to make changes that result in stronger paragraphs.

Part 3

Paragraphs for Discussion and Analysis

Student Writing

Summer at Aunt Clara and Uncle Frank's Farm

Phyllis J. Hilding, *student*

My favorite memories from my past have to be the summers I spent on my Aunt Clara and Uncle Frank's farm. From the time I was ten years old until I turned sixteen, at which age I had to get a job, I spent every summer on the farm, along with at least eighteen other nieces and nephews. My aunt and uncle had no children of their own, and so, my cousins and I, plus other assorted kids, became their children for the summers, to work and play, and have the best times of our young lives. We all did the chores, household chores and farm chores alike. We girls did cooking, cleaning, and washing, while my boy cousins helped my uncle with the bulk of the heavier farm work. All of us fed and watered the farm stock, milked cows, and mucked out the pig and cow stalls, the last of which was never on the top of anybody's list of things to do. We had fun while we did our chores like riding the big boar called Pinky, squirting milk into the mouths of at least a dozen cats lined up at milking time, and shucking corn; it was all fun to me. We made friends with the neighboring farm kids, some of whom I still keep in contact with. We, including the real farm kids and my city cousins, had "parlor" parties, went on picnics and hay rides, went to county fairs and auctions, and even participated in barn-raisings where farm people got together and helped rebuild other farmers' burned-down barns. Every evening, after the farm chores were done, we all piled into the back of my uncle's old beat-up pickup and drove the mile or so to Bird Lake where we all jumped into the lake and rejoiced in the cool water, pleased with the day's work and happy with being young, healthy, and alive. There was a camaraderie among us that I haven't experienced since those long-ago summers on my aunt and uncle's farm. I'll always remember those idyllic summers I spent on the farm, the good and wonderful people I met and got to know, and the feelings of love and friendship I felt then.

Understanding Words
Briefly define the following words as they are used in the above paragraph.

1. mucked   *removed dirt and manure*

2. boar   *male pig*

3. camaraderie   *warm feelings and rapport among friends*

4. idyllic   *having natural charm, simple and pleasant*

Answers are in the Instructor's Manual, page 20.

Questions on Content

1. Why did the author spend summers on the farm?

2. Who was Pinky?

3. What were the lasting effects of these summers on the author?

Questions on Form

1. In what way did the author use logical or sensible order?

2. What makes the paragraph complete?

3. How does the concluding sentence add to the paragraph?

Playhouse under the Orange Tree

Peggy Scarbrough, *student*

The most comfortable, secure place that I can remember as a child was the playhouse I made under an orange tree. This tree was in a grove of orange trees next to my house. The tree wasn't trimmed, so the branches were thick and hung to the ground. I was five at the time, and the inside of the tree formed a quiet, cool, private place to play hide and watch. No one could see me from the outside of the tree, but I could see and hear what was going on outside. I watched through the holes in the branches of the tree as my dad and his friend repaired our car. I could hear the music coming from the radio in the kitchen where I knew my mom was fixing lunch for us. I could even hear the whooshing noise the car tires made on a paved road as they passed by. Occasionally as I leaned against the trunk of that tree, quiet, dazed, almost asleep, birds would come sit on the branches to preen their wings with their beaks and make small bird noises. Then with any slight movements on my part, they would take flight to another tree out of my sight. Yes, that playhouse under the tree provided me with a private place where I could be my own person and still be safe, comfortable, and secure.

Understanding Words

Briefly define the following word as it is used in the above paragraph.

1. preen   *clean and smooth feathers*

Questions on Content

1. What are the holes in the branches?

2. When the birds sat on the branches, what did they do?

3. What was she aware of outside her safe place?

Questions on Form

1. What is the topic sentence?

2. What makes the concluding sentence effective?

Concentration Camp

Jan-Georg Roesch, *student*

My visit to the concentration camp was a frightful and thoughtful experience. In the 1930s and 1940s under the regime of Adolf Hitler, this place ended many innocent people's lives. The building looked as unwelcoming as a graveyard by night. The heavy iron door, which slowly gave way to the pulling force, creaked as it was opened. Each footstep echoed through the chamber as each individual slowly pondered and walked from one end of the room to the other. Every unconscious mumble could be heard clearly. The smell was so sharp and distinct, yet I could not identify it with anything explicable. The glaring light which lit the room was unbearable, and for many it was the last sight of daylight before entering the execution room. The major impact this place had on me was that even the most negative thought could not describe the coldness of this place.

Understanding Words

Briefly define the following words as they are used in the above paragraph.

1. concentration camp   *a place of confinement for those considered dangerous to the regime, as in Nazi Germany*

2. regime   *a system of government or rule*

3. pondered   *thought*

4. explicable   *understandable*

Questions on Content

1. When was this concentration camp used?

2. What does the author compare this place to?

3. What was the overall feeling the author experienced at this place?

Questions on Form

1. Which senses does the author use?

2. What makes the topic sentence effective?

3. State the concluding sentence.

Fort Leonard Wood

Terry M. Donaldson, *student*

The first view of Fort Leonard Wood is very foreboding when seen from an incoming airplane. It appears to be a land decimated by war! The ground, pitted with craters, looks barren and lifeless. Scattered about the terrain are the remnants of the life it once held. The skeletal remains of a few trees stand like twisted spikes driven into the earth. Others lie rotting on the ground. All are victims of the constant volley of exploding shells. The solitary building has big holes in the walls, and a large part of the structure has been reduced to a pile of rubble. The burned-out shells of military vehicles are scattered about. A couple of dump trucks, a jeep, and farther off, what is left of an army tank are still there. The only movement is the parched sand blowing in the wind. Though only a grenade and ballistics firing range, this scene exposes the senseless devastation and vicious brutality of any war.

Understanding Words

Briefly define the following words as they are used in the above paragraph.

1. foreboding   *predicting something harmful*

2. decimated   *destroyed*

3. ballistics   *the science dealing with the motion of bullets*

Questions on Content

1. What is the author's first impression of Fort Leonard Wood?
2. What killed the trees?
3. What is the only movement?
4. What is the author actually describing?

Questions on Form

1. What makes the paragraph effective?
2. Why are the supporting details so effective?
3. What is effective about the closing sentence?

Munich

John Schulz, *student*

The most exciting city I have ever visited was Munich. There was always something going on. I think that they had a festival for just about everything. There were Maifests, Weinfests, and Oktoberfests, to name only a few. When they weren't going on, I had a lot of other sights to see, such as a castle, a palace, or a brewery. The majority of the places I visited stayed pretty crowded, but they still offered a lot of excitement. And if all else failed, I went shopping at the "Marktplatz," which consisted of a street that stretched for two or three miles and had stores, restaurants, and cafes. I plan on returning to Munich in the near future.

Questions on Content

1. Why did he enjoy Munich?
2. What did he do when all else failed?
3. How far did the Marktplatz stretch?

Questions on Form

1. Does the paragraph contain a topic sentence, support sentences, and a concluding sentence?
2. Is the topic sentence clear? In what way?

Professional Writing

An Eyewitness Account of the San Francisco Earthquake

Excerpt from an article in *Collier's* by **Jack London**

On Wednesday morning at a quarter past five came the earthquake. A minute later the flames were leaping upward. In a dozen different quarters south of Market Street, in the working-class ghetto, and in the factories, fires started. There was no opposing the flames. There was no organization, no communication. All the cunning adjustments of a twentieth-century city had been smashed by the earthquake. The streets were humped into ridges and depressions and piled with debris of fallen walls. The steel rails were twisted into perpendicular and horizontal angles. The telephone and telegraph systems were disrupted. And the great water mains had burst. All the shrewd contrivances and safeguards of man had been thrown out of gear by thirty seconds' twitching of the earth-crust.

Understanding Words
Briefly define the following words as they are used in the above paragraph.

1. ghetto   *part of a city where certain people are forced to live*
2. perpendicular   *at right angles to a given line*

3. shrewd   *clever*

4. contrivances   *devices or plans*

Questions on Content

1. What could be done about the earthquake?

2. What damage did the earthquake do?

3. At what time did the fire start?

Questions on Form

1. Do all the examples support the topic idea?

2. How is the topic idea stated?

3. Does the concluding sentence echo the topic idea?

Martin Luther King

Excerpt from *Martin Luther King* by **Rae Bains**

In Atlanta and other parts of the South, blacks were not treated the same as whites. For example, a white person who wanted to ride a bus simply got on, paid the fare, and took a seat. But a black person got on, paid the fare, got off again, walked to the rear door of the bus and got on there. Blacks could only sit in the back of the bus. If all the seats became filled, the blacks had to give up their seats to white people who got on.

Questions on Content

1. Where did blacks sit on a bus?

2. What did blacks do when the bus was full and a white person got on?

3. What part of the country is the author talking about?

Questions on Form

1. Does the idea of blacks sitting in the back support the topic sentence?

2. Where is the topic sentence stated?

3. How is the topic sentence supported?

Making a World of Difference

Excerpt from an article in the 1987 Spring/Summer issue of *Experienced Engineer*

Coming to terms with limited technology is one thing; acclimating to foreign living conditions and social customs is another. Though the Peace Corps makes sure its volunteers have adequate language and cultural training programs, there were a few cultural hurdles [Melissa] Lang had to overcome on her own—one of which was food. "The first week was really hard. It was the hot season, and I had serious doubts I could make it because I thought there's nothing I could eat. It was one tricky thing to face a dish of rice for breakfast. I lived with a family for the first few months, and there were many times I'd leave the breakfast table with my mouth burning." In retrospect, Lang found that the food was the easiest thing to get used to in Thailand.

Understanding Words
Briefly define the following words as they are used in the above paragraph.

1. acclimating   *getting used to a new climate or place*

2. retrospect   *a looking back or thinking about things past*

Questions on Content

1. What volunteer agency is mentioned in the paragraph?

2. What food does she remember eating?

3. What was the easiest thing to get used to in Thailand?

Questions on Form

1. Where is the topic sentence stated?

2. How does the example relate to the topic sentence?

3. Are the sentences in logical order?

Part 4

Grammar for Effective Writing: Basic Sentence Skills

Objectives

- Identify prepositional phrases to avoid confusing them with subjects.
- Identify subjects and verbs in sentences.
- Recognize sentence-structure errors.
- Maintain subject-verb agreement in sentences.
- Maintain consistent verb tense in paragraphs or essays.

Having a paragraph that focuses on one idea and stays with that one idea is the most important part of writing. Sometimes, however, the effectiveness of a paragraph is diminished because of simple grammatical errors that distract the reader from the ideas in the paragraph.

After writing your paragraph and making sure that all the information supports the topic sentence, you will need to do some editing. In this section, you can review parts of speech with special attention to prepositional phrases, subjects, and verbs. You will also be able to review basic sentence-structure errors. Emphasis is then placed on identifying subjects and verbs within a paragraph to make sure that they are both singular or both plural (subject-verb agreement). You will also practice checking the verbs in a paragraph to see if they are all in the present or all in the past (consistent verb tense).

However, before you can edit your paragraph for sentence-structure errors, subject-verb agreement, and consistent verb tense, you must be able to identify subjects and verbs in sentences. **Subjects** are words that function as nouns or pronouns; however, sometimes the nouns or pronouns in prepositional phrases are mistaken for the subject of a sentence. Because this is true and because prepositional phrases are easy to identify, you will find it easier to locate subjects if you identify prepositional phrases first. One of the most common problems students face in finding the subject of a sentence is to mistake the object of a preposition for the subject of the sentence.

Understanding Parts of Speech

Before you study subjects and verbs, a quick review of parts of speech may be useful. Sentences are made up of words, and each word in a sentence functions as a specific part of speech. The eight parts of speech follow:

nouns   adverbs

pronouns   prepositions

verbs   interjections

adjectives   conjunctions

Though not all sentences contain all eight parts of speech, being able to recognize these parts of speech can help you write effective papers and help you become a critical evaluator of your own work.

See ESL Appendix for more information on nouns.

Nouns

A noun is any word that names a person, place, or thing.

person   *person*   *thing* *place*
Jason Stevens became an **attorney** and practiced **law** in the **city.**

- **A noun can be common or proper.**

  Common nouns are general words and are capitalized only when they come at the beginning of a sentence.

  Proper nouns name particular people, places, or things. Proper nouns are always capitalized.

  proper   *common*
  Marie Williams is a wonderful **administrator.**

- **A noun can be concrete or abstract.**

  Concrete nouns refer to objects that can be visualized or touched. They can be either common or proper.

  Abstract nouns name a quality or idea. They are usually common nouns.

  concrete   *abstract*   *concrete*
  The college **student** felt that **success** meant driving a **Corvette.**

Pronouns

A pronoun is a word that takes the place of a noun. Using pronouns can keep you from repeating the same nouns over and over again.

  Katrina rode the giant rollercoaster three times. **It** roared down the steep dips and scared **her** as **it** hurtled around the curves.

- **Pronouns can be put into groups or categories.**

  personal

  possessive

  demonstrative

indefinite

interrogative

relative

intensive and reflexive

- **Personal pronouns are probably the most frequently used pronouns in English.**

Singular		Plural	
I	me	we	us
you	you	you	you
she	her	they	them
he	him		
it	it		

- **Possessive pronouns are also personal pronouns, but they show ownership. The personal possessive pronouns are shown in bold type.**

Singular			Plural		
I	me	**my, mine**	we	us	**our, ours**
you	you	**your, yours**	you	you	**your, yours**
she	her	**her, hers**	they	them	**their, theirs**
he	him	**his**			
it	it	**its**			

personal   *possessive*

She forgot to mail **our** letters.

- **Demonstrative pronouns point out persons, places, or things.**
  The most common demonstrative pronouns are **this, that, these,** and **those.** They may function as pronouns or as adjectives.

  This is the book I misplaced over ten years ago. (Pronoun)

  This book is the one I misplaced over ten years ago. (Adjective)

- **Indefinite pronouns, like demonstrative pronouns, point out persons, places, or things, but less clearly.**
  The most common indefinite pronouns are

all	each	few	none	several
another	either	many	one	some
both	everyone	neither	other	

  All feel that the pancake breakfast was a great success.

- **Interrogative pronouns are used when asking questions.**
  Interrogative pronouns include **who, whom, what, which,** and **whose.**

  Who will go with me to the celebration?

- **Relative pronouns function as connecting words.**
  Notice that some of the same words used as interrogative pronouns are also relative pronouns. Relative pronouns include **that, what, which, who, whom,** and **whose.**

My favorite puppy is the tiny one **that** I brought from Florida.

- **Intensive and reflexive pronouns are personal pronouns that end in** *-self* **or** *-selves.* Intensive pronouns refer to a noun or a pronoun to give emphasis. Reflexive pronouns refer to the subject. Common intensive and reflexive pronouns include **myself, yourself, himself, herself, itself, ourselves, yourselves, themselves.**

    I made the pizza **myself.** (*intensive*)

    I helped **myself** by studying more than usual. (*reflexive*)

Verbs

All sentences have a verb.

- **A verb can express action.**

    The wolf cubs **tumble** in the grass.

- **A verb can be a form of "be." (am, are, is, was, were, been, being)**

    The pale lavender orchid **is** superb.

- **The verb can show a "state of being."**

    The national park **seems** quiet and peaceful.

- **A verb can be more than one word.**

    Jerry **has been** a chef for over two years.

Adjectives

Adjectives are words that describe nouns and pronouns. Adjectives describe by answering "which one," "what kind," or "how many." The articles **a, an,** and **the** are adjectives. An adjective is usually found before the noun that it modifies; however, it may be located after this noun if a form of the verb **be** is used.

The **old** woman made **scrumptious Mexican** food.

The **old** woman's **Mexican** food was **scrumptious.**

Adverbs

An adverb is a word that describes or modifies a verb, an adjective, or another adverb. It answers "when," "where," "how," or "how much."

The young man serenaded his girlfriend **beautifully.** (Modifies verb)

The **extremely** tasteful music brought back old memories. (Modifies adjective)

Older people often drive **very** slowly. (Modifies another adverb)

Prepositions

A preposition is a word used with a noun or pronoun to form a phrase that shows location, time, ownership/identification, or exclusion. See pages 62–66 for further explanation.

During 1998, cold air **from** Alaska and warm air **from** El Niño combined and caused heavy storms **in** many states.

Note   At times, a preposition is used alone at the end of a sentence, but it should add meaning to the sentence.

  Acceptable: What do you want me to put the salad **in**?

 Unnecessary: Where do you live **at**?

  Less wordy: Where do you live?

Conjunctions

A conjunction joins items in a sentence. You will use coordinating conjunctions, subordinating conjunctions, and conjunctive adverbs.

- **Coordinating conjunctions join words, phrases, or sentences that are equal.**
  These joining words are

for	but
and	or
nor	yet
	so

  The game is over, **so** we will celebrate.

Note   The first letters of the coordinating conjunctions spell "fan boys."

- **Subordinating conjunctions join two sentences by making one sentence dependent on the other sentence for meaning.**
  The commonly used subordinators can be found on page 167.

  When the game is over, we will celebrate.

- **Conjunctive adverbs join two sentences together.**
  A list of commonly used conjunctive adverbs can be found on page 172.

  The game is over; **therefore,** we will celebrate.

Interjections

An interjection is an exclamatory word that shows strong feeling. These words are sometimes used alone and sometimes used in a sentence although they are always grammatically independent from the rest of the sentence. Some words often used as interjections are

awesome	wow	fantastic
help	hooray	fine

   Placed alone: **Fantastic!** Now let's close the deal.

 Placed with sentence: **Hooray,** we won the election!

Determining Parts of Speech

The way a word is used determines the part of speech it is. Some words, such as "of" and "gratitude," can be only one part of speech. However, other words, such as "down," can be used as five different parts of speech. Read the following sentences, paying attention to the way "down" is used in each one. How it is used determines what part of speech it is.

Preposition

The children tumbled **down** the hill.

Verb

Harold could **down** a pie at one meal.

Adjective

The **down** but not out Atlanta Braves rallied and won the game.

Noun

The team seemed to make a first **down** every time they had the ball.

The comforter contained goose **down.**

Adverb

The doctor struggled to get the child's temperature **down.**

Finding Prepositional Phrases

Generally, prepositional phrases begin with a preposition and end with a noun or pronoun. The noun or pronoun that ends the phrase is called the **object** of the preposition and can never be the subject of a sentence. The object of a preposition can be identified by asking a question consisting of the preposition and "what":

prep.   obj.
by the rider   (by what?)

prep.   obj.
with careful training   (with what?)

prep. obj.
into water   (into what?)

prep.   obj.
to the other   (to what?)

- **A prepositional phrase may show location.**

    The mother bird quickly hopped *from one baby to the other.*

    ("From one baby" and "to the other" show the location of the mother.)

- **A prepositional phrase may show exclusion.**

The baby birds had nothing on their minds *except food.*

("Except food" shows what was excluded.)

- **A prepositional phrase may show ownership or identification.**

  This spring a mother sparrow *with her two young sparrows* ventured forth.

  ("With her two young sparrows" explains that the young sparrows belong to the mother.)

- **A prepositional phrase may show time.**

  The mother sparrow and her babies ventured out *in the early morning.*

  ("In the early morning" tells when they ventured out.)

- **A prepositional phrase may have more than one object.**

  The mother sparrow and her babies searched *for food and water.*

The best way to identify a prepositional phrase is to look for a pattern that always includes the preposition and its object. It also includes any word(s) that come between the preposition and its object.

prep.   obj. (noun)
in high esteem

prep.   obj. (pronoun)
by no one

prep.   obj. (noun)
of the young boys

prep.   obj. (pronoun)
to the pretty one

prep.   obj. (noun) obj. (noun)
for his bow and arrow

Now, refer to the following list of prepositions until they become easy to recognize.

Prepositions

aboard	around	between
about	as	beyond
above	at	but
according to	because of	by
across	before	concerning
after	behind	down
against	below	during
along	beneath	except
along with	beside	for
among	besides	from

in	onto	toward
inside	out	under
into	out of	underneath
like	outside	until
near	over	unto
of	since	up
off	through	with
on	throughout	within
on account of	to	without

Note Some writers consider "in addition to," "in favor of," and "in spite of" to be single prepositions.

Study the following paragraph and notice the prepositional phrases. The preposition is printed in bold italic type, and the rest of the prepositional phrase is in italics.

Many nineteenth-century Native Americans were expert horse trainers. ***After*** *a wild horse catch*, trainers often could tame a horse ***in*** *one day*. They wrapped the lasso ***around*** *the horse's nose* and guided the horse ***into*** *water*. There one ***of*** *the young boys* mounted it. The horse, of course, began bucking, but after getting its head ***under*** *water* a few times, soon quit. Native Americans ***from*** *some tribes* also trained special horses ***for*** *the buffalo hunt*. ***With*** *careful training*, these horses could be guided ***to*** *the left or right* ***by*** *the rider* who applied pressure ***with*** *his knees*. As a result, the hunter had both hands free ***for*** *his bow and arrow* and could shoot the buffalo ***with*** *ease*. Other horses were trained as war horses and were ridden ***by*** *no one* ***except*** *the trainer*. Sometimes these horses were so well trained that ***during*** *battle* they would strike the enemy ***with*** *their hooves*. Consequently, Native Americans held their horses ***in*** *high esteem*.

To check your ability to identify prepositional phrases, work through the following exercises. In the first exercise, the sentences are isolated so that you can identify the prepositional phrases more easily. In the second exercise, paragraphs are used to help you see how prepositional phrases are a natural part of writing.

Exercise 1

Strike through the prepositional phrases in the following sentences.

Example:
Baskets ~~of all shapes and sizes~~ covered the shelves.

1. ~~Without thinking~~, the man spent his entire paycheck ~~in one night~~.

2. The associate ~~behind the desk~~ is looking ~~through the newspaper~~ ~~for another job~~.

3. Most ~~of Sara's creative ideas~~ occur ~~in the evening~~.

4. Flight attendants constantly check ~~for potential problems~~ and offer extra comforts ~~to their customers~~.

5. ~~After lunch,~~ we went ~~to the lab~~ and worked ~~on our project~~.

6. ~~For two weeks,~~ they stayed ~~in a tent~~ ~~near the Rocky Mountains~~.

7. All ~~of my cousins~~ ~~except Rene~~ decided to go ~~to the park~~.

8. The fire alarm sounded ~~throughout the campus~~.

9. ~~In spite of the snow,~~ they drove their jeep ~~to the airport~~.

10. The baseball game ended early ~~because of the rain~~.

11. The ingredients ~~for the cake~~ should be ~~at room temperature~~.

12. The redwood trees ~~near the cabin~~ provide homes ~~for many insects, birds, and animals~~.

13. I take desserts ~~like chocolate cake~~ ~~to my friend~~ ~~in the retirement center~~.

14. The Florida Everglades support a wide variety ~~of beautiful birds~~.

15. Seven inches ~~of new snow~~ fell ~~on the ski run~~ ~~during the night~~.

16. The fish ~~in the lake~~ were biting ~~beyond our expectations~~.

17. We floated ~~down the Salt River~~ ~~on an inner tube~~.

18. I bought two bird feeders ~~like this one~~.

19. The message ~~inside the fortune cookie~~ promised good luck ~~for seven years~~.

20. The information ~~concerning graduation~~ can be found ~~at the first desk~~ ~~inside the administration building~~.

Exercise 2

Strike through the prepositional phrases in the following paragraphs.

Paragraph 1

Parenting requires major commitments ~~for young couples~~. They must take the responsibility ~~for someone besides themselves~~. Staying ~~at home~~ to care ~~for a new infant~~ twenty-four hours a day demands love and dedication. Parents often spend their money ~~on the child's needs~~ rather than ~~on their own needs~~. They frequently must function ~~on less sleep~~ and be prepared to get up several times each night to feed, change, and comfort a small one. This commitment continues ~~for many years~~.

Paragraph 2

Today's students have many obligations. ~~In addition to classes,~~ many must work while they attend college. They must juggle their schedules, alternating ~~between work, classes, and homework~~. Many work ~~on campus~~, but they still must arrange classes ~~without conflicts~~ ~~with their work hours~~. Students ~~with children~~

must consider time ~~for their kids~~. ~~In spite of a heavy schedule~~, these students still give love and attention ~~to their children~~. Doctor visits and illnesses are not anticipated but must be worked ~~into the schedule~~. Some students take advantage ~~of every moment~~ and finish each day ~~without even one wasted minute~~. Though the lifestyles ~~of students~~ can be complicated, success is just a degree away ~~for determined individuals~~.

Finding Subjects and Verbs

As you gain skill at finding prepositional phrases, it becomes easier to identify subjects and verbs. Learning to edit for certain grammar problems is usually easier if you are able to identify subjects and verbs.

Subjects

A **subject** is the word that answers "who" or "what" to the main verb in the sentence. Some sentences have a simple subject, and other sentences have a compound subject. *Only* a word that functions as a noun or a pronoun (except the noun or pronoun in a prepositional phrase) may be the subject of a sentence.

- **A simple subject is a word that functions as a noun or pronoun and is what the sentence is about.**

  Here are two sentences in which a noun is the subject:

  Ron gave me a great idea. (Who gave me a great idea?)

  The **flowers** in the vase fell on the floor. (What fell on the floor?)

  Here are two sentences in which a pronoun is the subject:

  He gave me a great idea. (Who gave me a great idea?)

  Others were planted yesterday. (What was planted yesterday?)

- **A compound subject is two or more words that identify who or what the sentence is about.**

  Trisha and **Sam** are late. (Who are late?)

  Ron and **Carrie** gave me a great surprise. (Who gave me a great surprise?)

- **All sentences *must* have a main subject and a verb. However, when a command is used, the subject is understood to be *"you."***

v	*s* *v*
Close the door.	(You) close the door.

v	*s* *v*
Water the plants.	(You) water the plants.

v *v*	*s* *v* *v*
Come in and sit down.	(You) come in and sit down.

  "Here" and "there" can never be the subject of a sentence.

Here are the books.

There are five children in the van.

Study the following paragraph. The subjects have been underlined once; prepositions are in bold italic type and the rest of the prepositional phrases are in italics. Notice how much easier it is to identify the subject(s) of a sentence once the prepositional phrases have been identified.

Many nineteenth-century Native Americans were expert horse trainers. *After a wild horse catch,* trainers often were able to tame a horse *in one day.* They wrapped the lasso *around the horse's nose* and guided the horse *into water.* There one *of the young boys* mounted it. The horse, of course, began bucking, but after getting its head *under water* a few times, soon quit. Native Americans *from some tribes* also trained special horses *for the buffalo hunt.* *With careful training,* these horses could be guided *to the left or right by the rider* who applied pressure *with his knees.* As a result, the hunter had both hands free *for his bow and arrow* and could shoot the buffalo *with ease.* Other horses were trained *as war horses* and were ridden *by no one except the trainer.* Sometimes these horses were so well trained that *during battle* they would strike the enemy *with their hooves.* Consequently, Native Americans held their horses *in high esteem.*

To check your ability to identify subjects and prepositional phrases, do the following exercises. In the first exercise, the sentences are isolated so that you can identify the prepositional phrases more easily. Then paragraphs are used for further practice.

Exercise 3

In each sentence, strike through all prepositional phrases. Then underline the subject(s) once. Some sentences will have simple subjects, and others will have compound subjects.

Example:
Women, children, and men ~~of all ages~~ **enjoy holidays.**

1. There are no seats left ~~for the next basketball game~~.

2. Sondra pulled her car ~~into the garage~~, ran ~~into the house~~, and gave me a hug.

3. ~~After breakfast,~~ we jogged ~~around the lake~~.

4. Andri parked his car ~~across the street~~ ~~from the theater~~.

5. Many colleges provide fitness centers and recreational areas ~~for their students~~.

6. The English bulldog and the Siamese cat are playing together.

7. The assistants ~~in the geology lab~~ brought their lunches ~~to work~~.

8. ~~In the first quarter,~~ the rookie hit seven ~~of eight baskets~~.

9. ~~During the movie~~, the <u>father</u> and his <u>children</u> ate popcorn and drank pop.

10. Here are the <u>instructions</u> ~~for your next math assignment~~.

11. The <u>tomatoes</u>, <u>cucumbers</u>, and <u>lettuce</u> rotted ~~in the refrigerator~~.

You 12. Please leave your shoes ~~by the door~~.

13. ~~In spite of the fog~~, <u>we</u> drove the scenic route ~~around the glacier~~.

14. <u>Two</u> ~~of my friends~~ left ~~for vacation~~ ~~at the same time~~.

15. ~~In Colorado~~, the ski <u>resorts</u> ~~at Aspen and Vail~~ provide skiers ~~with many wide, groomed trails~~.

16. <u>Everyone</u> ~~in my house~~ got up ~~at 6:00 a.m.~~ and worked ~~in the yard~~ ~~until noon~~.

17. ~~After supper~~, the band <u>members</u> met ~~for two hours of practice~~.

18. <u>Everyone</u> ~~in my family~~ ~~except Phil~~ went ~~on the boat ride~~.

You 19. Please close the door.

20. ~~On international flights~~, <u>passengers</u> can meet people ~~with very interesting backgrounds~~.

Exercise 4

Strike through the prepositional phrases in the following paragraphs. Underline the subject of each sentence.

Paragraph 1

    <u>Mr. Socks</u>, Anne's cat, was an ideal visitor ~~at my home~~. <u>He</u> arrived ~~on a Monday night~~ and immediately found his favorite spot, ~~underneath my bed~~, ~~inside the box springs~~. Gradually ~~over the next couple of days~~, <u>he</u> emerged and walked ~~through the house~~, inspecting everything. <u>He</u> entertained himself playing ~~with a ping-pong ball and a thick black shoelace~~. Sometimes <u>he</u> walked ~~to his scratching post~~ and forcefully sharpened his claws, but <u>he</u> never clawed ~~at anything else~~. ~~After a few days~~, <u>Mr. Socks</u> napped ~~on top of my bed~~. One day my <u>dog</u> walked ~~into the room~~, and <u>Mr. Socks</u> jumped ~~to the floor~~, rubbed ~~against her fur~~, and began a friendship. <u>They</u> slept ~~in the same room~~, drank ~~from the same water dispenser~~, and ignored each other's food dishes. ~~After a couple of days~~, <u>Mr. Socks</u> progressed ~~to my lap~~. <u>I</u> scratched his ears, and <u>he</u> responded ~~with steady purring~~. This first <u>visit</u> ~~to my house~~ lasted ~~for a short period of time~~, but <u>it</u> was certainly pleasant and free ~~from stress~~.

Paragraph 2

    In the summer, <u>libraries</u> have many activities ~~for children~~. <u>Many</u> offer movie schedules ~~with educational, nonviolent classics~~. ~~Because of donations from public and private organizations~~, reading <u>programs</u> ~~with award prizes~~ can motivate young readers. ~~For excitement~~, <u>children</u> can set goals and meet them. ~~In most cases,~~

everyone is a winner. ~~During many hot days~~, happy <u>children</u> are found browsing ~~through books~~, looking ~~at special displays~~, watching fish ~~in the library aquarium~~, or searching the Internet ~~for current information~~. Cool, quiet learning <u>environments</u> ~~in a library~~ can be appealing ~~to children~~.

Verbs

A **verb** is what the subject of the sentence does. The verb may show action—"run" or "hit"; it may be a form of *be*—"is" or "am"; or it may be a state of being—"appears" or "sounds."

Action: Ralph **ran** through the woods.

Sara **hit** the car broadside.

Nonaction: form of *be*

Ralph **is** in the woods.

Sara **was** in her car.

state of being

Ralph **appears** cool and strong.

Sara **sounds** confident and impressive.

The iced tea **tastes** good.

- **The verb may consist of one word or several words.**

The simple verb is one action verb or nonaction verb that tells what the subject does. The simple verb may be this one action or nonaction word alone or may be combined with a helping verb.

Here are some helping verbs:

be (*all forms*)	does	might
can	had	shall
could	has	should
did	have	will
do	may	would

Action: Todd **blew** his horn. (action verb)

Todd **did blow** his horn. (helping verb + action verb)

Nonaction: form of *be*

Todd **is** a good brother. (nonaction verb)

Todd **has been** a good brother. (helping verb + nonaction verb)

state of being

Todd **appears** happy. (nonaction verb)

Todd **does appear** happy. (helping verb + nonaction verb)

Sometimes forms of *do (do, does, did)* and *have (have, has, had)* are the main verb in a sentence; other times these forms are used with another main verb to form the simple verb.

Main verb: Todd **did** his homework.

Helping verb: Todd **did finish** his homework.

- **Compound verbs** are two or more verbs that tell what the subject does.

> The man **looked** down and **found** a diamond ring.

> The camel **ate** the apple and then **snorted.**

The following paragraph can help you understand how subjects, verbs, and prepositional phrases appear in writing. In the paragraph below, which you studied earlier, the verbs are underlined twice, the subjects are underlined once, and the prepositional phrases are in italics.

> Many nineteenth-century Native Americans were expert horse trainers. *After a wild horse catch*, trainers often could break a horse *in one day*. They wrapped the lasso rope *around the horse's nose* and guided the horse *into water*. There one *of the young boys* mounted it. The horse, of course, began bucking, but after getting its head *under water* a few times, soon quit. Native Americans also trained special horses *for the buffalo hunt. With careful training*, these horses could be guided *to the left or right by the rider*, who applied pressure *with his knees*. As a result, the hunter had both hands free *for his bow and arrow* and shot the buffalo *with ease*. Other horses were trained as war horses. These horses were also well trained. Sometimes they would even strike the enemy *with their hooves*. Consequently, Native Americans held their horses *in high esteem*.

Recognizing Sentence-Structure Errors

Learning to identify subjects and verbs in a sentence is a skill that can help you edit your writing. For example, you can find and revise sentence problems so that your ideas are expressed in clear and complete sentences. Examine three sentence-structure errors: sentence fragments, comma splices, and run-on sentences.

Sentence Fragments

To be complete, a sentence needs a subject and a main verb that together form a completed idea. If one or more of these parts are missing, then the sentence is a **fragment.** Consider the following example of a complete sentence:

> People with loyalty to their country voted.

However, if you left out the verb, you would not have a complete sentence:

> People with loyalty to their country.

Leaving out "voted" makes the idea a **fragment.** Your readers might get some meaning out of the fragment, but they would not know the completed thought you wanted to express.

Likewise, if you left out the subject, "people," you would again have a fragment instead of a complete sentence:

> With loyalty to their country voted.

Here are other examples of incomplete thoughts that do not work as sentences because one or more parts are missing:

> Being honest and being loyal to each other.

> Without these qualities for a friendship.

To make complete sentences out of these fragments, you must revise them so that each one has a subject and a verb and, therefore, is a completed thought.

> Being honest and being loyal to each other are necessary for two people to be close friends.

> Without these qualities for a friendship, two people might not ever be close friends.

> Here is another kind of sentence fragment that needs to be revised:

> When we first met in high school.

> People who are loyal to their country.

"When we first met in high school" may sound all right because it has a subject and a verb, but the idea is still a fragment because "when" leaves the thought incomplete. The reader expects an explanation of what happened "When we first met in high school." Revised and completed, the thought might sound like this:

> When we first met in high school, we did not think of each other as friends.

In the second sentence, "who" makes the sentence a fragment because the reader hasn't been told what happens when "people are loyal to their country." The completed thought could sound like this:

> People who are loyal to their country probably vote.

Note This is a quick discussion of sentence fragments. Unit 3 provides more detailed help, including exercises.

You may have two other kinds of sentence problems that need to be eliminated: comma splices and run-on sentences.

Comma Splices

Comma splices are two complete sentences with just a comma to mark the end of one sentence and the beginning of the next.

> The speed skater raced across the frozen lake, he ignored the thin ice.

Revised to show where the first sentence ends and the next one begins, the separated sentences would look like one of these:

> The speed skater raced across the frozen lake. He ignored the thin ice.

> The speed skater raced across the frozen lake, and he ignored the thin ice.

Note Unit 3 provides additional help and exercises to eliminate comma splices.

Run-On Sentences

Run-on sentences are two or more complete ideas with no punctuation or connecting words to mark the end of one sentence and the beginning of the next one.

> The speed skater raced across the frozen lake he ignored the thin ice.

To eliminate the confusion of two ideas run together, you could mark the end of the first sentence with a comma and a connecting word, or you could use a period and start the new sentence with a capital letter. You may also use a semicolon to solve the problem.

The speed skater raced across the frozen lake, and he ignored the thin ice.

The speed skater raced across the frozen lake. He ignored the thin ice.

The speed skater raced across the frozen lake; he ignored the thin ice.

Note   Unit 3 provides additional help and exercises to eliminate run-on sentences.

These three kinds of sentence problems will confuse your reader. Sometimes they are hard to find in your own writing, but reading aloud or getting some feedback from another reader will help you identify and eliminate these confusing sentence-structure errors.

Tests covering subject-verb agreement are on pages 18–21 in the Test Bank.

See ESL Appendix for additional information.

Maintaining Subject-Verb Agreement

In addition to revising to eliminate sentence-structure problems, you will need to check for subject-verb agreement errors. The subject and the verb in a sentence must agree in number. In other words, they must both be singular (one) or must both be plural (more than one). For example, consider the following sentences:

  s   v
The dog likes to play in the sprinkler.

  s   v
The dogs like to play in the sprinkler.

In the first sentence, "dog" (which is singular) agrees with "likes" (which is also singular). In the second sentence, "dogs" (which is plural) agrees with "like" (which is also plural).

Forming Plural Nouns

Most nouns are made plural by adding an -s.

Singular	Plural
dog	dogs
book	books
car	cars
rock	rocks
plate	plates

A few nouns are made plural in other ways.

Singular	Plural
box	boxes
child	children
mouse	mice

foot	feet
man	men
woman	women
tooth	teeth
ox	oxen

A few nouns have the same form for both singular and plural.

Singular	Plural
deer	deer
moose	moose
sheep	sheep

When in doubt about how to make a word plural, check your dictionary.

Forming Plural Verbs

Adding -s to a noun makes it plural; however, adding -s to a verb makes it singular. Singular verbs should be used when the subject is a singular noun or one of the pronouns *she, he,* or *it.*

Incorrect: The book seem interesting.

Correct: The books seem interesting.

Correct: The book seems interesting.

Correct: It seems interesting.

Exercise 5

In each sentence, strike through the prepositional phrases. Then underline the subject once, and fill in the blank with the verb that agrees in number with the subject.

Example:
The lions ~~at the zoo~~ ___*sleep*___ peacefully. (sleep, sleeps).

1. The automobile mechanics must ___*explain*___ their bills ~~to their customers~~. (explain, explains)

2. The bread baking ~~in the oven~~ ___*fills*___ the house ~~with a delicious aroma~~. (fill, fills)

3. One ~~in ten drivers~~ ___*suffers*___ ~~from fatigue~~. (suffer, suffers)

4. The snow-covered branches ~~on the tree~~ ___*look*___ beautiful. (look, looks)

5. All links ~~on the website~~ ___*are*___ updated ~~by the students~~. (are, is)

6. The trainers of the Clydesdale horses ___*have*___ many responsibilities. (have, has)

7. The elementary school teacher ___*rewards*___ students with gold stickers. (reward, rewards)

8. Cell phones sometimes ___*ring*___ during the symphony. (ring, rings)

9. The President of the United States ___*arrives*___ at 6:00 tonight. (arrive, arrives)

10. One of my cars ___*breaks*___ down during every snowstorm. (break, breaks)

11. The ice on the roads ___*makes*___ driving on the highway dangerous. (make, makes)

12. The leader of the group project ___*helps*___ the team stay organized. (help, helps)

13. The owner of the Honda Accord often ___*leaves*___ his keys in the car. (leave, leaves)

14. One step in gardening ___*involves*___ buying plants at the nursery. (involve, involves)

15. The student fine arts magazine often ___*receives*___ many awards. (receive, receives)

Exercise 6

Strike through all prepositional phrases. Underline the subject once and the verb twice. Then change both the subject and the verb from singular to plural form.

Example:

geese   *bring*
The goose with golden feathers brings him fortune.

sheep   enjoys
1. The bighorn sheep enjoy climbing the mountain.

sounds   help
2. The steady sound of falling rain helps me sleep.

workers   listen
3. The worker on the roof listens to the radio.

boxes   weigh
4. The box on the picnic table weighs ten pounds.

women   their   dogs walk
5. The blind woman with her guide dog walks confidently down the street.

daughters   eat
6. My daughter seldom eats lunch in the school cafeteria.

windows   are
7. The stained-glass window in that old chapel is beautiful.

deer   are
8. The deer at the zoo is very tame.

Mice live
9. A mouse lives in the basement of the abandoned building.

statues   *weather*
10. The statue ~~at the east side of the park~~ weathers gradually.
       ───────   ════════

       answers   *surprise*
11. His answer ~~on the math test on fractions~~ surprises me.
       ──────   ════════

       Pairs   *need*
12. A pair ~~of scissors~~ needs to be sharpened.
       ────   ═════

       churches   need
13. The church needs new paint and landscaping.
       ──────   ═════

       grades   *reflect*
14. The grade ~~on his essay~~ reflects his careful revision.
       ─────   ═══════

       children   remember
15. The child remembers last summer's trip ~~to Alaska~~.
       ─────   ════════

Checking for Subject-Verb Agreement

1. Identify all prepositional phrases; place them in parentheses.

2. Identify the subject and verb of each sentence; underline the subject once and the verb twice.

3. Check whether the verb agrees in number with its subject.

4. If not, change the verb to agree in number with the subject.

Exercise 7

Strike through each prepositional phrase. Underline each subject once and verb twice. Then, if necessary, correct the verb to agree in number with the subject. Write "C" to the left of the number if there is no error.

Example:

Raspberry bushes ~~in the wild~~ produce a new crop ~~of berries~~ each year.
          ────────   ═══════

          provide
1. The trees ~~by Big Lake~~ provides shade ~~for the campground~~.
       ─────   ════════

C 2. The coyotes help ~~with the balance of nature~~.
          ────── ════

          are
3. Blue herons is abundant ~~on the lakes of northern Colorado~~.
       ────── ══

                              cause
4. The people ~~in the cabin~~ causes no alarm ~~to the young skunks~~.
       ─────   ═════

          prune
5. My neighbors prunes their rose bushes every February.
       ──────── ═════

C 6. A ranch ~~in the mountains~~ boards horses.
          ─────   ══════

                      sits
7. The well-dressed old man sit ~~on the park bench by the fountain~~.
                        ─── ═══

cause
8. Frequently, <u>mudslides</u> <u><u>causes</u></u> more damage ~~after wildfires~~.

pitch
9. We often <u>pitches</u> our tent ~~among the Ponderosa pine trees~~.

leave
10. ~~In the winter~~, snow <u>skiers</u> <u><u>leaves</u></u> tracks ~~down the slope~~.

keep
11. The wild <u>cats</u> ~~at the farm~~ <u><u>keeps</u></u> the mouse population ~~under control~~.

have
12. The peach <u>trees</u> lining the street <u><u>has</u></u> fragrant flowers.

cause
13. Speeding <u>drivers</u> <u><u>causes</u></u> roll-over accidents ~~at intersections~~.

drink
14. <u>Hummingbirds</u> ~~with their long beaks~~ <u><u>drinks</u></u> ~~from feeders~~ suspended ~~from tree branches~~.

walk
15. The <u>turtles</u> <u>walks</u> freely ~~through Golden Gate Park~~.

Recognizing Singular and Plural Pronouns

Because a pronoun can be the subject of a sentence, it is helpful to know which pronouns are singular, which are plural, and which can be either singular or plural.

- **Some indefinite pronouns are always singular even though we often think of them as plural.**

anybody	everybody	no one
anyone	everyone	nothing
anything	everything	somebody
each	neither	someone
each one	nobody	something
either		

s   v v
Everything is working out quite well.

s   v
No one wants to work late.

v s
There is something on the table for you.

- **When "each," "every," or "any" modifies the subject, the verb is singular.**

n   v v
Each person is asked to contribute to the United Way.

n   *v*

Any carpenter knows the answer.

- **Some pronouns are always plural.**

  few

  many

  s   *v*

  A few of my friends are happy about the decision.

  s   *v*

  Many are willing to work.

- **Some pronouns may be singular or plural.**

  When one of these pronouns is the subject of a sentence and is immediately followed by a prepositional phrase, the verb agrees in number with the object in the prepositional phrase.

all	half	more
any	most	some

  s   *v*

  Some of the books are very old.

  s   *v*

  Some of the candy is on the table.

  s   *v* *v*

  Most of my homework is finished.

  s   *v*

  Most of the boys live in the dorm.

  s   *v* *v*

  All of the work is completed.

  s   *v* *v*

  All of the assignments are completed.

  s   *v* *v*

  More of the pie was eaten.

  s   *v* *v*

  More of the cookies were eaten.

  Noun: name of a person, place, or thing

  Pronoun: word that takes the place of a noun

  Verb: word that tells what the subject of a sentence does

  Subject: word that answers who or what to the main verb in the sentence

Exercise 8

In each sentence, strike through the prepositional phrases. Then underline the subject once, and fill in the blank with the verb that agrees in number with the subject.

Example:

Everyone ~~at the park~~ _endures_ the hot, humid weather. (endure, endures)

1. After graduation, most ~~of the students~~ _find_ challenging jobs. (find, finds)

2. All ~~of the honeysuckle vines in the backyard~~ _provide_ nectar ~~for the bees~~. (provide, provides)

3. All ~~of the tennis players~~ _wear_ comfortable clothes. (wear, wears)

4. More ~~of the inmates~~ _learn_ life skills ~~for living in the outside world~~. (learn, learns)

5. ~~After a touchdown~~ somebody ~~in the crowd~~ always _yells_ , "Go ~~for two~~!" (yell, yells)

6. Nothing _makes_ a team happier than winning. (make, makes)

7. Some ~~of the melons~~ _are_ too expensive ~~for my family~~. (is, are)

8. Dozens ~~of shooting stars~~ _streak_ ~~through the northern sky~~. (streak, streaks)

9. Each play _makes_ a difference ~~in the outcome of the game~~. (make, makes)

10. Everybody ~~in the small town~~ _comes_ ~~to the fireworks display~~. (come, comes).

11. The gray wolf _slides_ ~~under the electric fence~~. (slide, slides)

12. Most ~~of the teachers~~ _work_ many hours ~~beyond accountability~~ each day. (work, works)

13. More ~~of the fish in the pond~~ _die_ ~~during the winter~~. (die, dies)

14. Some ~~of the professional ball players~~ actually _feel_ underpaid. (feel, feels)

15. Thousands ~~of bats~~ _swarm_ ~~from the cave at dusk~~. (swarm, swarms)

16. ~~Without hesitation~~, a few players _come_ early ~~for practice~~. (come, comes)

17. ~~According to the coach~~, there _is_ something special ~~about this year's team~~. (are, is)

18. Each one ~~of the hotels~~ _offers_ special room rates ~~in the spring~~. (offer, offers)

19. Few ~~of the children~~ _like_ school ~~without recess~~. (like, likes)

20. People _enjoy_ baseball whether ~~at the ballpark~~ or ~~at home in front of the television set~~. (enjoy, enjoys)

Strike through all prepositional phrases. Underline each subject once. Then find the verb in each sentence, and, if necessary, correct it to agree in number with the subject. Write "C" to the left of the number if there is no error.

Example:

is

Each person ~~on the fishing boat~~ **are guaranteed one fish.**

likes
1. Everybody like time ~~for relaxation and reflection~~.

has
2. Nobody have any complaints ~~about the food~~.

close
3. Some ~~of the vendors~~ closes their booths early.

learn
4. Many young boys and girls learns computer skills easily.

survives
5. Nothing ~~below the dam~~ survive a major flood.

need
6. Young people needs to plan early ~~for retirement~~.

are
7. Children ~~in the pool~~ is supervised ~~by lifeguards~~.

leaves
8. Almost everyone leave ~~before the end of the game~~.

C 9. All ~~of my class projects~~ take hours ~~of hard work~~.

is
10. All ~~of the medicine~~ are covered ~~by insurance~~.

has
11. Each ~~of the committee members~~ have time ~~for an afternoon meeting~~.

stick
12. A few ~~of the blueberry muffins~~ sticks ~~to the pan~~.

love
13. Most ~~of my friends~~ loves shopping ~~at the factory outlet stores~~.

C 14. Others spend Saturday working ~~in the yard~~.

love
15. ~~Without a doubt~~, most of my dogs loves to go ~~for walks in the evenings~~.

needs
16. Everything ~~in the newspaper~~ need careful editing.

are
17. All ~~of my friends~~ is going ~~to the museum with their families~~.

18. Everyone ~~in the neighborhood~~ help *helps* each other.

19. Any diversion ~~from routine activities~~ are *is* refreshing.

20. Half ~~of the employees~~ receives *receive* overtime pay.

Exercise 10

Edit the following paragraphs for subject-verb agreement. Underline the subject(s) in each sentence once and the verb(s) twice. Then find any incorrect verb forms and correct them to agree in number with the subject.

Paragraph 1

The people in the jury assembly room reports *report* for jury duty in clothing that they ordinarily wears *wear* to work. Several looks *look* like students or service workers. They wears *wear* casual dresses or sport shirts and jeans. Some in work uniforms appears *appear* to be truck drivers or repair people. A large number of professional men and women sits *sit* in more formal suits. One gentleman apparently does not know the dress code for jurors, and he walk *walks* around in shorts and a bright blue T-shirt. This scene is a good example of the variety of people on juries.

Paragraph 2

As Vincent grows up, he explores many personal interests. His first experience include *includes* the care of gerbils that he sell *sells* for pets. This hobby proves unsatisfying, so with his gerbil money, he buy *buys* a Sheltie puppy and take *takes* her to obedience classes. Soon, he takes her to dog shows and enter *enters* the competitive world of obedience and conformation. Before long, he joins a specialty dog club, and he become *becomes* editor of their newsletter. At the shows, he watches as the photographers take pictures of the champion dogs, and Vincent decide *decides* he can learn the art of photography. At the same time, his love of dogs keep *keeps* him reading many articles about dogs, including medical materials, so he considers a career in veterinary medicine. He also

volunteers
volunteer at Phoenix Baptist Hospital and *experiences* the excitement of watching
several surgeries. Perhaps, exploration of these interests may some day help him to
decide on a career.

Paragraph 3

Kenting Park is at the southernmost part of Taiwan. It is surrounded by a beach

are
and high cliffs. Luxurious, high-priced hotels is available for those able to afford

are *look*
approximately $200 a day. When people is tired of playing on the beach, they looks

through little shops for seashells, costume jewelry, hats, and other tourist trinkets.

has
The park north of the beach have exotic tropical plants. For example, a 300-year-old

illustrates
bonsai-like tree with old, exposed roots illustrate the coastal park's antiquity. In

addition, a small cave with a stalactite forming an imaginative, fossil-like figure

brings *offers*
bring relief from the sun and offer the passing tourists a peaceful rest. Kenting Park

has many attractions for visitors.

Paragraph 4

Early Native Americans used the buffalo wisely. They ate the meat fresh or

were
dried it in strips to use throughout the year. Some of the dried strips was eaten the

were
way they were, and other times they was ground into powder to be cooked. When the

were
meat was scraped off the bones, the large bones was used for tools. Likewise, a few

were *were*
of the small bones was made into needles. The skins of the buffalo was used for

was
warm clothing, rugs, or coverings for their homes. Some history of the tribe were

written on the dried buffalo skins. Even the sinews were saved to be used as thread,

and the Native Americans even boiled the hooves to make glue. Very little of the

buffalo was wasted.

Tests covering consistent verb tense are on pages 22–25 in the Test Bank.

Maintaining Consistent Verb Tense

Another important skill you can master once you can identify subjects and verbs is keeping verbs consistent in your writing. What does "consistent" mean in this case?

Keeping two or more verbs in a sentence or paragraph consistent means keeping them in the same time or "tense"—most of the time in either the **present tense** or the **past tense.**

Read the following sentences, and note the **time** (tense) of each of the verbs.

> The old man **fished** in the lake every day. Even on rainy days, he **walks** to the lake and **throws** out his line at the same spot. He seldom **caught** a fish, but he never **stopped** going until he **broke** his fishing pole.

The description begins in the past tense ("fished") because all the events happened in the past. The last sentence clearly indicates this. The verbs in the second sentence, though, shift to the present tense ("walks" and "throws"). The present tense suggests to the reader that these events are still going on. The last sentence then moves back to the past tense. All the verbs should be in the past tense, so "walks" and "throws" should be changed to "walked" and "threw." All the sentences would then be a description of events in the past. Present-tense verbs would not be appropriate in this description because the man stopped going fishing when he broke his pole. These events are *not* happening now.

Here is the easiest way to eliminate the verb shift:

> The old man **fished** in the lake every day. Even on rainy days, he **walked** to the lake and **threw** out his line at the same spot. He seldom **caught** a fish, but he never **stopped** going until he **broke** his pole.

Because all the verbs are now in the past tense, they are *consistent*.

Present-tense verbs are used to describe something that is still true in the present. For example, one way to show activities that go on regularly would be to use the present tense consistently to describe these events. If the old man *had not broken* his pole, he might still be fishing *regularly*.

> The old man **fishes** in the lake every day. Even on rainy days, he **walks** to the lake and **throws** out his line at the same spot. He seldom **catches** a fish, but he never **stops** going unless he **breaks** his pole.

Using the present tense *consistently* in this way is appropriate. Your writing will be clearer and will convey your ideas more accurately if you make an effort to use the right time signals for your reader. One such signal is consistent verb tense that is appropriate for your intended meaning.

Checking Consistent Verb Tense

1. Find the first verb in a paragraph, and determine whether it is in the present tense or the past tense.

2. Check whether all other verbs in the paragraph are in the same tense as the first verb.

3. If not, change the verbs so that they are all in the same tense.

Note   A list of irregular verbs can be found in Appendix C.

Identify the tense of the verb in the first sentence as either present or past, and then make the remaining sentences match that tense.

Paragraph 1

Tense: _____*Present*_____

David's best friend is Stormy, his pet dog. Every night she goes to bed with him

stays

and ~~stayed~~ with him until he gets up the next morning. She sits outside the shower

door until he finishes. She also eats breakfast with him and then sees him off at the

play   *race*

front door. After school, they ~~played~~ catch or ~~raced~~ through the yard. She always

bother   *showers*

knows when things ~~bothered~~ him, and she gently ~~showered~~ him with "kisses." She

practice

becomes his when he ~~practiced~~ his piano or his companion as he builds his Lego

share

structures. They even ~~shared~~ an afternoon snack of cheese and crackers. Best of all,

they are always there for each other.

Paragraph 2

Tense: _____*Past*_____

The above paragraph would require past tense if Stormy were no longer alive. Edit the above paragraph to reflect this change in time. The first sentence needs to be "David's best friend was Stormy, his pet dog."

was   *went*

David's best friend ~~is~~ Stormy, his pet dog. Every night she ~~goes~~ to bed with him

got   *sat*

and stayed with him until he ~~gets~~ up the next morning. She ~~sits~~ outside the shower

finished   *ate*   *saw*

door until he ~~finishes~~. She also ~~eats~~ breakfast with him and then ~~sees~~ him off at the

front door. After school, they played catch or raced through the yard. She always

knew

~~knows~~ when things bothered him, and she gently showered him with "kisses." She

became   *built*

~~becomes~~ his audience when he practiced his piano or his companion as he ~~builds~~

his Lego structures. They even shared an afternoon snack of cheese and crackers.

were

Best of all, they ~~are~~ always there for each other.

Paragraph 3

Tense: ___Present___

      A large city like San Francisco offers visitors many kinds of exciting activities.

         wants   *has*
If someone ~~wanted~~ to attend sporting events, a large city usually ~~have~~ college

basketball and football teams as well as professional basketball and football teams.

        do   *fill*
If visitors ~~did~~ not care for sports, perhaps museums ~~filled~~ the bill. A large city

usually has art museums as well as historical and scientific museums. For the

          likes   *provides*
visitor who ~~liked~~ shopping, the large city ~~provided~~ a range of stores from small

specialty shops to large department stores. Since San Francisco is near the water, it

 offers
~~offered~~ fishing, a harbor cruise, surfing, an aquarium, and other waterfront

                                give
activities. Theaters and nightclubs also ~~gave~~ visitors a chance to experience evening

                do
entertainment they ~~did~~ not have at home. A large city usually gives an out-of-town

visitor a wide range of activities for excitement and fun.

Paragraph 4

Tense: ___Present___

      Senior citizens receive many recreational opportunities by living in retirement

                           attend
communities. Retired men and women ~~attended~~ craft classes that range from

                                 frequent
needlecraft to woodworking. Community members ~~frequented~~ one or more

recreational halls that are usually equipped with pool tables and shuffleboard

                       stay   *receive*
courts. In the evenings, they ~~stayed~~ busy attending dances or parties. They ~~received~~

exercise in indoor or outdoor swimming pools, depending on the specific region of

                         tee   *play*
the country. Fervent golfers ~~teed~~ off on well-manicured greens or ~~played~~ tennis on

clean courts any time of the day. No matter what activity people enjoy, they find

         enjoy
many others who ~~enjoyed~~ doing the same type of things.

When you edit and revise your writing, do not try to eliminate all the problems at the same time. Read for one kind of difficulty at a time.

To check for verb consistency in your own writing, read the first sentence in your paragraph. What tense is the verb? Are you describing or discussing an event that happened in the past? Are you talking about something in the future or the present? Make the verbs in the rest of the paragraph consistent with the time established in that first sentence.

Concentrate on the time signals as you read from sentence to sentence. Add other appropriate "time" words ("yesterday" or "last week" or "ten years ago" or "tomorrow" or "now" or "currently") that will clarify meaning for the reader.

The extra **time** spent on **tense** will pay off!

Part 5

Putting It All Together

 ## *Cumulative Unit Exercise*

Now that you are acquainted with ideas for reading your paragraphs critically, practice your skills on the following paragraph.

Transparency of uncorrected cumulative exercise is on page 47 in the Instructor's Manual.

1. Read the paragraph carefully. Identify the topic sentence for the paragraph. Read the first support sentence. Reread the topic sentence. Does this sentence support the topic sentence? Read the second support sentence and reread the topic sentence. Do this for every sentence within the paragraph. Consciously ask yourself if each sentence supports the topic sentence. Give the number of one sentence that does not support the topic idea.

2. Then check to see if the sentences seem to be in the best possible order. Only one sentence is out of order. Find that sentence, and indicate where it should go.

3. Check to see if the ending sentence completes the idea presented in the topic sentence. Be prepared to discuss your answer.

4. Then check the paragraph for subject-verb agreement and consistent verb tense. Correct any errors.

Alzheimer's Disease

(1) Alzheimer's disease, a form of dementia that usually strikes older people, slowly destroys their abilities. (2) At first, victims ~~loses~~ *lose* short-term memory and ~~were~~ *are* unable to learn new information. (3) These frustrating signs progress to a more frightening stage where adults with this disease may forget who they are and may also lose their ability to recognize other people, even loved ones like husbands, wives, and children. (4) Before long, it ~~was~~ *is* not unusual for these afflicted people to become confused and misplace items. (5) Also, they often ~~neglects~~ *neglect* personal hygiene such as brushing their teeth, combing their hair, or even taking a bath. (6) ~~Alzheimer's disease is a sad disease for the victims and their caretakers.~~

(7) Skills they once took for granted, such as paying a bill or balancing a checkbook, are no longer possible. (8) In the last stages of Alzheimer's disease, victims often ~~lost~~ *lose* their ability to communicate with others as well as to control bodily functions, so full-time nursing care becomes inevitable. (9) These symptoms progress for many years, but the results are ultimately fatal.

Collaborative Writing Project: Working and Learning Together

Writing Assignment

Write a paragraph on one of the following topics. Explain how you feel about this activity.

1. Going to a concert
2. Visiting a relative
3. Walking through a cemetery
4. Watching a fireworks display
5. Shopping at the mall
6. Riding a bus
7. Driving a car
8. Eating at home
9. Eating out
10. Playing a musical instrument

As you learned in Introduction to Writing, **talking** can help you begin a writing assignment when the topic does not have an obvious direction. Talking about a topic can focus your thinking and help you come to a clear direction so that you can write a topic sentence for your paragraph.

Working in a Group

1. **Choose** a topic. After you have chosen something to write about, **break into groups of three.** The three of you can discuss your experiences and impressions of the activity you have chosen. Avoid telling a story or describing how to do this activity.

2. Choose one of your group to be responsible for keeping you on track.

3. **Discuss your topic for 10 minutes. Make notes** of ideas that would help you come to an overall opinion about your topic that could then be the direction for your paragraph. For example, if you have chosen "going to a concert," talk about one or two of the exciting concerts you have been to recently. In your discussion, offer the overall impression you would like to make about going to a concert. Listen to the ideas from the other members of your group. Be sure to write down notes as you go along.

4. When the discussion time is up, focus your thinking on your own assignment. Decide on the **direction** for your paragraph, then **write a possible topic sentence.**

5. When all of you have written topic sentences, work together again to arrive at clearly stated, smooth topic sentences. **Read aloud** each topic sentence in turn. Be sure each topic sentence has a topic and a clear direction. Be prepared to show your topic sentence to your instructor or to the rest of the class for general discussion.

Working Individually

1. At this point, **freewrite or brainstorm with direction from your topic sentence** to help you come up with more specific information and ideas to put into your paragraph.

2. **Sort** the information to eliminate ideas that do not support the topic and the direction.

3. **Organize** the ideas you want to use by making a rough outline like the model on pages 34–35 in Part 1 of this unit.

4. **Draft** your paragraph. Remember not to tell a story or describe how to do this activity. Explain how you feel about this activity.

5. **Reread** carefully for adequate support for your main idea and for clear logical order.

6. Make **three** clear copies of your paragraph for peer review, one for yourself and one for each of the other members of your group.

Peer Review

Be positive in your review of each other's paragraphs, and be open to suggestions for revising your own paragraph. Write on the drafts so you can consider revision more easily.

In your group, be sure everybody has copies of each other's paragraphs. **Ask one person to help you stay on track**, especially if your instructor has set a time limit for you. **Read** the first paragraph aloud, and go through the following review. Then read the other paragraphs in turn and check for the same points.

1. **Identify** the topic sentence and decide if the direction is clear. Mark the word or words that show the direction.

2. **Check** to see that each support sentence clearly refers to the topic and the direction.

3. **Decide** if each sentence flows clearly from the one before it. If there seems to be a "gap" in the flow, offer a suggestion to bridge the gap.

4. **Check** to see if the ideas are in the best order. Offer suggestions if necessary.

5. **Mark** subject-verb agreement errors.

6. **Mark** any examples of inconsistent verb tense.

When you have completed the review and returned papers to the owners, you will each be ready to reread your own paragraph and make possible revisions.

Final Checklist

Content

Revise the paragraph so it has a clear topic sentence.

Include four to six supporting sentences.

Include a closing sentence.

Mechanics

Check for subject-verb agreement.

Check for consistent verb tense.

 Internet Activities

Activity 1   Finding Handouts on Writing

The Internet has a lot of information that can help you improve your writing skills. Exploring this information can reinforce what you learn in this text.

Please note: Internet addresses are constantly changing. The Internet addresses listed here were determined to be active at the time of printing.

a. Go to Purdue University's Online Writing Lab, which you marked or saved earlier. If you do not have the bookmark or the favorite, type the address. (Type all Internet addresses exactly as they appear.)

   http://owl.english.purdue.edu

b. Halfway down the middle of the initial page under the pencil link "Handouts and Materials," you can see "General writing concerns" as a link. Click on this link. Which handouts would be the most helpful in learning about the writing process in Unit 1? Review the handouts that can help you with the writing process, especially sentences and paragraphs.

c. Write down the elements that are emphasized here, and share them with your class or a collaborative group.

starting to write

———

effective writing

———

revising, editing, and proofreading

———

types or genres of writing

———

d. What resources are available here to help writers compose strong sentences and paragraphs?

handout on constructing paragraphs

———

handout on improving sentence clarity

———

Activity 2   Writing Topic Sentences

In this unit, you learned how to write clear paragraphs that contain an effective topic sentence, four to eight support sentences, and a strong concluding sentence. In this activity, you will read and use information on the Internet and then apply it to what you have learned in this unit.

a. Using one of the search engines listed on page 147, type the following words in the appropriate box: Elizabeth Kirk evaluating information Internet

b. Read the information included in the article "Evaluating Information Found on the Internet" by Elizabeth Kirk. Then work individually or in groups to develop a topic sentence for a strong paragraph. Give two examples on the lines below.

Evaluating Internet sources is important.

———

A writer must determine the validity of an Internet source before using the material.

———

Activity 3   Reviewing Basic Grammar

The following is a valuable website for general grammar assistance.

a. Type in the following address. (Type all Internet addresses exactly as they appear.) You may want to bookmark the site or save it as a favorite for future reference.

http://webster.commnet.edu/grammar/index.htm

b. Note the "Guide to Grammar & Writing" and all the subdirectories. Explore the topics under the three major levels of this site: "Word & Sentence Level," "Paragraph Level," and "Essay & Research Paper Level." Look at "Ask Grammar, Quizzes, Search Devices" to get a feel for the organizational layout.

c. In Unit 1 of *Writing Paragraphs and Essays,* review the topics in Part 4, "Grammar for Effective Writing: Basic Sentence Skills." Which of these topics from Unit 1 are also listed at this site?

subject-verb agreement

prepositional phrases

consistent verb tense

Singular and plural pronouns are discussed under the heading "Pronoun and Pronoun-Antecedent Agreement." If students look at this handout, they will see a matrix under number 5 that shows singular and plural pronouns. Sentence-structure errors: Students may not recognize this one unless they know the specific error because the listing shows "Sentence Fragments, Run-on Sentences, and Parallel Structure."

Activity 4   Reinforcing Subject-Verb Agreement

Here is a way to get feedback on how well you are learning subject-verb agreement.

a. Type in the following address. (Type all Internet addresses exactly as they appear.) You may want to bookmark the site or save it as a favorite for future reference, especially if you want to take other quizzes.

http://webster.commnet.edu/grammar/index.htm

b. At the "Guide to Grammar & Writing" web page, click on the pull-down menu under "Word & Sentence Level." Scroll down until you find "subjects." Read through the information.

c. Take a practice quiz by clicking on "Quiz" at the bottom of this page. You can print by clicking on "Print" on the browser toolbar. You may turn this in to your instructor if requested.

Unit 2

Being a Sensitive Writer

Writing Skills: Interaction of Topic, Purpose, Audience, and Voice

Objectives

Pretest over Unit 2, Parts 1 and 4, is on page 4 of the Test Bank.

- Understand the interaction of topic, purpose, audience, and voice.
- Identify topic, purpose, audience, and voice in a given situation.
- Identify changes in wording needed when writing for different audiences.
- Compose paragraphs with predetermined topic, purpose, audience, and voice.
- Revise a paragraph when one of the four elements has been changed.

The diagram labeled "WRITING" shows the interaction of topic, purpose, audience, and voice in your writing. **Topic** is the subject or focus of your paper and helps to establish your **purpose**, which is essentially your reason for writing the paper. Your purpose and your **audience**, the intended reader, determine what voice you use. **Voice** is the way you "sound" to your reader. If any one of these is ignored, miscommunication occurs, and your message is misunderstood.

The following example shows how such miscommunication can occur. Dr. Wilson Riles, a well-known California educator, tells of an incident in which a father received the following note from his son's principal:

> Our school's cross-graded, multi-ethnic, individualized learning program is designed to enhance the concept of an open-ended learning program with emphasis on a continuum of multi-ethnic, academically enriched learning, using the identified intellectually gifted child as the agent or director of his own learning.

According to Riles, the father replied with his own note:

> I have a college degree, speak two foreign languages and four Indian dialects, have been to a number of county fairs and three goat ropings, but I haven't the faintest idea as to what the hell you are talking about. Do you?

The principal had a purpose and topic but ignored his voice and his audience. Consequently, his note resulted in misunderstanding and anger. The father also had a topic and purpose, but he considered his voice and audience. He used a straightforward, clear, yet angry voice to achieve his purpose—communicating the principal's failure to explain his message clearly.

The principal's note seems pretentious, written with the purpose of impressing the father rather than communicating with him. The father, on the other hand, responds simply and honestly, and his son's principal probably understood the message.

How do you want your reader to respond to what you have to say? If your purpose for writing is to entertain, then you want your reader to react lightheartedly. If your purpose is to inform, you want your reader to take you seriously and to have a clear understanding of your message. If your purpose is to persuade, you may want your reader to take some action or to acknowledge a problem.

To review, then, here are the four elements of writing:

Topic:	focus of the paper
Purpose:	reason for writing the paper
Audience:	intended reader
Voice:	the way writing "sounds" to the reader

The following situations show how topic, purpose, audience, and voice work together.

Situation 1

Mr. Latham has worked hard at his job as a newspaper editor for six years. He has demonstrated creativity and journalistic talent. In those years, he has received favorable evaluations but not a significant raise. He is writing a memo to his boss to convince him that he deserves a raise.

Topic:	Mr. Latham's raise
Purpose:	to persuade his boss to give him a raise
Audience:	Mr. Latham's boss
Voice:	formal, polite, respectful, yet forceful

Situation 2

Mary Jones is a nurse in an elementary school. Recently a measles epidemic has swept through the community. Ms. Jones is responsible for the health and well-being of the children. Therefore, she is writing a notice to be taken home to explain to the children and their parents why the children must be vaccinated and why it is important not to be afraid to have this done.

Topic: measles vaccination

Purpose: to inform them of the facts and persuade them to participate

Audience: children and parents

Voice: simple but serious, knowledgeable

Situation 3

Tessie's friend has just had a skiing accident that has kept her from trying out for the Winter Olympics. Tessie is going to write her friend a note to let her know what has happened at school while she was gone.

Topic: school activities

Purpose: to cheer her friend up with accounts of funny happenings

Audience: Tessie's friend

Voice: humorous, light, sincere, informal

Each of these situations requires clear, effective communication to accomplish the desired purpose. To get the message to the audience, consider how topic, purpose, audience, and voice interact. Try working through the following exercise with this interaction in mind.

Exercise 1

Read each situation and identify the topic, purpose, audience, and voice.

Situation 1

A young man has just been offered a job at another company with more benefits and higher salary. He needs to write a letter to his current employer notifying her of his resignation. However, he wants to leave with an option to return if necessary.

Topic: *resignation*

Purpose: *notification of resignation with option to return to current employment*

Audience: *boss*

Voice: *serious, honest, sincere*

Situation 2

Debra Kim's psychology instructor wrote her letters of recommendation to seven different pharmacy schools. Debra would like to buy her a gift and send her a thank-you note.

Topic: *letters of recommendation*

Purpose: *show appreciation for the letters*

Audience: *psychology instructor*

Voice: *polite and appreciative*

Situation 3

Dee is writing a letter to her mother-in-law to tell her about the plans she and her husband have made regarding their new baby's birth. After the new baby is born, they would like her to wait a week before she comes to visit because Dee's mother will be there when Dee's baby is born and will stay for the first week.

Topic:	*mother-in-law's visit after the baby is born*
Purpose:	*have the mother-in-law stay with them the second week rather than the first week*
Audience:	*mother-in-law*
Voice:	*diplomatic, warm, friendly*

Situation 4

Jane Culver has just learned that her friend recently lost her mother. She sits down to write her a note.

Topic:	*death of friend's mother*
Purpose:	*show sympathy, understanding*
Audience:	*friend*
Voice:	*personal, serious, warm, comforting*

As you become a more experienced writer, you will become more aware of how you can adjust your writing to suit your topic, purpose, audience, and voice. You will see how these elements work together to convey ideas effectively.

Purpose Influences Organization

Why you are writing a particular paragraph determines how you organize the ideas in the paragraph. There are key points to keep in mind when you are organizing your ideas. Most of these points are already familiar to you, such as putting ideas into logical order and putting ideas into the most effective order. For example, you have already learned to decide which supporting ideas or examples are the most important and which are the least important. However, in this section, you will learn how to organize a paragraph when your purpose is to show how things are alike or different or to show how things have changed over a period of time. For this purpose, you can choose between two patterns. Also, you will see a sample paragraph that shows you how to use a narrative to support a topic sentence. In addition, you will learn about giving directions to do something and explain how a procedure is done.

After you have chosen a topic and decided on your purpose, you are ready to think about a pattern of organization and a topic sentence for your paragraph. Remember that **purpose determines the way you organize your ideas, and this purpose will be reflected in your topic sentence.** You need to think about your topic sentence as the one thing you want to support or prove in your paragraph. Following are some of the most common types of organization you might use.

Types of Organization Based on Purpose:

1. how something is true (illustration with examples)
2. how something has changed; how two things are alike or different (comparison/contrast)
3. why someone should do something (persuasion)
4. what happened (narrative)
5. what happened afterward (the effects or results of an event)
6. why something happened (cause/s)
7. what something means (definition)
8. how things can be sorted into groups (classification)
9. how to do something (process/give directions)
10. how something is done (process/describe the procedure)

One important point to remember is that all the paragraphs you write need to have a topic sentence and that all paragraphs will use supporting examples and details to show "in what way" that topic sentence is true. As you read through the possible types of organization, be aware that not all paragraphs fit into a set pattern. Identifying your purpose and your audience will help you decide on the best way to write your paragraph.

(1) How something is true (illustration with examples)

Topic: showing grief in different ways

Purpose: to show how people spontaneously express their grief

Audience: general reader

Choose a pattern of organization: use examples.

Topic sentence: **People can show grief by establishing an informal, spontaneous memorial.**

Brainstorm examples: to illustrate your topic sentence.

death of a young person in an accident

take flowers

take candles

just go to the place and stand in sadness or talk about their friend

other kinds of gifts, stuffed animals

speaking publicly about the friend

writing notes or poems

Arrange the examples in the order that seems most effective to you:

expressions of grief

taking flowers

taking candles

being at the spot of the accident

writing notes or poems

leaving other objects as gifts

talking to reporters

speaking publicly about the loss

Draft the paragraph:

Creating a Memorial

People can show grief by establishing an informal, spontaneous memorial. When a young person dies in an automobile accident, the friends of the person killed often set up a display of flowers and candles at the spot where the accident happened. Someone may write his or her feelings in a poem to share how important the friend's death is, so the poem appears spontaneously alongside the flowers. The usually sad poem becomes a display for all to read. Still others leave personal objects that are especially meaningful to them, so perhaps small stuffed animals and other mementos take their place near the site. Others may go to the site and hang out with their friends to express their grief just by being there. Sometimes, if the event is covered by a local television crew, those at the scene may talk to a reporter about their friend and openly express how they feel. Many, however, are crying and are too upset to speak at all. Hour by hour, a small unplanned memorial grows by the side of the street, and this memorial helps people cope with the loss of a friend.

(2) How something has changed; how two things are alike or different (comparison/contrast)

To show how something has changed, you first need to explain what something was like before the change occurred. For example, to show how communication or transportation has changed, you must first show what communication or transportation was like twenty, forty, or more years ago. Then, you can use the way things once were as a basis for change. Now, think about how the roles of husbands and wives have changed in the last forty years. Once you know what the roles were like forty years ago, then you can show how those things have changed.

> *Topic:* marriage
>
> *Purpose:* to show how the roles of husbands and wives have changed in the last forty years
>
> *Audience:* general reader

Choose a pattern of organization: show how things have changed.

> *Topic sentence:* **The responsibilities within a family today are much different than they were forty years ago.**

The topic sentence shows that you are talking about responsibilities in two different time periods, so you will need to sort your ideas into two groups: the responsibilities forty years ago and the responsibilities today.

Now **brainstorm** for ideas. You might even start brainstorming with **two lists of ideas and details** that you will need to help you explain your topic sentence.

In the **first half** of the paragraph, you could explain what the roles of husbands and wives were forty years ago:

husband's role	**wife's role**
provided money for family	usually did not work
was primary disciplinarian	deferred to husband as disciplinarian
did outside work, yard work	did cooking, cleaning, laundry

In the **second half** of the paragraph, you could explain how those roles are different today:

both may earn income

both may discipline children, whoever is around at any particular time, or may sit down together and work out what is best for the child

husband may cook, and wife may clean up afterward

both do laundry, wife does yard work

running a household now a shared effort for both partners

Draft the paragraph. (To show how the roles have changed, first you need to establish what the roles once were.)

Changing Responsibilities in a Family

Today, the responsibilities within a family are much different than they were forty years ago. At that time in American history, when two people were married, each partner took on a very defined role. The husband was expected to provide for the financial needs of the family, and the wife usually did not work outside the house. The husband was often the primary disciplinarian. If the children misbehaved, the wife might say, "Just wait until your father gets home." On weekends, he was responsible for keeping the yard looking nice, but he seldom had to worry about cooking, doing the laundry, or cleaning the house because his wife did those things. Today, however, husbands and wives share the responsibilities of earning the income, and both often work outside the home. When children misbehave, whatever parent is closest will correct the situation, or the parents may sit down together and decide on the most effective discipline for the child. Also, the husband and wife will often share the responsibilities of keeping the household running smoothly. The husband may cook the meals, but the wife might clean up the kitchen or work in the yard. Running a household has become more of a team effort where both partners pitch in and do whatever is best for everyone.

For another example of this pattern of organization, read the paragraph on page 32 about the way the responsibilities of administrative assistants have changed. This is an additional example of how this pattern of organization can be used effectively. In the administrative assistants paragraph, you can see how ideas are also divided into two groups. All the **former responsibilities** are discussed in the first half of the paragraph. All the **current responsibilities** are in the second half.

Another way to show how two things are different   Now look at a paragraph that shows another way to explain two different things. In the following paragraph Deborah Tannen explains the two different styles of communication that women and men, for the most part, use. Again, the two sets of ideas are first put into two groups: women's style of communication and men's style of communication. This time, notice that the ideas **alternate back and forth in a consistent manner.**

Women	eye contact, stick to a topic longer, personal topics
Men	less eye contact, do not stay on a topic long, impersonal topics
Women	look for emotional meanings underlying words
Men	usually use direct language

Women	use language to achieve personal cooperation
Men	use language to compete
Women	concerned with being "in tune" with partner; use interrupters like "really, gosh, wow"
Men	tend to avoid these kinds of interrupters
Women	better at personal talk
Men	tend to dominate public, formal communication

Gender Communication

Debra Tannen's research on gender communication reveals many differences in female—male communication. For example, women use more eye contact and usually stick to a topic longer. Men usually have less eye contact, select more impersonal topics, and don't stay on a topic for a long duration. Women may look for hidden, emotional meanings in and between words; however, men usually use direct language. Women focus on the personal cooperation that language encourages, but men may use language, perhaps, to compete. A woman uses interrupters—"really, gosh, wow"—to let the other person know that she is "in tune" with her verbal partner. Women are better at personal, private talk while men dominate the public, formal scene. All in all, Debra Tannen makes it clear that one gender is not necessarily better at communicating; they simply have different styles.

(3) Why someone should do something (persuasion)

You can easily understand how important the purpose becomes in this kind of writing situation. Whether you have chosen the topic first or have thought of the purpose first does not matter because topic and purpose soon become closely interrelated. Also, once you start your prewriting, you probably will not have any trouble identifying the audience for your writing. The example that follows shows you that a first-person point of view can be very convincing without being openly emotional.

> *Topic:* Shawn Stevens
>
> *Purpose:* to inform and persuade the fire department to admit Shawn Stevens to its training academy
>
> *Audience:* personnel at the fire department

Choose a pattern of organization: persuasion.

> *Topic sentence:* **On behalf of Shawn Stevens, I would like to make you aware of his ability to do the job of a firefighter.**

Then **brainstorm** for ideas.

Because you are trying to convince someone to do something, you need to brainstorm all the ideas you can think of to support your topic sentence.

Abilities to do job of a firefighter

dedication, self-discipline—builds his body at the gym

lifeguard—rescued four near-drowning victims

CPR—can react in an emergency

leadership—swim instructor for 200 youths, swim coach

Again, put the examples in the most effective order, and be aware of how your voice will sound. Word choice becomes very important because you want to be persuasive but not emotional in a negative way.

Draft the paragraph:

Recommendation for Shawn Stevens

To Whom It May Concern:

Everyone realizes the extreme importance of the qualities a firefighter must possess. **On behalf of Shawn Stevens, I would like to make you aware of his ability to do the job of a firefighter.** His strongest asset is his dedication. He has shown an ability to commit himself with great self-discipline. For example, five years ago, Shawn decided to build his body and has put in the time and energy on a routine basis to achieve that goal. Also, Shawn has experienced panic situations and has remained clear-headed. As a lifeguard for the city of Phoenix, he rescued four near-drowning victims. He knows how to administer CPR and how to react in an emergency. Finally, Shawn has demonstrated leadership. As a swim instructor, he taught approximately two hundred youths to swim, and as a swim coach, he directed and inspired several youths on his team to work hard and achieve their swimming goals. Dedication, calmness in an emergency, and leadership are three qualities I imagine you would like your firefighters to possess. I recommend Shawn Stevens because he has proven he has all these characteristics.

Sincerely,

Rebecca Ivans, English Instructor and Counselor

(4) What happened (narrative)

When you narrate an event, you still need to begin your paragraph with a topic sentence. Then, as you explain what happened, include only the examples and details that support the topic sentence. In the following paragraph, you will only include why the day at Slide Rock State Park makes you smile today.

> *Topic:* Adventure at Slide Rock State Park
>
> *Purpose:* to reminisce about adventure
>
> *Audience:* family, friends

Choose a pattern of organization: what happened, narrative.

> *Topic sentence:* **I still have to smile when I think about our adventure at Slide Rock State Park in Oak Creek Canyon.**

Remember that a narrative supports a main idea or topic sentence. To tell the story of something that happened, put events into logical time order. Use time words like *now, then,* and *later* so that your reader can clearly follow what happened. You need details so that your reader can feel and visualize the events that support the topic sentence.

Then, **brainstorm** for details and examples.

> I wanted my son to experience something I had enjoyed as a child
>
> Beauty of Slide Rock State Park
>
> Thrill of sliding down the natural water slide shared with my son

Draft the paragraph:

Adventure at Slide Rock

I still have to smile when I think about our adventure at Slide Rock State Park in Oak Creek Canyon. My son was ten years old, and I thought that he should enjoy the same fun I had experienced years ago when sliding down this natural water slide, a natural indentation that had formed in the red rock as the flowing water eroded the sandstone. I was excited as I explained how the creek would swiftly carry us forty or so feet into the little pool of water at the end of this amazing "slide." As the three of us, my husband, son, and I, walked toward this famous attraction, we saw at least twenty young people in bathing suits sitting around on the beautiful red rock, admiring the natural water slide that seemed chiseled out of the red rocks surrounding them. My husband soon joined them, but I lured my son over to the entrance of the slide and convinced him to "test the water" by sticking his toes in the water. We both did this, only to feel how cold the water really was. I told him how much fun it would be to jump in and let the water carry us down to the pool. My son immediately decided that he really wanted no part of this ritual, and when I realized he was not going to slide down alone, I grabbed his hand and pulled him in with me. I still remember my body hitting the freezing cold water that rapidly carried us down to the equally cold pond. I was laughing, telling him how great it was when I noticed that all the people who had once been admiring the water were now jumping in, one by one, enjoying this fast ride to the pond at the bottom.

(5) What happened afterward (the effects or results of an event)

> *Topic:* losing a job
>
> *Purpose:* to show what happens to a person when he/she loses a job
>
> *Audience:* general reader

Choose a pattern of organization: effects or results.

> *Topic sentence:* **Losing a job affects people in negative ways.**

Brainstorm as many **effects** or **results** as possible, and arrange them in what seems to you to be the most effective order.

From least important to most important

From most important to least important

From important to less important to most important

Effects or results

    Money worries

        House payment or monthly rent

        Car payment

        Utility bills

        Doctor bills

    Making changes in lifestyle

        Not going out to eat as often

        Not going to the movies

        No impulse buying at the grocery store

        Buying less expensive items for food

No shopping just for the fun of it

No weekend out-of-town trips just for fun

Sharing rides with friends

Draft the paragraph:

Losing a Job

Losing a job affects people in negative ways. Right away they begin to feel the effects of having no income. Discouragement comes along with money worries. Making the house payment or paying the rent becomes a primary concern. Soon fears also surface about not being able to pay the electric, gas, water, and phone bills. Then, when someone gets sick, money may not be available for a necessary trip to the doctor. At this stage, because people want to get through the situation all right, their thoughts begin to focus on cutting expenses. Losing a job results in people making different choices. They may stop going out to eat, instead choosing to cook and eat at home. At the grocery store, they put less expensive foods into the grocery cart and avoid buying anything on impulse. In addition, shopping trips to the mall just for fun are now impossible. People can no longer afford to go to the movies. If gasoline costs a lot, people drive less, walk to do errands, or may share rides with friends or other family members. All in all, the lack of money can be emotionally draining, but while looking for a new job, an individual will also learn how to use resources wisely.

(6) Why something happened (cause/s)

> *Topic:* a major, life-changing decision, the decision of a professional football player to give up money to serve as an Army Ranger
>
> *Purpose:* To explain why a professional football player gave up a multimillion-dollar contract to become an Army Ranger
>
> *Audience:* Any American citizen

Choose a pattern of organization: causes.

> *Topic sentence:* **Pat Tillman, a professional football player, gave up three million dollars to join the U.S. Army because his family background and his own character made a sports career no longer meaningful.**

Brainstorm to get information on what caused him to become an Army Ranger.
Brainstorm as many reasons as you can for the event, and then arrange them in what seems to you the logical or clearest order.

Tillman's reaction to the Sept. 11, 2001, terrorist attack

Knowledge of grandfather's and uncles' military experiences at Pearl Harbor

Decisions of other people his age to volunteer for military service

Realized he had never laid his life on the line for anything important

Personal character—did not feel right about what he saw in his life:

Enjoying the things that money can buy

Living life for pleasure and fun

Strong feeling that the effort and passion required for football were no longer meaningful

Draft the paragraph:

Pat Tillman's Decision

Pat Tillman, a professional football player, gave up three million dollars to join the U.S. Army Rangers because his family background and his own character made a sports career no longer meaningful. According to friends, the destruction of the World Trade Center on September 11, 2001, focused his thinking inward. He remembered the experiences of his grandfather and two uncles who had served at Pearl Harbor. They had laid their lives on the line to protect the freedom enjoyed by Americans. Also after 9/11, many young men and women were volunteering for the service because they wanted to give something back to America. In contrast to these examples, he found himself on the verge of enjoying a life of pleasure and excitement made possible by his new football contract. Many people noted at the time that Pat Tillman suddenly seemed to think that football was not the right place for him to put all his effort and passion. He needed to serve his country by following the examples of family and friends.

(7) What something means (definition)

When you write the definition for a word, you will want to show how your meaning of the word is different from other people's meaning. In doing this, you might want to expand or narrow your term. You might begin with the ordinary, everyday meaning of a term and then show how your definition differs from this meaning. The best way to make your meaning clear is to use specific examples so that your reader can understand your meaning.

> *Topic:* stubbornness as a positive trait
>
> *Purpose:* to define the word "stubborn"
>
> *Audience:* parents, childcare workers

Choose a pattern of organization: definition.

> *Topic sentence:* **Today I think of the word "stubborn" positively.**

Then, **brainstorm** to find examples that will make your definition clear to your reader.

> Ordinary meaning of the word "stubborn"
>> Negative meaning of the word—unreasonable, refuses to give in, difficult
>>> Example: when I gave my son medicine
>> Positive meaning of the word—son's car accident
>>> Bought school clothes even though he could not go to school
>>> Took 6 hours to do something that used to take him 20 minutes
>>> Graduated from high school
>> Asset for people to have this quality—refusal to yield as a strength and positive part of his existence

Draft the paragraph:

Is Being Stubborn All Right?

At one time, when I thought of the word "stubborn," I thought about someone who refused to yield, someone who was unreasonable, someone who refused to give in, basically someone difficult to be around. When my son was a baby, I did not know what to do with him sometimes. For example, the only way to get him to take his medicine was to hold his arms down, pry open his mouth, pour the medicine into his mouth, and hold it open until he swallowed. At best, he was stubborn, difficult, impossible. He did not want the medicine, so he would not take the medicine. Once he decided not to do something, there was no way I could convince him to do otherwise. Later, when he was seventeen, he was critically injured in a car accident; again, he was "stubborn." When the doctors told him that he would most likely never graduate from high school, he refused to hear them. Nine weeks after his accident, it was time for school to start. Though his arms were bandaged like two huge tree trunks and he was physically and mentally unable to start classes, he insisted that we go to the store and buy school clothes because he could not fit into any of his shirts. Trying them on was no small task for someone whose arms did not bend, but he persisted until we found some shirts he could wear. Then, for the next few years, his doctors considered him unreasonable because he refused to give in to his injuries. His persistent determination never changed. At first, he spent six hours doing what he had once done in twenty minutes, but he did graduate from high school with honors; he did graduate from college cum laude; he did go on to graduate school, earning a doctorate. Was he stubborn? Yes, he was. **Today, I think of the word "stubborn" positively.** I see my son's stubborn acts and his refusal to yield as a strength and a positive part of his existence. To me, stubbornness is not a negative trait; rather, it is an asset that parents should cherish and channel in a positive direction because that same trait may someday serve their children well.

(8) How things can be sorted into groups (classification)

Topic: Mexican folk music

Purpose: to show the different types of Mexican folk music

Audience: anyone who loves music

Choose a pattern of organization: classification.

Topic sentence: **Folk music and dance are more than an expression of art to Mexicans.**

Then, **brainstorm** to get ideas that will fit into categories. The example below illustrates how the music of Mexico is classified by its place of origin and by the identifiable costumes.

State of Jalisco

   China Poblana

   Charro

State of Oaxaca

   La Tehuana

Port of Veracruz

   La Jarocha

      huapangos

         La Bamba

Draft the paragraph:

Music in Mexico

Folk music and dance are more than an expression of art to Mexicans. This *Baile Folklorico,* as it is called, defines a certain group of people, region, and folkloric history as well as a national spirit. The best-known category is identified as *Charro* and *China Poblana* songs and dances. This type comes from the state of Jalisco, which includes Mexico City and is perhaps the most famous of all the Mexican music and regional dancing. The *China Poblana* costume consists of a white blouse with a square or round low neck adorned with embroideries, stitched in vivid colors. The skirt is red flannel with sequins and two green satin stripes at the waist and lower part of the skirt. The male partner is the *Charro,* whose costume resembles the dress of typical Mariachis. Another identifiable category comes from the state of Oaxaca, which is the most southern coast of southern Mexico in the area of Tehuantepec, hence the name *La Tehuana.* The traditional dress is a short blouse with a round or square neck and a skirt that is an extension of the blouse and hangs below the knee. A pleated white lace skirt then covers down to the feet. Traditionally, the *tehuana* woman dances barefooted and may have a brilliantly colored flower decoration carried on her head or in her hands as she moves to the rhythm of the music. Finally, another famous and distinct dance and music category is called *La Jarocha,* which comes from Mexico's Port of Veracruz. The folk dances and songs in this state are extremely happy, and they are called *huapangos.* One example, *La Bamba,* is known worldwide, including a rendition that made the pop charts in the '60s in the United States. The performers sing and dance at the same time, improvising short, amusing verses. The costume for the dancers is a white skirt for the women or pants for the men. The woman's skirt is adorned with beautiful laces. Over the skirt is a black apron embroidered with flowers and surrounded by black lace. Music to Mexicans is the thread that weaves them together in time, and though each region has a distinct folk dance, all regions are connected through their unique and beautiful Mexican music.

(9) How to do something (process/give directions)

Perhaps you have been asked to describe how to become a caregiver for an elderly person. You will want to be clear in your directions and suggestions. You will also want to be sure you cover everything that a new employee would need to know to do the job well and with the least amount of stress on everybody concerned.

Topic: becoming a caregiver for an elderly woman

Purpose: to show clearly and comprehensively what someone needs to do before becoming a caregiver for an elderly woman in her home

Audience: prospective employee, male or female

Choose a pattern of organization: process/give directions.

Topic sentence: **Before becoming a caregiver for an elderly woman, you must prepare ahead of time for the job.**

Because you will be describing the **steps** someone needs to go through to become a caregiver, you will be doing a **process** paragraph. Ask yourself or others in small group discussion what someone would need to be able to do to perform this job effectively. You will probably find out as you go along that the steps will fall into two or three major groups, so you can organize them logically.

Brainstorm the steps that a person will need to go through.

Assess her overall physical abilities and activities:

Find out if she has any health problems, such as heart or kidney disease or cancer

Find out if she takes any medication

Special diet needs; cooking her meals, providing food she needs

Taking care of her own personal needs

Walking by herself or needing a cane or a wheelchair

Getting into and out of bed by herself, sitting down and getting up from a chair alone

Hearing—hearing aid?

Eyesight—glasses or severe vision problems, such as macular degeneration

Mental capabilities:

Able to follow requests or directions

Reliable short-term memory for daily events

Carries on a conversation

Takes medicine by herself

Your own mental and physical preparation:

Be patient and caring and always positive

Do things at her pace, not at yours—for example, get her ready for a doctor appointment

Keep family and/or emergency phone numbers you might need

Be thorough and accurate

Keep a daily log, an outline at least, of her care

Draft the paragraph:

Preparing to Become a Caregiver

Before becoming a caregiver for an elderly woman, you must prepare ahead of time for the job. Begin by finding out if she has any health problems, such as heart or kidney disease or cancer, because you may be taking her to doctor appointments or to dialysis for treatment. You need to find out if she takes any medications and if she is on any special diets. Be willing to cook her nutritious meals that she will enjoy. Then, determine if she can dress and feed herself as well as take care of her personal needs in the bathroom. Find out if she can walk by herself or if she needs a cane or a wheelchair to get around. Find out if she can get into and out of bed by herself, sit down and get up out of a chair alone. If she needs assistance in doing these things, you will have to help her. Evaluate her hearing to see if she uses a hearing aid or if she needs to get one. Evaluate her eyesight to determine if she needs glasses or if she has serious vision problems such as macular degeneration. When you have covered the physical abilities, you need to determine what to expect about her mental capabilities. Again, ask if she can follow directions, if she has reliable short-term memory for daily events, or if she can carry on a conversation. If she is on any medication, see if she can take it on her own or if she needs reminders. Once you have this information, you must prepare yourself for being a caregiver by being patient, caring, and always positive. Take time to do things at her pace rather than yours. Start well ahead, for example, to get her ready for doctor appointments. At all times, keep emergency phone numbers you might need handy. Be thorough and accurate when you talk to her family or to whoever is supervising your work. Most important of all, keep a daily log and outline, at least, of her care, whether you are working independently or for an agency. You must be flexible, open-minded, and prepared for the unexpected.

(10) How something is done (process/describe the procedure)

When you do this kind of paragraph, you will not actually be giving directions to do the process or procedure but will be describing how someone else does it. Sometimes, there will be a definite step-by-step series of actions that you will describe. At other times, you may be describing something that does not have a definite chronological series of steps. You may not have to explain in any certain order how someone does the procedure. Of course, you will have to be sure to cover everything necessary for another person to understand how the activity is performed.

> *Topic:* Car repair
>
> *Purpose:* Explain the process for having a car repaired
>
> *Audience:* Car owners

Choose a pattern of organization: procedure for doing something.

> *Topic sentence:* **Every service department at a car dealer has a procedure for handling maintenance and repairs.**

Because you will be telling how a car dealership serves customers, you will be describing a process, but you will have to put the steps of the **process** in chronological order.

Brainstorm the typical procedures at the service department of a car dealership.

> Service department makes appointment for customer
>
> Verify the model and year of the vehicle
>
> Determine the problem
>
> Issue an identification tag
>
> Check car for dents or dings
>
> Determine previous service
>
> Draft work order and estimate costs
>
> Keep customer informed
>
> Notify customer that car is fixed

Draft the paragraph:

Customer Service

Every service department at a car dealer has a procedure for handling maintenance and repairs. The process begins when the service department makes an appointment for a customer to have a vehicle repaired or serviced. Then, as soon as the customer pulls into the service area, the same service adviser greets the customer courteously and begins to fill out the draft work orders. As the driver gets out of the car, the service adviser verifies the model and year of the vehicle. The customer begins to describe the problem to the service adviser, who also asks questions to help pinpoint all of the customer's concerns. He or she then attaches to the car an identification tag that may also be a claim number which the customer may use later to check on the car. Before taking the car back to the garage area, an employee usually walks around the car and makes note of any dents or dings on the car. The service adviser then checks the service department's database to determine when or if the vehicle has been serviced there before. The service adviser then records the car's mileage and types the work order into the computer and may advise the customer of other regularly scheduled maintenance that needs to be done. The service adviser then estimates the cost of the repair and the time when the car will be ready. The customer then signs the work order. The adviser asks if the customer wants to wait for the vehicle. As part of their customer service, most dealerships have a lounge or other facility where customers may read, watch television, or enjoy snacks while they wait. If the customer does not want to or cannot wait, the dealer usually provides a complimentary shuttle ride to work or elsewhere. The service adviser then thanks the customer and promises to call when the car is ready or if any additional work needs to be done. Once the car is ready, the service adviser notifies the customer and directs him or her to the cashier for payment and key pickup.

Being aware of your purpose will help you decide on the best way to organize material for your paper. As you gain experience in writing, it will become natural for you to choose the best pattern of development as well as the voice that is appropriate for the topic and purpose you have identified.

Topic and Purpose Influence Voice

Often the **topic** may be given to you, or you may find it fairly soon when brainstorming or freewriting. If so, you might know right away how you want your voice to sound to your audience. For example, it would be difficult to write a humorous paper about cancer or AIDS. You would probably want to sound serious so your reader would take you seriously. On the other hand, if you were writing about raising children, you might want to sound lighthearted rather than serious.

Sometimes topic and **purpose** for writing may come to you almost simultaneously. If your topic were cancer, for instance, you might soon discover that you wanted to persuade your audience to have annual physical checkups. To be *persuasive,* you would certainly want your writing voice to sound knowledgeable and convincing. If you wanted to *inform* your reader about facts concerning AIDS, you would want to sound honest and informed. If you were writing about raising children, you might want to *inform and entertain* the reader at the same time. Then your writing voice could be informative as well as humorous.

Now work through the following exercise.

Exercise 2

Read the following paragraphs, and identify the topic, audience, and organizational pattern. The purpose for each paragraph is given.

Paragraph 1
Purpose: to show similarities and differences between two kinds of childcare options

After receiving a degree in early childhood education, students must decide to open their own home-based childcare center or work in someone else's childcare facility. If they do decide to work out of their own homes, they must not only recruit the children but will be responsible for the safety of each child. They must also be responsible for providing all the materials the children might need. This will include toys, craft supplies, snacks, and special furniture such as strollers, high chairs, or even cribs. They must be sure their homes are safe. However, if they decide to work for a childcare facility, they will be working for someone else and will have less liability. They will still be responsible for a certain number of children, and they might have to prepare lessons for the children, but they will not have to provide the toys or the furniture that they need. The daycare center will provide the snacks, toys, and even the playground equipment. One job is not better than the other. Both involve responsibility, and both allow childcare workers to interact with and help youngsters.

Topic: _employment for childcare workers_

Audience: _people who want to work with children_

Organizational pattern: _how two things are alike or different (comparison / contrast)_

Paragraph 2

Purpose: to make the homeowners aware of a problem

After purchasing a home here at the Rose Terrace Condominiums, I have become aware of a possibly dangerous situation that needs to be changed. A common swimming pool in the center of the courtyard poses a threat because the self-closing, locking gate at the west entry to the pool is bolted open because John, a resident who is confined to an electric wheelchair, has access to his home only when the gate is open. The city has required that the pool be covered when the gate is open, but the cover is not always in place because people are constantly using the pool in the summertime. The open gate to the pool is a potentially dangerous situation, especially if a child walks through that open gate when someone is not looking. Two little boys, both under the age of five, live in the complex, and if they try hard enough, I am sure they could find their way into this pool. As a member of this homeowners' association, I believe we should meet to discuss the best way to maintain wheelchair access as well as provide a safe environment for the children. We should not wait until a child drowns or until we are sued before taking action.

Topic: _potential danger of the swimming pool_

Audience: _homeowners' association_

Organizational pattern: _persuasion, why someone should do something_

Paragraph 3

Purpose: to help people understand the educational challenges faced by some immigrant people

In 1996, when the General Education Class (GED) met for the first time, it provided an opportunity to many migrant people. One man in his late 40s, perhaps early 50s, was one of the students. His name was Cuyatino Acosta, and he entered with unrestrained enthusiasm as he told of his greatest ambition, to get an education. When he was a young boy, he came to America with his family, but because he was the oldest, he could only wave each day as the school bus drove by his house. He had to work so his family could eat, but now GED classes were starting, and his opportunity had arrived. When the classes were over and he had passed his test, he was a proud man as he held his equivalency diploma in his hand. The next year, he went on to college and eventually graduated with a teaching degree at the age of 55. His success in obtaining an education made him an example for his small community of migrant workers.

Topic: _GED classes and Cuyatino Acosta's education_

Audience: _anyone worrying about returning to school_

Organizational pattern: _illustration / example_

Paragraph 4

Purpose: to explain why one person is not going to patronize Crestview Mall anymore

For the first time in my life, I have made a decision to stop shopping at Crestview Mall. Yesterday, when I was walking through the mall, I saw the traditional bell-ringer from the Salvation Army. As I approached, a man suddenly stopped by the woman ringing the bell and told her she would have to leave the mall because no solicitors were allowed there. A volunteer who was seeking help for the less fortunate in our city was not allowed to stay in the mall and seek donations. The bell-ringer represents the spirit of giving that, from my point of view, has just about disappeared from the holiday season. The merchants want all the dollars they can get from us, but they have forgotten the original meaning of the holidays. I for one will not patronize Crestview Mall to buy presents for my family!

Topic: _ban on holiday bell-ringers_

Audience: _general population_

Organizational pattern: _causes for not going to the mall / reasons why something happened_

Paragraph 5

Purpose: to show gratitude to a teacher for having written a letter of recommendation

Dear Professor Kalucha,

Thank you so much for taking the time to help me get accepted into the college of medicine at this university. Being in your class helped me gain the skills I needed to be competitive in getting into a medical program. Also, your encouragement gave me confidence that if someone with your background felt that I could do it, then maybe it was really possible. Your letter of recommendation, I am sure, was extremely important in my acceptance. Having your support will help me stay focused as I complete my graduate work. Once I receive my degree, you will be the first person I notify. Again, thanks for all of your help, and I hope we can stay in touch.

Sincerely,

Rene Carpenter, your former student

Topic: _express appreciation for help in getting into pharmacy school_

Audience: _Professor Kalucha_

Organizational pattern: _effects / results of an event_

Paragraph 6

Purpose: to share information about himself and his present conflict

I often wonder what my future life will be. I live on the reservation near Indian Wells, where my little brother and I spend time in the summer taking care of the sheep and the small field of corn that my family owns. In the wintertime, I go to school away from the reservation, and when I am at Lakeside Community College, I still think of the quiet hours we spend watching the sheep eat the little sprigs of grass and weeds. As we work in the corn, we talk about what will happen when I get out of school. He will still be at home and thinks that living in the city all the time will not be good for me. We would have no peaceful times together with the sheep anymore. We couldn't walk down the corn rows and feel the earth. I wish I could live in the city and still have a flock of sheep and a field of corn.

Topic: <u>*personal conflict about the future*</u>

Audience: <u>*counselor, friend, teacher*</u>

Organizational pattern: <u>*illustration / example*</u>

As you gain experience in writing, you will learn to choose a writing voice that is appropriate for the topic and purpose you have identified.

Collaborative Writing Project: Working and Learning Together

Writing Assignment

Read through the following possible topics for a paragraph, and then work with one or two other students to discuss the topics.

1. How has communication changed since your grandparents' day?

2. How has transportation changed since your grandparents' day?

3. How has technology made household chores easier in the last sixty years?

4. How has one particular job changed since your grandparents were young?

5. How has one particular job changed since you started working there?

6. What are the primary reasons you did not do well in a class?

7. What are the primary reasons you did well in a class?

8. Explain why a particular party was a success.

9. Explain how your definition of a word is different from another person's definition of that same word.

10. Explain the effects of being called up for military service.

11. Explain the effects of spending time in the service of your country.

12. Describe an unusual or enjoyable or negative experience you have had.

13. How has being a parent changed your life?

In your group, brainstorm together to identify the purpose you want to achieve. Then identify the pattern of organization that best suits your purpose.

Working Individually

1. Continue to brainstorm to develop ideas for your paragraph.

2. Draft a topic sentence that includes a topic and direction and reflects the purpose you have identified.

3. Draft a paragraph, arranging the ideas in the most effective organization.

4. Be sure your paragraph has a topic sentence, support sentences, and a concluding sentence.

Purpose and Audience Influence Voice

Frequently, purpose and audience interact and become major influences on voice. After you have chosen a topic and have identified a purpose, you should ask yourself, "Who is my **audience**?" If you wanted to persuade children to do something, you would use words that children could understand. If you wanted to entertain your peers, you would choose words that would be appropriate for this situation. If you were writing to someone in authority over you because you needed that person to do something for you, you most certainly would choose your words carefully to accomplish your purpose.

Read the following notes, each written with a different audience in mind. In the first note, the topic for the writer is permission to make up a quiz. The audience is the instructor, so the purpose is to persuade the instructor to let the student make up the quiz. Consequently, the student's voice is polite, somewhat formal, and respectful. The italicized words are especially appropriate words for this situation.

Note to Teacher

Ms. Mathews:

Please accept my apology for being absent on Friday, November 8. I stayed up very late the night before doing *some homework* that I was having *a hard time understanding. Consequently,* I overslept the next morning. *Please allow me* to make up the quiz that was given. *I will try* to catch up with the class by *borrowing the notes* from someone in the class.

Thank you.

In a second note, the purpose is the same—to persuade someone to do something. However, because the topic and the audience are different, the voice has changed to match the situation. The topic is missed lecture notes, and the audience is a fellow student. So the voice is informal, friendly, and honest. In the student's note to a friend, the italicized words were chosen to sound informal—simpler phrasing throughout sounds less formal and more appropriate for the fellow student.

Note to Friend

Carla, I *missed math* yesterday because I overslept. Bill came over, and after he left, I still had to do my biology homework. The *stuff* was so hard I had a hard time reading it, and I stayed up until 2:00 this morning studying. I left a note on Ms. Mathews's door *asking her to let me make up the quiz* we had. *Anyhow,* I told Ms. Mathews I would borrow the notes from someone in the class, *so can you let me borrow yours?*

Word Choice Alters Voice

The preceding notes show how word choice changed when the audience changed. The note to the student especially shows how changing the words made the voice sound very different. Word choice often determines whether or not you get your message across. Making poor word choices and not writing appropriately for the audience can distract the reader so much that the message you intended to convey is missed. Recall the situation introduced at the beginning of this chapter:

> Mr. Latham has worked hard at his job as a newspaper editor for six years. He has demonstrated creativity and journalistic talent. In those years, he has received favorable evaluations but not a significant raise. He is writing a memo to his boss to convince him that he deserves a raise.

Consider the following memos written by Mr. Latham to his boss. The words used in each memo will affect the boss in very different ways, even though both are written for the same purpose of requesting a raise. The words in italics emphasize how the voice sounds to Mr. Latham's boss.

Memo 1 to Boss

Dear Mr. Stevens,

As you well know, I have worked for this company for six years as a newspaper editor. *Obviously* you haven't *seemed to notice* that you owe me a raise. You *can't help but notice* that I have received favorable evaluations, and it is *long past time to give me a raise.* I have gotten awards, but these awards *don't help me pay my bills any easier. I am sick and tired* of watching other people get raises instead of me. Everyone else thinks that I am doing a good job, so *what is wrong with you?*

In this first memo, Mr. Latham uses words like "obviously" and "you owe me a raise" that distract his boss from hearing a fair request for a raise. Instead, Mr. Stevens is going to feel angry and upset that one of his employees has the nerve to use a condescending, demanding voice. Now read the second memo.

Memo 2 to Boss

Dear Mr. Stevens,

I have worked for this company for six years as an *effective newspaper editor* and have devoted these years to quality work. In this time, I have watched the circulation of this newspaper grow tremendously. I have never missed a deadline, and during the time that I have been here, I have received two awards, one of which was authorized by you. My evaluations reflect a *hardworking, serious employee.* I plan to continue with the same dedicated performance. At the same time, I hope that you will *seriously consider my request for a raise in pay.*

In this memo, Mr. Latham has changed his voice by putting in different information. He has used more factual information about his job and about the newspaper. This second memo is directed toward ideas that highlight his own ability or performance. In the first memo, the emphasis was on accusing the boss of wrongdoing. In the second memo, however, word choices like "effective newspaper editor" and "hardworking, serious employee" emphasize Mr. Latham's performance and enhance his image. His voice, then, is polite rather than arrogant or nervy.

Which memo do you think is more likely to accomplish its purpose? Clearly, the second memo is more appropriate for the purpose intended by the writer. It is also important to be aware that words not only can create negative feelings but can also create negative images. For instance, if you describe a chair as being a "dull, drab, dirty brown," the chair may be perceived as being ugly. On the other hand, if you describe a chair as being "soft beige," the chair is probably perceived as being attractive. These word choices are very important because the negative words result in a negative voice, whereas the positive words result in a positive voice.

A positive voice (like Mr. Latham's in memo 2) is more apt to get the message across because the reader is not distracted by negative or offensive words. Changing words to suit your purpose and audience is an important goal of revision.

Now it is time to get some practice in creating different voices—whether angry, humorous, sad, or informative.

Exercise 3

Read the following sentences and then write words to describe the voice or voices reflected by each statement.

Examples:

a. **Roberto was so perceptive that he understood what I was saying.**

Voice/s: *positive, praising*

b. **Roberto weaseled the information out of me.**

Voice/s: *angry, resentful*

c. **Roberto obtained the information from me.**

Voice/s: *formal, neutral*

1. a. Three red carnations and four orchids mixed with small pine branches and red twist wire stood on the table.

   Voice/s: *positive*

   b. The wilted brown flowers reminded everyone of the passing holidays and the end to the festivities.

   Voice/s: *thoughtful and nostalgic*

   c. All who passed the rotting flowers smelled the moldy odor.

   Voice/s: *negative*

   d. She angrily smashed the flowers and threw the memory of them into the garbage.

   Voice/s: *negative, angry*

2. a. The passenger asked the flight attendant for more peanuts.

   Voice/s: *neutral*

   b. The passenger demanded a different seat from the flight attendant.

   Voice/s: *negative*

   c. The passenger complimented the flight attendant on his courteous, efficient service.

   Voice/s: *positive*

   d. I fondly remember my first airplane trip to Albuquerque.

   Voice/s: *nostalgic*

3. a. Francis always adhered to the traffic laws.

   Voice/s: *pleasant, positive*

   b. Francis zipped excessively fast through the city streets.

   Voice/s: *negative*

   c. For two years, Francis drove downtown to work.

   Voice/s: *neutral, factual*

   d. Francis screamed at the pedestrians and burned rubber as he zoomed around the corner.

   Voice/s: *angry, hostile*

4. a. Joe was hired for the job.

   Voice/s: *neutral*

   b. Joe's sharp thinking during the interview got him the job.

   Voice/s: *positive, complimentary*

   c. Joe got the job in spite of his muddled answers during the interview.

   Voice/s: *negative, derogatory*

5. a. The master of ceremonies rambled and made few points.

   Voice/s: *irritated, disgruntled*

b. The master of ceremonies was inspirational and motivational.

Voice/s: *positive, warm*

c. The master of ceremonies gave a brief talk.

Voice/s: *neutral*

d. The master of ceremonies made sarcastic responses to the audience's questions.

Voice/s: *negative, derogatory*

6. a. The Rocky Mountain Twin Peaks stood 10,000 feet.

Voice/s: *neutral*

b. The majestic mountain peak stood tall against the blue sky.

Voice/s: *positive, poetic*

c. The high mountaintop covered with snow invited those who loved the challenge.

Voice/s: *positive, inviting*

d. That treacherous mountain was the site of the avalanche that injured two skiers.

Voice/s: *ominous, negative*

7. a. I often think of the kindness that woman extended to me as a child.

Voice/s: *nostalgic, positive*

b. That woman took me, a poor child, to her store and helped me select new Easter clothes as a gift.

Voice/s: *complimentary, positive*

c. When I was a child, the women's organization dumped used, outdated clothes on me.

Voice/s: *negative, offensive*

d. On Easter morning, I admired my new clothes in the mirror and then skipped lightly down the hall.

Voice/s: *light, appreciative, positive*

8. a. The young people wolfed down their food as though they had not eaten in a week.

Voice/s: *offensive, rude*

b. The young people ate heartily, enjoying everything that had been prepared.

Voice/s: *positive, light, appreciative*

c. The young people savored the food that had been prepared, much as their parents had done many years before.

Voice/s: *nostalgic, factual, informative, formal*

d. The young prisoners had the food thrown at them as if they were animals.

Voice/s: *negative*

Maintaining the *same voice* within a paragraph or an entire essay is also an important goal of revision. To help you extend your ability to create and keep a consistent voice, try working through the following exercise to see how these elements work together to form a paragraph that will accomplish its purpose.

Exercise 4

Read each sentence and revise it to reflect the new voice given.

Example:

The building was tan. (neutral)

The building was painted in earth tones.
(positive)

The building was painted a boring tan.
(negative)

1. Their house was located in the older section of the city. (neutral)

They lived in the old, neglected, run-down section of the city.
(negative)

Their restored home was in the historic section of the city.
(positive)

2. The young man bought the old car so that he could restore it. (factual)

The young man loved the old car that he had transformed into a beautiful vehicle.
(positive)

The young man bought a beat-up, junky old car.
(negative)

The old car that the young man bought turned out to be a rip-off.
(angry)

3. The people's excited chatter grew louder as the concert began. *(positive)*

   The rude concert audience pushed and yelled obscenities.
   (negative)

   The golden-oldie songs echoed through the park as people recalled college memories.
   (nostalgic)

4. I remember the hillside covered with Texas bluebonnets. *(nostalgic)*

   The Texas bluebonnets that covered the hillside made my allergies worse.
   (negative)

   Texas bluebonnets covered the hill.
   (neutral)

5. Sara felt anxious and insecure as she walked into her 20th high school reunion. *(unsure, tentative)*

   Sara could hardly wait to greet her old friends at their 20th high school reunion.
   (happy, excited)

   Sara frowned at her old enemy classmates as she arrived at their 20th high school reunion.
   (negative)

6. The American bald eagle perched on the tall oak tree branch. *(neutral)*

   With hungry, greedy eyes, the American bald eagle stared from the tall oak tree branch.
   (negative)

   With quiet dignity, the American bald eagle sat on the tall oak tree branch.
   (positive)

7. The blue car had been in the parking lot for three days. *(neutral, informative)*

   "Old Blue" rusted away in the corner of the car lot.
   (nostalgic)

   Please be advised that no cars are allowed overnight in the parking lot.
   (polite)

8. The ecstatic soccer players jumped up and down, celebrating victory. *(enthusiastic)*

   The opposing team scowled at the referee and angrily shook the hands of their opponents.
   (angry)

   The game was a show of poor sportsmanship, inept coaching, and no game strategy.
   (negative)

9. As a fifteen-year-old, Briana felt that her bedroom was the seat of her soul and was off-limits to anyone else. *(arrogant)*

Briana felt that her bedroom was a special place where she could be alone with her thoughts.
(positive)

As a fifteen-year-old girl, Briana spit fire at anyone who came near her room.
(angry)

10. I remember the long, graceful skirts my grandmother wore. *(nostalgic)*

My grandmother's silk skirt was wrinkled and tattered.
(negative)

Look at my grandmother's beautiful lavender silk skirt.
(excited)

Exercise 5

Using the topic, purpose, audience, and voice described below, draft a paragraph that reflects the four elements in either A or B. Revise each paragraph to create the most effective voice for the intended purpose. (You may wish to prewrite on other paper first.)

A.

Topic: installation of speed bumps in a neighborhood with lots of children

Purpose: to convince residents to pay for speed bumps that will make the street safer for their children

Audience: neighborhood residents

Voice: friendly, lighthearted, factual

B.

Topic: installation of speed bumps in a neighborhood with lots of children

Purpose: to get permission to install several speed bumps in a local neighborhood

Audience: city traffic commission

Voice: persuasive, factual

_____

_____

_____

_____

_____

_____

_____

_____

_____

A.

Topic: improved technology for physically challenged students

Purpose: to inform the school what they need to provide

Audience: school board

Voice: authoritative, factual, persuasive, formal

B.

Topic: improved technology for physically challenged students

Purpose: To convince citizens that taxes need to be raised

Audience: parents

Voice: persuasive, factual, friendly

_____

_____

_____

_____

_____

_____

_____

_____

_____

Now, as you continue writing, you can be more conscious of and sensitive to your audience so that you achieve the purpose of your writing. Because voice often determines what kind of attitude your reader has while reading your paper, you can communicate more effectively by selecting the right words.

 ## Collaborative Activity

Divide into groups of three. Select one of the following situations. Collaboratively write a short note to the audience based on voice 1, 2, or 3. Then share the notes with the rest of the class.

Situation 1

A company with mandatory overtime for its assembly-line workers has reduced overtime pay from $20 an hour to $15 an hour.

Voice 1: supervisor to all employees

Voice 2: supervisor to friend who is scheduled to work twenty hours of overtime

Voice 3: supervisor to the president

Situation 2

A bond issue for an elementary school district did not pass. Budgets will have to be cut, and the computer labs for the schools will not be completed.

Voice 1: teachers to students

Voice 2: school board to parents

Voice 3: parents to the newspaper

Situation 3

A sixteen-year-old borrows her boyfriend's parents' car and dents the fender in an accident.

> *Voice 1:* young woman to her boyfriend
>
> *Voice 2:* young woman to her boyfriend's parents
>
> *Voice 3:* young woman to the insurance company

Situation 4

Julie has just moved out of her apartment, and the manager refuses to refund her security deposit even though she has cleaned the apartment thoroughly. She needs the security deposit to buy her college textbooks.

> *Voice 1:* Julie to the apartment manager
>
> *Voice 2:* Julie to one of her teachers
>
> *Voice 3:* Julie to the Better Business Bureau

Part 2

Something to Think About, Something to Write About

Professional Essay to Generate Ideas for Writing

Space to Sing

Letter by **Dean K. Terasaki**, *Faculty, Art/Photography Department, Glendale Community College*

1   Toward the end of each spring, the art department in which I teach at Glendale Community College (GCC) exhibits perhaps four or five hundred student artworks, in a salon-style exhibition. This year, amid charges of racism that forced the removal of a student's piece, the exhibit was closed down by the art department faculty. The art department faculty voted to close the exhibition as an act of solidarity with Julie Glaze, the first-year sculpture student whose piece was removed. It was closed to honor the contract we had with each student that no piece would be removed before the close of the exhibition. With tremendous sadness, I voted that the show be closed. I write because I am concerned for my community and this conflict between expression and political correctness.

2   I am concerned for my peers who made the charges of racism because I, too, am a person of color. I am concerned for my students because they are the ones I repeatedly ask to show me in their photographs what they passionately believe to be important, to be the truth, to be worth loving. This is not the sentimental task of trying to please a parent; it is the vulnerable task of the creative endeavor. I am concerned that as this semester winds to a close, an opportunity for discussion of race, stereotype, and free expression will evaporate in the long summer heat.

3   I appreciate the expression of outrage toward Julie Glaze's sculpture, "Mother Earth," which was seen as a racist stereotype by some members of the GCC educational community. In the midst of the racist graffiti that has been appearing on

campus, this community has been sensitized to racial conflict. It is in this atmosphere that the artwork was threatened with destruction and subsequently taken from the exhibition. But something very important was lost with the forced removal of this artwork and the subsequent closing of the Student Art Show. Art is about conversation. It is about intercourse. It is about learning what you and I feel. It's about our experience as separate individuals who share a community and walk on the same ground. This breath of life, this exchange of what is personal, these hopes and fears, laughter and anger are the very things that artists hunger for.

4   Glaze's piece was motivated by love. "Mother Earth" is a sculptural portrait of an outgoing, humorous, black woman whom Glaze spoke and laughed with many times as they rode together on an Atlanta city bus. The removal of this piece from the exhibition in essence sends a message to Glaze. The message essentially states that Glaze's memories of this woman, her feelings of love and respect, indeed her own biography are not valid territories for the expression of art. I fear that every time Glaze or any other student moves to create something in the future it will be tempered by her fear that she will anger someone. I'm wondering if castrated might be a better word than tempered because if she decides not to make her vision a reality, then that is, in fact, what will have happened to that thought, that idea, that love which will not be given its artistic manifestation.

5   Notwithstanding this possible future, the issues of free speech and academic freedom, and the problems of having to remove each and every piece that offends someone for its lack of political correctness, because "Mother Earth" was removed, a voice was silenced. There was no discussion. That was to be the end of the story.

6   I can speak from personal experience that racist stereotypes are a fiction, a lie, a blasphemous, scurrilous oversimplification that deny the humanity and the individuality of those they purport to describe. Those stereotypes deny the very things that art and artists seek to reveal. Could there be some irony here? I believe that catalyzed by this work of art, just at the point when discussion about the vicious nature of racial stereotypes could start to take place in the wider arena of this full community, a conversation clearly needed here at GCC, the germinating seed was nipped in the bud.

7   It must be understood that artistic expression is vulnerable. While this student may claim to have made this work out of love, her piece, like any artwork, had a life of its own. Like any child learning to socialize, this piece said something very rude to some although I would argue it was out of pure innocence. However, because of the larger context of the white supremacist graffiti that has been appearing on campus, a state of fear exists for all minority members of the GCC community.

8   That fear turns to anger when given a chance. My experience of going home confused in the second grade to ask my mother, "What's a Jap?" played no small part in forming the rage that is at the core of my being. I believe this rage must be part of my art. I learned of the emotional power of at least one of my pictures this semester when I retrieved from the Faculty Art Exhibition a photograph that had been spat upon twice during the show. Once I got past my anger and powerlessness, I truly felt that my photograph had succeeded. It somehow represented something so strongly to one or two people out there that they were compelled to express themselves as well with my photograph as the target. While I would have preferred a cup of coffee and some conversation, this story will have to suffice.

9   "Mother Earth" was simply a convenient target as well. It was tangible, both ugly and beautiful in its truthfulness. The solution was not to remove it, denying an innocent voice the space to sing, and forcing the closure of the Student Art Show. The solution was to talk, maybe even scream, to validate Julie Glaze's experience, and at

the same time help her understand that she does not live in a vacuum. The solution was to let people know.

"Can't we all just get along?"

Understanding Words

Briefly define the following words as they are used in the above paragraph.

1. solidarity   *being strongly united*

2. vulnerable   *easily hurt*

3. stereotype   *a fixed picture of a person, usually negative*

4. castrate   *to remove the vitality or force of*

5. manifestation   *real form*

6. blasphemous   *lacking respect for something considered sacred*

7. scurrilous   *abusive, as in language*

8. catalyzed   *caused change without changing its own form*

Collaborative Writing Project: Working and Learning Together

1. Divide into groups of three, and select someone to keep the group on task and someone to keep notes.

2. Select one of the following quotes. For ten to fifteen minutes, discuss the meaning of the quote. Also, discuss what happens to people who are victims of these ideas.

Quotations: Additional Ideas on Prejudice

"Ageism is a prejudiced outlook toward (or treatment of) people who are deemed too young or too old to be regarded as fully human." *Virginia Ramey Mollenkott*

"Like an unchecked cancer, hate corrodes the personality and eats away its vital unity. . . . Hate cannot drive out hate; only love can do that." *Martin Luther King Jr.*

In China, a woman's "worth is 'measured by the loudness of her husband's belch.'" *Amy Tan*

"Interestingly, prejudice penalizes not only the child who is hated but also the child who hates." *Bruce A. Epstein, M.D.*

"When refugees flee their homeland because of 'ethnic cleansing,' they aspire to come to the United States. These exiles have heard that the strength of America comes from people living together despite differences in culture, race, and religion." *Bruce A. Epstein, M.D.*

"So how did a nice person like you get to be overweight?" *Richard Simmons*

"There is something deeply disturbing about a culture that insists on glorifying one extreme physical type [thin] while portraying even moderately large women as either neurotic freaks or boring losers." *W. Charisse Goodman*

3. At the appropriate time, have the notetaker report the results of your discussion to the class.

Writing Assignment

Now that you have read the article and discussed the quotations about prejudice, write a paragraph about one of the following topics.

1. Where have you experienced prejudice in society?

2. Where have you seen prejudice in society?

3. What can people do individually to decrease or eliminate prejudice?

4. Why are people prejudiced?

5. Should public art shows be censored?

6. Discuss society's attitude toward older people.

7. How can children learn to be open-minded?

8. What determines the ideal appearance of people? How might this result in prejudice?

After reading through these topics, begin working on your writing assignment by following these steps:

1. Brainstorm or freewrite, using one of the above topics.

2. Decide on the audience and purpose for your paragraph. Think about a voice that is appropriate for this audience.

3. Develop a topic sentence that includes a subject and a direction.

4. Following the model shown on page 34 in Unit 1 under "Outline the Paragraph," make a rough outline of the ideas that will go into your paragraph.

5. Draft a paragraph, using your outline. As you are working, use any other related thoughts or details that occur to you. Be sure to include a closing sentence that brings your reader back to the main idea in your topic sentence.

6. When you have finished your draft, reread it, paying particular attention to the voice you have used.

7. Make sure you have two copies of your draft so that you will have one for yourself and one for your partner for peer review.

Peer Review

Choose a partner and exchange paragraphs. Carefully read one of the paragraphs out loud. Then answer the following questions. Just as in the previous peer review, write directly on the paper so the author can consider the responses later. Then read the other person's paragraph, following the same procedure.

1. Identify both the topic and the direction in the topic sentence.

2. Check to see if key words in the topic and direction are used throughout the paragraph. Discuss any more information that could be added.

3. Write at least two words that describe the voice used by the author.

4. For what audience was this paragraph written?

5. Is the voice appropriate for the purpose and the audience?

6. In what way does the paragraph accomplish the purpose?

7. Check to see if the ideas are in clear, logical order. If a sentence seems out of place, suggest a change.

8. Does the last sentence bring the paragraph to a sense of closure? Does it seem to sum up the main idea?

9. If you are not sure about any of the comments, include your instructor in the discussion.

10. Revise your paragraph, including any of the suggestions you feel will strengthen your paper.

Part 3
Paragraphs and Essays for Discussion and Analysis

Student Writing

The Nursing Home

Steve Bostrom, *student*

I love my grandmother very much, but visiting her in the nursing home is a sad and uncomfortable experience. When I walk in, I see many old, sick people who stare or say weird, crude things. They make me feel that I am intruding and do not belong. My grandmother is suffering from Alzheimer's disease, so it always takes a little time to explain who I am. This also gives me time to mentally orient myself after seeing how the disease has taken a toll on her mind and body. Then another problem appears, what to do while I am there. Conversation is hard because she cannot keep her mind on what the conversation is about although sometimes she will get a thought and will not let it go. For example, she will start yelling, "Take me for a walk!" Because she has a broken hip, walking is very painful for her. I will try to get her mind on another subject, but it does not always work. She keeps insisting on going for a walk until I remind her that she has a broken hip. She then will argue about it and tell me that I'm an "asshole" or "full of shit." She never talked like this before she got sick, so I understand, but it still hurts to hear her talk like that. One of the biggest problems is saying good-bye. I know she likes having people there to visit, but I am so uncomfortable I can hardly stand to stay too long. So I leave, knowing that in a few minutes she will forget that I was even there. Going to visit Grandmother is not fun, but I know it is important, so I'll continue to put myself in that uncomfortable position.

Understanding Words

Briefly define the following word as it is used in the above paragraph.

1. Alzheimer's disease   *A disease that causes severe mental deterioration*

Questions on Content

1. Explain the conflict in the author's mind when he visits his grandmother.

2. What disease has changed his grandmother?

3. How is her behavior different now compared to how she acted in her earlier life?

Questions on Form

1. Describe the author's voice.

2. What is the author's purpose?

3. Who do you think is his audience?

Subways

Muriel Gray, *student*

When I was a child, traveling on the New York subway system to and from school was sheer torture for me. I was sure that every insane, perverted drunk in the world traveled only by train. It seemed that I would run into one every day. Some would threaten me with bodily harm while others would hound me until I would give them my lunch money. When the train entered a tunnel, the hair stood up all over my body. The lights in each car went completely out, and I was sure that the weirdo in this car had staked me out for this precise moment. My heart pounded wildly until I reached my stop. The torments of the subway system are still vivid in my mind today.

Understanding Words

Briefly define the following word as it is used in the above paragraph.

1. perverted   *turned away from what is good or right*

Questions on Content

1. In what city did these incidents take place?

2. What does the author dislike about the subways?

3. What happened when the train entered a tunnel?

Questions on Form

1. What is the author's purpose? How well does she accomplish her purpose?

2. The author has successfully captured a distinct voice in this paragraph. How would you describe it?

3. Why is this experience so easy for the reader to relate to? What phrases or support sentences make this experience believable?

4. Who could be an appropriate audience for this paragraph?

Professional Writing

Growing Up Latina

Eva Montoya, *College Administrator*

1   In college in 1967, I decided to join my roommate's sorority. It seemed like the thing to do at the time, even though for me it was expensive. So I went through the party invitation process. Rushing a sorority meant that I could attend only those parties whose members, after scrutinizing me, would reinvite me. I made it through

all the parties until the last crucial invitation. When I went to the Dean of Women's office, I noticed that I was not reinvited to the particular sorority I wanted. That afternoon, against all Panhellenic rules, my roommate called me in tears, explaining that a sorority alumna would not approve my membership because of my surname. It was Hispanic. I cannot really explain the futile dismay or defenselessness I felt in this experience. In high school, I had been an honor student, a cheerleader, a girls' state representative, a class officer, and a homecoming and prom princess, yet because of my surname, I could not be a Chi Omega. I could control other aspects of my life, but I could not control my heritage. I went through years feeling misfortune until I reached adulthood and realized the beauty of my Hispanic culture and its influence on my perception: it helped me to gain the strength to be different and to speak a second language, to appreciate people over material items, to make a celebration out of nothing.

2   I was, in today's vernacular, an exceptional or diverse child; however, because I attended a school with a large Hispanic population, I never noticed my "diversification." However, I do remember having my English teacher correct my pronunciation of various words. This guidance was not unusual except that the incorrect pronunciation was correct at home, so I had to learn which pronunciation to use at school and which to use at home. Again, looking back as an adult, I see now that at an early age I unconsciously perceived myself as being different. Fortunately, because I had no control over my uniqueness, I gave myself permission to be unique, and this has, I believe, been a source of later creative individuality for me. Every day, as an educator, I see inflexible minds that have never had the push to be different. Growing up different can be difficult at times, but the distinction remolds perception in an advantageous way, too.

3   "Mi casa es tu casa," is a very familiar "dicho" among Hispanics as well as "Gabachos" (whites). The phrase denotes an unlimited welcome, an open-door policy, or a boundless generosity. I remember a visit from friends on the Fourth of July. This family had several children, and the mother was pregnant. During the visit, the mother started labor, and my parents, of course, offered their bedroom. Playing the midwife role, my mother assisted in the birth of a baby boy, and because it was July, he was named Julio. The young parents were so indebted that they offered the baby to my parents. My parents appreciated this gracious offer, but they felt they had enough children. This Hispanic hospitality was not an exceptional happening. Almost every Saturday, three to four separate family visits were not unusual, and the minute a foot stepped into our home, the hospitality began. Potatoes were peeled. The beans were warmed; the chili was begun, and the tortillas were rolled for a hot meal. Everyone was unconditionally welcomed and fed, and they usually left with the extra tortillas or fresh produce from the garden. As a child, I thought everyone participated in this unlimited giving and sharing, and it wasn't until I left my childhood inner circle that I learned some people do not open their doors in this way.

4   Most families remember get-togethers as quiet meals and conversations. For me, holidays meant about fifteen Hispanics gathering together. Everyone brought a few basic cultural similarities like red or green chili, a pot of beans, or tamales, and each family brought a specialty like a pineapple upside-down cake. We ate, and, later, adults and children mixed and played baseball or volleyball. Then, as evening neared, guitars and accordions emerged, and we gathered by an open fire and listened to the traditional Mexican songs. Women and men would sing, and some would dance together with the children. I especially have fond memories of my father playing the guitar and being the center of entertainment. As a child, I never really appreciated these times. Not until I became an adult did I realize the wonderful messages that

came from those experiences. To this day, I realize that good times do not have to be expensive or involved.

5   I am a product of my past. Growing up Latina has made me realize that differences are all right and are to be celebrated, not shunned. Whatever material possessions we have should be shared with our friends, relatives, and, yes, even strangers. The best of times can be spontaneous, cheap, and simple, and, most of all, my childhood was extraordinarily wonderful.

Understanding Words

Briefly define the following words as they are used in the above essay.

1. sorority   *a club of women with something in common, as in college*

2. scrutinizing   *examining or looking at carefully*

3. dismay   *discouragement, fear, dread*

4. vernacular   *everyday language of common people*

5. denotes   *signifies*

Questions on Content

1. What was the biggest hurt the author experienced during her college years?

2. What are the fond memories she has of her dad?

3. What is the source of her later creative individuality?

Questions on Form

1. How old do you think the author was when she wrote this article? Why is this perspective effective?

2. How would you describe the tone of voice in this essay?

3. In what way is this essay forceful for different audiences?

4. For what purpose do you think this essay was written?

I Am Not a Disease

Excerpt from the article "On Being a Cripple," in *Plain Text* by **Nancy Mairs**, poet and essayist

1   I am not a disease [multiple sclerosis].

2   . . . a disease is not—at least not singlehandedly—going to determine who I am, though at first it seemed to be going to. Adjusting to a chronic incurable illness, I have moved through a process similar to that outlined by Elizabeth Kübler-Ross in *On Death and Dying*. The major difference—and it is far more significant than most people recognize—is that I can't be sure of the outcome, as the terminally ill cancer patient can. Research studies indicate that, with proper medical care, I may achieve a "normal" life span. And in our society, with its vision of death as the ultimate evil, worse even than decrepitude, the response to such news is, "Oh well, at least you're not going to *die*." Are there worse things than dying? I think that there may be.

3   I think of two women I know, both with MS, both enough older than I to have served me as models. One took to her bed several years ago and has been there ever since. Although she can sit in a high-backed wheelchair, because she is incontinent she refuses to go out at all, even though incontinence pants, which are readily available at any pharmacy, could protect her from embarrassment. Instead, she stays at home and insists that her husband, a small, quiet man, a retired civil servant, stay there with her except for a quick weekly foray to the supermarket. The other woman,

whose illness was diagnosed when she was eighteen, a nursing student engaged to a young doctor, finished her training, married her doctor, accompanied him to Germany when he was in the service, bore three sons and a daughter, now grown and gone. When she can, she travels with her husband; she plays bridge, embroiders, swims regularly; she works, like me, as a symptomatic-patient instructor of medical students in neurology. Guess which woman I hope to be.

Understanding Words

Briefly define the following words as they are used in the above paragraphs.

1. decrepitude   *state of deterioration*
2. incontinent   *unable to control bodily functions*
3. foray   *short trip*

Questions on Content	Questions on Form
1. What does the author say is NOT going to determine who she is?	1. What pattern of organization is used in paragraph 2?
2. With "proper medical care," what can she hope to achieve?	2. How does the author use the reference to *On Death and Dying*?
3. What two types of women were models for her?	3. Name some details that make the example effective.

An American Soldier

Excerpt from "The Casualty" by **Dan Baum**, freelance journalist

1   When people talk about the Army being good for a certain kind of young man, it's boys like Michael Cain they have in mind. . . .

2   To Charlene's [Michael's mother] amazement, Michael thrived under military discipline. The unity of purpose, the clarity of authority, and the hard physical work all gave him hope of becoming the man he wanted to be—serious, competent, respected. His biggest gripe in calls home was that other soldiers were insufficiently respectful to the drill sergeant—a complaint that left his mother speechless. His score on the Army entrance exam wasn't high enough to get him into electronics, but it qualified him to be an "eighty-eight mike"—a truck driver. For Private Cain, barreling along in a thirty-eight-thousand-pound transport at highway speeds was more fun than arranging displays of toaster ovens. He twice wrote to his recruiter, describing how he was getting his "ass kicked" so hard he'd lost twenty-eight pounds, but also to thank him for helping him "fulfill a life long dream, being AN AMERICAN SOLDIER!!!" After basic, he was sent to Vicenza, Italy, and spent two years driving trucks and taking parachute training in order to get his jump wings. The Army worked its traditional alchemy. Michael rose smoothly to the rank of specialist and was sent to Fort Hood, Texas. He met an attractive woman named Leslie Lantz, who worked at a Denny's restaurant in the nearby town of Killeen, and they began seeing each other. On April 1st of last year [2003], Cain departed for Kuwait and left in her care his most precious possession—a new Dodge Ram pickup.

3   Two decorations hold particular fascination for soldiers who are shipping out. The Combat Infantryman Badge, or C.I.B., is awarded for spending at least sixty days under fire. The Purple Heart goes to soldiers wounded by enemy action. Together, they mean that a soldier has experienced the essence of warfare. What soldiers want when they envision the Purple Heart is to get shot, patched up, and returned to their

platoons in one piece. When Cain [eventually] left for Iraq, he knew he'd get his C.I.B. But he also boasted to his mother that he'd win a Purple Heart.

Understanding Words

Briefly define the following words as they are used in the above paragraphs.

1. alchemy   *transformation*

2. platoons   *military groups, each containing 2–3 squads led by a lieutenant*

Questions on Content

1. How did Michael react to military discipline?

2. After basic training, what rank did he achieve?

3. What did Michael do to earn his jump wings?

4. In the last paragraph, what did Michael boast to his mother?

Questions on Form

1. Give an example of the results of his military training.

2. What is the topic sentence in the last paragraph?

3. What does the author do to develop this topic sentence?

Etiquette, What to Say When You Can't Find the Words

Susan P. Halpern, psychotherapist, founder of the New York Cancer Help Program, and author of *The Etiquette of Illness*

Usually etiquette means simply a correct form of speech and behavior to be used in predictable situations. I use the word in a different sense in this book. I intend etiquette to mean thoughtful and compassionate behaviors, influenced by the specifics of care and relationship. When I use the word, I mean speaking our sincere inner truth from our heart and mind. It's not a set of rules and manners that can be learned and should be performed, but it is the true underlying kindness and engagement with other people in a way that is helpful to both parties. If we took the care to do it well, the world would be a better place. There is no *one* way to write the perfect card or say the perfect words of condolence. What is important is to be able to write the card, when we are so moved, and once we have written [the card], to send the card, to make the call, to ask our questions, and to give voice to our feelings of love.

Understanding Words

Briefly define the following words as they are used in the above paragraph.

1. predictable   *expected*

2. engagement   *caring interaction*

3. condolence   *expression of care and concern*

Questions on Content

1. What is the dictionary or ordinary meaning of "etiquette"?

2. When does Halpern say we should write a card?

3. What is also important when we are moved to do something kind?

Questions on Form

1. What is the pattern of organization in this paragraph?

2. How does Halpern clarify the meaning of "etiquette"?

Being a Leader

Excerpt from *Talking from 9 to 5* by **Deborah Tannen**, professor of linguistics at Georgetown University and author

1   Similar [cultural] expectations constrain how girls express leadership. Being a leader often involves giving directions to others, but girls who tell other girls what to do are called "bossy." It is not that girls do not exert influence on their group—of course they do—but, as anthropologists like Marjorie Harness Goodwin have found, many girls discover they get better results if they phrase their ideas as suggestions rather than orders, and if they give reasons for their suggestions in terms of the good of the group. But while these ways of talking make girls—and, later, women—more likable, they make women seem less competent and self-assured in the world of work. And women who do seem competent and self-assured are as much in danger of being negatively labeled as are girls. After her retirement, Margaret Thatcher was described in the press as "bossy." Whereas girls are ready to stick this label on each other because they don't think any girl should boss the others around, it seems odd to apply it to Thatcher, who, after all, was the boss. And this is the rub: Standards of behavior applied to women are based on roles that do not include being boss.

2   Boys are expected to play by different rules, since the social organization of boys is different. Boys' groups tend to be more obviously hierarchical: Someone is one-up, and someone is one-down. Boys don't typically accuse each other of being "bossy" because the high-status boys are expected to give orders and push the low-status boys around. Daniel Maltz and Ruth Borker summarize research by many scholars showing that boys tend to jockey for center stage, challenge those who get it, and deflect challenges. Giving orders and telling the others what to do are ways of getting and keeping the high-status role. Another way of getting high status is taking center stage by telling stories, jokes, and information. Along with this, many boys learn to state their opinions in the strongest possible terms and find out if they're wrong by seeing if others challenge them. These ways of talking translate into an impression of confidence.

Understanding Words
Briefly define the following words as they are used in the above paragraphs.

    1. anthropologists   *people who study humans and their culture*

    2. Margaret Thatcher   *first woman prime minister of Great Britain from 1979 to 1990*

    3. hierarchical   *organized by rank*

    4. jockey   *maneuver*

    5. deflect   *push away*

Questions on Content

1. What are girls sometimes called when they give direction to others?

2. Why don't boys accuse one another of being bossy?

3. What is one way boys take center stage?

Questions on Form

1. What pattern of organization is used in these paragraphs?

2. Why does the author refer to Margaret Thatcher?

Dear Dad

Excerpt from *Dear Dad* by **Louie Anderson**, comedian and actor

God, what I would have given to hear and see you play. I never did, you know. I've never even seen a photo of you playing the horn. I remember a few times when there was a trumpet resting beside the platform rocker in the living room. But you didn't play it. I wonder, though, if when you performed it was the same as when I'm on stage? You're up there in front of the crowd and every moment is very real. Your heart seems connected to a light, and the truer you are to your heart, the brighter the light gets and the stronger your heart feels, and your eyes see the world spinning at its absolute clearest.

Questions on Content

1. What instrument did Louie Anderson's dad play?

2. What did the author wonder about?

Questions on Form

1. How would you describe the voice of the author?

2. What comparison does Louie Anderson make?

3. Who is Louie Anderson's audience?

Getting Off the Roller Coaster

Jerry L. Palmer, former utility worker first-class, Palo Verde Nuclear Generating Station, presently studying to be a rehabilitation counselor for alcoholics

1   "Hi, my name is Jerry, and I'm an alcoholic." I'll never forget the day I stood up and said that. It was not easy after twenty years of being an alcoholic to change my life around, yet there I stood at Chit Chat Rehabilitation Hospital saying those words to Group Ten, the support group of twelve people who helped me understand what alcohol did to me. These people, along with the doctor, helped me, a very depressed and insecure person, take the first step on the road back to recovery. However, in order to recover, I had to turn my life completely around emotionally, physically, mentally, and socially.

2   Emotionally, life as an alcoholic is a roller-coaster ride. The only problem is the ride never ends. When I was high, I felt more confident, more relaxed, and happier. I could make everyone laugh, and I was always the life of the party. I would never think of going to a party unless I was high on something. But, when I was down, I was very shy, very insecure, and very depressed. I was afraid of life, responsibility, and most people. I needed a crutch in life, and I found it in alcohol. I kept that crutch for twenty years or more. Then on Sunday, April 10, 1986, I found my world closing in around me. I was very unhappy and totally confused about my life. I didn't know which way to turn or whom to turn to. I told my wife I was going to check out of this world and today was just as good as any other day. It was very clear to my wife that I was headed toward a nervous breakdown. The next day my wife had me admitted into Chit Chat Rehab Hospital. Chit Chat was different from the usual twenty-eight-day rehab hospital. At Chit Chat I had to stay until the doctors said I could go home. I didn't know it then, but my life was about to change.

3   When I entered the hospital ward at Chit Chat, the first rule I was taught was that to make the mind healthy, I must first make the body healthy. That meant that before I could start their program and be physically able to handle all the pressure, all the alcohol in my body had to be removed. I spent eight agonizing days in that dreadful hospital ward while my body became accustomed to functioning without alcohol in it.

I went through terrible withdrawal (because of the drugs inside me) the first three days, and though I tried, I just could not keep anything down. The fourth day the sweating and shaking stopped, and I had lost eleven pounds. Still I wouldn't eat. All I wanted was a drink of alcohol. I knew without alcohol or drugs in my system I could not function. The doctors told me that alcohol and drugs were the reason that my family put me in there, and if I didn't start eating, they would have no other choice but to force-feed me. I was really determined to get out of that hospital, but at last I realized that no matter what I did or said I wasn't going anywhere. So on the eighth day I stopped fighting them and started eating. I had taken my first step.

4   When I went through detoxification and had all the alcohol and drugs removed from my body, it was like waking up from a twenty-year sleep. Even though the alcohol and drugs were out of my system, mentally I was still sick. When I tried to remember things about my life, I found out I couldn't. I didn't realize that while I was under the influence of alcohol, I was just existing in this world. Sure, I knew a lot of things, but I didn't know anything about me as a person. When I had started drinking alcohol, I had stopped thinking about myself. All I thought about was getting that next drink; mentally I had stopped growing. I was so thankful that the doctors and the people of Group Ten were there to help me when reality set in and I had that nervous breakdown. Without them, I would have never made it, emotionally or mentally, through one of the hardest times of my life. They helped me turn my life completely around by showing me how to get off and stay off that roller-coaster ride, how to believe in myself as a person, how to deal with the pressure when I become nervous and shy around people, and how being myself is more fulfilling than trying to be someone I am not. It took a lot of tears, argument, and hard work to pull me through, but I made it. I was the only black person in that hospital; therefore, I was called "The Soul Survivor." They used a lot of tricks on me that kept me emotionally and mentally strong. They really cared about me, and I knew it.

5   Except for a two-hour visit each Saturday from my family, for seven months the people at Chit Chat were the only people I came in contact with. They told me that changing socially would be very difficult, especially toward family and friends. Socially all my friends were alcoholics. If they didn't drink, I didn't want to hang around them. I have four brothers who are all alcoholics. I knew that if I wanted to stay sober, I had to get away from all of them. It really hurt me to say good-bye to everyone, but I did, and I moved my family out West to Phoenix, Arizona. Out here in Phoenix, I have a new start in life, and my family has adjusted very well to the changes that they had to make. Though I travel back East once a year at Superbowl time to visit Harve, my only friend back home who doesn't drink, I still don't have the confidence in myself to be around my brothers and other friends when they are drinking. So, I sneak in and out of town without anyone knowing I am there. For now, even though it hurts me deep down inside, I know for me to stay sober things must stay this way. Some day, one day, I hope to be able to go home for a visit.

6   Every day I continue to fight a disease that took twenty years out of my life the same way someone would take a bite out of an apple. It is a disease that a lot of people know about, but only a few really understand. I must live with the fact that this disease will never die inside me until the day I die. This disease is called alcoholism. "Hi, my name is Jerry, and I'm an alcoholic, but I've been sober for three years."

Understanding Words

Briefly define the following word as it is used in the above essay.

    1. detoxification   *The removal of the effects of poison or drugs*

Questions on Content

1. How long was the author a practicing alcoholic?

2. Why was the author admitted to Chit Chat Rehab Hospital?

3. How did Mr. Palmer get the name "The Soul Survivor"?

4. After he left the hospital, what did he realize he had to do to stay sober?

Questions on Form

1. Who is the audience?

2. What is the purpose for this article?

3. What is the voice?

Part 4

Grammar for Effective Writing: Consistent Point of View

Objectives

- Understand point of view.
- Identify shifts in point of view.
- Make point of view consistent in a paragraph or essay.

Point of view is the way you as the writer present ideas in a paragraph or an essay. You can talk from your own experience, can speak directly to the reader (such as giving directions), or can relate someone else's experience.

When you talk from your own experience, the pronouns *I* or *we* can be used. When you speak directly to the reader, *you* is used for either singular or plural. When you relate someone else's experience, *she, he, it,* or *they* is used.

When you use *I* or *we,* you are using **1st person.** When you use *you,* you are using **2nd person.** When you use *she, he, it,* or *they,* you are using **3rd person.**

	Singular	Plural
1st person	I	we
2nd person	you	you
3rd person	she, he, it	they

In other words, you can write from different **points of view.** The 1st person point of view ("I," "we") allows you to write as if an experience happened directly to you.

I will take Psychology 201 next semester.

We will take Psychology 201 next semester.

The 2nd person point of view ("you") gives directions to your reader or allows you to speak directly to your reader.

You will take Psychology 201 next semester.

You will enjoy Psychology 201 next semester.

The 3rd person point of view ("she," "he," "it," "they") allows you, the writer, to be less personal and to discuss someone else's experience.

She will take Psychology 201 next semester.

He will take Psychology 201 next semester.

Helen will take Psychology 201 next semester.

They will take Psychology 201 next semester.

They will take **it** next semester.

Determining Point of View

Determining person or point of view is very simple. All you have to do is locate the main subject in a sentence and then decide which pronoun can be used in place of this subject.

For example, in the sentence "Bob and his stereo go everywhere together," the subject is "Bob" and "stereo." The only pronoun that can replace this subject is "they," so the point of view is 3rd person plural.

In the sentence "Janet and I often go hiking," the subject is "Janet" and "I." The pronoun used to replace this subject must be "we," so the point of view is 1st person plural.

In the sentence "The manager of the company hired new employees," the subject of the sentence is "manager." The pronoun that replaces this subject must be either "she" or "he," so the point of view is 3rd person singular.

In the sentence "For a high school graduate, summer work in a large city is generally easy to find," the subject of the sentence is "work." The pronoun that replaces this subject can only be "it," so the point of view is 3rd person singular.

In the sentence "Bill needs to go on a vacation," the subject is "Bill," and if you were speaking directly to Bill, you would use the pronoun "you" instead of "Bill." "You need to go on a vacation" is 2nd person singular.

Now try identifying the point of view in the following exercise.

Exercise 1

Underline the subject, and then, above the subject, put the pronoun that could be used to replace the subject.

Example:

They

~~The children~~ walked home from school every day.

He
1. ~~Fernando~~ is doing well in chemistry this semester.

It
2. ~~Using digital cameras~~ can be exciting.

We
3. ~~Roger, Stephanie, and I~~ watched the Fourth of July parade, and we enjoyed it.

It
4. ~~Maintaining a consistent point of view~~ is really quite simple.

They
5. ~~The electricians~~ had to rewire the entire building.

She
6. ~~Juanita~~ returns to Mexico for a vacation every year.

He
7. ~~Keshawn~~ played a leading role in the musical production.

They
8. ~~The bicyclists~~ moved through the streets at a rapid pace.

It
9. ~~Eating hot dogs at baseball games~~ is an American tradition.

They
10. ~~Amy Tan and Sandra Cisneros~~ both write prose that portrays an understanding of different cultures.

Maintaining Consistent Point of View

Tests on consistent point of view are on pages 26–29 in the Test Bank.

Maintaining a consistent point of view means that you establish the person (1st, 2nd, or 3rd person) in the first sentence of your paragraph and then continue to use that same person throughout the paragraph unless there is a logical reason to change. For instance, if you say, "Parents are often surprised by the many unpredictable games their children play," you will use the 3rd person plural because the subject is "parents" (*they*). You would continue to use nouns that are consistent with 3rd person pronouns (*she, he, it,* or *they*) or any of these pronouns throughout the remainder of the paragraph. As you read through the following paragraph, pay close attention to the 3rd person nouns and pronouns in bold type. Notice that *they are all in the same person.* Not all 3rd person nouns and pronouns have been marked.

> **Parents (they)** are often surprised by the many unpredictable games **their** children play. **Their** children often imitate activities that **they** have seen grownups do, or **they** simply want to be helpful. **Ann and her sister (they)** did just this when **they** decided to improve the neighbor's lawn chairs by covering them in a nice coating of mud. Not only did the **neighbor (she)** get a grand surprise, but so did the girls' **father (he)** when **he** found out that **they** had used his new paint brush. Another time their **brother Bobby (he)** set up a candy shop in the basement where **he** made a fresh batch of divinity with his **mother's (her)** laundry soap. Working hard to be a great chef, **he** whipped the mixture into a smooth consistency with his mother's eggbeater. Their **mother (she)** was the one who was upset this time when **she** went to wash **her** clothes and found that the detergent box was empty. The **children (they)** decided to make lemonade one afternoon but used lemon detergent as the base. Fortunately, **their** effort to help was discovered before anybody drank any of this sparkling drink. Though **parents (they)** can be upset and frustrated when the **children (they)** are so helpful, **they** can also appreciate **their** efforts to be grown up.

Occasionally, you may have a logical reason to shift the point of view in your paragraph. Be careful, however, because you can accidentally change the meaning. For example, if you change the first sentence in the previous paragraph to "Parents are often surprised by the many unpredictable games *your* children play," you are implying that the readers' children, not the parents' children, are unpredictable. That is probably not what you intended to say.

Note Perhaps the most common writing difficulty you will run into is a shift from 1st or 3rd person to 2nd person. Therefore, be certain that when you use "you," you are really addressing the reader and not just shifting your point of view.

Once again, use the following table to help you examine the preceding paragraph for consistent point of view in each sentence:

	Singular			Plural		
	Subj.	Obj.	Possessive	Subj.	Obj.	Possessive
1st person	I	me	my, mine	we	us	our, ours
2nd person	you	you	your, yours	you	you	your, yours
3rd person	she	her	her, hers	they	them	their, theirs
	he	him	his			
	it	it	its			

The following exercise will help you change point of view so that you can find and change point-of-view shifts in your own paragraphs.

Exercise 2

Underline the subject and change the word(s) to a different person or point of view as shown. Refer to the table if necessary. (Be sure to change any pronouns that follow in the sentence. Some sentences require verb changes as well.)

Example:

Change to 3rd person

Their   *their*
~~Your~~ <u>assignments</u> are always typed on ~~your~~ computer.

1. *Change to 1st person.*

   I   *volunteer*
   <u>~~Antonio~~</u> often ~~volunteers~~ at the local food bank.

2. *Change to 3rd person.*

   They
   ~~I~~ put away the tools before leaving for the day.

3. *Change to 1st person.*

   I
   ~~The children~~ found a ten-dollar bill on the sidewalk.

4. *Change to 3rd person.*

   They   *their*
   <u>~~My sister and I~~</u> have always tried to take ~~our~~ vacations at the same time.

5. *Change to 1st person.*

   I   *play*
   <u>~~Isabella~~</u> ~~plays~~ trumpet in the band.

6. *Change to 3rd person plural.*

     they

For exercise, ~~I~~ walk in the neighborhood mall.

7. *Change to 1st person.*

    I   *my*

Last year, ~~you~~ began the research on ~~your~~ family genealogy.

8. *Change to 3rd person.*

 Robert is/Rosa is   *his/her*

~~I am~~ anxious to start ~~my~~ new job as a consultant.

9. *Change to 1st person.*

   I

~~Others~~ have procrastinated until the last minute.

10. *Change to 3rd person.*

 Josh buys his

~~I buy my~~ airline tickets over the Internet.

Revising Inconsistent Point of View

In the following paragraph, the point of view shifts several times in a confusing way. These shifts are marked for you in bold type. Read the paragraph. Then study the sentence-by-sentence analysis that follows so that you can understand how and why the point of view should be revised throughout.

UPS

 (1) The hardest **job** is working at United Parcel Service. (2) **They** pay well, but it is hard work. (3) **You** have to be able to lift seventy pounds into a truck. (4) **They** require that you load up to three hundred and fifty packages an hour. (5) The **hours** I work are weird, and **that** makes it difficult, too. (6) I work third shift, which is three to nine in the morning. (7) There are no **breaks.** (8) **You** work until all the work is done. (9) I have four trucks to load. (10) I have to run and grab as many packages as I can off the slide and load them into the truck. (11) I am running constantly. (12) If **it** weren't for the money, there is no way I would work that hard.

Sentence 1: The hardest **job** is working at United Parcel Service.

 The subject in the first sentence is "job." The correct subject pronoun to use in place of "job" is "it." By looking at the table, you can find "it" listed as 3rd person singular. The 3rd person singular sets the point of view for this sentence and, consequently, for the entire paragraph. In using this point of view, the writer is speaking *about* something.

Sentence 2: **They** pay well, but **it** is hard work.

The second sentence uses the subject pronoun "they" rather than a noun for a subject, so to determine the point of view for this sentence, you simply find the subject pronoun "they" in the table. As you see from the table, "they" is 3rd person, but because it is *plural*, it does not refer to "job" in sentence 1. To clear up the vague reference, "the company" might be used instead because it is more specific.

Revision: The company pays well.

Sentence 3: **You** have to be able to lift seventy pounds into a truck.

Here the writer uses the subject pronoun "you." As the table indicates, this is a shift to the 2nd person, but the preceding sentences use 3rd person singular. "Jobs" is a better choice than a pronoun because it is specific.

Revision: Jobs require lifting up to seventy pounds into a truck.

Sentences 4 and 5: **They** require that you load up to three hundred and fifty packages an hour.

The **hours** I work are weird, and **that** makes it difficult, too.

The fourth and fifth sentences shift back to the 3rd person plural. The writer is speaking *about* something.

Revision: Employees are required to load. . . . The work hours are at odd times, too.

Sentence 6: **I** work third shift, which is three to nine in the morning.

In the sixth sentence, the subject is "I," so the writer has shifted to 1st person and is speaking from a personal perspective.

Revision: The third shift works three to nine.

Sentence 7: There are no **breaks.**

Now the writer shifts to the 3rd person *plural* point of view.

Revision: Third shift has no breaks.

Sentence 8: **You** work until all the work is done.

Here the writer shifts back to "you" and addresses the reader directly again.

Revision: Employees are expected to stay until all the work is done.

Sentences 9–12: **I** have four trucks to load.

I have to run and grab as many packages as **I** can off the slide and load them into the truck.

I am running constantly.

If **it** weren't for the money, there is no way **I** would work that hard.

In the remainder of the paragraph, the writer shifts again to "I." The writer shifts the experience from 2nd person ("you"), which directs the reader, to 1st person ("I"), which indicates that the writer is sharing his or her own personal experience.

Revision: It is not unusual for employees to load four trucks. They have to run and grab. . . . They are running constantly. . . .

The shifting point of view in the UPS paragraph makes it difficult to follow. At times, the reader may lose sight of who is speaking and who is being spoken to. The paragraph, in effect, lacks an extremely important component—coherence. By using a consistent point of view, coherence is strengthened. Also, this shift in point of view makes it difficult to determine an audience and purpose. Now read a thorough revision of this paragraph and compare it to the first draft.

Consistent 3rd Person Point of View

UPS

Working at United Parcel Service is strenuous, demanding work. The **company** pays well, but the **work** is hard. First of all, entry-level **jobs** require lifting up to seventy pounds into the bed of a truck. Along with this, **employees** are required to load three hundred and fifty packages an hour. The work **hours** are at odd times, too. The third **shift** works three to nine in the morning with no breaks. In addition, **employees** are expected to stay until all the work is done. It is not unusual for **employees** to load three trucks in one day. **They** have to run and grab as many packages as **they** can off the slide and load them into the truck. Because the **money** is good, **United Parcel Service** is always looking for **people** to do this type of demanding work.

By keeping a consistent 3rd person point of view (*she, he, it, they*), the writer is able to use a variety of nouns as well as the four subject pronouns. Also, the voice now sounds more objective and more convincing. Because of this consistent 3rd person point of view, this paragraph might be used as a job description with an intended audience of potential employees.

As a contrast to the 3rd person point of view, the 1st person (*I*) allows the writer to personalize his or her experience and make the tone of the writing more informal. Read the following paragraph and notice how the 1st person (*I*) point of view helps the reader identify with the writer's experience.

Consistent 1st Person Point of View

UPS

The hardest job I ever had was working at United Parcel Service. I was pleased with my salary, but I thought it was hard work. First of all, I had to be able to lift seventy pounds into a truck and load up to three hundred and fifty packages an hour. Besides this, I had a difficult schedule, too. I worked the third shift, which was from three to nine in the morning, with no breaks. At times I had to stay longer until all the work was done. Often, I had three trucks to load, and I would have to run and grab as many packages as I could off the conveyor and load them into the transporting truck. I was running constantly. I believe that if I hadn't been getting good money, there is no way I would ever have worked that hard.

This paragraph maintains the 1st person point of view. It allows the writer to identify all the experiences as his or her own. This paragraph might easily be a journal entry or a reflection.

Now read the same paragraph written from the "you" point of view, the 2nd person. Generally, the "you" point of view is found in papers that give instructions to a reader or in an explanation or discussion (like those in this textbook) that speaks directly to the reader. Notice how the 2nd person point of view affects the tone of voice of the paragraph.

Consistent 2nd Person Point of View

UPS

If **you** enjoy hard work, **you** might like working at United Parcel Service. **You** will enjoy the salary because it pays well, but **you** will probably find the work demanding. First of all, **you** have to be able to lift seventy pounds into the bed of a truck, as well as load three hundred and fifty packages an hour. **You** will also discover that the work hours are at very odd times. If **you** are on the third shift, **you** have to work from three to nine o'clock in the morning with no breaks. In addition, **you** have to stay until all the trucks are loaded. **You** often load three trucks in one day. **You** have to run and grab as many packages as **you** can off the conveyor and load them into the truck. However, the pay is good. If this sounds appealing to **you,** fill out **your** W4 form and show up at 3:00 tomorrow morning.

This paragraph has a consistent 2nd person point of view and may be effective at a job orientation. However, unless you are giving instructions to someone or are speaking directly to your audience, you may want to choose another point of view. Keep in mind that different points of view create different impressions on your reader. Because you can learn to control point of view, you have one more way to control how you sound in your own writing. As a result, you can feel more confident about how your reader will react.

Maintaining a consistent point of view keeps your paragraph focused and brings your many sentences together as one piece of writing. For longer papers, a consistent point of view is essential for clarity. Consequently, you should edit carefully for a point of view that is consistent and appropriate for your topic, purpose, and audience.

As a writer, you must decide what your writing purpose is and match your point of view to that purpose. Do you want to sound more authoritative or more personal? Do you want to inform or entertain? Do you want to remain distant or get close to your reader? Do you want to sound more formal or informal? Answering these questions will determine your point of view and give you greater control over a writing situation.

Exercise 3

Read the following paragraphs and identify the shifts in point of view. The first sentence establishes the point of view that should be maintained. Any deviation from the first sentence should be changed to an appropriate subject pronoun or noun that conforms to the point of view of the first sentence. Some sentences require verb changes as well. Revise each paragraph by making the point of view consistent. When you have finished revising each paragraph, identify the purpose, voice, and audience.

Paragraph 1

I love to haggle every time I go to a border town in Mexico. First of all, I make

out a list of the items I would like to have. Then I find a market square that has lots

I believe that competition

of vendors. ~~Competition~~ allows me to do some comparative scouting and may mean

I   *I*

lower-priced items. ~~You~~ should always go dressed in older clothes so that ~~you~~ don't

I   *I*

look like the rich American tourist. As ~~you~~ enter the store, ~~you~~ should not appear anxious. Next, with a maximum price in my mind, I casually saunter to the object

that I most want. If the vendor's price is way above my price, I go to the next store. If

not, I smile and offer him a price lower than my set price, and we begin haggling

we can
from that point. Usually, a~~compromise is struck,~~ and we both go away happy.

Purpose: _to explain shopping in Mexico_

Audience: _general reader_   Voice: _honest, frank_

Paragraph 2

Renee loves to haggle every time she goes to a border town in Mexico. First of
she makes   *she*   *she finds*
all, ~~I make~~ out a list of the items ~~I~~ would like to have. Then ~~I find~~ a market square
her
that has lots of vendors. Competition allows ~~me~~ to do some comparative scouting
She   *goes*
and may mean lower-priced items. ~~You should~~ always ~~go~~ dressed in older clothes so
she doesn't   *she enters*   *she does*
that ~~you don't~~ look like the rich American tourist. As ~~you enter~~ the store, ~~you should~~
                              her   *she*   *saunters*
not appear anxious. Next, with a maximum price in ~~my~~ mind, ~~I~~ casually ~~saunter~~ to
            she   *wants*   *her*   *she goes*
the object that ~~I~~ most ~~want.~~ If the vendor's price is way above ~~my~~ price, ~~I go~~ to the
                she smiles   *offers*   *her*   *they*
next store. If not, ~~I smile~~ and ~~offer~~ him a price lower than ~~my~~ set price, and ~~we~~ begin
                              they strike a compromise   *they*
haggling from that point. Usually, ~~a compromise is struck,~~ and ~~we~~ both go away happy.

Purpose: _to explain shopping in Mexico_

Audience: _general reader_   Voice: _honest, frank_

Paragraph 3

The long-time Mexican luminaria tradition warms Christmas Eve in many

neighborhoods in the United States. The tradition of luminarias—paper bags, each

one containing a small candle anchored in a little sand—was imported into the

United States many years ago as Mexicans brought their simple means to light up
their   *people*   *their*
~~your~~ haciendas. To participate in the tradition, ~~you~~ line ~~your~~ driveways and

sidewalks with many small paper bags, each one holding a flickering candle,
they   *their*
anchored in sand. In this way, ~~I~~ turn ~~my~~ neighborhood into an enchanted

wonderland. Taking part in this activity provides a way for ~~you~~ *neighbors* to celebrate the

season together and greet visitors. The luminarias provide a brilliant transformation

from darkness to a magical lighted maze. This primitive version of Christmas lights

has expanded, and now ~~you~~ *people* can buy artificial luminarias, bulbs that are placed in

small plastic bags and lit by electricity. However, the old authentic use of bag, sand,

and candle is still popular and provides ~~me~~ *them* not only with light but a connection with

~~your~~ *their* past and a way to bring people together toward a common Christmas goal—

harmony and beauty.

Purpose: _to explain the tradition of luminarias_

Audience: _general reader_   Voice: _informative, factual, nostalgic_

Paragraph 4

Reentry students enroll in college for a variety of reasons. Sometimes women

have not worked outside the home and have recently been through a divorce. ~~I~~ *They*

realize that the responsibility of finding a job to support ~~me~~ *themselves* and ~~your~~ *their* children is

crucial to survival, so ~~we~~ *they* enroll in college to gain career skills. Some students may

have been involved in an accident or may have a debilitating disease so ~~you~~ *they* are no

longer physically able to continue with ~~your~~ *their* present occupation and must learn a

new way of life. ~~We~~ *Others* are victims of downsizing by business, and ~~you~~ *they* lack skills

required for today's industry. These reentry students return with the goal of

acquiring specialized technical skills. Community colleges welcome them all and

provide training that will allow ~~you~~ *these individuals* to become successful, productive members of

the workplace.

Purpose: _to explain why students go back to college_

Audience: _people interested in education_   Voice: _informative_

Paragraph 5

Changing the oil and the oil filter in an automobile can be a simple task for car

they

owners. By referring to the car manual, ~~I~~ know the correct kind and amount of oil as

They

well as the correct size of oil filter to purchase. ~~You~~ then begin the job by loosening

the engine oil cap on the top of the engine so a little air goes into the oil cavity,

they

making the oil drain more thoroughly. When ~~I~~ loosen and remove the drain plug at

they

the bottom of the oil pan, ~~I~~ notice that the used oil will easily drain into a separate

container that should be disposed of according to environmentally safe standards.

They

The owners can now easily remove the used oil filter. ~~You~~ then put a light coat of

They

fresh oil on the new filter's rubber seal and put in the new filter. ~~I~~ then replace the

They

drain plug, remove the oil cap on top of the engine, and put in the fresh oil. ~~You~~

then put the oil cap back on, and the job is done for at least another three months.

Purpose: _to tell how to change an oil filter_

Audience: _car owner_   Voice: _informative, objective_

Part 5

Putting It All Together

Cumulative Unit Exercise

Now that you are aware of voice and realize the importance of maintaining a consistent point of view, practice your skills on the following paragraph.

1. Read the paragraph carefully.

2. Now read the first sentence again and identify the point of view. Determine if this point of view results in the desired voice. If the point of view seems appropriate, check the second sentence to be sure that the point of view has not changed. Then read the remaining sentences to be sure the paragraph has maintained a consistent point of view. Revise to make the point of view consistent.

3. The voice in this paragraph is positive and praising. Underline words that you feel develop this positive voice.

4. Then check to see if there are any subject-verb agreement errors or inconsistencies in verb tense. If you find any, correct them.

5. Check to see if all the sentences support the topic sentence.

6. Check to see if the concluding sentence completes the idea presented in the topic sentence. Be prepared to discuss your answer.

Overcoming Challenges

Transparency of uncorrected cumulative exercise is on page 48 in the Instructor's Manual.

(1) Two American teenagers who live in different parts of the country are overcoming major challenges in their lives. (2) Born with no arms below the elbows and no legs below the knees, both of these young men have strong supporting families who ~~made~~ *make* every effort to help them become <u>happy and confident</u>. (3) Having learned at an early age, ~~you~~ *they* set goals for ~~yourself~~ *themselves* and work hard every day to meet them. (4) Each teenager plays positions on the defensive line for his high school football team and makes <u>valuable contributions</u> to the team. (5) In fact, they both have game balls, given to them during the season for making tackles and recovering fumbles. (6) These young men also <u>make an</u> impression off the playing field. (7) They make above-average grades in all their classes and ~~looks~~ *look* forward to going to college. (8) When they have to do the equivalent of a lot of walking, ~~you see them~~ *they* use motorized wheelchairs and <u>cruise around campus</u> from class to class. (9) They seldom need help and <u>do not</u> expect special favors. (10) Perhaps most amazing of all, they always ~~seems~~ *seem* to be <u>energetic and upbeat</u> as they face the ventures ahead of them.

Collaborative Writing Project: Working and Learning Together

Writing Assignment

As you have learned in this unit, a piece of writing has a voice. A paragraph can be nostalgic, angry, sad, happy, or neutral. Your attitude as a writer toward your subject and the words you choose to express your feelings are reflected in the voice or tone of the paragraph. What happens if you consciously select your voice **before** you write? This exercise will help you answer this question.

1. Use one of the following ideas to generate a topic sentence for this exercise.

The best/worst _____ I ever had was. . . .

Using the above phrase, circle either **best** or **worst** and then complete the idea with whatever topic you choose. Some suggestions might be **car, pet, class,** or **meal.**

What I appreciate/dislike most about my _____ is. . . .

Using the above phrase, circle either **appreciate** or **dislike** and then complete the idea with whatever topic you choose. Some suggestions might be **neighbor, girlfriend, boyfriend, sister, brother, mother, father** (or another relative).

2. Based on your topic sentence above, write your overall feeling toward the subject.

3. Brainstorm for ideas and words that capture this voice.

4. On the other side of the paper, using your selected topic sentence, draft a paragraph that describes your subject. As you write, keep your selected voice and purpose in mind. Your purpose is to show how you feel about this subject. Identify an audience for your paragraph.

Working in a Group

1. Team up with another student. Read your rough draft out loud, but **do not reveal the tone of voice you intended for the paragraph.** This activity will not work if you tell your reader ahead of time what voice you intended to use in the paragraph.

2. Then ask your listener to guess the tone of voice, the purpose, and the audience you had in mind when you wrote the paragraph.

3. If your listener cannot guess your tone of voice, purpose, or audience, you may then share it.

4. Discuss words, sentences, or ideas that will make the voice more obvious or more appropriate for the audience and purpose.

5. Repeat the same steps for your partner's paragraph.

If you consider voice before you write a paragraph, you will have to consider your purpose and audience. By doing this, you will write a stronger paragraph.

Working Individually

1. Using your partner's suggestions, revise your draft.

2. When you are satisfied with the content, check the subject-verb agreement in each of your sentences.

3. Check for consistent verb tense.

4. Use a 1st person point of view in your topic sentence. Check your point of view throughout the paragraph, and make sure it is consistent. Eliminate any inconsistencies in point of view, especially any use of the 2nd person "you."

Final Checklist

Content

Revise the paragraph so it has a clear topic sentence.

Include four to six supporting sentences.

Include a closing sentence.

Check to see that the voice is appropriate for purpose and audience.

Mechanics

Check for subject-verb agreement.

Check for consistent verb tense.

Check for a consistent point of view.

 Internet Activities

Activity 1   Learning About Internet Sources

If you want to search the Internet successfully, you need to know how to find credible information online. You may use one or more of the following search engines, but always keep in mind what you learned earlier about evaluating websites.

About
http://www.about.com

AltaVista
http://www.altavista.com

Ask Jeeves!
http://ask.com

Dogpile
http://www.dogpile.com

Excite
http://www.excite.com

Findwhat
http://www.findwhat.com

Google
http://www.google.com

HotBot
http://hotbot.com

Infoseek
http://www.go.com

LookSmart
http://www.looksmart.com

Metacrawler
http://www.metacrawler.com

Monstercrawl
http://www.monstercrawl.com

NorthernLight
http://www.nlsearch.com

Overture
http://www.overture.com

Teoma
http://www.teoma.com

WebCrawler
http://www.webcrawler.com

Yahoo!
http://www.yahoo.com

Bruce Maxwell, a leading journalist, author, and editor of several newsletters, has written twelve tips for searching the Internet successfully.

a. Read through his suggestions.

1. If your subject is broad (cancer, archaeology, politics), start with a directory—such as Yahoo!—that categorizes websites by subject. Just pick the most likely subject, and then drill down through layers of subcategories until you find what you want.

2. If your subject is narrow (such as a particular bed-and-breakfast you want to try), choose a search engine such as AltaVista, HotBot, Excite, Infoseek, or NorthernLight.

3. For comprehensive research, use several search engines or try a meta-search engine such as Metacrawler that simultaneously queries numerous engines.

4. Before using a search engine, read any instructions it offers. Yes, these documents can be snoozers, but each engine has its quirks, and knowing them will help you craft a more accurate search.

5. When choosing keywords for a search engine, select six to eight words to help narrow your search. If you type just one or two words, you'll likely get thousands or even millions of documents. Use nouns whenever possible, and put the most important words first. Put a "+" before any word you want to include, and a "−" before any word you want to exclude. (This works with most engines.)

6. To increase your search's accuracy, use phrases instead of single words. Put quotation marks around the phrase.

7. Many search engines will let you refine the results of your initial query. Do it.

8. When you find a good website about your topic, check whether it provides links to similar sites.

9. You may be able to guess the address of specific sites. Many are "www," a period, the name or acronym of the site's operator, a period, and three letters denoting the site's type. Thus: www.microsoft.com (commercial), www.fbi.gov (federal government), and www.harvard.edu (education).

10. Double-check your spelling. You'd be amazed at how many people misspell words in their queries.

11. Keep in mind that even if you type a precise query, many of the documents returned won't be applicable. Computers (and search engines) aren't perfect.

12. Remember: The Internet does not contain the sum of all knowledge. You may still need to hit the library.

b. After reading through these suggestions, list three that seem the most helpful to you in doing web searches.

Answers will vary.

_____

_____

c. For further exploration, go to Bruce Maxwell's website. (Type all Internet addresses exactly as they appear.)

http://bmaxwell.home.mindspring.com

Activity 2   Doing a Search on the Internet

In this activity, you will have an opportunity to practice what you have learned about doing successful searches.

   a. Select one of the following authors: Ernest Hemingway, John Steinbeck, Amy Tan, Sandra Cisneros, Larry McMurtry, Frank McCourt, or Charles Dickens. Proceed through the steps below to find a critique of your author's work.

   b. Select a search engine such as Alta Vista, HotBot, Excite, Google, or Infoseek. Type in the address of your search engine. Once you are at the website, locate the search box, and type in your author's name and the word/s "evaluation," "critique," or "critic."

   c. Then, once you have a suitable critique, evaluate the critiquer's voice and audience. Look for words that highlight or defend your opinion. Write a paragraph, and share your evaluation with the class or with your collaborative group.

Activity 3   Practicing Consistent Point of View

Visit Capital Community College's writing support page to learn more on consistent point of view and take a quiz.

   a. Go to the following website. (Type all Internet addresses exactly as they appear, or use a bookmark or favorite for quick access.)

   http://webster.commnet.edu/grammar/index.htm

   b. You will arrive at the "Guide to Grammar & Writing" page. Look at the right-hand side and pull down the menu for "Paragraph Level."

   c. Select "Tense/Pronoun Consistency." Read through the information on this page, including the information concerning Toni Morrison's *The Bluest Eye*. If your instructor asks you to, take the quiz on "Consistency in Tense and Pronouns."

Unit 3

Organizing Ideas and Writing Them Clearly

Writing Skills: The Thesis Sentence

Pretest over Unit 3, Parts 1 and 4, is on page 5 of the Test Bank.

Objectives

- Write a thesis sentence that states the direction of the paper.
- Write a thesis sentence that previews the points to be covered in the paper. Be sure that all divisions are coordinate with each other, subordinate to the general direction in the thesis sentence, and parallel to each other.
- Brainstorm to generate ideas.
- Cluster the related ideas.
- Identify and write the divisions in sequential order.
- Include the key word of each division in the topic sentence of each support paragraph.

Just as a paragraph depends on a topic sentence to restrict and control the paragraph, so an essay depends on a thesis sentence to restrict and control the ideas covered in the longer paper. You have just learned that the most general statement in the paragraph is the topic sentence. Similarly, the most general statement in an essay is the **thesis sentence,** which directs and determines the topic sentences that will be used to support the thesis sentence. For example, if your topic sentence states, "Learning disabilities can create problems for students," you can use supporting details to develop a paragraph. Read the following sample paragraph.

> Learning disabilities can create challenges for students. *Often academic challenges arise when learning-disabled students have a difficult time reading the textbook because they are reading two or more years below grade level. Also, the students may have trouble putting into writing what they know well. *This can lead to social challenges because students with learning disabilities often spend two or three times longer doing their homework than other students do, leaving little time to spend with others. *Personal challenges may emerge because they feel inferior to other students who can spell every word right the first time. *The least noticeable of all might be physical challenges like coordination or balance that the average person will not even notice. Though these learning disabilities are difficult for others to detect, they certainly can make life difficult for many students.

If you wish to expand this paragraph into a longer paper, you must discuss the specific ways in which learning disabilities create problems for students. A thesis sentence helps you organize your challenges.

You may write the thesis sentence in two ways: one that clearly states the direction for the longer paper or one that states the direction *and* specifies the points to be covered.

Thesis Sentence That States the Direction

In the sample paragraph, the topic sentence, **"Learning disabilities can create challenges for students,"** could also serve as the thesis sentence for a longer paper. Although it does not preview the main points to be covered in the essay, specific "chal-

---

*These sentences could be developed into separate paragraphs for a longer paper.

lenges" still have to be discussed in a logical, organized manner. Brainstorming could give you these points. Perhaps you would use the four problems included in the sample paragraph (academic, social, personal, and physical) and develop each idea in one (or more) support paragraphs. Each support paragraph will need a strong topic sentence, clarifying the point being discussed.

Look at the following list of topic sentences for the four support paragraphs. Each topic sentence will be the most general statement in the paragraph.

Students with learning disabilities may encounter many academic challenges.

Students with learning disabilities also encounter many social challenges.

Other problems that learning-disabled students experience are personal.

The least noticeable challenges of all might be physical.

Tests covering thesis sentences are on pages 30–37 in the Test Bank.

Thesis Sentence That States the Direction and Previews Main Points

If you preview the main points in your thesis sentence, it might read:

$$\quad\quad\quad\quad\quad\quad\quad\quad \#1 \quad\quad \#2 \quad\quad \#3 \quad\quad\quad \#4$$

Learning disabilities can create academic, social, personal, and physical challenges for students.

(Again, the thesis sentence will be the most general statement in the paper.)

Using the points previewed in this thesis sentence, you can write a topic sentence for each support paragraph. The same topic sentences presented in the previous list could be used in this paper as well.

Support paragraph 1: **Students with learning disabilities may encounter many academic challenges.**

Support paragraph 2: **Students with learning disabilities also encounter many social challenges.**

Support paragraph 3: **Other challenges that learning-disabled students experience are personal.**

Support paragraph 4: **The least noticeable challenges of all might be physical.**

Coordinate and Subordinate Ideas in Thesis Sentences

Whether or not you preview the supporting ideas in the thesis sentence, you need to organize your paper logically. To do this, you need supporting ideas that are **coordinate,** which means that the two or more divisions in the paper must be of equal value. This degree of equality is determined by the restriction and direction of the thesis statement. If in one paper you are writing about working in the yard, having a party, sleeping late, and doing homework, your readers might wonder what these activities have in common. However, if you write

"I look forward to spring break because I enjoy

working in the yard,

having a party,

sleeping late, and

doing homework,"

the reader is then aware that these activities are what you enjoy doing when school is in recess. Even though you might enjoy one activity more than the others, they are all equal.

On the other hand, if you write

"I look forward to spring break because I enjoy

working in the yard and

pulling weeds,"

then your thesis statement is faulty because pulling weeds is not equal to working in the yard. Rather, it is one of the activities you might do when you work in the yard. Furthermore, if you write

"During my spring break, I enjoyed

my personal life,

my social life,

my spiritual life, and

picking flowers,"

it is easy to see that "picking flowers" is too restricted and narrow and, therefore, is not coordinate with the other ideas in the group.

Also, all of these divisions must be **subordinate** to one idea. In this case they must all be activities you enjoy doing during spring break. These divisions might be different for different people. For example, someone else might say, "But I do not enjoy doing homework." Then that person could substitute "working on a car" or "cooking gourmet meals" or "going on a trip." It really doesn't matter as long as all the points you want to make are *coordinate* (equal) and also *subordinate* (under) to the main idea of the paper. Whether or not you preview the points in your thesis sentence, you need to decide on your supporting ideas before writing your paper.

The following exercises will help you determine which ideas are equal to each other and will also help you realize that these coordinate ideas must be subordinate to the thesis statement. These exercises will help you think about how ideas fit together into a paper.

Exercise 1

Read the following words or phrases that could be generated through brainstorming. First, determine which word or phrase is the most general. Second, decide which words or phrases are coordinate or equal to each other. Finally, decide which words or phrases are unrelated or part of another group.

Example:

a. playing croquet

b. hitting the ball with the mallet   ___*a*___ is the most general word or statement.

c. going through the wickets   ___*b, c, d*___ are equal to each other.

d. hitting the post   ___*e*___ is unrelated or part of another group.

e. drinking water

1. a. learning Spanish vocabulary

   b. doing homework   _b_   is the most general word or phrase.

   c. drafting an essay   _a, c, d_   are equal to each other.

   d. studying chemistry   _e_   is unrelated or part of another group.

   e. paying bills

2. a. laughing at the clowns

   b. waiting in the rain   _c_   is the most general word or phrase.

   c. enjoying a parade   _a, d, e_   are equal to each other.

   d. applauding the floats   _b_   is unrelated or part of another group.

   e. humming along with the bands

3. a. getting a cup of coffee

   b. finding counter space   _d_   is the most general word or phrase.

   c. locating an electrical outlet   _b,c,e_   are equal to each other.

   d. setting up a workstation   _a_   is unrelated or part of another group.

   e. plugging in a laptop computer

4. a. eat nutritious food

   b. maintain good health   _b_   is the most general word or phrase.

   c. exercise   _a, c, d_   are equal to each other.

   d. reduce stress   _e_   is unrelated or part of another group.

   e. watch the news

5. a. practicing soccer

   b. passing out snacks   _a_   is the most general word or phrase.

   c. running sprints   _c, d, e_   are equal to each other.

   d. kicking the ball into the net   _b_   is unrelated or part of another group.

   e. playing one-on-one

6. a. educational plan

    b. tax reform   _____*e*_____ is the most general word or phrase.

    c. the First Lady's influence   _*a, b, d*_ are equal to each other.

    d. foreign policy   _____*c*_____ is unrelated or part of another group.

    e. Presidential agenda

7. a. experienced detectives

    b. fingerprints   _____*c*_____ is the most general word or phrase.

    c. police department evidence   _*b, d, e*_ are equal to each other.

    d. DNA tests   _____*a*_____ is unrelated or part of another group.

    e. clothing fibers

8. a. aircraft carrier

    b. canoe   _____*e*_____ is the most general word or phrase.

    c. battleship   _*a, c, d*_ are equal to each other.

    d. submarine   _____*b*_____ is unrelated or part of another group.

    e. naval ships

Exercise 2

Study the following sentences. Identify the most general idea in each sentence.
Then identify which words are coordinate.

Example:

**The mountains are beautiful in the spring because of the new growth, the rains, and
the animal activities.**

mountains are beautiful in the spring
_____
(most general idea)

new growth, rains, animal activities
_____
(words that are coordinate)

1. Most firefighters are trained to put out fires, administer emergency medical
care, and handle hazardous materials.

Most firefighters are trained to
_____
(most general idea)

put out fires, administer emergency medical care, handle hazardous materials
_____
(words that are coordinate)

2. The Grand Canyon offers tourists striking views, exciting mule rides, and comfortable hotels.

The Grand Canyon offers tourists
_____
(most general idea)

striking views, exciting mule rides, comfortable hotels
_____
(words that are coordinate)

3. Special Olympics can give physically and mentally challenged people the thrill of competition, a sense of self-worth, and pride in reaching a goal.

Special Olympics can give physically and mentally challenged people
_____
(most general idea)

the thrill of competition, a sense of self-worth, pride in reaching a goal
_____
(words that are coordinate)

4. Security doors, alarm systems, and floodlights help Americans feel safer in their neighborhoods.

help Americans feel safer in their neighborhoods
_____
(most general idea)

Security doors, alarm systems, floodlights
_____
(words that are coordinate)

5. People in New York City get around by walking, taking taxis, or riding on subways.

People in New York City get around by
_____
(most general idea)

walking, taking taxis, riding on subways
_____
(words that are coordinate)

6. The Internet gives people access to music, email, travel information, and merchandise sales.

The Internet gives people access to
_____
(most general idea)

music, email, travel information, merchandise sales
_____
(words that are coordinate)

7. Having surgery is difficult because it can be expensive, painful, and frightening.

Having surgery is difficult because it can be
_____
(most general idea)

expensive, painful, frightening
_____
(words that are coordinate)

8. Pets aid the elderly by providing security, companionship, and self-esteem.

Pets aid the elderly by providing
_____
(most general idea)

security, companionship, self-esteem
_____
(words that are coordinate)

9. People with diabetes must be concerned with exercise, diet, and stress.

People with diabetes must be concerned with
_____
(most general idea)

exercise, diet, stress
_____
(words that are coordinate)

10. Lack of parental skills, media violence, availability of weapons, and school bullying may play a role in current teen problems.

may play a role in current teen problems
_____
(most general idea)

Lack of parental skills, media violence, availability of weapons, school bullying
_____
(words that are coordinate)

Overlapping Coordinate Ideas

When you write thesis sentences, be sure that the coordinate ideas do not overlap. **Overlapping** occurs when two or more coordinate ideas have approximately the same meaning. For example, the following sentence shows two coordinate ideas with similar meanings.

Redecorating a house requires *creativity*, time, *talent*, and money.

"Creativity" and "talent" are so close in meaning that it would be hard to write separate support paragraphs about them. When you try to write the essay, the two support paragraphs will end up being about the same idea. For example, if people are talented, they are able to figure out color schemes for remodeling a room, or maybe they are able to rearrange the furniture to make the room look more appealing. They might also suggest a few accessories that would accent or highlight the old furniture. If people are creative, they are able to do these same things. Consequently, these coordinate ideas overlap. Now consider a less obvious coordination problem in a thesis sentence:

While raising children, parents try to be *sensitive*, *understanding*, and cheerful.

Though it is not quite as apparent as in the previous example, "sensitive" and "understanding" also overlap in meaning. Parents may understand a child's outburst of temper if they are sensitive enough to know that the child has just been through a frustrating experience. These two ideas are simply too close in meaning to write separate paragraphs about them. As you will see in the model essays in this unit, each support paragraph must explain a different coordinate idea in the thesis sentence.

Read each thesis sentence carefully. Some of the coordinate ideas are faulty because they overlap (have almost the same meaning). Cross out one of the overlapping ideas.

1. People who love pets are usually caring, patient, and ~~kind.~~ *(or ~~caring~~)*

2. A good coach motivates players, ~~plans strategy,~~ recruits rookies, and designs plays. *(or ~~designs plays~~)*

3. DVDs are preferable to videotapes because they have easy search features, clear resolution, durability, ~~sharp display,~~ and compact size. *(or ~~clear resolution~~)*

4. Students respond to teachers who are fair, understanding, smart, knowledgeable, and ~~intelligent.~~ *(or ~~smart~~)*

5. Many young people gain an education through traveling, ~~attending college,~~ volunteering in the community, and going to school. *(or ~~going to school~~)*

6. A beneficial health plan should include a balanced diet, exercise, meditation, ~~healthy food,~~ and doctor supervision. *(or ~~a balanced diet~~)*

7. Businesses that thrive in America provide ~~quality products,~~ excellent service, reasonable prices, and outstanding merchandise. *(or ~~outstanding merchandise~~)*

8. The plumber ~~evaluated the problem,~~ estimated time and cost for the work, figured out what should be done, and then scheduled the job. *(or ~~figured out what should be done~~)*

9. Acquiring computer skills requires ~~persistence,~~ proper equipment, perseverance, clear directions, and time to practice. *(or ~~perseverance~~)*

10. Skiing is dangerous, ~~fatiguing,~~ expensive, and exhausting. *(or ~~exhausting~~)*

Parallel Grammatical Form in Thesis Sentences

If your thesis sentence previews the points to be covered in your paper, be sure that each point is written in the same grammatical form. This similar grammatical structure is called **parallel form.** You may choose whatever grammatical structure you like, such as nouns, verbs, phrases, or clauses. Study the following list to help you understand parallel form.

- **If an "-ing" verb form is used, all divisions must be in an "-ing" form.**

    For the elderly, having a pet means receiving companionship, getting exercise, having protection, and feeling useful.

    receiving companionship

    getting exercise

    having protection

    feeling useful

- **If the present tense of the verb is used, all divisions must be in the present tense.**

  Elderly people with pets receive companionship, get exercise, have protection, and feel useful.

  receive companionship

  get exercise

  have protection

  feel useful

- **If a noun is used, all divisions must be nouns.**

  Having a pet can provide companionship, exercise, protection, and usefulness to the elderly.

  companionship

  exercise

  protection

  usefulness

- **If "to" is used before the verb, all divisions must have "to" written or understood before the verb.**

  Elderly people often own a pet to receive companionship, get exercise, have protection, and feel useful.

  to receive companionship

  to get exercise

  to have protection

  to feel useful

- **If a prepositional phrase is used, all divisions must be prepositional phrases. (If the same preposition is used, it does not need to be repeated.)**

  Elderly people often own pets for companionship, exercise, protection, and a sense of usefulness.

  for companionship

  for exercise

  for protection

  for a sense of usefulness

It really doesn't matter which form is used; however, the thesis sentence will flow smoothly when all divisions are grammatically equal.

Exercise 4

In each group below, some ideas are not in parallel form. Revise the wording to make the parts parallel. Try more than one pattern. You may also change the order of the items within each group.

Example:

a. **to eat pie**

b. **drinking milk**

c. **read a book**

a. *to eat pie, to drink milk, to read a book*

b. *eating pie, drinking milk, reading a book*

c. *ate pie, drank milk, read a book*

1. a. play cards

   b. reading stories

   c. did crossword puzzles

   d. to sort pictures

   a. *play cards, read stories, do crossword puzzles, sort pictures*

   b. *reading stories, playing cards, doing crossword puzzles, sorting pictures*

   c. *did crossword puzzles, played cards, read stories, sorted pictures*

   d. *to sort pictures, to play cards, to read stories, to do crossword puzzles*

2. a. polished the chrome

   b. changing the oil

   c. to clean the windows

   d. put air in the tires

   a. *polished the chrome, changed the oil, cleaned the windows, put air in the tires*

   b. *polishing the chrome, changing the oil, cleaning the windows, putting air in the tires*

   c. *to polish the chrome, to change the oil, to clean the windows, to put air in the tires*

   d. *polish the chrome, change the oil, clean the windows, put air in the tires*

3. a. visiting cousins

b. talk to Grandma

c. to hug favorite aunts

d. listened to Grandpa

a. *visiting cousins, talking to Grandma, hugging favorite aunts, listening to Grandpa* ___

b. *talk to Grandma, visit cousins, hug favorite aunts, listen to Grandpa* ___

c. *to hug favorite aunts, to visit cousins, to talk to Grandma, to listen to Grandpa* ___

d. *listened to Grandpa, visited cousins, talked to Grandma, hugged favorite aunts* ___

4. a. uses a cell phone

b. bought a Palm Pilot

c. burning a CD

a. *uses a cell phone, buys a Palm Pilot, burns a CD* ___

b. *bought a Palm Pilot, used a cell phone, burned a CD* ___

c. *burning a CD, using a cell phone, buying a Palm Pilot* ___

5. a. formed the bowl

b. drawing the design

c. to fire the vase

a. *formed the bowl, drew the design, fired the vase* ___

b. *drawing the design, forming the bowl, firing the vase* ___

c. *to fire the vase, to form the bowl, to draw the design* ___

6. a. camp in the forest

b. to ride a raft

c. hiked the trails

d. eating by the campfire

a. *camp in the forest, ride a raft, hike the trails, eat by the campfire* ___

b. *to ride a raft, to camp in the forest, to hike the trails, to eat by the campfire* ___

c. *hiked the trails, camped in the forest, rode a raft, ate by the campfire* ___

d. *eating by the campfire, camping in the forest, riding a raft, hiking the trails* ___

Exercise 5

Revise each thesis sentence so that the points previewed are in parallel form.

Example:

The flower garden provides a colorful sidewalk border, fresh table arrangements,
and gifts for my neighbors
~~and my neighbors enjoy receiving them as gifts.~~

1. Most people celebrate New Year's Eve by eating a special meal, celebrating with
   making
   friends until midnight, and ~~to make~~ future resolutions.

2. Alternative fuel vehicles are powered by electricity, hydrogen, propane, and

   ~~others run on~~ natural gas.
                                                        obey
3. For safe driving, one must drive under control, ~~obeying~~ the speed limit, and

   never ~~to~~ drive under the influence of alcohol.

4. The office supply store sells digital cameras, fax machines, computers, and ~~it~~

   ~~also has~~ Palm organizers.

5. My winter spent in Maine brings pleasant memories of socializing with friends,
   making
   ^extra money, buying my first car, and surviving my first ice storm.
                                                                    reviews
6. *Time* magazine reports current news, analyzes political campaigns, and^movies

   ~~are also reviewed~~.

7. I enjoy going to that restaurant because the prices are reasonable, the food is
                the service is good
   excellent, and ~~good service~~.
                                             receive
8. Snowboarding enthusiasts enjoy beautiful scenery, ~~receiving~~ healthy exercise,

   and improve physical agility.

9. The gardener mowed the lawns, trimmed the hedges, and ~~he also~~ watered the

   flowers.

10. Servers in restaurants who receive the biggest tips help customers with the
            provide
    menu, ~~providing~~ beverage refills, and politely correct kitchen errors.

11. Playing the piano provides an opportunity to relax, ~~to~~ entertain friends,
    develop
    ~~developing~~ a talent, and ~~to~~ learn new songs.

12. Individuals who experience kidney failure must be concerned with following a
restricting
diet, ~~restrict~~ fluids, getting exercise, and having dialysis.

13. Making a career change often requires a positive attitude, determination, and ~~to learn~~ new skills.

14. Nurses, doctors, and ~~working with~~ therapists are all important to hospitalized patients.

If you do not preview the subtopics in the thesis sentence, be sure that your subtopics are coordinate and identified clearly in your prewriting before drafting the paper.

Generating a Thesis Sentence

Now that you know what a thesis sentence is, you need to learn how to generate ideas that can be used to formulate this thesis sentence. The following steps can help you.

1. **State your topic.**

2. **Brainstorm to find a direction.** Type or write anything that comes to your mind. This is like a game of free association. Continue to jot down ideas as rapidly as they come to mind. Remember, now is the time to use your resources. Generate ideas that come from your personal experiences. Include your feelings. These feelings may be positive or negative; it really doesn't matter so long as they reflect what you have seen or felt.

3. **Find a direction.** Because it is impossible to write everything you know about a subject, it is important to find the direction you want to take. As soon as you are aware of a direction in your brainstorming, write it down. If your topic is "divorce," you might write the following entries:

   a. My divorce has left me with many problems.

   b. My divorce was the best thing that ever happened to me.

   c. My divorce changed my life.

   d. My parents' divorce created many problems for me.

   e. My parents' divorce solved many of my problems.

   f. My parents' divorce changed my life.

   The direction you choose may be either positive (b,e), negative (a,d), or a combination of both (c,f).

4. **Brainstorm with direction.** Once again, jot down everything that comes to mind; however, this time your entries will be more specific because you already have a direction. Continue to brainstorm until you have ten to twelve entries.

5. **Cluster entries that fit together.** Carefully look over all the entries you made while brainstorming. Combine these entries into clusters until you have two to five separate areas that support the focused topic. **The key word and**

direction with two to five support groups form the thesis sentence. Even if you do not preview the points of the paper in the thesis sentence, you will still have coordinate groups of ideas to guide the paper.

6. **Formulate the thesis sentence.** Write it with a clear direction, or write it with a clear direction and previewed subtopics.

Carefully examine the following examples of stating the topic, finding the direction, brainstorming with direction, and sorting related ideas into groups.

Example 1

Topic: Divorce

Brainstorm to find direction:

my divorce   parents divorced

Being divorced has caused me many problems.

divorce is widespread   sister divorced

Direction: Being divorced has caused me many problems.

Brainstorm with direction:

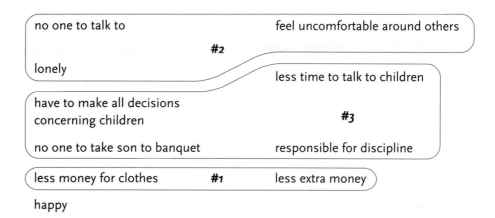

Clusters (topic outline):

1.   money problems (financial)

2.   personal problems (emotional)

3.   responsibilities for son (parental)

Thesis sentence with clear direction:

Being divorced has caused me many problems that I did not face when I was married.

Thesis sentence with clear direction and previewed subtopics:

Being divorced has caused me financial, emotional, and parenting problems that I did not face when I was married.

Note   The groups can serve as a topic outline or as part of the thesis sentence.

Example 2

Topic: pets

Brainstorm to find direction:

dogs	fun for children
need love	good for old people

Direction: beneficial to old people

Brainstorm with direction:

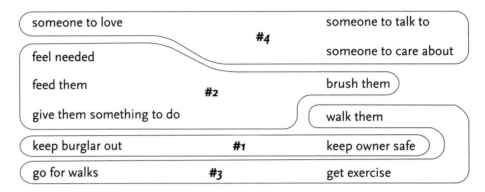

Clusters (topic outline):

1. provide protection

2. make them feel needed

3. get exercise

4. have companionship

Thesis sentence with clear direction:

For the elderly, having a pet can be very beneficial.

Thesis sentence with clear direction and previewed subtopics:

For the elderly, having a pet means receiving companionship, getting exercise, having protection, and feeling useful.

Note   The groups can serve as a topic outline or as part of the thesis sentence.

Exercise 6

Master for the transparency is in the Instructor's Manual, pages 31–32.

Using the process shown in Examples 1 and 2 above, develop a thesis statement for *three* of the following subjects:

tour of your city	*horses*
weight room	*swimming*
football game	*art museums*
a particular restaurant	*stock market*

1. *Topic:* _____

Brainstorm to find direction:

_____
_____
_____
_____
_____

Direction:

_____
_____

Brainstorm with direction:

_____
_____
_____
_____
_____
_____
_____

Clusters (topic outline):

_____
_____
_____
_____

Thesis sentence:

_____
_____
_____

2. *Topic:* _____

Brainstorm to find direction:

_____
_____
_____
_____
_____

Direction:

_____
_____

Brainstorm with direction:

_____
_____
_____

_____
_____
_____
_____

Clusters (topic outline):

_____
_____
_____
_____

Thesis sentence:

_____
_____
_____

3. *Topic:* _____

Brainstorm to find direction:

_____
_____
_____
_____
_____

Direction:

_____
_____

Brainstorm with direction:

_____
_____
_____
_____
_____
_____
_____

Clusters (topic outline):

_____
_____
_____
_____

Thesis sentence:

_____
_____
_____

Arranging the Order of Divisions or Subtopics

One last item you need to consider before writing your thesis sentence is the order in which to present your coordinate ideas. Sometimes there is more than one way to arrange the divisions in a paper, so use your best judgment to decide which order is most effective for the overall development of your essay. Even during drafting, you may discover that you need to rearrange the order of the subtopics. When the thesis sentence does not preview the points to be covered in the paper, the points generated through prewriting can serve as a rough outline. Remember, though, that **the divisions must be presented in some logical order.** Here are some possible arrangements for subtopics.

1. **Place the divisions in order of *increasing importance*, as *you* see them.** Put the most important last.

   Example: Before buying a used car, a person must consider special features desired, type of car needed, cost, and condition of the car.

   Before buying a used car, a person must consider several factors.

   1. special features desired

   2. type of car needed

   3. cost

   4. condition of the car

2. **Place the divisions in order of *decreasing importance*, as *you* see them.** Put the most important first.

   Example: Before buying a used car, a person must consider condition of the car, cost, type of car needed, and special features desired.

   Before buying a used car, a person must consider several important factors.

   1. condition of the car

   2. cost

   3. type of car needed

   4. special features desired

3. **Place the second most important division first and the most important one last, as *you* see them.** Arrange the weaker points in the middle. This order begins and ends on a strong note.

   Example: A nurse must care for patients, fill out charts, and talk to family members.

   A nurse has many duties.

   1. care for patients

   2. fill out charts

   3. talk to family members

4. Place in order of increasing interest, as *you* see them.

Example: Being divorced has caused financial, emotional, and parenting problems.

Being divorced has caused many problems.

1. financial

2. emotional

3. parenting

5. Place in *chronological order*. This is similar to historical progression.

Example: Transportation has progressed from trains to cars to jet planes.

Transportation has progressed rapidly.

1. trains

2. cars

3. jet planes

6. Place in *sequential progression* (one idea naturally follows the other).

Example: To produce good essays, writers brainstorm, sort related ideas into groups, and formulate a thesis sentence.

To produce good essays, writers use an organized process.

1. brainstorm

2. group

3. formulate a thesis sentence

These steps will become automatic as you write more papers. No one method is used by all writers, and some steps may come more easily than others. Just continue to work hard and have confidence in yourself.

 ## Collaborative Activity

Option 1
Divide into groups of three to five. In each group, brainstorm the topic "making a home safe" or "making a home childproof." On self-stick notes, jot down ideas, using only one idea per note. Then, stick the notes on a surface where everybody in your group can see them. Next, group the like ideas together. As a group, compose a thesis sentence that includes a topic and direction. Either preview the main points in the thesis sentence or include a topic outline on a transparency to be shared with the class. Be prepared to discuss each group's thesis sentence.

Option 2
Divide into two age groups: those twenty-five years of age and over and those under twenty-five years of age. Then brainstorm, group related ideas, and develop a thesis sentence based on the following topics.

Group twenty-five years of age and older: Advantages of going to college right out of high school.

Group under twenty-five years of age: Advantages of going to college after waiting ten or more years.

Share the thesis sentences with the other group. Discuss the perspective taken by each group.

Part 2

Something to Think About, Something to Write About

Professional Essays to Generate Ideas for Writing

Drawing the Lines

Liz Hufford, *Chairperson, professor of English at Glendale Community College, and freelance writer*

1   According to tattoo mythology, these ink drawings appeared on brawny arms after a night of hard drinking. In recent years, however, nontraditional groups have undergone the needle, stone sober and in impressive numbers. One tattoo artist reports that female clients, who made up only 5 percent of his practice in the sixties, now account for 60 percent of his business. A recent study reveals that one of ten adolescents has a tattoo, and half are interested in obtaining one. Why does a person become a dermal canvas? The reasons to tattoo vary as much as the designs, but three prominent motivations are the bond, the statement, and the cover-up.

2   Ritual tattooing is still practiced in some parts of the world to mark members of a particular clan or class. This desire to visualize a group bond is alive in the industrialized world as well. Sailors, as stereotyped by Popeye, often assert their profession with appropriate tattoos; in the 1980s some loyal Nike employees sported the company logo. Avocations as well as vocations provide the impetus. Motorcycle club members and their women sport slave bracelets and PROPERTY OF HELL'S ANGELS verbiage. Some tattoos reflect the desire to bond rather than an actual tie. Appreciating the success or appeal of another may explain the demand for celebrity tattoos like Janis Joplin's heart or Pamela Anderson's barbed wire bracelet.

3   The second reason to tattoo contradicts the first. Some tattoos make a personal statement, asserting not commonality but individuality. Aaron, for example, is a quiet honors student and a self-professed computer geek. But a discreet bloody dagger asserts that he will not be stereotyped. Statements of individuality may represent deep personal beliefs; Lucy, a feminist, chose Shiva, a female god, to literally back her. Finally, personal statements may reveal intimate feelings, I LOVE MOM or, more recklessly, I LOVE SHANNA.

4   Over the course of time, name tattoos often provide the motive for the third reason to tattoo, the cover-up. Having now-insignificant others literally under a person's skin can be a difficult situation, especially when a new spouse or lover is involved. Though tattoos can be removed, the process is expensive, and the results not always pretty. Witness Johnny Depp's black triangle on a shoulder where Winona used to rest. Homemade, shabby, or name tattoos can be obscured by more professional, usually more complex, designs.

5   Not all cover-ups mask a physical condition, however. Some tattoos bandage emotional trauma. Deborah Strouse relates the story of her daughter, who was sexually abused as a child but healed herself through tattooing. Her daughter explained her feelings this way: "I was in pain before and had only misery to show for it. Now I choose the pain and have something beautiful and meaningful."

6   Since women and youths are choosing tattoos, some see the act as a tangible manifestation of the empowerment of these individuals and groups. Whatever the reason for the interest in this ancient practice, tattoo parlors were the sixth-fastest-growing business in 1996. Obviously, discomfort, health concerns, and possible adverse societal response no longer dissuade potential customers. Still, cautionary information is available on the Internet and from such an unlikely source as Axl Rose, the heavily tattooed rock singer. What is his advice? "Think before you ink."

Understanding Words

Briefly define the following words as they are used in the above essay.

1. dermal   *relating to the skin*

2. impetus   *driving force*

3. verbiage   *expression in words*

4. manifestation   *display*

Your College Years

Dr. Bob Hartman, *president, BHIM*

1   Have you ever considered the changes that are taking place and will take place in your life as a college student? Has it ever occurred to you that your professors and other school personnel have certain goals for your growth and maturity during your college years? Has it ever dawned on you that certain developmental changes will occur in your life as you move from adolescence to young adulthood? Though college students seldom think about them, key changes will probably happen to them during their college years.

2   During this time, students are going through an identity crisis and are endeavoring to find out who they are and what their strengths and weaknesses are. They have, of course, plenty of both. It is important to know how people perceive themselves as well as how other people perceive them. According to Piers and Landau, in an article discussing the theories of Erik H. Erikson in *International Encyclopedia of Social Sciences* (1979), identity is determined by genetic endowment (what is inherited from parents), shaped by environment, and influenced by chance events. People are influenced by their environment and, in turn, influence their environment. How people see themselves in both roles is unquestionably a part of their identity.

3   While students are going through an identity crisis, they are becoming independent from their parents yet are probably still very dependent on them. This independence/dependence struggle is very much a part of the later adolescence stage. In fact, it may be heightened by their choice to pursue a college education. Immediately after graduating from high school, some graduates choose to enter the work world. As a result of this choice, they may become financially independent from their parents. But college students have chosen to grow and learn new skills that take years to develop, so they probably need at least some degree of dependence on their parents.

4   In his April 1984 article "Psychological Separation of Late Adolescents from Their Parents" in the *Journal of Counseling Psychology*, Jeffery A. Hoffman observed that there are four distinct aspects to psychological separation from one's parents. First, there is functional independence, which involves the capability of individuals to take care of practical and personal affairs, such as handling finances, choosing their own wardrobes, and determining their daily agenda. Second, there is attitudinal independence, which means that individuals learn to see and accept the difference between their own attitudes, values, and beliefs and those of their parents. The third process of psychological separation is emotional independence. Hoffman defines this process as "freedom from an excessive need for approval, closeness, togetherness, and emotional support in relation to the mother and father." For example, college students would feel free to select the major that they want to pursue without feeling they must have parental approval. Fourth is freedom from "excessive guilt, anxiety, mistrust, responsibility, inhibition, resentment, and anger in relation to the mother and father." College students need to stand back and see where they are in the independence/dependence struggle.

5   Probably one of the most stressful matters for young college students is establishing their sexual identity, which includes relating to the opposite sex and projecting their future roles as men or women. Each must define her or his sexual identity in a feminine or masculine role. These are exciting times yet frustrating times. Probably nothing can make students feel lower or higher emotionally than the way they are relating to whomever they are having a romantic relationship with. For example, when I was working with a young college student, he bounced into my office once with a smile on his face and excitement in his voice. The young man declared, "I've just had the best day of my life!" He went on to explain how he had met an extraordinary young woman and how this relationship was all he had dreamed a romantic relationship should be. That same young man came into my office less than a week later, dragging his feet with a dismayed, dejected look on his face. He sat down in the same chair, sighed deeply, and declared, "I've just had the worst day of my life!" He and the young woman had just had an argument, and their relationship was no longer going well. Thus, the way students are relating to those of the opposite sex has a definite influence on their emotions.

6   At the same time, these young adults are learning how to give and receive affection in the adult world. This aspect of growth deals not only with interaction with the opposite sex but with friends of both sexes and all ages. As they grow and reach young adulthood, the way they relate to others changes. It is a time when they as adults should think about how they relate to and show proper respect for peers, how they relate to the children and young adolescents in their lives, and how they relate to their parents and show them affection. For example, when I was a graduate student at Southwestern Baptist Theological Seminary, I visited my parents after I had just finished a course in counseling. During the course I had come to realize that while my world was expanding and new options were opening for me, my father, who was in his sixties, was seeing his world shrink and his options narrow. During my visit home, my father and I had several conversations in which we discussed the content of my course and how it applied to our lives. I found myself seeing my father in a different way and relating to him as a friend whom I could encourage. I was consciously encouraging the man who over the years had encouraged me. I was relating to my father in a different way.

7   Another change for college students is internalizing their religious faith, their values, and their morals. Since birth, one or more parents have been modeling for them and teaching them certain beliefs, values, and morals. In their adolescent years,

however, these matters are questioned and in some cases rebelled against. Now, as young adults, they have the opportunity to decide for themselves what beliefs, values, and morals they are going to accept for their lives. In the late sixties, a young woman from a background that was extremely prejudiced against people from other races came to college convinced that her race was superior. She was distressed because she had been put into a dorm that had people from a variety of ethnic backgrounds. Over the next four years, this student, who considered herself intelligent, found herself in classes and social events in which people of other races performed as well as or more competently than she did. As she finished her senior year, she had grown to realize that people of other races were not only equal to her but were people who could be her friends and from whom she could learn. These religious, moral, and ethical values that are set during the college years often last a lifetime.

8   In addition to affirming personal values, college students develop new ways to organize and use knowledge. The challenges of academic life not only introduce them to new knowledge but force them to evaluate how they gather, process, and apply knowledge in their lives. For some, this will be a painful experience, but for all it will be a growing experience. One student with whom I had worked went on to become an English teacher. She shared with me how her attitude toward literature changed during her college years. "In high school I made good grades in English," she observed, "but the material meant very little to me." She then went on to explain how in college she came to realize that literature is one of the best ways to understand a culture. Her way of learning had changed. All students should be aware of how they react to new knowledge and new ways of learning, how they process the knowledge presented to them, and how they organize this knowledge.

9   And last of all, these young adults are becoming world citizens, are becoming aware not only of other groups in their own culture but also of people of other cultures. As they meet these people and interact with them, they find themselves being introduced to new ways of life and new ways of interpreting life. As they do so, they grow and become more mature people. A student attending a community college in his home town explained how as a student he came to know a student from a Third World country—a country he had not even heard of before. The international student, who expected to be appointed to an important governmental position when he returned home, had a brother who taught law at the major university of his country. The American student and the international student became close friends and spent many hours sharing their thoughts and dreams. The American student observed, "Because of our friendship, I have come to understand people of Third World countries in a way I never realized possible. I can no longer read the newspaper or watch a television newscast without seeing the people from other countries in a different light. They are now real people who have dreams, hopes, and struggles, just as I do." Because of the opportunities he had while attending college, this young man, like many other students, experienced a new understanding of the world and of himself.

10   College is designed to be a time of personal growth and expansion. At times it can be threatening. For certain, it is an experience that contributes to young adults' growth and maturity. Not only are they being introduced to new people and new knowledge, but they are also acquiring new ways of assembling and processing information. Just as profoundly, they are growing in their understanding of themselves, others, and the world in which they live.

Understanding Words

Briefly define the following words as they are used in the above essay.

1. endeavoring   *trying or striving*

2. genetic   *related to the science of studying genes*

3. endowment   *talent, ability*

4. internalizing   *taking in and making an integral part of one's attitude and beliefs*

5. ethical   *pertaining to standards of conduct or moral judgment*

6. Third World country   *the underdeveloped or emergent countries of the world, especially of Africa or Asia*

Collaborative Writing Project: Working and Learning Together

To start your first essay assignment, work in groups of three or four to discuss one or more of the following quotations. Explore the ideas, and see how they might relate to the two previous articles. Your discussion may generate ideas to help you when you choose a topic below.

Quotations: Additional Ideas on Independence

"While few kids want to stay home forever, more of them aren't leaving home without good reasons." *Marcia Mogelonsky*

"The process of separation from parents continues over the entire life course. It is never completed." *Daniel J. Levinson*

"Relationships, and particularly issues of dependency, are experienced differently by women and men." *Carol Gilligan*

"A man has to blaze his own trail, and mine was to the west." *Jubal Sackett*

"One lives so long to learn so little." *Louis L'Amour*

"Young people are responding to the disadvantages of the sexual revolution by returning to more conservative courtship behaviors of the past." *Mark Gauvreau Judge*

"Generation Xers take longer to make job choices. They look upon a job as temporary instead of as a career, partly because they want to keep their options open. They are always looking to jump ship when they can upgrade their situation." *Bob Loysk*

Writing Assignment

1. After you have discussed the articles and quotations as a group, choose one of the following topics:

   What are the advantages or disadvantages of serving in the military?

   How has your job changed in the last five years?

   How have your family responsibilities changed in the last few years?

   How has a divorce changed your life?

How has a change in employment altered your life?

Explain how your life is different now from what it was in high school.

Discuss how a friend has changed since graduating from high school.

Give the biggest challenges that college students face.

Explain types of support that are important to college students.

How is your life different from that of your peers who are working rather than going to school?

In what ways are you dependent upon your parents?

In what ways are you independent from your parents?

How have your values changed in the last few years?

In what ways do young people express their independence from their parents?

Explain the adjustments parents have to make when their children become independent.

2. Work within the time limits suggested by your instructor.

3. Brainstorm to develop a clear direction for a thesis sentence. Using related ideas from your previous discussions, develop one thesis sentence for each group.

4. Consider the purpose and an appropriate audience for the essay.

5. Have someone write down the list of ideas. Encourage each member to contribute to the brainstorming. Be prepared to share your list with the class or turn it in to your instructor.

6. As you learned earlier in this unit, sort the list into three or four groups of related ideas. Choose a general word that includes the related ideas in each group. These words will be the previewed points in the thesis sentence.

7. Write your thesis sentence with a clear direction, and preview the main points for your paper. If your instructor prefers that you do not preview the main points for your essay, write a topic outline so that the support paragraphs will be in logical, effective order.

8. Choose a member from your group to write the thesis sentence on the board. Let the class critique each thesis sentence and decide if an essay could be developed using this thesis sentence. If you have an outline, write it on the board also.

Working Individually

1. Using the thesis sentence developed in your group, begin to draft your own essay. Remember that you will need a topic sentence for each paragraph and that each topic sentence should be developed from one of the points previewed in your thesis sentence or one of the points in your topic outline.

2. Brainstorm further to get enough specific information to develop an adequate support paragraph for each topic sentence.

3. Draft an essay that includes a thesis sentence and three to four support paragraphs.

Peer Review

1. Working with a partner, exchange essays and read one essay aloud.

2. Discuss the purpose and the audience.

3. Decide if the voice is appropriate for the purpose and the audience. Discuss changes in wording that would make the voice more effective.

4. Check the organization of the essay by underlining each topic sentence. Be sure that each topic sentence includes a previewed point from the thesis sentence and goes back to the main idea and direction for the essay.

5. Decide if each support paragraph has enough information to explain the topic sentence.

6. Check for subject-verb agreement, consistent verb tense, and consistent point of view.

7. Repeat the same steps with your partner's paper.

Part 3

Essays for Discussion and Analysis

Student Writing

Respect

Phyllis J. Hilding, *student*

1   "I get no respect!" The comedian Rodney Dangerfield has made many of his fans laugh at this famous remark of his. In truth, however, respect for other people and their property is not a laughing matter. In our world as it is today, respect for other people has taken a back seat to flagrant disrespect of people's feelings, their property, and even their very lives.

2   Respect for other people's feelings seems to be out-of-date in today's world. Children and teenagers are growing into adulthood learning not to "Do unto others as you would have them do unto you," but to do unto others before they do unto you. Movies, television, and today's books most probably have all played a part in forming the younger generation's attitudes. Most parents, regardless of how hard it is, have tried to raise their children to be respectful of their elders and their peers. Besides the outside influences like movies, television, and wanting to be like everyone else, being brought up in a disrespectful family environment where family members talk and act badly toward one another can encourage people to grow up without a sense of value and respect for other people. If parents would treat each other and their children in a caring and courteous way, perhaps they could instill in their children a respect for other people's feelings that would stay with them throughout their lives, regardless of what they see or hear in the world at large.

3   Disrespect is shown every day when Americans see or hear of people stealing or damaging other people's property without feeling any guilt. Thievery and vandalism have always existed, but in today's world, they seem to be prevalent, not from need

and the frustration of being poor, but because of the current generation's sense of values. Thieves and vandals see no wrong in taking or damaging what does not belong to them because they have never learned to respect people in general.

4   Disrespect for human life seems to be at an all-time high. The movies many kids watch portray cold-blooded killers who take lives without blinking an eye. The so-called good guy in the movie who takes out half a dozen people in the name of justice or retribution is considered an idol by impressionable children and adults alike, and respect for human life is nowhere to be seen or heard. The television news and the newspapers all tell of murder in the first degree, premeditated killing of human beings without any sense of guilt. Television presents street gangs killing one another without remorse. Killing a person is nothing more to them than swatting at a fly. In stories and in real life, depicted in movies and on television, and in newspapers and magazines, viewers see soldiers or mercenaries nonchalantly standing over the dead bodies of people they have just cold-bloodedly killed, calmly smoking a cigarette, as if the bodies were nothing more than a grease spot in the road. The world must learn to value human life again, whether at war or at peace.

5   If mankind can learn to respect other human beings in thoughts, words, and actions, humanity may survive on this planet, Earth. If parents teach children clearly not only to respect their elders but to treat everyone with respect and courtesy, children may grow up to be responsible adults who influence other people to respect human feelings, rights, and property. They may grow up to cherish human life, not annihilate it. All people want respect, and so they must give it to earn it.

Understanding Words
Briefly define the following words as they are used in the above essay.

1. flagrant   *shocking*

2. retribution   *a deserved punishment*

3. mercenaries   *people who will fight wars for any country that will pay them*

Answers for Unit 3 are on page 22 in the Instructor's Manual.

Questions on Content

1. In the author's opinion, how do people treat other people today?

2. What do television, movies, and newspapers do that depicts a disrespect for human life?

3. How might family life contribute to a loss of respect for human beings?

Questions on Form

1. Identify the thesis sentence.

2. Show how the support paragraphs relate to the thesis sentence.

3. Why does the author use the 3rd person point of view rather than the 1st or 2nd person point of view?

Being a Student

YoungMi Dauer, *student*

1   "I'm so tired of high heels and business suits! I wish I could go back to school," I often grumbled in a cushy chair in my office. My wish came true, and today I once again wear blue jeans and T-shirts, carry a backpack, and hold heavy textbooks in my arms as I had dreamed. But being an older student is not so much fun; socially, financially, and psychologically I am a handicapped person.

2   I used to enjoy the rainy campus in a school cafeteria, hang out with classmates between and after classes, and go backpacking for a long summer break, experiences that are not available for me anymore. Studying time eats most of my day! My social

life is zero since I have become a student again. My important assets such as invitations from friends for a party, a potluck, bowling, and camping are now a liability. I can't gladly greet a relative who calls me on the phone to tell me in a bright voice that she will visit me for a week during final exams!!! I murmur for God's mercy on me.

3   I am definitely not ready to be a social butterfly, and I am also limping financially, which is humbling me quite a bit. Without my contribution to the budget, I'm just another item on the expense account. My tuition, expensive books, and other expenses have put my home economy in a recession. Even though I have restrained my personal spending on entertainment, clothing, and gifts for friends, my eyes still flash red lights as chunks of cash fly out for me to buy things. I prefer to be a contributor over being a dependent number on a tax form.

4   An older student isn't a healthy person psychologically; stress, anxiety, confusion, and nervousness are the words that surround my daily life. I can't be just a student as I had dreamed; consequently, my emotions are responsibilities that are divided between family and student life. Yes, I have things to be faced as a wife at home; I get a headache when thinking about buying a house, dealing with my husband on his bad days, and making a decision on starting a family. On my student side, pressures are not less. Reading the books for each class, meeting the due day for my computer program, doing math homework, and taking the tests make my days pretty rough.

5   School life as an older student isn't as romantic as it was in my old days. Too many responsibilities, pressures, and different priorities are interrupting my concentration just on schoolwork. Maybe I'd rather wear my high heels and business suits than blue jeans and T-shirts.

Understanding Words

Briefly define the following words as they are used in the above essay.

1. assets   *things of value*

2. liability   *a disadvantage*

Questions on Content

1. How has the author cut down on spending?

2. What pressures does she refer to?

3. What new expenses does she have?

Questions on Form

1. Where is the thesis sentence located?

2. How does the author support the thesis sentence?

3. What makes this essay enjoyable to read?

Golf

Kathy Bagby, *student*

1   "I can't believe anyone would even want to try to hit a dumb little golf ball with one of those skinny little sticks, much less chase it all around a golf course." These were the exact words I had used before the summer I decided to take golf lessons. My daughter was playing on the junior golf team, and I thought it would be nice if we could play together. Much to my surprise and delight, after the first lesson I was hooked! I learned golf can be a terrific challenge, a very humbling game, and, most of all, a great family sport.

2   First of all, I learned that in playing golf, it is me against the course and Mother Nature. Naturally, it's great fun to play the game with friends; however, the real challenge comes when I tee off. I must tackle a fairway covered with innumerable obstacles such as hills, sand traps, rough grassy areas, and ponds. To make matters

worse, I usually have only three or four chances to "plunk" the ball into a hole on the green if I want to make par. Then, of course, there is the weather. On a windy day my ball can be thrown in an off-direction or slowed down. Then there are the sandstorms that blind me or perhaps the up-and-coming rainstorm that I'm trying desperately to beat as I race to the ninth hole. It seems the challenges are never-ending, making the game so addictive.

3   Next, golf is a humbling game! I'll never forget the time I set up to tee off. I took my practice swing, stepped up, took form, felt confident, brought down my swing, and hit the ball, only to watch it go a foot! My face was as red as the ball I had just hit. Another example of humility came the day I was playing the front nine at the Bellaire Golf Course. I had just birdied my first hole. It was hole seven. I must have jumped ten feet in the air. I let everyone near and far know what I had done! I was ready for the pro circuit now! Then came the ninth hole with a long, tough par 4. "A cinch for this old pro," I thought to myself as I stepped up to tee off—1st stroke, 2nd stroke, 3rd stroke, etc., etc., etc. With ten strokes on my card and my head between my knees, I headed for the ninth hole. In addition to these kinds of things, I've had my humbling moments at the water hole. I hit one ball after another, trying any way possible to get over or around the water, only to end up in it. I have definitely eaten a few pieces of humble pie playing this game!

4   The most important part of golf, however, is the pleasurable time I'm able to spend with my family playing together. As an example, we have found it is a great time to share our thoughts and ideas with each other as we walk the course. We will sometimes laugh, tell jokes, or just tease each other. My nine-year-old son loves to show off to his dad just how far he can hit the ball with his custom-made club. My husband and I enjoy moments of closeness as we just walk together quietly. Watching the beautiful grace and form with which my daughter plays swells up a pride within me. Playing together has really helped knit a special closeness in our family.

5   In conclusion, I have found playing golf to be a very positive and rewarding experience. It has taught me many things, such as patience, humility, and perseverance. To anyone who has never given the game a fair chance, I say, "Don't knock it until you try it!"

Understanding Words
Briefly define the following words as they are used in the above essay.

1. innumerable   *countless*

2. perseverance   *persistence in spite of difficulty*

Questions on Content

1. What do sandstorms do to the player?

2. At Bellaire Golf Course, how did the author do on hole seven? On hole nine?

3. How old is her son?

4. Does it appear as if the writer is a beginning golfer or an experienced player?

5. What does the author mean when she writes, "With ten strokes on my card and my head between my knees, I headed for the ninth hole"?

Questions on Form

1. This essay on golf is well written. However, of the three parts of the essay—introduction, support, and conclusion—which part could use a bit more development? What would you suggest to the writer?

2. Does the essay have a distinct thesis sentence? What makes it effective?

Professional Writing

Building a Better Home

John K. Terres, a roving editor for *National Wildlife*

1   A bird's nest is its home—a house without a mortgage, as one ornithological wag said. Products of avian ingenuity and tireless labor, nests and nesting places come in a bewildering variety of sizes, shapes, and styles; each is a marvel of longtime evolution and adaptation of birds in response to the basic need to protect their eggs and young.

2   The most obvious difference between nests is size, which usually varies in proportion to the size of the builder. Two- to three-inch-long calliope hummingbirds, the smallest birds in temperate North America, build tiny cups of mosses and lichens only about one and a half inches across, balanced on small dead pine twigs up to 70 feet above the ground. Even more delicate is the tiny spoonlike nest of the Asiatic crested swift. It is made of bark and glued with the swift's saliva to the side of a lofty, slender forest limb.

3   Compare these with nests of larger birds. A bald eagle's nest in the upper branches of a longleaf pine near St. Petersburg, Florida, was the largest known nest ever built in a tree by a single pair of birds. Sticks, grasses, and debris were added annually for many years by the adult eagles. The nest grew to be 20 feet deep and 9 1/2 feet across—and was estimated to weigh several tons.

4   The tall, stately white storks of Europe and Asia construct huge stick nests, usually on roofs or chimney tops. One nest in Holland, built on a huge wagon wheel atop a stable, blew down in a high wind. It was 12 feet across, weighed several thousand pounds and could easily have accommodated six storks standing along the rim of one side of the nest. It was so tightly woven that it could not be torn apart but had to be burned to be disposed of.

5   The largest bird nests in the world, however, are built on the ground by Australasian megapodes—hen- to turkey-sized "incubator birds." Using their big feet to scratch up leaves, sticks, and earth from the forest floor, they fashion huge, conical mounds, 5 to 7 feet high and 20 to 50 feet across. Large mounds may weigh up to five tons. The birds' eggs are incubated by the internal heat of the decomposing litter in the mounds. . . .

6   The African hammerhead, a storklike bird only 12 inches tall, builds a massive, ball-shaped, clay-lined nest of sticks, usually low in the fork of a tree. Six feet deep and six feet across, the nest is so well built it can bear the weight of a man. Building takes six weeks; one pair watched by an American ornithologist made more than 8,000 trips carrying nesting material in their bills.

7   A tropical Wagler's oriole observed in a Panama tree colony took nearly four weeks to weave its three-foot-long, pouchlike nest. In contrast, most small American songbirds—bluebirds, wrens, catbirds, cardinals, robins, warblers—need a few days to a week to build their nests. Natural selection seems to have speeded up nest-building in temperate regions where the nesting season is shorter and most nests are simpler.

8   Yet some birds labor much longer than seems necessary. Energetic male house wrens, marsh wrens, and prothonotary warblers, as part of their courtship, build extra "dummy" nests—up to six or more in marsh wrens. Each male displays his nests to a female, allowing her to choose among them.

9   One of the most astonishing examples of extra nest-building has been shown by the American robin. A pair in Willoughby, Ohio, once decided to nest on a long girder in a partly finished factory building. The problem was that the girder had 26 identical openings. The birds' solution? They began building 26 nests. The pair finally finished one of the nests and successfully raised a brood.

10   Another pair of robins built nine partly finished nests on nine successive steps of a fire escape at the Bronx Zoo. One local newspaper called it the "Case of the Confused Robin." The birds began by bringing nesting material to each of the steps. Then, explained the zoo director, "when the female robin sits on her nest, she looks up, sees those other nests over her head, and flies off for mud and straw to finish them." . . .

11   Some birds nest together, apartment style. In one tree, a flicker, a bluebird and a kestrel (sparrow hawk) live harmoniously in separate nesting holes, even though the hawk is normally a predator of the other two birds. House sparrows, night herons, and grackles that nest in the lower parts of the nest of eagles apparently gain protection from the large, fierce raptors.

12   Perhaps the most spectacular nests of all are the gigantic apartment-style structures of the sociable weavers of Africa. Up to 30 feet long, with thatched roofs of grasses and twigs that are 3 to 6 feet thick, the enormous nests are usually found high on the branches of isolated trees in open grassland. From a distance, they are sometimes mistaken for native huts. From 100 to 300 pairs of the sparrow-sized birds work together to build the dwelling in which they live throughout the year and sleep in at night. . . .

13   Normally, nest building ends once the eggs are laid. But some birds continue to add to the nest, especially the lining. Female Costa's hummingbirds often build up the sides of their nests while incubating their eggs. Chimney swifts even continue to gather twigs and glue them in place on the nests with sticky saliva. They stop only after the young have made their first flight from the nest. Such behavior is just one of the many marvels of birds and their nests.

Understanding Words

Briefly define the following words as they are used in the above essay.

1. ornithological   *having to do with the study of birds*

2. avian   *pertaining to the characteristics of birds*

3. ingenuity   *cleverness*

4. megapodes   *certain birds in Australia and the South Pacific*

5. predator   *hunter of prey*

Questions on Content

1. What is the most obvious difference among nests?

2. How much did the largest-known nest ever built in a tree by a single pair of birds weigh?

3. When does nest building usually end?

Questions on Form

1. Where does the author state the thesis sentence? What is the thesis sentence?

2. Does each paragraph stay with one idea?

3. Does the entire essay stay with the main idea?

Part 4

Grammar for Effective Writing: Eliminating Fragments, Run-On Sentences, and Comma Splices

Objectives

- Recognize and correct fragments.
- Recognize and correct run-on sentences.
- Recognize and correct comma splices.

To be clearly understood, writing is organized into sentences. Each sentence must be complete, which means that it must contain at least a main subject and a main verb. If a sentence does not have these basic parts, it is a **fragment.**

Sentences must also be separated by clear punctuation. If sentences are not properly separated from one another, **run-on sentences** and **comma splices** are created. These sentence problems can confuse and distract the reader from the content of your writing.

Fragments, run-on sentences, and comma splices are major sentence-structure problems that you can learn to eliminate from your writing. The following explanations, examples, and exercises will help you identify and revise your own writing so that you can write clearly on your job or for your college classes.

Tests covering fragments, run-on sentences, and comma splices are on pages 38–41 in the Test Bank.

Fragments

A sentence is a group of words that has a main subject and a main verb and states a complete thought. If a group of words lacks one of these parts, it is a **fragment.**

Types of Fragments

1. fragments that contain no subject
2. fragments that have no verb
3. fragments with verb forms that cannot be the main verb

   "-ing" form of the verb used alone

   "to" before a verb

4. fragments that have both a subject and a verb but are preceded by a subordinator

Fragments That Contain No Subject

Examples: Runs two miles every morning. (fragment)

Ate all of the pizza herself. (fragment)

You can change these fragments to sentences simply by *adding a subject*—someone who "runs" or someone who "ate."

Steve runs two miles every morning. (sentence)

Theresa ate all of the pizza herself. (sentence)

Note   A command is a sentence, not a fragment, although the subject "you" is not stated.

(You) Close the door, please. (sentence)

Exercise 1

Change each fragment to a sentence by adding a subject.

Example:

We can
~~Can~~ hear the freeway traffic from our backyard.

1. Out in the lake, *we* watched the moon rise.
2. In addition, *they* bought a four-wheel-drive vehicle.
3. Then *we* joined the company softball team.
4. ~~Never~~ *I never* did balance the checkbook.
5. ~~Also~~ *The family also* toured the Carlsbad Caverns.

Fragments That Have No Verb

Some fragments have no verb and can often be thought of as "tag-ons" or "after-thoughts."

> *Examples:*   The soft, furry kitten. (fragment)
>
> The soft, furry kitten in the basket. (fragment)

To correct these fragments, **add a verb** (and other words, if needed).

The soft, furry kitten in the basket **cried.**

The soft, furry kitten **was** in the basket.

Very often when you are writing, fragments without verbs become "tag-on" thoughts that belong with another sentence. The words in bold type in the following examples are fragments that could easily be added to the previous sentence.

He did not give us a number. **An exact number.**

The child looked longingly at the kitten. **The kitten in the basket.**

Rusty opened a store. **Her own store.**

The best way to correct these "tag-on" thoughts is to **combine the fragment with a complete sentence** (usually the one before or after it).

He did not give us **an exact number.**

The child looked longingly at the soft, furry **kitten in the basket.**

Rusty opened **her own store.**

Note   Eliminating these fragments also eliminates a kind of wordiness that distracts from your writing.

Exercise 2

Revise the "tag-on" thoughts in each paragraph by combining them with another sentence.

Paragraph 1

Large daily newspapers usually present information in the same order each day. Section A usually provides an overview of events. *world and national* ~~World and national events.~~ This section may also include local stories with *national or worldwide* appeal. ~~With national or worldwide appeal.~~ Then, Section B updates readers on local news. The last page of Section B usually includes general weather for the nation and more detailed weather forecasts for the *entire* state. ~~The entire state.~~ Another section, business, includes *national, international, and local* information related to the economy. ~~National, international, and local information.~~ Another important section, the sports news, is about athletes, games, and *other sporting* events. ~~Other sporting events.~~ Many newspapers include special sections on the weekends, and these sections may specialize in home *and garden* issues. ~~And garden issues.~~ Sometimes sections may be mixed by delivery carriers, or a reader may want to skip or ignore one part, but the *content and implied* order of the sections usually remains the same. ~~Content and the implied order of the sections.~~ Knowing the order can be helpful for readers, and predictability in this age of constant change is always reassuring.

Paragraph 2

Citizens can do their part to help the environment. They can crush, save, and take aluminum cans to ~~centers. To~~ recycling centers. In addition, people can reuse *glass and plastic* containers rather than throw them away. ~~Glass and plastic containers.~~ Gardeners can use natural ecological defenses such as ladybugs, water sprays, and beer solutions. ~~Rather~~ *rather* than *harmful* pesticides. ~~Harmful pesticides~~ to eliminate insects. Car owners who service their own cars should properly dispose of used *motor* oil ~~and filters.~~ ~~Motor oil~~ and oil filters. Saving the earth is like preserving America's future.

Fragments with Verb Forms That Cannot Be the Main Verb

Some verb forms cannot be used as main verbs in a sentence. If you use them as main verbs, you create fragments.

Verb Forms That Cannot Be Main Verbs

1. the "-ing" form of a verb used alone
2. "to" before a verb

- **The "-ing" form of a verb used alone cannot be the main verb in a sentence.**

    Bill going to the gym after school. (fragment)

    Going to the yogurt shop. (fragment)

    To be used as a main verb, this "-ing" form must be linked to some "be" verb.

"Be" Verbs

is	are	were	has been
am	was	had been	have been

For example, if you convert the fragment "Bill going to the gym after school" to "Bill is going to the gym after school," you have a complete sentence, and the fragment has been eliminated.

These fragments can be corrected in a variety of ways. How you revise them depends on the meaning you would like to communicate in your sentence. Here are some ways to correct the fragment "Going to the yogurt shop."

First, you could **add a subject and some form of the verb "be."**

Bill is going to the yogurt shop.

You could **make the fragment the subject and add a main verb.** (You may want to add other words to make the meaning clear.)

Going to the yogurt shop **makes** the children happy.

Or you could **add a complete sentence (subject and a verb) after the "-ing" verb form.**

Going to the yogurt shop, **Bill met his girlfriend.**

Note   In the above example, the "-ing" verb form must refer to the subject in the sentence that it is linked to.

Exercise 3

Revise each fragment using these same patterns.

Example:

Walking to the bus stop.

Lori is walking to the bus stop.

Add a subject and some form of the verb "be."

Walking to the bus stop invigorates me.

Make the fragment the subject and add a main verb. (Add other words if needed.)

Walking to the bus stop, I counted six rabbits.

Add a sentence (subject and a verb) after the fragment.

1. Looking for an apartment to rent.

   My mother is looking for an apartment to rent.

   Add a subject and an appropriate form of the verb "be."

   Looking for an apartment to rent became frustrating.

   Make the fragment the subject and add a main verb. (Add other words if needed.)

   Looking for an apartment to rent, my mother lost her patience.

   Add a sentence (subject and a verb) after the fragment.

2. Collecting aluminum cans.

   Harvey is collecting aluminum cans.

   Add a subject and an appropriate form of the verb "be."

   Collecting aluminum cans can be a profitable hobby.

   Make the fragment the subject and add a main verb. (Add other words if needed.)

   Collecting aluminum cans, Pete found a diamond ring.

   Add a sentence (subject and a verb) after the fragment.

3. Enjoying a cappuccino after the theater.

   We were enjoying a cappuccino after the theater.

   Add a subject and an appropriate form of the verb "be."

   Enjoying a cappuccino after the theater ended a lovely evening.

   Make the fragment the subject and add a main verb. (Add other words if needed.)

   Enjoying a cappuccino after the theater, we discussed the play.

   Add a sentence (subject and a verb) after the fragment.

4. Arriving at the concert.

   The teenagers were arriving at the concert early.

   Add a subject and an appropriate form of the verb "be."

   Arriving at the concert generated a lot of excitement.

   Make the fragment the subject and add a main verb. (Add other words if needed.)

   Arriving at the concert, the teenagers began to look for their friends.

   Add a sentence (subject and a verb) after the fragment.

5. Restoring the old furniture.

   My neighbor is restoring the old furniture.

   Add a subject and an appropriate form of the verb "be."

   Restoring the old furniture was her project for the summer.

   Make the fragment the subject and add a main verb. (Add other words if needed.)

   Restoring the old furniture, my neighbor spent many enjoyable hours.

   Add a sentence (subject and a verb) after the fragment.

6. Exploring the Internet.

Students in the class were exploring the Internet.

Add a subject and an appropriate form of the verb "be."

Exploring the Internet fascinated the students.

Make the fragment the subject and add a main verb. (Add other words if needed.)

Exploring the Internet, the students found information they could use.

Add a sentence (subject and a verb) after the fragment.

- **"To" plus a verb cannot be the main verb in a sentence.**

  To fish at the lake. (fragment)

  Based on your meaning, you may revise this fragment in any of the following ways. First, you can **link the fragment to a complex sentence.**

  To fish at the lake, **Rene bought a fishing license.**

  You can **add both a subject and a verb.**

  Bill likes to fish at the lake.

  Or you can **make the fragment the subject and add a verb.** Be sure to add any other needed words.

  To fish at the lake is relaxing.

Exercise 4

Revise each fragment using the given patterns.

Example:

To get the work done.

To get the work done, Ralph hired new men.

Link the fragment to a complete sentence.

Ralph worked to get the work done.

Add both a subject and a verb.

To get the work done cost a lot of money.

Make the fragment the subject and add a verb. (Add other words if needed.)

1. To learn a new skill.

To learn a new skill, the employees attended the conference.

Link the fragment to a complete sentence.

The employees wanted to learn a new skill.

Add both a subject and a verb before the fragment.

To learn a new skill meant a pay raise.

Make the fragment the subject and add a verb. (Add other words if needed.)

2. To curtail binge drinking of college students.

   To curtail binge drinking of college students, the president established a curfew.

   Link the fragment to a complete sentence.

   The president wanted to curtail binge drinking of college students.

   Add both a subject and a verb before the fragment.

   To curtail binge drinking of college students was difficult.

   Make the fragment the subject and add a verb. (Add other words if needed.)

3. To buy a new camera phone.

   To buy a new camera phone, Jasnia traded in her old phone.

   Link the fragment to a complete sentence.

   Jasnia wanted to buy a new camera phone.

   Add both a subject and a verb before the fragment.

   To buy a new camera phone was expensive.

   Make the fragment the subject and add a verb. (Add other words if needed.)

4. To qualify for the race.

   To qualify for the race, Jack trained many hours.

   Link the fragment to a complete sentence.

   Jack hoped to qualify for the race.

   Add both a subject and a verb before the fragment.

   To qualify for the race became Jack's goal.

   Make the fragment the subject and add a verb. (Add other words if needed.)

5. To shop on the Internet.

   To shop on the Internet, Jason bought a computer.

   Link the fragment to a complete sentence.

   Jason learned to shop on the Internet.

   Add both a subject and a verb before the fragment.

   To shop on the Internet simplified Jason's life.

   Make the fragment the subject and add a verb. (Add other words if needed.)

6. To become president of the company.

   To become president of the company, Jordan had to work his way up the ranks.

   Link the fragment to a complete sentence.

   Jordan wanted to became president of the company.

   Add both a subject and a verb before the fragment.

   To become president of the company required years of hard work.

   Make the fragment the subject and add a verb. (Add other words if needed.)

**Fragments That Have Both a Subject and a Verb
but Are Preceded by a Subordinator**

Some fragments have both a subject and a verb but are preceded by a subordinator.

Example: **When** I get my paycheck. (fragment)

This fragment does not state a complete thought. For example, if you walked into a room and said to a friend, "When I get my paycheck," the person you are speaking to would want to know, "What *about* 'when I get my paycheck'?"

However, if you complete this thought by adding a sentence, your meaning will be clear.

When I get my paycheck, **we will go shopping.** *Or:*

We will go shopping when I get my paycheck.

("We will go shopping" is a complete sentence that can stand alone.)

In these fragments, the subordinator makes the thought incomplete. (You will learn more about subordinators later in this unit.) Here is a list of subordinators that change a complete sentence into a fragment:

Subordinators

after	if	where
although	in order that	whether
as	since	which
as if	so that	whichever
as long as	that	while
as soon as	though	who
as though	till	whoever
as well as	unless	whom
because	until	whomever
before	what	whose
even though	whatever	whosoever
how	when	why

Exercise 5

Revise each fragment by linking it to a complete sentence.

Example:

When I go on a diet, *I am grumpy.*

1. If Jim finishes his degree, *he will get a good job offer.*

2. After I learn to cook, *I will make lasagna./I will save money.*

3. After the game was over, *everyone decided to go for pizza.*

4. If Carla is going to cook the spaghetti, *I will make the salad.*

5. When the power went off, *everyone stayed inside.*

6. Before we left for vacation, *we had to arrange for a pet sitter.*

7. Unless I finish my schoolwork, *I will not be able to go to the play.*

8. Because my DVD is broken, _we might want to go to the movies._

9. Until the lake thaws, _we will be unable to go fishing._

10. So that Veronica would not arrive late, _she got up earlier than usual._

The best practice for revising fragments is to work on your own paragraphs. However, you can practice by correcting the following sample paragraphs and then applying the practice to your own paragraphs.

Exercise 6

For the following sample paragraphs, do one or more of the following: (1) add a subject, a verb, or both a subject and a verb, or (2) combine the fragment with a sentence before it or with a sentence after it.

Paragraph 1

With the discovery of penicillin in 1928. ~~Scientists~~ *, scientists* and citizens alike believed that the battle *over infectious diseases* was won and that no one would die from an infection again. ~~The battle over infectious diseases.~~ Americans breathed a sigh of relief. However, *they* did not know that other organisms that had survived for thousands of years could not be conquered that easily. These organisms simply produced mutant ~~strains. That~~ *strains that* were resistant to various antibiotics. Today, scientists realize that once again Americans may become ill from *deadly* outbreaks of infections that have no cure. ~~Deadly outbreaks.~~ Because scientists are aware of the serious threats of these mutant ~~strains. Hopefully~~ *strains, hopefully they* will discover new ways of wiping out these infectious diseases soon.

Paragraph 2

Diabetes is a disease that requires ~~control. Dietary~~ *dietary* control. People with diabetes need to balance the insulin and sugar level in their blood. Most of the time, *they* need to avoid foods that contain sugar. They also need to eat smaller meals more often throughout the day. However, if they have not eaten enough and their insulin level ~~rises. Must~~ rises*, they must* eat or drink something with sugar so that the insulin level in their blood will be balanced. For example, when they feel ~~shaky. They~~ shaky*, they* may eat a candy bar or drink a soda pop. Diabetics can be ~~healthier. If~~ healthier *if* they watch their diet.

Run-On Sentences

A second type of sentence-structure problem is the **run-on sentence.** The term "run-on" explains the mistake; two sentences have been run together. In other words, no punctuation mark separates the independent thoughts.

The assignment was easy it took only a couple of hours to complete.

(run-on sentence)

In this run-on sentence, there are two independent thoughts about the assignment. One is that it was easy, and the other is that it took only a couple of hours to complete. Two sentences have been written as one sentence. Adding punctuation clears up the problem. Here is one way these two thoughts could be written:

The assignment was easy. It took only a couple of hours to complete.

One misunderstanding that some writers have is that if ideas are related to each other, they should be written as one sentence. Look at the following ideas.

My cousin is coming to Arizona she wants to visit the Grand Canyon.

(run-on sentence)

These ideas (coming to Arizona and visiting the Grand Canyon) are related, but they should be two separate sentences. Each idea has a subject and a verb and is an independent thought:

My cousin is coming to Arizona. She wants to visit the Grand Canyon.

Another misunderstanding writers have concerning run-on sentences is that if the idea is short, it cannot be two sentences. However, sentences are determined by whether or not they have a subject and a verb, not by length.

When you write "We should hurry we are late," you have two sentences. "We should hurry" is one sentence with its own subject and verb. "We are late" is another sentence with its own subject and verb.

We should hurry. We are late.

It is important to write without using run-on sentences. When you do not identify where one sentence ends and another begins, your reader has a hard time following your thoughts. Run-on sentences may be revised in several ways.

Ways to Revise Run-On Sentences

1. Add a period at the end of each complete thought.
2. Use a comma and a connecting word called a coordinate conjunction.
3. Use a semicolon.
4. Use a semicolon, a connecting word called a conjunctive adverb, and a comma.
5. Use a subordinator.

Note A list of conjunctive adverbs precedes Exercise 10 on page 195, and a list of subordinators precedes Exercise 5 on page 190.

Add a Period at the End of Each Complete Thought

The simplest way to deal with this problem is to add a period at the end of each complete thought. For practice, complete the following exercise.

Exercise 7

Find the place where the first sentence ends and the second sentence begins. Then revise each run-on sentence by adding a period after the first sentence and by beginning the second sentence with a capital letter.

Example:

chores. They

The girls chose their ~~chores they~~ did them rapidly.

health. Without

1. Humor is important to people's ~~health without~~ humor, they become tired and depressed.

pets. They

2. Black Labs can be loyal ~~pets they~~ are also good with children.

newspaper. Then

3. Every morning, Trent read the ~~newspaper then~~ he left for work.

competition. He

4. Armondo entered the Olympic ~~competition he~~ won a silver medal.

position. She

5. Kanisha applied for the ~~position she~~ met all the qualifications.

contractors. They

6. Building houses requires licensed ~~contractors they~~ know regulations and codes.

outdoors. It

7. They look forward to spending the day ~~outdoors it~~ takes them away from stress.

again. She

8. The champion show dog won ~~again she~~ was best of show.

literature. The

9. Toni Morrison won the Nobel Prize in ~~literature the~~ award was $818,000.

taxes. Her

10. Marsha used her computer to figure her ~~taxes her~~ return was accurate.

Use a Comma and a Coordinate Conjunction

You can also revise run-on sentences by connecting them with a comma and an appropriate coordinate conjunction.

Coordinate Conjunctions

for	but
and	or
nor	yet
	so

I enjoy my job the rewards are great.   (run-on sentence)

I enjoy my job, **and** the rewards are great.   (correct)

Note   The first letters of the coordinate conjunctions spell **fan boys**.

Exercise 8

Revise each of the following sentences by finding the place where the sentences should be separated. Then add a comma and a coordinate conjunction between the two sentences.

Example:

lunch, and they
The boys ate pizza for ~~lunch they~~ enjoyed it.

1. Firefighters spend many hours training for emergencies ^*, so* they are well prepared.

2. Jeremy keeps his tools in excellent condition ^*, and* he cleans them regularly.

3. The hikers walked quietly ^*, but* they disturbed a rattlesnake.

4. Rita works as a photographer ^*, so* she often works weekends.

5. A broken water pipe stalled traffic ^*, and* drivers were irate.

6. The dishwasher flooded the kitchen ^*, so* floor tile was ruined.

7. Many people went to the coin show ^*, for* they wanted to sell their collections.

8. The security guard was alert ^*, for* he heard the glass break.

9. The newest school board member is a paramedic for the fire department ^*, and* he is involved in community activities.

10. Hank found a lost kitten ^*, and* he could keep it ^*, or* he could take it to the Humane Society.

Use a Semicolon (;)

You may also revise run-on sentences by separating the complete thoughts with a semi-colon.

I enjoy my job the rewards are great. (run-on sentence)

I enjoy my job; the rewards are great. (correct)

Exercise 9

Revise each of the following sentences by finding the place where the sentences should be separated. Then add a semicolon to separate the sentences.

Example:

me; I
Seven cars were in front of ~~me I~~ needed to turn left.

1. After school, Kayla played soccer ^*;* she did her homework later.

2. The book was unusually interesting ; I could not put it down.

3. The cardiologist has four boys ; the youngest three are triplets.

4. Baseball players travel often ; they are constantly away from their families.

5. Farmers depend heavily on nature ; weather conditions are important to them.

6. Automobile technicians require specialized training ; they must know computers and other electronic equipment.

7. Many older people discover a talent for painting ; they produce outstanding pictures.

8. Politicians seldom have private lives ; they can expect constant scrutiny.

9. Chan signed a contract for the job ; he promised to start the project immediately.

10. Airplane travel is safer than automobile travel ; air accidents are just more publicized.

Use a Semicolon, a Conjunctive Adverb, and a Comma
Run-on sentences may also be revised by joining the two complete thoughts with a semicolon, a conjunctive adverb, and a comma.

Frequently Used Conjunctive Adverbs

moreover	consequently
in addition	however
therefore	in fact
thus	nevertheless
	as a result
otherwise	
futhermore	

Note   The first letters of the conjunctive adverbs spell **Mitt of China.**

I enjoy my job the rewards are great. (run-on sentence)

I enjoy my job**; moreover,** the rewards are great. (correct)

Exercise 10

Revise each of the following sentences by finding the place where the sentences should be separated. Then add a semicolon, a conjunctive adverb, and a comma between the two sentences.

Example:

delicious; in fact, it
The spaghetti was ~~delicious it~~ was homemade.

                          ; however,

1. Kristin bought a new digital camera ^ she had trouble using it.

                        ; consequently,

2. Justine prepared for the hike ^ she was ready for any emergency.

                      ; in fact,

3. Traffic over the bridge is heavy ^ thousands of cars cross daily.

                    ; moreover,

4. Training a puppy takes lots of time ^ it also requires lots of patience.

                    ; however,

5. Starting a new job can be exciting ^ it can also be stressful.

                  ; nevertheless,

6. Sandra lost one of her contacts ^ she has a spare lens.

                  ; in addition,

7. Peanuts are high in protein ^ they taste good.

                 ; therefore,

8. I lost my traveler's checks ^ I had to go to the bank to replace them.

                        ; in fact,

9. Keeping rivers clean should be a priority ^ children can even get involved.

                       ; however,

10. Raymond drove his sport utility vehicle fast ^ he was careful.

Use a Subordinator

Another way to revise run-on sentences is to join them by using a subordinator. You can easily achieve sentence variety in this way. (Refer to the list on page 190.)

> I enjoy my job the rewards are great. (run-on sentence)

> I enjoy my job **when** the rewards are great. (correct)

Exercise 11

Revise each of the following sentences by finding the place where the sentences should be separated. Then add a subordinator from the list on page 190. (Use a comma when needed.)

Example:

             because

I want to go to the store ^ I need to buy some new tennis shoes.

                        although

1. My cousin and his girlfriend plan to have children ^ they are not married.

                so that

2. I helped my mother find a new doctor ^ she could get the care she needed.

           because

3. I enjoy listening to music ^ it is relaxing.

            before

4. The bear was given a tranquilizer ^ he was examined by the veterinarian.

            unless

5. Visitors cannot see the special exhibit ^ they have reservations.

until
6. The young man does not get up in the morning ^ the alarm goes off.

after
7. Jesus built a pond in his backyard ^ he bought his new house.

if
8. People might like to move to a cold climate ^ they like winter sports.

when
9. The dog knocked over Aunt Harriet's lamp ^ he ran into the room.

because
10. I enjoyed Kartchner Caverns ^ the rock formations were spectacular.

Comma Splices

Another sentence-structure problem similar to the run-on sentence is the **comma splice**.

> We spent the day at the beach, we came home sunburned. (comma splice)

In this case, the writer has separated two sentences with a comma. Using only a comma, however, is *not* an acceptable way to divide two independent thoughts. The easiest way is to substitute a period for the comma and begin the next word with a capital letter.

> We spent the day at the beach. We came home sunburned. (correct)

Sometimes this method creates too many short sentences in a row. In such cases, other kinds of revision can help your sentences flow better. To correct comma splices and still retain sentence variety, do the following:

Ways to Revise Comma Splices

1. **Use a comma and a coordinate conjunction.**

   We spent the day at the beach, **and** we came home sunburned. (correct)

2. **Use a semicolon.**

   We spent the day at the beach; we came home sunburned. (correct)

3. **Use a semicolon and a conjunctive adverb.** (See the list that precedes Exercise 10 in this unit, page 195.)

   We spent the day at the beach; **as a result,** we came home sunburned. (correct)

4. **Use a subordinator that logically links the two sentences.**

   Because we spent the day at the beach, we came home sunburned. (correct)

Note   When the subordinator is added to the first sentence, this introductory idea is separated from the rest of the sentence with a comma. For more detailed explanation, see Unit 5.

Exercise 12

Revise each comma splice. Try using several of the methods explained in the text.

Example:

cats. Then
cats, and then
Mary often took in hungry, stray ~~cats, then~~ she tried to find homes for them.

; consequently,
1. The turtle hibernated for many months,‸he emerged famished and began to eat his way through the garden.

. Then
, and then
2. After removing the rocks from the yard, we leveled the ground ~~then~~‸we put in a sprinkler system.

;
3. When the stone mason finished the wall, he cleaned up the area,‸the homeowner was happy with the results.

. Then
4. While we were on the beach, we collected shells,‸~~then~~ we built a sand castle.

; however,
5. When a tornado touches down, it may destroy everything in its path‸the American Red Cross assists the victims.

and
6. As soon as Jacob gets off work, he grabs a bite to eat,‸then he goes to class.

because
;
7. Every evening, Toni checks her email messages,‸she loves hearing from her friends.

and
8. During a severe winter storm in the desert, snow covered the cactus,‸muddy roads froze.

because
9. Sara enjoys growing herbs in her garden‸she loves to use them in her cooking.

; in addition, he
10. Harry read the three articles about drug abuse in the newspaper,‸~~he~~ took notes for his history report.

Note If you want further practice on these types of combinations, review the materials in Units 4 and 5.

Exercise 13

Revise the fragments, run-on sentences, and comma splices in the following paragraphs. Be creative by using as many different methods as possible.

Paragraph 1

The forest service is becoming more sensitive to the needs of physically

challenged people who like the outdoors. Braille hiking trails offer a way for the

remarkable

visually impaired to tramp through America's forests without fear. ~~America's~~
             ^

~~remarkable forests.~~ Blind hikers can begin to experience what others take for

as

granted. Braille signs identify the surrounding trees and plants. ~~As~~ well as mark the

trails. These trails are carefully constructed and twist their way through wooded

and   *;*

valleys. ~~And~~ onto safe hillsides. Some paths are only a quarter of a mile others
                                                                                  ^

so

stretch for almost a mile. ~~So~~ that hikers can choose a long or short route. Some

and

campgrounds have wheelchair-accessible paths throughout the area, some even
                                                                  ^

include ramps to lakes where the campers can fish from the bank. Each

campground is calm, serene, and accommodating to the physically challenged.

Paragraph 2

as

Being aware of differences in languages can help students. ~~As~~ they study to

;

become bilingual. For example, English has many different sounds for the letter *a*
                                                                                   ^

a. This

Spanish, however, has only one sound for the letter ~~*a* this~~ means that Spanish

and

students must learn English's unique rules for changes. ~~And~~ exceptions. Another

and

distinction is that English is spoken from the back of the mouth, Spanish uses the
                                                                  ^

. This

front of the tongue and mouth, ~~this~~ allows an opportunity for the speakers to use

noun

different motor skills. Another important idea is the construction of forms. ~~Noun~~
                                                                             ^

~~forms.~~ English does not label items such chairs and clocks as masculine (*he*) or

; however,

feminine (*she*) ~~however~~ all Spanish nouns are preceded and identified with gender

if

articles. Students must know. ~~If~~ a word is masculine or feminine. "The chair" in

. "The

English is *la silla* in Spanish, which is a feminine noun, ~~"the~~ clock" in English is *el*

reloj in Spanish, which is a masculine noun. No matter what two languages people

, they   *, they*

may speak. ~~They~~ have two ways of expression. By knowing two languages. ~~They~~ can

see and understand the world differently.

Paragraph 3

Because pizza is so versatile. *, it* ~~It~~ is no wonder that it is one of America's favorite foods. Pizza is available frozen at the grocery store or piping hot from a variety of pizza restaurants. It can be bought with thin crust ~~or~~ *,* thick crust, *or* ~~it can be~~ sandwiched between two crusts. Plain pizza crust can be bought frozen ~~or~~ *,* already baked in packages much like bread, or mixed at home. Almost every person's individual taste can be satisfied because of the variety of toppings. ~~Toppings~~ spread on the sauce. Pepperoni leads the list of favorites, but jalapeño, anchovies, olives, and sausages are some of the other options *. Even* ~~, even~~ sausage comes in different types. For a real "like-home" Italian taste. *, the* ~~The~~ pizza can be topped with garlic bits and a little Parmesan cheese without the sauce. Since pizza can be varied, almost everyone can be satisfied.

Paragraph 4

Owning cats can be a frustrating experience. Sometimes they want to be affectionate and even sit in their owner's lap *. Other* ~~, other~~ times, they treat their owner like a second-class citizen and turn away. ~~Turn away~~ saucily. A person who does not know cats may be frustrated by their cautiousness. *and* ~~And~~ mistake it for a lack of affection. For example, a lazy-looking cat gazing out the window may really be a lonesome pet *. He* ~~, he~~ may really be eagerly waiting for the owner to come home. When the owner does come home. *, the* ~~The~~ cat probably will not immediately jump down like a dog and run to greet the owner *. The* ~~the~~ cat may cautiously turn his head and look the other way. He is not ignoring his owner but just showing caution in case the owner ignores him. This is the kind of lukewarm "hello" that frustrates people who do not understand. ~~Understand~~ cats.

It is easy to identify fragments, run-ons, and comma splices when the sentences have been isolated and you are looking for a specific kind of sentence-structure problem. However, in your own writing this major problem may be hidden within your ideas and may be overlooked. If you are having a problem identifying run-ons, comma splices, or fragments, read backward through your paper. Going backward through your paper will help you concentrate on the structure of your sentences rather than on the ideas.

Exercise 14

Identify the sentence-structure problems in the following paragraph. Start with the last sentence and read each sentence individually, moving backward through the text. Identify each sentence as a fragment (F), a comma splice (CS), a run-on sentence (RO), or a proper sentence (OK) in the blanks provided after the paragraph.

(1) Alamogordo, New Mexico, and its outlying area offer its residents variety. (2) The image of a sleeping lady is carved by the sloping Sacramento foothills this image identifies from a distance the location of Alamogordo. (3) A city of approximately 36,000 people. (4) It is located ninety-five miles north of the Texas/Mexican border in the south-central part of the state. (5) Consequently, it has a rich Hispanic influence that is reflected in its architecture, history, and people. (6) Adding another ethnic exposure to the city. (7) Alamogordo welcomes yet another group of people, two thousand Germans who are fulfilling a ten-year U.S. contract as part of the German Flying Training Center, they bring a distinct culture as German signs identify their presence. (8) Approximately fifty miles north in the beautiful Sacramento Mountains with tall pines, noisy streams, and wild horses is the Mescalero Apache Indian Reservation. (9) Resting twenty miles west of the city. (10) White Sands National Monument with dunes of snow-white gypsum for sand surfing, picnicking, or sunset viewing. (11) Due northeast, Cloudcroft is a quaint little village. (12) This area resembles the Swiss Alps with its 5,000-foot elevation and its rustic shops. (13) Described as a hidden city. (14) Alamogordo is a progressive city with the International Space Hall of Fame, it represents the old West as well as new scientific achievements. (15) Alamogordo is indeed a versatile city.

15.	OK	10.	F	5.	OK
14.	CS	9.	F	4.	OK
13.	F	8.	OK	3.	F
12.	OK	7.	CS	2.	RO
11.	OK	6.	F	1.	OK

Part 5

Putting It All Together

 ## Cumulative Unit Exercise

Now that you know how to write a thesis sentence, read the following essay. (Complete introductory and concluding paragraphs are covered in Unit 5.)

1. Read the essay carefully.
2. Read the thesis sentence. Then identify the topic sentence in each support paragraph and underline the key words that show a clear link to the thesis sentence.
3. Check to see if each paragraph has adequate support and a concluding sentence.
4. Check for consistent verb tense and consistent point of view. If you find any errors, correct them.
5. Correct the one fragment, one run-on sentence, and one comma splice.

Hummers

Transparency of uncorrected cumulative exercise is on pages 49–50 in the Instructor's Manual.

"Hummers," the word's smallest birds, are amazing creatures because of their movements, appearance, and tame nature.

Support paragraph #1

The <u>movements</u> of these <u>small wonders</u> have <u>intrigued</u> people for years.

Hummingbirds can hover in the air, fly backward, forward, to the left, to the

                                                   move

right, and upside down as they ~~moved~~ through the air with agility and speed,

outmaneuvering other birds. Hummingbirds love to bathe or frolic in the rain or

in sprinklers where their darting flight can be observed. These jewels or rainbows

of color hover in the water droplets, suddenly fly upward or to the side, and then

move back into the water as they enjoy an afternoon shower. Unique birds,

"hummers" have the ability to zoom through the air at top speed and then stop

                                     . The

CS   suddenly to land gracefully,~~ the~~ tiny marvels move about so fast that they are

hard to follow, and because of their wing structure, they are able to make a quick

                                           get

getaway by flying upside down. Their bodies ~~gets~~ lift on both the upstroke and

the downstroke, making their wings move in what appears to be a figure eight.

This movement gives the birds the ability to hover and change directions fast, an

                                      people

aerial proficiency that simply captivates ~~you~~.

Support paragraph #2

What <u>delights</u> so many individuals is the <u>fascinating appearance</u> of <u>these</u> <u>astonishing birds</u>. More than three hundred varieties exist, some plain, some with fancy tails, some with colorful crests, some with brilliantly colored throats, but all beautiful to watch. Some hummingbirds are as small as two inches and others as large as eight and a half inches long. Their long, slim bills are often longer than the bird's head itself. Though their unique bills are generally black,

RO they may also be yellow or red ~~their~~ **. Their** plumage may include iridescent pinks, violets, blues, and greens. When viewed in the sunlight, the crown and gorget of some hummingbirds simply glow. Their tiny little feet ~~made~~ **make** them look as if they may have no feet at all, but they do, and because their feet are so small, the birds are kept airborne or perched. Their tail feathers, spread in flight, ~~completes~~ **complete** a beautiful creature that fascinates people throughout the world.

Support paragraph #3

Perhaps part of the <u>hummingbirds' fascination</u> comes from their <u>tame</u> <u>behavior</u> that makes them seem like <u>pets</u> to some people. They seem to become tame as they eat from feeders that are often just outside people's windows. When they see people moving around, they seem to recognize them and even enjoy being around them. When gardeners work in their yard~~.~~ **, these** ~~These~~ small creatures may perch on a tree limb and "hum" to the people whom they seem to recognize. When feeders become empty, these tiny birds may scold the landlords until they replenish the supply of nectar. Also, it is not unusual for hummingbirds to light on the shoulder of the person who fills the feeders. Some "hummers" may also notice when ~~you~~ **people** come into the backyard and set up sprinklers. These birds, who have wonderful memories, are waiting for the chance to play in the water, knowing that they will not be harmed. Once a hummingbird finds a home, though it may migrate during some seasons of the year, it remembers ~~your~~ **the** friendly backyard and returns year after year. It is no wonder that human friends hang feeders so they can enjoy interacting with these birds who swoop in for a drink, hover near the feeder, or perch on a tree branch.

Collaborative Writing Project: Working and Learning Together

Working in a Group

As you learned in Unit 3, a thesis sentence helps you organize a longer paper just as the topic sentence helps you organize a paragraph. The topic sentence has a topic and a direction, but the thesis sentence has a topic and direction and previews the main points to be covered in the essay. The following collaborative exercise will show you how a paragraph can be expanded into a full essay.

1. Divide into groups of three or four.

2. Have one person in your group read the following paragraph aloud.

"Hummers," the world's smallest birds, are amazing creatures. They can hover in the air, fly backward, forward, to the left or right, and upside down as they move through the air with agility and speed, outmaneuvering other birds. Hummingbirds love to bathe or frolic in the rain or in sprinklers where their darting flight can be watched. These jewels or rainbows of color hover in the water droplets, suddenly fly upward or to the side, and then move back into the water as they enjoy an after-noon shower. More than three hundred varieties exist, some plain, some with fancy tails, some with colorful crests, some with brilliantly colored throats, but all beauti-ful to watch. Some hummingbirds are as small as two inches, but their long bills, along with a tongue that extends beyond the bill, allow these birds to obtain nectar from such flowering plants as bird of paradise or trumpet creepers. It is no wonder that human admirers hang feeders so they can enjoy watching their "pets" swoop in for a drink or admire them as they perch on the feeder or a tree branch.

3. As a group, mark the ideas in the above paragraph that support "movement, appearance, or tame nature."

4. Work in one of the following groups:

Group one

Read the first support paragraph in the **previous essay** on hummingbirds. List the details that are included in both the single paragraph above and the first support paragraph in the essay. Then list new details that have been added to the essay's first support paragraph.

Support paragraph 1

Details that are in both the single paragraph and the first support paragraph:

_____

_____

Details that have been added to the support paragraph:

_____

_____

Group two

Read the second support paragraph in the **previous essay** on hummingbirds. List the details that are included in both the single paragraph and the second support paragraph in the essay. Then list new details that have been added to the second support paragraph.

Support paragraph 2

Details that are in both the single paragraph and the second support paragraph:

_____

_____

Details that have been added to the support paragraph:

_____

_____

Group three

Read the third support paragraph in the **previous essay** on hummingbirds. List the details that are included in both the single paragraph and the third support paragraph in the essay. Then list new details that have been added to the third support paragraph.

Support paragraph 3

Details that are in both the single paragraph and the third support paragraph:

_____

_____

Details that have been added to the support paragraph:

_____

_____

> **5.** Report your results to the class.

Note that the paragraph was expanded into three support paragraphs that originated from the idea that "hummingbirds are amazing creatures."

 ## Writing Assignment/Working in a Group

> **1.** Return to the same groups and collaborate on a paragraph explaining what a person must consider before undertaking one of the following actions.

Having a baby

Working in a foreign country

Retiring from a job

Marrying a person of a different ethnicity

Moving out on one's own

Moving in with a mate or roommate

Resuming a broken relationship

Becoming a college student

Participating in extracurricular activities in college

Joining a club on campus

Playing sports in school

Or, collaborate on a paragraph discussing the advantages or disadvantages of one of the following.

Having a hobby

Being a coach

Having a mother or father as a coach

Changing jobs

2. Be sure to begin with a strong topic sentence that includes both the topic and a direction.

3. Brainstorm to generate support for the topic sentence.

4. Include a concluding sentence.

5. Appoint a group member to write the paragraph on the board for class analysis.

Working Individually

Using the ideas from the paragraph you wrote as a group, develop a thesis sentence on your own, and then draft an essay. If you do not have enough information to develop a longer essay, research other sources of information about your topic. Remember that research can include talking, reading, or searching the Internet.

Final Checklist

Content

Essay

Check to see that the thesis sentence states a clear direction or previews the points to be covered in the paper.

Check to see that the voice is appropriate for purpose and audience.

Paragraphs

Revise so each paragraph has a clear topic sentence that develops an idea suggested by or previewed in the thesis sentence.

Include four to six supporting sentences.

Include a closing sentence in each paragraph.

Internet Activities

Activity 1   Using Parallel Structure in Thesis Sentences

Unit 3 stresses the importance of parallel structure in thesis statements. The "Guide to Grammar & Writing" website will give you more practice in this area.

    a. Go to the following website. (Type all Internet addresses exactly as they appear, or use your bookmark or favorite for quick access.)

       http://webster.commnet.edu/grammar/index.htm

    b. From the start page, scroll down under "Word & Sentence Level" until you find "Parallel Structures." Read through this material to learn more about parallel form.

    c. Click at the bottom of the page to take a quiz. How did you do? Write down the items about parallel structure that you need to review.
       Answers will vary.

Activity 2   Finding More Information on Thesis Sentences

    a. Go to the following website. (Type all Internet addresses exactly as they appear.)

       http://web.uvic.ca/wguide/Pages/EssaysToc.html

    b. From the start page, look at "Writing Your Essay: Getting Started." Select and read "The Thesis." Notice how this information supports the material you have learned in *Writing Paragraphs and Essays*.

    c. Now click "Back" on your toolbar, and return to "The Essay" page. Click on "Narrowing Your Topic," and read the material.

    d. Click "Back" on your toolbar, and return to "The Essay" page. Click on "The Statement of Your Thesis." Read through this information. Then list one or two main ideas that support what you read in your textbook about strong thesis sentences.
       Answers will vary.

Activity 3   Correcting Fragments

Visit Capital Community College's Online Writing Textbook to practice, do an interactive activity, and have fun with a partner.

a. Go to the following website. (Type all Internet addresses exactly as they appear, or use your bookmark or favorite for quick access.)

http://webster.commnet.edu/sensen/exp2/mainmenu_exp.html

b. Review the information on this first web page. Scroll your mouse over each chapter listed on the right-hand side of the page, and a summary will appear. Scroll over to heading 2, "Usage," and click on 8.

c. A submenu will appear under the "Inside This Chapter" box. Go to 7, "Review and Practice." Take the quiz, and compare your responses to the correct answers. Print pages for your instructor if requested.

d. For more fun, click "Back" on your toolbar and select 8 once more. The same submenu, "Inside This Chapter," will appear. This time, select 8, "Fun with Grammar: Unpolished Lyrics." With a partner, read the directions, and do the "Lost and Found in Translation" activity.

Unit 4 Writing with More Depth and Variety

Part 1

Writing Skills: Writing with Examples

A pretest over Unit 4, Parts 1 and 4, is on page 6 of the Test Bank.

Objectives

- Understand the purpose of an example.
- Recognize sources of examples.
- Generate examples through freewriting or brainstorming.
- Recognize and write both extended and short, interrelated examples.
- Use only relevant examples.
- Determine the number of examples needed to clarify the topic idea.

Master for transparencies is in the Instructor's Manual, pages 33–34.

In composition writing, an **example** is a specific reference to an experience you have had, have witnessed, have read about, or have seen in a movie or on television. Such a reference helps you clarify or illustrate a point, fact, or opinion you wish to make in your paper.

The Purpose of Examples

Just as your paragraphs need specific details for good, solid support, they also can be more fully developed through relevant, well-selected examples. Examples in writing are based on life experiences that can be used to support your focused thesis, and by presenting carefully selected examples, you add credibility to your writing. Think of examples as a "defense for your case" as you state it in your thesis. With strong examples, you can convince your reader and present your essay as trustworthy rather than as weak and unbelievable.

As you learned in Unit 1 on topic sentences and paragraphs, the following sentences are not sufficient for a paragraph.

> Many people have pet dogs that become heroes because these companions show their bravery in life-threatening situations. **When a family member is in danger, these beloved pets do not run to safety. Instead, they instinctively know what to do to save the lives of their owners.**

The first sentence expresses the main idea. The two sentences in bold type give support to the main idea, but you still need more information. You might want to "show" how this is true through *specific examples* that clarify the point being made. What is needed is one or more detailed examples—*incidents* or *pictures*—to show and support the topic idea. Now read the revised paragraph. Four specific examples have been added.

> Many people have pet dogs that become heroes because these companions show their bravery in life-threatening situations. When a family member is in danger, these beloved pets do not run to safety. Instead, they instinctively know what to do to save the lives of their owners. Just last week, a toddler wandered out of the yard and across the railroad tracks with his dog. His parents could not find him anywhere, and they became frantic because just as a train came

shooting past, they caught a glimpse of their little boy on the other side of the tracks. After the train had gone by, they saw their son with his dog still holding him by his shirt. The little boy was scared but safe. On another occasion, a man was inside his kitchen when an armed robber broke into his home. His dog silently moved behind the kitchen door, but when the intruder went through the doorway, the dog sprang at him, knocking the gun from his hand and saving his owner's life. In another incident, an eighty-year-old woman went on her back porch to get something before locking her door for the night. She slipped on the icy floor and was unable to get up. Her two dogs lay down, one on each side of her. They spent the night together like this, preventing the woman from freezing to death. Another woman, who suffered from diabetes, programmed her telephone so that the pound sign would ring emergency. She then trained her little dog to nudge the receiver off the hook and hit the pound sign, hoping he could do this if she got sick. Several weeks later, the woman went into a diabetic coma, and her dog was able to reach 911. He then continued to bark until help arrived. These and many other times, dogs have rescued their owners from harm's way.

This paragraph shows the reader "in what way" pet dogs become heroes by stating that "these companions show their bravery in life-threatening situations." This statement is explained and then clarified by four supporting examples: one in which a pet dog keeps a toddler away from a moving train; one in which a dog disarms an intruder; one in which a dog keeps an elderly woman from freezing; and one in which a dog reaches emergency help. In your writing, you too can give specific examples to illustrate your main idea.

Sources of Examples

Finding appropriate examples for your writing involves discovering various sources through freewriting, brainstorming, or other prewriting activities.

Sources That Provide Examples

1. personal experiences
2. personal observations of other people
3. short stories, novels, television, or movies
4. facts, statistics, or reports from authoritative sources

Personal Experiences

A personal experience can add convincing information to support your thesis. Frequently, personal experiences that you can recall in detail can help you clarify the main point for the reader. The more specific your example, the clearer the topic idea becomes to the reader. Freewriting and brainstorming can help you remember details of events in your life. If these events are important enough for you to remember, then perhaps your reader will also be able to relate to these examples. Suppose your topic idea for a paragraph is the following:

Topic: Taking a child shopping can be embarrassing.

Perhaps during freewriting or brainstorming, you remember the following incident:

When I took my four-year-old child shopping at Metrocenter, he decided to "check out" the mannequin wearing a beautiful black, slinky dress, and somehow he managed to knock it over with a thud. Instantly a salesperson appeared to see if my child was hurt. He wasn't hurt, but he was scared. People began to gather from all directions. I wasn't sure what to do, so we quietly slipped away.

Notice that this incident "shows" the reader "in what way" taking a child shopping can be embarrassing. This *incident* or *picture* that you have created for the reader is a strong, *specific example.*

Realistic examples make the topic idea clearer to the reader. *Made-up stories often sound fake,* adding little or no credibility to your writing. It is much easier to remember the time your child knocked over a mannequin than it is to make up an example that never happened. In the earlier paragraph, it would be very difficult to make up a story about a dog that had been trained to alert 911. Therefore, by recalling real events that have happened, you can "show" what it is you want to prove. "Showing" makes writing stronger and more interesting than "telling about" an idea.

Observations of Other People

Observations that you have made of other people can illustrate the topic you are discussing and add more credibility to your paragraphs. Perhaps you are writing about fatherhood, but you are not a father. Maybe your brother, husband, or neighbor is a father, and you have observed him with his children. After freewriting or brainstorming, you might have decided to begin with this topic idea:

Topic: Many fathers in the United States are becoming involved in all aspects of their children's lives.

During additional freewriting or brainstorming, you might remember when you saw a father becoming involved in his children's lives:

Last summer I always knew it was 5:30 P.M. because I could see Hugh Dobson and his son, equipped with a bat, gloves, and a baseball, emerge from their front door. Sometimes they would practice catching, sometimes pitching, and other times batting.

Even though these are not your personal experiences, they are events that you have witnessed. They will sound more convincing to your reader than a made-up incident.

Short Stories, Novels, Television, or Movies

Examples that come from short stories, novels, television, or movies can also support or "show" topic ideas. This extensive source for examples can include characters and events from stories that you have read in books or seen in the movies or on television.

If you are writing an essay about how the meaning of life can change for a person, you might use an incident from Orwell's *1984* as an example. In that novel the change that the main character, Winston, feels regarding sex could be an example of your topic idea. You could summarize the incident and use it to support your topic idea:

Winston's sexual encounter with a prostitute is very degrading to him. The prostitute is repulsive, and he feels that the sexual act itself has been lowered to only a mechanical act. Winston feels no love as he performs a loveless, almost disgusting act. (*This would be considered one example.*)

On the other hand, if you are writing an essay about the realistic depiction of strong, assertive individuals, you might draw from a source like *Erin Brockovich,* a movie based on a true story. The topic idea might be that there still are people in America who are willing to stand up and fight when they see an injustice done to others. You might use specific examples as follows:

> Erin went from house to house, convincing the people of Hinkley, California, to stand up to the giant corporation, Pacific Gas and Electric Company. She convinced Ed Masry, the owner of a small law firm, to take on the case. When she needed to obtain legal documents, she used her sexuality to persuade the records clerk to let her go through the files, and she refused to stop until she got the evidence she needed. Erin actually went out into the property of the Pacific Gas and Electric Company to gather evidence, including a dead frog and various water samples. (*This would be considered four examples.*)

Or, if you are writing a paper about humorous events in family life, you could use a current television program for appropriate examples.

Facts, Statistics, or Reports from Authoritative Sources

Research studies, verifiable facts, or current news stories can provide examples to support your thesis. To use these kinds of examples, you may have to read material in the library, search the Internet, or talk to someone who is an expert on your topic. If you want to write a paper about aquariums but do not have one, you can still write about them if you read books or articles about aquariums or if you go to a fish store and talk to someone who is knowledgeable in the field. You would want to know if this "authority in the field" is or has been a breeder and/or has been working with fish for a long time. You need this background to decide if you can trust the source of your information, whether it comes from a book, an article, an Internet source, or a personal interview.

Once you have read about or talked to someone about your topic, your freewriting or brainstorming might give you this topic idea for one paragraph in your essay:

Topic: When an aquarium is set up correctly, a natural balance results.

Your conversation at a fish store with an expert has given you a specific example of a natural balance. You could use the information like this:

> According to the owner of the Coral Reef fish store, catfish clean up the waste from the bottom of the fish tank. In this way, the catfish help to create a natural balance.

The catfish would be only one example in your paragraph. Your reading, your Internet exploration, and your conversation with the store owner would give you other examples.

In a different essay, you might be working on a paragraph to support the topic that technology has provided improved treatments for people with congestive heart failure. You could recall some factual information you have read, or you could go to the library or search the Internet. As a result of your reading in the June 25, 2001, issue of *Newsweek,* you found an article by Geoffrey Cowley and Anne Underwood about a new artificial heart. If you decide to use this example, you might write something like this in your paragraph:

> In the June 25, 2001, issue of *Newsweek,* the article "New Heart, New Hope" describes the AbioCor, a mechanical, battery-powered heart made of titanium, plastic, and glue that can beat as efficiently and regularly as a human heart.

This specific example could be used in your paragraph; however, as you can see, you need to let the reader know where you got the information. This is one kind of authoritative example that can give credibility to your writing.

In each of the previous writing situations, you would also need other examples in each paragraph to support the topic idea. These examples could come from your personal experience or from observations of people you know. As you have learned, one of your goals in each paragraph is to support the topic sentence with enough specific information to convince your reader. (For more information on documentation, see Appendix F.)

Generating Examples Through Freewriting and Brainstorming

As you have already learned, freewriting and brainstorming are important steps that you can use at different times in the writing process. You can freewrite or brainstorm to get started in a writing situation. You can also use these strategies to help you think of or "discover" more or better examples needed to support your thesis sentence and/or topic sentences.

Suppose you have developed the following thesis sentence:

Returning to school has been a rewarding experience because I have found that I have abilities I never knew I had before, have changed the way I dress, and have met new friends.

In looking over your freewriting or brainstorming, you probably realize that you do not yet have enough specific information to write strong paragraphs. Using each topic idea previewed in the thesis sentence, then, you would do more freewriting and/or brainstorming to find the examples you need. For instance, freewriting and brainstorming on "I have found that I have abilities I never knew I had before" might produce the following ideas. (Remember that in freewriting or brainstorming you do not stop to correct errors!)

Freewriting for Examples

Going to school can be rewarding. I need to come up with some examples of times when I found I had new abilities I didn't know I had before. There are many times that I have found that I could do things that I didn't think I could do before. I haven't been to school in ten years, and I didn't even know how to use the Internet and I thought that the kids just out of high school would do circles around me or make me feel inferior. I still think it is hard. But I am really not in that bad of shape. I am doing pretty good in my English class and in my Psychology class. I hope that my grade point average is an A. I am more concerned about learning though. I studied for my grammar test. It came out pretty good too. I made 95 percent on that test. It was on consistent point of view. Most of the kids made around 70 percent, so that really made me feel like I could do alright. No one has made fun of me yet. Some of the younger kids think I am an old lady, but that is ok. Jim didn't seem to think I was so dumb when the teacher asked me to help him with the topic sentence. He began to get it too. I felt real proud when I could show him how to write one. You know, it made it easier for me too. I guess showing someone else how to do things is good for me. It made me feel better, and now I think I'll make it. Maybe I'll even decide to be a teacher. I had a little trouble when I wrote my first essay. The next time I wrote one the teacher told me I had an effective thesis sentence and that my support was good. That really made me feel good. I wasn't sure I could do all that when I came back to school.

When you reread the freewriting, you can see three distinct examples that show you are doing well in your English class. They show *in what way* you discovered abilities you didn't know you had. These three examples would help you write a strong support paragraph for this part of your essay.

Study the following list to see how the ideas underlined in the previous freewriting have been rewritten as specific examples that support the topic sentence "I have abilities I never knew I had before." The topic sentence, in turn, clearly relates to the main idea in your thesis sentence.

Thesis sentence:	Returning to school has been a rewarding experience because I have found that I have abilities I never knew I had before, have changed the way I dress, and have met new friends.
Topic sentence:	I have found that I have abilities I never knew I had before.
Linking sentence:	I did well in my English class.
Specific example 1:	When I wrote my second essay using my job as the topic, my instructor told me that my thesis sentence was well written and that I had followed through well on my paragraphs.
Specific example 2:	My English instructor asked me to help a student who was having trouble with the topic sentence, and as I helped him, I felt good because he understood what I was saying.
Specific example 3:	I took my first grammar test on consistent point of view and scored 95 percent on it.
Specific example 4:	I feel more comfortable using the Internet.

Notice that a linking sentence, "I did well in my English class," has been put in. Sometimes in the freewriting you can also find a suitable sentence to link the examples to the topic sentence. Also notice that a lot of unnecessary or "warm-up" information from the freewriting has been left out.

Brainstorming for Examples

Topic sentence: I have abilities I never knew I had before.

> did well on grammar test: 95 percent
>
> helped other student with topic sentence
>
> wrote good essay
>
> did well in English class
>
> learned how to use the Internet

Sometimes it is easier to freewrite before you brainstorm and then pull the ideas from the freewriting. Others prefer just to brainstorm in order to generate ideas.

The other two support paragraphs can also be developed through freewriting or brainstorming. The choice is yours.

How Finding Examples Fits into the Writing Process

At this point, you may find it helpful to review the writing process. Study the following review of the writing process for a longer paper—from selecting a topic to finding examples.

Steps in the Writing Process to Generate Ideas for a Paper

1. selecting a topic
2. freewriting/brainstorming for direction
3. identifying direction
4. freewriting/brainstorming and clustering for thesis sentence
5. writing the thesis sentence
6. freewriting/brainstorming again to recall specific examples

Suppose you have selected "driving on ice" as the topic for your essay, and you decide to brainstorm to find a direction and develop a thesis sentence. Now follow this process from selecting the topic of "driving on ice" to writing a support paragraph in a longer paper.

Choose a topic:	driving on ice
Brainstorm for direction:	hazardous
	dangerous
	could get hurt
Identify direction:	hazards of driving on ice

Brainstorm and group for thesis sentence:

black ice is scary	braking
nothing can be done to prevent it	weather conditions
causes skidding	driving too fast
shiny, clear, invisible	drive slower
freezes at 32 degrees F	chains
learn from experienced driver	warnings
salt on road	

Next, cluster similar ideas, rewrite them, and give each group a "label."

learning to control the car
    realize that braking causes the skid
    know how to bring the car out of a skid
        turn in the direction of the skid
    drive with someone who is used to driving in icy weather
understanding dangerous conditions
    black ice is shiny, clear, invisible
    occurs at 32 degrees F
following safety precautions
    using chains
    driving only on roads that have been salted
    obeying warnings
    listening to weather reports
    driving at slower speeds

Write the thesis sentence: Driving safely on ice involves learning to control the car, understanding dangerous conditions, and following safety precautions.

At this point in the process, you know that you need more specific examples to write strong paragraphs, so you may either freewrite or brainstorm to find these examples.

Freewrite to recall specific example(s):

I need to remember examples that show driving on ice safely involves learning to control the car. I am a pretty good driver but ice still scares me. I guess it scares me because of the time I almost hit another car because I put on the brakes and went into a skid. That was really scary. I remember that I was near my house and since I thought I was a pretty good driver in winter weather, I wasn't paying too much attention to how fast I was going. It is a good thing I did know how to bring the car out of a skid. I remembered Mr. Lopez, but that really didn't have anything to do with controlling the car. That was more because he didn't have time to bring his car out of a skid.

Brainstorm to recall specific example(s):

Mr. Lopez, who was fatally injured

the time I almost got into a wreck

Either of these two incidents, whether generated through freewriting or through brainstorming, could provide convincing details. You may choose one or both of them to support your topic idea. Each incident you select will be *one detailed example* that helps you develop the topic idea that learning to control the car is important when driving on ice. You might write the paragraph this way:

Being able to control the car is important when I drive on dangerous ice. Being a native of Colorado, I am comfortable with my ability to drive in the winter months, but each year I get shocked into reality. This winter was no different. A week after the worst snowstorm, I thought things were getting better because the snow was beginning to melt. Suddenly, without warning, a cold night froze the melting snow at a busy intersection close to my house. As I came to the stop sign, I applied the brakes as usual, but my Bronco seemed to accelerate into the flow of traffic. I quickly took my foot off the brake and concentrated on turning into the skid. Thanks to my guardian angel, I missed running into an innocent motorist, but just barely. Next year I hope I can remember this near miss as vividly as I do now and can avoid an ice accident.

The following exercise will give you practice in generating examples to support a topic idea. Either freewrite or brainstorm to find these ideas.

Exercise 1

Using the following topics, or one you have chosen for your next writing assignment, write a personal example, a personal observation of someone else, a fictionalized example, and a fact, statistic, or incident from an authoritative source. (To obtain an authoritative example, you may need to go to the library, search the Internet, or talk to an expert on your topic.)

1. Pets comfort their owners.

_____

_____

_____

(personal example)

_____

_____

_____

(personal observation of someone else)

_____

_____

_____

(example from a short story, novel, television show, or movie)

_____

_____

_____

(fact, statistic, or incident from an authoritative source from the library or the Internet)

2. Email has changed communication.

_____

_____

_____

(personal example)

_____

_____

_____

(personal observation of someone else)

_____

_____

_____

(example from a short story, novel, television show, or movie)

_____

_____

_____

_____

(fact, statistic, or incident from an authoritative source from the library or the Internet)

Extended Examples and Shorter, Interrelated Examples

Examples can appear in basically two forms:

1. extended examples

2. series of shorter, detailed, interrelated examples

Extended Examples

An extended example illustrates one person, one experience, or one significant incident developed fully so that the reader has not only a clear picture of the example but also its relationship to the topic idea. After brainstorming, you might have written the extended example in the following paragraph.

> **Driving on ice can be dangerous because it is invisible and can catch motorists unaware.** Mr. Lopez was one of these unsuspecting motorists. As a UPS inspector, he had to take his turn on the graveyard shift. When he drove to work in the early evening, the roads were fine, but when he left at 2:00 in the morning, black ice had formed. Because he was anxious to get home to his warm bed and no traffic slowed him down, he came upon an unexpectedly busy intersection too rapidly. As he applied the brakes, his tires slid on the ice, and his car slammed into a big diesel. Mr. Lopez, who never knew what hit him, died unnecessarily. No driver should ever underestimate icy winter conditions.

This paragraph uses an **extended example** to support the topic sentence in bold type. The second sentence—"Mr. Lopez was one of these unsuspecting motorists"—is the link between the topic idea and the extended example of Mr. Lopez's accident.

You do not need to relate everything that you know about Mr. Lopez, only the information that supports the topic sentence. Your reader does not need to know if Mr. Lopez was single or married, if he was rich or poor, if he liked to fish or play football. That information is irrelevant to the topic sentence.

Remember the pattern:

topic sentence

linking sentence

extended example

The following exercise will help you write extended examples and their linking sentences.

Exercise 2

For each topic sentence, write a sentence that links the topic idea to an appropriate extended example. Then write an extended example that clarifies the topic sentence. (You may find it easier to write the example first and then think of an appropriate linking sentence.)

1. *Topic sentence:* Motherhood/fatherhood can be a frustrating experience.

_____

_____

(linking sentence)

_____

_____

_____

_____

(extended example)

2. *Topic sentence:* Student athletes or working students must organize their time carefully.

_____

_____

(linking sentence)

_____

_____

_____

_____

(extended example)

3. *Topic sentence:* Proper maintenance can increase the life of a car.

_____

_____

(linking sentence)

_____

_____

_____

_____

(extended example)

After you have recalled the extended example by freewriting or brainstorming, you need to decide how much of the freewriting/brainstorming you actually need to use in the paragraph. Sometimes in freewriting, you get carried away and put in details that are not related to the topic sentence. You may remember many more details than you need. Just keep in mind the requirements for a good paragraph: topic sentence, related support sentences, and a related concluding sentence.

The following exercise will help you sort out unrelated details in an extended example.

Exercise 3

Read the following paragraphs and decide if there is any extra information that is not needed to support the topic. First, underline the topic sentence and the linking sentence. Then strike out the sentences in each extended example that do not support the topic sentence.

Paragraph 1

<u>Cell phone users often ignore the people that they are around.</u> They are even distracted from paying attention to their own children. At the grocery store, one mother, cradling her phone to her ear, shopped with her two young daughters. She spent the entire thirty minutes talking to whoever was on the other end of her cell phone. ~~Several other people kept staring at her and her daughters.~~ Her main focus was on her conversation, and at one point, without even interrupting her chatting, she glanced at one of her daughters and told her to get off the side of the grocery basket. ~~The girls added four boxes of Froot Loops to the basket.~~ Several minutes later, as she stood in the checkout line, she realized that her daughters were not with her. Alarmed, she quickly glanced around, spotted one daughter, and called to her. Still holding the phone to her ear, she told the little girl she was supposed to stay with her sister and then suddenly realized that the other little girl was still missing. Momentarily distracted from her call, she repeated three times, "Where is your sister?" When the little girl pointed to her sister in another part of the store, the mother motioned with her free hand for her other daughter to come back, and then she continued her phone conversation. Even when the clerk was checking them out, the mother kept her mind on her call. ~~She spent $142 on the groceries.~~ <u>Then she walked her cell phone and her two daughters out the door.</u>

Paragraph 2

<u>When my child first learned to read, short-term rewards were often more important than the actual ability to read.</u> He wanted to be a good reader. When he realized he needed to work hard and practice, he wasn't sure reading was as important as watching "Mr. Wizzard's World" to obtain his knowledge about the scientific world. However, he was willing to sit down and plan a strategy. Because he also wanted to set up an aquarium that had been unused for many years, together we decided that for every fifty pages he read aloud to me, he could either buy a fish or have two dollars of in-store credit. ~~He had two other pets.~~ With this agreed upon, he assembled the aquarium, filled it with water, and went to the fish store to wish. As soon as we got home and he walked through the door, he said, "Let's read." And read we did. Even though the first book was below his grade level, it took him four days to finish fifty pages. However, it only took twenty minutes to get the first inhabitant for his tank. That one fish looked lonely, and the only solution was to read another fifty pages. Soon he had earned another fish and another fish. ~~The fish cost me anywhere from eighty-nine cents to two dollars.~~ Moving up to grade-level books brought a little resistance because there were NO pictures. But soon these books, too, seemed easier and easier until he was able to select books way above grade level. Now he was enjoying reading for the sake of reading, and he began to read extra books on his own. ~~Of all the books he read, he enjoyed the one about a kid who ended up with jars and jars of goldfish with no place to put them.~~ As he earned fish, he began to love reading for the sake of knowledge, and he seldom found reading a chore because every page brought him closer to a new fish.

Paragraph 3

<u>Being hospitalized for an illness can cause a person to suffer a financial setback. The extensive bills can mount up.</u> Bo Lewis suffered a severe financial setback when he spent several weeks in the hospital. The seven days in intensive care and four additional weeks in the hospital resulted in astronomical costs. Even though he had insurance, he had to pay a $500 deductible and 20 percent of the bill. Because the hospital bill alone was over $54,000, his responsibilities were $10,700. ~~Also, his wife went on a shopping spree for new summer clothes.~~ On top of this, he had to purchase several hundred dollars' worth of medicine. He also had to purchase medical supplies that were not covered by insurance. Because Bo Lewis was unable to work, he was eligible for disability, but this amount was much less than his regular salary. ~~Before his illness, he smoked only one carton of cigarettes a week, but because of the stress during and after his illness, he smoked two cartons.~~ In just a few weeks, he found himself owing $11,200 in medical expenses. It is scary to think how fast medical bills can accumulate when an extended illness occurs.

Shorter, Detailed, Interrelated Examples

In addition to one extended example, your brainstorming may give you a series of shorter, detailed, interrelated examples that can be used in your support paragraphs. After brainstorming for examples, you may write a paragraph like the following that uses these shorter, detailed, interrelated examples.

> When an aquarium is set up correctly, a natural balance results. Choosing the correct plant and animal life provides an opportunity for these two forces to live harmoniously. Not only do plants put oxygen into the water, but they also provide a place for baby fish to hide so they won't be eaten. Selection of animal life is just as important to the owner of the aquarium. Catfish are scavengers that clean up the waste from the bottom and sides of the fish tank. Plecostomus, which are a type of catfish, even clean plants that have become slimy from algae. Snails can be seen removing the algae and slime or eating fish that have died and settled on the bottom of the tank. At the same time, all of these fish return carbon dioxide to the water. If proper thought is put into starting an aquarium, a harmonious balance can be achieved.

This paragraph has a clear topic sentence and a linking sentence to introduce the short, interrelated examples. Four separate examples support the topic sentence: (1) plants, (2) catfish, (3) plecostomus, and (4) snails.

The following exercise will give you practice in generating short, interrelated examples and the appropriate linking sentences.

Exercise 4

For each topic sentence, write a sentence that links the topic idea to appropriate short, interrelated examples. You may use the same linking sentences that you wrote in Exercise 2. Then write the short, interrelated examples that clarify the topic sentence. If it is easier for you, write the series of short examples first; then write a sentence to link them to the topic sentence.

1. *Topic sentence:* Motherhood/fatherhood can be a frustrating experience.

_____

_____

(linking sentence)

_____

_____

_____

(short, interrelated examples)

2. *Topic sentence:* Student athletes or working students must organize their time carefully.

_____

_____

(linking sentence)

_____

_____

_____

(short, interrelated examples)

3. *Topic sentence:* Proper maintenance can increase the life of a car.

_____

_____

(linking sentence)

_____

_____

_____

(short, interrelated examples)

Stressing Relevance in Short, Interrelated Examples

You have learned that strong paragraphs are unified, that all the sentences relate to the topic sentence. Whenever you use examples to develop your paragraph, be sure that every example is related to the topic idea.

In the previous paragraph about setting up a balanced aquarium, all of the sentences support one topic idea. Suppose, in further reading, you find that "dojos are Chinese weather fish that change color with the weather" and that "African frogs are nocturnal aquatic creatures that come out to play at night when the fish are sleeping."

This information sounds so interesting that you decide to include it. Here is your new paragraph:

> When an aquarium is set up correctly, a natural balance results. Choosing the correct plant and animal life provides an opportunity for these two forces to live harmoniously. Not only do plants put oxygen into the water, but they also provide a place for baby fish to hide so they won't be eaten. Selection of animal life is just as important to the owner of the aquarium. Catfish are scavengers that clean up the waste from the bottom and sides of the fish tank. Plecostomus, which are a type of catfish, even clean plants that have become slimy from algae. Snails can be seen removing the algae and slime or eating fish that have died and settled on the bottom of the tank. At the same time, all of these fish return carbon dioxide to the water. **Dojos are Chinese weather fish that change color with the weather, and African frogs are nocturnal aquatic creatures that come out to play at night when the fish are sleeping.** If proper thought is put into starting an aquarium, a harmonious balance can be achieved.

Even though these two new examples are appealing, *you should not add them* to the paragraph because they do *not* support the topic idea of a balanced aquarium. When you are drafting or revising a paragraph, you have time to think through how well your examples support the topic sentence. Do not hesitate to cut examples that are interesting but are not directly related to the topic idea.

The following exercise will give you practice in finding examples that are not relevant to the topic sentence.

Exercise 5

In each paragraph, decide which examples are relevant to the topic sentence and which examples are not. Then cross out the examples that do not support the topic idea.

Paragraph 1

Early Americans had to rely on their own ingenuity to make life comfortable or even to survive. They turned survival skills into a type of art that was passed down from generation to generation. Some of these art forms, which may no longer be practical in today's society, were a part of living for our great-grandparents. In the West, sturdy houses could be made from adobe brick, but first the brick had to be made from mud and straw. Making clothes was also an art of the past that few people could accomplish today. Even buying material for clothes was a luxury few knew. The process of making a new dress or shirt or pants involved shearing sheep, carding wool, spinning yarn, and weaving cloth. Sometimes the clothing maker dyed the yarn different colors, using natural materials like walnut shells. ~~The women enjoyed growing flowers to make the home look more attractive.~~ Tatting—making lace by hand—became an art form that was used to decorate collars or to bring beauty to something as necessary as pillowcases. ~~People loved to get together in the evenings and have dances.~~ Since there were no refrigerators, families found that making beef jerky was a way to preserve meat and have a year-round supply. And if they wanted to take a bath, they needed soap, but making soap at home, an art almost unheard-of today, was required before that bath could take place. When the supply of candles, the source of night light, became low, there was one solution—making more from melted lard. ~~Sometimes the men and women would work from sunup to sundown so they could take a day off for celebration.~~ Today, we talk of "the good old days" when life was simple, but maybe we should say when families were resourceful and used art in order to survive.

Paragraph 2

For the millions of people using cell phones, many drawbacks exist, not only for the users but for the people around them. As people talk on these phones, they are exposing their bodies to electromagnetic waves that might damage their brains, possibly resulting in brain tumors. Researchers are especially concerned about the impact on young, developing minds. Just as cell phones may harm the users, their danger could spread to include those around them. For example, when individuals decide to drive and talk at the same time, they can be distracted while dialing or talking on the phones. The results can be accidents, sometimes even fatal ones. ~~Of course, if they do get in an accident, they can immediately call for help.~~ Other times, when people are in line waiting for services, they may try to place orders and talk at the same time, slowing the transaction down and causing other customers to wait longer than normal. Sometimes people can be sitting inside a theater, completely enthralled in the most exciting part of a movie, only to have a cell phone ring, ruining the mood. ~~If the movie is longer than they anticipate or their friends do not know where they are, their friends can get hold of them.~~ Perhaps people are in a classroom or at a church service when the cell phone rings. Not only is the speaker rudely interrupted, but others in the room are annoyed. A parent and child can be out for an enjoyable afternoon, only to have the child's special time spoiled by the parent talking nonstop on the phone. Cell phones have become a way of life for many people, but as more and more people use these cell phones, the negative side effects seem to increase.

Deciding How Many Short Examples to Use

Usually after you have drafted your paragraph, you need to decide how many short, interrelated examples are needed to clarify the topic sentence. This is something you have to think through logically. You want to provide as many different types of examples as you can. You do not, however, want to refer to the same types of examples over and over again. Read again the sample paragraph about the balanced aquarium:

> When an aquarium is set up correctly, a natural balance results. Choosing the correct plant and animal life provides an opportunity for these two forces to live harmoniously. Not only do plants put oxygen into the water, but they also provide a place for baby fish to hide so they won't be eaten. Selection of animal life is just as important to the owner of the aquarium. Catfish are scavengers that clean up the waste from the bottom and sides of the fish tank. Plecostomus, which are a type of catfish, even clean plants that have become slimy from algae. Snails can be seen removing the algae and slime or eating fish that have died and settled on the bottom of the tank. At the same time, all of these fish return carbon dioxide to the water. If proper thought is put into starting an aquarium, a harmonious balance can be achieved.

Catfish are chosen as an example because catfish clean up the wastes. Plecostomus are added because they do one additional thing—they clean the algae slime from the plants. There are many more varieties of algae eaters, but they are not needed to make the point that an aquarium that is set up properly can result in a natural balance between plants and animals. The four examples clearly and forcefully support the topic idea. All four add something *different* to the supporting details.

Look at the following paragraph on special-interest classes offered by a community college.

The special-interest classes offered by many community colleges meet the needs of all members of a society. The classes are varied in scope and content depending on the population living around the college. "Remodeling Your Own Kitchen" offers an opportunity for people to equip themselves with information before investing thousands of dollars on a remodeling job. "Quilting for Fun" enables men and women to learn an art that is no longer passed down from generation to generation. "Making Animals from Balloons" is a course offered to children and provides hours of creative enjoyment. "Living with an Elderly Parent or Handicapped Child" eases the responsibility felt by adults in charge. These courses are as varied as the community itself and provide enrichment for the public.

Four *different* types of courses are included. More examples could have been added. You would not, however, add an example like "Remodeling Your Bathroom" or "Simple Needlecraft" because these types of examples have already been used. You might, though, use a different type of example, such as "Camping Made Easy."

Deciding how many examples to use is up to you. Three or four is usually a good number to put into each paragraph. Remember, though, that each one should add *something different* to support the topic sentence. Each one should show in a different way "how the topic sentence is true."

The following exercise will give you practice in finding duplicate examples in a paragraph that is developed with a series of short, interrelated examples.

Exercise 6

Read each paragraph carefully and decide which examples duplicate a type of example already used and which examples show different ways in which the topic idea is true. Strike out any example that duplicates a type already used. Be prepared to explain your answer.

Paragraph 1

In order to avoid the high cost of living, many retired couples have become full-time recreational vehicle travelers ("RVers"). After selling or renting their homes, they literally spend all their time traveling. One couple sold their home and bought a fully equipped van. They now pull a boat that provides recreation, and, when the boat is not being used on the water, it provides storage. Another couple sold their home and now spend several months in an Indiana resort area trading a few hours of work for a place to stay and free hookups. When summer comes, they do the same thing at an RV resort in Florida. Another retired couple spend their time working at national and state parks in exchange for a place to live and modest pay. ~~Likewise, a couple who lived in New Mexico now spend all their time moving from one national park to another serving as a host to the RV campground.~~ In this way, these retired people reduce their living costs and are able to live on moderate retirement funds.

Paragraph 2

Today in America, medical researchers are realizing the many ways pets are helping physically handicapped adults. These pets are an extension of these adults because they perform tasks that are often impossible for the handicapped adult to do alone. Seeing Eye dogs are used to guide visually handicapped people so that these individuals can experience some of the freedom their blindness has taken from them. Trained monkeys are used to perform simple manual tasks like turning light switches on and off or holding the telephone receiver for adults with limited or no use of their hands and arms. Parrots are used to bring companionship to handicapped adults who are confined to their homes. The parrot and master can sing songs together and can even talk to each other. ~~Cats are also being used for companionship so that the handicapped adult doesn't feel so lonely.~~ All of these pets and their owners become great friends as they lean on each other for support.

When adding examples to your writing, use your judgment to decide whether you want one longer, extended example or many shorter examples. Remember, *both* types of development are effective because they contain specific details that provide strong support for a topic idea.

Exercise 7

Read each paragraph and decide whether it is developed by using several short, interrelated examples or one longer, extended example. Identify the kind of example used by writing "SIE" (short, interrelated example) or "Ext" (extended) in the margin to the left of the paragraph.

Paragraph 1

SIE

From May to July of 2002, drought in Arizona's national forests created disappointments for people who wanted to enjoy the outdoors. Because of the extreme fire danger, all public hiking trails were closed. Many fishing spots were inaccessible because roads into the wilderness areas were also closed. No campfires were allowed anywhere in the forests, including official campgrounds, where only propane gas stoves could be used for cooking. Smoking was allowed only in automobiles, trucks, or recreational vehicles, including trailers where smokers had easy access to ashtrays. They could not smoke in such places as private trails in resorts, picnic areas, or campgrounds. Vacationers in Arizona were constantly aware of the fire dangers in the forests.

Paragraph 2

Ext

For many years, the human touch has been used successfully by medical personnel to improve the health of patients. Today, nurses are more than ever aware that touching their patients provides emotional support during difficult times. When these health providers place their hands on patients' shoulders, touch their foreheads, or even take their hands into their comforting grasps, they are often reducing stress and helping their patients accept a medical procedure or condition more easily. As nurses care for their patients during their hospital stay, some may take a few minutes to make skin contact as they perform such tasks as brush their hair, massage their backs, change bandages, or even dispense their medications. These simple acts let patients know that they are important and that someone cares about them. Some hospitals even go a step further and train their nurses in touch therapy because they realize the importance of human contact. Though having a few minutes or even a few seconds to do anything extra for a patient is difficult for busy nurses who have so many responsibilities, these simple acts of kindness can actually help patients recover faster or deal with their medical condition better because they know someone cares about them.

Paragraph 3

Ext

The persecution of Jewish children was a tragedy that has been captured in the Holocaust Museum in Washington, D.C. The museum features a thought-provoking exhibit entitled "Remember the Children." It is the story of Daniel, dramatizing one child's life as it changed from freedom, then to a Polish ghetto, and finally to Auschwitz, a concentration camp. Daniel's life is pictured in a series of rooms with excerpts from his diary to show his life's progressive deterioration. The first room illustrates Daniel's home full of bright lights, laughter, and good food. Daniel's displayed diary shows how the persecution of Jews increased, how Daniel, his mother, and his sister were moved to a Polish ghetto. Through Daniel's diary, the exhibit shows that his father was sent away to a camp. Daniel's life then became barren and more difficult. The last phase of Daniel's life was depicted by a dark, silent room with a dirt floor closed in by barbed wire. His life portrayed a part of history that many Jewish children experienced.

Paragraph 4

Ext

Though depression descends on many men, women, and children each year, medication and psychoanalysis have allowed some of those who seek help to return to their normal productive lives. Andrew Solomon, an accomplished author, moved into depression and was eventually unable to perform even routine activities such as showering. His sleep pattern was skewed, and he found that on some days he slept all day, only to wake in the evenings, yet he was not able to enjoy the normal social activities that had once been a part of his evenings. Nothing brought him pleasure. He knew he needed help, so he sought professional therapy. He tried different medications and combinations of medications, experiencing side effects, but he never quit trying. Through talking to the right psychotherapist, finding the right medication, and wanting to get better, he finally did manage to shake this depression. He did not stop there, however; he went on to write about this depression and share his story with others throughout the world.

Paragraph 5

Ext

Cats are bright animals. Most people consider them fur-brained, but if closely observed and nurtured, a household cat can demonstrate intelligence. A precocious pet named Ashes knows how to communicate and assert herself. When she's hungry and her bowl is empty in the morning, she patiently stands at the foot of the bed and eyes her owner. She doesn't meow until she hears her friend stir. She then knows that her owner is awake. At other times, if Ashes can't make eye contact, she sounds a particular cry for help. She has learned where to find her owner, what tone to use, and when to speak, and this learning has been reinforced—a remarkable feat for a being that can't talk. Because cats are subtle, quiet creatures, many people fail to recognize their intellect.

Paragraph 6

SIE

Many times students believe that teachers are callous and don't care when the students have problems. Teachers may not be callous or uncaring. They simply may have been taken in by one too many sob stories. For example, a student came in after missing a test plus two other days of class. He said he had had some personal problems—his mother had died. The teacher began to worry about him, and the next day she called to see if there was anything she could do. His mother answered the phone. Another time a student left a message telling his teacher that he was too sick to come to class. Later that afternoon when the teacher was working out at the fitness center, she saw the student working out there, too. When she asked him how he was feeling, he looked embarrassed. Another time a student came in to say that he hadn't been to class the week before because it was raining too hard for him to catch the bus. The teacher thought he might have some special type of problem and asked why he couldn't ride the bus when she had seen other students getting off the same bus. These teachers are not callous, but rather they do not want to be unfair to the rest of their students by giving special privileges to irresponsible students.

Exercise 8

Carefully consider the following thesis sentences. Then develop a topic sentence for each division in the thesis sentence. Brainstorm on a separate sheet of paper to generate examples. Decide whether an extended example or several shorter examples would be the most effective way to develop each paragraph. Then write each paragraph, using one extended example or several short, interrelated examples.

1. *Thesis sentence:* During my first years in college, I met deadlines, cut back on expenses, and found new friends.

Paragraph 1

_____

_____

_____

(topic sentence)

_____

_____

_____

(extended example or several shorter examples)

Paragraph 2

_____

_____

_____

(topic sentence)

_____

_____

_____

(extended example or several shorter examples)

Paragraph 3

_____

_____

(topic sentence)

_____

_____

_____

(extended example or several shorter examples)

2. *Thesis sentence:* Families visit zoos so they can observe wild animals, interact with the animals at the petting zoo, and learn about endangered species.

Paragraph 1

_____

_____

(topic sentence)

_____

_____

_____

(extended example or several shorter examples)

Paragraph 2

_____

_____

(topic sentence)

_____

_____

_____

(extended example or several shorter examples)

Paragraph 3

_____

_____

(topic sentence)

_____

_____

_____

_____

(extended example or several shorter examples)

3. *Thesis sentence:* I have experienced satisfaction at work because of my new skills, my supportive boss, and my friendly coworkers.

Paragraph 1

_____

_____

_____

(topic sentence)

_____

_____

_____

(extended example or several shorter examples)

Paragraph 2

_____

_____

_____

(topic sentence)

_____

_____

_____

(extended example or several shorter examples)

Paragraph 3

_____

_____

_____

(topic sentence)

_____

_____

_____

(extended example or several shorter examples)

Collaborative Activity

In groups of three, discuss one major problem on your campus. Then brainstorm as many examples as possible that illustrate the problem. Generate short, interrelated examples that come from personal experience, observation, or authoritative sources. Have one person from each group report the results of the discussion.

Part 2

Something to Think About, Something to Write About

Professional Essay to Generate Ideas for Writing

Refuge for Animals in Distress

Susan Husemoller-Bailor, *professor of English, Front Range Community College*

1   Taylor, a happy black Great Dane, ambles through the front door of the Larimer Humane Society, pulling a small woman behind him. She's bringing him to the shelter because she can't provide a home for him anymore. A young girl with long black braids tenderly holds the small gray kitten her father has just adopted. An older husband and wife both wring their hands with worry as they inquire about their missing hounds. In another room, a three-year-old Labrador retriever is being euthanized after being hit by a car, his injuries too severe to save him. In a nearby room, a veterinarian is setting the broken bone of a mature tabby cat. Every day, the dedicated people who work at the Larimer Humane Society experience myriad emotions as they witness joyful and distressing events like these. At times, the sounds of dogs barking and howling, cats meowing, and people coming and going create a frenzied atmosphere, but the trained staff and volunteers stay on a steady pace to complete their important tasks. It is this remarkable effort by volunteers and staff that make the Larimer Humane Society an outstanding refuge for animals in distress.

2   Like many nonprofit organizations, the Larimer Humane Society relies heavily on its volunteers. People of all ages enjoy their jobs as volunteers because they know that in small and large ways, they are helping animals. For example, as a retiree, Jepp Anderson has found his niche grooming dogs and cats for adoption. While it may seem like an insignificant job, clean and friendly dogs and cats have a better chance for adoption than animals who might look unkempt. Other volunteers take dogs and cats to local businesses where they are more visible as well as more accessible to the public. After being released from their crates or kennels, the animals are transported to the businesses where they enjoy attention from others. Many pets will meet their future guardians through endeavors like this, thanks to hardworking and dedicated volunteers.

3   Through the efforts of volunteer foster families, young animals are nurtured in a friendly and warm home until they are ready for adoption. Often, litters of kittens or

puppies who need immediate care are brought to the shelter. Because the Larimer Humane Society has a cadre of trained volunteers who are ready to provide homes, these furry and round youngsters can begin their lives with good medical attention, nutritious food, and loving hands that will help to socialize them. When the puppies and kittens reach the age of adoption, the foster families, with mixed feelings, must return them to the shelter. While they are happy to see their charges healthy and ready to begin life in a new home, the families are often sad to say goodbye to their little companions.

4 Not only are volunteers integral to the successful operation of the Larimer Humane Society, staff members provide loving care to animals on a daily basis. For example, veterinary technicians assist the veterinarians with surgeries and routine animal care such as removing sutures, bandaging wounds, and maintaining sterilized work areas and equipment. Also, Animal Protection and Control officers must be prepared for any situation they might encounter as they cover a vast county in their vans. These professionals, who receive certification from the state, must understand the laws associated with animal protection, and they must have expertise in working with other law enforcement agencies. Because they are on the front lines of many animal mishaps, they must always keep a cool head and be able to work amicably with both humans and animals under stress.

5 Other staff members fulfill the educational and financial missions of the Larimer Humane Society. The development director is constantly looking for ways to receive grants from various sources. The marketing director ensures that the organization stays prominent in the community, and the volunteer coordinator organizes people and events throughout the year. Additionally, information technology specialists ensure efficient communication throughout the establishment. An animal behaviorist provides necessary training classes for members of the community and their canine companions and writes a weekly column in the local newspaper. She continually teaches others how to be more understanding, compassionate, and knowledgeable while sharing a life with an animal that has joined their family. Each of these professional positions contributes to better animal welfare.

6 While many people would label these workers as "animal lovers," their dedication and passion demonstrate that they regard their work much the same as any caregiver would. They are constantly thrilled and energized by the beauty and complexity of animals and feel privileged to be a part of their well-being. They are happy to try to speak for a species that has no voice, being respectful in every way of their grace and dignity. The people of the Larimer Humane Society work hard at what they do: they foster a powerful bond of love and devotion that enriches the lives of both humans and animals.

Understanding Words
Briefly define the following words as they are used in the above essay.

1. myriad *numerous*

2. refuge *safe place*

3. niche *place where a person feels he or she belongs*

4. foster families *families that temporarily take in children or animals*

5. cadre *small, enthusiastic group of people with similar training and interests*

6. integral *central to*

7. foster a powerful bond *promote emotional attachments between people and animals*

Collaborative Writing Project: Working and Learning Together

To start your next essay assignment, work in groups of three or four to discuss one or more of the following quotations. Explore the ideas, and see how they might relate to the ideas in the preceding article. Your discussion may generate ideas to help you when you choose a topic below.

Quotations: Additional Ideas on Being Humane to Animals

"I hope to make people realize how totally helpless animals are, how dependent on us, trusting as a child must that we will be kind and take care of their needs. . ." *James Herriot*

"The question is not can they reason, nor can they talk, but can they suffer?" *Jeremy Bentham*

"No one loves you unconditionally as your beloved pet." *Cynthia S. Dobesk*

"Which of us has not been stunned by the beauty of an animal's skin or its flexibility in motion?" *Marianne Moore*

"Animals are reliable, many full of love, true in their affections, predictable in their actions, grateful and loyal. [These are] difficult standards for people to live up to." *Alfred A. Montapert*

"The soul is the same in all living creatures, although the body of each is different." *Hippocrates*

"The fingerprint of God is often a pawprint." *Susan Chernak McElroy*

"Until one has loved an animal, a part of one's soul remains unawakened." *Anatole France*

"Until we have the courage to recognize cruelty for what it is—whether its victim is human or animal—we cannot expect things to be much better in this world. . . . We cannot have peace among men whose hearts delight in killing any living creature." *Rachel Carson*

"If you are patient in one moment of anger, you will escape a hundred days of sorrow." *Chinese proverb*

"The smallest feline is a masterpiece." *Leonardo DaVinci*

Writing Assignment

After your discussion of the article and quotations, read and discuss the following topics with your group.

1. Advantages or disadvantages of having a pet such as a dog, cat, or horse

2. Reasons people work without pay (such as volunteer on their own, fulfill a requirement)

3. Greatest rewards of volunteering

4. Most important ways animals aid people in society (such as providing service animals, research animals, income)

5. Most important ways animals aid their owners

6. Who benefits when people volunteer?

7. What can people do to strengthen a friendship?

Working Individually

1. Choose a topic for your essay.

2. Freewrite or brainstorm ideas for a thesis sentence. Follow the process you practiced in Unit 3 for developing a thesis sentence.

3. Draft a possible thesis sentence, keeping in mind your purpose, audience, and voice.

4. Check your thesis sentence for a main idea, a clear direction, and previewed subpoints.

5. Check to see if the subpoints are parallel and coordinate (equal). Be sure they do not overlap in meaning.

6. Then draft your essay. Pay particular attention to the examples in each support paragraph. If you use short, interrelated examples, try to have three or four different ones in each paragraph.

7. Be sure to use your own words to link the examples to the topic sentence.

8. Have your draft ready for peer review.

Peer Review

1. Exchange drafts and, in turn, read each essay aloud.

2. Underline the thesis sentence. Be sure that each topic sentence includes key words that go back to the topic, direction, and one of the previewed ideas.

3. Identify the examples in each support paragraph and decide if each example clarifies the topic sentence.

4. Underline the words or sentences that link the examples to the topic sentence.

5. Check to make sure the point of view and verb tense are consistent throughout the essay.

6. Check for fragments, run-on sentences, and comma splices.

Part 3

Paragraphs and Essays for Discussion and Analysis

Student Writing

Legacy

Renee Robbe, *student*

1   I had a wonderful friend who was older than I was, but that was all right with me. I had been with her ever since I could remember, so I watched my best friend grow up through the years. I thought of her as my role model, and she thought of me as her little sister. Why was she my role model? I admired her because she was smart, artistic, and determined.

2   Everything came easy to my sister; therefore, I thought she was very smart. She had no problems in school; in fact, she was a straight "A" student. I always asked her for help with my homework because she explained it better than my teachers; as a result, I became a "B" student. Not only that, but my sister had a job working with computers, and she was very good at using them. Because I did not even know how to turn a computer on, she taught me the basics about computers, but I am still not as expert at them as she was. I admired the knowledge she had about computers because computers are the way of the future. My sister was smart in another way that helped me to solve my problems because she gave smart advice. She was like my own personal psychiatrist, but she did not charge me by the hour. I often wish I had my sister's brain.

3   Another quality I liked about my sister was her artistic talents. She was great at drawing cars, landscapes, and portraits. I was jealous of her drawing abilities because when I was little, I wanted to be an artist; however, I was never any good at art. Because decorating was something that she also loved to do, she wanted to open her own interior design business. It was amazing how she could put together colors to make a room have its own personality. I was inspired to follow in her footsteps and make interior design my career. Her artistic ability also appeared in her talent for sculpting nails. It might look easy, but if a person does not have a steady hand and is not artistic, the nails will look fake. My sister had the talent to make the nails look real. I know from experience because she used to do my nails. I have always admired my sister because she had so much artistic talent.

4   Having determination helped my sister get through life. When she found out that she had cancer, she was determined to survive it. She went through several operations, and no matter how much pain she had to endure, she held on. After seeing what my sister had to go through, I do not think that I could even try. Even though my sister had cancer, she was determined to live a normal life. She lost all her hair due to radiation; therefore, she wore a wig, but it never bothered her. She even went bald sometimes. She had made up her mind that she was not going to hide in her bedroom just because she had no hair. My sister was also determined to follow through with school. She knew she was going to die, but she did not let that stop her from living the rest of her life fully. My sister taught me that having determination will get a person through life, good or bad.

5   My sister taught me many things in her lifetime. She gave me knowledge about things I never knew about, and she taught me a little about art, but most important, she taught me never to give up on life. I think I was lucky to have a role model like my sister to watch and learn from while I was growing up.

Understanding Words

Briefly define the following word as it is used in the above essay.

   1. legacy   *inheritance*

Answers are in the Instructor's Manual, starting on page 20.

Questions on Content

1. What did the author learn from her older sister?

2. What artistic talents did her sister have?

3. What was the older sister's reaction to her illness?

Questions on Form

1. In paragraph 3, what kinds of examples are used?

2. Describe the voice in paragraph 4.

3. What is the purpose of the essay?

A Surprising Experience

Mauro Guzman, *student*

1   It was our first child, and my wife and I could hardly wait for her to be born. However, when my daughter was born, the feeling of happiness and excitement that a newborn is supposed to bring was mixed with confusion, sadness, and desperation. Diana was born three months prematurely. Her chances of survival were minimal, and there were no predictions on her future if she made it through. We were definitely not ready to face this problem; however, we had no choice, and for three months we did not know if she would survive. I found that being a parent to my tiny premature daughter was difficult emotionally, physically, and financially.

2   The most difficult part of having my child born prematurely was the terrible emotional suffering that my wife and I went through. I was waiting and getting ready for my baby to come, like every father in the world would do, shopping, decorating her room, thinking of names. . . . The news that she was going to be born too early was devastating. I remember the first time I saw her when she was being carried in an incubator. She was so small; her face was covered with an oxygen mask, and her whole body was covered with wires and bandages. When she passed by, she opened her tiny eyes and looked at me. I knew she was suffering and did not want to be in there. I felt guilty, speechless, powerless. The nurse who was transporting her to the pediatric intensive care unit tried to cheer me up. "It's a girl. Don't be sad. She is alive," she said. I went back to my wife and hugged her. We both cried. "Don't worry," I said. "Everything is going to be okay." From that moment I knew I had to prepare myself to deal with the situation. It was going to be the longest three months of my life. Having to tell the news to the rest of the family, to friends, and to people at work was also very frustrating, though everybody was very supportive, making things a lot better. The more we prayed, the more faith we had, the more hopeful everything became.

3   The situation was also physically exhausting for me, and I can imagine it was extremely painful for my child. I had an obligation to go to the hospital every day, most of the time before or after working hours. The hospital became a labyrinth where I walked up and down, right and left, to fill out paperwork, to see doctors, to get tests done, doing whatever I had to do to save my little girl. My child had to endure daily cleanings, checkups, and tests that were so painful that sometimes I could not watch. An oxygen mask covered her small face for almost two months until she was ready to breathe on her own. IVs and shots were necessary almost every day, and two blood transfusions also had to be done, adding even more pain and suffering to my "poor little one." Regardless of the physical struggle she was going through, Diana was a fighter, a strong child who wanted to survive. The most dangerous part of all was over after the second month. Again I was able to continue the preparation for my baby to come home, just as if she were going to be born the next month. Thank God things were becoming all right. The everyday reports from specialists and nurses were finally satisfactory.

4   The financial predicament is perhaps the last thing we could think of at that moment, but it could not be ignored. My wife, of course, had to be out of work for a long period of time, affecting our economic situation. Soon the bills started to come, and even though my insurance covered the majority, I still had to pay a large sum. We had to purchase an expensive medical apparatus when our baby was out of the hospital, and most of it was not covered by insurance. Later on I found out that the insurance company paid a total of a quarter of a million dollars in hospital and other

medical bills. It was definitely a bad moment in my life, but again, money was not the issue at that point. The life of my child was the only concern we had.

5   Today I'm glad it is all behind us. The "miracle girl," as the doctors called Diana, is now five years old, and she is a lovely, normal child. We are also relieved to have recuperated from the financial part of this experience. All the struggling and suffering was necessary for her to survive, and the results were surely worth it. I love my daughter more each day, and though she is no longer tiny or tied to wires, I will always carry that first image of my little girl in my heart.

Questions on Content

1. How long was the baby in the hospital?

2. Why was the baby in the hospital?

3. What is his lasting memory from her birth?

Questions on Form

1. What are some examples of emotional suffering given in paragraph 2?

2. Describe the voice in this essay.

What Have You Done to Help Someone?

Gudrun Waltraud Lorke, *student*

1   When my mother was 76 years old, I made the decision to take better care of her because I saw that she needed help. She lived alone in a residence in another city, and always when I visited her I realized that she had lost interest in important things. I thought one reason for this was her age, but mostly it was the loneliness. I talked with my sisters and brothers about this problem and hoped that they would spend more time taking care of our mother and that they would integrate her more into their families on weekends because they lived very close to her. They promised to think about this, but they did not do anything; therefore, I was determined to solve the problem. First, I spoke with my mother to see if she was willing to move to my city, but it wasn't easy to find a place for her. Sometimes it was very frustrating to know what people thought about old people. They were afraid that an elderly person could die soon or create problems. Finally, I found a nice place for her, and my mother moved to the same city where I lived with my family. As a result of this, my mother was busy, ate well, and became closer to my family.

2   From this time on, my mother was busy and made plans because I explained to her that she needed goals and a schedule for the day or the week. She never stayed in bed until noon but was interested in new things. I took her to meet other people her age at senior centers and took her to craft classes. She had fun and counted the days until she could go again. She was busy with handicrafts and embroidered tablecloths in different sizes. This was very difficult for her because her eyesight was getting worse, but I encouraged her to make work on simple cross-stitch pieces. For that, I divided the embroidery cotton and threaded some needles for her. Every day she showed me how much she worked, and when some cross-stitches were not so accurate, I told her that she made it very well for her age. Another activity of hers was to help an old woman who lived in the same house and who couldn't see well. For example, she picked up the mail for her and brought her the newspapers. She stayed much busier than ever.

3   Another way to help her was that I cooked for her because she was diabetic and did not take enough care of herself. Every day during my lunch break from work, I went to her house and prepared her a lunch that she enjoyed. She liked watching me prepare the food and helped me decide what foods she could have and which foods

had too much sugar. We often prepared potatoes and even made whole grain bread. I made sure that she always had fresh fruits, and I always avoided giving her food with high-fat, high-sugar content. After my work, I went to her home again, and we took a little walk together so that she would be hungry before supper. In the evening, we prepared her dinner for that night and breakfast for the next morning. She ate her balanced meals on schedule. Her diabetes was much more under control and getting better because she was eating right.

4   Besides this help, we integrated my mother more into our family life. Most weekends she was in our home; moreover, when we went on a short trip, she came with us. She was very happy to stay with us at the lake for a picnic, and she enjoyed the outing. In our home, sometimes, she helped me to peel potatoes for lunch. She dusted the room for my daughters, and when she saw that they had new things, she had something to talk about with them. These were little things that she could do, but they gave her the feeling that she was needed. My daughters played games with their grandmother or told her what happened in their school life. Being a close part of our family was important for her.

5   Six years later, at 82, she died after a heart attack, but I still have a good feeling about her last years. Most of the time she was very grateful and often said, "You do so much for me." But for me it was wonderful to be able to help her and make life easier for her. Because she took care of me when I was a child, I was able to pay her back in some small way.

Questions on Content

1. What illness did her mother have?

2. What did she do to help her mother?

3. How often did she go to her mother's house?

Questions on Form

1. In paragraph 2, what are some of the things she did to keep her mother busy?

2. Does the author use short, interrelated examples or extended examples?

Responsibility

Charles Marchbanks, *student*

1   Recently, I spent four years living with my uncle. I was a little apprehensive about living with him because I had not met him, and I had heard that he was very mean and nasty. My first encounter with him proved no different. I was sleeping, and a rude voice came bellowing down the hallway. "Wake up! Get up!" I had a feeling that I was about to come face to face with my uncle for the first time. He walked into my room screaming, "You better get out of that bunk before I drop you." I was so startled that I didn't know what to think. Meanwhile, he continued to yell and scream, and I was wishing that I could transform into a speck of dust and blow away. The first impression I received of my uncle was not very good; however, I later found him to be very fair and giving. My uncle has altered my life in a positive way. He has done this by instilling in me discipline, self-pride, and responsibility.

2   While staying with my uncle, I received a fair amount of what he called justice and I called punishment. When I graduated from high school, I thought that I was ready for the world; I thought incorrectly. I had a fair amount of discipline while growing up, but I totally lacked self-discipline. Well, my uncle filled in the void. If I got into trouble, I was disciplined, and the discipline was strictly enforced. Staying with my uncle, I found there was no room for slack. For instance, I accidentally called my uncle "Dude." He didn't like that; consequently, I was outside for fourteen days painting curbs, trimming bushes, and sweeping rocks. The discipline was effective to say the least.

3   Self-esteem is also a quality that I did not possess before living with my uncle. It was something that I had to work on, and my uncle helped me a great deal. He helped me by rewarding and praising me for doing a good job. I remember the first time that he ever praised me. It was when I had stayed late at work while all my coworkers had gone home. I had done this because there was a piece of equipment that was broken, and it needed to be fixed as soon as possible. Well, I stayed there until I had repaired it. My uncle was very pleased, and he praised me for my work. Through his encouragement and positive reinforcement on this and other occasions, I was able to build confidence and pride.

4   Responsibility is one of the major attributes that were implanted in me. I was fortunate to have an uncle who was more than happy to force responsibility on me. He always gave me a job that was a challenge, and he would see how well I performed the task. If I didn't perform to his satisfaction, he did not give me any responsibilities for a long time. I can see now why he tried so hard to make me more responsible. He knew that if I was irresponsible in the future I could not make it in the job market. Now I accept responsibility with the greatest of ease. Being with my uncle gave me a chance to accept responsibilities that might not have come my way. I find that being a responsible person can make a job or even my life a lot easier to handle.

5   In summary, these three attributes—discipline, pride, and responsibility—are qualities that will make my life flow a little more smoothly. I now feel that my decision to live with my uncle was one of the wisest that I have made, and if I had the choice, I would do it all over again.

Understanding Words

Briefly define the following words as they are used in the above essay.

1. apprehensive   *anxious, uneasy, fearful*

2. void   *empty space*

3. attributes   *natural qualities of a person*

Questions on Content

1. What was the author's first impression of his uncle?

2. What did he learn from his uncle?

3. Why did his uncle stress responsibility?

Questions on Form

1. Identify the topic sentence in paragraph 2.

2. Which paragraph, in your opinion, has the strongest support?

3. Do the support paragraphs contain short, interrelated examples or an extended example?

Professional Writing

Wandering Through Winter

Excerpt from the chapter "Summer in January" by **Edwin Way Teale**

In the folklore of the country, numerous superstitions relate to winter weather. Back-country farmers examine their corn husks—the thicker the husk, the colder the winter. They watch the acorn crop—the more acorns, the more severe the season. They observe where white-faced hornets place their paper nests—the higher they are, the deeper will be the snow. They examine the size and shape and color of the spleens of butchered hogs for clues to the severity of the seasons. They keep track of the blooming of dogwood in the spring—the more abundant the blooms, the more bitter the cold in January. When chipmunks carry their tails high and squirrels have heavier fur and mice come into country houses early in the fall, the superstitious gird themselves for a long, hard winter. Without any scientific basis, a wider-than-usual black band on a woolly-bear caterpillar is accepted as a sign that winter will arrive early and stay late. Even the way a cat sits beside the stove carries its message to the credulous. According to a belief once widely held in the Ozarks, a cat sitting with its tail to the fire indicates very cold weather is on the way.

Understanding Words

Briefly define the following words as they are used in the above paragraph.

1. folklore   *traditional beliefs*

2. severity   *gravity or seriousness*

3. credulous   *easily convinced*

Questions on Content

1. What does the author call the ideas that farmers and country people have about judging a coming winter?

2. What kind of "basis" or proof is lacking for these ideas?

3. In what part of the United States was there a belief about cats sitting close to the fire?

Questions on Form

1. What makes the paragraph well developed?

2. Identify the kinds of examples used.

Overheard on a Train Trip Through England

Excerpt from *Kingdom by the Sea* by **Paul Theroux**

Once, from behind a closed door, I heard an Englishwoman exclaim with real pleasure, "They are *funny,* the Yanks!" And I crept away and laughed to think that an English person was saying such a thing. And I thought: They wallpaper their ceilings! They put little knitted bobble-hats on their soft-boiled eggs to keep them warm! They don't give you bags in supermarkets! They say sorry when you step on their toes! Their government makes them get a hundred-dollar license every year for watching television! They issue drivers' licenses that are valid for thirty or forty years—mine expires in the year 2011! They charge you for matches when you buy cigarettes! They smoke on buses! They drive on the left! They spy for the Russians! They say "nigger" and "Jewboy" without flinching! They call their houses Holmleigh and Sparrow View! They sunbathe in their underwear! They don't say "You're welcome"! They still have milk bottles and milkmen, and junk-dealers with horsedrawn wagons! They love candy and Lucozade and leftovers called bubble-and-squeak! They live in Barking and Dorking and Shellow Bowells! They have amazing names, like Mr. Eatwell and Lady Inkpen and Major Twaddle and Miss Tosh! And they think *we're* funny?

Understanding Words

Briefly define the following word as it is used in the above paragraph.

1. flinching   *drawing away or moving away from as if in pain*

Questions on Content

1. What two nationalities are the focus of this paragraph?

2. What is the author replying to in the paragraph?

3. What is the author really saying in the question in the end?

Questions on Form

1. What makes the supporting examples effective in this paragraph?

2. How many examples are given?

3. What is the implied topic sentence?

Part 4

Grammar for Effective Writing: Sentence Variety—Forming and Punctuating Compound Sentences

Objectives

- Combine simple sentences using coordinate conjunctions.
- Combine simple sentences using conjunctive adverbs.
- Combine simple sentences using semicolons.

Tests covering compound sentences are on pages 42–53 in the Test Bank.

One of the first steps in good revision is to change short, choppy sentences into compound sentences. You may write good compound sentences now but may not be aware of them. On the other hand, perhaps you could strengthen your writing by learning to revise short, choppy sentences into effective compound sentences. In this way, you will achieve some sentence variety. Additional types of sentence patterns will be covered in Unit 5.

A **compound sentence** is two or more simple sentences combined in a variety of ways. They may be joined by a comma and a coordinate conjunction, a semicolon followed by a conjunctive adverb and a comma, or just a semicolon.

Using a Comma and a Coordinate Conjunction

Coordinate conjunctions join two sentences that are of equal value or are "coordinate" with each other. The coordinate conjunctions you choose depend upon the meaning you want to achieve in your writing.

Coordinate Conjunctions

for	but
and	or
nor	yet
	so

Note   Remembering the words **fan boys** can help you memorize the list of coordinate conjunctions.

Here are some examples of the use of coordinate conjunctions to join two simple sentences.

and (adds)

Mike enjoys his job.

He performs well.

Mike enjoys his job, **and** he performs well.

but (contrasts)

Mike enjoys his job.

He has a long drive each day.

Mike enjoys his job, **but** he has a long drive each day.

for (gives a reason)

Mike enjoys his job.

It offers a challenge.

Mike enjoys his job, **for** it offers a challenge.

nor (adds another negative idea)

Mike does not enjoy his job.

He does not perform well.

Mike does not enjoy his job, **nor** does he perform well.

or (gives a choice)

Mike can choose to work four ten-hour days.

He can work five eight-hour days.

Mike can choose to work four ten-hour days, **or** he can work five eight-hour days.

so (shows result)

Mike enjoys his job.

He works hard.

Mike enjoys his job, **so** he works hard.

yet (shows change or contrast)

Mike works hard.

He also makes time for recreation.

Mike works hard, **yet** he also makes time for recreation.

Combine each pair of simple sentences into one compound sentence by adding a comma and a coordinate conjunction.

Example:

refreshing, so we

The day was cool and ~~refreshing. We~~ **went on a picnic.**

, yet Paula

1. Positive reinforcement motivates people. ~~Paula~~ seldom uses it.

, nor did I

2. I did not enjoy the food. ~~I did not~~ care for the entertainment .

, yet

3. Ariana was short on time. ~~Rudolph~~ kept talking.

, for we

4. We bought a used truck. ~~We~~ did not have enough money for a new one.

, but their

5. The restaurant cooked healthful food. ~~Their~~ prices were high.

, for he

6. Ross climbs the mountain three times a week. ~~He~~ is training for the marathon.

Using a Conjunctive Adverb

You can combine two simple sentences by placing a conjunctive adverb between them. Place a semicolon at the end of the first sentence to separate the two sentences, and then put a comma after the conjunctive adverb.

> The clerk offended the customer; **consequently,** the customer did not shop at that store again.

When you put a conjunctive adverb *within* a sentence rather than between two simple sentences, put a comma *before and after* the conjunctive adverb.

> The clerk offended the customer. The customer, **consequently,** did not shop at that store again.

> Helen hates the heat; she, **however,** is coming to Phoenix in July.

Note   In the second example, which is a compound sentence, a semicolon still separates the two complete sentences.

Conjunctive Adverbs

moreover	consequently
in addition	however
therefore	in fact
thus	nevertheless
	as a result
otherwise	
furthermore	

Note   The first letters of the conjunctive adverbs spell **Mitt of China.**

Just as you choose a coordinate conjunction to express a particular meaning, so you must pay close attention to the conjunctive adverb you select. Here are some examples of conjunctive adverbs in compound sentences.

as a result (shows a result)

Mike enjoys his job; **as a result,** he works very hard.

consequently (shows a result)

Mike does not enjoy his job; **consequently,** he does not work very hard.

furthermore (shows an additional idea)

Mike plans to quit his job; **furthermore,** he plans to change his career.

however (shows a contrast)

Mike likes his job; **however,** he plans to find a better one.

in addition (adds an equally important idea)

Mike likes his job; **in addition,** he likes his coworkers.

moreover (adds an equally important idea)

Mike likes his job; **moreover,** he likes his coworkers.

nevertheless (shows a contrast)

Mike enjoys his job; **nevertheless,** he finds time for other things.

otherwise (indicates a result if the first situation did not occur)

Mike enjoys his job; **otherwise,** he would look for a new job.

therefore (shows a result)

Mike wants more money; **therefore,** he will ask his boss for a raise.

thus (shows a result)

Mike has saved money from his job; **thus,** he will be able to go to school.

Exercise 2

Combine each pair of simple sentences into one compound sentence by adding a semicolon, a conjunctive adverb, and a comma.

Example:

salty; however, we

The stew was too ~~salty. We~~ ate it anyway.

; nevertheless, they

1. At first, the students were reluctant to do community service. ~~They~~ found it very rewarding.

; however, she

2. He resists commitment. ~~She~~ would like to marry.

; consequently, she

3. Hope graduated from the community college. ~~She~~ found a good job.

; as a result, she
4. The doctor prescribed a diet for my neighbor. ~~She~~ lost twenty pounds.

; however, they
5. Traditional encyclopedias are losing popularity. ~~They~~ are offered online.

; in addition, it
6. Learning to use a digital camera can be frustrating. ~~It~~ can be expensive.

Using a Semicolon

Two simple sentences can also be connected by using a semicolon. However, when they are joined by a semicolon, the second sentence does *not* begin with a capital letter.

The clerk offended the customer.

The customer did not shop at that store again.

The clerk offended the customer; the customer did not shop at that store again.

Exercise 3

Combine each pair of simple sentences into one compound sentence by adding a semicolon. Remember to begin the second sentence with a lowercase letter.

Example:

females; two
Five of the puppies were ~~females. Two~~ were males.

; they
1. Prison guards have dangerous jobs. ~~They~~ must be alert at all times.

; jambalaya
2. Louisiana has many unique dishes. ~~Jambalaya~~ and gumbo both use spicy sauces.

; the
3. We enjoyed going to the ocean. ~~The~~ children collected seashells.

; they
4. Europeans enjoy their strong coffee. ~~They~~ drink it like espresso.

; she
5. The old dog trembled. ~~She~~ was afraid of thunder and lightning.

; it
6. I saw the movie *The Passion of the Christ.* ~~It~~ was very realistic.

Exercise 4

Combine each pair of simple sentences into one compound sentence as indicated. Punctuate correctly.

Example:

Sara trains dogs well. She is always busy.

Sara trains dogs well, so she is always busy.

(coordinate conjunction)

Sara trains dogs well; she is always busy.

(semicolon)

Sara trains dogs well; consequently, she is always busy.

(conjunctive adverb)

1. Savannah admired butterflies. She had a butterfly tattoo put on her ankle.

   Savannah admired butterflies, so she had a butterfly tattoo put on her ankle.

   (coordinate conjunction)

   Savannah admired butterflies; she had a butterfly tattoo put on her ankle.

   (semicolon)

   Savannah admired butterflies; therefore, she had a butterfly tattoo put on her ankle.

   (conjunctive adverb)

2. Flavio makes delicious enchiladas. He makes good salsa, too.

   Flavio makes delicious enchiladas, and he makes good salsa, too.

   (coordinate conjunction)

   Flavio makes delicious enchiladas; he makes good salsa, too.

   (semicolon)

   Flavio makes delicious enchiladas; in addition, he makes good salsa.

   (conjunctive adverb)

3. Kristen works for a professional baseball team. She seldom attends their games.

   Kristen works for a professional baseball team, yet she seldom attends their games.

   (coordinate conjunction)

   Kristen works for a professional baseball team; she seldom attends their games.

   (semicolon)

   Kristen works for a professional baseball team; however, she seldom attends their games.

   (conjunctive adverb)

4. Alicia's peach tree had an abundant crop. She made fresh peach preserves.

   Alicia's peach tree had an abundant crop, so she made fresh peach preserves.

   (coordinate conjunction)

   Alicia's peach tree had an abundant crop; she made fresh peach preserves.

   (semicolon)

   Alicia's peach tree had an abundant crop; as a result, she made fresh peach preserves.

   (conjunctive adverb)

5. The attorney worked hard on the divorce case. He won it.

The attorney worked hard on the divorce case, so he won it.
(coordinate conjunction)

The attorney worked hard on the divorce case; he won it.
(semicolon)

The attorney worked hard on the divorce case; furthermore, he won it.
(conjunctive adverb)

6. Albert had his tongue pierced. Biting on the metal resulted in a cracked tooth.

Albert had his tongue pierced, but biting on the metal resulted in a cracked tooth.
(coordinate conjunction)

Albert had his tongue pierced; biting on the metal resulted in a cracked tooth.
(semicolon)

Albert had his tongue pierced; however, biting on the metal resulted in a cracked tooth.
(conjunctive adverb)

7. Keta and Bede live in Alaska. They often fish for salmon.

Keta and Bede live in Alaska, so they often fish for salmon.
(coordinate conjunction)

Keta and Bede live in Alaska; they often fish for salmon.
(semicolon)

Keta and Bede live in Alaska; consequently, they often fish for salmon.
(conjunctive adverb)

8. Dave's car broke down four times last month. He decided to sell it.

Dave's car broke down four times last month, so he decided to sell it.
(coordinate conjunction)

Dave's car broke down four times last month; he decided to sell it.
(semicolon)

Dave's car broke down four times last month; therefore, he decided to sell it.
(conjunctive adverb)

Exercise 5

Revise the following paragraphs by changing the short, choppy sentences into compound sentences. Use a variety of ways to combine the sentences.

Paragraph 1

Last Saturday, the weather seemed impulsive. One side of the sky was a brilliant
, but the
blue mixed with soft white clouds. ~~The~~ other side was a mass of streaked charcoal

gray clouds. However, right in the middle of the darkest clouds, bright blue patches
, and the
of sky appeared like little lakes in the sky. One minute the air was still. ~~The~~ sun

broke through the clouds and poured sunshine over everything. At these times, the
; in addition, the
warmth of the sun took over. Then, within minutes, the sun retreated. ~~The~~ wind
, and then
whipped everything around. It twirled leaves and twigs in a circle. ~~Then~~ it beat them

against tree trunks or whatever came across its path. At the same time, the clouds
, but they
released raindrops everywhere. ~~They~~ only dampened the earth. Just moments later,
, and the
the rain suddenly stopped. ~~The~~ peacefulness of the sun appeared once more. All day

long, the sky played like this.

Paragraph 2

The "give and take" involved in the job of firefighter-paramedic appeals to many

young people. Firefighters may have to sit around the station with nothing to do
, but once
while waiting for a call. ~~Once~~ they are en route to an emergency, they do not have
; every
time to be bored. Every call is different. ~~Every~~ day is different. A constant stress for
, but they
them is being sure the routing is the quickest way to the emergency. ~~They~~ feel pride

when their response time makes them first on the scene. On one call, they may need
, and on
to remove a trapped baby from a burning building. ~~On~~ the next call, they may need

to help an elderly person who fell and cannot get back into bed. They work away
, so the
from their families on 24-hour shifts. ~~The~~ other firefighters provide a second family

with whom they spend a third of their life. They become a part of two families.

, but their

Sometimes they have to spend holidays at the station. ~~Their~~ spouses and children

are free to visit the station when the firefighters are not on call. They take

, and they

responsibility for people's lives. ~~Paramedics~~ have the opportunity to save people's

lives as well as their belongings. These firefighter-paramedics must remember all

of their training because they never know when they are going to need that

; however, they

knowledge. ~~They~~ also feel the satisfaction of seeing someone survive who was

moments away from death.

Paragraph 3

Throughout their adult years, people must adjust to many changes in their

, and often

lives. Technology may require people to retrain for a new job. ~~Often~~ company

; sometimes

restructuring causes change. Sometimes promotion causes change. ~~Sometimes~~ job

loss causes change. Other major changes occur in people's personal lives, too. For

, so they

various reasons, some married adults separate from their mates. ~~They~~ must take on

total responsibility for the household. Many adults must deal with having the last

; however, some

child leave home. ~~Some~~ people must cope with adult children returning home.

, and other

Sometimes they return alone. ~~Other~~ times they return with children. Once in a

, or they

while, they return with a mate. ~~They~~ return with a mate and children. All these

situations cause adults to make shifts in their lifestyles.

Paragraph 4

; nevertheless, they

American people do not want to eat less. ~~They~~ want to consume fewer calories.

, and they

Food companies know this. ~~They~~ are coming out with reduced- or low-calorie food

products. Powdered "butter" substitutes boast of having the same taste as real

; furthermore, ice

butter with a fraction of the calories. ~~Ice~~ cream is appearing in "light" form also.

Producers use fat substitutes and sugar substitutes that add up to fewer calories but

have "the same great taste" for the consumer. Even potato chips come with the "light" option. Not only single items but many prepackaged microwave meals

, and the

specialize in meals with under three hundred calories. ~~The~~ meal can be topped off

with a variety of pastries with "less than half the calories of other baked goods." Food

, so consumers

producers keep churning out new alternatives. ~~Consumers~~ keep "eating them up."

Part 5
Putting It All Together

Cumulative Unit Exercise

Be ready to apply the writing skills you have learned so far in this text.

Master for transparency of Cumulative Unit Exercise is in the Instructor's Manual, pages 51–52.

1. Read this essay carefully, and identify the thesis sentence. Revise the thesis sentence so that the previewed points are written in parallel form.

2. In each paragraph, underline the examples that support the topic sentence. Mark each paragraph as having short interrelated or extended examples.

3. Check sentence variety. In each support paragraph, combine short sentences into compound sentences. (You should make one or two combinations in each paragraph.)

4. Make any changes necessary to maintain consistent point of view, subject-verb agreement, and consistent verb tense.

5. Correct the two fragments, one run-on sentence, and one comma splice.

Investment, Anyone?

judgment

1   Investing for one's future takes time, ~~knowing what to judge,~~ and knowledge.

2   Time can be a young investor's best friend. An illustration that clearly points

out the concept of time and compound interest involves two people. Gen Frugal

at age 22 puts $2,000 per year into an Individual Retirement Account (IRA), a

government-sponsored tax-deferred plan that allows people to deduct and invest

RO   up to $2,000 from their taxable income. She invests a total of $16,000 for eight

, and then

years ~~then~~ she stops. When she retires at age 65, she will have $642,750,

grows

assuming Gen reinvests her gains and the investment ~~grew~~ an average of 10

Gen can be contrasted

percent a year. ~~Contrast Gen~~ to John Lately. He waits until he is 30 to start

investing. He puts $2,000 a year into an IRA until his retirement at age 65. John

invests a total of $70,000 over 35 years and accumulates $542,050, assuming

, but at

the same 10 percent annual growth. He invests $54,000 more than Gen. ~~At~~ age

65, he has made $100,700 less. Gen has used investment time more wisely.

3   Another factor in investing money is judgment. Experienced investors are

usually concerned with deciding when to buy, when to sell, and when to hold

investments, but this is not always an easy task. Less-experienced investors are

exist

SIE probably more concerned with where to invest. Lots of choices ~~exists~~. Savings in

a bank are considered quite safe and generally yield about 3 percent. Money

market funds, which are another type of low-risk savings, yield about 6 percent.

A conservatively managed mutual fund, which is a type of relatively safe investment,

CS can yield from 10 to 15 percent. A high-risk mutual fund might yield 25 percent on

the

invested money. Of course, anyone wants to get the most return for ~~your~~ invested

so   *a person*

money, determining how much risk ~~you~~ can handle is crucial in investment

     ^

selections. Depending on judgments, investors may lose all or a portion of their

; consequently, good

investment. ~~Good~~ decisions are extremely important when money is involved.

4   Finally, an investor must be knowledgeable. Reading and research are essential

before investing any money. The library is an excellent place to start. Information on

mutual funds, money market funds, stocks, and bonds is available in every library.

Also, newsletters, such as *Morningstar Investor,* Louis Rukeyser's *Mutual Funds,*

SIE Richard F. Band's *Profitable Investing,* or Jack Adamo's *Inside Track,* can be

purchased for approximately $100 a year. The business section of most

provides

newspapers ~~provided~~ basic information. A financial expert may have a daily or

weekly column in these newspapers to supplement the technical information

Frag   that appears regularly. Weekly magazines such as *Newsweek*, *Time*, and *U.S.*

                                                 have

Frag   *News and World Report.* ~~Have~~ business sections that deal with specific events as

well as trends. Some exclusive magazines that deal only with money investment

abound. *Money Magazine, Smart Money, Moneysworth, Your Money, Worth*

Magazine, and *Money World* are just a few. Finally, today's investor, whether new

or experienced, should have access to the Internet. It provides information

                    , but the   *the investor*

similar to that in print. ~~The~~ Internet gives ~~you~~ more direct access to individual

mutual fund companies and stock and bond brokers. Whatever someone

chooses as sources, a wise investor is a wise reader and researcher.

Collaborative Writing Project: Working and Learning Together

This collaborative exercise is designed to help you generate thesis sentences and recall and pool relevant examples that can be used to develop a longer paper. The final group outcome will be a collectively written thesis sentence and enough extended or interrelated examples to help you draft your essay.

Writing Assignment/Working in a Group

1. Work with two or three other students and discuss the following topics. Select one topic of common interest; then follow the remaining directions.

   Qualities of a perfect mate

   Reasons people buy clothes

   Issues facing your city government, state government, or federal government

   Reasons cars are important to people

   Reasons vacations are important to people

   Information people can learn by reading a newspaper

   Reasons children or adults find television appealing

   Reasons music appeals to people

   Reasons people ride bicycles rather than drive cars

   Reasons people drive cars rather than ride bicycles

2. Select someone to share the results with the class, but all group members need to take notes.

3. Brainstorm to develop a thesis sentence that includes a topic, a direction, and three to four previewed subtopics.

4. Begin to share short interrelated or extended examples that support the thesis sentence. Then decide which previewed point each example supports.

5. Continue to pool examples until you have at least one extended example or four or five short interrelated examples for each previewed point.

6. Be prepared to write your thesis sentence on the board and have the group representative share the examples your group has generated for each point.

Working Individually to Write an Essay

Using the thesis sentence from your group and the examples written by your group, draft your individual essay.

1. Write topic sentences, being sure to include the main idea, direction, and one of the previewed points in each topic sentence.

2. As you write each paragraph, blend the examples together, linking each example to the topic sentence.

3. Close each paragraph with a concluding sentence that refers to, but does not repeat, the topic sentence.

Peer Review

1. Bring four copies of your finished essay, and return to the same group you used to generate the thesis sentence and examples.

2. Each essay will probably have the same thesis sentence and examples, so you will be concerned with the support paragraphs.

3. Analyze one support paragraph at a time.

   Does the paragraph have a topic sentence that includes the main idea, direction, and one of the previewed points in the thesis sentence?

   Are the examples blended into each support paragraph smoothly?

   Underline the words or sentences that tie the examples back to the topic sentence.

4. Check for subject-verb agreement, consistent verb tense, and consistent point of view.

5. Check for fragments, run-on sentences, and comma splices.

Final Checklist

Content

Essay

Check to see that the thesis sentence states a clear direction or previews the points to be covered in the paper.

Check to see that the voice is appropriate for purpose and audience.

Paragraphs

Revise so each paragraph has a clear topic sentence that develops an idea suggested in the thesis sentence.

Include four to six supporting sentences that are developed using short interrelated examples or an extended example.

Include a closing sentence in each paragraph.

Mechanics

Check for subject-verb agreement.

Check for consistent verb tense.

Check for a consistent point of view.

Check for fragments, run-on sentences, and comma splices.

Check punctuation of compound sentences.

Sentence variety

Revise short sentences into compound sentences.

 Internet Activities

Activity 1   Writing with Examples

In Unit 4 you have learned about how to expand and strengthen your writing by providing specific examples. In this web activity, you will have the opportunity to read Martin Luther King Jr.'s "I Have a Dream" speech—a masterpiece. Even though Dr. King uses a unique style that doesn't comply with the standard thesis and support model, note his creative use of examples and descriptions.

a. Use any one of the search engines listed on page 147 of your text and enter "Martin Luther King Dream Speech" in the appropriate text box for the search.

b. Read Martin Luther King Jr.'s speech, and answer the following questions:

c. Does King tend to use more extended examples or short, interrelated examples to make his points?
Short, interrelated examples. Paragraphs 9 and 10 give examples of specific states. Each part that starts with "I have a dream . . ." is a specific example. Each part that starts with "Let freedom ring . . ." is a specific example. (These are just a few of the examples that can be found.)

d. How does he use the hypothetical example of the check to carry forward his message?
The country made a promise of freedom to every American, but the country has failed to pay what it owes to African-Americans.

e. "I have a dream" is repeated several times. How does this add to the effectiveness of his speech?
It emphasizes or underlines his main point.

Activity 2

Now look at another speech by a famous president, John F. Kennedy. Use any one of the search engines listed on page 147 and enter "JFK 1961 Inaugural Address" in the appropriate text box for the search.

In the second paragraph of John F. Kennedy's speech, he says, "For man holds in his mortal hands the power to abolish all forms of human poverty and all forms of human life."

a. Does he give specific examples to clarify what he means by "human poverty"?

No

b. Can you provide examples of what he might mean specifically by human poverty?

Economically depressed areas, people without jobs, single mothers, homeless people

c. How do specific examples prevent confusion?

The people reading the speech either will have first-hand experience of these problems or will know people who have had these problems.

Unit 5

Reaching an Audience by Creating Interest

Part 1

Writing Skills: Introductory and Concluding Paragraphs

Pretest over Unit 5, Parts 1 and 4, is on page 7 of the Test Bank.

Objectives

- Understand the purpose of introductions.
- Recognize the parts of an introductory paragraph.
- Understand the types of hooks used in introductory paragraphs.
- Be aware of audience and purpose in relation to hook.
- Write an introductory paragraph that has a hook, a transition, and a thesis sentence.
- Understand the purpose of conclusions.
- Recognize and revise a weak conclusion.
- Recognize and write a strong conclusion.

After you are able to write both a thesis sentence and the support paragraphs necessary for the longer paper, you need to add an effective introductory paragraph. Because you already know how to write a thesis sentence, you only need to add a hook and a smooth transition to that thesis sentence.

Parts of an Introductory Paragraph

hook

transition

thesis sentence

The Purpose of Introductory Paragraphs

The purpose of an introductory paragraph is to get the reader's attention and to let the reader know what will be covered in the essay. Very often, it sets the tone for the entire essay. While reading your introduction, your audience might think, "This paper really sounds good," or "I can't figure out what this person is talking about." The first response is what you want from your reader. The introduction gives you a chance to "hook" your audience right away.

Developing Introductory Paragraphs

Writing an introductory paragraph can be simplified if you follow a step-by-step process.

Compose the thesis sentence.

Decide on the type of hook that is most effective.

Write the hook.

Write the transition.

Draft these three parts into an introductory paragraph.

Composing the Thesis Sentence

The part of the introductory paragraph that you write first is the thesis sentence. As you recall, the thesis sentence consists of either the topic and a clear direction, or a topic, a clear direction, and a preview of the points to be covered in the paper. Because the thesis sentence keeps you on track, it is composed first; however, it usually will be the *last* sentence in the introductory paragraph.

Developing the Hook

Transparencies for hooks and examples are on pages 35–39 in the Instructor's Manual.

After you have composed your thesis sentence, you need to write a strong hook. Even though the hook is usually the second part you write, it comes *first* in the actual introductory paragraph; consequently, it should be strong and should make the reader keep on reading. There are several ways to get the reader's attention. Your job is to be creative in finding the best way for each specific essay that you write. An effective introduction may contain *one or more* of the following hooks.

Types of Hooks

personal examples

quotations

facts or statistics

questions

current events

contrast to the thesis sentence

Using Personal Examples   Examples can be either a personal experience or an event that you witnessed happening to someone else.

Personal experience provides strong, sometimes even dramatic incidents to use. Writing about personal experiences may be difficult, but if you are honest in expressing your thoughts and feelings, you will establish a real connection with your reader. Sharing with the reader creates interest and forms a healthy bond that will last throughout the paper. The reader will want to read further because you are sharing a part of yourself, and that is what communication is all about. This personal experience should be one that really happened to you. If you make up the experience and the reader discovers you are pretending, you will lose your credibility as a writer, and you will lose your reader as an audience.

Another type of hook can come from your **personal observation** of an event that you saw happening to someone else. It must be something that really impressed you when you saw it, or the event will not impress anyone else. For example, if you saw a terrible accident, recalling facts or observations from this experience will likely grab your reader's attention immediately.

The following introductory paragraphs hook the reader by using personal experiences effectively. In each paragraph, the hook is in bold print, and the thesis sentence is underlined. First, read this example, which uses a personal experience as a hook.

On February 19, 2000, life changed for an eighteen-year-old young man. He became very ill from a bacterial infection. His body could not fight the infection. Why? After a week of tests and examinations by several specialists, the diagnosis was made. He had leukemia, a cancer in the bone marrow. I am that young man. When a person finds out that he has cancer, just as I did, his whole world changes. A cancer patient is affected physically, psychologically, and socially by the impact of cancer.

This paragraph captures the reader's attention immediately. Credibility is established when the author states the exact date, February 19, 2000, and when he notes that the specific type of infection was bacterial. The audience is taken by surprise to read "I am that young man." Probably every reader would be affected by this dramatic statement and would identify with the writer. (A shift in point of view is permissible if it is used for special effect.)

Anytime someone is told about a serious, life-threatening illness, the situation is emotional. Telling this incident in a straightforward way, however, makes the information all the more moving. Readers of all ages are able to identify with the young man and will listen to his ideas. The reader knows from this introduction that the experiences and ideas in the paper are real and believable.

Now read the following example, which uses a personal observation of someone else's experience as a hook.

> **One morning a young mother had her seven-month-old son in his stroller under the peach tree near their family swimming pool. She walked to her kitchen to get a knife so she could peel a peach for him. Ten seconds later, she found him face down with the stroller at the bottom of the pool. She immediately pulled him out and administered artificial respiration to him.** If she had been gone any longer, he might have become one of the statistics that plague our country every year when many children die needlessly in water-related accidents. These child drownings could, however, be greatly reduced if parents never left their children unattended around water, if pools were properly fenced, and if other safety devices were installed in or by the pool.

This example is also very moving because the writer saw and remembered the scene vividly. It helps the reader recognize the fear that comes with a near tragedy. This example brings home the reality of the dangers of a swimming pool. The incident is very appropriate to get the reader interested in ways to keep children from drowning or from becoming permanently disabled in family swimming-pool accidents.

You may think that you do not have experiences as dramatic and emotionally appealing as these, but you do. Be detailed and thorough when you think about ways to get your audience caught up in your topic, and you will discover effective experiences that will make good hooks.

The following exercise helps you use a personal experience as a hook for an introductory paragraph.

Exercise 1

Using the thesis sentences given or the thesis sentence for your next writing assignment, write a personal example that you feel would get the reader's attention. Use either a personal experience or a personal observation.

1. _____

_____

_____

_____

Eating at ethnic restaurants can be educational, satisfying, and occasionally expensive.

2. _____

_____

_____

_____

Helping a son or daughter plan a wedding can create family unity, leave pleasant memories, yet create unexpected expenses.

3. _____

_____

_____

_____

Attending college allows students to acquire new information, make lifetime friends, and prepare for a career.

Using Quotations   Another way to get your reader's attention is to quote an effective line or two from someone famous or even someone not so famous. Just as the personal examples were dramatic or surprising, the content of the **quotation** should also be dramatic or in some way emotionally appealing, surprising, or humorous. You might choose a humorous quotation from Ben Franklin, like "Fish and visitors smell in three days." Or perhaps you might choose a line of poetry, like "Come live with me and be my love,/and we will all the pleasures prove. . . ." Another might be a phrase like "Born in the USA." If the quotation is relevant to the thesis sentence and the connection between the quotation and the thesis sentence is established, your reader will be not only willing but eager to continue.

Look at another sample introductory paragraph. This time the student writer began with the topic "facing life." After freewriting/brainstorming, she composed the following thesis sentence: "Individuals can control their attitude about life by facing issues, looking at the bright side, and reducing stress." The student then wanted to use a quotation to get the attention of the reader and found one in a book of famous quotations. The student writer wanted to stress how a person's mental outlook can bring success or failure, so she looked up "mind" in the book of quotations. She found a sentence with a captivating message in it. Notice how she put the introductory paragraph together, starting with the quotation.

> **"The mind is its own place, and itself can make a heaven of hell, a hell of heaven."** This thought by John Milton was recorded over three hundred years ago, but it is still timely today. He seems to be saying that people are the ones to control their lives. They can be miserable when things are going well, just as they can be happy when things are going wrong. <u>With this thought in mind, individuals can control their attitude about life by facing issues, looking at the bright side, and reducing stress.</u>

The quotation is effective because it is thought-provoking. Although it was written many years ago, it is still applicable today. Also, the writer is quoting a famous man, John Milton, a great English poet. Readers pay attention to profound comments made by famous people.

Sometimes a quotation used with a personal example makes both more effective. To see how this works, first look at this paragraph.

As the parents of a learning-disabled child, Jason and Erica often felt unprepared to help their child with his handicap and were frustrated in their attempts to seek the proper placement of him in the public school system. They, along with their son, felt the frustration that school presented. Because their son reversed his letters and numbers, both he and his papers were at the mercy of teachers who did not understand the situation. The experience of school can be overwhelming for children who have trouble learning. Learning-disabled students in the public education system must deal with academic, social, and emotional problems.

The previous paragraph uses only a personal example for the hook, but the following paragraph is stronger because it combines a quotation with a personal example.

Master for transparency of these two introductory paragraphs is in the Instructor's Manual, page 36.

"I am stupid. I am never going back to school," Micah said when he was in the first grade. With his eyes downcast, he slowly walked to his bedroom, silently crying as he shredded his schoolwork into small pieces. Then both he and his mother cried. This was the first of many times when they would feel the frustration that school presented. Because he reversed his letters and numbers, both Micah and his papers were at the mercy of teachers who did not understand the situation. The experience of school can be overwhelming for children who have trouble learning. Learning-disabled students in the public educational system must deal with academic, social, and emotional problems.

The above introduction includes a personal example written using the third-person point of view. However, sometimes you will want to write your hook using the first-person point of view. As a result, the hook might be much more effective because it includes details that make the experience come to life for the reader. Now read the following paragraph.

"I am stupid. I am never going back to school." These are the words spoken by my learning-disabled child when he was in the first grade. He cried as he slowly walked down the hall, shredding his schoolwork into small pieces. Then we both cried. This was the first of many times when I would feel frustrated because there was nothing I could do to help him. I often felt frustrated when I saw him make low scores on his papers and tests because he reversed his letters and numbers. It was not unusual for him to work a math problem correctly, only to reverse the numbers in the answer. This put him at the mercy of teachers who did not understand the situation. Many other children like him have difficulties that make the experience of school overwhelming. Learning-disabled students in the public educational system must deal with academic, social, and emotional problems.

This quotation and personal example will attract the attention of anyone who has had to cope with a disability of any type or anyone who has had a family member with a disability. It will also get the attention of individuals who can empathize with the situation even though they have had no experience with disabilities. The quotation blended with the personal example makes the introduction more effective.

If a paper is going to be written using the "I" point of view, it will include a hook and thesis that are written in 1st person point of view. On the other hand, if the paper is going to be about learning-disabled children in general, but the personal example is written in 1st person, the introduction needs to include a transition that moves the point of view from 1st to 3rd person in the thesis sentence. The point of view used in the thesis sentence will control the point of view in the paper. You might want to practice this kind of introductory paragraph in one of your papers.

Note   Quotations you might want to use in your introductions are included in each unit. Look in the index under "quotations" to find page numbers.

Exercise 2

Using the thesis sentence given or the thesis sentence for your next writing assignment, write a direct quotation that you think would get the reader's attention. Use either a quotation that you have heard, looked up in a book, or found on the Internet. (See Internet Activity 1 on page 310.) If you wish, combine it with a personal example.

1. _____

   _____

   _____

   _____

   Healthy dieting requires accurate medical information, appropriate exercise, and nutritious food.

2. _____

   _____

   _____

   _____

   Hobbies can provide a mental escape, a creative outlet, and a social opportunity.

3. _____

   _____

   _____

   _____

   Smoking is detrimental because it costs money, creates pollution, and results in medical problems.

Using Facts or Statistics   To generate interest, you may also use a fact or a statistic as your hook. To work well, the fact or statistic must be startling or unusual. You do, however, need to be sure that it really is a fact and that it comes from a credible source. When you are reading the newspaper or reading for your other classes, be alert for information that catches your attention. If you keep a journal, jot these facts down to use in future writing.

The following introductory paragraphs use facts or statistics to hook the reader.

Master for transparency of introductory paragraph is in the Instructor's Manual, page 37.

> **In the desert regions of Arizona, solar homes date back to the pre-Colombian Indians. These people carefully designed their homes in the recesses of south-facing cliffs to receive the warmth of the winter sun. In the summer, shade was provided by the overhanging cliffs.** Today, as then, the desert-region solar home

must be carefully designed to use the sun efficiently in the orientation, the exterior, and the interior.

In this paragraph, the hook creates curiosity because it brings out a fact that is probably not known to most people outside the Southwest. Because the student lived in the Southwest, she knew about the solar homes of pre-Colombian Indians. The association between ancient Indian homes and modern solar homes makes this introduction unique and effective.

In the next example, the student writer quotes some statistics gathered from outside reading.

> **"Every 45 seconds a fire breaks out in an American home—700,000 residences aflame each year. And 16 times a day somebody dies in one of these burning homes," according to an article in *Family Safety & First Aid* published by Berkley Books.** These statistics are frightening and should not be taken lightly. The best way to deal with the possibility of loss from fire is to plan ahead before it happens. Otherwise, it is too late. In order not to become one of these statistics, Americans need to equip their homes with safety devices, set and adhere to safety rules, learn safety procedures in case of a fire, and practice a family escape plan.

Such statistics are shocking, and they get the reader's attention because these fires happen so often, every 45 seconds, and to so many people, 700,000 homes a year. These statistics should make the reader stop and think about how prevalent fires are and would, therefore, make the reader more willing to listen to the advice given in the thesis sentence.

In another example, the writer combines a personal experience with statistics:

> **"In the year 2000, the City of Phoenix responded to 210 calls of water-related incidents, and of the 210, 64 resulted in death, including 28 children," according to Carolyn Mayberry, recreational/safety coordinator for the Central Arizona Chapter of the American Red Cross. She went on to say that of these near drownings, approximately "30 percent never really recover." Also, neighborhood drownings occur often. Just yesterday a seven-month-old child fell into a swimming pool, but he was pulled out a few seconds later when his mother found him. He was lucky,** but what about the many other children who die or are permanently disabled needlessly in water-related accidents? The number of child drownings and near drownings could, however, be greatly reduced if parents never left their children unattended around water, if pools were properly fenced, and if safety devices were installed in or by the pool.

Note that the writer has taken time to check out the facts from a very creditable source, the recreational/safety coordinator for the Central Arizona Chapter of the American Red Cross.

Exercise 3

Using the thesis sentence given or the thesis sentence for your next writing assignment, write a fact or statistic intended to get the reader's attention. Use something that you recently heard, looked up in a book or periodical, or found on the Internet. If you wish, combine it with a personal example.

1. _____

_____

_____

_____

Selecting a mate, getting an education, and deciding on a place to live are major decisions that young adults must make.

2. _____

_____

_____

_____

Small businesses usually succeed when the owners are adventuresome, creative, and well organized.

3. _____

_____

_____

_____

Visitors to foreign countries experience new foods, a different language, and unique architecture.

Using Rhetorical Questions Rhetorical questions are asked for effect or for emphasis because no answer is actually expected. For example, if an essay is about adult children who return home, the writer might ask, "Would anyone disagree that once children are grown, they should not be allowed to move back in with their parents just to make their own lives easier?" No answer is expected because most people would agree that adult children who have been on their own need to solve their own problems and be responsible for their own lives.

An introductory paragraph may include one rhetorical question, or it may include a series of questions. Using a series of rhetorical questions can be effective if each question draws the reader deeper into the focus of the essay. The purpose, then, of one or several rhetorical questions is to generate thought about an idea before it is presented in the essay.

In the following introductory paragraph, the student writer effectively uses several rhetorical questions to hook the reader.

Master for transparency of introductory paragraph is in the Instructor's Manual, page 37.

> When people think ahead to the year 2050, many different questions come to mind. **Does germ warfare have the potential to destroy the world? Does the medical profession have the knowledge and technology to make gene therapy a natural part of medical care? Will the cloning of humans be successfully accomplished in the next few years? Will terrorist attacks and other violent acts lead to more stringent security precautions in the future? Do people need to have a renewed respect for the environment?** If the answer to all these questions is "yes," then it is only logical that <u>in the next fifty years people will experience major differences in medicine, transportation, lifestyles, and living environments.</u>

In the hook, the author asks rhetorical questions and provokes curiosity about possible changes in society that might occur by the year 2050. These questions are used to inspire the reader to think about how different life might be in fifty years. The thesis sentence then connects these questions with major ideas to be presented in the paper.

Exercise 4

Using the thesis sentence given or the thesis sentence for your next writing assignment, write one or more rhetorical questions that you think will get the reader's attention.

1. _____

_____

_____

_____

Old automobiles can be costly and dangerous.

2. _____

_____

_____

_____

Heavy flooding drives people from their homes, destroys crops, and interrupts business activities.

3. _____

_____

_____

_____

High school athletes who go directly into professional football must consider the possibility of injury, the length of their playing careers, and their chances to make a lot of money.

Using Current Events　A **current event** is a recent, important incident or series of incidents made public by newspapers, magazines, television, or radio. Everyone who reads newspapers or watches television should then be familiar with current events. Your job is to use the occurrence to lead into the thesis sentence.

In the following introductory paragraph, the student writer effectively uses a current event to hook the reader.

Master for transparency of introductory paragraph is in the Instructor's Manual, page 38.

An article in this morning's *Arizona Republic* reported the story about migrant workers who contract AIDS while working in the United States and then infect others when they return to Mexico. Jaime Lopez, a twenty-three-year-old migrant worker, spent time in California trying to save money for his future. When he found out he had AIDS, he returned home to the rural area near Guadalajara, Mexico, but never told anyone about his illness, including his girlfriend. After their marriage, he suffered symptoms of AIDS, but he did not seek medical attention because of the stigma this disease carries there. The disease weakened him, and he eventually died; however, it was not until after his death that his wife learned that the illness had been caused by AIDS. It was too late for her and her infant son who was born after her husband's death. Today, both she and the child are HIV positive, but now she keeps the same devastating secret. This unfortunate incident is far from being an isolated case in this rural area where people know little about AIDS. However, the one thing that they do know is that in this area, people who are infected with this disease quickly become outcasts from their neighbors, jobs, and schools.

This hook contains an extended example related to AIDS, a topic that is prevalent in the news today. This example surprises the reader because it is hard to believe that these events can happen in today's society, that fear and lack of knowledge can ruin people's lives. If the reader becomes involved emotionally, the hook works.

Exercise 5

Using the thesis sentence given or the thesis sentence for your next writing assignment, briefly describe a current event that you think would get the reader involved right away. If you wish, combine this current event with one of the other hooks explained previously.

1. _____

_____

_____

_____

Irresponsible and illegal activities of athletic role models usually include illicit drug use, illegal gambling, and socially unacceptable lifestyles.

2. _____

_____

_____

_____

Digital cameras bring pleasure to families, provide hobbies for people, and even make law-enforcement officers more accountable.

3. _____

_____

_____

_____

Coming to a decision about the abortion issue involves legal, physical, and mental considerations.

Using Contrast to the Thesis Sentence   Sometimes the thesis sentence contains an idea that might be surprising to the reader or might be different from what is expected. An introduction can be effective when the hook contains information that is in direct **contrast to the main idea in the thesis sentence.**

In the following introductory paragraph, the student writer uses contrast to hook the reader.

Master for transparency of introductory paragraph is in the Instructor's Manual, page 39.

> **Since the middle of the 1940s, the female *Cannabis sativa* plant, commonly known as marijuana, has been classified by the United States government as a Schedule I drug. This classification recognizes marijuana as a dangerous narcotic, similar in potency to heroin and possessing no redeeming medicinal**

qualities. Research in the last few years, however, has brought many new discoveries in medicine relating to the possible uses of marijuana to treat many different illnesses, including glaucoma, cancer, asthma, and phantom limb pain.

This hook reaffirms the reader's opinion because most people think of marijuana as an illegal drug that causes problems. The general public often identifies marijuana use with negative results. Because the main idea in the paper is that this drug may be *useful* in treating certain health problems, the hook directly contrasts with what is stated in the thesis sentence.

Exercise 6

Using the thesis sentence given or the thesis sentence for your next writing assignment, write a contrasting idea for a hook that you think will get the attention of the reader. If you wish, combine it with one of the other types of hooks.

1. _____
   _____
   _____
   _____

   Having out-of-state guests can be enjoyable because of the excitement of planning for their arrival, the opportunity for catching up on each other's lives, and the fun of breaking the normal routine.

2. _____
   _____
   _____
   _____

   Self-awareness, information about particular job skills, and knowledge of future job opportunities help people choose careers.

3. _____
   _____
   _____
   _____

   Having a family member in the hospital can be stressful, expensive, and frightening.

As you have seen in this unit, an effective introduction may contain one hook or a combination of hooks. Use the hook that will be most appealing to your audience and most appropriate to help you meet your purpose.

Creating a Transition to the Thesis Sentence

Regardless of what you use, the hook must be clearly connected to the thesis sentence in your essay. Nothing jars a reader more than a disjointed introduction—one with no connection between the hook and the thesis sentence. The hook will seem mechanical and artificial if it is not clearly related to the thesis sentence.

Transition is the clear *connection* between the hook and the thesis sentence and is the part of the introduction that you write *last*. The transition may be a word, a phrase, or a sentence or sentences between the hook and the thesis sentence that clearly relates the hook to the broader thesis so that the reader understands the connection.

For instance, if you use a specific quotation as your hook, you will need to take the reader from that specific quotation to a more general thesis sentence. Look at the following introductory paragraph. The specific quotation is about one person, whereas the thesis statement is about a larger group of people.

> *Hook:* "Why try? The white kids get all the jobs!" That is what Ken used to say whenever he tried to find a job.
>
> *Thesis:* Current research indicates that black unemployment is a result of racial discrimination, economic conditions, and a failure in educational systems.

Remember, the thesis sentence was written first and the hook second. Now a logical transition is needed to bridge the gap from the quotation, "Why try? The white kids get all the jobs!" to the broader thesis sentence about black unemployment. The sentences in bold type in the following paragraph show how the writer bridged this gap.

> "Why try? The white kids get all the jobs!" That is what Ken used to say whenever he tried to find a job. **It seemed that the jobs were out there, but only the white teenagers, not the black teenagers, got those jobs. This problem could not be something that developed overnight but rather evolved over many years.** Current research indicates that black unemployment is a result of racial discrimination, economic conditions, and a failure in educational systems.

Each of the introductory paragraphs presented earlier has a logical transition that shows the relationship between the thesis sentence and the hook. Note the transitions in the following introductory paragraphs to see how the transitions tie the paragraphs together. The transitions are highlighted in bold type.

Transition from Personal Example to Thesis Sentence

> On February 19, 2000, life changed for an eighteen-year-old young man. He became very ill from a bacterial infection. His body could not fight the infection. Why? After a week of tests and examinations by several specialists, the diagnosis was made. He had leukemia, a cancer in the bone marrow. I am that young man. **When a person finds out that he has cancer, just as I did, his whole world changes.** A cancer patient is affected physically, psychologically, and socially by the impact of cancer.

In one simple sentence, this transition transfers the reader from one specific personal example of a young man who discovers he has cancer to all cancer patients.

Transition from Quotation to Thesis Sentence

> "The mind is its own place, and itself can make a heaven of hell, a hell of heaven." **This thought by John Milton was recorded over three hundred years ago, but it is still timely today. He seems to be saying that people are the ones to control their lives. They can be miserable when things are going well, just as they can be happy when things are going wrong.** With this thought in mind, individuals can control their attitude about life by facing issues, looking at the bright side, and reducing stress.

In this transition, the student explains the meaning of the quotation and its relationship to the thesis sentence. The author also bridges the gap between today and over three hundred years ago. The transition between a quotation and the thesis almost always begins with a phrase like "this quotation" or "this thought" (as underlined above).

Transition from Fact to Thesis Sentence

In the desert regions of Arizona, solar homes date back to the pre-Colombian Indians. These people carefully designed their homes in the recesses of south-facing cliffs to receive the warmth of the winter sun. In the summer, shade was provided by the overhanging cliffs. **Today, as then,** the desert-region solar home must be carefully designed to use the sun efficiently in the orientation, the exterior, and the interior.

Here the student uses "Today, as then," to draw a parallel between the construction of homes in pre-Colombian times and the construction of homes today.

Transition from Statistic to Thesis Sentence

"Every 45 seconds a fire breaks out in an American home—700,000 residences aflame each year. And 16 times a day somebody dies in one of these burning homes," according to an article in *Family Safety & First Aid* published by Berkley Books. **These statistics are frightening and should not be taken lightly. The best way to deal with the possibility of loss from fire is to plan ahead before it happens. Otherwise, it is too late. In order not to become one of these statistics,** Americans need to equip their homes with safety devices, set and adhere to safety rules, learn safety procedures in case of a fire, and practice a family escape plan.

The transition interprets the meaning of the statistics and makes a suggestion about preventing this disaster. "These statistics" starts the shift that the reader must make to understand the connection between the startling numbers and the conclusion that the author is going to state in the thesis sentence.

Because the transition is the clear connection between the hook and the thesis sentence, *if the thesis is changed, then the transition must also change.* Now look at the following paragraph. Instead of being about home safety, the thesis sentence deals with firefighters. The statistic used in the hook is the same, but the transition to the thesis sentence needs to show the connection between the hook and firefighters.

"Every 45 seconds a fire breaks out in an American home—700,000 residences aflame each year. And 16 times a day somebody dies in one of these burning homes," according to an article in *Family Safety & First Aid* published by Berkley Books. **The dangers from fires can never be underestimated, but for every fire that breaks out, someone must be on call to put out that fire and treat anyone who is injured. Every day thousands of firefighters throughout the United States respond to emergencies, many times working under dangerous conditions; however, this is only one of their many responsibilities.** Firefighters serve citizens by fighting fires, performing emergency medical procedures, and helping out with community service.

This transition shows the relationship between the statistics and the firefighters, and it takes the reader from firefighters fighting fires to having other responsibilities.

Exercise 7

The following introductory paragraphs lack a transition from the hook to the thesis sentence. Try to bridge the gap logically so that your reader understands the connection between the hook and the thesis sentence.

Paragraph 1

The *Rocky Mountain News,* January 3, 2004, reported, "An estimated 54,000 Colorado children ages 11 or under have 'serious emotional disturbances.'" The article goes on to discuss how families attempt to cope alone.

_____

_____

_____

Though raising a mentally ill child can be fulfilling, it can also be costly and depressing.

Paragraph 2

According to Richard Alfred in his article titled "Positioning Alternatives and New Partnerships," a worker entering the labor force "would have to relearn his job seven times in a forty-year career."

_____

_____

_____

To aid students who are retraining, community colleges offer assessment and advisement, financial aid, and updated curricula.

Paragraph 3

Last year I lost my driver's license. I planned to get another one the next day. However, a week later, when I got a ticket for speeding, I realized that I had not yet gotten another driver's license. Instead of just one ticket for speeding, I got two tickets, one for speeding and one for driving without a driver's license. Instead of paying $95 for one ticket, I had to pay $175 for two tickets.

_____

_____

_____

Putting responsibilities off can be expensive, inconvenient, and embarrassing.

Exercise 8

In the following introductory paragraphs, underline the hook, circle the transition, and underline the thesis sentence.

Paragraph 1

Williamsburg, Virginia, offers a time-travel visit to 1775, a year before the American

Revolutionary War. The city was restored in the 1930s to its 1775 appearance, so it

resembles the town as it was in the 18th century. The governor's palace that housed the royal ruling power exhibits impressive 18th-century guns and swords on the walls and ceiling in organized, decorative patterns. In another historic area near Gentryville and Dale, Indiana, the Lincoln Boyhood National Memorial contains a log cabin that is an approximation of the original log cabin where Lincoln once lived. The area also includes a living historic farm where early 19th-century life is portrayed. Such realistic depictions and information that take people back to earlier times can be obtained by visiting restored historic landmarks. Through these moving re-creations, visitors obtain historical information and gain a feeling for bygone times.

Paragraph 2

Why are some people self-directed, confident, and personable? Why do some people have high standards and honorable values? Why are some people optimists and others pessimists? The answers to these questions are complex. Home environment, socioeconomic level, and genetic background are some of the factors that make people what they are. However, one constant in all of these influences is parents. Parents affect children's self-confidence, attitude toward others, and general outlook toward life.

Paragraph 3

"Reading is to the mind, what exercise is to the body," Sir Richard Steele wisely stated. Steele's quotation draws an analogy between the importance of exercise to tone the body and reading to stimulate the mind. If people do not exercise, they become fat, sluggish, unhealthy, and weak, and this condition is readily visible. When people do not exercise their minds, they become mentally unhealthy and weak, yet this situation is even more dangerous because it is not noticeable. This is especially true for children in their formative years when habits are developing. Reading can make the difference between a strong or a weak mind. Encouraging children to read improves their vocabulary, expands their understanding, and increases their creativity.

Exercise 9

Using one of the topics listed below, write an introductory paragraph that includes a hook, a logical transition, and a thesis sentence. You may use several types of hooks. Develop the thesis sentence first, the hook second, and the transition third.

food	weight training
music	political movements
shopping	technology's effect on shopping
new food trends	new music trends

Paragraph

_____

_____

_____

_____

_____

_____

_____

Here is one final piece of advice: For successful introductory paragraphs, **do not**

repeat the wording the instructor has used for the assignment

apologize for your paper

claim a lack of interest in the topic

use an inappropriate tone

write "In this essay, I will. . . ."

The Purpose of Concluding Paragraphs

The last part of your essay is the concluding paragraph. This final paragraph gives you a chance to reemphasize the thesis you have supported throughout the paper. The conclusion should be thorough, not cut off prematurely. At the end of the paper, the reader should *not* ask, "Where is the rest of the paper?" or "What did the author mean?" Rather, the reader should say, "Now I see how nicely everything fits together and how it applies to me."

The purpose of the introduction is to get the attention of the reader; the purpose of the support paragraphs is to focus on the thesis and develop that main idea thoroughly. The purpose of the conclusion is unique. It brings all of the thesis points together in a reflective way. In your concluding paragraph, you don't have to worry about building up lots of support. For this reason, conclusions are fun to write because most of the work has been done. Your only concerns are blending together the main points, providing a feeling of closure, and reinforcing your main points. If your reader has drifted away at any time during the paper or lost his or her concentration, you can recap the main points.

Recognizing Weak Conclusions

After you have written the support paragraphs in your paper, it is not time to ease up. It is time to be forceful to keep the reader with you. Sometimes you may feel rushed when you get to the end of your paper and may be tempted to finish it in a hurry so you can turn it in. This is like constructing a beautiful house and then deciding that you do not have time to put on a roof because you want to move in "right now."

The following essay includes an introductory paragraph and three support paragraphs but no conclusion. Read the essay and the conclusions that follow. All four endings illustrate weaknesses to avoid.

Family Weekend Vacations

1   "More than 2.1 million children from ages 5 to 13 have no adult supervision after school, and many are alone at other times of the day and night," according to a column by Abigail Van Buren. These children come from families in which both parents work or there is only one parent, and that one parent must work full-time. Even though these children must come home alone after school each day, the parents are often home on the weekends. If everyone is willing to cooperate and get the work done during the week, these weekends can be filled with short vacations that can help family members come together whether the household is headed by two parents or one parent. These weekend vacations can provide many rewarding activities for family members, including family togetherness, knowledge, and exercise.

2   Family togetherness is strengthened when the members participate in weekend vacations. Before families go away for the weekend, they often spend time planning what they are going to be doing for the next two days. When a weekend trip includes sightseeing, family members have time to communicate with one another as they go from place to place. When camping, families often hike together, exploring rivers or streams as they share their thoughts with one another. When visiting relatives, families experience a broader sense of togetherness as time is shared "catching up" with cousins, grandparents, and other relatives, or finding out what Mom and Dad did when they were young. When it is time for dinner, everyone sits down together and discusses the comedies or tragedies of the day. Whether they have been camping, sightseeing, or seeing relatives, they become a stronger unit.

3   On these treasured weekend vacations, family members often find themselves gaining and sharing knowledge. Combing the beach in the early morning as the light slowly appears, children and adults alike realize that shells washed onto the shore are more than treasures to be taken home. They bring food to the many sea gulls and other birds that live there. In addition, visiting Indian ruins teaches how the early inhabitants lived on the land that we now enjoy. Visiting Amish villages helps each member of the family see what America was like before it became so technologically oriented. There is no end to the educational opportunities offered by simple weekend vacations.

4   An additional benefit that cannot be overlooked is the exercise obtained during these weekend vacations. Many occasions require more physical activity than just spending time at home being a couch potato. Amusement parks like Disneyland are large and keep everyone walking from one attraction to another. Jet skiing or waterskiing seems to work every muscle of the body. Surfing in the ocean or simply swimming in the salt water provides an extensive workout. Some of the beaches, like

Laguna Beach, are equipped with gymnastic apparatuses that let adults and children test muscles as they fly through the air. Even shopping at resorts or quaint towns or ghost towns like Jerome requires a lot of walking, if no more than simply window shopping or sightseeing. The best part of all is that all of these activities can be shared by all members of the family.

Following, you will find several weak conclusions that add little to the effectiveness of the essay.

> These weekend vacations provide many rewarding activities for family members, including family togetherness, knowledge, and exercise.

Notice how this first conclusion does nothing for the essay. It simply repeats the thesis sentence and leaves the reader hanging.

> These weekend vacations provide many rewarding activities for family members, including family togetherness, knowledge, and exercise. First, family togetherness is strengthened. Second, family members learn a lot on these trips. And last of all, these same family members get a lot of exercise.

This conclusion shows no creativity. It simply copies the thesis sentence and mechanically repeats what has already been said in the essay. It is artificial and redundant.

> So guys, let's put our heads together and chat about ways to spend the weekends. Well, you only live once, so why not forget the dishes and floors. The dirt won't go away. Just party long and hard. The weekends will be so much fun that you may never want to come back home or back to the drudgery of work and school.

This conclusion throws the reader off because instead of ending on a serious note consistent with the essay, it attempts to be humorous and flippant. The point that should be stressed in the conclusion is lost. Consequently, the unity of the essay has been destroyed. If you are ironical throughout an essay, you may want to make the most biting statement in the conclusion. If you are humorous, end on a humorous note. For best effect, do not change to a different tone of voice in the concluding paragraph.

> Time is a precious commodity, and certainly Mom and Dad can find other tasks to do instead of taking the family out for a weekend trip. However, these weekend trips are important for unifying the family, educating the family, and keeping the family physically active. If this is done, many problems are avoided, like juvenile delinquency and divorce. Consequently, this time is worth it.

This conclusion also throws the reader off. Although it reiterates the main points of the essay, it then goes off on a tangent about major problems like delinquency and divorce. These issues can be mentioned in the conclusion only if they have been mentioned in the introduction and discussed in the paper. This ending leaves the reader with the feeling that the writer is not clear about the point to be made. A strong conclusion does not suddenly introduce a new idea.

The Conclusion Should *Not*

- repeat the thesis sentence exactly as it appeared in the introduction
- repeat the thesis sentence and mechanically repeat the topic sentences
- change the tone of the essay
- introduce a new idea in the conclusion

Recognizing and Writing Strong Conclusions

Just as a weak conclusion leaves the reader confused and unsatisfied, a strong conclusion leaves the reader informed and emotionally gratified. You have flexibility in writing a conclusion because many choices are available.

The Conclusion *Should*

- summarize main points made in the paper and creatively restate the ideas in the thesis sentence
- end with an obvious closure that leaves the essay with a sense of completeness

Read the following concluding paragraph, which includes both a summary and an obvious closure.

> The mind, the body, and the soul of a family unit can be invigorated simply by spending precious days together taking weekend vacations. Teenagers, small children, and adults have quality time together as they share the many opportunities offered simply by being alive and enjoying each other's company doing little things. While these family members are strengthening the bond they feel for one another, they are also gaining valuable knowledge and healthy exercise. Weekend vacations provide these opportunities for families.

This concluding paragraph shows creativity. The writer addresses the family as if it is a living being when she speaks of "The mind, the body, and the soul." Family members are identified in "Teenagers, small children, and adults." The thesis idea is repeated but is not redundant because the author has chosen different words. This conclusion links to the introduction as well as to the support paragraphs. It is not rushed and does not cut off abruptly. The writer shows sincerity and maintains a consistent tone.

Additional strategies, however, can be used to add to or enhance a conclusion.

Strong Conclusions

- refer to an example, fact, or statistic mentioned in the introduction
- end with a question that leaves the reader thinking about what was said
- comment about the future

- **For added emphasis, recall an example, fact, or statistic mentioned in the introduction.**

> The mind, the body, and the soul of a family unit can be invigorated simply by spending precious days together taking weekend vacations. Teenagers, small children, and adults have quality time together as they share the many opportunities offered simply by being alive and enjoying each other's company doing little things. While these family members are strengthening the bond they feel for one another, they are also gaining valuable knowledge and healthy exercise. **Even though nothing can be done about the fact that so many children from ages five to thirteen get home from school before their parents get home, something can be done about the weekend that will leave lasting memories for these children.** Weekend vacations can provide these memories for them.

The idea in bold type adds to the effectiveness of this conclusion because it goes back to and reinforces the emotional appeal made in the introductory paragraph. The statistic that "children from ages five to thirteen get home from school before their parents" is smoothly linked to the thesis sentence that "these weekend vacations can provide many rewarding activities. . . ." Without introducing any new ideas, the conclusion is uplifting and optimistic because it reassures the reader that something can be done about the future.

- **Use an appropriate question to leave the reader thinking.**

> The mind, the body, and the soul of a family unit can be invigorated simply by spending precious days together taking weekend vacations. Teenagers, small children, and adults have quality time together as they share the many opportunities offered simply by being alive and enjoying each other's company doing little things. While these family members are strengthening the bond they feel for one another, they are also gaining valuable knowledge and healthy exercise. Even though nothing can be done about the fact that so many children from ages five to thirteen get home from school before their parents get home, something can be done about the weekend that will leave lasting memories for these children. **Aren't these wonderful memories that these parents are leaving for their children?**

The preceding paragraph ends with a different kind of emotional reaction. It causes the reader to search her/his conscience. This strategy might prompt some parents to spend more time with their children.

- **Comment about the future.**

> The mind, the body, and the soul of a family unit can be invigorated simply by spending precious days together taking weekend vacations. Teenagers, small children, and adults have quality time together as they share the many opportunities offered simply by being alive and enjoying each other's company doing little things. While these family members are strengthening the bond they feel for one another, they are also gaining valuable knowledge and healthy exercise. Even though nothing can be done about the fact that so many children from ages five to thirteen are getting home from school before their parents get home, something can be done about the weekend that will leave lasting memories for these children. What kind of memories are these parents leaving for their children? **Instead of checking out the TV schedule this weekend, maybe more families should be checking out the adventurous opportunities waiting to be taken.**

This concluding paragraph ends with a recommendation for the future. Parents are called upon to make a change in their lives. Instead of being vague, this conclusion gives the reader a definite action to take.

Exercise 10

In the following paragraphs, the introductions are followed by weak conclusions. Revise each conclusion. Use a combination of strategies.

1. **Introduction**

    "Every 45 seconds a fire breaks out in an American home—700,000 residences aflame each year. And 16 times a day somebody dies in one of these burning homes," according to an article in *Family Safety & First Aid* published by Berkley Books. These statistics are frightening and should not be taken lightly. The best way to deal with the possibility of loss from fire is to plan ahead before it happens. Otherwise, it is too late. In order not to become one of these statistics, Americans need to equip their homes with safety devices, set and adhere to safety rules, learn safety procedures in case of a fire, and practice a family escape plan.

Conclusion

Americans need to equip their homes with safety devices, set and adhere to safety rules, learn safety procedures in case of a fire, and practice a family escape plan. If these things are done, maybe we will not have as many people killed in fires.

_____

_____

_____

_____

_____

_____

2. **Introduction**

"Why try? The white kids get all the jobs!" That is what Ken used to say whenever he tried to find a job. It seemed that the jobs were out there, but only the white teenagers, not the black teenagers, got those jobs. This problem could not be something that developed overnight but rather evolved over many years. Current research indicates that black unemployment is a result of racial discrimination, economic conditions, and the educational system.

Conclusion

In conclusion, black unemployment is an obviously bad condition. The first reason is all the racial discrimination in society. Another reason is the economic conditions that blacks are subjected to. The third reason is the educational system. All these reasons together result in black unemployment.

_____

_____

_____

_____

_____

_____

3. **Introduction**

An article in this morning's *Arizona Republic* reported the story about migrant workers who contract AIDS while working in the United States and then infect others when they return to Mexico. Jaime Lopez, a twenty-three-year-old migrant worker, spent time in California trying to save money for his future. When he found out he had AIDS, he returned home to the rural area near Guadalajara, Mexico, but never told anyone about his illness, including his girlfriend. After their marriage, he suffered symptoms of AIDS, but he did not seek medical attention because of the stigma this disease carries there. The disease weakened him, and he eventually died; however, it was not until after his death that his wife learned that the illness had been caused by AIDS. It was too late for her and her infant son who was born after her husband's death. Today, both she and the child are HIV positive, but now she keeps the same devastating secret. This unfortunate incident is far from being an isolated case in this rural area where people know little about AIDS. However, the one thing that they do know is that in this area, people who are infected with this disease quickly become outcasts from their neighbors, jobs, and schools.

Conclusion

AIDS is the tragedy of the century. It is sweeping from country to country and killing thousands of innocent victims. The most tragic of all are the small children who come into this world already affected by the AIDS virus. Only education about AIDS can help people prevent this tragedy from destroying so many lives.

_____

_____

_____

_____

_____

_____

Exercise 11

Write an effective conclusion for each introduction. Use a combination of strategies.

1. **Introduction**

Williamsburg, Virginia, offers a time-travel visit to 1775, a year before the American Revolutionary War. The city was restored in the 1930s to its 1775 appearance, so it resembles the town as it was in the 18th century. The governor's palace that housed the royal ruling power exhibits impressive 18th-century guns and swords on the walls and ceiling in organized, decorative patterns. In another historic area near Gentryville and Dale, Indiana, the Lincoln Boyhood National Memorial contains a log cabin like the original cabin where Lincoln once lived. The area also includes a living historic farm where early 19th-century life is portrayed. Such realistic depictions and information that take people back to earlier times can be obtained by visiting restored historic landmarks. Through these moving re-creations, visitors obtain historical information and gain a feeling for bygone times.

Concluding paragraph

_____

_____

_____

_____

_____

_____

2. Introduction

    Why are some people self-directed, confident, and personable? Why do some people have high standards and honorable values? Why are some people optimists and others pessimists? The answers to these questions are complex. Home environment, socioeconomic level, and genetic background are some of the factors that make people what they are. However, one constant in all of these influences is parents. Parents affect children's self-confidence, attitude toward others, and general outlook toward life.

Concluding paragraph

_____

_____

_____

_____

_____

_____

 Collaborative Activity

As a class, select a thesis sentence from any of the examples given in the exercises in this unit. Then divide into six groups. Within each group, using the same thesis sentence, select a different type of hook from the following list to compose an introductory paragraph:

    1. personal example

    2. quotation

    3. fact or statistic

    4. rhetorical question

    5. current example

    6. contrast to the thesis sentence

    Share the introductions, and post them on a bulletin board for future reference as a reminder of the many choices you have for possible introductions to the same thesis sentence.

Part 2

Something to Think About, Something to Write About

Professional Essay to Generate Ideas for Writing

Women in Science and Engineering

Shyrl Emhoff, *retired aeronautical engineer, instructor of technical writing*

1   Throughout history, and even as we move through the 21st century, women have not been given credit for possessing any technical ability. However, records reveal that in the 19th century, and more so in the 20th century, the achievements of women particularly merit recognition equivalent to their male colleagues' in science and engineering. Moreover, during the first 100 years of recorded patents, more than 8,000 patents were issued to women. Among the awards was a patent to Margaret Knight who, although she had only a high school education, designed and made a mechanism for paper-feeding machines to fold square-bottomed paper bags. This device was just one of her many inventions that involved heavy equipment and won her the accolade of being called the "Woman Edison." There are many other role models for women in science and engineering whose names are not recognized as well as those of their male colleagues but who have been in the forefront of extending the frontiers of science and engineering during the past 100-plus years.

2   Among those women in the 1800s was Emily Roebling. When the Brooklyn Bridge was opened May 24, 1883, Emily Roebling should have been given at least some credit for the design and construction supervision of the 1,595-foot suspension bridge across the East River in New York City. A few days into the project, her husband became paralyzed, and Emily assumed full responsibility. The construction crews were fully aware of her achievement, but the public and politicians never gave her the recognition she deserved.

3   On the other hand, the name Marya Sklodovska, for most people, would not project an image of anyone of importance. Now add the title Professor at the Sorbonne, and the receipt of a Nobel Prize in physics and a Nobel Prize in chemistry, and you have the only woman who has won two Nobel Prizes—Madame Marie Curie. Her work with her husband, Pierre, in the discovery of radium is well known, but lesser known, until you think about the second Nobel Prize, is her discovery of the 84th element in the periodic table—polonium, which is named after her native country Poland.

4   Again, among those distinguished women in science in the early part of the 20th century was one of the atomic pioneers. Lise Meitner was the first woman to earn a Ph.D. in physics from the University of Vienna. She devoted her life to the exploration of the elements, and working with the famous German scientist Dr. Otto Hahn, they discovered a new element—the 91st element in the periodic table, now known as protactinium. But Dr. Meitner's work, accomplished while in exile in 1938 in Sweden, deserves the most attention. Without her discovery of the loss of mass in the splitting of an atom, the United States would not have been able to complete the atomic bomb in the time frame that it did. It all began while Hitler was in power. Through her correspondence with Hahn, who, because he was not Jewish, remained at the Kaiser Wilhelm Institute in Germany experimenting with uranium, she learned about his

experiment of obtaining barium from uranium. This experiment prompted Lise to calculate the conversion of a particular loss of mass into energy. The result of her reasoning and analysis was the stepping-stone that provided Bohr and Fermi the key to perform the simple experiment that would show them fission. From that point, Fermi was able to continue his research and see something related to fission that proved to be more important than splitting the atom—chain reaction. This, of course, led to the atomic bomb for which Lise Meitner claimed no part, but when asked what peaceful purposes could be served, she was quick to reply "for driving submarines, aircraft, and industrial power." Her predictions have proven true.

5   And then in 1963, an educator and nuclear physicist, Maria Goeppert Mayer, who had been born in Poland but became an American citizen in 1933, was the first American woman to win the Nobel Prize in physics. The concept of the atom at that time was based on her research in quantum mechanics. She developed the nuclear shell theory, which detailed the activity inside the nucleus of an atom.

6   Diverging from physics and chemistry, and looking at the field of industrial engineering in the early 1920s, one name stands out—Dr. Lillian Moller Gilbreth. She is recognized immediately when *Cheaper by the Dozen* is mentioned. As the parents of twelve children, she and husband Frank planned the operation of their household according to the efficiency procedures they recommended to their industrial clients. Five days after Frank's death in 1924, Dr. Gilbreth attended the First International Management Congress in Prague, Czechoslovakia, which they had helped organize. Not only did she read the paper he was to present, but she presided over the sessions he was assigned. Upon returning home, she assumed the presidency of their company, and Gilbreth, Inc., subsequently became highly respected in the field of time and motion study. Among her other notable achievements was the instigation of the formation of the Society of Women Engineers (SWE). In 1946, while a member of the faculty at Purdue University, and with the approval and full support of Dr. Andre A. Potter, Dean of Engineering, Dr. Gilbreth and a nucleus of thirteen women engineering students formed the engineering group known as Pi Omicron. Thus, when she returned to her home in New Jersey with this recent achievement fresh in her mind, she set into motion the formation of a national organization (later to become international) based on some of the ideas promulgated at Purdue University. There were forty-eight charter members, with Dr. Gilbreth listed as an honorary member, and four charter sections: Boston, New York, Philadelphia, and Washington, D.C.

7   Today there are more than ten thousand students and members of SWE throughout the fifty states. Although composed predominantly of women, SWE now boasts of nondiscrimination by having men among its membership; Dr. Gilbreth would certainly approve wholeheartedly. Besides all her accomplishments, perhaps the culminating recognition of her contribution to engineering and society in general is her appearance on the forty-cent stamp in the Great American Series.

8   Many, many young women today are finding exciting careers in the field of computing, but in the 1950s the situation was different. Nevertheless, in the early fifties, Grace Murray Hopper, whose career within the computer science field is legendary, developed the world's first compiler and Common Business Oriented Language (COBOL). She was the last World War II WAVE to leave active duty. Moreover, after having been recalled twice by the U.S. Navy because of her expertise in computing, she retired as a rear admiral. Her departure at the age of seventy-nine was an auspicious occasion aboard the *USS Constitution* in August 1986.

9   Although the Soviets can claim to have had the first woman in space in 1963, when Valentina Tereshkova flew a 48-orbit mission in Vostok-6, twenty years later, the youngest American astronaut to go into orbit was Dr. Sally Ride. The five other women admitted to the U.S. space program in 1978 with Sally, who has her doctorate

in astrophysics, were Anna Fisher and Rhea Seddon, both medical doctors; Kathryn Sullivan, marine geophysicist; Shannon Lucid, chemist and biochemist; and Judith Resnik, electrical engineer. Dr. Resnik became the second American woman in space in May 1984 aboard the space shuttle *Discovery*. Tragically, she was one of the crew on the *Challenger* when it exploded after it left the launch pad on January 28, 1986. However, she left a legacy behind for all women when she stated in *U.S. Woman Engineer* (April 1984) that "women who make breakthroughs in space or other horizons must pursue their endeavors to the end of full equality." Perhaps this full equality was illustrated in 1995 when Eileen Marie Collins was appointed the first woman to command a space mission when she guided the shuttle *Discovery* on an eight-day mission.

10   Because women make up more than 50 percent of today's population and little more than 10 percent of women are working scientists and engineers in the United States, the bank of talent offered by women has hardly been tapped. Probably the greatest obstacle to their underutilized talent is the ancient mental attitude of a "woman's place." This attitude was addressed beautifully by the late Dr. Gilbreth, who in 1967 set the tone for SWE's Second International Conference at Cambridge University, England, with these words:

> The world needs the contribution that women engineers and scientists are able to make, and we, in turn, need to be needed. . . . It is a universal need. People of all ages, all walks of life, and every country on earth need to be needed. Life becomes exciting and worthwhile when our skills are applied to needed tasks. . . .

Understanding Words
Briefly define the following words as they are used in the above essay.

1. patents   *rights given by a government to an inventor to make, use, or sell an invention*

2. accolade   *approval or praise*

3. exile   *banishment*

4. fission   *splitting apart*

5. nucleus   *a central part around which other parts are grouped*

6. instigation   *bringing about the start of something*

7. culminating   *reaching highest point or climax*

8. auspicious   *favorable*

Collaborative Writing Project: Working and Learning Together

This exercise will help you get started on your next writing assignment. As in previous assignments, you have the chance here to work with someone because sharing ideas makes the writing process easier. The collaborative exercise will help you write a thesis sentence and an introduction for an essay. Then you will work on your own to draft your essay and a suitable conclusion. Begin by reading the following quotations.

Quotations: Additional Ideas on Personal Challenges

"Even when the path is nominally open—when there is nothing to prevent a woman from being a doctor, a lawyer, a civil servant—there are many phantoms and obstacles, as I believe, looming in her way." *Virginia Woolf*

"Whatever women do they must do twice as well as men to be thought half as good. Luckily, this is not difficult." *Charlotte Whitton*

"I was dating a man for several months who basically said, 'You know what? You work too hard.' When he ended it [the relationship], I thought, 'Is he right?. . . Am I always going to have to choose between a career and a relationship?'"
Dawn Alexander

"Courage and perseverance are the most important of all human virtues. Courage gives you the mental clarity to see the right thing to do and to do it, even if it's unpopular or difficult. Perseverance gives you the determination to keep on doing the right thing." *J. Tye*

"The stronger the belief we have in ourselves, the more staying power we have!" *Prevention* magazine

"When you are really deep in alligators, it is hard to remember that the goal was to drain the swamp. But remember too, that when we focus only on obstacles, we've lost sight of our goals." *Steve Tackitt*

"You may encounter defeats, but you must not be defeated." *Maya Angelou*

"And she had nothing to fall back on; not maleness, not whiteness, not ladyhood, not anything. And out of the profound desolation of her reality she may very well have invented herself." *Toni Morrison*

"The reward is not so great without the struggle." *Wilma Rudolph*

"Oh, warm is the waiting for joys, my dears!/and it cannot be too long." *Gwendolyn Brooks*

"The whole idea of a man who'll take care of you—it makes you feel feminine." *Katie Roiphe*

1. Work with one other person and discuss the quotations.

2. Explain what they mean to you and how they relate to the ideas in the preceding article.

3. Both you and your partner should keep notes.

 ## Writing Assignment/Working with a Partner

Working with your partner, discuss the following topics and choose one for your next essay. Find one that interests both you and your partner.

1. What makes a person outstanding?

2. What have you accomplished in the last five years?

3. What do you plan to accomplish in the next five years?

4. Describe your role model.

5. How has the role of women changed in the last twenty years?

6. How has the role of men changed in the last ten years?

7. Why is it difficult to be a woman today?

8. What are the advantages of being a woman today?

9. What can schools do to encourage young women to pursue careers in technological fields?

10. How does serving in the military change people?

At this point, it will be easier if you work with someone who wants to write about the same topic as you. If necessary, your instructor can help you switch partners. You may even work with two people rather than one, depending on the circumstances of the class.

1. Working with your partner(s), develop a thesis sentence. Before you write your sentence, brainstorm together to come up with as many ideas as possible.

2. As you learned previously, sort the information from your brainstorming into groups of related ideas, and label each group with a general word that summarizes the ideas in the group. Also, discuss the purpose and audience for this essay.

3. Write your thesis sentence so that it previews the main subpoints to be covered in your essay. Be sure that it matches the purpose and audience you have chosen. Are the previewed points in the most effective order?

4. Be prepared to share your thesis sentence with your instructor and with the class.

Because this may be the first essay you have done with a full introduction, continue working with your partner(s) to draft a full introduction. Each of you may use this introduction for your paper. Remember that an introduction has a hook and linking or transitional words or sentence(s) to connect the hook very clearly to the thesis sentence.

5. If possible, choose a quotation from the list above to be the hook for your introduction. If you cannot use one of these, you and your partner should work to find something appropriate. Refer to the list of possible hooks given earlier in this unit. Remember that the hook should be so interesting or dramatic that your reader wants to read the whole essay!

6. Write down that hook, and then, with your partner(s), write words or sentences that connect the hook to the thesis sentence. This transition will explain to your reader how the hook is related to the main idea in your thesis sentence.

7. Make sure your thesis sentence is the last sentence in the introduction.

8. Read this draft of your introduction out loud several times. Try to listen for a smooth flow of ideas from the hook all the way to the thesis sentence.

9. Be prepared to share your introduction with your instructor and with the rest of the class.

Working on Your Own

1. Now that you have a good start on your essay, you can go ahead on your own to draft the rest of your paper.

2. Using the brainstormed groups of related ideas and examples, write a clear topic sentence for each support paragraph and put in enough examples to make the point clear. If necessary, brainstorm for more examples.

3. When you have finished all the support paragraphs for your essay, you are ready to bring your paper to a close. Write a conclusion.

4. Finally, have your essay ready for peer review.

Peer Review

Work with a different partner or partners for peer review so that you will have a new perspective for your paper and can give a new point for someone else's paper. If possible, have a highlighter to use in part of the review.

1. Exchange drafts with your new partner(s) and read each essay out loud.

2. Pay particular attention to the introduction. First, underline the thesis sentence.

3. Then, underline the hook. With a highlighter, mark the transitional words or sentences that connect the hook to the thesis.

4. Decide if the ideas flow smoothly in the introduction. If your partner asks for help, offer a positive suggestion for change in wording.

5. Discuss the flow of ideas in the rest of the paper:

   - Check each topic sentence for a key word (or a variation of it) from the thesis statement.

   - Mark the examples in the support paragraphs. Decide if there is enough information to support each topic sentence.

   - Look for the author's own words that link the examples to each topic sentence.

   - In each support paragraph, decide if the last sentence links to the topic sentence.

6. Check the conclusion carefully. How does this final paragraph bring closure to the essay? Refer to the section in this unit on writing strong conclusions. If necessary, suggest a change.

7. Make any other positive suggestions for revision in point of view, verb tenses, subject-verb agreement, and sentence structure.

Part 3

Essays for Discussion and Analysis

Student Writing

Dancer

Nancy Chandler, *student*

1   "She is the fool who ruined our recital" rang in my ears as I looked up to see the whole dressing room looking at my nakedness as Margaruite Swartz pointed her finger at me. At nine years old, I felt that I was never going to dance again in a group. But twenty years later, that's exactly what I was doing professionally. In fact, I was not only dancing but creating dances and leading a troupe. Leading, choreographing, and dancing in a troupe have been rewarding for me emotionally, physically, and personally.

2   The emotional stimulation of creating, teaching, and performing dance numbers was the most uplifting experience in my life. I especially enjoyed choreographing the dance routines that our troupe performed because of the recognition I got from my fellow dancers and the management. I remember one time in particular when this was true. The manager of the club in which we performed gave me a song, a favorite of his, to create a dance number with. When I performed this number for him and the dancers so it could be critiqued, they gave me a standing ovation. They also said that if we chose this particular number in a competition we were considering entering, we would surely win. The feeling of accomplishment and respect I got from my colleagues is one of my most cherished memories.

3   The physical benefits of performing regularly in a dance troupe were an outstanding plus for my physical being. I do not think I have ever been in such top shape as when I was dancing professionally. The troupe not only performed on Friday and Saturday

nights, but we also practiced Monday through Friday for about five hours. I never needed to worry about dieting in my days of dance. Even teaching aerobics, as I had in the past, did not sculpture my body in quite the manner that dancing did. Performing regularly in a troupe was definitely the most physically demanding and physically beneficial job I have ever been involved in.

4   Not only was my physical body in shape, but my personal life became more satisfying as a direct result of being involved in the troupe. The troupe itself was more like a family to me than anyone else. They were a support system for me because I was going through a hard time in my marriage. I remember an especially memorable time when one of my dancers came to my rescue on a particular evening when I was in need of a hero. I had had a bad fight with my husband, and he had thrown me out of the house into the rain. I did not know what to do, so I called Raynard, one of the dancers, and he was there in a flash. Raynard was so understanding and diplomatic when it came to getting my daughter out of the house that my husband let me back into the house and apologized. I never knew what the conversation was between the two men, but my husband was much more civil to me for quite a while afterward. I got many benefits as a result of being involved with the dance troupe, such as courage, self-respect, and self-assurance, but most of all I cherished the friendships.

5   Dancing in a troupe was definitely my favorite job, but it did not seem like a job at all to me. Dancing was an outlet for my inner emotions and my physical expression, and a social activity for me. When I was nine years old and red-faced with embarrassment, I would have never guessed that I would end up becoming a dancer and falling so much in love with it as I did.

Understanding Words

Briefly define the following words as they are used in the above essay.

Answers to Unit 5 are on page 23 in the Instructor's Manual.

1. troupe *company or group of actors or singers or dancers*

2. choreographing *planning the dance steps and movements of the ballet*

3. critiqued *analyzed and judged*

4. ovation *enthusiastic outburst of applause or public welcome*

5. diplomatic *tactful*

Questions on Content

1. How many hours a day did the author practice dance?

2. What happened when she performed a special number?

3. What was the most physically demanding thing she had ever done?

Questions on Form

1. What makes the introduction so effective?

2. What is effective about the conclusion?

Qualities I Appreciate about My Dad

Agustin Rojas, *student*

1   As the little boy lay in bed, his stomach growling from the hunger pains that would not subside, his mind took him from the hunger and cold to different faraway places. He dreamed of places where he would never be hungry or cold again, places

where his own family would not feel the hunger pains he felt every day and every night as he lay in bed. He imagined giving his family the things he could only dream of, while his mind tried to put aside the hunger and fight the cold. I never met this little boy when he was a child. When I was born, he was already a family man with six children of his own, and now he had one more to take care of. This now-grown man is my father, and he has the qualities that I appreciate a lot and can only dream that I will one day be able to possess, including becoming a family man, a person driven to succeed, and a great musician.

2   My father was born to a poor Mexican family in Mexico. He was the second and last child born to a local town blacksmith. At the age of eleven, my father dropped out of school because he wanted to find a better way of life in the United States. He was determined to give his future family the opportunities he himself had never received. He left his mother and father behind, not knowing what he would encounter in the new country his future family would call home. He crossed the border at McAllen, Texas, where he eventually married and raised his own family. As the years went by, my father and mother had eight boys and three girls, a total of eleven kids. Even though the years were lean and we felt the same hunger pains he felt as a child, my father had not forgotten his dream of making a better life for us. Without any knowledge of what lay ahead in the future, my father packed us up, all eleven kids, into our family car. He had been told that he would find the fruits of life in the state of Oregon. To this day, I can remember the trip to Oregon. Our family car was not in the best condition (we had to use tie-downs to keep the doors closed, and we could see the highway through the car floor). Many of my childhood friends were raised only by their mothers because their fathers had walked away from raising a family through the rough times. My father could have walked away very easily, but in his heart he knew that if he left, his family would just struggle more, find life in the streets, or maybe in jail. Through all the struggles and tribulations, I will always remember that my father was there for us. Leaving his family behind would have been the easiest thing to do, but then if he had, he would not have been true to his dream of giving his family the things he never had.

3   Anybody can walk away from struggles and tribulations. It takes a driven man with a dream to stay and fight through all the hardships life throws in front of his path where his life's dream lay. After spending over half his life working as a farm laborer, my father reentered the school system at the age of forty. He became aware that without the proper education he would not be able to provide his family the dreams and hopes he wanted to instill in them. My father graduated from Chemeketa Community College at the age of forty-four. The years he put himself through school were hard on the family, but his drive and determination to better himself eventually bettered our lives. If my father had not driven himself to get an education, I know for a fact that I would not be here at the age of thirty-seven trying to get a degree. I am not the only one in my family who has been affected by my father's determination and drive. All my brothers and sisters have learned that any dream worth obtaining has hardships and obstacles. For this drive, I will forever be thankful to my father.

4   I have met very few individuals who can pick up a musical instrument and after a few minutes of stroking the chords or keys can start playing a song. My father is one of these individuals. (Unfortunately, I have my mother's ears when it comes to music.) I remember the time when one of my older brothers was in high school. My brother got involved in high school band because he wanted to learn how to play the trumpet. He brought the instrument home to practice. My father had never played the trumpet before, but the next thing I knew, my father was belting out some tunes from the trumpet. I have seen my father do the same thing with the organ,

harmonica, piano, and drums. He can play just about any instrument, and he can also carry a tune. I will never forget the nights he would sing and play his guitar for us kids. Those are memories I plan to share with my own family.

5   As a child, I could never see how great a man my father was, but as life throws its obstacles in my own path, it has opened my eyes to the struggles and tribulations my father endured. I watched my father graduate from college and become successful, and through this gift that my father has given me, I have learned that if I have a dream, I must fight to make my dream come true. Otherwise, the dream will never become a reality.

Understanding Words
Briefly define the following word as it is used in the above essay.

　　1. tribulations　　*hardships, trials*

Questions on Content

1. What are the qualities the author admires most about his father?

2. What did his father do at 44?

3. What does the author remember most about the trip to Oregon?

Questions on Form

1. What kind of hook does the author use?

2. Which sentence in the introduction begins the transition?

3. How does the conclusion give a sense of closure?

A Good Manager

Marlene Reed, *student*

1   What qualities make a good manager? Should a manager be a "good buddy" or be stern and strict? Should a manager have a combination of these traits? Because the majority of the population is working-class, many people may work under the authority of a manager. They certainly hope to work under managers who know their jobs and know how to work with people. Paul Eweres, a manager at Safeway, is an excellent manager because he is disciplined, intelligent, and fair.

2   There is a special, admirable quality in Mr. Eweres: his self-discipline. Mr. Eweres is one of the most disciplined people that anyone could work for. Safeway managers must work with district managers, the constant threat of losing their jobs, and very long hours. Many managers with pressures such as these lose their cool—not Mr. Eweres. He can take all that the job dishes out, get the work done, and not once blame his problems on someone else, much less take these problems out on the employees. This is a sign of considerable maturity, and more managers should have self-discipline such as this.

3   Of equal importance, a manager needs to be intelligent. Without knowing his I.Q., one can tell that Mr. Eweres is very bright. The ease with which he solves complex problems is noteworthy. For example, when his store recently received new scanner registers, Mr. Eweres had no problems adjusting to the new system, as most managers might. Any problem that came up he knew instantly how to fix. In addition, Mr. Eweres knows how to make a schedule that works well. This has proven to be a problem for many managers because it takes considerable savvy to know when help is needed and to keep hours within the amount allotted. Managers most often do not schedule enough help at the right times, or they schedule too much help when it is not needed, yet this has never been a problem for Mr. Eweres. His schedules are accurate, and his store runs smoothly because he has the needed intelligence.

4   Above all else, Mr. Eweres is fair. He does not let his personal preferences guide his decisions, and he always tries to work with his employees. Managers sometimes use intimidation to get work done. Though the use of intimidation might get the job done, it only breeds contempt and ill feelings. When people are treated like animals, they grow to hate their jobs and begin to call in sick. Paul Eweres doesn't use intimidation because he does not have to. His employees respect him; therefore, they not only do their jobs, but they do their best. He makes employees feel important to the store, not like cogs in a machine.

5   It is the opinion of this writer that, without these three qualities—discipline, intelligence, and fairness—the manager at Safeway on 19th Avenue and Northern would be just a manager, nothing special. Yet, because he possesses these qualities he is so much more effective. No, Paul Eweres is not just a manager; he is the best manager Safeway has.

Understanding Words

Briefly define the following words as they are used in the above essay.

1. intimidation   *deterring with threats or fear*

2. contempt   *feeling someone has toward someone considered lower; scorn*

Questions on Content

1. What does Mr. Eweres manage?

2. What does Mr. Eweres do that illustrates his intelligence?

3. Why does he not have to rely on intimidation to get employees to work?

Questions on Form

1. What is the hook used in the introduction? Is it effective?

2. Comment on the force of the conclusion. Is it consistent with the rest of the essay?

3. Has the student used any specific examples to support her opinion of Mr. Eweres's character? If so, what are they?

The Right Thing to Do

Jeff Collins, *student*

1   I had to think for a long time before getting married; however, many people didn't understand the thought and preparation it took to decide I could not live with my wife anymore. How would my son handle it? Was it the right thing for my child? When my marriage broke up, doing the right thing for my son took a great deal of thought, some value rearranging, and not doing necessarily what everyone else wanted me to do.

2   When my marriage broke up, the toughest decision I had to make was doing the right thing for my son—for example, deciding with whom, when, and where my child was going to live. This decision took a long time because sometimes I did not like the answer. The wrong decision would have left my son misunderstanding the entire situation and put him in a tailspin for the rest of his life. The last thing I wanted my child thinking was he was not loved or did not belong anywhere. He had to know where he lived was his home, and his home was where he should go if he had any problems. I had to decide who could make a better home for my son—my ex-spouse or me? Should both of us be able to visit our son? Should I move far away and keep visitation limited? I personally had to make these decisions, and they took a large toll on my life.

3   In deciding the future of my son, I needed to do some value rearranging. I had to set goals and decide what I was going to do for the rest of my life, what I wanted for my son, and what means would provide the things I wanted for my son. The hardest decision I have ever made was to decide I could not provide for my son as well as my ex-spouse could. She had a house for the two of them to live in, a good job to fall back on, and parents that lived nearby for support. These assets helped me make this difficult decision. It took months of thought and many sleepless nights before I decided to give up my son. I was his father, but a court battle for custody was not going to be good for anyone. I gave him a home and sense of belonging I never had, a chance to be happy with life, and a strong home to build his future with.

4   The decisions I made for my son were not necessarily what everyone else wanted me to do. These decisions took away my right to be part of my family and my right to take part in my son's growing up. My mother, whom I was very close to, disowned me. My father decided I was wrong to give up my son and did not think I was doing the right thing for him, although I think he understood the pain I was going through. My mother decided I was no longer part of the family if I could give up her first grandson. This was heartbreaking to me, and it will take years for me to understand her selfishness.

5   I miss seeing my son and watching him learn new things, but I know down deep in my heart I did the right thing for him, and it may take a long time for everyone to understand the parts of my life I had to give up in doing so. But the boy now has the chance to grow up in a strong home with parents who love him and a chance to figure out the tough things, like which shoe to put on which foot and whether to be right-handed or left.

Questions on Content

1. What major decision did the author have to make?

2. Why was this decision so hard for him?

3. What was one negative result for the author?

Questions on Form

1. The author is very honest and feeling in this essay. How does this add to the effectiveness of the essay?

2. In what way is the concluding paragraph effective?

Living in Another Country

Alberto Montaño Hernandez, *student*

1   My name is Alberto Montaño. I am 20 years old, and I am from Chihuahua, Mexico. Five years ago, my mom came from Mexico to visit my two sisters. After five days of being there, she did not feel very well, so my sisters took her to the hospital. At the hospital, the doctors discovered that she had a tumor in her head and that it was necessary to have surgery. After she had the surgery, the doctor said that she would have to remain in the United States because she was going to have appointments regularly. At the same time, I had just graduated secondary school in Mexico, so my mom suggested that I move to the United States so we could be together. When I came here, I thought everything was going to be really easy, but living in another country could be very challenging. Some of the challenges I faced moving to the United States were the migrant status, the language, and the environment.

2   First of all, one of the biggest challenges I faced moving to the United States was my migrant status. When I came from Mexico, I just had a tourist visa; it was not enough for me because with that visa, I could only stay in the United States for a certain period of time and I was not going to be able to work. After two months, I was not a visitor any more because my permit was over, so I turned into an illegal immigrant. Later on, I started working at McDonald's, using a name that was not mine, in order to help my father and to pay for my school materials. It was really hard for me because I attended high school while I had a full-time job. I did not have any free time to spend with my friends because if I was not doing my homework, I was working, but it was worth it because my mom and I were together. Getting a different visa so I could stay here was also difficult.

3   Another challenge that I faced moving to the United States was the language. When I came from Mexico, I knew little English, so it was very difficult for me to understand what people were saying and to communicate with them when they were talking to me. For example, one time I went to the store to buy a watch for my father. I observed every single one of them, and suddenly I saw the perfect timepiece for him. I asked the lady, "How many is for that clock?" She just looked at me and said, "What? I did not understand what you just said. Can you say that again please?" I did not say anything, and I left. Also, because of the language situation, when I first started my job at McDonald's, a lot of the words that they used I did not know. For example, one customer asked for a cheeseburger with extra pickles and catsup, well done, so I just made it with extra pickles and catsup, but with regular meat. Two minutes later, the customer brought the cheeseburger back to my counter and told my manager that it was not right. My manager came back to the grill area and explained to me what well done meant. However, as time went by, my ability to understand and speak the language became much better.

4   Finally, another challenge that I faced moving to the United States was the environment. In Mexico, I used to live in a small town with no more than 100 families in it. I attended a small school and enjoyed cool weather. When I came here, I saw a lot of different people everywhere, enormous schools, and very hot weather. For example, when I went to Wal-Mart the first time, I got lost because of the many people who go there all the time. Also, the first week of school, I could not find my classroom, so I had to go to the attendance office to ask them where my classes were. In addition, when I just got here, I stayed home all the time because I could not handle the burning air that Arizona has. As time went by, I became accustomed to these changes.

5   In conclusion, the place where I live, the idioms that I speak, and my immigrant status created many challenges that I had to face after moving to the United States. Today, however, I am close to having my citizenship, and I have almost completed my college degree. Though I am sad because I lost my mother, I will always remember that my mother and I spent the last part of her life together. I know that she would be proud of my accomplishments.

Questions on Content

1. Why did Alberto come to the United States?

2. What challenges did he face in the United States?

3. How did he finally resolve his challenges?

Questions on Form

1. What hook does the author use?

2. What is the transition between the hook and the thesis sentence?

3. How effective is the conclusion?

Part 4

Grammar for Effective Writing: Sentence Variety—Using Complex Sentences

Objectives

- Combine simple sentences using subordinators.
- Practice revising sentences.

Sometimes writing becomes less interesting to the reader if the sentences are too much alike. A series of short, simple sentences is monotonous, and too many sentences joined with "and" or "but" also sound monotonous.

The following draft paragraph contains only simple sentences.

> All the players in the basketball game played very hard. They ran up and down the court. They frequently jumped and moved around quickly. They dodged back and forth. The guards dribbled the ball all around the court. They also passed the ball hard to other members of their team. Sometimes the players even knocked opposing team members to the floor. They twisted, turned, and bumped into each other. Occasionally, they ran into the referees. All the activity caused the players to exert lots of energy throughout the game.

As you learned earlier, one way to make writing more interesting is to combine simple sentences into compound sentences.

> They ran up and down the court, **and** they frequently jumped and moved around quickly.

However, too many compound sentences also sound monotonous and somewhat elementary. When you revise a draft, you may want to use other kinds of connecting words to combine ideas in a paragraph. For instance, if one sentence gives a reason for something, a word like "because" can make one stronger sentence out of two shorter related sentences.

> Sometimes the players even knocked opposing team members to the floor **because** they twisted, turned, and bumped into each other.

This kind of sentence is called a **complex sentence.** The simple sentence "They twisted, turned, and bumped into each other" has now become an idea that is *dependent* upon the idea in the first part of the sentence. To understand more clearly how complex sentences are used, study the following discussion carefully.

Independent and Dependent Clauses

Tests on complex sentences are on pages 54–65 in the Test Bank.

A complex sentence contains two kinds of clauses: one independent clause and one or more dependent clauses.

A **clause** is a group of words with a subject and a complete verb. An **independent clause** can stand by itself and be a sentence because it contains a complete idea. A **dependent clause** cannot stand by itself and cannot be a sentence. Combining two independent clauses with "because" makes one of them dependent on, or *subordinate to,* the other. The word "because" is called a subordinator. Thus, the new sentence formed has become a complex sentence. It now has two clauses—one independent and one dependent. The "because" idea now has become a dependent clause subordinate to the other idea in the sentence. The idea in a subordinate clause receives *less emphasis* than the idea in the independent clause. Consider the same complex sentence:

Sometimes the players even knocked opposing team members to the floor **because** they twisted, turned, and bumped into each other.

Now, "because they twisted, turned, and bumped into each other" cannot stand by itself as a sentence. The word "because" makes this part a dependent clause, and it also clearly shows why players are sometimes knocked down in a basketball game.

Many common words are used to combine ideas into more mature sentences. Most of these connecting words you probably already know and use. These words are called **subordinators.** Here is a list of subordinators (you may already have studied them in Unit 3, Part 4, concerning fragments).

Subordinators

after	if	where
although	in order that	whether
as	since	which
as if	so that	whichever
as long as	that	while
as soon as	though	who
as though	till	whoever
as well as	unless	whom
because	until	whomever
before	what	whose
even though	whatever	whosoever
how	when	why

Using Subordinators to Form Complex Sentences

Even more important, however, is knowing how to use the subordinators to combine simple sentences into stronger, more mature ideas. These stronger, revised sentences clearly show how ideas relate to each other. Consider the following list of uses of subordinators.

after

I will finish this chapter.

I will treat myself to some fudge cake.

After I finish this chapter, I will treat myself to some fudge cake.*

I will treat myself to some fudge cake **after I finish this chapter.**

Note When the dependent clause is an introductory expression in the sentence, put a comma after it.

---

*You sometimes need to change wording when you build complex sentences.

as soon as

John is coming.

I am leaving.

As soon as John comes, I am leaving.*

I am leaving **as soon as** John comes.

before

Rick needs to study.

He needs to take his test.

Rick needs to study **before he takes his test.***

Before he takes his test, Rick needs to study.

when

The river dries up.

The fish will die.

When the river dries up, the fish will die.

The fish will die **when the river dries up.**

while

The bride walked with her father.

The groom waited.

While the bride walked with her father, the groom waited.

The groom waited **while the bride walked with her father.**

where

The students stood there.

There was shade.

The students stood **where there was shade.**

The students stood **where the shade was.***

as

She took the medicine.

The doctor had prescribed it.

She took the medicine **as the doctor had prescribed it.***

---

*You sometimes need to change wording when you build complex sentences.

if

We will not have the picnic.

It might rain on Saturday.

We will not have the picnic *if* **it rains on Saturday.**

If **it rains on Saturday,** we will not have the picnic.

although

The coach had a winning season.

He cut six players.

Although **the coach had a winning season,** he cut six players.

The coach cut six players *although* **he had a winning season.**

because

We needed the extra money.

Mom decided to get a job.

Mom decided to get a job *because* **we needed the extra money.**

Because **we needed the extra money,** Mom decided to get a job.

so that

Mary raked the leaves.

Clay could burn them.

Mary raked the leaves *so that* **Clay could burn them.**

So that **Clay could burn the leaves,** Mary raked them.

as long as

The girls were content.

They had games to play.

The girls were content *as long as* **they had games to play.**

As long as **the girls had games to play,** they were content.

as well as

Mary Duncan did not run well.

She could have run better.

Mary Duncan did not run *as well as* **she could have.** *

---

*Sometimes it does not sound natural to put the dependent clause first.

Exercise 1

Using words from the list, choose a subordinator that logically connects each pair of simple sentences. Then combine them into a complex sentence. More than one subordinator may fit, depending upon the meaning you want to express. Also, you may need to make some changes in wording. Reminder: When the dependent clause is an introductory expression in the sentence, put a comma after it.

Example:

The game was over.

The players went into the locker room to change clothes.

The players went into the locker room to change clothes after the game was over.

After the game was over, the players went into the locker room to change clothes.

1. Rachel earned a college degree.

   She became the manager at a retail store.

   After Rachel earned a college degree, she became the manager at a retail store.

   Rachel became the manager at a retail store after she earned a college degree.

2. The rookie threw a wild pitch.

   The manager took him out of the game.

   After the rookie threw a wild pitch, the manager took him out of the game.

   The manager took the rookie out of the game after he threw a wild pitch.

3. Fresh Idaho snow covered the high mountaintops.

   The scouts continued to hike up the trail.

   Even though fresh Idaho snow covered the high mountaintops, the scouts continued to hike up the trail.

   The scouts continued to hike up the trail even though fresh Idaho snow covered the high mountaintops.

4. The sunbathers and the surfers left the beach.

   The storm began.

   When the storm began, the sunbathers and the surfers left the beach.

   The sunbathers and the surfers left the beach when the storm began.

5. The manager resigned his position.

   It created too much stress in his life.

   The manager resigned his position because it created too much stress in his life.

   Because his job created too much stress in his life, the manager resigned.

6. Mike wants to fly to Montana.

He renews his pilot's license.

As soon as Mike renews his pilot's license, he wants to fly to Montana.

Mike wants to fly to Montana as soon as he renews his pilot's license.

Words like "who," "whose," "whom," "which," and "that" are also subordinators and can be used to combine simple sentences into more mature sentence patterns. These more mature sentences are also complex sentences because they have an independent clause and one or more dependent clauses. These connecting words are probably familiar to you.

Cindy saw the herd at the gate.

The gate had been left open.

Cindy saw the herd at the gate *that* **had been left open.**

Jason admires Mr. Winters.

Mr. Winters requires his teams to train hard for their games.

Jason admires Mr. Winters, *who* **requires his teams to train hard for their games.**

The sentences may not always fit end to end. To combine them logically, you may have to put one idea inside the other and make changes in wording. More than one revision may be possible, depending upon the idea you want to emphasize. The important point to remember is that you are revising to make stronger sentences.

The car was stolen from the driveway.

The car belonged to my mother.

The car *that* **belonged to my mother** was stolen from the driveway.

Joseph was the best-qualified candidate.

The company hired him after one interview.

Joseph, *who* **was the best-qualified candidate,** was hired after one interview.

Note   The commas are required because the "who" clause does not identify Joseph. If the man's name had not been given, no commas would be used, as in this sentence: The man who was the best-qualified candidate was hired after one interview.

Joseph, *who* **was hired after one interview,** was the best-qualified candidate.

Joseph, *whom* **the company hired after one interview,** was the best candidate.

Note   The second sentence is a more formal sentence. To learn how to use "whom" appropriately, see the special section on page 302 called "Choosing *Who* or *Whom*."

Exercise 2

Practice combining simple sentences using "who," "whose," "which," or "that." You may have to make some changes in wording to construct the sentences smoothly and logically.

Example:

The novel was *Moby Dick*.

We all liked that book the best.

The novel that we all liked the best was Moby Dick.

Moby Dick was the novel that we all liked the best.

1. The children loved the playground.

   It was filled with bright, colorful equipment.
   The children loved the playground that was filled with bright, colorful equipment.

2. The hikers were rescued.

   They were taken to the hospital.
   The hikers who were rescued were taken to the hospital.

3. My brother works as a carpenter.

   My brother built his new home next to the mountain preserve.
   My brother, who works as a carpenter, built his new home next to the mountain preserve.
   My brother, who built his new home next to the mountain preserve, is a carpenter.

4. The climbers made it to the top of the lighthouse.

   The climbers' training had been intense.
   The climbers whose training had been intense made it to the top of the lighthouse.

5. Nick teaches math online.

   He is semi-retired.
   Nick, who is semi-retired, teaches math online.
   Nick, who teaches math online, is semi-retired.

6. Kana learned to bake a chocolate cake.

   His dad liked this cake the best.
   Kana learned to bake a chocolate cake that his dad liked the best.
   His dad liked the chocolate cake that Kana learned to bake.

Putting the Dependent Clause First Once in a while for variety, you may want to use a sentence in which the dependent clause comes first and actually functions as the subject of the sentence. Try varying your sentence patterns by using this kind of sentence. The words that begin these dependent clauses are also in the previous list of subordinators. Each new, revised sentence will be stronger than the original sentences. Here are some examples showing possible revisions:

You are going on vacation.

Where, depends on you.

***Where* you go on vacation** depends on you.

People watch that program.

It is a mystery to me.

***Why* people watch that program** is a mystery to me.

The committee will vote on the proposal.

It must be reported to the public.

***How* the committee votes on the proposal** must be reported to the public.

Exercise 3

Use "who," "why," "how," or "that" to combine each pair of simple sentences into a stronger, complex sentence. To make your revised sentences clear and logical, make any changes in wording you think are necessary. Put the dependent clause at the beginning of the sentence, and eliminate vague words at the same time.

Example:

I want to buy a motorcycle.

It does not thrill my mom.

Why I want to buy a motorcycle does not thrill my mom.

That I want to buy a motorcycle does not thrill my mom.

1. He cares about a clean house.

   It is surprising to his mother.

   That he even cares about a clean house is surprising to his mother.

2. The money was gone.

   This upset us.

   That the money was gone upset us.

3. The house escaped the forest fire.

It seemed to be a miracle.

How the house escaped the forest fire seemed to be a miracle.

_____

4. I earn my own money.

It is my business.

How I earn my own money is my business.

_____

5. My dog got loose.

No one seems to know how.

How my dog got loose no one seems to know.

_____

6. Ruby, the painting elephant, died in childbirth.

It shocked zoo members.

That Ruby, the painting elephant, died in childbirth shocked zoo members.

_____

Putting the Dependent Clause Last   When revising a paragraph or an essay, you may want to eliminate short, ineffective sentences in other ways. Try putting the dependent clause at the end of the sentence and eliminate vague words at the same time.

The director's employees can solve the problem.

He has learned this.

The director has learned **_how_ his employees can solve the problem.**

We know the answer.

At least, we could find it at the library.

We know **_that_ we can find the answer at the library.**

Exercise 4

Use "who," "why," "how," or "that" to combine each pair of simple sentences into a stronger, complex sentence. Again, to make your revised sentences clear and logical, make any changes in wording you think are necessary. Put the dependent clause at the end of the revised sentence, and eliminate vague words at the same time.

Example:

The attorney recalled the information.

Her client told her the facts.

The attorney recalled what her client told her.

The attorney recalled the information that her client told her.

1. I do not understand.

   He is always late.

   I do not understand why he is always late.

2. We watched the hummingbirds.

   They played in the sprinkler.

   We watched how the hummingbirds played in the sprinkler.

3. The elderly man was confused and lost.

   The police officer realized the situation.

   The police officer realized that the elderly man was confused and lost.

4. Everyone is amazed.

   Andrea can always find a parking space.

   Everyone is amazed that Andrea can always find a parking space.

5. We know the difficulties.

   They can be overcome by hard work.

   We know that the difficulties can be overcome by hard work.

6. My cat did not understand.

   I could not let her out.

   My cat did not understand why I could not let her out.

Choosing *Who* or *Whom*

Occasionally you may have difficulty knowing whether to use "who" or "whom" in your writing. If the subordinator is used as the subject of your dependent clause and it refers to a person, you should select the subject pronoun "who."

Bob will marry Marsha next June.

Marsha is an airline pilot.

Next June, Bob will marry Marsha, ***who* is an airline pilot.**

In this sentence, "who" refers to a person and acts as the subordinator and the subject of the dependent clause. However, if the dependent clause already has a subject, then the subordinator has to be "whom."

Bob will marry an airline pilot.

He met the airline pilot in Peru.

Bob will marry an airline pilot **whom** he met in Peru.

An easier way that might help you choose between "who" or "whom" is a simple substitution.

- **If you can substitute "he" or "she" in the sentence, use "who."**
- **If you can substitute "him" or "her" in the sentence, use "whom."**

Who (he) is coming for lunch?

Josh, **who** (he) is my good friend, will be here soon.

In these examples, you would not use "whom" because neither "him is coming" nor "him is my good friend" is correct.

Josh is the person **whom** we selected (him) for the job.

Master for transparency to review sentence combining is on page 41 in the Instructor's Manual.

Note   At times you may have to rearrange the dependent clause to see how the substitution works. Thus, in the previous example, "whom we selected for the job" becomes "we selected whom for the job"; using "whom" is correct because you would say "we selected *him*," not "we selected *he*."

You can remember whether to use "who" or "whom" more easily if you remember that the two words that end in "m" substitute for each other:

her/him   ⟷   whom

she/he   ⟷   who

Exercise 5

Revise the following draft paragraphs by combining simple sentences into complex sentences. Try to use a variety of complex sentences.

Paragraph 1

who
People remodel their home. ~~They~~ can save a lot of money by being their own general
  ^
                                      that
contractor. They do not have to pay someone to subcontract out the various jobs. ~~These~~
                                       If homeowners
~~jobs~~ require an electrician, plumber, or general carpenter. ~~Homeowners~~ have three
                                     , then
or four licensed and bonded subcontractors bid on a job. ~~Then~~ they can select the

most favorable bid. Also, they do not need to hire an expensive architect to create a
        that
plan. ~~This kind of plan~~ can run into hundreds of dollars. Instead, homeowners can
                                   who
look into finding a house designer. ~~The designer~~ will simply put their remodeling

ideas into a standard blueprint. Sometimes they can also save money by doing some

of the jobs themselves. For example, they might want to install the appliances

because it   *If they*   *, they*
themselves. ~~It~~ can be done very easily. ~~They might~~ paint the house themselves. ~~They~~

will save the often high cost of a professional subcontractor. Remodeling can be a

fun project, and saving money can make it even more pleasurable.

Paragraph 2

Because stamina
Basketball requires a variety of physical skills. ~~Stamina~~ is a stringent requirement
^
, many
for this highly active sport. ~~Many~~ times the victory goes to the team with the greatest

because they
physical endurance. Agility is another important factor for basketball players. ~~They~~
so that they
must be able to move smoothly and quickly. ~~They~~ can coordinate their moves. Kevin

Garnett's finesse on the court is a great example of winning, aerobic-like moves.

If players
Sheer aggression defines the dribbling path of his drives to the basket. ~~Players~~ have
^
, they
good peripheral vision. ~~They~~ can pass without looking at the players receiving the
Because jumping   *, great*
ball. ~~Jumping~~ ability is important. ~~Great~~ basketball players can slam-dunk and get
^   ^

many rebounds. These physical skills can lead to a winning team.

Paragraph 3

who
Bodybuilding is a sport that demands discipline. Bodybuilders push themselves
^

until their muscles won't work anymore. ~~They~~ build muscle mass. Serious athletes
until they
must work out at the gym five to seven hours a day. ~~They~~ feel a burning sensation in
If the   *, they*
their muscles. ~~The~~ muscles are sore the next morning. ~~They~~ know they had a good
In which they
workout. Athletes must also have the willpower to adhere to a strict diet. ~~They~~ eat no
When they   *, they*
fatty foods, especially hamburgers and french fries. ~~They~~ need to cut fat. ~~They~~ must
When they
stay on an even stricter diet than normal. They also must get plenty of sleep. ~~They~~
, dedicated
are at a party with their friends and everyone else wants to stay late. ~~Dedicated~~

athletes will have enough control to go home early. This dedication, however, will

result in a body they can take pride in.

Part 5

Putting It All Together

 ## Cumulative Unit Exercise

Now that you have studied the format for essays, analyze "Homeward Bound."

1. After reading the essay carefully, find and identify the hooks used in the introductory paragraph.

2. Underline the topic sentence in each support paragraph, and circle the key words that show a clear link to the thesis sentence.

3. Use brackets to enclose the linking sentences that tie the examples to the topic sentence in each paragraph.

4. Check to see if each paragraph has adequate support and a concluding sentence.

5. Combine each pair of italicized sentences into a more sophisticated sentence, using a subordinator.

6. How does the conclusion link to the introductory paragraph?

Transparency of uncorrected cumulative exercise is on pages 53–56 of the Instructor's Manual.

Homeward Bound

quotation and question

1   "Mom, Dad, I have a favor to ask. Do you think I could move back home for a little while?" Twenty years ago this question would never have been asked because kids grew up, graduated from high school, and then got married or went off to college, leaving a home empty of offspring. However, today many young people live at home and attend a community college. They also wait until they are older to get married, or they move out and become independent, but they no sooner leave

rhetorical question

than they move back home. Do parents really want their adult children to return home, especially when they bring kids and pets with them? However, whether or not parents want them to move back home, adult children are doing so in record numbers. Living at home allows them an opportunity to get back on their feet, save for the future, and lessen their personal obligations.

2   In today's society, young people may find themselves (in debt or unable to) (support themselves) on their current income, and one way to deal with this situation is to (move home) with Mom and Dad until they can (get back on their feet) [Perhaps

they are working at jobs that pay minimum wage, and they want to go back to college and earn a degree or receive specialized training so they can get a job that pays more money. These young adults find it very difficult to work, go to school, and pay for their independent living, so they move back home where they find inexpensive rent or, in some cases, no rent at all while they are attending college.]

Stacy found that moving back home eliminated her rent, and the money she saved was put toward college tuition. Though she continued to work at her $6.10 an hour job, she was able to pay her bills and pay off her credit card, and two years later when she moved out, she was making over twice that as a computer technician. [Sometimes adults may have just graduated from college and they are left with a debt such as a student loan. Having shrewd minds, they figure the best way to get this debt out of the way is to return to their childhood home while they recover financially.]That is exactly what happened to Brian. *He graduated from college. He* **After he** , **he** *moved home for three years until he had paid off not only his college expenses but a three-month tour of Europe that followed his graduation.* Many parents are overjoyed to see their offspring shed themselves of debt and face life with a better future.

3   Many young adults today want to be financially secure so they return to a nurturing environment before they move out permanently.[The personal sacrifices of losing their complete freedom seem to be minute compared to the future rewards.]Eric received his paramedic training and was hired as a firefighter/ paramedic, but no sooner had this happy news reached his parents than he asked to move back home so he could save most of his paycheck. He paid his parents for room and board and helped out around the house, but before long he bought a condo. Did he move in? No, he rented the condo out for profit and stayed with his parents for several more months until he could put a hefty down payment on a new home. *He helped out his parents by paying rent. By the time he became financially* **After he** , **by**

independent, he owned a big black truck, a condo, and a house, not to mention a

big-screen television set and living room furniture.[It isn't just guys who save to

purchase the extras they want.]Robin moved back in with her parents so that she

could save money for the extras she wanted for her wedding. Her parents helped

with the expenses for the wedding, but because she was not paying rent, Robin was

able to pay for most of the expenses, and she even used her own money to rent an

exclusive resort facility for the reception. ~~*She*~~ **When she** *left home.* ~~*Neither she*~~ **, neither** *nor her parents*

were left with any debts. These two young people represent the future-mindedness

of today's society.

4   [Even though some young adults are doing quite well financially,]they

move back home to ease their personal obligations.Marti had been living on her

own for seven years, and she had a high-paying job, but she spent so much time

traveling that she found it simpler just to rent the basement from her parents.

When she was gone, her parents took care of her dog and watered her plants. This

was a perfect arrangement. She still had her freedom, and her parents willingly took

on part of their daughter's personal responsibilities.[In some cases, complex

obligations play a significant role in an adult child's decision to return home.]*Todd*

had been married for nine years. ~~*He*~~ **before he** *became the divorced parent of two children,*

ages five and seven. He shared custody of his children with his ex-wife, but he found

he could have more time with his children if he moved back in with his parents. Of

course, his parents welcomed him and their grandchildren with open arms, at least

for a while, and Todd had the perfect babysitters who loved his children and were

home for them when they got home from school.[Sometimes the conveniences are

even simpler than this.]Adrian moved back with her parents for two months, but

when she found how much she enjoyed doing things with her parents, including four-

wheeling, and not having to worry about clean clothes or a messy house, she settled

> *Though none*
in for four years before venturing out on her own again. ~~None~~ of these young people
> *, they*
were suffering hardships. ~~They~~ teamed up with their parents to make life better.

reinforces thesis

5   Becoming established in today's society is extremely complex, but families are reaching out to help one another, trying to make life easier. At a time when fast-paced living is the norm, shared households have become more than permissible; they have become acceptable and even desirable. When adult children move back home, they are simply finding workable solutions to existing problems or are seeking a better life for themselves and sometimes for their families. Maybe someday the parents will feel just as comfortable saying to their adult children, "Do you think we could move in for a little while?"

goes back to hook

Collaborative Writing Project: Working and Learning Together

Writing Assignment

This exercise will help you practice writing an essay, complete with an introductory and a concluding paragraph.

1. For this writing assignment, work with another person in the class to discuss a personal experience that was a major event in your life. It can be a positive or a negative experience, but it must have altered your life in several ways.

   Events might include a divorce, death of someone close to you, a move to another country or another part of the same country, the birth of a child, a marriage, or a major incident such as a car accident, a fire, or an illness.

2. Explain to your partner how this experience changed your life. Jot down notes so that you will have ideas to work from later when you develop a thesis sentence.

3. Now repeat the same procedure for the other group member.

4. Help each other develop thesis sentences. The thesis sentence will express at least three ways your life is now different because of this event.

Working Individually

1. Start the introduction for your essay by summarizing the event that happened to you. This will be the hook.

2. Write one or more words or sentences that connect this personal experience to the thesis sentence. The previewed points in the thesis sentence will include how your life was changed by this particular event.

3. Be sure the thesis sentence is the last sentence in your introductory paragraph.

4. Write a support paragraph for each point previewed in your thesis sentence. Each paragraph needs a topic sentence, support sentences, and a concluding sentence.

5. Write a concluding paragraph that captures the idea of the thesis sentence without using the same words. At the end of this paragraph, you may want to refer to the hook to add closure to your paper.

6. Revise simple, short sentences into compound or complex sentences.

Final Checklist

Content

Essay

Check the introductory paragraph for an effective hook.

Check for a smooth transition between hook and thesis.

Check to see that the thesis sentence states a clear direction or previews the points to be covered in the paper.

Check to see that the voice is appropriate for pupose and audience.

Check for a strong concluding paragraph.

Paragraphs

Revise so each paragraph has a clear topic sentence that develops an idea suggested in the thesis sentence.

Include four to six supporting sentences that are developed using short interrelated examples or an extended example.

Include a strong closing sentence in each paragraph.

Mechanics

Check for subject-verb agreement.

Check for consistent verb tense.

Check for a consistent point of view.

Check for fragments, run-on sentences, and comma splices.

Check punctuation of complex sentences.

Check punctuation of compound sentences.

Sentence variety

Revise short sentences into compound sentences.

Revise sentences to include complex sentences.

Internet Activities

Activity 1   Locating Quotations, Facts, and Current Events

In this unit, you learned the importance of creating interest with quotations, startling facts, or current events. This web activity will give you an opportunity to find resources on the Internet that can help you in writing introductory paragraphs.

a. Visit the following website for *Bartlett's Familiar Quotations*. (Type all Internet addresses exactly as they appear. Bookmark this site, or save it as a favorite for future reference.)

http://www.bartleby.com/100/

b. Scroll down, and fill in the search box for your particular topic. Select a quotation, and write it below. Click "Back" on your browser toolbar.

Answers will vary.

_____

c. Visit the following website for the top 10 sites for locating statistical facts, research, and tips on how to research facts. (Type all Internet addresses exactly as they appear. Bookmark this site or save it as a favorite for future reference.)

http://www.onlinemag.net/OL1998/berinstein3.html

d. Name three of the top ten sites below:

Statistical Abstract of the U.S.; U.S. Bureau of the Census; U.S. Bureau of Labor

Statistics; Fedstats; A Matter of Fact; World Almanac, Information Please Almanac;

American Demographics; The CIA's World Factbook; Major Business Journals; Newspapers

e. Visit this site to find magazine articles that might supply specific examples. Search articles by subject. (Type all Internet addresses exactly as they appear. Bookmark this site or save it as a favorite for future reference.)

http://www.findarticles.com/

f. Do a search on a particular topic, and write the name of one or two articles that you found.

Answers will vary.

_____

Activity 2   Reinforcing Compound and Complex Sentences

a. Visit Purdue University's Online Writing Lab, and see a summary of sentence patterns studied in *Writing Paragraphs and Essays,* Unit 4 and Unit 5.

http://owl.english.purdue.edu/

b. On the base page, scroll down until you find a pencil-link subheading titled "Handouts and Materials." Click on this link and you will come to a page titled "Handouts and Materials for Students and Teachers." Scroll down this page and click on the box "Grammar, Punctuation, Spelling." On the left-hand side navigational bar, under "contents," click on "Grammar." Scroll down this new page until you see "Sentence Structure." Click on "Sentence

Punctuation Patterns." Note the first 4 patterns of development from simple sentences to compound sentences. Note patterns 5 through 8 that illustrate complex sentences. Close this website.

c. Go to the following home page to take an interactive quiz on independent clauses. The quiz has explanations for correct answers. (Type all Internet addresses exactly as they appear. Bookmark this site or save it as a favorite for future reference.)

http://webster.commnet.edu/grammar/index.htm

d. Go to "Ask Grammar, Quizzes, Search Devices." Select "170+ Interactive Quizzes." Scroll down until you reach number 59, "Independent Clauses." Test your knowledge, and use the explanation option for those you do not understand. Click on your browser toolbar to print out a copy if requested by your instructor.

Unit **6** | *Making Ideas Flow Clearly*

Part 1

Writing Skills: Coherence

Objectives

Pretest over Unit 6, Parts 1 and 4, is on page 8 of the Test Bank.

- Use transitions effectively.
- Repeat key words to add coherence.
- Use time words and other transitional words to add coherence.
- Use pronouns to add coherence.
- Revise a given paragraph using appropriate transitional words and phrases.
- Recognize how the ideas in the thesis sentence provide the key words for transition in the topic sentences.
- Given a thesis sentence, write topic sentences containing appropriate key words.
- Add coherence within and among paragraphs in an essay.

Clear and interesting writing has logical connections between sentences and between paragraphs, and these clear connections make the writing flow smoothly. Sometimes the relationship is so obvious to you that you do not realize that you still need to make the connection obvious to the reader. Writing that flows smoothly contains specific words that make the connections between ideas so the reader does not have to fill in the gaps. These connections help to clarify meaning.

Creating Coherence Within Paragraphs

The following paragraph is choppy because it does not have clear connections between the sentences.

> When I was growing up, I had many responsibilities around my house after school and on Saturdays. I took care of my cats. I picked up the fallen sour oranges from the front yard. Trimming the juniper bushes in the back was my job. Cleaning my room was something I did once a week. Working around the house is one of my clearest memories of growing up.

Each sentence is *isolated* from the next. The sentences might just as well be in a list:

1. When I was growing up, I had many responsibilities around my house after school and on Saturdays.
2. I took care of my cats.
3. I picked up the fallen sour oranges from the front yard.
4. Trimming the juniper bushes in the back was my job.
5. Cleaning my room was something I did once a week.
6. Working around the house is one of my clearest memories of growing up.

What idea ties all these sentences together? Sentences 2, 3, 4, and 5 are all "responsibilities around my house" referred to in the topic sentence, but the sentences have no obvious connections to each other. If the connections were clearer, the information would be more meaningful to the reader.

Clear connecting words make these sentences flow more smoothly. A revised paragraph might read as follows:

> When I was growing up, I had several responsibilities around the house. I took care of my cats every day. After school each day in the spring, I had to pick up the fallen sour oranges from the front yard. I usually had to do this chore first because my mom wanted the front yard clean. In addition to these jobs, I spent many Saturday mornings trimming the juniper bushes in the back. After finishing the trimming (or any other work I had to do), I would then clean my room. Working around the house is one of my clearest memories of growing up.

Specific words and phrases have been added to the first draft to make clear *when* the activities occurred in relation to each other, to establish a coherent sequence of events.

These additional words and phrases are called **transitions.** When you write, choose transitions that make clear, logical connections between sentences.

There are several kinds of words and phrases that can be used to create **coherence** in a paragraph:

1. **repeated key words** that refer to the *topic* idea in the paragraph: "responsibilities," "this chore," "these jobs," "the trimming."

2. special **time words** and other **transitional words** or phrases that add definite meaning to link sentences logically into a coherent whole: "every day," "after school each day in the spring," "in addition," "then."

3. **pronouns,** including possessive pronouns ("my" mom) and **words that point out** ("this" and "that"). Avoid "it," "they," and "this" whenever they do not refer to specific nouns in the paragraph.

The following paragraph lacks coherence.

> **Learning how to drive a car with a stick shift is difficult.** The location of each gear and the best speed to drive in for each gear must be learned. How to push in the clutch and change the gear to obtain the best speed can be tricky until the driver discovers just where the clutch accelerates the gear speed. Bouncing and jerking can occur until this maneuver is mastered. This "sweet spot" is different in all cars. Downshifting has to be learned to allow for turns and slowing. The clutch and gear speed work together again, but the gear is shifted to slow down, not to speed up. When shifting and downshifting are learned, usually driving is easy.

Now consider the following steps for creating coherence within paragraphs.

Repeating Key Words

Repeating **key words** that refer to the topic idea and direction is the easiest way to create coherence in a paragraph. You may want to list words that come to you or refer to a dictionary or thesaurus for variations of the key words. You do not want to look for more complicated words but simply for other common words that will repeat the topic idea without repeating the same word over and over.

The key words in the topic sentence are "learning how to shift a car" and "difficult." Here are other words that could replace "learning how to shift a car":

shifting

changing speeds

changing gears

slowing down

procedure

Other words could replace "difficult":

hard

frustrating

demanding

complicated

tiring

bothersome

Here is the revised paragraph showing how new key words were added:

Learning how to drive a car with a stick shift is difficult. The location of each

gear and the best speed to drive in for each gear must be learned. How to push
tricky and frustrating until
in the clutch and change the gear to obtain the best speed can be ~~tricky until~~ the

driver discovers just where the clutch accelerates the gear speed. Bouncing and
this complicated manuever   To make matters more challenging, this
jerking can occur until ~~this maneuver~~ is mastered. ~~This~~ "sweet spot" is different
Though downshifting is bothersome, it
in all cars. ~~Down shifting~~ has to be learned to allow for turns and slowing. The
the procedure is harder because the
clutch and gear speed work together again, but ~~the~~ gear is shifted to slow down, not

to speed up. When shifting and downshifting are learned, usually driving is easy.

Using Time Words and Transitional Words

Special **time words and other transitional words** or phrases add definite meaning to link sentences logically into a coherent whole. Here are some examples of time words and other transitional words that add coherence to the paragraph:

To add something:	also, too, in addition, equally important, furthermore, similarly, again, besides
To show a contrast:	but, yet, however, in contrast to, on the other hand, nevertheless
To give an example:	for example, for instance, thus, in particular, in other words
To compare or show similarity:	similarly, in the same way
To show time sequence:	then, next, first, second, later, finally, previously, afterward, after, yesterday, today, the day (or week or year) before, as, now

To emphasize:	in fact, to repeat
To show space relationship:	above, beyond, below, near, next to, here, there, to the left, to the right, behind, in front of
To acknowledge a point that may be opposite of the one you are making:	although, though, even though, in spite of, no doubt, of course
To summarize:	finally, in conclusion, in summary, consequently, thus, therefore, as a result of, on the whole, to conclude

Here is the revised paragraph after time words and transitional words have been added:

Learning how to drive a car with a stick shift is difficult. The location of each
before changing   *learned first.*
gear and the speed to drive in ~~for~~ each gear must be ~~learned.~~ How to push in the

clutch and change the gear to obtain the best speed can be tricky and frustrating
until after the
~~until the~~ driver discovers just where the clutch accelerates the gear speed.
Furthermore, bouncing
~~Bouncing~~ and jerking can occur until this complicated maneuver is mastered. To

make matters more challenging, this "sweet spot" is different in all cars.
In addition,   *but it*
~~Though~~ downshifting is bothersome, ~~it~~ has to be learned to allow for turns and
    In the same way, the
slowing. ~~The~~ clutch and gear speed work together, but the procedure is harder

because the gear is shifted to slow down, not to speed up. When shifting and

downshifting are learned, usually driving is easy.

Using Pronouns and Words That Point Out

Pronouns, including possessive pronouns, **and words that point out** also create coherence. Possessive pronouns are words like "our," "my," "his," or "their." Words that point out are "this," "that," "these," and "those."

Now look again at the fully revised paragraph. (All the words that point out are highlighted in bold italics.) This paragraph is now coherent.

Learning how to drive a car with a stick shift is difficult. The location of each gear and the speed to drive before changing each gear must be learned first. How to push in the clutch and change the gear to obtain the best speed can be tricky and frustrating until after the driver discovers just where the clutch accelerates the gear speed. Furthermore, bouncing and jerking can occur until ***this*** complicated maneuver is mastered. To make matters more challenging, ***this*** "sweet spot" is different in all cars. In addition, downshifting is bothersome, but ***it*** has to be learned to allow for turns and slowing. In the same way, the clutch and gear speed work together, but the procedure is harder because the gear is shifted to slow down, not to speed up. When shifting and downshifting are learned, usually driving is easy.

Revise the following paragraphs by adding key words derived from the topic idea, time and other transitional words, and pronouns that make each paragraph a coherent whole.

Paragraph 1

As part of their job, they

Pharmacy technicians have very responsible jobs. ~~They~~ must make sure that the

drugs and supplies in the pharmacy are stocked in the right place and in the right order.
When patients come into the store, technicians
~~Technicians~~ are responsible for typing prescriptions into the computer database and
In addition, technicians   *However, they*
filling prescriptions. ~~Technicians~~ are often asked to count out and pour drugs. ~~They~~
then
must check with the pharmacist, who verifies that they have the right medications and
Also, technicians   *be trusted to*
have put the correct dosage into the bottles. ~~Technicians~~ must not counsel customers

or give advice on prescription medications or even over-the-counter drugs. Having
that are efficient, capable, and reliable
technicians ensures that the pharmacists and interns are free to do their jobs well.

Paragraph 2

The spacious swings

A small park can be a haven for children. ~~Swings~~ are big and sturdy so
safely soar   *Children love to feed the ducks that*
children can ~~swing~~, seemingly to the tops of trees. ~~Ducks~~ swim close to the
At the same time, older
shore to eat whatever the small visitors bring. ~~Older~~ children canoe through
peaceful, rippling water while others safely
~~rippling water. Others~~ stand or sit at the edges of the lake and throw out fishing
are content as they
lines complete with worms. The children wait for some hungry fish to bite the
They feel comfortable, knowing their parents are relaxing
hook, ~~Parents of the children relax~~ under the shade of nearby trees. Here the world

feels safe as children enjoy spending time at this sanctuary with their families.

Paragraph 3

Prepackaged, microwavable dishes are a way of life for people on the go.
For example, prepackaged
~~Prepackaged~~ entrees for babies help working mothers serve nutritional meals to the
soon learn to
small members of the family. Older children can microwave their own dinners.

then

When Mom and Dad are unable to prepare lunch, children can heat up such items

Also, entrees

as spaghetti and meatballs or chicken and rice. ~~Entrees~~ that appeal to the whole

family can be stored in the freezer and popped into the microwave while the cook

throws together a quick salad and sets the table. Chicken and dumplings,

of these dishes

vegetable lasagna, or pork back ribs are a few of the many varieties available.

In addition, evening

~~Evening~~ snacks can include popcorn in minutes or milk shakes that defrost in

Therefore, people

seconds. ~~People~~ with a microwave oven no longer have a reason for skipping a meal.

Paragraph 4

Before starting, the

Driving a school bus is a job with many responsibilities. ~~The~~ driver may be

A dependable driver knows that tires

expected to make all the safety checks to see that the bus is in top shape. ~~Tires all~~

Another important safeguard is making sure

need to be checked for proper inflation. ~~Making sure~~ all the children are safely

to   *In addition, if*

seated ~~helps~~ prevent falls and tumbles. ~~If~~ seat belts have been installed, all children

In fact, the

should be properly secured. ~~The~~ driver needs to be alert at all times to prevent

who ride the bus.

accidents and injuries. Responsible people ensure safety for schoolchildren.

Creating Coherence Between Paragraphs

Just as the sentences within each paragraph must be connected smoothly, so the paragraphs within an essay must be connected smoothly to each other. Each paragraph must flow logically to the next one.

When you write an essay, you can use the three previously explained methods for connecting ideas: **key words** (repeated topic words or ideas), appropriate **time** and **transitional words** and **phrases**, and **pronouns.**

Read the following thesis sentence and topic sentences for an essay on a family's experiences at the beach. Notice the coherence provided by the words in bold type: key words (*kw*), time (*t*), other transitional words (*tw*), and pronouns (*p*).

Thesis sentence:

My family and I always look forward to going to the beach at Oceanside because of the many smells, sights, and sounds that abound there.

Topic sentence for the first support paragraph:

>   *p*   *kw*   *p*
> As soon as **we** walk onto the **beach, we** notice a multitude of both good and
>
> *kw*
> bad **smells.**

Topic sentence for the second support paragraph:

>   *tw*   *kw*   *kw*   *p*   *tw*   *kw*
> **In addition to fragrances** and **odors, we also** observe unusual **sights**—
> especially people.

Topic sentence for the third support paragraph:

>   *kw*   *kw*   *tw*   *kw*
> Our **memories** of the **beach also** include a whole array of **sounds**—from
> small, insignificant ones to the pounding roar of the waves.

Concluding sentence:

>   *t*   *t*   *p*   *kw*
> **Over the years, whenever we** have stayed at **Oceanside,** we have come away
>
>   *tw*
> with very special memories of our vacations **there.**

Exercise 2

Using the thesis sentences given, construct three topic sentences with key words
that provide transition. Then construct an appropriate concluding sentence.

1. Even though visiting a zoo can be educational and relaxing, it can be expensive.

   Topic sentence 1:

   _____

   _____

   _____

   Topic sentence 2:

   _____

   _____

   _____

   Topic sentence 3:

   _____

   _____

   _____

Concluding sentence to begin the last paragraph:

_____

_____

_____

2. Neighborhood parks provide places to play, picnic, exercise, and read.

Topic sentence 1:

_____

_____

_____

Topic sentence 2:

_____

_____

_____

Topic sentence 3:

_____

_____

_____

Concluding sentence to begin the last paragraph:

_____

_____

_____

Exercise 3

Read this essay and add coherence in the form of key words, time and other transitional words, and pronouns.

During my morning jog, I stopped and talked to a man who was carefully tending his garden. When I expressed interest in the luscious garden, he replied, "I got over six five-gallon buckets of strawberries alone this summer." I was taken by surprise because the strawberry patch was only about six feet by five feet. His green-bean vines that were growing along the fence were loaded with long, healthy beans, and I could only wonder how many of those he had harvested. Seeing his garden made me think of all the benefits that gardening can bring to anyone who is willing to put in the time and effort. Although having a small garden can be hard work, it

can result in pleasure and savings.

The benefits of a garden *, however,* do not come without work. ~~S/he~~ *First, the gardener* must select a
location for the garden. *After the plot of ground is selected, it* ~~It~~ needs to be dug out and loosened. ~~Sawdust,~~ *Next, sawdust,* peat, and
fertilizer mixed and added will allow the seeds to grow easily. ~~Growing~~ *Just as important, growing* instructions
need to be followed when the seeds are planted. ~~The~~ *Finally, the* garden must be watered,
weeded, and debugged daily. Watering at the correct time of day *sometimes can be difficult, but* is necessary.
Keeping the weeds to a minimum *is hard work but* makes the garden vegetables stronger. A good

gardener prepares a good place and watches the plants as if they were helpless,

defenseless creatures.
With a little dirt, water, and sunshine, a
~~A~~ garden can bring many pleasures. The sight of small sprigs reaching up
through the soil toward the sun gives the *warm* feeling of capturing a small part of nature
and getting in touch with the earth. *the enjoyment of* What greater satisfaction is there for the
gardener than to know that s/he has used the elements to produce food? *Usually more* ~~More~~ than
enough is produced, and the gardener can *proudly* share the crisp flavor of fresh produce
with a neighbor. *delighted* In view of the much-publicized use of insecticides on commercial

produce, the gardener can use natural combatants such as ladybugs or praying

mantises or ingenuity to preserve the vegetables *, and feel comfortable* knowing the products from the

garden are healthy. A garden can be the source not only of food and pride, but also

of peace of mind.
After the initial work is done, having
~~Having~~ a small garden to bring in fresh vegetables provides a savings. Each

year grocery prices slowly creep up on such items as lettuce and tomatoes.
For example, tomatoes
~~Tomatoes~~ that last year cost 98 cents a pound *now* cost $1.49. *Likewise, lettuce* ~~Lettuce~~ is sold at
99 cents a pound instead of 99 cents a head. ~~The~~ *These* gradual price *increases make* ~~increase makes~~
one wonder if the consumer will ever see the end. *The savings are easy to see because a* ~~A~~ package of tomato or lettuce

seeds costs about $1.29 total, and these seeds can provide enough tomatoes and lettuce

for an entire summer. *Moreover, extra* ~~Extra~~ vegetables can be frozen or canned to provide a year-

round supply of fresh food. *Additional savings occur when surplus* ~~Surplus~~ vegetables can be sold to bring in extra money. *The gardener also saves money by trading* ~~Trading~~ produce with other gardeners *to avoid* ~~avoids~~ buying so much at the grocery store.

Gardens can add much-needed pocket change and give the *positive* feeling of defeating the

inflationary war.

Work, time, and patience ~~One~~ can transform a tiny seed into baskets of delicious, healthy food. By

gardening, a person can experience a miracle of nature and can save money at the

same time. *Though a* ~~A~~ person may not be able to get thirty gallons of strawberries in a five-

by-six plot of ground, ~~but~~ that same person may be able to find *satisfaction and* happiness, knowing

his/her *hard* work is being rewarded.

Collaborative Activity

Read the essay by Cynthia L. Vinzant (on page 328 of this unit), and, in groups of four, evaluate two paragraphs for coherence. Mark the words or phrases that provide coherence. Return to the class as a whole and share your findings.

Part 2

Something to Think About, Something to Write About

Professional Essay to Generate Ideas for Writing

Harley a Bad Word to Say

Patrick Haas, *English instructor and perennial searcher for the fountain of youth, Glendale Community College*

1   As was always the case when I rode my Harley, the words of a well-known classic rock-n-roll tune played in my head. It was January 3, 1995, and I was on my Harley running a few errands on a cool but sunny day in Phoenix, Arizona. As I prepared to exit the parking lot of a store on the corner of two very busy streets, I rolled to a stop and looked to my left. A city bus had just stopped to let some passengers off, so I

said to myself, "Pat, you've got to be very careful pulling out since you can't see around the bus until you're almost in the roadway." With this thought in mind, I released the clutch and began moving forward. In a moment, I knew I had gone too far, too quickly. I sensed more than saw the car approaching from my left. I swerved to my right as far as I could. My memory of what happened next is sketchy at best. I felt a strong burst of air as the car sped by. At about that same instant, I felt a slight bump. The next thing I remembered was awakening flat on my back, in the road, with my left leg pinned painfully between the front fork and the gas tank of my Harley. Though I would rather forget this incident, what will stay with me forever was the compassion of the strangers who stopped to help me, the patience I learned, and the love of my family and friends.

2   As I lay pinned by my Harley, people suddenly began appearing out of nowhere. A man leaned over and said, "Take it easy, buddy. You'll be fine." I know I looked at this man, but I can't remember his face. A lady came to me and said, "I'm a nurse. Lie still. An ambulance is on the way." I don't remember her face either. About this time, I became aware of the crushing pain around my left knee. As I tried to sit up, I called out, "My leg—I think I've broken my leg." Some person or persons whom I do not recall at all must have helped pull me out of the wreckage because the crushing sensation eased as I was placed flat on my back. In what seemed just a few minutes, the ambulance arrived, and I was on my way to a local hospital. As a citizen of Phoenix, the sixth-largest city in the United States, I was as doubtful as anyone of other people's compassion. However, since the accident, one thought I have had again and again is how nice it was that so many people stopped and offered their assistance through kind words and gestures. I learned on that day that my fellow Phoenicians are much more compassionate than I had ever suspected.

3   In the months that followed my accident, I was to learn a great deal about patience. As a result of the accident, I ended up in the hospital for four days. I had two very serious blood clots in my left leg, which caused it to turn a very nasty-looking grey-black color. While in the hospital, I noticed a pain in my right side. When the doctor examined this, he discovered a blood clot in my right lung. My destiny for the next six months was set. I was on blood-thinning drugs for the entire time I was in the hospital. I also had to stay on another blood thinner for six months after I left the hospital. Because of the danger of hemorrhaging while on the blood thinners, I was forced to curtail activities that might cause any serious bruises, cuts, or abrasions. I even had to shift from a safety razor to an electric razor. Since I am a jogger, this inactivity bothered me physically, mentally, and emotionally. It was weeks before the doctor permitted my return to the fitness center, and then I was only allowed to ride a stationary bicycle. This proved to be very boring and caused my left leg to swell, especially around my ankle. The doctor assured me on my weekly visits that this was normal, but he also warned me not to overdo my exercising. While this was all very frustrating to me, I eventually began to get adjusted to my restrictions, and I was able to work my way through my rehabilitation. The seven months that passed between my accident and my final release from my doctor really tried my patience time and time again.

4   After the accident, I wondered how my family, especially my wife, would react. Soon, however, I learned how important my family and friends were at this time. As I rode to the hospital in the ambulance, the paramedic asked if there was anyone he could notify once we reached the hospital. I told him my wife's phone number, but I asked him, when he called, if he could please tell my wife that I was okay. My wife had ridden with me on my Harley just once, and then she had nothing to do with it. She saw it as a very dangerous means of transportation, and she was not at all in favor of my riding on the streets of Phoenix. Through my days in the hospital and my weeks

and months of rehabilitation, my wife never once said anything negative about what had happened. I know she was angry and upset, but she took care of me and made me feel as comfortable as possible. My children were also a blessing. My oldest daughter was especially traumatized by this accident since one of her friends in her high school class had just lost her father, and this brush with fate was almost too much for her to deal with, but each day my children made the trip to the hospital to see me and wish me well. They also made a very large get-well card and brought it to me in the hospital. Their love for me was very clear, and this made me feel blessed. My friends showed their love by dropping by the hospital for visits, phoning me both in the hospital and at home once I was released, and by offering to help my wife if she needed anything. This outpouring of support was very touching, and I felt very comforted knowing that I had such caring friends who were willing to help my family and me in our hour of need. Their love helped me to overcome the consequences of my motorcycle accident.

5   Having a motorcycle accident helped to bring into focus some very important factors in my life that I once took for granted. I found that total strangers were not as callous as I thought, but rather that they would stop and help me, someone they had never seen before. I learned that I could be patient with myself when I needed to be. And more importantly, I felt the outpouring of love from my family and friends and realized that they are truly blessings. I still love to ride my motorcycle and feel the wind in my face, and I even go on weekend rides, but I never venture onto streets unless I have visibility on all sides.

Collaborative Writing Project: Working and Learning Together

To start your next essay assignment, work in groups of three or four to discuss one or more of the following quotations. Then, keeping "Harley a Bad Word to Say" in mind, discuss ideas that will help you develop a thesis sentence.

Quotations: Additional Ideas on Kindness and Gratitude

"The gift is to the giver and comes/back most to him—/it cannot fail."
Walt Whitman

"We didn't think twice about helping that boy. I just thought of him as someone else's child. If you were in that situation, what would you do?" *Denise Terry*

"When you see misery in your brother's face, let him see mercy in yours."
Anonymous

"Gifts travel far in the hands of giving people." *Anonymous*

"Giving is a way to honor receipt of past kindness." *Andrew Jacobs Jr.*

"Heroes are just ordinary folk who seek to render service to humanity." *Anonymous*

"It is more blessed to give than to receive." *Bible*

"Mistakes are a fact of life. It is the response to the error that counts."
Nikki Giovanni

"To bring up a child in the way he should go, travel that way yourself once in a while." *John Billings*

"When I was a boy of fourteen, my father was so ignorant I could hardly stand to have the old man around. But when I got to be twenty-one, I was astonished at how much he had learned in seven years. (It never occurs to a boy that he will someday be as dumb as his father.)" *Mark Twain*

Writing Assignment

1. Recall the qualities of someone who has helped you.

2. Why do people volunteer in hospitals, in schools, in jails, or in charitable organizations?

3. What have you done to help someone? (elderly person, child, parent, or other relative)

4. In what way can people restore a relationship with their parents or children?

5. What can be done to help people who have experienced a tragic event?

6. How can husbands and wives improve their relationships?

7. What can people do to improve a relationship with someone outside the family?

8. What are the rewards of giving to other people?

9. Discuss your family's tradition of gift giving.

10. How is the value of a gift determined?

Working Together

1. Choose a topic from the list above. Work with two other people who want to write on the same topic. Brainstorm, and continue to discuss the ideas generated by the previous article and quotations.

2. As you have done in the past, work together, but record ideas so that each of you can form your own thesis sentence.

3. Exchange thesis sentences. Check for previewed subpoints that are parallel, equal to each other (coordinate), and **not** overlapping. Be prepared to share thesis sentences with your instructor and the class.

Working Individually

This time, along with the other skills you have practiced, focus on strong **coherence** in your essay. This means that as you draft your essay, put in appropriate transition words (from the list in this unit) and key words or variations of them from the thesis sentence.

1. Draft each part of your essay carefully. Write an introduction, the support paragraphs to explain and clarify each previewed point in your thesis sentence, and a strong conclusion.

2. As you revise each support paragraph, check to see if your topic sentence includes the key word (or a variation of it) from the topic and direction as well as the previewed point. These repeated words create needed **coherence between** paragraphs, helping the parts of your essay flow smoothly.

3. Also, as you revise support paragraphs, be sure that you have linked each sentence directly to the one before it and after it. This will create coherence **within** each paragraph. One of the easiest ways to create a smoothly

connected paragraph is to use clear **pronouns** and other **transition** words that link your thoughts into a seemingly effortless flow of ideas.

4. Be prepared during peer review to find these words that create clear links **between** and **within** paragraphs.

5. In the conclusion, restate the main idea, but use words that are not exactly the same as those in your original thesis sentence. You may also want to refer to the hook you used in the introduction. In this way, you can bring a well-thought-out unity to your paper.

Peer Review

This activity will help you focus on **coherence.** Use a highlighter as well as a pen or pencil. Exchange essays with another person, and read each paper aloud. Then analyze each essay.

1. Read the introduction again. Find the **hook,** the **transition,** and the **thesis sentence.** (If you cannot find any one of the parts, suggest some revision.) Underline the thesis sentence. Then decide if the transition adequately explains how the hook relates to the thesis sentence. A strong introductory paragraph sets the stage for good coherence.

2. In the thesis sentence, highlight the main idea and each subpoint that will appear in a support paragraph. Remember that the words for the main idea and subpoint are **key words.**

3. Choose one support paragraph, and check it in a detailed analysis:

   Underline the topic sentence. Highlight the key word(s) from the thesis sentence. In the topic sentence, highlight any other words that link to the paragraph immediately before it.

   Then go through each sentence in the support paragraph and highlight every word or phrase you can find that directly links each sentence to the next. Look for the time-signal words, repeated key words, and clear pronouns.

   If you cannot find many of these, discuss with the author how some change in wording might make the flow of ideas smoother.

   Be sure the ideas are in logical order with no gaps in thought.

   Check for a concluding sentence to bring closure to the paragraph.

4. Choose a different support paragraph, and check for sentence variety. Highlight a compound or complex sentence.

5. Check for transition in the conclusion. Highlight the word(s) that signal closure to the reader. Underline the sentence or sentences that restate the main idea. If the conclusion does not refer to the hook in the introductory paragraph, decide if the conclusion can be strengthened by doing so.

6. Finally, check for any problems in subject-verb agreement, verb tense, point of view, and sentence structure.

Part 3

Essays for Discussion and Analysis

Student Writing

Home: Just How Safe Is It?

Cynthia L. Vinzant, *student*

1   According to an article in *The Front Page*, "An estimated four of five sexual abuse victims know their abusers, who often are their fathers, mothers, uncles, grandparents, clergy, or family friends." This statement by Ward Harkay is supported by the statistics, which show that one of every three girls and one of every four boys are sexually molested before the age of eighteen. To begin addressing the enormous problems associated with sexual abuse of children, Americans must recognize the denial that fuels it, educate themselves on the problems that victims develop, and develop programs that will prevent further abuse as well as aid those already afflicted.

2   Denial fuels the cycle of sexual abuse of children. Reports, statistics, and case histories have proven, with shocking detail, the existence of such crimes. And yet the cycle continues, passing from one generation to the next. In one case history, a woman reported that she was sexually molested by nine members of her family by the age of fifteen. During five years of recovery work, including therapy and twelve-step programs, she discovered many more sexual abuse victims within her family. All four siblings that she was raised with, two girls and two boys, were molested as well. Her mother also reported having been molested as a child. One of her brothers in turn molested a niece and nephew. Yet the majority of her family members continue to minimize or deny the sexual abuse cycle within the family. Once at the age of fourteen, she said she reported the abuse to juvenile authorities. Besides not believing her, they sent her back home assuming that it was a safe place. This is only one of many case histories where denial allowed the abuse to continue.

3   To cope with sexual abuse, victims often develop survival skills that can lead to further emotional and mental problems. While aging chronologically, emotionally they remain fixed at their current developmental level. Not having been protected, trusted, or validated, they develop several defense mechanisms in order to survive their traumatic childhood. One common defense mechanism of such victims is depersonalization. In depersonalization, the victim temporarily experiences loss of reality including "feelings of being in a 'dreamlike state,' 'out of the body,' 'mechanical,' or 'bizarre' in appearance," according to *Basic Concepts of Psychiatric–Mental Health Nursing*. It may take years or even decades for such victims to get to the place where they can reach out for help in dealing with their problems.

4   Programs and treatment centers are clearly needed not only to aid those already afflicted but also to prevent further abuse as well. Perhaps such programs could be modeled after the widespread drug-prevention programs currently sweeping the country. Children who chant, "Just say no" to drugs could also be taught to chant, "Just don't touch" to perpetrators. Prevention has always been the most effective weapon against crime. However, emergency centers and foster home care can provide support services to abusive families within the community. Treatment centers must be concerned with the entire family unit, not just the victims of abuse.

5   Since sexual abuse is so widespread, it is imperative that individuals become united in a mass effort to wake themselves from the perpetuating circle of denial.

They must take aggressive action to assist those already victimized and implement effective prevention programs to protect the children of tomorrow from becoming sexual-abuse victims.

Understanding Words
Briefly define the following words as they are used in the above essay.

1. perpetrators   *offenders*

2. imperative   *urgent, necessary*

3. perpetuating   *constant*

Answers to Unit 6 are on pages 23–24 in the Instructor's Manual.

Questions on Content

1. How does the author think denial harms families?

2. How do victims cope with sexual abuse?

3. What will provide support services to abusive families?

Questions on Form

1. Give examples of good sentence variety.

2. Give examples of words or phrases that create coherence.

3. What is the purpose of this essay?

Education

Jan-Georg Roesch, *student*

1   Only fifteen months ago I was sitting in a typical German classroom daydreaming through the lecture and hoping for a miracle that my grades would improve. All the help I got came too late because I had already wasted too much time in the first semester. My goal was to finish *Abitur* and then continue going to a university. The goal just seemed to vanish in thin air, and how was I going to do my master's degree? Fortunately, my father was going to retire soon, and plans were made to make a permanent settlement in Phoenix because my grandmother lived there. Hence, I was given the opportunity to continue my educational goal in America, skip the draft in Germany, and enjoy the warm Arizona climate.

2   In Germany, I would have to complete thirteen years of school and attain the diploma in order to go to a university. I had completed twelve of the thirteen years and didn't have enough points to get into the last year. Furthermore, the conditions I was facing made it more or less impossible for me to repeat the class, and I did not want to take the risk of losing the prediploma. The only solution left was to come to the United States and try to finish my educational goal. Again, I was very fortunate to have friends in Phoenix who made my entrance into Arizona State University very easy. Although I knew that much of what I had learned over the past two years was going to be repeated, I accepted the challenge because I did not really have a choice.

3   Yet, finishing the educational goal was not the only reason for my coming here. At the age of eighteen every male teenager who had completed school was picked for the draft. This meant I had to serve for fifteen months and receive a wage of $70 a month. The alternatives were either to sign up for a longer period, either for four or six years, or do social work for the same period. I was not too crazy about the idea of serving fifteen months; I felt that it was a waste of time because the program does not offer any real educational use. Of course, the service does provide people with good educational service; however, I would have to sign up for a longer time period.

4   Finally, my last criterion for coming to Phoenix was the warm climate. I had spent over eighteen years of my life living in countries where the climate was mild, damp, wet, and sometimes very cold. Having the flu five times a year was not uncommon

and seemed more or less to be part of daily life. In addition, it would sometimes rain for days nonstop and flood all the rivers, which normally resulted in flooding the cellar or creating total chaos in the streets. The so-called summer was usually brief. The warm weather might have stayed for two weeks when the next rain clouds were already expected. The winter period was mainly characterized by residents watching tourists streaming out to see warmer places or sitting next to the warm fireplace and sipping hot chocolate.

5   It is close to one year now since I moved, and I do not regret living the eighteen years in countries with colder climates. However, I also feel that moving to Phoenix will bring me new experiences that I could not have encountered if I had stayed in Germany. I will learn new cultural traits and behaviors that differ from the European heartland. Yet, most important of all, I can achieve my educational goals that I once dreamed of fifteen months ago.

Understanding Words

Briefly define the following word as it is used in the above essay.

   1. criterion   *standard, rule, or test by which a judgment can be formed*

Questions on Content

1. Why could the author not go to a university in his native country?

2. What were two reasons for his move to Phoenix?

3. How long has he lived in the United States?

Questions on Form

1. What key words from the thesis sentence does the author use for coherence in each topic sentence?

2. What is the transition that links paragraphs 2 and 3?

3. How does the author use time words to provide coherence in paragraph 4?

Never Again Homeless

Kimberly Adair, *student*

1   As I sat at the bus stop, I saw an old woman picking food out of a garbage can. My heart was so heavy that I had to go into my workplace and purchase her some food. After I handed her the meal, I wondered how she got herself into this situation. Never would I have imagined that I would be in her shoes, but a year later I was. I married at seventeen and left my parents' home to venture out into newly wed life. Shortly after my marriage, I contracted a bad case of pneumonia, but unfortunately my employer had no sympathy for me. I lost my job, and it wasn't more than a month until I lost my home and a bit later my husband. It seemed like a nightmare, but it wasn't. It was real, and it was happening to me. As the days went by, my life changed dramatically. When I was homeless, I experienced many situations, such as feeling unstable, being hungry, and experiencing the dangers of living on the street.

2   Being in an unstable environment, for me, was like not being given the chance to have a future. I had grown up protected from the elements of the outside world, only to find myself thrust into homelessness. I worked temporary day jobs in order to buy food, but still I did not make enough money. I was unable to get a permanent job because no one wanted to hire someone who didn't have an address. Soon I had to sell my car just to survive. I lived from one place to the next, in parks, behind buildings, and in trees. I never knew where I was going to be sleeping the next night. I seldom had a way to take baths or wash my clothes. Once in a while, when I had enough money I could afford to go to the public swimming pool where I could shower

and wash all my clothing in the showers. I never had enough time just to relax or go swimming. During this time of uncertainty, I was truly trapped with no hope for the future. I was unable to get a job, had no place I could call home, and was constantly moving from place to place. Life was getting worse.

3   The fact that I was facing hunger on a daily basis made things unbearable. Not being able to find employment meant not having any money to purchase food. I soon felt the burning in my stomach and the pain of my body craving nourishment. I had never known how badly the pain of not eating really felt. I would sit in one spot with my arms wrapped tightly around my midriff. Putting pressure on it would make the pain seem lighter. Once in a while I would collect cans for the refund money so that I could eat a sandwich. I would also frequent small restaurants and offer to help in any way possible. Every now and again I could earn food for my work. I quickly learned what time all these restaurants threw away their leftovers. I waited for them to dump their leftover food, then rushed over, and grabbed it before anyone saw me. I started visiting churches where they help the homeless. I would get a sandwich or two a day. I guess after a long time of being hungry my body got used to it. I started not to have hunger pains anymore. If I didn't eat for a day or two, it wouldn't bother me. I did end up moving to rougher parts of town because that's where most of the places were that assisted people like me. I received more food, but I was putting my life on the line at the same time.

4   The dangers of living on the street became very real to me for the next ten months. My idea of what the world was like was shattered by reality. The hazards I faced were like none I could have imagined. The worst danger of all was not hunger or instability, believe it or not; it was people. In school I was taught about plant and animal life; I learned that humans were considered to be animals. I really never thought of people as a kind of animal until I became a vagrant. When I lived on the streets, I had to use my animal instincts to survive the exposure. I learned quickly that people on the street could sense fear much as a dog does. If I showed fear, I would become easy prey to an unknown evil. Once I fell victim to a man who sold women to make his living. I didn't know his friendship was a ploy to catch me off guard. I was beaten and tied up in an alley for not cooperating with him. I can still remember that I was beaten so badly I could barely feel the pain any more. I kept drifting off, and my thoughts were that I was dying. Time did escape me since I still don't remember how long I was there. An old man untied me and just ran off without saying anything. I learned humans would take my life if I were careless enough to let my guard down. I experienced more abuse and learned more about living on the streets. I was determined not to live like that any more, and I was determined that my street-living days would be over. I went door to door offering my skills of housecleaning and live-in baby-sitting. I was employed by an elderly couple who were winter visitors. I was finally off the streets and safe.

5   My life changed in those eighteen months I was homeless; I had changed. I was not able to be social with people any more. I always watched my back wherever I went. I still have a sense of that world that follows me every day of my life. I will never live like that again. Being homeless has to be the worst thing that could happen to anyone. Are people really homeless because they want to be? I say no because it could happen to anyone at any time. Can homeless people find a way to get back on their feet? I say yes if the will to survive or have a better life is strong enough. Until society walks in the shoes of a homeless person, they will never understand how all the other homeless people and I lived. When I was homeless, I never knew where I was going to sleep, where my next meal would come from, or if I was going to live long enough to worry about it.

Questions on Content

1. How long was the author homeless?

2. Where did she live?

3. How old was the author when she first became homeless?

Questions on Form

1. What makes the introduction effective?

2. How did the author end the essay with a sense of closure?

3. How does the author create coherence in the last sentence of paragraph 3?

Professional Writing

"I Don't Like What You're Wearing"

David Updike, *English instructor at Roxbury Community College in Boston*

1   My reaction to my 9-year-old son's clothes leaves both of us wondering: what's my problem?

2   My son turned 9 recently, and I am surprised to find myself party to a subtle, low-grade tussle with him over his clothes. In the last few months he has taken up a style of dressing that, for reasons not entirely clear to me, I do not particularly like: large, baggy pants; big sneakers that bear the name of famous young basketball players; any shirt or sweat shirt with writing on it. Hats, too, he loves, and wears constantly—baseball hats, usually, though recently he has become enamored of a blue, camouflage number, pulled tightly onto his head, visor curled ominously around his eyes. No matter which corner of the cluttered closet I throw it into with my private hopes, it always reappears on his head.

3   Attempts to get him to wear shirts without writing on them—nice, simple, collared shirts from the Gap, for example—are all for naught. They remain neatly folded in his top drawer. Nice khaki pants remain untouched for weeks, then months, until, one morning after the usual struggle, he pulls them out and triumphantly announces, "Dad, they don't fit anymore. They're too tight!" (Time is on his side.)

4   The struggle, I realize, is an ancient one, and I am surprised to find myself cast in the role of a doughty Ward Cleaver to the rebellious young Beaver. It's odd, as I've never been held up as a paragon of fashion myself. As a child I tended toward the conservative, and I remember a couple of titanic struggles with my parents over a pair of pants that seemed to me a half inch too short. And I was heartbroken to discover that the blue camping shorts and plaid shirt that I begged my mother to order out of a catalog did not turn me into the cherubic blond boy in the photograph. In college I grew my hair long and took on a look that now I recognize as a precursor to grunge—baggy polyester work pants and ill-fitting coats that I bought at the old-men's store.

5   My wife does not fully share my anxieties about our son's clothes. It was she who caved in and bought him the Iverson sneakers ($69.99) and, in a moment of weakness and flagging judgment, succumbed to the camouflage hat. She is less bothered by the sight of him playing basketball with his hat on sideways, one pants leg halfway up his shin, Iversons barely attached to his feet. But she was on the front lines of a struggle the other day at the mall, where the only coats for sale featured, in large, bold letters, the name of their manufacturer: ADIDAS, NIKE or HILFIGER.

6   Am I actually a cultural conservative dressed in liberal tweed, out of step with the times, nervous that my son is affecting the style of a hip-hop culture that makes me nervous? Is there a racial aspect to my ambivalence? Am I overly sensitive to the remarks of the playground moms who, as we watch our children play basketball, observe, "He's really changed!" followed by meaningful silence? Am I fearful of his going the way of the shy, smiling boys I knew when they were children, and have watched slowly turn

into cigarette-smoking teenagers who glower at me? When I say hello, sometimes, they look up, surprised, and the shy smile of their childhood briefly returns.

7   But what I once took as a largely urban phenomenon clearly is not: we went out to the small town where I grew up, the other day, an hour from the city, and as we played in the yard three or four boys strolled by, their enormous pants billowing like sails in the warm spring wind. I don't want to be an old stick-in-the-mud, but I draw the line at pants trying to slide down the backside. "Dad," he protests, "I have no belt!" Nor do I want my good-looking son turned into an unpaid walking billboard for Nike, or Adidas or Hilfiger. Beyond that, I've probably got some work to do myself, updating my own antiquated and overly mythologized sense of fashion and cultural iconography.

8   The baseball hat, after all, is as American as apple pie, emblematic of virility and a peculiar brand of American male self-satisfaction. The fact that he likes to wear his sideways shouldn't send shivers of dread and alarm down my spine, should it? I was driven from the sport myself in the late 1960s by an overzealous coach who thought he was going to save America from communists by making me get my hair cut. When I did, finally, he said "shorter," and I quit instead.

9   Baseball catchers wear their hats backward, and football players in postgame interviews, and half the male college students in America, drifting around in their smug little packs, looking for a woman or a beer. But sideways? What does it mean? Why does it bother me?

10   "Dad!" my son asks during one of our morning skirmishes, rejected garments strewn around the floor, his hands raised and shoulders shrugged in an eternal gesture of astonishment and dismay. "What's your problem?"

Understanding Words
Briefly define the following words as they are used in the above essay.

1. tussle   *struggle*
2. enamored   *very fond of*
3. ominously   *evilly*
4. naught   *nothing*
5. khaki   *tough, beige-colored fabric*
6. doughty   *brave and determined*
7. paragon   *held up as an example*
8. titanic   *gigantic*
9. cherubic   *sweet and innocent*
10. precursor   *something coming before*
11. flagging   *weakening*
12. succumbed   *gave into*
13. tweed   *rough, thick woolen fabric*
14. ambivalence   *two contrasting ways of feeling*
15. glower   *angrily stare*
16. phenomenon   *something extraordinary, marvelous*
17. billowing   *swelling with air*
18. antiquated   *outdated*
19. mythologized   *imaginary*
20. iconography   *images*
21. emblematic   *symbolic*
22. virility   *manliness*
23. skirmishes   *battles*

Questions on Content

1. What upsets the author about his son?

2. How did the author look and where did he buy his clothes when he was in college?

3. What is the father afraid might be a part of his ambivalence?

Questions on Form

1. In paragraph 2, what word in the topic sentence creates coherence or makes a connection to paragraph 1?

2. What examples support the topic sentence in paragraph 2?

3. How is the author's ambivalence toward the way his son dresses repeated throughout the essay?

Part 4

Mechanics for Effective Writing: Reviewing Punctuation

Objectives

- Review the uses of the comma.
- Learn the proper use of quotation marks.
- Learn the use of the apostrophe.
- Learn the use of underlining.
- Learn the use of parentheses.
- Review ways of marking sentences.

Mastering the art of written communication means being able to use appropriate punctuation. Think of appropriate punctuation as traffic signals guiding you through a city. The traffic signs help you know when to stop or slow down, when to be aware of dangers, when to pause, and when to go on. Without accurate road signs, your journey through the city would be dangerous. Reading compositions with inappropriate or confusing punctuation makes understanding just as risky.

Using Commas

Tests on punctuation are on pages 66–69 in the Test Bank.

Using a comma correctly is *not* a matter of guesswork. If you follow some very simple rules and use commas only when you know the rules, you will be able to use commas correctly.

Uses of Commas

items in a series

introductory expressions

clarity

    identifying and nonidentifying expressions

    interrupters

    misunderstandings

addresses and dates

direct address

Items in a Series

- A comma is used to separate three or more items in a series of words, phrases, or clauses.

A series uses the same grammatical construction—for example, three or more nouns, verbs, phrases, or dependent clauses.

Series of Words

John had a **hamburger, french fries, and a milk shake** for lunch.

Jerry noticed that the dog was **cold, wet, and hungry.**

Books, pens, and papers must be brought to class.

The **blue, yellow, and green** tablecloth is new.

Series of Phrases

People brought aid **to the elderly, to the homeless, and to the sick.**

Playing blackjack, eating Chinese food, and sleeping late in the morning are all activities that Trent enjoys.

The child was guilty of **kicking the nurse, biting the thermometer, and writing on the wall.**

Series of Dependent Clauses

Because the weather turned bad, because the park became crowded, and because we had no more money, we left Disneyland.

I know **why you came, who sent you, and when you will leave.**

The quality of a product is judged by **how long it will last, what it is made of, and who makes it.**

- A comma is *not* used between two words, two phrases, or two dependent clauses that are joined by a coordinating conjunction.

  Randy received a raise in pay and better working hours.

- A comma is *not* used to separate three or more items in a series if a coordinating conjunction is used to separate these items.

  My date told me he did not like my hairstyle or my makeup or my dress.

Exercise 1

Punctuate each sentence by adding the necessary commas. Look for items in a series. If no punctuation is needed, write "None" beside the sentence.

Example:

The material was written to be read to be absorbed and to be understood.

1. My cousin Jessica can go on vacation with us if she can get off work, save enough money, and find a house sitter.

2. While employed at the parks and recreation department, Shane learned sign language, coached a softball team, and worked at the concession stand.

3. Today's auto mechanics must have computer, management, and interpersonal skills.

None 4. The playful mule needs to be fed and watered.

5. College counselors help students solve family problems, build self-esteem, and explore career possibilities.

None 6. My ex-husband did not care for my cooking or my housekeeping or my job.

Exercise 2

Punctuate each paragraph by adding commas where necessary. Look for items in a series. Do not remove any commas already in the paragraphs.

Paragraph 1

Grandparents, aunts, uncles, and cousins gathered for the annual picnic at the park. Together they ate the attractive and well-prepared food, which smelled delicious, tasted great, and satisfied everyone. Then the older children took turns playing volleyball, tennis, and tetherball. Some of the grandparents spread blankets on the green grass for the little ones to take their bottles, to nap, or just to rest. Sometimes the adults, too, fell asleep. Later they took turns riding on the park's train, looking through the model-train exhibits, and reading about the history of trains. Soon, however, everyone returned to the picnic tables to munch on leftovers and talk about last year's picnic.

Paragraph 2

The cavy or guinea-pig breeder took excellent care of her animals. Every morning she gave them pellets, water, carrots, and alfalfa. Every day she also checked the hutches for newborn babies, for any signs of illness, and for any guinea pigs that needed to be put into different cages. Every other day she cleaned each hutch and put in new bedding. Once a week she added vitamin C to their water bottles to make sure there were no pigs with a vitamin-C deficiency. Because she did not want young boars to create problems in the hutches, she separated them at four weeks of age from the females, the older boars, and the young babies. Customers who bought pets from her knew that they had purchased guinea pigs that had healthy coats, were free from disease, and would tame easily.

Introductory Expressions

- Use a comma to set off introductory expressions that are single words, phrases, or dependent clauses.

Single Words

Silently, the man walked through the park.

Effortlessly, the ice skaters performed their new routine.

Phrases

In the morning, I will work in the yard.

Running in the yard, the puppy stumbled over her own feet.

Stung by a bee, the child began to cry.

Dependent Clauses

When I get to the lake, I will put up the tent.

After he got to work, he realized he had left the papers at home.

Because I am not hungry, I will not go out to eat.

Note   If the expression is placed somewhere else in the sentence, it is not set off by a comma.

The man walked **silently** through the park.

I will work in the yard **in the morning.**

I will put up the tent **when I get to the lake.**

Exercise 3

Punctuate each sentence by adding commas where necessary. Look for introductory expressions. If no comma is needed, write "None" beside the sentence.

Example:

Carefully, the father placed the baby in her crib.

1. Without thinking, we locked the keys in our car.
2. In April, the wildflowers bloomed in thick rows along the interstate.
3. As soon as we pack the truck, we can head for the mountains.
4. Fortunately, I was able to pay all my credit card bills.
5. To solve the conflict, the flight attendant seated the passenger by the window.
6. Incidentally, having professional networking skills always helps in a person's career.

Exercise 4

Punctuate each paragraph by adding commas where necessary. Look for introductory expressions first, and then look for items in a series. Do not remove any commas already in the paragraph.

Paragraph 1

People with good credit ratings fear identity theft and spend time every day trying to protect their financial reputation. Usually, they are afraid to throw away anything that contains personal information. For protection, people use cross-cut or confetti shredders to destroy papers with their names, addresses, social security numbers, and any other personal information. In addition, they like to shred unwanted credit card offers that arrive almost daily in the mail. Also, they carefully shred outdated medical records, paid bills, and other personal records no longer needed. In fact, many people spend time every day destroying this information because they do not want anyone to have access to all the personal information needed to open new charge accounts, drain money from their checking account, or apply for large loans in their names. In many cases, people keep in a safe place at home any papers that cannot be destroyed. Though doing these things might become tedious at times, it is a way to make sure that their assets are safe.

Paragraph 2

According to Luigi Ciulla, the biggest challenge he faced when he came to America in 1961 was to find a job. Because he had trouble filling out an application, people would say, "I'm sorry. We don't have a job for you. When you learn to speak English, then we can hire you." Just to work on an assembly line, employees were required to pass IQ tests. Because the tests were in English and because they were timed, it was almost impossible for a person who spoke very little English to pass them. Luigi said that even though some words are learned by studying books, some words just cannot be learned without living in a country. He also said that he didn't know anyone, so it was hard to find people to use as references on application forms. Because he had never worked in this country, he had no references from previous employers either. One other obstacle in finding a job was lack of any "connections." There was no one who could help him "get a foot in the door." He also had to face the reality that many jobs were far away and getting transportation to these jobs was hard. He said, "Even if I knew how to drive, it was hard to pass the written test for a driver's license." That was twenty-nine years ago, and today he is hiring people to work for him in his own business.

Commas for Clarity

The need for a clear set of road signs referred to previously really becomes evident when you want your meaning to be clearly understood by the reader. Knowing for sure whether or not to use commas helps you to write exactly what you mean. As a result, your reader is more likely to understand your meaning right away and not have to reread your sentences several times.

Identifying and Nonidentifying Expressions

- **If an expression is necessary to identify the noun that comes before it, it is called an identifying expression, and no commas are used to set it off.**

    The dogs **that have had their shots** will be allowed in the mall.

    The chickens **that got out of their pen** laid eggs all over the yard.

    The elephant **with twins** is in the next exhibit.

No commas are used because each expression in bold type identifies the noun before it. The expression could not be left out without creating confusion or changing the meaning entirely.

- **If the noun is already specifically identified, the expression that comes after it is nonidentifying, and commas are used to set it off.**

Using commas means that this nonidentifying expression adds more information to the sentence and could be left out without creating confusion. Names (proper nouns) provide specific identification.

    Lester, **who left town yesterday,** took my fishing rod with him.

    Leroy, **my cousin,** will be in town tomorrow.

However, if you put "cousin" first, *no* comma is used because "Leroy" identifies which cousin.

    My cousin Leroy will be in town tomorrow.

Interrupters   A comma is used before and after an expression that is not really a part of the sentence structure. If the word or expression is not part of the basic structure, the expression is probably an **interrupter.** Taking these interrupters out of the sentence still leaves a complete idea. However, these interrupters often serve as transitions and can be necessary for clarity and a smooth flow of ideas.

    Yes, I finished a long time ago.

    I will, **of course,** be on time.

"Yes" and "of course" could be left out, leaving complete sentences, but these interrupters would help these sentences connect more smoothly with others in a paragraph.

Words or Phrases Often Used as Interrupters

as a matter of fact	no
for example	of course
for instance	well
however	yes
nevertheless	

Misunderstandings   In some sentences, commas are necessary to prevent confusion and misunderstanding. Without a comma, the exact meaning of the following sentence is not clear.

Besides Mary Lou Anne is the only experienced driver.

Notice how adding a comma not only makes the meaning clear right away, but also changes the meaning in each sentence.

Besides, Mary Lou Anne is the only experienced driver.

Besides Mary, Lou Anne is the only experienced driver.

Besides Mary Lou, Anne is the only experienced driver.

Exercise 5

Punctuate each sentence by adding commas where necessary. Look for nonidentifying expressions, interrupters, and possible misunderstandings. If no comma is needed, write "None" beside the sentence.

Example:

None   **The employee who received the award has a special parking space.**

Zebras, on the other hand, are feisty.

1. Patches, who is my favorite cat, came to my house as an orphan.

2. The book is, I believe, the leading authority on genetics.

3. Rochester, however, is known for its cool summers.

4. My brother Jim, as a matter of fact, lives in Aspen during the winter months.

5. For instance, Steve is an expert plumber.

6. Reyna looked, without expression, at the shocking film on abortion.

7. The museum was filled with outstanding exhibits, some more valuable than others.

None   8. The girl who is a gymnast is from Salt Lake City.

Exercise 6

Punctuate each paragraph by adding commas where necessary. Look first for interrupters, nonidentifying expressions, and expressions that can only be understood with commas. Then look for items in a series and introductory expressions. Do not remove any commas already in the paragraph.

Paragraph 1

The sign reads "No skating, biking, running, or loud music." A granite wall progressively emerges from the ground. From one-sixteenth of an inch and one name, the wall grows to one-half inch, then to a foot. Two names appear, then three, five, ten. With no logical mathematical sequence, the names increase on the wall until at midpoint it reaches approximately eight feet tall with hundreds of names tightly embedded one after another. The time depicted by the wall was, of course, the 1960s, and the names represent the soldiers killed or missing in Southeast

Asia during the Vietnam War. The visual representation of heartfelt American deaths turns the tourist chatter to silence. Experiencing the Vietnam Veterans Memorial it seems makes visitors realize the sacrifices of American youth.

Paragraph 2

The trend of the 1990s to rely heavily on "disposables" has created a throwaway society. Everywhere we look trash that has to be disposed of is piling up. Americans litter the countryside with plastic aluminum cans and glass bottles. At home disposable plates cups plastic ware and of course diapers are filling the plastic bags that must be transported to the local landfill. At hospitals paper gowns disposable thermometers towels used in surgery and miles of plastic tubing cannot be resterilized and reused and as a result are being sent to special landfills for medical wastes. Whereas it takes many years for the paper products to break down in the landfills scientists predict that the plastics will take several hundred years to break down. Styrofoam especially takes an inordinately long time to degrade. These nonbiodegradable plastics are petroleum-based and keep us importing oil to make them. Making aluminum cans likewise uses up our natural resources. Not only does it use up natural resources to make new plastic products aluminum cans and bottles, but it takes energy to manufacture these products. Reusing aluminum cans and glass bottles will save resources and energy. Recycling can help cities and towns that are filling up their landfills and running out of room to construct more of them. Fortunately we as Americans are making an effort to reverse the trend and use products more than once before throwing them away.

Addresses and Dates

- **A comma is used to set off the name of a city, county, state, or zip code in a sentence. There is, however, no comma *between* the state and zip code.**

  His work in **Phoenix, Arizona,** was of monumental value to all.

  Jason's home at 2482 North 16th Street, **Phoenix, Arizona 85521,** burned to the ground.

- **A comma is used to set off the month, day, and year in a sentence. However, when the day is omitted, a comma is not used.**

  On **June 4, 2004,** I fell in love.

  I went to Rocky Point in **July of 1999.**

  The company opened for business in **November 2003.**

Direct Address

- **Use a comma when you use a name in speaking directly to someone.**

  "**Dave,** will you please finish this work?"

  "When, **Theresa,** do you think this work will be done?"

- **Do not use a comma when you are speaking about someone.**

  Sam wants to try out for the elite soccer team.

Exercise 7

Punctuate each sentence by adding commas where necessary. Look for addresses, dates, and direct address. If no punctuation is needed, write "None" beside the sentence.

None **1.** Jesse worked at that restaurant for fifteen years.

2. Only correspondence sent to 620 Main Street, Akwesasne, New York 13655, will be accepted.

3. On November 8, 2003, the nine black lab puppies were born on my cousin's farm near Loveland, Colorado.

4. In our backyard, May 12, 2004, we celebrated our parents' fiftieth anniversary.

None **5.** July 4th is a national holiday.

6. Jody, when do you plan to leave?

7. What I want to know, Ruby, is how you do your art so well.

8. Address the card to 138 West Maple Drive, Portland, Oregon, 94031.

Exercise 8

Punctuate each paragraph by adding commas where necessary. Look first for addresses and dates. Then look for items in a series, introductory expressions, interrupters, and nonidentifying expressions. Do not remove any commas already in the paragraphs.

Paragraph 1

On September 1, 1939, Germany invaded Poland and started World War II. Beginning in 1940, Hitler invaded Belgium, Luxembourg, Denmark, Norway, and France. On April 9, 1940, the Germans seized Denmark and invaded Norway. Just one month later, on May 10, 1940, Germany invaded Belgium. Just a few days later, on May 14, 1940, the Netherlands surrendered. Because England had treaties with France, she made good her commitment, and on September 3, 1940, Great Britain and France declared war on Germany. On May 26, 1940, the Allied Powers began their heroic evacuation at Dunkirk, a seaport in northern France. By 1940, the entire

European continent was at war. Then on June 22͵1941͵Germany invaded the Soviet Union. On December 7͵1941͵Japan attacked Pearl Harbor͵bringing the United States into the war. By now͵almost all countries in the world were involved in this devastating war.

Paragraph 2

During my childhood͵I moved many times. On July 2͵1968͵my family and I moved to El Paso͵Texas͵where my mother attended the nursing program at the university. When she graduated on June 2͵1971͵we moved to Lubbock͵Texas͵where she got a job working for the hospital there. However͵we moved again in March of 1974 because my mom got a better job. We stayed there for a little over two years, and on November 7͵1976͵we moved to West Frier Drive͵Plainville͵Texas. We stayed in that house for a year and a half but moved for what I hoped would be the last time when my mom remarried on May 14͵1978. But as fate would have it͵only a few months later we moved again, and on October 3͵1978͵we moved to a house in the country.

Using Quotation Marks

- Use quotation marks to enclose the exact words (direct quotation) of a speaker. A comma is used to set the direct quotation off from the rest of the sentence.

    Tom said, **"The house that I like is for sale."**

    "The house that I like," Tom said, **"is for sale."**

However, if you are summarizing or using the word "that," quotation marks are *not* used.

    Tom said **that we could move in tomorrow.**

    Mom said **that we would be going on vacation soon.**

Other Punctuation with Quotation Marks

- Periods and commas are always placed *inside* quotation marks.

    Margarita said, "I want a hot fudge sundae."

    "I want a hot fudge sundae," Margarita said.

- Semicolons are *always* placed *outside* quotation marks.

    Janice said, "I believe we will buy that house"; then she left.

- Question marks and exclamation points are placed inside or outside quotation marks. Place them *inside* if the direct quotation is the question or exclamation.

    Tom asked, "When can we move into the house?"

    Carolyn yelled, "Run for shelter!"

Place them *outside* if the entire sentence is the question or exclamation.

Did Tom say, "We can move in in three weeks"**?**

Quotations Within Quotations

- Single quotation marks are used inside double marks when a quotation exists within another quotation.

  "I heard Keith say, **'Be careful,'** before the board fell," said Stan.

  Stan said, "Before the board fell, I heard Keith say, **'Be careful.'"**

Words or Phrases That Require Special Attention

- Quotation marks or italics are used to set off words that are referred to as words and are not a part of the basic sentence structure.

  When you use the word "**clever,**" use it carefully.

  Try not to use "**very**" too often.

- Quotation marks are sometimes used to set off words that are slang or that are used ironically.

  That was a "**cool**" movie.

  Would you like to drive the "**green bomber**"?

Titles Contained Within Larger Works

- Use quotation marks around the title of any selection that has been published within a larger work. Underline or italicize the name of the larger work.

  "**Learning to See**" is the title of the second chapter in Eudora Welty's book <u>One Writer's Beginnings.</u>

  Milton's "**On His Blindness**" is a poem that has been included in many anthologies.

Using Apostrophes

An apostrophe is used to show ownership. An apostrophe is also used in contractions, which are informal.

Possessive Nouns

- Form the possessive of singular nouns by adding an apostrophe and *-s*.

  Put **John's** book on the **car's** fender.

- Plural nouns that end in *-s* form the possessive by adding just an apostrophe.

  The **books'** edges have been torn.

  The **students'** assignments were all completed on time.

- **Plural nouns that end in any letter other than *-s* form the possessive form by adding an apostrophe and *-s*.**

    The **workmen's** wages were paid by the company.

    The puppy played with the **children's** toys.

Note   Do not confuse a possessive noun with a plural noun that ends in *-s*.

    The **books** (plural noun) have not been torn.
    (The books do not own anything.)

    The **books'** edges (ownership) have not been torn.
    (The edges belong to the books; therefore, an apostrophe is used.)

Possessive Pronouns

- **An apostrophe is *not* used to form the possessive of personal pronouns.**

    His book was left on the floor.

    This book is **hers.**

    It's time for us to look at **its** internal structure.

Note   "**It's**" with an apostrophe is a contraction for "it is." The "**its**" (without an apostrophe) is a possessive pronoun.

However, an apostrophe is used to form the possessive form of indefinite pronouns.

    One's work must be done well.

    He is **everybody's** favorite trumpet player.

    The smoke from **somebody's** barbecue drifted through the neighborhood.

Contractions

- **In contractions, an apostrophe indicates that one or more letters have been left out.**

    He'll have to get there early to get a parking spot.

    That's a nice place to go on vacation.

Using Underlining

- **The title of any piece of writing that has been published by itself should be underlined or put in italics. If it has been published within a larger collection or magazine, use quotation marks.**

    I read the article "Building Solar Homes" that appeared in the <u>Builders' Guide</u>.

    <u>Of Mice and Men</u> is a novel that appeals to many people.

    I enjoy reading <u>New Times</u>.

Using Parentheses

- Parentheses are used to enclose expressions or sentences that are separate from the main thought of the writing. If the entire sentence is set off by parentheses, the end punctuation mark is inside the closing parenthesis. If the expression is part of a sentence, the punctuation is outside the closing parenthesis.

  (The first part needs to be read carefully.)

  Please read all of the first chapter carefully (especially the first part).

Exercise 9

Edit each sentence by adding the necessary punctuation. Look for missing quotation marks, for words showing ownership, and for contractions. Add any other punctuation marks that are needed.

1. I enjoyed reading Leif Enger's novel <u>Peace Like a River</u>.

2. "If Lisa gets a promotion," said Kevin, "she will stay with that company."

3. "You need to get your car's oil changed every 3,000 miles," said Phil, "so that the car will last longer."

4. "Everybody's favorite dessert is homemade ice cream," said Susan's mother.

5. "It's a fact about our dog," said Trudy. "Its nose is a million times more sensitive than ours."

6. The poem "Civics" by Robert Wrigley was published in the March 15, 2004, issue of <u>The New Yorker</u> magazine.

7. <u>The Call of the Wild</u> by Jack London is a survival story about a perceptive dog.

None 8. Keith said that he needs to have his car inspected on his way home from work.

Exercise 10

Punctuate each paragraph. Look first for quotations, words that show ownership, titles, and contractions. Then insert any other commas that are needed. Do not remove any punctuation marks already in the paragraphs.

Paragraph 1

My family's trip to the Grand Canyon northwest of Flagstaff, Arizona, was an unforgettable experience. On June 17, 2003, we boarded the steam train in Williams, Arizona, and headed for the canyon. The train moved across the Kaibab Plateau, which was rolling hills covered with scrub cedar. Once there, we got off the train and walked to Bright Angel Lodge, where we bought a lunch that we enjoyed under a tree at the South Rim of the canyon. There we could see the colorful layers of rock shadows made by clouds and distant evergreen trees. We were impressed by the vastness of the canyon and from the canyons edge we could see part of Bright Angel Trail. Soon however we needed to walk back to the train for the trip back to Williams. Although we were tired we were inspired by what we had seen.

Paragraph 2

Surgeons who operate on patients who are not put to sleep sometimes say things that can upset their patients. They forget that the patients are already anxious about having surgery. When Dr. Madox operated on a patient he tuned in some fast music and jokingly commented There, thats good. It helps me cut faster. When he started sewing up the incision before getting the lab results the patient asked if he had gotten all of the cancer. He replied I hope so. Later on when he was putting in the sutures he stated Oh no the nurse is going to be upset with me when she takes this stitch out. I snipped the ends too close. He then headed for the door and said Ill see you later. The patient asked him if he was coming back, and he just bounced on out the door. Fortunately one of the nurses told the patient that the doctor was going to the lab to get the results. Although the surgery was over the patient dreaded the return visit to the doctors office to have the surgeons "closely snipped" sutures removed.

Paragraph 3

The Epcot Center in Orlando Florida authentically portrays the atmosphere of various countries throughout the world. For example as visitors arrive at the Japanese pavilion they are welcomed by the large red torii gate similar to the one at the Itsukushima shrine at Hiroshima Bay. At they walk closer to the pavilion they can hear traditional Japanese folk melodies. At the same time visitors are drawn to the five-story pagodas distinct architecture. Japanese taiko drummers entertain visitors by performing just as they do in their home festivals. The pagoda and a Japanese castle are surrounded by a beautiful flower garden with well-tended red and yellow flowers and peaceful ponds filled with koi and water lilies. Inside the castle people can stop at the Japanese tea shop or shop for Japanese clothing porcelain dishes bonsai trees paper fans and many other authentic items. At the pavilion's restaurants the smell of Japanese food fills the air and people can purchase full meals or simply get a quick bite at the sushi bar. Visitors to the Epcot Center can then continue to the next exhibits that also feature architecture costumes customs foods and entertainment from around the world.

Punctuating Sentences

To maintain clarity, you must mark your sentences clearly. Though all sentences in a paragraph revolve around one main idea, you must separate ideas into sentences.

Simple Sentences

- **All simple sentences must end with an end mark like a period, exclamation point, or question mark.**

    We went to the store.

    We bought new school clothes.

    We bought the best school clothes ever!

    Would you like to go shopping with us?

Compound Sentences

- **Simple sentences are combined into compound sentences by using a semicolon, a comma and a coordinate conjunction, or a semicolon followed by a conjunctive adverb and a comma.**

    #### A Semicolon

    We went to the store; we bought new school clothes.

    #### A Comma and a Coordinate Conjunction

    We went to the store, and we bought new school clothes.

    #### A Semicolon Followed by a Conjunctive Adverb and a Comma

    We needed new school clothes; therefore, we went to the store.

Compound-Complex Sentences

- **Complex sentences can also be joined to simple sentences by using a comma and a coordinate conjunction or by using a semicolon followed by a conjunctive adverb and a comma.**

    #### A Comma and a Coordinate Conjunction

    After we got paid, we went to the store, and we bought new school clothes.

    #### A Semicolon Followed by a Conjunctive Adverb and a Comma

    Before classes started, we needed to buy new clothes; consequently, we went to the store.

Using all the punctuating skills covered in this section, punctuate each paragraph. Do not remove any punctuation marks already in the paragraphs.

Paragraph 1

During World War II average American citizens experienced many difficulties buying products they wanted or needed. The ability to buy products was restricted by monthly ration stamps for such items as gasoline shoes sugar and meat. Though people had ration stamps meat was especially hard to find because it was put into products like Spam and sent to the soldiers overseas. Even with stamps citizens might not be able to buy the products they wanted. Often the shelves were empty because it seemed as though everything was channeled into Americas defense system. For example shoes were difficult to obtain because the shoe producers needed to supply boots for the army. Likewise cloth was difficult to purchase because fabrics were shipped to factories to make uniforms for the Armed Forces. Jim and Alice Basham who owned their own upholstery business said We could not buy goods to upholster furniture because material was shipped to the Armed Forces. They also said that women were unable to buy nylons because the fabric needed to make them went into making parachutes to be used in the war. Imported items like coffee tea sugar and rubber were scarce. The little rubber that the United States could import went into the production of tires for the Armed Forces. For four years no automobiles were made because all American energies were channeled into the production of military vehicles. American citizens who lived through World War II will always remember those hard times.

Paragraph 2

Summertime offers many opportunities for children of all ages with extra time on their hands. Kids can spend their days at a local boys or girls club, where they can swim play supervised sports and even go on field trips. If there is no boys club or girls club for a small fee they can swim in public pools. There they can join swim teams take swimming lessons or just swim for pleasure. Often libraries that offer summer reading programs are close by. There children can attend story time to hear such storybooks as <u>Bears on Wheels</u> or <u>The Honey Hunt</u> check out videotapes or books or leisurely look through magazines. In the evenings these same children can play Little League baseball or watch other children play ball. If they want to earn extra money they can collect aluminum cans glass plastic or paper to recycle. Also a great potential exists for a lawn service that can bring in money for school. Older children can also earn extra money babysitting or working for the city supervising younger children in recreational programs. Opportunities abound for kids everywhere therefore all they need to do is look around.

Paragraph 3

Transparency of Paragraph 3 is on page 42 of the Instructor's Manual.

Poetry is an art form that can be enjoyed sometimes because of the meaning sometimes because of the way it is written and other times because of both. Can anyone read Walt Whitmans Leaves of Grass without saying That is nice really nice Lines that seem to stick in the mind are often written with a strong message. For instance the lines from Anne Sextons poem The Abortion Somebody who should have been born is gone stay in the mind long after the poem has been read. Whenever the question of abortion arises, these lines are recalled in the mind again and again. Thomas Hood wanted to change labor laws in England. In his poem The Song of the Shirt he wrote With fingers weary and worn,/With eyelids heavy and red,/A woman sat, in unwomanly rags,/Plying her needle and thread—John Milton, married but miserable, spent much effort inserting lines about divorce into his poetry in an attempt to change the laws that forbade divorce. Some poets however do not moralize but simply present things the way they are. James Dickey a well-known American poet wrote of adultery objectively without making any judgment of its wrongness or rightness. On the other hand Joyce Peseroff expresses her ideas in The Hardness Scale a poem in which she seems to be relating a womans feelings about a man who is not such a perfect man. Diane Wakoski writes of revenge in her poem You, Letting the Trees Stand as My Betrayer In this poem nature will pay back someone who loved her and then left her. The meaning is there in these and many other poems but the way they are written makes the lines recur over and over in the readers mind.

Putting It All Together

 Cumulative Unit Exercise

Now that you have studied the format for the longer essay, analyze "A Better Tomorrow."

1. After reading the essay carefully, circle the transition between the hook and the thesis sentence.

2. Underline the topic sentence in each support paragraph and circle the key words that show a clear link to the thesis sentence.

3. Check to see if each paragraph has adequate support and a concluding sentence.

4. A well-written paragraph contains coherence so that the ideas flow smoothly. Read through paragraph 3 carefully and write one of the following transitional words or phrases in each blank. Use each word or phrase only once.

similarly	further discussions show
as time passes	from the beginning of the illness
too	these
prior to the assisted suicides	although different from the MS victim

5. How does this conclusion link to the introductory paragraph?

6. Correct the inconsistent point of view in paragraphs 3, 4, and 5.

7. Correct the sentence-structure errors in paragraph 2.

8. Correct the punctuation in paragraph 4. (8 changes)

A Better Tomorrow

Transparency of uncorrected cumulative exercise is on pages 57–60 of the Instructor's Manual.

1   He is called Doctor Death. In Michigan, he has been tried twice for murder but acquitted both times. He has become the subject of jokes on late-night TV shows. He is Dr. Jack Kevorkian, a physician who helps terminally ill patients take their own lives. He objects to the kind of life some terminally ill patients have described, a lingering, painful life without meaning, without dignity. He has stated that quality of life and the "right to die with dignity" are important for all people. When terminal illness forces patients into circumstances that make not only living but dying with dignity impossible, more and more of these patients, in recent years, have

asked for Dr. Kevorkian to arrange assisted suicides. Estimates exist that he has responded to at least a hundred of these requests. Why have these requests occurred? The reality is that a steadily deteriorating quality of life brought inevitably by a terminal illness creates heartbreaking conditions for the patient, the family, and the health care professionals involved with the patient.

2   Some people think death is far in the future and of little concern, but terminally ill patients consider dying to be a release from hopelessness, pain, and despair. Their lives have no comfort, no joy because daily life has no dignity. In many cases, the patients have lived through many years of gradually diminishing abilities, the patients may face complete paralysis. Once in a while, the person is *. The*
fully conscious but cannot swallow food comes through intravenous feeding tubes. *, so*
In severe instances, a patient may have only head movement and cannot walk or provide self care in any way. In other cases, the patient is in constant pain and may be taking increasingly larger doses of painkillers. After life has turned into darkness. The calls have gone to Dr. Jack Kevorkian. *, the*

3   Terminal illness also directly affects the lives of family members. Having to see a loved one in pain and despair brings anguish to mothers, fathers, brothers, sisters, and children. _____ From the beginning of the illness _____, you have been in *they*
daily contact with the patient, and, _____ as time passes _____, you often realize that *they*
living has become an intolerable experience. Though they have done all they can to help their family member handle the situation, they are hurt and ultimately in despair as you watch your loved one's life slowly deteriorate. As they accept the *they   their*
reality of the decision, family members may participate in a discussion with Dr. Kevorkian concerning the patient's request for assisted suicide. For example, _____ prior to the assisted suicides _____ of Sherry Miller and Marjorie Wantz, Dr. Kevorkian recorded these discussions. (They are on the Internet for anyone to

read.) They indicate that the patients and their families did not decide easily or quickly. _Further discussions show_ that everyone understood why Sherry Miller, suffering from multiple sclerosis (MS), wanted Dr. Kevorkian's help. Her brother stated he could not help his sister take her own life but would not interfere in the process. He felt her despair, and he respected her decision. Her father said he would even carry his daughter to the place chosen by Dr. Kevorkian for the event. _Similarly,_, Marjorie Wantz and her husband also talked honestly about her situation. _Although different from the MS victim_, she, _too_, had no future free of pain or suffering. _These_ families confronted their own emotions about their loved one's quality of life and played a role, even if indirectly, in the decision to call Dr. Kevorkian for help.

4   Time after time, health care professionals clearly are aware of the pain and despair patients with terminal, debilitating diseases face. Because they have taken oaths to save lives, to restore the quality of life, they have to balance in their own minds and hearts the integrity of their profession and the patients' need for peace. How ~~you~~ _they_ handle these emotional situations varies. After many experiences, some simply block emotion and arrange medication and feeding tubes to prolong life until the patient dies "normally." On May 7, 1998, a 91-year-old woman, having suffered a paralyzing stroke, was lying in a nursing home, receiving morphine and other medication to make her final days comfortable, but she was not hooked to feeding tubes or life support. Her doctors and nurses knew she could not live long. Her twin sister spent literally every possible waking hour by her sister's bedside. They were so close that they were described as having separate bodies but one heart. An attending nurse who observed the death said, "This is the way it is supposed to be." She went on to say that there is no reason to hasten the final event. When all hope is gone, other professionals undoubtedly have eased the final days of dying patients by convincing family members not to order intravenous feeding or

other life-support systems. However‸actively helping a person take his or her

own life is another situation entirely. Some health care professionals believe

they
~~you~~ can manage terminal patients in such sophisticated ways now that

excruciating pain and suffering no longer have to be a part of the picture. They

provide a high level of comfort to quiet the frustration‸anxieties, and fears of

patients themselves and their families. They are convinced that no one like Dr‸

Kevorkian ever has to be involved.

5   When a terminal illness or a debilitating disease progresses, everyone around

the patient suffers. Not everybody is fortunate enough to die a simple death, free of

suffering and pain. When the suffering is worse than living, when people have

their
exhausted their own strength and that of ~~your~~ families, the natural release from

despair is a quick and dignified death. Even though families would continue to

love and care for the terminally ill, the patients themselves realize there is

their
nothing better in the future for themselves and ~~your~~ families. They no longer

want to exist in this way, so they ask for Dr. Jack Kevorkian.

 ## *Collaborative Activity*

This activity is designed to help you practice sequential order to maintain coherence
in your essays.

1. Form five groups. Each group will work with the scrambled sentences from
   one paragraph.
2. Put the sentences into logical, coherent order. If members disagree on the
   order, then discuss your reasons for the order.
3. As soon as your group is satisfied that the sentences are in the correct order,
   be prepared to read the paragraph to the class.

Memory Made Manageable

Introductory paragraph:

1. However, one special person, Shreshevskii, or "S," as psychologist Alexander
   Luria called him, has a remarkable memory and can repeat up to 70 digits or
   words that are read about three seconds apart with no other time allowances.
2. For many people, "89, 71, 30, 24, 18, 2, 14, 29, 65, 10" may not be a difficult
   string of numbers to repeat.

Introduction
2, 7, 1, 4, 6, 5, 3

3. Some of these memory tricks are mnemonics, acronyms, and hierarchies.

4. Moreover, he can recall the number series backward as easily as forward and recall them even as long as fifteen years later, after having memorized hundreds of other lists.

5. With a few techniques, many people can train their minds to use imagery or mental pictures to retain information.

6. In contrast to "S," most people have to concentrate and put in substantial mental effort to recall unfamiliar information such as formulas, definitions, dates, and facts.

7. In fact, they probably could learn and repeat two or three similar series of numbers if given enough time to work the numbers into their long-term memory.

Support paragraph 1:

Support
paragraph 1
6, 1, 3, 4, 7, 11,
8, 5, 9, 2, 10

1. This method was developed by ancient Greek scholars and orators as aids to remember long speeches, stories, and dramas.

2. This illustration is a simplified example, but the method can still be used with longer, more abstract information.

3. Capitalizing on basic step-by-step mental pictures, they sequentially cued long passages in their minds, and they imagined themselves moving through a familiar series of locations, associating each place with a visual representation of the material.

4. Thus, when calling up the information, the orator would revisit each location mentally and retrieve the stored image.

5. For example, a person has a grocery list of carrots, milk, butter, and peanut butter to recall.

6. A mnemonic, which means "memory" in Greek, is simply forming mental pictures in a series.

7. A concrete method of applying this principle is the use of peg words.

8. One is a bun; two is a shoe; three is a tree; four is a door.

9. To do this, the person can imagine carrots stuck in a bun, milk filling a shoe, a tree dripping with butter, and a door held ajar by a container of peanut butter.

10. When the mnemonic becomes established in people's minds, long series become much easier to recall.

11. First, the person must mentally establish a linear foundation such as numbers attached to images.

Support paragraph 2:

Support
paragraph 2
8, 3, 5, 1, 6, 7, 9,
10, 2, 4

1. Another common acronym, "REM," denotes the "rapid eye movement" stage of sleep.

2. By thinking of this "apple-elevator" image, the students remember the words for the psychological stages of classical conditions.

3. Many abbreviations exist in the English language.

4. People soon find that using acronyms can be intriguing as well as worthwhile.

5. Originating from the military, "radar" stands for "radio detecting and ranging," and "snafu" translates quickly into "situation normal all fouled up."

6. An additional way of using letters to form memory cues is creating the words to help recall a list of words.

7. For example, "Roy G. Biv" can help a person remember the colors of ultraviolet light, and "fan boys" is a great way to remember coordinating conjunctions.

8. Equally effective for memorizing information is the use of acronyms or abbreviations.

9. Another version of forming letter cues is by creating sentences to remember information.

10. For example, if students have to remember the psychological stages of classical conditions—acquisition, generalization, distinction, extinction, and spontaneous recovery—they can create the sentence, "Apples going down elevator, stop."

Support paragraph 3:

Support paragraph 3
3, 2, 4, 9, 5, 6, 7, 10, 1, 8, 11

1. Alcohol and valium are both depressants; nicotine, cocaine, and speed are stimulants; and marijuana, LSD, and GHB are hallucinogens.

2. An outline, which is familiar to most people, is an organized hierarchy.

3. Another extremely useful method for remembering information is the implementation of hierarchies.

4. Coordinate levels and sublevels for arranging information can greatly simplify the remembering process.

5. For example, a student may be studying a unit on drugs.

6. Many types may be presented in the textbook, including depressants, alcohol, valium, stimulants, nicotine, cocaine, speed, hallucinogens, marijuana, LSD, and GHB.

7. This list can be organized in such a way that recall is easier.

8. A textbook might even have headings and subheadings that help students organize the drug information or any other information into hierarchies.

9. Structuring information into general levels, to subgeneral, to specific, to subspecific and so on and on sets a framework so that if one can recall the general item, the other information will come more easily.

10. By finding general categories such as depressants, stimulants, and hallucinogens, the other words can be placed under those categories, and the remembering of the general words brings up the specific drugs that go into each list.

11. Once information is streamlined into hierarchies, general cues can bring out the specific sublists and topics, enhancing memory.

Concluding paragraph:

Conclusion
1, 3, 2, 4

1. Whatever methods for remembering information are applied, memory techniques are important.

2. Mnemonics, acronyms, or hierarchies can become part of people's study technique, and in time these routines will become natural as they store information in such a way that recall will become easier and easier.

3. At first, students may not wish to take the time to use these devices to imprint the information into long-term memory; however, using a memory trick can be well worth the few minutes needed to develop a process.

4. A good memory is not always a given ability; a good memory is practiced and developed.

Collaborative Writing Project: Working and Learning Together

Writing Assignment/Working Individually

1. Prepare to write an essay about a movie, a play, or a book that you enjoyed very much. Choose one that you remember very well. Then think about what made it so enjoyable. Your essay must be a discussion about the movie, play, or book. *Do not just retell the story.*

   A **movie** discussion might include such items as sound effects, visual effects, acting, realism of the story, time period, or action.

   A **play** discussion might include such items as sound effects, props, special lighting, scenery, acting, realism, message, make-up, or costumes.

   A **book** discussion might include such items as vivid descriptions, characters, humor, historical background, reality, theme, or atmosphere.

2. After making your selection, brainstorm on the above ideas, and then write your thesis sentence.

3. Brainstorm each previewed point in your thesis sentence so that you will have enough ideas to write strong support paragraphs.

4. Complete the introductory paragraph by adding a hook and a transition before the thesis sentence.

5. Draft a support paragraph for each previewed idea in your thesis sentence. Remember that each support paragraph must have a topic sentence, support sentences, and an ending sentence. Concentrate on key words, time words, and other transitional words to create coherence.

6. Write the concluding paragraph. Remember to refer to the main idea in your thesis sentence, but do not use the exact words you used in your original thesis. If possible, refer also to the hook to provide closure.

7. Edit carefully for fragments, run-ons, and comma splices. Check for consistent point of view, consistent verb tense, and subject-verb agreement.

8. Check punctuation carefully, especially commas.

Peer Review

1. Exchange papers with another class member.

2. Read each essay aloud in turn, and use a highlighter to mark the following:

   In the introductory paragraph, mark the words used to create coherence between the hook and the thesis sentence.

   At the beginning of each support paragraph, highlight the key word or words in the topic sentence that refer back to the thesis sentence.

   Within each paragraph, highlight the key words, time words, and other transitional words used to create coherence.

3. Make any other positive suggestions for strengthening the essay.

Final Checklist

Content

Essay

Check the introductory paragraph for an effective hook.

Check for a smooth transition between hook and thesis.

Check to see that the thesis sentence states a clear direction or previews the points to be covered in the paper.

Check to see that the voice is appropriate for purpose and audience.

Check for a strong concluding paragraph.

Paragraphs

Revise so each paragraph has a clear topic sentence that develops an idea suggested in the thesis sentence.

Include four to six supporting sentences that are developed using short interrelated examples or an extended example.

Include a strong closing sentence in each paragraph.

Mechanics

Check for subject-verb agreement.

Check for consistent verb tense.

Check for a consistent point of view.

Check for fragments, run-on sentences, and comma splices.

Check for correct punctuation.

Sentence variety

Revise short sentences into compound sentences.

Revise sentences to include complex sentences.

Check for coherence between and within paragraphs.

 ## Internet Activities

The sites listed for this unit include the Purdue Online Writing Lab, an online thesaurus, and an online dictionary.

As you learn about repeating key words for coherence, you may also want to use other words with similar meanings to give your sentences variety. How do you think up all of these words? Don't worry. There is a writer's helper called a thesaurus, which lists both similar words and words with opposite meanings—in other words, synonyms and antonyms.

To make it easier for you, there are online thesauruses that will look up the word for you and suggest other words you can use to replace the key words.

Activity 1 Revising, Editing, and Proofreading

Visit Purdue University's Online Writing Lab, and evaluate the editing and proof-reading information.

a. Type in the following website. (Type all Internet addresses exactly as they appear. Bookmark this site or save it as a favorite for future reference.)

http://owl.english.purdue.edu/

b. On the base page, scroll down to the pencil-link subheading "Handouts and Materials" to a pencil link on the left-hand side of the page. Click on "General Writing Concerns."

c. Scroll down this page, and click on the box "Revising/Editing/Proofreading." Then click on "Editing and Proofreading Strategies for Revision." Scroll down until you see "Steps in Editing," and click on that option. Read through the material, and then click "Back" on your toolbar.

d. Now click, and look at "Proofreading Strategies." Pay particular attention to "Organization and Paragraphing." Read through the material. Click "Back" on your toolbar.

e. Finally, read "Proofreading Your Paper." Based on your reading, make a list of possible editing checks for yourself.

Answers will vary.

_____

_____

_____

_____

_____

_____

Activity 2 Using an Online Thesaurus to Find Alternatives to Key Words

In an earlier exercise, you were given the word "expensive" in the sentence "Even though visiting a zoo can be educational and relaxing, it can also be expensive."

a. Type in one of the following websites. These sites are similar, so you can use either one. (Type all Internet addresses exactly as they appear. Bookmark this site or save it as a favorite for future reference.)

http://www.thesaurus.com

http://Bartleby.com/62/

b. Type the word "expensive" in the box at the top of the page. Then click on "OK" or "Return." Then list other words that you could use that mean the same thing and that will provide possible transitions and coherence in your writing.

high-priced, of great price, costly, precious, dear

_____

_____

c. Choose a keyword that you will be using in your next writing assignment. Then, using one of the above websites, type in that word at the top of the page to find words with similar meanings. List these words below.

Answers will vary. _____

_____

_____

_____

Activity 3 Using Online Dictionaries to Understand Words

When you are not sure what a word means, you may try to figure out its meaning by looking at the context. You may also look up the word in the dictionary for guidance and then come back to your reading to see which meaning fits. Try this with three online dictionaries.

Earlier in this unit, you read Cynthia L. Vinzant's essay, "Home: Just How Safe Is It?" Immediately following the essay are three words that need to be defined. Look up each word to determine which definition best fits the meaning in the essay.

a. Type in the following website for the *Merriam-Webster Dictionary*. (Type all Internet addresses exactly as they appear. Bookmark this site or save it as a favorite for future reference.)

http://www.m-w.com/netdict.htm

The *Merriam-Webster Dictionary* lists the oldest meaning first, so you may want to move down the list to find the most recent meaning and then come back to your reading to see which meaning fits best.

perpetrators _____

imperative _____

perpetuating (perpetuate) _____

b. Once again, try the same activity, this time using the *Cambridge Dictionary*. Type in the following website. (Type all Internet addresses exactly as they appear. Bookmark this site or save it as a favorite for future reference.)

http://dictionary.cambridge.org

perpetrators _____

imperative _____

perpetuating (perpetuate) _____

Unit 7

Composing with Effective Alternate Patterns

Part 1

Writing Skills: Patterns of Development

Pretest over
Unit 7, Parts 1
and 4 is on
page 9 of the
Test Bank.

Objectives

Develop an essay using

- Illustration

- Comparison/contrast

- Classification

- Definition

- Cause/effect analysis

- Process analysis

- Argumentation

When you master the essay using examples, you are well on your way to becoming an effective writer. You have learned a basic skill that you will use many times. However, it is vital that you understand the *connection between the precise form of this essay,* as you have practiced it, *and the other types of writing* that you will need to do.

Mastering a basic plan for an essay is similar to mastering the art of home building because becoming a good builder requires certain skills, just as becoming an effective writer requires precise skills. The following chart shows how both building a house and writing an essay are similar.

Building a Home	Writing an Essay
Planning	Planning
gather house-plan ideas	prewrite
design home for owner	consider audience and purpose
make drawings	outline
Building	Writing
pour foundation	draft a thesis sentence
erect frame	draft support paragraphs
put on roof	draft an introduction and a conclusion

Completing the Process

add finishing touches	revise and edit

If you want to write an effective essay, you need to understand each step of the process. You may think of these components of the essay as a building code to be followed. This building code keeps you from doing shoddy work; however, it does not keep you from being creative and adding variety to your writing. If you drove into a town and saw that every house was built exactly alike, you might wonder whether the people who lived there possessed any creativity at all. Similarly, if you learned to write an essay using examples and never learned to go beyond that point, people might wonder whether you, too, lacked creativity. Always remember that *every* completed house has a foundation, a frame, a roof, and finishing touches. It may also have a fireplace, an upper story, picture windows, or whatever the builder adds to make the house more appealing. You, too, will want to have that something extra in your essays even though *every* essay you write needs an introduction, support paragraphs, a conclusion, and finishing touches.

Once you have learned to write a thesis sentence and support it with examples, you can learn other methods to organize ideas in an essay. You always begin by planning, using freewriting, brainstorming, or another prewriting activity to generate ideas. Then the organization, no matter what pattern you select, will include an introduction, support, and a conclusion.

Developing a paper can be done in different ways that are usually called **patterns of development.** These patterns are ways of developing and organizing the support paragraphs that explain the thesis sentence. There are many patterns of development; all of the following patterns are important for basic writers to learn.

Patterns of Development

illustration

comparison/contrast

classification

definition

cause/effect analysis

process analysis

argumentation

Your purpose in writing a paper determines the method you use to develop your essay. If your purpose is to show how home builders can create energy-efficient homes, you could **illustrate** the way different houses are built to conserve energy. If you are writing an article for home buyers, your purpose might be to **compare/contrast** two different kinds of homes available so that the reader can then decide which kind is better. If your purpose is to inform the population about the types of homes available to them, your job would be to **classify** the types of homes available in a certain area. If you want to **define** the word "home," you might include not just the physical structure but the emotions associated with a home. If you want to explain *why* someone decides to build a home, your purpose would be to explain the **causes** of that event. If you want to discuss remodeling parts of an existing home rather than buying a new home, your purpose would be to explain *how* to remodel or explain the **process** of remodeling. If you are a person who sells homes, your purpose might be to use an **argument** that would persuade a first-time home buyer that purchasing a repossessed home in need of repair is more advantageous than buying a new home.

This unit shows how the general subject "homes" can be developed into different kinds of essays, depending upon the particular purpose of the essay. Using the same topic, homes, each of the seven patterns of development is explained and illustrated.

Illustration

In Unit 4, "Writing with More Depth and Variety," you studied how to use examples to clarify and support topic ideas in paragraphs and essays. This use of examples is also the pattern of development called **illustration.** Previously, you practiced writing paragraphs and essays by supporting a topic sentence or a thesis sentence with clarifying details and examples. These examples were also illustrations.

To use illustration well in writing a longer paper, you do not need to learn a new way of generating ideas. The simple writing process you used earlier in this text is appropriate in this part, too.

Freewrite/brainstorm your topic.

Cluster ideas to find a direction or point of view for your topic.

Freewrite/brainstorm again for more details and examples.

Arrange similar details and examples into groups, and compose your thesis sentence.

Draft the support paragraphs for your essay.

Draft an introduction and a conclusion.

Revise and edit.

The *purpose* of an illustration paper is to explain or clarify by giving specific examples that show the reader "in what way" the thesis is true. If you say that "when building a new home, structural changes can be made to make the home energy-efficient," then you need to follow up with specific examples. The paper should contain examples and illustrations that show how structural changes make the home more energy-efficient.

The *topic* for an illustration paper can be any subject you can convincingly explain by giving examples or illustrations. It is one of the most frequently used kinds of writing. Basically, the *organization* for an illustration paper looks like this:

1. The introductory paragraph includes a hook, a transition, and a thesis sentence.

2. Each support paragraph includes a topic sentence and examples or illustrations.

3. The conclusion includes a restatement of the main idea that the examples have illustrated.

When you use this pattern for an essay, each supporting paragraph is developed with examples or illustrations. During drafting, you may choose short, interrelated examples or a single, extended example or illustration.

In this section, you are *not* learning a new pattern of development. You are learning that you can use the same process and pattern that you have already practiced in many writing assignments. You have simply learned a new descriptive phrase for it— *development by illustration.*

Suppose you want to write a paper to explain or illustrate the ways in which a house can be energy-efficient. Through brainstorming/freewriting, you have written the following possible thesis sentence:

A homeowner can have an energy-efficient home by changing certain features in construction, installing energy-efficient devices inside the home, and planning landscaping to control the amount of heat or cold coming into the home.

The following essay shows how you could use illustrations to support this thesis.

A Home for the 21st Century

hook

1   Thirty years ago, homeowners believed that there were no limits to the energy needed for them to live comfortably. They assumed the American Dream meant the right to own a home without even thinking about how much energy the house required. For most Americans today, part of the American Dream still

transition	includes owning a home complete with modern appliances. This dream, however, can turn into a financial nightmare if careful attention is not given to using energy wisely. Having a home that uses too much energy can be a financial
thesis sentence	drain on the owner and, in the long run, on the country. However, a homeowner can have an energy-efficient home by making certain changes in construction, by installing energy-efficient devices inside the home, and by planning landscaping to control the amount of heat or cold coming into the home.
topic sentence #1 2 *illustration #1*	When the house is built, the homeowner can change or add certain features to make the home energy-efficient. For example, in the desert Southwest, the roof overhang should be wide enough to keep the high summer sun from shining on most of the walls. In the winter, because of the changing position of the sun, the low winter sun can warm the house by shining on the walls under
illustration #2	the overhanging roof. When plans are being made for the house, the owner can consider block or brick construction. Using two-by-six boards for framing to
illustration #3	allow for thicker layers of insulation in the walls will save energy in both hot and cold climates. According to the April 1999 issue of *Professional Builder,* the builders who won the Energy Value Housing Award also incorporated sophisticated techniques such as air-sealing packages to prevent outside heat or cold from
illustration #4 *concluding sentence*	leaking into the home. Although they may cost more money to put in, special double-paned windows and weather stripping will save energy, too. All these structural features add up to long-range energy savings.
topic sentence #2 3 *illustration #1* *illustration #2* *illustration #3*	One of the best ways to save energy in the 21st century is to install energy-efficient devices inside the house. Even small changes can be made, such as adding an insulating blanket to the hot-water tank. Putting up blinds that block the heat also helps save energy. The most energy can be saved, however, by the type of heating-cooling unit installed in the home. Most recently, the "seasonal energy efficiency ratio" (SEER) provides the best guide as to the type of unit to install for heating or air conditioning. These ratios are given in numbers like 9, 10, or 11, and by selecting a unit with a high number, the homeowner saves energy as well as money. As pointed out in *Professional Builder,* air-conditioning units now can be rated at 16, a very energy-efficient unit for the 21st century.
concluding sentence	Installing energy-efficient devices like these can help a homeowner conserve energy.
topic sentence #3 4 *illustration #1*	After considering these ways of conserving energy in a home, the owner can plan the landscaping so that it helps the house become energy-efficient. If the house is new, the owner can plant trees and shrubs around the home so that
illustration #2 *illustration #3*	they shade the walls and the roof from the sun. Grass that requires little water can be planted close to the house to absorb heat from the sun. In the wintertime, people who live in the desert can trim their trees and shrubs to allow the sun to
illustration #4	shine on the house. In colder parts of the country, landscaping can be planted to give shade in the summer, but trees and shrubs that lose their leaves in the winter can be chosen so that the sun shines into the house. Landscaping provides more
concluding sentence	than an attractive appearance for a home. It becomes one more way for the homeowner to save money in day-to-day operating costs and, at the same time, to save energy for the country.
concluding paragraph 5	In the 1960s, Americans used as much energy as they wanted without concern for the future. In the 21st century, though, Americans have learned that sources of energy are limited and that some kind of conservation is needed if they are going to have enough energy in the future to live in the same kinds of comfortable homes they have always dreamed about. Owning a home today carries the responsibility to reduce the amount of energy required to operate a

house and live a comfortable life at the same time. By paying attention to the energy-saving devices now available, homeowners can save money for today and natural resources for tomorrow.

 Writing Assignment

Use illustration to develop an essay on one of the following topics. During revision and editing, refer to the checklist on the inside back cover.

1. Problems with transportation in your city
2. Ways to keep a body healthy
3. Factors to consider before buying a puppy
4. Summer projects for the family
5. Reasons people enjoy vacationing in national parks
6. Reasons people dread or look forward to holidays
7. Reasons discipline is important at home or at school

Comparison/Contrast

Another useful way to develop an essay is to explain how two items relate to each other. This kind of essay is called a **comparison/contrast** paper. The *purpose* of a comparison/contrast paper is to show how two things are alike or different. A paper may be primarily a comparison (how two items are alike) or primarily a contrast (how two items are different).

The *subject* for a comparison/contrast paper is two people, objects, or places that have both similarities and differences. Two children, two lakes, or two types of flowers would probably be contrasted because their similarities are obvious. A donkey and a person or a flower and a person would probably be compared because it is not so easy to see how they are alike. There is no point in contrasting two objects if they are not alike in any way. Likewise, there is no point in comparing two objects that do not differ. In your other college classes, you may be asked to explain the similarities or differences between ideas: two opinions, two philosophical theories, two personalities, or two political candidates.

In a true comparison/contrast essay, both sides are treated fairly, with equal amounts of information given for each side. However, one side may appear to have the advantage over the other. If one side does have an advantage, it should be discussed *last*. The side with more disadvantages should be covered *first* or should start the discussion. For instance, if you were to write a paper about two political leaders, Colin Powell and Malcolm X, you might want to start your essay with Malcolm X because he did not achieve the widespread appeal and influence Powell has achieved.

If the paper is a true comparison/contrast, it will present the same characteristics for both sides. For example, if you talk about Malcolm X's appearance, you must also talk about Powell's appearance. If you talk about Malcolm X's family, you must talk about Powell's family, also. In this way, you balance your paper equally between the two sides.

The process you have been using for essays can be modified as you *organize* the comparison/contrast paper. Your freewriting or brainstorming is done in two separate parts. One section should be labeled "comparisons" or "similarities." The other section should be labeled "contrasts" or "differences."

Suppose you were writing an essay comparing and contrasting the costs of buying either a new or a "fix-up" home. In this case, "item #1" under consideration might be "fix-up homes," and "item #2" might be "new homes." Your brainstorming might be done in lists like the ones that follow.

Similarities
Item #1 (fix-up homes) and Item # 2 (new homes)

_____

_____

Differences

Item #1 (fix-up homes)   Item #2 (new homes)

_____   _____

_____   _____

_____   _____

The next step is to *cluster* ideas and decide whether the information you have generated can be explained best in a paper that presents contrasts (differences) between the two items or in a paper that presents comparisons (similarities) between the two items. The clustering of ideas should lead to an outline that includes a thesis sentence and a preview of the main points to be covered in the paper. There is no definite, correct number of similarities or differences, but more points create more paragraphs to support your thesis.

If the paper is a *comparison*, it will focus primarily on *similarities*, but to be realistic and effective, it may begin and end with significant differences. On the other hand, if the paper is a *contrast*, it will focus primarily on *differences*, but, again, to be realistic and effective, it may begin and end with significant similarities.

You now have one more decision to make: how to present your explanation. Choose one of the following patterns:

1. items discussed in alternate paragraphs
2. items discussed in two distinct parts within each paragraph
3. items discussed in alternate sentences within each paragraph

On the following pages, you will find outlines of these patterns; a draft of an essay written according to that pattern then follows.

Items Discussed in Alternate Paragraphs

1. The **introductory paragraph** previews major differences (with brief reference to a major similarity) **or** previews major similarities (with brief reference to a major difference).
2. **Support paragraphs** include points of contrast (or comparison) in an alternating pattern.
3. The **concluding paragraph** reemphasizes major differences (with a brief reference to a major similarity referred to in the introduction) **or** reemphasizes major similarities (with a brief reference to a major difference referred to in the introduction).

Here is a sample format for the contrast essay that follows.

Introduction

Paragraph 1: Hook, brief reference to similarity, and thesis sentence

First point

    Paragraph 2: Item #1 (fix-up homes)

    Paragraph 3: Item #2 (new homes)

Second point

    Paragraph 4: Item #1 (fix-up homes)

    Paragraph 5: Item #2 (new homes)

Third point

    Paragraph 6: Item #1 (fix-up homes)

    Paragraph 7: Item #2 (new homes)

Conclusion

    Paragraph 8: Summary of main points with a brief reference to similarity

Here is an essay in which the paragraphs illustrate the above pattern.

Saving Money on a New Home

hook

1   Jason and Jennifer had been married for two years when they decided that they were ready to start a family. But they also decided that they should buy a house before they had children. On their combined income of $72,000 a year, they felt they could afford a home of their own. After they contacted a real estate agent and read articles about home buying, they narrowed their options to buying either a new home or a "fix-up" home. The decision would be difficult. As many other Americans have learned, the initial money invested, the continuing costs, and the return on the investment vary according to the option selected.

brief reference to similarity
thesis sentence

first point of contrast
item #1 discussed

2   **Probably the most marked difference between buying a new home and a "fix-up" home is the initial costs involved.** A "fix-up" home does not always have a fixed down payment and sometimes can be purchased at the rate of interest paid by the previous homeowners. The cost of a "fix-up" home is set by the current homeowner, but many times an offer of a few thousand dollars less will be accepted. A "fix-up" home is often sold "as is" with an opportunity for the buyer to check everything out before signing the closing papers. Anything that is defective can be negotiated to be repaired or to lower the cost to the buyer. Anything that breaks after the final papers are signed, though, becomes the responsibility of the new owner. A "fix-up" home often needs landscaping but usually has grass, shrubs, and trees that are already established.

first point of contrast

item #2 discussed

3   **On the other hand,** a new home has higher initial costs and often requires a 10–20 percent down payment with interest rates set by current bank regulations. The initial cost of a new home is set, and an offer at a few thousand dollars less will be met with rejection or even laughter from the salesperson. A new home is not equipped with all of the appliances that will be needed, for example, a washer and dryer, and purchasing new appliances may mean paying extra for extended warranties. Another initial cost could be upgrading any standard feature that comes with the home, including carpeting or even paint and roofing materials. A new home may be sold with standard landscaping that includes leveling the yard, seeding the lawn, and planting one or two trees, but the buyers may find that they have to spend additional money in the beginning for landscaping.

second point of contrast	4	**Once the house is purchased, the costs do not end. There are still payments to be made each month.** Buying a "fix-up" house means that payments are less than they would have been had the home been purchased new at the current house prices. In addition to house payments, owners of "fix-up" homes often need to spend money on major renovations, such as restoration of walls or replacement of plumbing lines. Remodeling, however, is done to please the owners, and they can often save money by doing the work themselves or getting several bids to keep costs down. Another cost would be taxes, but they may be lower on a "fix-up" home.
item #1 discussed		

second point of contrast

item #2 discussed

5   **In contrast,** when a new home is purchased, house payments are generally higher by at least 10–15 percent over house payments for "fix-up" homes, which might amount to several hundred dollars. However, owners of new homes seldom need to spend additional money repairing fixtures or appliances for the first five to six years, nor do they usually spend money altering the structure of the new home. Buyers of brand-new homes do spend money decorating their homes; however, the decorating is not so extensive or so expensive as the remodeling that is needed in a "fix-up" home. Owners of new homes also pay taxes, which may be higher than the taxes on a "fix-up" home.

third point of contrast

item #1 discussed

6   **Though there are many costs, these homes also represent a return to buyers because they both appreciate in value within a certain time frame and they both bring satisfaction.** A "fix-up" house, especially an ugly duckling among swans, can appreciate rapidly, following repairs. If the home is bought at half the going price of the surrounding homes, it can equal or surpass the other homes in assessed value within a year. Owners of "fix-up" homes often need to spend months cleaning up and fixing both the interior and exterior of their new home but are able to give the home a distinct personality of its own.

third point of contrast
item #2 discussed

7   **During the same time frame,** a new home will appreciate slowly at the same rate as the other homes in the neighborhood. The home is bought at the same price as the other homes in the neighborhood, and its value will not change substantially unless it is not taken care of properly. Buyers of brand-new homes are often pleased with their home when they move in and can enjoy it immediately. They do need to spend time and money, though, getting a lawn started and caring for the outside of the home.

concluding paragraph
brief reference to
similarity

8   Both types of homes are available in a wide range of sizes, styles, and locations that appeal to many people. Some people enjoy spending their spare time working on their homes, whereas others do not. Whether buying a new home or a "fix-up" home, all new homeowners can feel a sense of pride in their investment. And, like Jason and Jennifer, they have an ideal place to raise a family.

Items Discussed in Two Distinct Parts Within Each Paragraph

1. The **introductory paragraph** previews major differences (with brief reference to a major similarity) **or** previews major similarities (with brief reference to a major difference).

2. **Support paragraphs** include points of contrast (or comparison) in an alternating pattern.

3. The **concluding paragraph** reemphasizes major differences (with a brief reference to a major similarity referred to in the introduction) **or** reemphasizes major similarities (with a brief reference to a major difference referred to in the introduction).

Here is a sample format for the contrast essay that follows.

Introduction
>Paragraph 1: Hook, brief reference to similarity, and thesis sentence

First point
>Paragraph 2: Item #1 (fix-up homes)
>Item #2 (new homes)

Second point
>Paragraph 3: Item #1 (fix-up homes)
>Item #2 (new homes)

Third point
>Paragraph 4: Item #1 (fix-up homes)
>Item #2 (new homes)

Conclusion
>Paragraph 5: Summary of main points with a brief reference to similarity

Here is an essay in which the paragraphs illustrate the above pattern.

Saving Money on a New Home

hook

1   Jason and Jennifer had been married for two years when they decided that they were ready to start a family, but they also decided that they should buy a house before they had children. On their combined income of $72,000 a year, they felt they could afford a home of their own. After they contacted a real estate agent and read articles about home buying, they narrowed their options to buying either a new home or a "fix-up" home. The decision would be difficult. As other Americans have learned, the initial money invested, the continuing costs, and the return on the investment vary according to the option selected.

brief reference to similarity
thesis sentence

first point of contrast
item #1 discussed

2   **Probably the most marked difference between buying a new home and a "fix-up" home is the initial costs involved.** A "fix-up" home does not always have a fixed down payment and sometimes can be purchased at the rate of interest paid by the previous homeowners. The cost of a "fix-up" home is set by the current homeowner, but many times an offer of a few thousand dollars less will be accepted. A "fix-up" home is often sold "as is" with an opportunity for the buyer to check everything out before signing the closing papers. Anything that is defective can be negotiated to be repaired or to lower the cost to the buyer. Anything that breaks after the final papers are signed, though, becomes the responsibility of the new owner. A "fix-up" home often needs landscaping but usually has grass, shrubs, and trees that are already established. **On the other hand,** a new home has higher initial costs and often requires a 10–20 percent down payment with interest rates set by current bank regulations. The initial cost of a new home is set, and an offer at a few thousand dollars less will be met with rejection or even laughter from the salesperson. A new home is not equipped with all of the appliances that will be needed, for example, a washer and dryer, and purchasing new appliances may mean paying extra for extended warranties. Another initial cost could be upgrading any standard feature that comes with the home, including carpeting or even paint and roofing materials. A new home may be sold with a standard landscaping that includes leveling the yard, seeding the lawn, and planting one or two trees, but the buyers may find that they have to spend additional money in the beginning for landscaping.

item #2 discussed

Once the house is purchased, the costs do not end. There are still payments to be made each month. Buying a "fix-up" house means that payments are less than they would have been had the home been purchased new at the current house prices. In addition to house payments, owners of "fix-up" homes often need to spend money on major renovations, such as restoration of walls or replacement of plumbing lines. Remodeling, however, is done to please the owners, and they can often save money by doing the work themselves or getting several bids to keep costs down. Another cost would be taxes, but they may be

lower on a "fix-up" home. **In contrast,** when a new home is purchased, house payments are generally higher by at least 10–15 percent over house payments for "fix-up" homes, which might amount to several hundred dollars. However, owners of new homes seldom need to spend additional money repairing fixtures or appliances for the first five to six years, nor do they usually spend money altering the structure of the new home. Buyers of brand-new homes do spend money decorating their homes; however, the decorating is not so extensive or so expensive as the remodeling that is needed in a "fix-up" home. Owners of new homes also pay taxes, which may be higher than the taxes on a "fix-up" home.

Though there are many costs, these homes also represent a return to buyers because they both appreciate in value within a certain time frame and they both bring satisfaction. A "fix-up" house, especially an ugly duckling among swans,

can appreciate rapidly, following repairs. If the home is bought at half the going price of the surrounding homes, it can equal or surpass the other homes in assessed value within a year. Owners of "fix-up" homes often need to spend months cleaning up and fixing both the interior and exterior of their new home but are able to give the home a distinct personality that is its own. **During the**

same time frame, a new home will appreciate slowly at the same time as the other homes in the neighborhood. The home is bought at the same price as the other homes in the neighborhood, and its value will not change substantially unless it is not taken care of properly. Buyers of brand-new homes are often pleased with their home when they move in and can enjoy it immediately. They do need to spend time and money, though, getting a lawn started and caring for the outside of the home.

Both types of homes are available in a wide range of sizes, styles, and locations that appeal to many people. Some people enjoy spending their spare

time working on their homes, whereas others do not. Whether buying a new home or a "fix-up" home, all new homeowners can feel a sense of pride in their investment. And, like Jason and Jennifer, they have an ideal place to raise a family.

Items Discussed in Alternate Sentences Within Each Paragraph

1. The **introductory paragraph** previews major differences (with brief reference to a major similarity) **or** previews major similarities (with brief reference to a major difference).

2. **Support paragraphs** include points of contrast (or comparison) in an alternating pattern.

3. The **concluding paragraph** reemphasizes major differences (with a brief reference to a major similarity referred to in the introduction) **or** reemphasizes major similarities (with a brief reference to a major difference referred to in the introduction).

Here is a sample format for the contrast essay that follows.

Introduction

Paragraph 1: Hook, brief reference to similarity, and thesis sentence

First point

Paragraph 2: Item #1 (fix-up homes)

Item #2 (new homes)

Item #1 (fix-up homes)

Item #2 (new homes)

Second point

Paragraph 3: Item #1 (fix-up homes)

Item #2 (new homes)

Item #1 (fix-up homes)

Item #2 (new homes)

Third point

Paragraph 4: Item #1 (fix-up homes)

Item #2 (new homes)

Item #1 (fix-up homes)

Item #2 (new homes)

Conclusion

Paragraph 5: Summary of main points with a brief reference to similarity

Here is an essay that illustrates the above pattern.

Saving Money on a New Home

hook

1   Jason and Jennifer had been married for two years when they decided that they were ready to start a family. But they also decided that they should buy a house before they had children. On their combined income of $72,000 a year, they felt they could afford a home of their own. After they contacted a real estate agency and read articles about home buying, they narrowed their options to buying either a new home or a "fix-up" home. The decision would be difficult. As many other Americans have learned, the initial money invested, the continuing costs, and the return on the investment vary according to the option selected.

brief reference to similarity
thesis sentence

first point of contrast
item #1 discussed

2   **Probably the most marked difference between buying a new home and a "fix-up" home is the initial costs involved.** A "fix-up" home does not always have a fixed down payment and sometimes can be purchased at the rate of interest paid by the previous homeowners. A new home has higher initial costs and often requires a 10–20 percent down payment with interest rates set by current bank regulations. The cost of a "fix-up" home is set by the current homeowner, but many times an offer of a few thousand dollars less will be accepted. The initial cost of a new home is set, and an offer at a few thousand dollars less will be met with rejection or even laughter from the salesperson. A "fix-up" home is often sold "as is" with an opportunity for the buyer to check everything out before signing the closing papers. Anything that is defective can be negotiated

item #2 discussed

item #1 discussed
item #2 discussed

item #1 discussed

to be repaired or to lower the cost to the buyer. Anything that breaks after the final papers are signed, though, becomes the responsibility of the new owner. A new home is not equipped with all of the appliances that will be needed, for example, a washer and dryer, and purchasing new appliances may mean paying extra for extended warranties. Another initial cost could be upgrading any standard feature that comes with the home, including carpeting or even paint or roofing materials. A "fix-up" home often needs landscaping but usually has grass, shrubs, and trees that are already established. A new home may be sold with standard landscaping that includes leveling the yard, seeding the lawn, and planting one or two trees, but the buyers may find that they have to spend additional money in the beginning for landscaping.

item #2 discussed

item #1 discussed
item #2 discussed

second point of contrast
item #1 discussed

3   **Once the house is purchased, the costs do not end. There are still payments to be made each month.** Buying a "fix-up" house means that payments are less than they would have been had the home been purchased new at the current house prices. When a new home is purchased, house payments are generally higher by at least 10–15 percent over house payments for "fix-up" homes, which might amount to several hundred dollars. In addition to house payments, owners of "fix-up" homes often need to spend money on major renovations, such as restoration of walls or replacement of plumbing lines. Remodeling, however, is done to please the owners, and they can often save money by doing the work themselves or getting several bids to keep costs down. However, owners of new homes seldom need to spend additional money repairing fixtures or appliances for the first five to six years, nor do they usually spend money altering the structure of the new home. Buyers of brand-new homes do spend money decorating their homes; however, the decorating is not so extensive or so expensive as the remodeling that is needed in a "fix-up" home. Another cost would be taxes, but they may be lower on a "fix-up" home. Owners of new homes also pay taxes, which may be higher than the taxes on a "fix-up" home.

item #2 discussed

item #1 discussed

item #2 discussed

item #1 discussed
item #2 discussed

third point of contrast

item #1 discussed

4   **Though there are many costs, these homes also represent a return to buyers because they both appreciate in value within a certain time frame and they both bring satisfaction.** A "fix-up" house, especially an ugly duckling among swans, can appreciate rapidly, following repairs. If the home is bought at half the going price of the surrounding homes, it can equal or surpass the other homes in assessed value within a year. A new home will appreciate slowly at the same rate as the other homes in the neighborhood. The home is bought at the same price as the other homes in the neighborhood, and its value will not change substantially unless it is not taken care of properly. Owners of "fix-up" homes often need to spend months cleaning up and fixing both the interior and exterior of their new home but are able to give the home a distinct personality that is its own. Buyers of brand-new homes are often pleased with their home when they move in and can enjoy it immediately. They do need to spend time and money, though, getting a lawn started and caring for the outside of the home.

item #2 discussed

item #1 discussed

item #2 discussed

concluding paragraph

brief reference to similarity

5   Both types of homes are available in a wide range of sizes, styles, and locations that appeal to many people. Some people enjoy spending their spare time working on their homes, whereas others do not. Whether buying a new home or a "fix-up" home, all new homeowners can feel a sense of pride in their investment. And, like Jason and Jennifer, they have an ideal place to raise a family.

The previous patterns reflect a paper that is primarily a contrast. A *comparison* paper would also follow one of these patterns; however, it would begin and end with differences, and the support paragraphs would focus on similarities.

Writing Assignment

Use comparison/contrast to develop an essay on one of the following topics. During revision and editing, refer to the checklist on the inside back cover.

1. Show how two holidays are alike or different.
2. Show how physical and mental abuse are alike or different.
3. Show how a vacation in the city and a vacation at a national park are alike or different.
4. Show how a living pet and a stuffed animal are alike or different to a child.
5. Show how two children are alike or different.
6. Show how competitive swimming and football are alike or different.
7. Show how owning an old car or owning a new car are alike or different.
8. Show how nursing homes and home health care are alike or different.
9. Show how neglect of children and abuse of children are alike or different.

Classification

Another method of organizing information is called classification. **Classification** means clustering objects, people, or events on the basis of similarities or characteristics they have in common. Each of the groups formed on this basis would be a *category*.

For example, if you wanted to open a small clothing store, it would be much easier for your customers to find what they wanted to buy if items were clustered in logical categories. Your customers would understand categories like children's clothing, women's clothing, and men's clothing. If you did not form these categories or groups, your customers would have to hunt for a boy's shirt among dresses, men's shirts, ties, or women's shoes—and go searching on and on for what they needed to buy. One way, then, to *classify* the items in the store would be by the age and/or sex of the people the clothing is appropriate for. Other logical categories within each of these clusters would be underwear and sportswear. By providing your customers with logical categories or clusters of items, you make it easier for them to find their way around and you will manage the store better.

Classification can be a useful way to present information clearly, but this way of thinking is not really new to you. When you learned to cluster the items in your brainstorming, you were also classifying them into clusters that have characteristics in common. Classifying and clustering, then, are two words for the same kind of thinking.

The *purpose* for classifying items in a paragraph or an essay works in two ways. First, classification helps you, as the writer, clarify for yourself and explain in writing what many separate items have in common. Second, your reader can in turn better understand the information you are presenting.

One important point to remember about classification, however, is that it is a way of thinking about *similar* characteristics of objects or people or events. The items within each category should have many characteristics in common if the clusters are to be useful in your writing. The categories should not ignore so many differences that the classification becomes illogical.

The *topic* for a classification paper is any group of things that have characteristics in common and can be put into categories. You can classify people by age, sex, occupation, or interests. You can classify cities by size or location. You can classify schools by size or types of programs.

Here are the distinct parts of a classification paper:

1. The introduction contains the thesis sentence, which includes the categories to be discussed in the essay and establishes the basis for the classification.

2. Each support paragraph discusses a separate category established in the introduction. (Each paragraph explains how the items in each category are alike. Each paragraph may also explain how each category is different from the other categories rather than having the reader figure out what the differences are.)

3. The conclusion reaffirms the categories established in the thesis sentence.

The following essay shows how *classification* has been used to organize the information needed by someone who is going to buy a house for the first time.

Buying a House for the First Time

hook 1 Why in the world do so many people every year want to buy a home? Why do they want to take on the often difficult-to-reach goals of paying for and maintaining their own homes? The answers are related to "being a success" or "having a real part of the American Dream" or "always wanting to own a home of their own." Whatever their reasons at the beginning, people thinking about buying a home for the first time usually try to find out what kinds are available and how much they cost. If they know very little about real estate, they may soon *transition* become overwhelmed by the whole process. If they start with some basic *thesis sentence* knowledge, however, they can find the process of buying a home to be fun and educational. The basic knowledge that the first-time buyer should have is an understanding of the three main categories of homes available for purchase— town houses, condominiums, and single-family residences.

support paragraph 1; 2 When a young person or a young couple starts thinking of buying a home, *discusses category #1* the idea of owning a town house seems appealing. Town houses are places of residence where the owner buys not only the building but also the land the building sits on. They are not like houses, though, because usually only a very small patio or terrace or courtyard goes with the building. Some town houses may have only a small plot of ground for a little flower garden by the front door. If there is a community pool or TV satellite dish, it is usually there when a person purchases the town house. Town-house owners do not have to belong to an association that requires fees and monthly meetings. In size, town houses can be similar to other medium-sized houses. They can contain a living and/or dining room, one or more bedrooms, a kitchen, and various storage areas like closets and cupboards. In one way, having a town house can seem like being in an apartment, but the town-house buyer owns the property, is responsible for its upkeep, and has a solid, long-term investment.

support paragraph 2; 3 The first-time buyer might also consider currently popular residences called *discusses category #2* condominiums. The condominium owner buys the building walls, floors, and ceilings but, unlike the town-house buyer, does not own the land the building sits on. In contrast to owning a town house, owning a condo, as they are frequently called, means that the owner must belong to an association that requires monthly fees for exterior maintenance and for the support of group recreational facilities, such as a pool or tennis or racquetball courts. If the association does not own a pool or a TV satellite dish, the members must vote on the purchase of these items, which then belong to the association rather than to an individual owner. The owner of the condo does not have any exterior area for flowers or a small yard. Instead, the condo may be one of several that are built like apartments in a high rise. Although there is no beautiful yard around their individual home, condo owners may still find that living in a condominium provides a glamorous, carefree life that provides a long-term investment and pride of ownership.

support paragraph 3; discusses category #3

4   The third option a first-time buyer may consider is a single-family residence because, in most cases, it provides more privacy and space for the money invested. Buying a single-family residence means buying the land under and around the house as well as the house itself. Decisions like putting in a swimming pool or a TV satellite dish are made by the individual homeowner, who would then own them. A single-family residence usually includes a living room, a dining room, perhaps a family room, as many bedrooms as the owner needs or can afford, a kitchen, and various storage areas including either a carport or a garage. The house can be as large as the owner wishes. The owner of this type of house does not belong to an association requiring fees for upkeep. Rather s/he is responsible for maintaining the yard as well as any other purchased land surrounding the house. S/he may have more responsibilities than the owner of a town house or condominium, but s/he enjoys more privacy and space.

concluding paragraph

5   When the first-time home buyer finally decides to go house shopping, knowing the basic kinds of homes available makes the process easier and less frustrating. Regardless of what the outcome is—town house, condominium, or single-family residence—the new owner will have made an informed decision.

 Writing Assignment

Use classification to develop an essay on one of the following topics. During revision and editing, refer to the checklist on the inside back cover.

1. Types of transportation for the elderly
2. Types of transportation in the city
3. Types of transportation in the country
4. Types of pets
5. Special uses for pets
6. Types of activities to keep children busy
7. Sports activities for children
8. Sports activities for handicapped adults
9. Sports activities for college students
10. Sports activities for people who work

Definition

Your *purpose* in writing a **definition** paper is to explain what you mean by a certain word or concept that could have more than one meaning. When you establish the definition at the beginning of the paper, the reader understands how your definition is different from those of others. You want the reader to understand your definition, which is based on your own experiences or thoughts.

In your college courses, you will need to write definitions that are primarily objective and based on a dictionary meaning. You may also be asked to write definitions that are subjective or based on your own feelings or experiences. These two types of definitions, with which you need to be familiar, are *denotation* and *connotation*.

The **denotation** of a word is a *general, objective definition* that might be found in a dictionary or in a science class like biology or chemistry.

A house is a building used as a place to live by one or more people.

An apple is the fruit of any *Pyres malus* tree.

The **connotation** of a word is a more *subjective, emotional definition* of a word or concept whose meaning may differ among people. To one person, an "educated person" might be someone who has read the *Encyclopaedia Britannica* from A to Z. Certainly, few people would agree with this definition, and this definition does not exist in the dictionary. Another person might consider an "educated person" to be someone who has a degree from a university or someone who has acquired knowledge through experimentation and experience. It would be your job, as the writer, to let the reader know what your definition of "educated person" is. If you were to write an essay defining "educated person," here is a possible thesis sentence: "An educated person is one who has attained knowledge through study, experimentation, and experience and is able to convey it to other people."

The *subject* of a definition paper, then, is any word or concept that has or can have more than one definition.

Here are the distinct parts of a definition paper:

1. The introduction gives the denotation of a word and your own personal connotation of the word. (This connotation either limits or extends the denotation.)

2. Support paragraphs contain example(s) that clearly show the difference between the denotation and the connotation of the word. (The emphasis is placed on the connotation because this clarifies the writer's definition.)

3. The conclusion reinforces the distinction between the denotation and connotation of the word or concept.

The following essay develops a definition of the word "home." It includes both the denotation and the connotation of the word.

A Home

denotation

1   When many people think about a home, they think about the physical place where they live. This definition restricts a home to a mere physical setting where people reside. Those who consider a home to be a place filled with possessions used solely to impress other people become "married to their home" and forget that a home should be a place where they can retreat from the pressures in life.

connotation

A home is more than just a place in which to dwell. Instead, it is a physical place with a psychological feeling that allows a person or people to feel comfortable and safe from the outside world, whether they live in a hogan or in the house next door. This place allows people to enjoy life by themselves or with other members of their family.

2   All members of a family should feel they belong in a home and are free to do the things they enjoy. A home is not a place where the children are forbidden to go into the living room for fear they will mess things up or are unable to play with their toys anywhere except in their own rooms. Nor is it a place where children are always asked to play outside or at a neighbor's home.

examples that emphasize what a home is not

Rather, it is a place where people are able to do the things that they enjoy doing, whether working on a model airplane or painting on canvas. A home is not a residence with antique silk sofa cushions that no one is allowed to sit on. This is not to say that the home cannot be expensive or that it should become a pigpen. Members of a home learn to take care of their sanctuary and treat it with great love and respect.

specific example of a home

3   Some Native Americans living on reservations in the Southwest still live in the most cherished homes of all—hogans. Because the hogan has only one room, all activities center in this room. Here the family members cook, converse with each other, and enjoy life with one another. They are protected from the outside world and find safety around a warm stove. When evening comes, they spread their thick blankets on the floor and sleep close to one another. There is great love and camaraderie in this one room that is home. Though the physical surroundings are limited, the psychological feeling of spaciousness exists, and the family members experience a harmony with the natural world.

example of an ideal home

4   Sometimes the house next door is a wonderful home because it is more than just a physical structure. Whenever there are family gatherings, everyone prefers to go to this home. The children are provided with art items and are allowed to cut, paste, and paint to create anything they wish. Their efforts never go unnoticed and are rewarded with praise. When they finish, they clean everything up and then head for the pool table. The smell of food is present as the adults cook, play cards, and share parts of each other's lives. Someone who drives by the home might say that it is an ordinary home in a middle-class neighborhood, but this home is anything but ordinary. The remarkable part of this home is not the physical boundaries but the psychological freedom that provides the love and concern that seem to be everywhere.

conclusion that reinforces distinction between denotation and connotation

5   A home is not just a physical structure where people reside, but rather it is also a place where people feel comfortable and can enjoy "doing their own thing." Here they experience freedom and security in their own sanctuary.

Writing Assignment

Use definition to develop an essay. Show how your meaning is different from the dictionary meaning for one of the following words. During revision and editing, refer to the checklist on the inside back cover.

1. discipline
2. loyalty
3. religion
4. brother/sister
5. creativity
6. beauty
7. sincerity

Cause/Effect Analysis

This may be the first time you have seen the term **cause/effect analysis**; however, you use this type of reasoning every day. You get up in the morning and ask yourself, "Why does it have to rain today of all days?" If your car doesn't start, you wonder, "Why isn't it starting?" As you rush through traffic, you unconsciously think, "Why do I live in such a busy city?" You may also think about the effects of these events: "What will happen next because it is raining?" "What are the results of my having a stalled car?" "What are the effects of my living in such a busy city?" Almost everyone instinctively analyzes day-to-day problems to find the causes and effects. This type of reasoning is similar to the kind of thinking you will do when you write a cause/effect paper. The *purpose,* then, is to explain causes or effects of something that happens.

The *topic* for a cause/effect analysis is any event or occurrence for which you want to find all the causes or effects. For example, if you want to build a custom home, you might want to examine the underlying reasons. Your examination will show that some causes uncover other causes. At times, reasons can be hidden, so when you are analyzing a complex question, spend time seeking all the reasons. Careful thinking and brainstorming will pay off. If you want to examine the effects of an event, you must also do thorough thinking and brainstorming.

For a causal analysis, the *thesis sentence* can start as a question but must be in statement form when you draft your paper. For instance, if you want to write an analysis of the causes for the subject "why build a custom home," the thesis sentence, to start with, could be, "Why would anyone want to build a custom home?"

Next, *gather information* to help you discuss and explain the reasons discovered in your brainstorming. In your paper, you want to provide your reader with examples, statistics if needed, and authoritative verification of the causes. Then, *draft your paper.*

The pattern of *organization* for a cause/effect paper is as follows:

1. The introductory paragraph summarizes the causes (or effects) of the subject being analyzed.

2. Support paragraphs clearly explain the causes (or effects) of the event or occurrence being analyzed. (Each support paragraph usually explains one cause or one effect.)

3. The concluding paragraph reinforces the main idea.

The following essay is an example of causal analysis. For an essay that discusses *effects,* see "Parenting: Singular" on page 401.

To Build or Not to Build

hook 1   Building permits, water and sewer taps, architectural drawings, delayed schedules, construction mishaps, and disreputable builders are a few of the horrors that race through a person's mind when thinking of building a house. Those who have never tried it would probably hesitate or at best think it over for several days. Some people who have dared to build their own homes swear that
transition   they would never do it again. So then, why is it that some still choose to enter
thesis sentence into this uncelebrated, unfamiliar experience? The reasons vary, but the common ones are that building a home may be a necessity, may have a financial advantage, and can provide personal satisfaction in a unique design.

necessity 2   In some cases, necessity underlies the decision to build a home. Unless people have beautiful property and plenty of money, they usually purchase a preconstructed home when they are in the market for a house. However, when the housing market does not offer the house they want or need, then potential buyers may be forced to construct the house for themselves. For instance, if a family moves to a small town where land is reasonable and the housing market is poor, building is the only choice. If the buyers have a special need, like four baths or a walk-out basement for a business, there is no alternative but to build.

If a family wants to move into a certain area where the choice of homes is limited, then construction of a custom home becomes unavoidable.

financial causes   3   Another important reason for building a home is financial. Building a home keeps an owner from paying a large real estate commission. Currently, a real estate commission is 6 percent, so if someone buys a ready-made $170,000 home, the buyer will pay close to $10,200 in real estate fees. Also, a prospective home builder has some control over the total cost of the construction. "Sweat equity" means that the homeowner and the home builder enter into a partnership in which the owner can do some of the labor to defray costs. Painting, tiling, landscaping, or any labor the owner chooses can be done on weekends to save dollars. In the same way, if the builders have plenty of time and are flexible, they can find bargains for lumber, concrete, appliances, carpet, or any other major items. The buyers have no control over most of these items in an already-constructed house. More control over finances can be a significant underlying reason for deciding in favor of building a home instead of purchasing a preconstructed home.

personal/psychological   4   Other important reasons for building a home are psychological. The challenge
causes   of accomplishing a major project can bring a person satisfaction when the job is completed. Also, the prospective home builders feel as though they are the creators of the home and immediately take on the pride of ownership. Because they have a better idea of the struggle and time that went into the home, they have a deep sense of appreciation. Another emotion that might cause a person to build a home is obtaining a sense of individuality. Because the homeowner-builders have the opportunity to create and change the floor plan, they know that no other home exists that is exactly like their own. To those people who feel strongly about having a unique design, this motive may be a very strong incentive for building. Even though emotional causes may not be very obvious at first, they are usually very strong influencing forces.

conclusion   5   A person's home is an extremely important place. It represents not only shelter but personal tastes and satisfactions. It is also the most valuable item a person ever owns. Deciding to build this valuable possession can be frightening and frustrating. Many people would never choose to take on such a major responsibility and task. However, some people are forced into the decision and find that there are advantages. Financial benefits, an opportunity to exhibit creativity, and a deep enjoyment and satisfaction in having a unique design all cause people to undertake this creative and satisfying project.

 Writing Assignment

Use cause/effect analysis to develop an essay on one of the following topics. During revision and editing, refer to the checklist on the inside back cover.

1. Why we have funerals

2. Results of a particular disappointment

3. Reasons for being successful in an activity

4. Results of being successful in an activity

5. Reasons people get a divorce

6. Reasons cities levy taxes

7. Reasons the state government or federal government levies taxes

8. Impact (effects) of taxes on citizens

9. Reasons people change jobs

10. Reasons young people move away from parents

11. Effects of moving away from parents

Process Analysis

Many times in your life, both in and out of school, you are going to be asked to explain how something is done or how to do something. How well you handle this request will depend on how clearly you can sort out the steps of a process or procedure and present them in a clear, logical way. Your audience, whether listening to you or reading your explanation, needs to be able to understand your information clearly and, if necessary, follow your directions precisely. The easiest way to practice these skills is to think through and write a **process** essay.

The *purpose* of a process essay is to tell how to do something (give a set of directions) or how something occurs or how something works.

These are important skills in school because your instructors expect you to show how well you understand basic concepts in your classes. Sometimes they want you to demonstrate that you can do something, telling on paper how to go through a particular procedure if that skill is part of your learning in the class. You could be asked to write about a variety of *topics*. For example, you may be asked in your environmental geology class to explain the process of topsoil erosion in the West. Your history professor may ask you to explain how a tax bill becomes law in the U.S. Congress. Your automotive technology professor may ask you to explain how to overhaul a carburetor.

These kinds of thinking and writing skills are also important in the world outside of school. In the business world, you cannot become a supervisor, a manager, or a director if you cannot understand how processes work or cannot explain them to someone else. You may be asked to explain a procedure to a superior or to someone under you. For example, if a vice president asks you to make a presentation to new employees summarizing how your department works within the entire operation of the company, you can do this effectively only if you practice these kinds of thinking and writing skills beforehand. If you are responsible for training new employees, you must be able to explain clearly and logically what they need to do by giving them clear directions. You might even get so good at this that you become the head of an entire department devoted to training.

Regardless of what the project or assignment is, before you start, be sure you know the parts of the process you are going to explain. You know the process because you have either read about it or have done it yourself. Most of the time, there is no substitute for firsthand information, information gained from your own hands-on experience. Being able to explain a process or give directions means that you must first break down the process into steps to be sure you understand all that is involved and to see which steps are most important. Breaking down the process or procedure into steps also helps you to decide the best order to put them in to explain them clearly. Again, you cannot explain anything that you do not thoroughly understand.

Be prepared to do some careful thinking to get the information in clear, logical order and to write a paper that can be understood easily. As for any kind of paper, producing a process paper follows a series of steps. The following discussion pertains to explaining how to do something.

Decide the purpose of the essay.

Brainstorm or **list the steps** as they occur to you.

Rearrange the list in the order in which the steps must be done.

Draft your paper, using command verbs.

With respect to the essay's purpose, decide what you want the reader to understand clearly. The reader should be able to follow the steps you explain and to undertake the project you are giving directions for. The reader should know what to do to get the desired results. If your topic is "remodeling a kitchen," then your reader should learn how to create an efficient, new kitchen with new appliances—carefully and professionally.

Looking at the rearranged list, begin thinking about drafting support paragraphs for your main idea. Write a *topic sentence* for each major step, and use command verbs to tell the reader clearly what to do at each stage of the process. Stay on track, and your reader will follow you. Obviously, the number of topic sentences you write will also be the number of support paragraphs for your paper.

Here is the pattern of *organization* for the process paper:

1. The introduction clearly states that this paper will give directions for doing something.

2. Support paragraphs guide the reader step-by-step through the process. (Each paragraph is a separate step.)

3. The concluding paragraph completes the process.

The following essay shows the steps that can be followed to remodel a kitchen.

How to Remodel Your Kitchen

hook 1   After several years of living in the same house, people find that remodeling must be done if the house is to be kept in "livable" condition. The one room that many people decide to remodel first is the kitchen. Many times all the appliances go at once: the refrigerator leaks when it defrosts; the dishwasher does not get the dishes clean; the thermostat in the oven does not work; and the garbage *transition* disposal quit. The kitchen suddenly seems too small for the family. It is time to *thesis sentence* remodel. Remodeling to have the kitchen of your dreams can be done without disappointments if you follow some simple steps.

first major step 2   Before you do anything else, **gather information from all available sources.** Purchase a book on kitchen remodeling or go to the library to check out a book or gather magazine articles on the subject. Take a class on remodeling a kitchen. One very valuable resource is stores that specialize in custom kitchen cabinets. Talk to the people at the stores' showrooms. Remember, though, you are still gathering information at this time, so do not sign any contracts. Another excellent source for getting ideas is to look at model homes, so look at as many as possible. Also talk to friends who have remodeled their kitchens recently. Ask them for their ideas or biggest regrets. Profit from other people's mistakes. When you feel you know everything about kitchens, move on to the next step.

second major step 3   This next step is to **decide on exactly which new appliances to buy.** Usually stoves, refrigerators, and dishwashers are replaced. Decide if you want a built-in stove or a drop-in stove. Also consider a range top built into an island and an oven and microwave built into the wall. Because refrigerators come in many sizes and varieties, choose the size and brand you plan to buy before you go on. Also, consider whether or not you want it built into the wall. After looking at the different kinds of dishwashers available, choose one that will not only clean the dishes well, but is energy-efficient. Get the exact measurements of the stove, refrigerator, and dishwasher you have selected and move on to the next step.

| *third major step* | 4 | Now the fun begins. **Get a visual idea of your new kitchen.** Buy a package of graph paper and draw the dimensions of your kitchen walls to scale. Be accurate, because appliances and cabinets need to fit snugly. Then, using the same scale, cut out a paper representation of each appliance, including the sink. Once this is done, rearrange the appliances on the piece of graph paper, mentally adding possible counter space as you go. If you plan to include an island, be sure that the dishwasher door or refrigerator door can swing open easily and that the traffic pattern meets your needs. It could be disastrous if you planned the kitchen so the back door opened into the refrigerator or dishwasher. Also, be sure you have ample counter space near the refrigerator and stove. Then keep shuffling the "puzzle" pieces until you are satisfied with the outcome. |

| *fourth major step* | 5 | Possibly the least enjoyable but most profitable part comes next: getting the bids and choosing the contractor or subcontractors. **Get bids from at least three different sources.** Of course, if you have one company responsible for all of the remodeling, go to at least three different companies and ask for comparable bids on your scale drawing. If possible, do the subcontracting yourself. Hire your own cabinetmaker, carpenter, electrician, and tile person. The price on any specific job can vary greatly. Three different licensed electricians may give you three different bids on the needed electrical work—for example, $2,400, $1,600, and $800. Before you decide on which bid to take, however, ask for and check out references for their previous jobs, and check with the local registrar of contractors. If possible, look at some work that they have done. Though this step is time-consuming, you will be glad that you made the effort to do this evaluation. |

| *conclusion* | 6 | The final step is the simplest. **Sign the contract or subcontracts with the most qualified bidders, and relax.** In a matter of weeks, your inadequate kitchen will be transformed into a functional, beautiful kitchen that will be enjoyed by every member of the family. The refrigerator will bring forth ice cubes rather than leak on the floor; the oven will cook without burning; and the dishwasher will get the dishes clean. Ask yourself, "Can I afford to put this off any longer? Is it time to 'go for it'?" |

Writing Assignment

Use process analysis to develop an essay on one of the following activities. Show how to do the activity successfully. During revision and editing, refer to the checklist on the inside back cover.

1. Eat well
2. Discipline children
3. Raise a puppy
4. Celebrate a holiday
5. Choose a mate
6. Put on a play
7. Keep peace in a family
8. Prepare for a vacation
9. Vacation with children
10. Buy a new car

Argumentation

The *purpose* of an **argumentative paper** is to persuade the reader to your way of thinking. Your audience is usually the uncommitted reader, one who is not strongly committed to one side or the other. You probably would not even attempt to convince a presidential campaign manager to move to the other side in an election. You do not want to alienate anyone who is committed to the other side, but you do want to appeal to someone who is willing to listen to what you have to say. You would try hardest, though, to appeal to the many people from the general population who are uncommitted or are not strongly affiliated with the other side.

The *topic* for an argumentative paper must be an issue that has two sides. If your topic involves homes, one side might be that "foreclosed homes are beneficial to people," and the other side might be that "foreclosed homes are harmful to society." After reading and researching, you must decide what your position will be and what the opponent's position will be.

Here are the *parts* of an argumentative paper:

1. The introduction states the writer's position and the opponent's position objectively.

2. Support paragraphs include statistics and authorities in the field to support each point in the argument.

3. The conclusion includes a restatement of the writer's position.

The writer's position and the opponent's position may function as the introductory paragraph for the argumentative paper. The important part to remember is that you as the writer need to be fair in presenting both positions. Do *not* set up the opponent unfairly. Sometimes a writer deliberately sets up a "straw man," someone presented just so he or she can be knocked down. For instance, you may state your position as "Buying a new home is advantageous to a young couple just starting out." If you state the opponent's position as "Young people who buy new homes right after they start out are greedy and impatient for the good life," you are being unfair and distracting the reader from the real issue. The real issue for the opponent should be that "For young people just starting out, renting a home is more practical than buying a home."

The introduction, then, consists of objectively presenting both the writer's position and the opponent's position (in one or two paragraphs). There is no room to be unfair or to present the introduction from a distorted viewpoint.

Some instructors will require you to preview your main arguments when you state your position in your thesis sentence. Others do not require you to do this. Previewing the main points helps you know in your own mind what your arguments are before you begin the paper.

If you take the position that "buying foreclosed homes has a devastating effect on society," you might preview the main points by stating that it has a devastating effect on "individuals, on the neighborhoods where the foreclosure occurs, and on both the local and federal governments." This maps out your entire argument, and each paragraph that follows will prove these points.

The next part of the argumentative paper is the support paragraphs. These paragraphs need to persuade the reader that what is presented in the introduction is true. In order to be persuasive, you must avoid using your own opinion anywhere except in stating your own position. Because the thesis sentence (position) is your opinion, the support paragraphs establish that this opinion is valid. You can do this by using statistics or direct quotations from authorities in the field. An authority in the field is someone who has studied the field thoroughly, has received recognition for her/his ideas, and has experience working in the field.

One way to support your position would be to use a quotation like the following: "HUD abandoned properties cost the government over $1 million a day." The readers should be told that this quotation came from Grace Jackson in a March 1999 transcript of her testimony published by the Committee on Government Reform, titled "HUD Losing $1 Million per Day—Promised 'Reforms' Slow in Coming." Her testimony would be considered a credible statistic. If you do not name your source, you could be accused of plagiarism, which means that you have used someone else's ideas as though they were your own.

After you feel you have supported your thesis convincingly, you are ready to end your paper. This last part of the argumentative paper is a simple restatement of your position. You have the opportunity to reinforce your opinion (position) given in the thesis sentence.

In the following essay, the author uses arguments to convince the reader to accept his position (opinion).

Foreclosed Homes

hook

1 In the first quarter of 2000, almost four percent of all home loans became delinquent, and of these, close to one in four went into foreclosure, according to the Mortgage Bankers Association of America. What happens to these foreclosed homes? Do they provide an opportunity for individuals to purchase a home at a reduced cost, or do they create incredible problems? Many people feel

opponent's position

that foreclosure homes, even if "neglected" or "run-down," can be transformed into attractive, comfortable homes if they take the time to find houses that they are willing to fix up. Investors may see it as an exciting opportunity to buy a

thesis sentence

home, renovate it, and then sell it for a profit. However, in the long run, these same foreclosures can have a devastating effect on individuals, on the neighborhoods where the foreclosures occur, and on both local and federal governments.

support paragraph 1

2 When foreclosures occur, both the people losing a home and the people purchasing the home often experience negative results. Losing a home means they lose everything they have invested in the home, including their initial down payment, their monthly payments, and any improvements they have made to the house. Unable to make payments or even keep up their home, they simply walk away, still owing back house payments but now carrying destroyed credit. The people purchasing these foreclosed homes can inherit problems, especially when the homes need major repairs. Additional problems occur when foreclosure homes fall into the hands of real estate investors who are dishonest. Opportunists see foreclosure homes as a chance to make some easy money. They purchase these homes, make cosmetic repairs, and then resell them at inflated prices. The new owner buys a foreclosed home, believing that it has been renovated, only to find an untold number of repairs that need to be made to

authoritative source

the home. In the July/August 2000 issue of *Mother Jones*, Kathryn Wallace gives the example of Tabatha Evans, an "unemployed single mother living on $12,000 a year in government assistance." Eager to own a home for her two boys, Evans found a foreclosed home that she could secure through a government loan. She

facts

paid $78,000 for a home that was worth much less. The investor had just purchased the home for $6,672 and then completed work that consisted of "a paint job and a drop ceiling to hide structural damage." Wallace went on to point out that "the gas leaked, and kitchen cabinets fell from the wall. When it rained, water poured into the kitchen." Tabatha was unable to pay for the needed repairs, and now she herself is facing foreclosure. Just like the homeowners before her, she will lose everything she has invested in this home.

support paragraph 2 3   When a foreclosure happens, the other homeowners in the neighborhood are also negatively impacted. In the May 21, 2001, issue of *Chicago Business*, Anthony Boylan quotes Daniel Burke, Illinois representative, as saying that foreclosure is "demoralizing for a community. It depletes the value of a home. It invites crime." A single empty home in a neighborhood can become a center for illegal activities, pulling in drug dealers and even runaways. These uninvited people who have no responsibilities toward the neighborhood destroy the home *authoritative support* "beyond redemption, stripped of doors, windows, cabinets, toilets—even copper plumbing," reports Laura Meyers in "The Home Rangers," published in *Los Angeles*. When a foreclosure occurs, neighbors must watch the empty house next door as the paint peels, the shingles fall off, and the shrubs and grass *facts* either die or grow out of control. When several foreclosures occur in the same area, the problems escalate. The boarded-up houses with roofs coming loose and litter piling up in the yards push property values down in the whole area as well as bring crime to the community. As foreclosure homes become more common, neighborhoods will continue to suffer.

support paragraph 3 4   Individuals lose their homes, and neighborhoods are forced to watch foreclosed homes affect their communities, but the problems do not end there. All taxpayers become victims when the costs are passed on to the city, state, and federal governments. When a foreclosed home sits empty, the costs to city police increase because officers must patrol the area and deal with increased drug activities. The city must also respond to complaints from responsible homeowners in the neighborhood, requiring even more money to take care of the problems. Millions of dollars may be lost when prospective buyers do not want to buy a home near boarded-up houses. New businesses do not want to locate near an area of foreclosed homes, and this, in turn, further decreases property values. Also, tax revenue decreases significantly when no one is paying property taxes on these vacant houses. When a homeowner defaults on a *authoritative source* Federal Housing Administration loan, then it is the taxpayers who must pay off the defaulted loan. In 1999, the Federal Housing Administration spent "\$6.5 million to bail out 78,890 home loans that went bad," according to Kathryn *authoritative source* Wallace. In a congressional hearing on March 23, 1999, Grace Jackson testified before the Committee on Government Reform and reaffirmed this when she said, "HUD [Housing and Urban Development] abandoned properties cost the government over \$1 million a day." Every time a home goes into foreclosure, the costs to taxpayers increase.

concluding paragraph 5   Being in debt is nothing new to Americans, but when they really get behind on their payments, they can find themselves in serious financial debt, including losing their homes. When they get five to six months behind in their mortgage payments, the lender can start foreclosure on their home. Once they are notified of a foreclosure, they have only 30 days to come up with enough money to save their home. Unfortunately, by the time they realize what is happening, it is too late to do anything about it. Foreclosure on their homes means that they lose *restatement of position* everything they have worked so hard to obtain, but they are not the only losers in the situation. The losses of these foreclosures spread to neighborhoods and eventually to all taxpayers in general.

Writing Assignment

Use argument to develop an essay. Persuade a particular audience that

1. Taxes are necessary.
2. Taxes make people poorer.
3. Divorce is harmful to children.
4. Divorce is good for children.
5. Nursing homes meet the needs of the elderly.
6. Nursing homes do not meet the needs of the elderly.
7. Photo radar should be used by police.
8. Photo radar should not be used by police.
9. Savings accounts should be started when children are young.
10. Mandatory use of seat belts saves lives.
11. Marriage should be abolished.
12. Marriage should be discouraged until both people graduate from college.
13. Custody of children should be given to fathers more often than currently occurs.
14. Custody of children should be equally split between parents.
15. Sex should be reserved for a permanent relationship.
16. Home health care has many advantages.

One of the most important skills you need is being able to decide which pattern of development is most effective for your topic. The possibilities are as varied as the number of people writing the essays. **There is no one correct pattern of development. Choose the one that helps you achieve your purpose and seems the most interesting.** Sometimes the assignment specifies the pattern of development; other times, depending on your purpose, you will need to think about how the subject can be explained in different ways.

The following list shows how different patterns can be used to write about the same subject but with different purposes.

Topic: The Circus

reasons people should not attend a circus: argumentation

kinds of events at a circus: illustration

types of animals at a circus: classification

types of people at a circus: classification

how to enjoy a circus: process analysis

ways a dog act is different from a tiger act: contrast

Sometimes you can write about a topic by combining several patterns within one essay. When your writing project does not specify the pattern of development to be used, you might discover that a blend of patterns expresses your ideas more convincingly. The commencement address "Did You Do Your Best?" (on the next page) illustrates how the author achieved his purpose with more than one pattern. In this unit, "The Mutt Who Saved Mr. Lambert" also illustrates more than one pattern of development.

Collaborative Activity

Read the selection by Dr. Reed, "Did You Do Your Best?" Then break into small groups and identify the different methods used in this selection. Be prepared to share your findings with the class.

Writing Assignment

Using the topics given, decide on a particular method of development and develop an essay. Decide what points you want to express. Choose the method that permits you to do this most effectively.

1. Garbage
2. Recycling
3. Historic buildings
4. Movies
5. Custom cars
6. Dates
7. Jobs
8. Gambling
9. Art
10. Investments

Part 2

Something to Think About, Something to Write About

Professional Essay to Generate Ideas for Writing

Did You Do Your Best?

James W. Reed, Ph.D., *commencement address given at Glendale Community College's 25th Anniversary*

1   On behalf of the faculty here at Glendale Community College, I want to congratulate each of you this evening on your achievement.

2   While putting this talk together, I began to suffer much the same flight behavior I experienced while writing as an undergraduate. And I found myself doing several of the things I did as a freshman and sophomore—walking back and forth to the refrigerator, tidying my apartment, and looking at *Auto Trader*. Because I've always loved Corvettes—the dream of owning one is probably why I initially enrolled in college—before long my eyes were scanning that section. One ad for a '78 'Vette caught my eye, and I called the owner. As the phone rang, I felt the air blowing through my hair; I smelled the salt air of the surf; and I accelerated out of a curve on Highway 1 south of Carmel, California. Well, we talked for a few minutes. He told me about all the options, including special Indy 500 Pace Car paint. I then asked, "Well,

how much do you want for it?" As he gave me the figure, the sleek little car—which was running full throttle across a beautiful suspension bridge—immediately turned into my little red Jeep. I asked the gentleman why he wanted so much, and he simply said, "Don't you understand how special this car is? It's a Silver Anniversary Edition." Today, I want you to know that you're making history. You see, you're GCC's Silver Anniversary Edition as well, and for that reason alone you'll always be a little bit special. Anniversaries make people reflect and reminisce. When you have a chance to look back at your own past, you may understand why it is important to think about what kind of purpose you want for your life and how you work to fulfill that purpose.

3   As faculty, we have recently been looking back to our world twenty-five years ago. Our world's been full of surprising changes. As I sat looking at the silver anniversary pictures during our celebration several weeks ago, my mind traveled back to that world, a world where we sang about our cars—409's, GTO's, and little deuce coupes. We could still romanticize with Rock Hudson and Doris Day, and many of us pursued that dream through marriage before ever reaching our twentieth birthday. Terror for us was a memory of a small roadside motel run by Anthony Perkins, which, I might add, made taking a shower a near impossibility for years. We started to see some new attitudes, too. No one over thirty was to be trusted, and people began chanting slogans such as "Black is beautiful!" Many were admonished for letting their hair grow over their ears and for acting so crazy about John, Paul, George, and Ringo. While some moved in this direction—peace signs, love beads, and turtlenecks— others said goodbye to school, donned military uniforms, and prepared to defend freedom in the tiny and little-known country of Vietnam. That was the world of Glendale Community College twenty-five years ago.

4   That was indeed quite a different world from yours today, one in which television shows arrange dates and people later return telling Chuck every detail—right down to their making love at the end of the evening. In today's world, an unemployed man can scrape together a couple of bucks and win a twenty-million-dollar jackpot. (We counted on a visit from Michael Anthony.) Or just think about how Japanese sports cars are everywhere, and the people who drive them are actually proud. We've come a long way, baby, all the way from the world of Donna Reed to that of Roseanne Barr and from "I wanna hold your hand" to "I want your sex."

5   I hesitate to generate any earthshaking contrasts between these two cultures, but if you were to look back at those slides of twenty-five years ago, we were a naive, funny-looking bunch. Hawks and doves alike—we went out into the world to change it, to make it a better place in our own individual way. Reading "Dear Abby" recently (April 29)—I believe in heavy research—I thought I had returned to that era. A St. Cloud University undergraduate wrote the following: "Hundreds upon thousands of men, women, and children die anonymously each and every day in heaps of bloated stomachs and brittle bones for want of food. The industrialized nations continue to belch noxious filth into the air and water of Mother Earth. The rain forests are dying. The oceans are dying." He then moves into the area of racial and class discrimination, talks about the "haves" and "have-nots," and concludes by asking readers to open their eyes regarding future generations. I couldn't help thinking how his message seemed a little out of date, his concern most unlike what I hear from many of you as I move across campus.

6   In order to get a little better handle on just how GCC students view the world, as well as what they plan to do with their future, I began asking several classes questions that addressed their reasons for attending college. Here's what I got. Many want a home—the favorites were Continental Homes at Arrowhead Ranch complete with Paddock Pools and 103-degree Jacuzzis. For cars, I heard the names Lexus, Infiniti, and BMW. There were others equally expensive. For a family, the goal

was two to three children enrolled at a preschool. Tickets seemed to be a hot item—season tickets to the Suns, the Phoenix Open, and The Tradition. (I didn't know this one until my poll.) Technology was extremely popular. There was a lot of call—no pun intended—for cellular phones, personal fax machines, modems linking into office computers. Some, believe it or not, can't wait to wear their own beeper. Memberships scored equally high, with the Arrowhead Country Club and the local Rotary ranking highest. As far as recreation goes, a Winnebago, a cabin in Prescott, and a week each year in places like Aspen, Tahoe, and Puerto Vallarta represent the run-of-the-mill answers. Some were not, however, without altruism because quite a few wanted to buy a home for Mom and Dad in Sun City—two even specified that it be close to Boswell Hospital.

7   I don't doubt for a second that you can have this lifestyle. You've been exposed to a tremendous learning opportunity. During your days here at GCC, you've written papers—some of them quite good—worked in groups, discussed philosophical concepts, studied the natural and behavioral sciences, and read many of the great books. However, as I talk to many of you, I often feel that the purpose for understanding Maslow's hierarchy of needs has been reduced to simply answering a true-false or essay question—and its application to your lives remains relatively untapped. No, I'm not going to ask you to join the Peace Corps, go into community legal service, or become a teacher. That was another era. But I do ask that you reflect the liberal arts education you've been exposed to. There's more to life than earning a living. You serve a higher purpose, I believe, than just to eat, sleep, have sex, and die.

8   When many of us graduated from college, "liberal arts" meant that we were liberated from being a cog in an organizational machine. We stood up straight—unlike our prehistoric forerunners—we looked around, our minds liberated, and we decided to use our education to do more than forage for food day in and day out. Instead of going into plastics, an offer made to Dustin Hoffman in *The Graduate,* we set out to right the world, *to create positive change.* Some of us even left the United States and went to remote parts of the earth. Now I'm not so sure how well we did. The Hunger Project hasn't been an overwhelming success. We still catch too many dolphins for each tuna, and we continue to make an unforgivable mess of the environment. We committed way too many errors—even though we were well intentioned, and, in the end, I guess many of us have become at least part-time foragers.

9   So where does that leave you? Well, I've got some good news and some bad news. The bad news is—we've got some mighty tall problems, maybe bigger than when we graduated twenty-five years ago. But the good news is—you won't have to leave the area if you want to do something about them. I can't wait to hear the nation's news each morning or read the paper to learn how we Arizonans have distinguished ourselves most recently. I read last week that we graduate fewer individuals from high school than most other states. Imagine that. We're not a dumb lot, though, especially when you consider land acquisitions by elected officials. They seem to know just where and when to make purchases so as to realize tremendous windfall profits. In private industry, we seem to be right in the middle of the savings-and-loan boondoggle. And in the nation's newest "off the record" business—drugs—we rank fourth from the top in cocaine usage.

10   When I told a colleague about my talk, he remarked, "That's not only undignified, it's depressing. I thought you were a motivational speaker." Well, I do motivational speaking, but I see motivation a little differently than most. It's best defined, I believe, as providing someone with a motive to act. If what you've heard here isn't

motive, I don't know what is. But frankly, I'm somewhat excited about the future. You are the ones who will be building the homes, arranging the loans, investigating "drive-by" shootings, serving in elected office, and working in our educational system. Whatever your career, you will be involved in the picture, our picture. And you will be called upon to make decisions, *choices*. What will you do?

11   I always turn to philosophers for answers to such questions, and the one I want to turn to this evening is Norda Ramona—that's my mother. As I was getting dressed one morning—while yet in high school—I began to put on a pair of underwear I found on the floor of my bedroom. Not certain if I'd worn them the day before, I yelled to my mother at the other end of the house, "Mama, are these shorts dirty?" She hollered back, "Yes!" At breakfast, I sat across from her wondering how she knew so much—she wasn't even in my room where she could see them. How did she know without even being there whether they were clean or dirty? When I finally asked her this question, she sat up straight, looked at me, and said, "James, if there's ever any question, they're dirty." And that's what I have to say to you this evening. If there's ever any question at all about the choice, it's dirty. You may not be carrying the torch of the sixties, I understand. But you may have an opportunity to carry a few tools home from work. After all, you've been there for five years. Or give someone an unearned grade, maybe fix a smog certificate, mistreat the ones you love, or show a gift to a nonexistent charitable organization on your IRS return. I hope each of these actions would make you pause and ask a question because they're all dirty.

12   A number of years ago, Admiral Rickover was interviewing candidates to head the nuclear submarine program. During a two-hour discussion with one of the officers he asked, "How did you stand in your class at the Naval Academy?" "Sir, I stood fifty-ninth in a class of 820!" The young officer sat back to wait for the congratulations, but they never came. Instead, the question, "Mr. Carter, did you do your best?" The soon-to-be senior officer of the *Sea Wolf* gulped and said, "No, sir, I didn't always do my best." Admiral Rickover then shifted in his chair, looked the young Carter in the eyes, and asked one final question: "Why not?"

13   During the time I was reading the Rickover autobiography, I paid a visit to my dentist. When I sat down in his chair, he must have detected my terror—I hate to go there—and began engaging me in a rather long and anxiety-relieving conversation. During our discussion he related that he was a graduate of GCC, and I wouldn't be editorializing too much to say that only a few years ago he was sitting where you are tonight. Finally, needle in hand, he became a man with a purpose. As he drew closer to inject the novocaine, I looked up into his eyes and wondered if he had done his best. Did he attend his classes, do his own work, respond with his own answers, and was he now keeping abreast of the latest techniques? I hoped he wasn't in practice because of a long-term friendship with the State Examiner.

14   As I, along with so many others, look into your eyes tonight, next week, next year—our Silver Anniversary Edition—we ask you the same question. Yes, we want you to have it all, but only if you've gone about it in the right way. We'll no doubt continue to have problems. *However, it's not so much the circumstances that count, but it's how you react to them. We're living in a world where your answer will probably not be heard through your individual expressions but through the community your choices help to create. Only through your making enough of the right choices will we reunite here to celebrate tomorrow's gold.*

15   My colleagues and I congratulate you on being an important part of the GCC tradition. We look forward to the community you will create and to reminiscing with you in 2015. Oh, one final word: *Do your best!*

Understanding Words

Briefly define the following words as they are used in the above essay.

1. reminisce   *to call past events to mind*

2. admonished   *scolded*

3. naive   *innocent, childlike*

4. noxious   *harmful, unhealthy, poisonous*

5. altruism   *unselfishness*

6. editorializing   *expressing an opinion, sometimes inappropriately*

Collaborative Writing Project: Working and Learning Together

As you have done previously, start your next essay assignment by working in groups of three or four to discuss the quotations below that are related to "Did You Do Your Best?" Your discussion may help you when you choose a topic. As your group works, take notes so that you can develop a thesis sentence.

Quotations: Additional Ideas on Success and the Future

". . . Young immigrants . . . along with children being born to immigrant boomers, will make the country more diverse than ever. These diverse young people will play, study, work, and grow up together. . . . This will be the key to less prejudice and better racial harmony in the future." *Bob Loysk*

"Success is a journey, not a destination." *Ben Sweetland*

"There is only one success—to be able to spend your life in your own way." *Christopher Morley*

"Failure is not an overnight experience, and neither is success." *J. Bruck Newellyn*

"Do the right thing even when it may seem like the hardest thing in the world." *Dave Thomas*

"Every time I've done something that doesn't feel right, it has ended up not being right." *Mario Cuomo*

"The best place to find a helping hand is at the end of your own arm." *Swedish proverb*

"You've got to do your own growing, no matter how tall your grandfather was." *Irish proverb*

"There are three types of baseball players—those who make it happen, those who watch it happen, and those who wonder what happened." *Tommy Lasorda*

"When I look at the future, it's so bright, it burns my eyes." *Oprah Winfrey*

"Where will I be five years from now? I delight in not knowing. That's one of the greatest things about life—its wonderful surprises." *Marlo Thomas*

Writing Assignment/Working in a Group

1. Still working in your group, choose a topic from the following list.

   What do you plan to accomplish after you graduate from college?

How do you want to spend the rest of your life?

What makes an effective employee?

What role does honesty play in the world today?

What could be done to reduce prejudice in the future?

What can people do to ensure success in their lives?

How does college prepare a person for the future?

Who influences the way people think about what is right and wrong?

Are people more or less materialistic than they have been in the past?

How have values changed in the last few years?

2. After your group members have chosen topics, discuss the purpose and audience for each essay in turn. Discuss the method of development that seems to fit each particular topic. Let the method come naturally from the topic.

Working Individually

1. Develop your thesis sentence.

2. Brainstorm for additional information you need to write strong support paragraphs.

3. Group ideas carefully and write an outline to check the logical order of your ideas.

4. When you write your introduction, try to use one of the quotations above as a hook. If you were writing about planning for the future, for example, the Marlo Thomas quotation about life's surprises would be a good contrast to the thesis.

5. Remember also that you may want to use more than one method as you saw illustrated in "Did You Do Your Best?"

6. As you write and revise each support paragraph, use transitional words and phrases, including key words from the topic and direction in your thesis sentence.

7. Draft a strong conclusion that reinforces your thesis sentence, and include a reference to the hook to give a sense of closure.

Peer Review

1. Work in groups of four or five. Read each paper aloud and discuss it carefully.

2. Does the paper have a strong introduction, adequately developed support paragraphs, and a powerful conclusion?

3. Without being told by the author, identify the method or methods used to develop the essay.

4. Decide if the method is effective for the purpose of the paper.

5. Describe the voice in each essay and decide if it is appropriate for the purpose of the essay.

6. Choose one paragraph from each paper, and discuss the coherence.

7. Edit for consistent point of view, subject-verb agreement, consistent verb tense, and correct punctuation.

Part 3

Paragraphs and Essays for Discussion and Analysis

Student Writing

Illustration

Heroes—"Sung" and "Unsung"

Lorena Acosta, *student*

1   Every nation, every family, every individual has heroes. These people have done something so outstanding that they are admired and respected for their actions. Usually, they have saved a life or lives, or they have done something else that has profoundly affected the beliefs and values of the people who look upon them as heroes. Most of the time these outstanding individuals get wide public recognition for their acts. Sometimes, though, heroic people do not receive any recognition for what they have done. These unrecognized heroes are the "unsung heroes" of our time. Whether they are publicly acknowledged or not, however, heroes are special people because of their ability to react quickly, calmly, and unselfishly.

2   People who become heroes may have saved someone's life by reacting quickly in circumstances that could lead an ordinary person to freeze or not react in time. Perhaps one of the best illustrations is a drowning child at the beach or in a swimming pool. The child is struggling and crying for help or, worse, is not making a sound. The person who quickly evaluates the situation and dives into the surf or the pool to save the child would certainly be a hero in the eyes of the public. Recently, a five-year-old child jumped into a swimming pool at an apartment complex because he had seen other children doing the same thing. The children at the other end of the pool noticed that he was floating below the surface of the water and quickly pulled him out. The child did not drown or sustain permanent damage because the rescuers quickly saw what was happening to the child and, instead of calling out for someone else to help, jumped in and did the job.

3   Sometimes, heroes are those who not only react quickly but also calmly under terrifying circumstances. In a 1989 airliner crash landing in Sioux City, Iowa, there were several heroes, one in particular. When the DC-10 crash-landed, it broke apart and caught fire. Although many people died, more than half of the passengers lived. Twenty-five or thirty lived because of one passenger who calmly took charge of one section of the burning plane. Without panic, he helped many people unbuckle their safety belts. He stood calmly and held up out of the way a heavy tangle of cables and wires blocking their way out of the plane. He gave directions to some who could not see because of the smoke, and he had to drop the cables to help some elderly people who fell while trying to get to the opening. After he had them on their feet, he pushed up the cables high enough so the people could get out. Although this hero was one of the "unsung" variety, he certainly deserves the name.

4   The pilot and the crew of the DC-10 described above are prime illustrations of the unselfish hero, who may be the first to deny any heroics. They reacted quickly, calmly, and—most important—unselfishly. They had to fly the large airliner after it had been

fatally crippled by a blown engine that had destroyed all the plane's hydraulic systems. While receiving as much help as possible from other experts and from the controllers at the Sioux City airport, the pilot repeatedly asked for instructions to help him keep the plane away from the city itself. Miraculously, having lived through the crash landing, the pilot said several times afterwards that they were not heroes, but had just done what they had to do under the circumstances. From the point of view of many, the public and other professional pilots, getting the plane to the end of the runway was a clear example of calm, unselfish heroism.

5   Whether "sung" or "unsung," special heroes save many lives in America every year. Not all heroes become well known, but they are heroes just the same. Their heroic actions display unselfish actions.

Understanding Words
Briefly define the following word as it is used in the above essay.

1. hydraulic   *operated by the force of liquid*

Answers are in the Instructor's Manual, starting on page 20.

Questions on Content

1. What makes heroes special people?

2. What happened to the five-year-old child who jumped into a swimming pool?

3. What did the hero in paragraph 3 do to save lives?

Questions on Form

1. What method of development is used in this essay?

2. Where is the thesis sentence?

3. Does paragraph 2 have short interrelated examples or one extended example? Paragraph 3? Paragraph 4?

Comparison/Contrast

The Baptism in Blood and the Beach Party

Lonnie B. Noah III, *student at Arizona State University, preparing to become an English teacher*

1   During the latter 1960s and early 1970s, the United States' involvement in Vietnam became what is considered to be the biggest black mark on American society to date. My uncle George was one of almost nine million men and women who were sent off like dirty little secrets to fight the most unpopular and hated military conflict ever, only to return to a nightmare of abuse at the hands of war protesters. Society at the time was wrapped up in great changes politically and spiritually, and it dealt with issues never before exposed in a public light.

2   In 1990, Operation Desert Shield, which later became Operation Desert Storm, was the quickest and most popular large-scale military victory in the history of the world. Soldiers of the Gulf War, myself included, were sent off in a hail of flag waving and National Anthem singing and returned to a heroes' welcome that would have made Ol' John Wayne himself envious. Our war took place at a time when American society needed to put a good ass-whipping on some other nation. It was a time of presidential election and frenzied patriotism.

3   I asked my uncle to compare war experiences with me, so as to get a better understanding of the huge social and political contrasts between our wars. He says he feels comfortable talking to me because only another war veteran can understand things that most of humanity can't. Truth be known, when he begins to let out his

demons, I can't even begin to comprehend the horror and fear that was Vietnam. Our wars happened in different places and times and took place under totally opposite situations. His war was one of surrealistic nightmares and sheer hell, and mine was a good time at a heavily armed beach party.

4   We sit on the sun-baked patio of my grandmother's house, drinking frosty, golden-brown bottles of Pacifico beer while watching a blazing fireball swing its arc toward the western sky. Talking about the war isn't easy for George. He strikes a flame and lights up another Marlboro, his hands exhibiting a nervous shake. He takes a healthy gulp of beer, washing down what is perhaps a little shot of courage that helps him free the past that clouds his soul. He lets out a deep sigh and begins to speak.

5   "When I first got there, I was assigned to this unit called The Motivation Station, where the Marine Corps got new people all fired up to kill the first thing in sight. There was this fat-ass lieutenant who used to preach fire and brimstone about Charlie not having souls and the Vietcong being the devil. We learned about 40 different ways to kill people each day, and he told us, 'When in doubt, pull the god-damn trigger. A dead gook is a safe gook!' Was I the only one over there wondering about the rights and wrongs of all this killing? My first night at my Recon unit, I heard all this yelling and carrying on. I ran out of my tent to see what was going on, and this little Vietnamese kid went running right towards me. All of a sudden, there's a bunch of shots, and this little kid's chest exploded in front of me, his heart blown right out of him. He died right there at my feet. His heart was still pumping. There was blood everywhere. This gung-ho asshole named McCarty blasted that little boy for stealing one of his C-ration biscuits. No one said a damn thing about it. I puked my guts out for two days after that."

6   To play on the words of Bob Dylan, "The times, they a-did some changin'." For three weeks before I was deployed to Kuwait with the 18th Airborne Corps, I was indoctrinated in the customs and practices of the Middle Eastern culture. The Army spent a great deal of time focusing on teaching us the good manners and respectable behavior necessary to deal with Kuwaitis, Saudis, and even those we were sent to kill, the Iraqis. We were taught such things as common courtesy, the proper way to sit, how to eat, the evils of using the left hand, observation of their holy days, and because we didn't want to offend the ones we were to kill, we were banned from all nudie books and alcoholic beverages. The closest I ever came to seeing someone losing it and killing a civilian was when this nerdy guy in my section named Geraghty got mad at the camels for eating our trash and shot at one with an AT-4 rocket. For that little stunt, he was brought up on charges, fined $1,500, and ordered to go to remedial indoctrination. I was one of the few people even issued ammunition prior to our attack on Iraq because there was too high a risk for more of that type of buffoonery taking place. While Vietnam was a war of the open promotion of wholesale killing, Desert Shield/Storm was one of proper manners and etiquette.

7   We have been talking for hours, and it is getting late. The sky is awash in an orgy of colors melting into one, and a blood-colored disc slowly begins to hide behind the western mountains like a shy child. We open two more bottles of beer and savor the icy libation, and most of all the light feelings of openness it brings.

8   We begin to talk of the political situations that sent us to the far reaches of the Earth to fulfill our duties. My uncle was trapped in a system of secrecy and blood oaths while I was merely a part of the biggest network TV ratings race ever televised. George lights up another smoke and laughs, "At the time, the Government was really secretive about what we were doing over there. Being that I was in a Recon battalion, we were totally cloak and dagger. We had guys from the Agency (CIA) assigned to us, and they watched us like hawks. When we went on missions into Laos, the Agency

guys changed the maps so they would show that we were still in Vietnam. We went so far into Laos that we couldn't get a resupply chopper for two weeks. Because of their politics, I had to survive by eating rats and maggots. My worst fear was starving to death, not being shot. We weren't allowed any off time, either. The Agency guys kept us pent up, and we couldn't even take a piss without them watching. No fun whatsoever, no catch, no football, no swimming, nothing."

9   I look away and think to myself that I wasn't in a war but instead in Disneyland. We had no secrets. Everywhere we went, we had a crew from CNN poking around, save for the actual invasion of Iraq. There were no supersecret infiltrations or Ramboesque techniques. We fought a so-called good war that was supposed to happen, televised for all to see, and blessed with all the comforts of home. We had Kentucky Fried Chicken, pizza, burritos, and corn dogs from the Wolf Wagons, not to mention the Meals, Ready to Eat (MREs) with such culinary masterpieces as the dehydrated pork pattie with powdered ketchup. My biggest concern in the desert war was how to get the most effective use out of my official ration of seven sheets of toilet paper per meal, especially after dealing with things like Army chicken à la king. Needless to say, I passed off most of my MREs on the starving Iraqis who surrendered to us. We didn't have CIA supervision but CNN supervision. If Wolf Blitzer wanted a particular shot, then we were ordered by our Battalion Commander to get dolled up in battle gear and go pose for it. As for recreation, our days were spent using the 125-millimeter main guns on M1A1 Abrams tanks as poles for our volleyball nets and throwing dirt clods at the Marines. The war I fought in was what America wanted to see, happy photo-ops for newscasters and never-ending victories, and my uncle's war was fought for the dark forgotten underbelly of American politics.

10   The changes in society are obvious in the way our wars ended. When my uncle was sent home from Vietnam, he was met at El Toro Marine Air Station in California by groups of war protesters. "This hippie spit in my face and called me a butcher. I hit him so god-damned hard I broke his jaw and eye socket and got locked up for 30 days for violating his right to protest. I survived 26 months in Nam just to come home and be treated like shit."

11   When I came home from the desert, we got nothing but the best of heroes' welcomes and all that fanfare. We didn't really do anything, but America was starved for heroes, and I guess that meant us. We were put on pedestals and treated like gods. On my first flight back to Arizona, an old man gave up his first-class seat to me and led the whole plane in a cheer for all Desert Storm veterans.

12   America was at a point in the 1960s when war was an extremely unpopular subject, and the people sent to fight it were treated like dirt. I was a part of what has become the most popular war in the history of the world while people like my uncle gave everything and ended up being made into scapegoats. Our wars took place under completely different circumstances: his was impossible to win, and mine was impossible to lose. The very same society that made his experience a living hell took only 15 years to turn mine into a walk on the beach.

Understanding Words
Briefly define the following words as they are used in the above essay.

1. frenzied   *agitated*

2. surrealistic   *having strange dreamlike incongruities*

3. gook   *negative slang term for Vietnamese*

4. deployed   *sent to a war zone*

5. libation   *drink*

Questions on Content

1. What two wars are being discussed?

2. Who are the narrators?

3. What conclusions does the essay present about the wars?

Questions on Form

1. What method of organization is used in the essay?

2. Does the essay use the block or the alternating pattern?

3. In what paragraph is the thesis sentence?

4. Describe the voices in the essay.

5. How does the author distinguish the two voices?

Classification

Which One Are You?

Kristi von Aspen, *student*

1   Midterms! Midterms! Midterms! The mere sound of that word sends chills down most spines. Why? Well, midterms translate into tests, and tests require studying—not the most favorable extracurricular activity on a student's agenda. But no matter what the subject may be, a person acquires certain methods of preparation over the years. I have observed these habits and concluded that there are three major types of students: The Perfectionists, the Naturalists, and the Procrastinators.

2   First of all, the Perfectionists are methodical people. They are always calculating and planning ahead for events in the future. One can usually find them making lists of things to do and then carefully arranging those items into well-thought-out time schedules. For example, if a test is to be given in two weeks and there are 140 pages of material to be covered, the Perfectionist immediately divides the days into the pages. The answer will give him the average number of pages he will need to read each night. There's even a good chance that this person will finish in advance and move on to something else. Perfectionists are high achievers and, on the whole, earn better grades than the other two groups.

3   The second category of students is the carefree spirits I like to call Naturalists. These people possess a casual, happy-go-lucky kind of attitude that is reflected in every aspect of their lives. For instance, when it comes to schoolwork, Naturalists study only when it is convenient for them. Their motto is, "If it gets done, it gets done." Don't get me wrong. Most Naturalists do have a conscience; in the back of their minds they know what they have to do, but they do their work in a nonconformist manner. They just refuse to allow academics to dominate their world.

4   Finally, there are the Procrastinators—the obvious choice to discuss last. Waiting until the final hour to study for that big test is one of the main traits of these people. As a result of their postponements, Procrastinators sometimes have to resort to cheating as a means of receiving an acceptable grade. Mothers of these students often have hoarse voices from constantly yelling at their children to do homework. Usually, a person of this nature never learned how to manage time and probably never will. Occasionally, some are able to break out of this rut and begin to lead normal lives.

5   Everyone, at one time or another, has experimented with all three of these studying methods. It's just a matter of discovering what works best for the individual and how to adapt to it. In the meantime, good luck on those midterms!

Understanding Words

Briefly define the following word as it is used in the above essay.

   1. procrastinators   *people who put off doing something until later*

Questions on Content

1. Who are the methodical people?

2. What characterizes the naturalists?

3. What does a procrastinator sometimes do to pass a test?

Questions on Form

1. What is the basis for the classification, and where is it made clear to the reader?

2. Where does the supporting information come from?

3. Identify a shift in point of view in the conclusion. Does it seem to work in this essay?

Definition

Wealth

Andrea Gonzales, *student*

    Wealth is quite often defined as a great quantity or store of money or property of value. However, wealth can be a great quantity of many other things acquired, not just material items. There are those who have had the good fortune to have seen many beautiful places throughout their lives. They have acquired many priceless memories. There is the man who is wealthy because he has many friends who are loyal and true, and to acquire friends like these makes a man rich. Perhaps the most wealthy man of all is the man who has a loving family around him. This alone can bring great happiness, which no amount of money can buy. Wealth is so much more than a great store of money. It can be any possession that is priceless to its owner.

Questions on Content

1. Who is perhaps the wealthiest person of all?

2. What is the denotation of wealth?

3. What is the connotation of wealth?

Questions on Form

1. What did the author do to make the connotation of wealth clear?

2. What makes the end of the paragraph effective?

Winter

Joan Papke, *student*

    The meaning of winter according to the dictionary is a period of inactivity and decay. However, to a desert dweller like me, it is not a time of inactivity and decay, but a time of new activities and growth. Many of the summer-scorched desert plants spring to new life from the gentle winter rains, and new species of desert growth bloom only in winter. To me it means the bright green of winter lawns and more traffic on the streets of Phoenix, more hustle and bustle in the stores, elbow-to-elbow crowds, and no room to park at the malls. To me it means people enjoying the park on weekends, jogging, playing handball, and trying unsuccessfully to get a tee time. It means thousands of "snowbirds" and many real snowbirds like mallards and pintails who also make their winter home here. No, to me, winter is not a time of inactivity and decay, but instead it is a time of new activity and a resurgence of life.

Understanding Words
Briefly define the following word as it is used in the above paragraph.

1. resurgence   *rebirth, forceful coming again*

Questions on Content

1. What is one dictionary meaning of winter?

2. What does winter mean to a desert dweller?

3. What do people in the desert enjoy doing in the winter?

Questions on Form

1. What kind of development does the author use to make the definition clear?

2. In what two places does the author state the denotation?

A Run

Tim Darcy, *student*

1   "I've decided to go on a run over the holiday weekend." This statement is simple enough and would be understood perfectly by millions of bikers and motorcycle enthusiasts throughout the English-speaking world. Why, then, out of no less than thirty-two noun definitions of the word "run" in one dictionary, do none of them apply? Apparently, lexicographers don't have the same kind of fun that bikers have because fun is what runs are all about. For the benefit of the uninitiated, a run is a planned motorcycle trip or destination that is meant to be attended by a group of riders.

2   It is interesting to wonder about how the word "run" came to be used by motorcyclists as it is today. The mere thought of a bunch of bearded, beer-bellied bikers in running shorts and Nikes, huffing and puffing down the road, is enough to rule out the most obvious literal connotation. Parallels could be drawn, if rather facetiously, to several standard uses of the word: "a run of good luck," "a dog run," "a beer run," and probably as many more as the imagination would allow. None of these meanings, however, really fit, so the question of why these events are called runs will just have to remain unanswered.

3   A run, as stated above, can be either a trip or a destination, and motorcycles are the common denominator. There are poker runs, in which riders stop at predetermined points along the way to pick up a playing card, and at the last stop, the rider with the best poker hand wins a prize. There are memorial runs, which bring people together to remember and honor departed friends. There are benefit and charity runs, in which bikers ride to bring toys, food, clothing, or money to try to help the needy. Finally, there is the classic run, which is really nothing more than an outdoor party. To qualify as a run, though, the party really should be an overnighter, and there must be travel involved. Riding to the local tavern and passing out in the alley until morning just doesn't constitute going on a run.

4   So what makes a run different from any other motorcycle ride or trip? First, a run is a planned happening; a spur-of-the-moment ride really couldn't be called a run. Runs are not something that are to be done alone, either. Individuals might ride to a run alone, but there must be a group at the destination. A ride to Florida from

Colorado could be a mighty long trip, but unless there is a purpose that is shared with other riders, it just isn't a run. In short, a run differs from any other type of ride because, large or small, far away or close by, it is a social event.

5   When a motorcycle enthusiast says that he is going on a run, he is not going for the aerobic exercise and he is not in training for a marathon. When he says that the run is five hundred miles, it is not a five-hundred-mile race. He is going for a ride, very probably with friends, and there is a definite purpose for that ride, even though that purpose may not be obvious to everyone.

Understanding Words

Briefly define the following words as they are used in the above essay.

1. lexicographers   *those who compile dictionaries*

2. literal   *concerned with facts, word for word*

Questions on Content

1. What is the author's definition of a run?

2. Where could he not find an appropriate definition?

3. Why aren't all motorcycle trips runs?

Questions on Form

1. Identify the hook in the introduction.

2. Describe the voice in this essay.

3. What transitional phrase links paragraph 3 to paragraph 2?

Cause and Effect Analysis

Parenting: Singular

Jenefer Radas, *student*

1   "Single parents" is a term heard more about every day. Statistically, the number of single-parent families is rising at the same rate as the divorce rate. The percentage of single-parent families may be as high as 50 percent in some areas of the country. The majority of single parents are women, even though in single-parent families, sometimes men raise their children on their own also. For several reasons, single parents are in this predicament. Alcohol and drug abuse can cause a parent to leave the family. Also, some unwed mothers decide not to marry. With all that is known about single parents, however, the number-one reason for a parent to raise a family alone is divorce. Regardless of the causes, the effects on both parents and children are serious. Single-parent families suffer financially, emotionally, physically, and sociologically.

2   As a country, people know about financial instability. America's economy experiences ups and downs, but the financial stability of single parents is even worse. On the average, single parents must survive in the lower-income group, yet they are willing to work hard for their family's existence. Not all single parents are able to work. Some must stay home with infants while others simply do not have the educational background to get well-paying jobs. Single parents who have high-paying jobs still have serious financial obligations to meet because they must pay every bill alone. These obligations usually include a high house payment or car payment. In the movie *Baby Boom,* Diane Keaton plays a businesswoman with an infant. Her male partner chooses not to help raise the child, leaving Diane alone to support and raise

her. Even with a well-paying job, she almost goes bankrupt because of her home repair costs. Eventually, she is asked to resign because of her parental responsibilities, leaving her to reevaluate her employment opportunities. This movie gives a clear picture of single parents' loss in financial status. Single parents, like the one played by Diane Keaton, can lose financial security and become destitute very quickly. The finances of a single-parent family can drop dramatically, within a few weeks of onset. Consequently, because of the financial strains put on single-parent families, many children from single-parent families are poorly fed, poorly dressed, and shunned by those more affluent. Furthermore, many of these families must depend on welfare or food programs for their mere existence. Because single-parent families make up such a large percentage of families in our country, their needs should be more seriously considered than they are now.

3   The emotional and physical effects of being a single parent are another serious issue. Looking at many single parents, a person would never know that they were in pain. Chances are those parents are hurting inside. Physical problems in these men and women can be caused by many different factors, but a major problem that exists for many single parents is depression, which leads to physical problems. Doctors found that infants who were refused any physical touch or intimate love became listless and depressed. After a time, the babies refuse to eat and become catatonic. Depression in the single parent is brought about in the same manner. These adults, who once had loving relationships, are now without any physical touch or love. This experience leaves them in a profound state of loneliness, which causes the debilitating illness depression. Depression causes feelings of exhaustion, anxiety, and tension that leaves its victims feeling listless. Single parents are more susceptible to all forms of illness. There are other physical problems for single parents. Compared to single adults without children, single parents usually contract many more childhood illnesses. They are exposed to these illnesses around the clock. Usually, single parents put their health needs second to their children's. This causes the parent to be sick longer and more frequently than nonsingle parents. Single parents carry the weight of the world on their backs. No wonder they are affected physically.

4   Equally important, the sociological effects on the single parent's life are hard to overcome. Society dictates what it considers a normal family: a mother and father and 2.5 children. The single-parent family consists of a mother or father and any number of children. Single parents are painfully reminded of this cultural ideal on a daily basis. These families are looked on as different; they are often excluded from neighborhood gatherings because of their family structure. Single-parent families are what society considers outcasts. Their children are continually reminded in storybooks and role-playing that they are missing a mother or father in their home. Children from two-parent families tell their mommy and daddy stories with proud exuberance. Quietly, one-parent children sit and listen to their stories but feel ashamed to tell their own stories. These feelings of inadequacy and humility are brought on by society. Even with this stigma, however, society is slowly turning around. Many in our society now recognize the strength and courage it takes to be a single parent.

5   Parenting is not for everyone. The impact of single parenthood on the family is serious and should be given more priority. It takes a strong person to raise a family alone with the financial, physical, emotional, and sociological pressures that exist. Such parents may fall short of perfection, but they work hard to make a good life for their children. These families are willing to overcome their problems but must be given a chance to do so.

Understanding Words

Briefly define the following words as they are used in the above essay.

1. statistically   *pertaining to numerical calculation of a group of people*
2. predicament   *a distressing situation*
3. destitute   *living in complete poverty*
4. affluent   *rich or wealthy*
5. listless   *without energy*
6. catatonic   *immobile, in a stupor*
7. debilitating   *making weak*
8. vulnerable   *easily hurt*
9. susceptible   *easily affected*
10. exuberance   *overflowing joy or enthusiasm*
11. stigma   *a mark of disgrace or disrepute*

Questions on Content

1. Why is the number of single-parent families increasing?
2. What is the ideal family in our culture?
3. How are children from single-parent families made to feel inferior?

Questions on Form

1. Why are causes given in the introduction even though the paper is about effects?
2. How are the effects organized for the reader?
3. What provides support for each effect?
4. Is the conclusion effective? Why or why not?

Process Analysis

Reducing Fear of a Hospital Stay for a Child

Eric Beach, *student*

1　Years ago, children were taken to the hospital, strapped down on a stretcher, and told to be good while the nurse slapped a gas mask on and the parent disappeared to another room. Little thought was given to the terrified child who didn't have the slightest idea what was going on. Those terrifying experiences do not have to happen. A caring parent can easily prepare a child for a surgical procedure. Though the process of getting a child ready for a hospital stay for the first time can still be scary for both the adult and the child, the stay can be made easier and much less stressful if some careful planning is done beforehand. Role playing, discussion with honest responses, and access to factual information help the child understand what is going on and, thus, keep her from imagining all sorts of scary experiences.

2　Tension can be reduced when preparation involves role playing. First, the child can pretend to be in the hospital and the adult can pretend to be the nurse or doctor. As a "nurse," the adult can fluff up the pillow, take the child's temperature, and take the child's blood pressure—all with a play doctor's kit. Then the "pretend" nurse can show the child how to ring for help or turn on the television set. The "nurse" can then set up a tray for lunch and say, "This is the way you will be served lunch in the hospital." The "nurse" can be resourceful by finding items around the house that they can pretend with. Then the adult and child might reverse the roles, with the child becoming the nurse and the adult becoming the patient. Then, when it is time for the child to check in at the hospital, she will have some idea of what to expect.

3   The most important part of the process might be to discuss with the child the fact that she will not be left alone in a strange place and forgotten. The child can be encouraged to take a favorite stuffed animal with her or maybe even her special blanket. The child needs to know that after she falls asleep for surgery, someone will be there waiting when she wakes up. The child needs to know that she will not be dropped off in a strange environment with no familiar items or faces. Rather, mom, dad, grandma, sister, or brother will be there as much as possible. Also, this is a good time to let the child know that a nurse will always be there when she needs anything and the stuffed animal can stay right there in bed with her the whole time.

4   Equally important is to allow the child the chance to ask questions. The adults should answer questions as honestly as possible. If the child wants to know if "it" will hurt, the adult should respond by saying, "Yes, it may hurt a little bit, but the nurse or doctor will be as gentle as possible." Then the benefits of the procedure should be explained. If it is the appendix that is being removed, then the adult can say, "But it won't hurt here (touching child's side) as much as it does now." If it is to repair a heart, then the adult might say, "But then you can play more. Remember how tired you get now?" The adult must be honest with the child. If the child asks, "Will I have to have a shot?" the adult should answer by saying, "Yes, and I am sorry." It is important for the child to know that the adult cares.

5   If time allows, the adult and child might visit a library and/or hospital for more specific information. At the library they can read children's books and view simple videos about hospitals. At the hospital, they might pick up a pamphlet that would show the child pictures of what to expect once in the hospital. A book that shows the internal parts of the body can also be useful. If a child is to have tonsils removed, a picture of the tonsils can be found. If the procedure is to be a complicated one, like heart surgery, the adult might show the child what will be fixed. The adult needs to explain only what the child is old enough to understand.

6   Following this process of preparing a child for surgery can benefit both the child and the adult. In today's world, it is unforgivable not to give the child information that she can understand and that will reduce anxiety and fear. Hospital stays do not need to be nightmares that are relived over and over again.

Questions on Content

1. What process is being explained?

2. What can the adult do to make this process easier?

3. What are the benefits of planning ahead?

4. What can a child take to the hospital with him or her?

Questions on Form

1. How does the writer organize the process?

2. What point of view is being used?

3. What makes the introduction effective?

Argumentation

Steroids and Bodybuilders

Samuel David, *student*

1   Steroids are hormones that are produced naturally in the human body. Anabolic steroids are based on testosterone that has been modified in a laboratory. These modified steroids increase the amount of nitrogen in the body, allowing the stored nitrogen to build muscle. Steroids also add to the production of red blood cells, which carry oxygen throughout the body. This extra oxygen flow allows athletes to work out longer and harder, adding intensity to a training session. Because of these positive effects of steroids, athletes use them to improve their workout by increasing muscle bulk as well as reducing recovery time. This means that it takes less time for a bodybuilder's muscles to recover from all the stress that was placed on the muscles. The bodybuilders who use anabolic steroids experience greater strength, less body fat, and enlarged muscles, allowing an advantage at competitions. Though anabolic steroids have useful purposes for bodybuilders, the side effects make them harmful; therefore, stricter laws are needed to regulate steroid use, and accurate tests should be mandated for competitions.

2   Anabolic steroids cause a variety of damaging side effects. Less threatening side effects include acne that appears all over the body, especially on the shoulders and the back. Anabolic steroids also result in the loss of hair, leading to baldness. A link also exits between anabolic steroid use and infertility. Men who take these drugs can suffer from shrunken testicles and may become sterile. Along with these problems, anabolic steroid users may experience "blood pressure elevations . . . [and] elevated levels of total cholesterol and depressed levels of high-density lipoprotein cholesterol," as pointed out by the American Academy of Pediatrics. The most serious side effects of anabolic steroids lead to life-threatening illnesses. According to Linn Goldberg, M.D., from the Department of Medicine at Oregon Health Sciences University in Portland, the problems that occur from anabolic steroid use, depending on the amount taken into the body, are "liver and kidney damage, swollen lymph glands, heart problems such as disease and strokes . . . and cancer." Since the liver is susceptible to damage from drugs, Jerry Brainum points out, "It's the steroid retention in the liver that causes problems, including cancer." Whether a bodybuilder experiences acne or baldness, cancer or liver failure, none of these would probably have occurred without the use of anabolic steroids.

3   Not only can the use of anabolic steroids lead to serious illnesses, but they can also result in aggressive behavior. This aggressive behavior is known as "roid rage." According to William Nack, from *Sports Illustrated,* "the ingestion of large quantities of anabolic steroids . . . can trigger episodes of violent rage in certain people." Many people who are normally calm and shy when not on anabolic steroids become short-tempered and violent when using them. According to Ellingrod, et al., in the *American Journal of Drug and Alcohol Abuse,* excessive steroid use leads to "aggression and dominance behavior." For example, Lou Ferrigno, the former Mr. Universe and the Incredible Hulk on television, saw a police officer writing him a ticket, so he "ran up to her scooter, loosed a Hulkian growl and shattered its windshield with a single punch." He later apologized for his violent act. Similarly, other bodybuilders have been involved in many other violent acts, and according to Nack, "Domestic violence among bodybuilders is unusually widespread," some episodes resulting in murder. Anabolic steroid use can trigger serious behavioral changes, causing these bodybuilders to act in ways contrary to their normal personality.

4   Anabolic steroids can destroy bodybuilders' health and have serious social consequences, but the steroids are easily accessible. According to *Release*, "Under the Misuse of Drugs Act in 1971, anabolic steroids are classified as a Class C, Schedule 4 drug (with modifications). It is not an offense to possess the drug or to import or export it providing it is in a medical form and for the person's own use. It is an offense to supply it or possess it with the intention of supplying." This means that anabolic steroids are readily available to bodybuilders and can be found in most gyms. To compensate for this, stricter laws should be enacted to make it more difficult for athletes to obtain this drug. Because anabolic steroids are so harmful to the human body, drug testing should also be required at the competitive level to reduce and eventually eliminate the use of steroids for bodybuilders. Bodybuilders should not be allowed to compete after using anabolic steroids. Though they may win in competition, their bodies and sometimes their lives are destroyed. If testing were done at all bodybuilding contests, it would also prevent bodybuilders from abusing their bodies just for the sake of winning.

Understanding Words

Briefly define the following words as they are used in the above essay.

1. testosterone   *male hormone*

2. ingestion   *absorption by the body*

3. mandated   *required*

Questions on Content

1. Why do bodybuilders use anabolic steroids?

2. Who shattered the police officer's windshield?

3. What are some of the physical problems associated with anabolic steroid use?

Questions on Form

1. What is the author proposing?

2. Where did he present the opponent's position?

3. What are his main arguments?

Professional Writing

Blend of Patterns

The Mutt Who Saved Mr. Lambert

William Thomas, M.D., from August 1997 *Guideposts*

1   The moment I met Mr. Lambert* that fall day in 1991, I knew my medical training wouldn't be much help to him.

2   Tall and frail, Mr. Lambert held onto his son's arm as he shuffled through the front door of Chase Memorial Nursing Home in New Berlin, N.Y., where I was medical director. Mr. Lambert had just been in an accident the police suspected was an attempted suicide. As I learned the old man's story, I could understand his depression. In three months he had lost his wife of 60 years, then, as his health failed, his independence. Mr. Lambert got into bed, turned his face to the wall, and refused to look at his dinner tray.

---

*Name has been changed.

3   "He doesn't have much to live for," I said to Roger Halbert, Chase's administrator. If Mr. Lambert remained in such despair, he was likely to die. Could the program I had just been given permission to try make a difference to him?

4   I had come to Chase six months earlier and still had trouble believing I was spending my time in a nursing home. I had graduated from Harvard Medical School without once setting foot in such a place. Later, during my residency, I did have to take my turn at various nursing homes. What an education those visits were! I would march into an old person's room with clipboard and stethoscope: "And how are you today, Mrs."—a quick glance at the chart—"Mrs. Walker?" Mrs. Walker would be asleep, medicated, or both. "Better today? Good, good."

5   When I finished my residency, I went into family practice in upstate New York, loving everything about my work except the occasional unavoidable stop-off at a nursing home. My wife, Judy, and I lived in the country where we surrounded ourselves with vigorous young growing things—plants and animals and soon two lively little boys. For Judy and me our hilltop homestead was our personal Eden.

6   Then one warm spring afternoon in 1991 came a phone call from Roger Halbert at Chase. "Would you consider becoming our medical director?" he asked.

7   I almost laughed aloud. But after I hung up, I found myself thinking about a phrase Roger had used. "We pride ourselves," he had said, "on the kind of care we provide here." What did it mean, I wondered, to *care* for patients? In medical school we had been taught treatment, not care. At our hilltop Eden, on the other hand, Judy and I were caring for our family, not treating them. The two things were quite different.

8   Days later Roger called again. "Why not come down just for a look?" he asked.

9   I saw at once Chase was well run. Still . . . it was not Chase, it seemed, but the nursing-home system that was wrong. The 80 residents lived in a setting that was a hospital in all but name. The rooms were spotless, the windows fitted with efficient venetian blinds, the pale-blue walls so antiseptically bare that there were echoes. Were America's nursing homes a setting for treatment instead of care?

10   As I walked through the halls, I found myself thinking of a Gospel commandment often quoted at our church: *Love your neighbor as yourself.* "Who is my neighbor?" Jesus was asked. In his answer the neighbor was a Samaritan, an unacceptable member of society. *Like the aged and infirm in our society?* I wondered. Shut out of sight, invisible though they might be to someone like me, weren't they still my neighbors? What would it mean to love *those* neighbors as myself, to want for them what others routinely enjoyed?

11   Right then I knew I was going to try to bring a bit of our Eden to Chase Memorial Nursing Home. It wasn't easy to change the way things had always been done. I'll never forget the day five months after I took the job when I asked for a meeting with Chase's board of directors. As my listeners sat with arms folded, I outlined my dream: "We'll have growing things everywhere! Plants in every room. Plants in the hallways. And birds!"

12   Scores of birds, I told them, will be singing away in their cages, cats and dogs wandering the halls, rabbits in hutches, and daily visits from children—there was a daycare center right next door. Curtains and pictures would help too, but mainly it would be the continuing close contact with living things that would make the difference.

13   There was a barrage of questions. What about allergies? Wouldn't we need different insurance? What if a resident didn't like animals, or the children made too much noise? And how about the staff—it would mean a lot more work for them. In the end, though, the board agreed our top priority was to do our best for the residents. If Roger and I could solve the various problems, we could go ahead.

14   Persuading the staff was more difficult. Nearly 130 men and women worked at Chase, and all were justifiably proud of the fact that year after year the state inspectors had given the home highest marks. Now here I came—a young doctor who rode to work on a bicycle, telling them they had to do things differently. One nurse in particular voiced the fears of many: Bring a bunch of children and animals into a nursing home? Play gardener when they had been hired only to look after the residents? Wouldn't it all create a mess—and more work for them?

15   Roger and I worked hard to gain the trust and support of staff and community members, and in the end the resident council voted yes. The outspoken nurse quit, but she was the only one to do so. The rest of the staff agreed to give the "Eden Alternative" a try. We received grant money, and New York State waived a regulation about animals for the experiment. Eight months after I came to Chase, we were ready to begin.

16   Mr. Lambert's depression became for me a test case for the new approach. Day after day he remained isolated in his room; most of his meals, even when concerned family members sat with him, were returned uneaten to the kitchen.

17   The maintenance staff had come up with what they called a life pole, a floor-to-ceiling steel rod fitted with arms for holding potted plants. As his was installed, Mr. Lambert glanced up with the first flicker of interest: Perhaps something in his farmer's heart had stirred at the sight of growing things. Next we hung from his pole a cage containing two bright-blue parakeets. The following day Mr. Lambert asked to have the pole moved closer to his bed.

18   Mr. Lambert had been at Chase for several weeks when one of our mutts, named Ginger, appeared in his room. A nurse reported that Mr. Lambert had raised himself in bed and reached out to scratch the dog's ears.

19   And then came the day when the nurse found Mr. Lambert sitting on the edge of his bed. "You know those dogs have to be walked, young lady," he said. "Maybe that's something I could help out with."

20   From that day forward, at four o'clock each afternoon Mr. Lambert was at the front door dressed and ready to take Ginger and a greyhound named Target for a stroll around the grounds. Week by week his strength and good spirits returned. Six months later Mr. Lambert said an affectionate good-bye to Ginger and Target and went back home to his family.

21   Such stories, less dramatic, were repeated many times at Chase over the next few years. The great enemies of the elderly, I came to believe, are loneliness, boredom and, above all, feeling unneeded. To that, compare Mr. Lambert walking the dogs; a blind woman carefully measuring out feed and water for her birds; another patient absorbed in pruning and watering plants while her neighbor reads to a smiling little boy. All those people, despite infirmities and disabilities, found they had something to give.

22   Quality of life cannot be measured, but other results of the Eden Alternative can be. We cut our pharmacy bills in half, slashed the infection rate by 50 percent, reduced mortality by 25 percent. And to everyone's surprise, staff turnover, always high in nursing homes, dropped by more than a quarter despite the extra work.

23   State surveyors on their regular inspection tours became enthusiastic about what was happening at Chase. A state law limiting nursing homes to the housing of only one animal was repealed. The inspectors too had enjoyed and seen the benefits of the more than 100 birds and animals in our Eden. They noted the flourishing jungle of plants, and the kids showing off their day's drawings to the elderly art connoisseurs who lived there. They saw the parakeets in the residents' rooms, the rabbits, the flock of laying hens, the dogs and cats. One day I saw the chief surveyor trying to fill out his report while a cat walked across his paperwork, her tail trailing slowly across his nose.

24   I stayed at Chase four years, then set out to introduce the Eden Alternative in neighboring areas. Our son Zachary—age five at the time—went along on one such trip, enthusiastic as we set out. "When we get to the home," he said, "I'll play with the other kids."

25   "I'm afraid there won't be any other children, Zach."

"I'll play with the dogs, then."

"There won't be any dogs there either, Zach."

"Cats?"

"No, Son."

"Gosh, Dad," Zach said. "I thought we were going to a *nursing* home."

Questions on Content

1. Where did the author graduate from medical school?

2. In what paragraph was the author's personal Eden described?

3. Why did one nurse quit?

4. Why was the author's son excited about going to the new home?

Questions on Form

1. What methods of development are used in this essay?

2. Where is the thesis sentence?

3. What were some of the statistics used to show effect?

Part 4

Mechanics for Effective Writing: Capitalization

Objectives

- Review the uses of capitalization.
- Practice capitalizing in paragraphs.

Capitalizing words is generally easy, but sometimes reviewing the rules for capitalization can help. Capitalization does not have any particular organization, but in this unit, you will practice capitalization grouped in the following way.

Tests on capitalization are on pages 70–73 of the Test Bank.

1. the first word of a sentence or a direct quotation; names

2. specific places, events, brand names, and dates

3. languages, ethnic groups, and other rules

Capitalizing First Words

- **Capitalize the first word of a sentence.**

   We returned the books.

   The concert began late.

   After the trial, the reporters hurried to turn in stories.

- **Capitalize the first word in a direct quotation.**

Frances said, "The neighborhood gang demands $30 payments in return for protection."

"The neighborhood gang," Frances said, "demands $30 payments in return for protection."

- **Do not capitalize the first word in a direct quotation if it is imbedded in or blended into your sentence.**

  Frances said that the neighborhood gang "demands $30 payments in return for protection."

- **Do not capitalize an indirect quotation.**

  Frances said that the neighborhood gang demands money in return for protection.

Capitalizing Names

- **Capitalize names, nicknames, and initials.**

  John Henry Carson, Ike, A. L. Smith

- **Capitalize titles when they appear before a name.**

  Mr. Sheridan, Professor Williams, Dr. James

  Captain Fischer, Coach Stevens, Aunt Mary

- **Capitalize the pronoun I.**

  I want to go.

  After school, I drove to the laundromat.

- **Capitalize words for family members if they are substitutions for their names.**

  Please help me with my homework, Mom.

  Can we go to the game, Dad?

- **Do not capitalize words for family members if they are preceded by a pronoun.**

  I asked my mom to call Aunt Mary before we left.

- **Capitalize any references to God, religious figures or groups, or sacred writings.**

  God, Jehovah, Buddha, Bible, Koran, Torah, Mennonite

Exercise 1

Using the above rules, capitalize words in the following paragraph.

      L   *M* *P* *R*
last year, mrs. polly reaves, an 87-year-old widow who lived alone, got lucky
              J   *M*
when her son james called her and told her, "mom, the family wants to remodel
          S
your home." she has five sons, three daughters, and numerous grandchildren, and
                           S
he told her that all of them wanted to help. she didn't want to put anyone out, but

she knew this would be a blessing. Two of her sons replaced the roof, and the other

sons worked inside fixing the plumbing and repairing the walls. Her daughters

helen and carol made new window coverings while the grandchildren painted first
H   *C*

the outside and then the inside of the home. chuck and beverly worked in her flower
     C   *B*

garden and even put in a new border. Everyone stayed busy, even her dog pj, who
     PJ

kept everyone company. Several months later, when mrs. reaves looked at her new
     M   *R*

home, she simply said, "i thank all of you for your hard work, and i thank god for my
     I   *I*   *G*

family." Everyone cheered.

Capitalizing Places, Events, Brand Names, and Dates

- **Capitalize names of specific places such as streets, cities, towns, states, countries, parks, buildings, and mountains.**

  Butler Drive, New Orleans, Sedona, Arizona, Great Britain, Golden Gate Park, Empire State Building, Mount Rushmore

- **Capitalize specific geographic areas but not directions.**

  Turn south after you get off the freeway.

  Stacy grew up in the South.

- **Capitalize the names of specific businesses, organizations, institutions, associations, and clubs.**

  Jake's Deli, Macy's, Arizona Diamondbacks, American Cancer Society, House of Representatives, Princeton, Optimist Club, Mercy Health Care, St. Joseph's Hospital

- **Capitalize abbreviations that stand for words that are capitalized.**

  IBM, USA, YMCA, ROTC

- **Capitalize specific historical events.**

  World War I, The Million Man March, Woodstock, American Revolution, Republican National Convention, Democratic National Convention

- **Capitalize brand names, but not the product itself.**

  Chevrolet sedan, Del Monte green beans, Tide detergent, Kodak film, Jeep off-road vehicle, Regal sedan, Corvette, Pepsi, Hershey chocolate bar, Fritos corn chips

- **Capitalize days, months, and holidays.**

  Thursday, April, Fourth of July, Labor Day

- **Do not capitalize the seasons of the year.**

  summer, autumn, fall, winter, spring

Exercise 2

Using the above rules, capitalize words in the following paragraph.

Wanting to break the daily routine of living and actually doing something
"different" or "exciting" are all too often unfulfilled wishes. In ~~march~~[M], some people want
to walk the hiking trails in the ~~south~~[S] ~~mountain~~[M] ~~park~~[P] with a backpack full of ~~doritos~~[D] and
~~snickers~~[S] bars. Others want to go to the ~~american~~[A] ~~automobile~~[A] ~~association~~[A] (~~aaa~~[AAA]) to plan a
trip to ~~alaska~~[A] and capture the wild on ~~kodak~~[K] film. Some people daydream about flying
to ~~washington~~[W] to climb ~~mount~~[M] ~~rainier~~[R], located in the ~~northwest~~[N]. Even a summer trip
to the ~~east~~[E] to remember ~~woodstock~~[W] seems exciting. When the time comes, though, to
make a "new" choice, breaking the routine and actually doing some of these things
means taking a risk that may be too difficult. In the spring, the ~~sonoran~~[S] ~~desert~~[D] may be
in the middle of snake season. ~~alaska~~[A] may cost too much, even in a ~~chevy~~[C] van. Climbing
~~mount~~[M] ~~rainier~~[R] is reserved for only the few with the skills and courage to make the
effort. Excuses for not breaking the routine all too frequently include "too expensive,"
"too dangerous," or "too busy" on holidays like ~~memorial~~[M] ~~day~~[D]. Perhaps after all, people
choose to do what they really want to do, in spite of their yearnings to the contrary.

More Capitalization Rules

- **Capitalize languages, ethnic groups, and words that come from the name of a country.**

  English, French, Spanish, Navajo, Apache, Native American

- **Capitalize adjectives that come from names that are capitalized by other rules.**

  French bread, English muffins, American citizen, Italian dressing, Shakespearean play

- **Capitalize titles of books, stories, movies, and television programs except for "a," "an," or "the," short prepositions, the infinitive "to," and conjunctions within the title.**

  The Game, The Practice, Bless the Beasts and the Children, "I Stand Here Ironing," *Epitaph for an Enemy, No Way to Go but Up*

- **Capitalize school subjects that name specific courses, especially those with numbers.**

  Algebra I, Chemistry 101, Psychology 211, Literature of Today

- **Do not capitalize classes that are not the specific names of the courses.**

  She is taking algebra this semester and will take chemistry and psychology next semester.

Exercise 3

Using the above rules, capitalize words in the following paragraph.

During one recent school year, the fourth grade class at Sunset Elementary

School had an exciting variety of experiences that inspired them to want to learn as

 W   *R*
much as possible about the world. In an issue of ~~weekly~~ ~~reader~~, an article about
A
~~african~~ elephants captured the students' attention. They learned how orphaned baby

elephants are cared for until they are ready to be sent back to the wild. In still
       S   *S*
another issue, "~~science~~ for ~~sale~~" told of scientists discovering in the hills of South

Dakota an almost complete dinosaur, whose bones were eventually auctioned for

more than 8 million dollars to a Chicago museum. These articles certainly inspired

the young readers to think about taking courses in working with wildlife or in

discovering and preserving relics or fossils from the ancient world. Along with

reading about animals current and past, the youngsters also heard enthralling
                                                                    Z
information about scorpions from a high school student taking ~~zoology~~ 112 and
                                 N *M*
about a summer spent on a ~~new~~ ~~mexican~~ "dig" from a community college student
        I   *A*   *T*   *K*
enrolled in ~~introduction~~ to ~~archeology~~. Later, students read in ~~time~~ ~~for~~ ~~kids~~ (the
                              T   *T*
children's version of ~~time~~ magazine) a heart-rending story of ~~tibetan~~ families and
                       C
their children fleeing ~~chinese~~ rule for more freedom in India. The youngsters from
S   *S*
~~sunset~~ ~~school~~, reading about these children, talked about how lucky they felt to be
A
~~americans~~. They seemed excited about wanting to know as much as possible about

other countries and cultures so they could help make the world a better place.

Exercise 4 (Review)

Using all the rules, capitalize words in the following paragraph.
 L *J*   *E*   *P*   *M*   *I*
~~last~~ ~~june~~, my family reunion at ~~encanto~~ ~~park~~ was relaxing. ~~my~~ family and ~~i~~
         B   *K*   *F* *C*
brought ~~boston~~ baked beans, potato salad, and ~~kentucky~~ ~~fried~~ ~~chicken~~ for a stress-
         M
free picnic. ~~my~~ aunts and uncles brought more and more food until we had a spread

no one could resist. ~~a~~**A**fter we ate, the kids had ~~c~~**C**arnation ice cream for dessert and set up a ~~m~~**M**onopoly game under the shade of a pine tree. ~~b~~**B**efore long, even ~~a~~**A**unt ~~m~~**M**artha joined the game by serving as the banker. My cousin ~~a~~**A**drian brought his ~~e~~**E**nglish and ~~m~~**M**ath books, but ~~i~~**I** noticed that he never opened either one. ~~o~~**O**n the other hand, ~~a~~**A**unt ~~m~~**M**argaret brought out ~~the kitchen god's wife~~ *The Kitchen God's Wife*, said "~~e~~**E**xcuse me," and began reading. ~~u~~**U**ncle ~~f~~**F**red and ~~u~~**U**ncle ~~b~~**B**ob had a lively discussion about the difference between the ~~v~~**V**ietnam ~~w~~**W**ar and the ~~p~~**P**ersian ~~g~~**G**ulf ~~w~~**W**ar when suddenly ~~g~~**G**randpa started telling us about ~~w~~**W**orld ~~w~~**W**ar II and his adventures with his good buddy, ~~s~~**S**ergeant ~~s~~**S**holam. ~~b~~**B**efore long, he opened his traditional package of ~~h~~**H**ershey ~~k~~**K**isses to share with us. "~~b~~**B**ack then," he said, "we looked forward to having ~~h~~**H**ershey candy bars. ~~e~~**E**veryone thought they were a real treat, especially when we handed them out during the war." ~~a~~**A**s ~~i~~**I** listened to him talk, ~~i~~**I** kept thinking how proud ~~i~~**I** was to have him as a grandfather. ~~i~~**I**n just a few days, my relatives, who had come from as far away as ~~h~~**H**awaii and ~~c~~**C**anada, would return to their homes, grateful that they knew a little more about each other, but today was ~~s~~**S**aturday, and we would finish the time enjoying each other's company and perhaps even planning for the family reunion next summer.

Part 5

Putting It All Together

Cumulative Unit Exercise

Now that you have studied the patterns of development, analyze the essay "Children with Confidence." Read the essay carefully, and then use the following questions to help you in your analysis.

1. The primary pattern of development for the essay is cause and effect. Mark the sentences in the introduction that indicate this paper is going to show cause and effect.

2. Within each support paragraph, other patterns are used. Paragraphs 2, 3, and 4 all include examples of cause and effect. Mark and label as many as you can find in each paragraph.

3. Paragraphs 3 and 4 include a definition. Mark and label the sentences that make up the definition.

4. Identify the type of hook used in the introductory paragraph.

5. In the conclusion, highlight and label the sentence or sentences that reinforce the thesis sentence.

6. Why does the article bring up Becky in the conclusion?

7. The development in each paragraph progresses from infancy to adulthood. How does this add coherence within paragraphs? *provides a logical time sequence*

8. The essay also has effective coherence between paragraphs. Mark and label as many examples as you can. *found in topic sentence of each paragraph*

Children with Confidence

example that serves as contrast to the thesis

1   When Becky was a little girl, her cat was lying next to the door with its tail under the opening. Becky could not see the cat, and she pulled its tail, making it cry loudly. Instead of stopping her and pointing out that the cat indeed was on the other side of the door hurting, her parents thought it was cute and laughed, but the situation was not funny because they lost a great opportunity to teach their child compassion. Many times, the way parents react in these situations determines the type of people their children become. If parents want to raise children who are well adjusted in life, they make time for their children, teach them kindness, and let them find their own way in life.

1st indication of cause/effect

2   When parents take time for their children, the end result is that the children grow up knowing their parents love them and are proud of them. As infants, babies know that when they cry, their parents will pick them up and comfort them, giving them a sense of security. As these tiny ones grow, they may test their parents and do anything for attention, but if parents just stop what they are doing for five or ten minutes and talk to their children, the unruly children become happy, content kids who return to playing with their toys, satisfied that their parents care about them. Even though parents are often busy trying hard to provide a secure life for their children, scheduling time for each individual child can work miracles. When Bo was a little boy, he and his mom had plans to go to a movie at 3:00 P.M. As he listened to his mom on the phone, he heard her say, "I can't do that because I already have a three o'clock appointment." As soon as she got off the phone, disappointment showed in his face, and he said, "I thought we were going to the movies." When he heard his mom say, "You are my appointment. You are important, too," the disappointment in his eyes changed to self-worth and importance. At this age, little kids are excited to go on outings or just spend time with their parents; however, as they get older, they still need their parents to listen to their problems or make suggestions about their choices. When parents take advantage of these few early years, they, along with their children, become winners.

example

3   When parents teach their children to be thoughtful of others, they are nurturing them into becoming outstanding adults. If parents see their children do something that hurts someone else's feelings, they can teach them to say, "I'm sorry." From the time children are small, when someone gives them a gift, parents can teach them to show their appreciation, either with a thank-you note or a phone call. If a friend, a neighbor, or a grandparent needs help, youngsters can learn from their parents the satisfaction of helping without expecting financial rewards. As the kids grow older, they might spend time volunteering in a nursing home or a hospital where they can practice compassion for others. As these children become

example

example

example

definition

adults and their grandparents are in the hospital, they will realize the importance of visiting them and making them feel better even though they might dread seeing their grandparents so helpless. Thoughtfulness is not something that suddenly appears one day; rather, it is a character trait that starts in the early years and continues throughout a child's lifetime.

4   Perhaps most difficult of all, parents who want to watch their children grow into self-sufficient adults let their children make their own decisions and gradually become independent. How parents define self-sufficiency is important. Helping sons and daughters learn to make their own choices does not mean letting children do whatever they want whenever they want. Rather, it means helping them understand the consequences of their actions so they can make intelligent decisions throughout their lifetime. A young child does not have the option of deciding whether or not to wear a seat belt, but that same child might decide if he or she wants to join a Little League ball team or take painting lessons. Sometimes it is difficult for parents to watch their children struggle as they learn to tie their shoes or later budget their money, but letting them try and try again until they are successful helps the children learn that they can "do it themselves." An opposite, perhaps detrimental, approach to creating self-sufficiency is using a command: "This is what you are going to do." Wise parents, however, point out the possible outcomes, but they also respect their children's right to make their own decisions. Though parents may want to see their children go to college and become architects, attorneys, or doctors, being supportive of their children's decisions to pursue their own career choices, such as writing, music, or carpentry, lets their children know that it is all right to pursue their life's dreams. When the time comes for marriage, parents may feel that their child is marrying the wrong person, but they accept the situation and the new family member. A bit later, if that child comes home and says, "I am getting a divorce," the insightful parent will spend time with that adult child and help him/her work through the divorce. Though it is not always easy for parents to understand this concept and support their children in their decisions rather than make the decisions for them, parents who create independent decision making will never be sorry, for they will have confident children who are not afraid to reach for their dreams.

definition

example

example

definition

example

example

reinforces thesis in intro.

5   Helping a child grow into an understanding, confident, and independent adult is not an easy job. However, if extra time, patience, and effort are invested in nurturing this special person, the emotional satisfaction is like no other in life. No parent is perfect, and no parent makes the right decision all the time, but parents must model what they teach and be willing to admit mistakes and learn patience. A couple of positive words, a few extra minutes, or some insightful advice can make a tremendous difference in a child's future life. Just because Becky's parents missed one opportunity does not mean that they missed others, but parents who take every opportunity to help their children grow into thoughtful adults will never be sorry.

reinforces hook and thesis

Collaborative Writing Project: Working and Learning Together

This exercise will help you decide on a pattern of organization for your essay. Review the information on illustration, comparison/contrast, classification, definition, cause/effect analysis, process analysis, and argumentation. Notice that the thesis sentence in each model essay in the preceding section suggests the pattern of development used.

Writing Assignment

1. Divide into groups of three or four and discuss the pattern of development that would be the most effective in the following situations:

c/c
- You already have a job, but you have been offered a job at a different place. You must decide what to do.

classification
argument
- You have had your driver's license only a few years and have noticed that not everyone drives the same way. Discuss your observations.

cause/effect
- You have been asked to speak at a high school assembly. Your topic is gangs.

process
illustration
- You are a college student, and your high school friends want to know what is involved in enrolling in college.

argument
- Your neighbors want to start organized sports activities for the kids. The neighbors are going to speak at the next block-watch meeting.

definition
- You are having trouble writing essays in your English class, and a friend offers you her papers. You have never done anything like this before and pride yourself on your honesty.

c/c
- An advertising salesman is writing up a sketch for his new client product, a deodorant called Dry. The competitive product has a bigger profit share, but laboratory research indicates that Dry actually works better and is longer lasting.

cause/effect
illustration
- A police officer must turn in an accident report for a serious crash that he investigated. After gathering all the details, he must now state in clear language his understanding of the accident, including the damages and the people at fault.

argument
- A parent has learned that her home-schooled daughter was not allowed to attend her friend's public school dance. She gave her daughter permission and thought the school office had cleared her visit. However, the principal turned her away at the door. She is writing him a letter to defend her daughter's right to attend a public school dance and to make the principal understand the embarrassment and emotional upset her daughter has endured.

cause/effect
argument
- An environmental biologist has become aware of dying fish in various lakes. After doing extensive investigative and laboratory research, he believes a chemical company is dumping hazardous wastes into the water. He is preparing a report to a state environmental control agency as well as the negligent company. He wants to make very clear the potential danger to fish and humans.

2. Select one primary method of development—illustration, comparison/contrast, classification, definition, cause/effect analysis, process analysis, or argumentation, and then collaboratively write a thesis sentence for a paper.

Option A: Using the thesis sentence developed by your group, write an individual essay that follows one of the methods of development. (Other methods of development may also be used.)

Bring a typed copy of your essay to class for peer review.

Option B: Collaboratively develop a sample essay that follows one method of development. (Other methods of development may also be used.)

Share and discuss your essay with other members of the class.

Peer Review for Option A

1. Depending on the pattern of development in the thesis sentence, check to see that the organization of the essay progresses logically.

2. Decide if the essay accomplishes the purpose suggested in the thesis sentence.

3. Discuss the conclusion, and decide if it is appropriate for the pattern of development and the purpose.

4. Identify other patterns of development used in writing the essay.

5. Edit carefully, using the checklist on the inside back cover of your book.

Final Checklist

Revise your essay so that it has an effective introduction that includes a hook, a transition, and a thesis sentence.

Be sure that each support paragraph has a strong topic sentence and ample supporting examples.

Check for sentence variety.

Check for unity and a smooth flow of ideas.

Revise to include a strong concluding paragraph.

Check for subject-verb agreement.

Check for consistent verb tense.

Check for consistent point of view.

Check for fragments, run-ons, and comma splices.

Check punctuation of compound sentences.

Check punctuation of complex sentences.

Check for proper use of capital letters.

 ## Internet Activities

Unit 7 focuses on patterns of development for essays. As you pull together the content for your essay, you can use the web as a resource. Each activity here is tied to a suggested writing for the patterns of development. Visit the text's website for this unit to get website links that you can use as starting points.

Activity 1   Writing an Illustration Essay

You could develop your illustration essay by recalling pictures of a place you have seen or visited. Sometimes visiting online will help you recall specific details and visual impressions from your experience.

a. To help you recall a trip to a national park, visit the park on the web by typing in the following address. (Type all Internet addresses exactly as they appear. Bookmark this site, or save it as a favorite for future reference.)

   www.nps.gov/parks.html

b. Once you are at the government site, select a park you have been to before, and search until you find pictures or other information that will help you remember your trip. Sometimes you might even find such multimedia elements as sounds and movies to help you remember why you or others enjoyed vacationing in the park.

c. By describing the details of your trip, you will be illustrating your essay. You can also find information on why others enjoy vacationing in national parks.

Activity 2 Comparison or Contrast

a. Use one of the search engines you explored in the Internet Activities in Unit 2.

b. Search for information on "abuse and neglect" of children. Read reputable and authoritative sources, noting the similarities and/or differences of each type of abuse. Make a rough outline, and then compose your paper.

c. Some articles will have information on both abuse and neglect. It will be your challenge to discover the similarities and/or differences.

Activity 3 Classification

a. Select a topic for your classification essay from the list in your text. To obtain information, use different search engines. (Various search engines and their web addresses can be found on page 147.)

b. Once you get to a search engine, type in key words from your selected topic. For example, if you use sports activities for children, you might type in exactly what is in the following brackets (Do not include the brackets.): ["sports activities" + children]. For "transportation for the elderly," you might type in [transportation + elderly]. If you do not find enough information by using one search engine, use a different one until you have enough information to organize a paper.

c. Read as many articles on your topic as possible, and then begin to organize your paper.

Activity 4 Definition

If you choose to do a definition essay, try to define an abstract word like "beauty." Defining beauty is not an easy task, especially since beauty has a very personal definition.

a. As you approach this topic, make a list of items you think are beautiful.
Answers will vary.
_____

_____

b. Check online in the combined dictionary/thesaurus for a definition of beauty, and write it here. Use one of the following addresses. (Type all Internet addresses exactly as they appear. Bookmark this site, or save it as a favorite for future reference.)

http://www.thesaurus.com
http://Bartleby.com/62/
Answers will vary.
_____

_____

Activity 5   Cause/Effect Analysis

a. Visit the following website for National Historic Landmarks (NHL). Use one of the search engines listed on page 147, and type in the words "national historic landmark" or go to the following site.

http://www.cr.nps.gov/nhl

(Bookmark this site, or save it as a favorite for future reference.)

b. Click on "Search for NHL." If you need help finding a site, click on "List of NHL" first. Notice that the listed NHL sites are categorized by state. Select one that interests you. Because the listing is so long, it may take a few minutes. Therefore, browsing takes patience, but most sites are incredibly interesting. Find one that inspires you, such as the New Mexico Trinity site, which was the location for the first atomic bomb testing ground. Read about what occurred at the location you have chosen. Why did it become a National Historic Landmark? What effect does this landmark have on people today?

Answers will vary.

Activity 6   Process Analysis

To write a process analysis, you need to know the parts of the process that you are going to describe. You can get the necessary information by searching online.

a. If you choose "Preparing for a Vacation," type in the following address. (Type all Internet addresses exactly as they appear. Bookmark this site, or save it as a favorite for future reference.)

http://www.maps.com/trip/

If you choose "Buying a New Car," type in the following address.

http://www.carbuyingtips.com/

b. Think about ideas that you find online, and decide which ones will be useful for your paper on "Preparing for a Vacation" or "Buying a New Car." Jot down the ideas that will support your thesis.

Answers will vary.

Activity 7   Argumentation

a. If you want to choose a topic different from the ones suggested in your text, go to the following website to help you develop your essay. (Type all Internet addresses exactly as they appear. Bookmark this site, or save it as a favorite for future reference.)

http://www.gc.maricopa.edu/English/topicarg.html

The above website, developed and maintained by Marla DeSoto, professor of English at Glendale Community College, includes a page called "Argumentative Topics." This page has suggested thesis statements, links to resources, and questions to get you thinking about the issues within the topics.

b. Another site that presents an excellent pro/con discussion of argumentative topics can be found by typing in the following address.

http://www.publicagenda.org/

c. When you go to this site, click on "Issue Guides" at the top. It will take you to a page with a list of the issues. Then, click on one of the issues, and you will see a page with two headings: "Understanding the Issues" and "Public Opinion." These summary sites help you understand the essential points of an issue, explore current opinions about the issue, and find additional reliable sources.

Appendix A: Confusing Words

This appendix will help you clarify and eliminate misunderstood words. These errors may seem minor, but they can distract your reader or change the meaning of a sentence.

Similar Words Misused

Some words are pronounced so similarly to another word or words that they are misspelled. You may want to learn and practice one or two a day, or you may want to practice only those that are troublesome to you. To learn the slight differences in the pairs of words shown below, study the meanings; then look at the spelling or construction of the word. Finally, practice the correct use of these words in sentences so that you can use them properly in your writing. If you still have difficulty with a pair of words, write them down and restudy them.

Definitions and Practice Sentences

Read each definition and the examples of confusing words. Work through the practice sentences by striking through the word errors. Then write the correct form above the words that are wrong. Write "C" if the sentence contains no errors.

Set 1

a lot: an acceptable (but overused) form meaning many or much. (You may want to consider alternative words that say the same thing, such as "many," "frequently," "much," or "often.")

A lot of my friends enjoy dancing.

alot: incorrect form, often a misspelling for "a lot"

allot: to give or assign as one's portion

He did not allot enough time to do the job properly.

a lot
1. Steve often has ~~alot~~ of figs on his tree.

allot
2. The employer will not ~~alot~~ any money for repairs.

a lot
3. Sonja often caught ~~alot~~ of fish at that lake.

allot
4. I was hoping he would ~~alot~~ us more time to get the work done.

Set 2

accept: receive

> I accept your apology for not calling.

except: excluding

> Everyone except Jason came home.

C   1. She accepted my apology and walked away with a frown on her face.

          except
2. Everyone went to the ball ~~accept~~ Cinderella.

C   3. She accepted the money greedily.

                                                except
4. When Natalie arrived in class, everyone was present ~~accept~~ Maria.

Set 3

adapt: to adjust or change to make usable (often followed by "to")

> Often students must learn to adapt to different instructors.

adopt: to accept as one's own

> The mother dog adopted both litters of puppies.

C   1. When people move to a new country, they must adapt to new customs.

          adopted
2. The organization ~~adapted~~ the constitution the way it was originally written.

          adopt
3. They hoped to ~~adapt~~ the little girl.

          adapt
4. They needed to ~~adopt~~ to the changing weather conditions.

Set 4

advise: (verb) to give valuable information

> Please advise John of the change.

advice: (noun) valuable information given

> John followed the advice.

C   1. John advised Butch not to hike the steep mountain.

          advice
2. Take the lifeguard's ~~advise~~, and don't swim if you hear thunder.

          advised
3. I ~~adviced~~ her to do her household chores early.

          advice
4. Margaret refused to take my ~~advise~~.

Set 5

affect: (verb) to change or influence

> One vote can affect the election results.

effect: (noun) a result
(verb) to accomplish or bring about

We felt the effects of the stock market decline.

Negotiation was the only way to effect change.

                    affect
1. His action cannot ~~effect~~ us.
                 effect
2. One ~~affect~~ of staying up late can be having a headache in the morning.

C   3. His honesty affected everyone around him.

C   4. The committee's work effected a satisfactory compromise.

Set 6

all ready: fully or completely ready

We are all ready for finals.

already: previously

Finals are already over.

              all ready
1. Are you ~~already~~?
              already
2. She is ~~all ready~~ at the soccer game.

C   3. When she got to the party, everyone was already there.
              all ready
4. We were ~~already~~ to take the test.

Set 7

all together: to indicate a group who performed an action collectively ("All together" can be used only if "all" and "together" can be separated in the sentence.)

The club members work all together.

All the club members work *together*.

altogether: completely, wholly (Always use "altogether" except in the above situation.)

Altogether, it was a strange event.

He was altogether surprised by the outcome of the election.

              altogether
1. Sharon was ~~all together~~ surprised by his comment.
             Altogether
2. ~~All together~~, I put in two weeks on that job.

C   3. The flowers were planted all together.

C   4. That summer, the young people were all together.

Set 8

among: (preposition) separates three or more things

She The tasks were divided among all five of the employees.

between: (preposition) separates two objects in space, time, or degree

The tasks were completed between two and six o'clock.

between
1. She divides her time ~~among~~ job and family.

among
2. I hope you will share the information ~~between~~ all employees.

C 3. That item was among the first ones to be considered.

between
4. I parked my boat ~~among~~ the house and the oak tree.

Set 9

are: (verb) form of "be"

My friends are usually willing to help me.

our: (pronoun) showing ownership

Everyone in our family enjoyed life.

Our
1. ~~Are~~ children are ready to go to the zoo.

are
2. When ~~our~~ you going to visit me?

are
3. The trees ~~our~~ growing faster than we had hoped.

C 4. Who is responsible for our future?

Set 10

brake: act of stopping or the device for stopping

I brake for animals.

break: separate into parts

I do not want to break the dishes.

brake
1. The bus driver slammed on the ~~break~~, and the passengers flew forward.

C 2. How did you break the lamp last night?

brake
3. When the car in front of us stopped, I hit the ~~break~~.

break
4. The karate expert will ~~brake~~ twenty boards in twenty-five seconds.

Set 11

by: a preposition indicating near, through, during, no later than, or with respect to

He parked his car by a fire hydrant.

buy: to purchase

I want to buy a new car.

buy
1. Mrs. Smith needed to ~~by~~ detergent for her washing machine.

C 2. The fishing gear is by the car in the garage.

C 3. Mick needs to be at church by 8:30 A.M.

C 4. Who put the *TV Guide* by the lamp?

Set 12

capital: punishable by death; excellent; place where the government is located; money or property

That was a capital offense.

The drama department put on a capital performance.

Sacramento is the capital of California.

He did not have enough capital.

capitol: building where a legislature meets

We visited the state capitol.

capitol
1. The field trip included a visit to the ~~capital~~ building.

C 2. Capital punishment is rare in all states.

C 3. When he gets enough capital, he plans to start his own business.

C 4. That was a capital performance.

Set 13

cite: to quote or mention

She cited Shakespeare in her talk.

sight: refers to seeing

I did not sight any new cars.

site: location

We particularly enjoyed that vacation site.

site
1. This is a wonderful ~~cite~~ for the new building.

site
2. Which ~~sight~~ would you prefer for the housing development?

sight
3. I was unable to catch any ~~site~~ of him.

cite
4. I would like to ~~site~~ your book in my next article.

Set 14

coarse: rough; not refined

> The boards were too coarse to use.

course: mental or physical path going from one point to another; complete series of
> studies

> His course in life was a challenge.

of course: as one expects

> Of course, I can be there on time.

C
1. The course I liked the best was not necessarily the easiest.
   course
2. Of ~~coarse~~, I enjoyed the play.
   course
3. The ~~coarse~~ he took was a challenge.
   coarse
4. The woman at the ball park appeared ~~course~~.

Set 15

conscience: (noun) moral value that guides behavior

> His conscience bothers him when he lies.

conscious: (adjective) aware

> He was conscious of his mistake.

C
1. The crowd sighed in relief when she became conscious.
   conscience
2. My ~~conscious~~ forced me to return the lost wallet.

C
3. I didn't want to study, but my conscience reminded me of the importance of making good grades.
   conscious
4. My grandmother is always ~~conscience~~ of my feelings.

Set 16

could of, must of, might of, should of: These are all incorrect forms and should not be
> used. Instead, use "could have," "must have," "might have," and "should have."

> I could have gone to the lake today.

   have
1. Everyone at the lake should ~~of~~ used sunblock.
   have
2. My mother must ~~of~~ cut the grass.

C
3. The street leading to the city could have been blocked off.
   have
4. When he fell asleep, he must ~~of~~ left the television on.

Set 17

council: group of persons, assembly

> The council will convene shortly.

counsel: advice or attorney

> He provided effective counsel for the young man.

> *counsel*
> 1. The ~~council~~ for the defense was an inexperienced attorney.

C   2. Every year the student body elects a new council.

> *counsel*
> 3. The father gave ~~council~~ to his son.

C   4. The city council voted on new ordinances.

Set 18

forth: forward

> He went forth into the battle.

fourth: referring to the number four

> She was only the fourth person to come into the store this morning.

C   1. He ate his fourth poppy-seed muffin.

> *fourth*
> 2. This is the ~~forth~~ time I have lost my keys.

> *forth*
> 3. From this day ~~fourth~~, the prime minister will be extremely cautious.

> *fourth*
> 4. Chip is working on his ~~forth~~ assignment.

Set 19

good: (adjective) better than average

> The president did a good job.

> "Good" is used when the verb refers to the senses (taste, feel, smell).

> Jessica feels good about her recent victory.

well: An adverb

> Sontos hit the ball well.

> "Well" used to introduce a sentence adds little meaning to your sentences. It is an expression that should not be used in more formal writing. It is frequently used in informal speech.

> Well, I'm broke.

> *good*
> 1. The flowers smell ~~well~~.

> *well*
> 2. The little boy wrote the story ~~good~~.

> *good*
> 3. The apple pie was ~~well~~.

> *well*
> 4. The apple pie was made ~~good~~.

Set 20

hear: ability to pick up sounds with one's ears

    She hears what she wants to hear.

here: location

    We can all gather here for lunch.

         hear
1. Didn't you ~~here~~ the car honking?

C   2. Come here and write your paper.

         hear
3. From our kitchen, we could ~~here~~ birds singing.

C   4. Here is my assignment.

Set 21

hole: an opening in something

    I have a hole in my shoe.

whole: entire

    He ate the whole pie.

         hole
1. Be careful; I think there's a ~~whole~~ around here.

    whole
2. The ~~hole~~ house was a mess.

         whole
3. Tall yellow weeds covered the ~~hole~~ field.

         holes
4. The yard was filled with small prairie-dog ~~wholes~~.

Set 22

imply: to suggest or hint

    The president implied that we need to save money.

infer: to conclude, based on what a speaker or writer says

    I inferred that he was talking about my department.

      infer
1. What did you ~~imply~~ from the speech?

      implied
2. The evidence ~~inferred~~ that she was guilty.

      implied
3. From what he ~~inferred~~, did you infer the right answer?

    inferred
4. She ~~implied~~ from the information provided that we had made the wrong decision.

Set 23

its: ownership or possession (3rd person singular)

    Its water bowl is empty.

it's: contraction for it is, it has

> It's been a long time since they visited Hawaii.

> *it's*
> 1. I believe ~~its~~ going to be a rainy day.

> *Its*
> 2. ~~It's~~ only purpose is to give directions.

> *its*
> 3. It's been a long time since ~~it's~~ beginnings.

> *it's*
> 4. I wonder if ~~its~~ in good shape.

Set 24
knew: understood

> We thought we knew the answers.

new: not old

> The puppy liked his new bed.

C   1. The meteorologist knew it was going to rain Wednesday.

> *new*
> 2. Mary was upset because she ripped her ~~knew~~ red dress.

> *knew*
> 3. I ~~new~~ the test would be difficult.

C   4. The new peach sweater looked terrific on Olivia.

Set 25
know: to understand

> I know what you are thinking.

no: a response in the negative

> There are no raisins in the oatmeal.

> *know*
> 1. Don't you ~~no~~ not to stick a fork into the toaster?

> *No*
> 2. ~~Know~~, you cannot play on the computer.

C   3. I know I shouldn't watch TV when I have homework.

C   4. Margaret asked her dad for $200, but he said, "No."

Set 26
lie: to recline or rest; to tell an untruth

> Please do not lie on the table.

lay: to put or to place (takes a direct object)

> Please lay the child on the table.

(The child receives the action of being placed on the table.)

Dr. Dries laid the child on the table.

Note "Lay" is also past tense of "lie."

Yesterday, Scott lay in bed all day.

Present	Past	Past Participle	Present Participle
lie	lay	lain	lying
lay	laid	laid	laying

C   1. The young man continued to lie throughout the investigation.

   laid
   2. The contractor ~~lay~~ the brick according to code.

   lie
   3. The doctor advised Chad not to ~~lay~~ in the sun.

C   4. We must lay a foundation before we can build the gazebo.

Set 27
lose: (verb) misplace or not win

They managed to lose only the last game.

loose: (adjective) not bound, free, not tight

The children were turned loose after school.

   lose
   1. Mom didn't want to ~~loose~~ Amy in the crowd, so she held her hand tightly.

   loose
   2. The fashion today is ~~lose~~ clothing.

C   3. The knot Bob made was too loose to hold the calf.

   loose
   4. Janet lost the ~~lose~~ ring Friday.

Set 28
passed: (verb) successfully completed; handed to; filed by or went by

She passed the bar exam.

past: time gone by, yesterday

In the past five years, they moved twice.

   passed
   1. My teammate ~~past~~ the ball to me, and I made a touchdown.

   past
   2. Susie was dreaming about her ~~passed~~ when she was awakened.

C   3. Mr. Van passed out the test at 8:00.

C   4. Karen sprinted past Matt to win the 50-meter dash.

Set 29

peace: quiet and calm

It is hard to keep world peace.

piece: a section or part

He ate a piece of fudge cake.

　　　　　　　piece
1. Pass Julio a ~~peace~~ of cherry pie.

　　　　　　　　　　peace
2. The Protestants made ~~piece~~ with the Catholics in Ireland.

　　　　　　　piece
3. Roger lost a ~~peace~~ of my science project, but I passed anyway.

　　　　peace
4. The ~~piece~~ symbol was part of the sixties generation.

Set 30

principal: main (adjective); head of a school; amount of money invested to earn interest

Money was his principal reason for quitting the job.

The school principal called a meeting.

principle: rule, law, or regulation

His answer was based on a simple principle.

　　　principal
1. Our ~~principle~~, Ms. Jones, is a sensitive woman.

C　　2. We learned the principles of good marketing.

　　　　　　　　　　principles
3. I called her and explained the new club's ~~principals~~.

　　　principal
4. The invested ~~principle~~ earned high interest.

Set 31

quiet: calm, peaceful

The baby was finally quiet.

quite: very, to a great extent, rather

He was quite sure of himself.

　　　quite
1. Laura is ~~quiet~~ a pretty girl.

　　　　　　　quiet
2. Grand Lake is always calm and ~~quite~~.

　　　　quite
3. The Russians were ~~quiet~~ surprised that they came in second in the gymnastics events.

　　　　　　　　　　　　quiet
4. After the children are put to bed, the Wagners' house is ~~quite~~.

Set 32

right: correct or opposite of left

He always seems to know the right answer.

rite: ceremony

The parents observed religious rites when they had their child baptized.

write: communicate with written words

She likes to write her thoughts in her journal.

        write
1. Beatrice started to ~~rite~~ her essay but was interrupted by another phone call.

       right
2. Henry turned ~~rite~~ at the intersection.

       right
3. I broke my ~~rite~~ hand when I fell.

         rite
4. Some communities have a ~~right~~ of passage into adulthood.

Set 33

than: used in comparisons

It is later than you think.

then: at that time; next in order; in that case

Then we can order two more books.

C   1. We will be through by then.

              than
2. I have more homework ~~then~~ I can complete.

           than
3. He has more money ~~then~~ I do.

C   4. If we go then, we can get a discount.

Set 34

there: location

He left his papers there.

their: ownership

Their papers were all turned in on time.

they're: contraction of "they are"

They're determined to finish first.

       their
1. They left ~~there~~ book in their car.

C   2. They're making excellent grades.

C   3. The puppy is hiding there in the grass.

      they're   *their*
4. Sam said ~~their~~ going to ~~there~~ favorite spot.

Set 35

though: (even), (although), however, nevertheless

He wants to buy a car even though he cannot afford one.

thought: thinking or an idea

I thought you would never ask.

C   **1.** Though Juana was tired, she stayed up and baked bread.
         thought
      2. The ~~though~~ of cooking another meal depressed the cook.

C   **3.** The Comets lost the game even though they played their best.

C   **4.** Her thought was to plan a surprise party for Jim.

Set 36

threw: tossed in air (past tense)

He threw the ball into the net.

through: from one side to the other

They passed through the city.
         through
      1. Sarah climbed ~~threw~~ the tunnel and ran for the slide.
            threw
      2. The muscular football player ~~through~~ a bullet pass to the receiver.
        through
      3. Ann ran ~~threw~~ the woods, jumping over logs and stones.
                through
      4. Janice accidentally poked the sharp pencil ~~threw~~ the soft Styrofoam.

Set 37

to: a preposition that shows direction toward; part of an infinitive (to sing, to act)

Sara wanted to go to the fair.

too: also, more than enough

Sharon wanted to go, too.

two: number two

The two women enjoyed the same types of activities.
         two
      1. The final score was three to ~~too~~.
        to
      2. The Fishers love ~~too~~ swim at night in the summer.
         too
      3. Nicki finished her paper, ~~to~~.
       Too
      4. ~~Two~~ many people were at the party in the small house.

Set 38

wander: to go from place to place aimlessly

He tends to wander in the summertime.

wonder: feel surprise, amazement; have doubts about; question mentally

I wonder if he will get off work on time.

        wanders
1. He ~~wonders~~ from one city to another.

      wonder
2. I will always ~~wander~~ about his decision.

C   3. I often wonder how my family is doing.

      wander
4. I like to ~~wonder~~ down the beach.

Set 39

weak: not strong

Sara is still weak from having the flu.

week: seven days

Eric stayed for three weeks.

      weak
1. Is she too ~~week~~ to go shopping?

      weak
2. Al's knee has been ~~week~~ since he broke it.

      week
3. The child gets an allowance every ~~weak~~.

      weeks
4. Every six ~~weaks~~, she goes to the doctor for a checkup.

Set 40

weather: outside temperature and conditions

The weather is beautiful.

whether: if, in case of

She wanted to know whether she needed to take a sweater.

      weather
1. The ~~whether~~ is great in Colorado in the summer.

C   2. Whether or not you apologize, Tracey's feelings are hurt.

C   3. The weather for tomorrow is predicted to be beautiful.

      whether
4. Tom was sorry ~~weather~~ he would admit it or not.

Set 41

were: past tense verb

Six flowers were placed in the vase.

where: place

Where can we find a good place to eat?

      Where
1. ~~Were~~ were you when I needed help?

               were
2. Fifteen of the students ~~where~~ going on a hike.

        where
3. Tanya went ~~were~~ the other students were playing volleyball.

C   4. They were moving into a new apartment.

Set 42

who's: contraction for "who is" or "who has"

Who's responsible for the vase of red roses?

whose: relating to possession of an object, frequently in a question

Whose pie is in the refrigerator?

      Who's
1. ~~Whose~~ at the door, John?

C   2. I forgot whose keys these are.
      Who's
3. ~~Whose~~ at the other end of the phone?
      Who's
4. ~~Whose~~ done the most work?

Set 43

who: refers to people

The people who live here are energetic.

which: should not be used to refer to people

We finished the assignment, which the teacher made on Monday.

that: can refer to people or things

The soup that I like is all gone.

          that
1. Cecil threw out the food ~~who~~ was spoiled.

        who or that
2. We like the neighbor ~~which~~ moved in across the street.

C   3. The people that came late to the concert could not get in.
         that
4. The programs ~~who~~ received the awards were purchased by the library.

Set 44

woman: one adult female human

She was the woman of his dreams.

women: two or more adult female humans

The women shared their concerns with one another.

         women
1. The three ~~woman~~ went through nurses' training together.

        woman
2. The ~~women~~ Jason married was his childhood sweetheart.

C   3. The most prestigious award was given to an outstanding woman student.

        women
4. Of all the ~~woman~~ he dated, that woman stole his heart.

Set 45

your: ownership or possession (2nd person singular or plural)

Janet, your speech was well received.

you're: contraction for "you are"

You're not feeling well, are you?

        you're
1. Jesse said that ~~your~~ not going.

C   2. Would you be willing to move your car?

        you're
3. I'm sorry, Jane, but ~~your~~ not going to be able to swim today.

C   4. Your assignment is not due until next Monday.

Appendix B: Keeping a Journal

Journal writing serves several purposes, none of which should be overlooked. It helps you:

work through emotions

make the words flow more freely

communicate with others

remember events in the past

make class notes clearer

Journal writing helps you *work through emotions* so you can back off and deal objectively with whatever is bothering you. Someone once said that you can become a journal writer only after you have written about the thing that hurt the most, and as you release your feelings on paper, you also release the tears that have been long overdue. For example, a man in his forties had not spoken to his mother and father for twenty years. He filled two journals in which he communicated with them only on paper. Eventually he wrote his mother and initiated some type of interaction. Though he could not change what had happened in his childhood, he was able to begin a new relationship with his parents.

When Ivan Lacore, a serious journal writer, was asked if journal writing helped him cope with life, he said, "Writing in my journal helps me face the future without the anger of the past."

One bonus to journal writing is that it *makes the words flow more freely*. The more you write, the easier it becomes. This can be compared to walking. If you stayed in bed for six weeks without ever walking, you would lose your ability to walk and would have to "learn" to walk all over again. Elementary school teachers often remind us that children who do not read over the summer cannot read as well in September as they did in June. Whether walking, reading, or writing, the more you do of it, the better you become at it. As you began this course, it might have been an effort to write one paragraph. However, by the end of the term you may be able to write a multiparagraph essay in the same length of time you once needed for one paragraph.

Journal writing can also help you *communicate with others*. What you write in your journal often involves your feelings about other people. Sometimes you may choose to write a letter to someone. Another time you may want to share parts of your journal with another person or with many people. Then editing and reworking the material become an important part of the writing. One woman wrote her memories of her childhood and her daughter's childhood. She then typed her journal and presented it to her grandchild. This journal became a treasure that will most likely be passed down from generation to generation.

Journal writing often allows you to *remember events in the past* that you have blocked from your mind. When you begin writing about these things, details surface and memories are renewed.

Another important purpose of journal writing is to *make class notes clearer*. Sometimes you may want to rework the notes that you took in this class or in another class. This reorganizing helps you understand ideas and concepts that your

Transparencies can be made from the sample journal entry, page 27, and the journal log, page 28, in the Instructor's Manual.

instructor wants you to grasp. Notes are often taken very rapidly in class. Rewriting and reworking them immediately after class makes the concepts "stick" in your mind.

Some instructors think that a notebook should be turned in and graded. Others think that these notebooks can be checked without the teacher reading the entries at all. These instructors do not check the entries because they feel that students should be able to write about their most personal feelings without worrying about an audience. If your instructor were to say that the journal is to be read and graded for grammar, you would be concerned with both form and content. On the other hand, if your instructor were to say that he or she would not read the contents, you would feel assured that you could write about anything you wanted to without worrying about form.

The actual journal may be a special composition book your instructor requires you to buy at the bookstore, a leather-bound book that costs twenty dollars, or a spiral notebook you bought for twenty-five cents on sale. What you use really does not matter. Unless your instructor requires a special type of writing instrument, you should use anything that feels comfortable. You can use a pencil, a pen, a typewriter, or a computer. You can write in neat lines and will want to if your instructor is going to read your journal. If not, you might find yourself writing from corner to corner, in circles, or whatever feels right. Likewise, you might have a special desk you like to sit at when you are writing, or you might like to sit on the floor. You might like everything quiet, or you might like both the radio and the TV going.

One last thought about journals is that you are not just meeting a requirement to pass a course. You are learning to feel on paper. Though writing how you feel about what is happening in your life may seem strange at first, you may find yourself keeping a journal years after this course is finished. This journal can help you improve your writing and thinking skills for many years to come.

Writing Assignment

1. Try writing in your journal about the most wonderful place you can remember as a child. Close your eyes until you can reenter this place. Then let the reader enter this place with you. What do you see, feel, touch, taste, smell? What is above you? What is around you? Begin to write when your mind can reenter this place, and continue to write as long as you can.

2. Try writing in your journal about the last time you got mad. Describe how you felt. Why did you feel that way? Who made you angry? Why were you angry? (Just continue to write until nothing more comes.)

3. In your journal, write a letter that is overdue. Perhaps you can write a letter to someone who might have reason to be upset with you. Or perhaps you can write a letter to someone whom you really dislike or like. (There is no need to mail this letter.)

4. In your journal, rework your notes in this class or another class immediately after the class is over.

5. In your journal, write about anything that bothers you. This can be prejudice, frustration, homelessness, your classes, or anything else. Try to recall a particular event that bothered you.

Appendix C: Irregular Verbs

Irregular verbs may cause a few problems because they have many different forms. Feel confident, however, that you probably use most of these verbs correctly.

You may find that you do not know some of the forms. Perhaps, in addition to not knowing them, you may say the verb forms correctly but not spell them correctly when you write them. In either case, you may need to refer to the following list.

What makes a verb "irregular"? It is irregular if it forms the past tense in any of the following ways.

Ways Verbs Are Irregular in the Past Tense

By changing the internal sound and/or spelling

> I *speak* now. I *spoke* yesterday.
>
> I *write* now. I *wrote* yesterday.

By changing most of the sound and most of the spelling

> I *bring* my lunch on Mondays.
>
> I *brought* it yesterday.

By changing to a different word

> I *go* today. I *went* yesterday.
>
> I *am* here now. I *was* here earlier.

You do not need to know these changes by name. Being able to use the verbs is much more important. Do not try to memorize all the forms in the following table; instead, use it as a reference when you are revising your writing.

Irregular Verbs

Present	Past	Past Participle*	Present Participle*
am	was	been	being
become	became	become	becoming
begin	began	begun	beginning
bite	bit	bitten	biting
blow	blew	blown	blowing
break	broke	broken	breaking
bring	brought	brought	bringing
buy	bought	bought	buying
catch	caught	caught	catching
choose	chose	chosen	choosing
come	came	come	coming

---

*When the past participle or present participle is used as a complete verb, a linking or *helping verb* is always used.

Present	Past	Past Participle*	Present Participle*
dig	dug	dug	digging
do	did	done	doing
draw	drew	drawn	drawing
drink	drank	drunk	drinking
drive	drove	driven	driving
eat	ate	eaten	eating
fall	fell	fallen	falling
fight	fought	fought	fighting
fly	flew	flown	flying
freeze	froze	frozen	freezing
get	got	gotten	getting
give	gave	given	giving
go	went	gone	going
grow	grew	grown	growing
hang†	hung	hung	hanging
have	had	had	having
hear	heard	heard	hearing
hide	hid	hidden	hiding
know	knew	known	knowing
lay (set something down)†	laid	laid	laying
lead	led	led	leading
lie (recline)‡	lay	lain	lying
lie (tell an untruth)	lied	lied	lying
pay	paid	paid	paying
read	read	read	reading
ride	rode	ridden	riding
ring	rang	rung	ringing
rise‡	rose	risen	rising
run	ran	run	running
see	saw	seen	seeing
set (put something down)†	set	set	setting
shine‡	shone	shone	shining
sing	sang	sung	singing
sit‡	sat	sat	sitting
speak	spoke	spoken	speaking
sting	stung	stung	stinging
steal	stole	stolen	stealing
swear	swore	sworn	swearing
swim	swam	swum	swimming
take	took	taken	taking
think	thought	thought	thinking
throw	threw	thrown	throwing
wake	woke	woken	waking
wear	wore	worn	wearing
win	won	won	winning
write	wrote	written	writing

*When the past participle or present participle is used as a complete verb, a linking or *helping verb* is always used.

†Takes a direct object.

‡Does not take a direct object.

Appendix D: Spelling

When you write a paper, it is important that all the words are spelled correctly. When you submit a paper with misspelled words, it seems as though you did not bother to take the time to proofread carefully or run a spell checker. You probably know some people who are excellent spellers and others who are extremely poor spellers. Research has shown that spelling skills have nothing to do with basic intelligence. On the other hand, since correct spelling is one of the characteristics of public writing, you need to spend time doing whatever is necessary to improve your spelling. If spelling is a problem for you, you will be happy to learn that it can be improved with practice. If you are willing to put in some time to review these pages and use the **Keys to Better Spelling,** your spelling should improve. Remember, though, that spelling is something that should not be a preoccupation until you do your final editing. To begin understanding spelling, you need to be aware of a few basic terms that follow.

Basic Terms

The main part of the word without a prefix or a suffix is the **root word.**

un **manage** able

One or more letters of a word that together form a unit for pronunciation make up a **syllable.**

va ca tion

A **vowel** forms the prominent sound in a syllable.

a, e, i, o, u, and sometimes y

Any letter of the alphabet that is **not** a vowel is identified as a **consonant.**

b, c, d, f, g, h, j, k, l, m, n, p, q, r, s, t, v, w, x, y, z

A syllable attached to the beginning of a word to extend the meaning of the root word is a prefix.

undo, **anti**government

A syllable attached to the end of a word to extend the meaning of the root word is a **suffix.**

govern**ment**, ski**ing**

Keys to Better Spelling

Here are a few basic patterns that can help with spelling. Read and study the keys, but more important, look at and pronounce the examples so that you can understand them. Then begin incorporating them into your spelling habits.

Key 1. If a one-syllable word ends in a consonant-vowel-consonant pattern, double the final consonant before adding a suffix that begins with a vowel.

Here are some words to study.

wrap	+er	=	wrapper
ton	+age	=	tonnage
hop	+ed	=	hopped

If the final consonant is an "x" or is not pronounced, do not double it.

box	+ing	=	boxing
row	+ing	=	rowing

Practice 1
To practice, add "ed" to the following words.

star	*starred*
tag	*tagged*
drug	*drugged*
wrap	*wrapped*
ship	*shipped*

Practice 2
To practice, add "ing" to the following words.

brag	*bragging*
swim	*swimming*
hum	*humming*
chat	*chatting*
lug	*lugging*

Key 2. If a two-syllable word ends in a consonant-vowel-consonant pattern and is accented on the second syllable, double the final consonant before adding a suffix that begins with a vowel.

Here are some words to study.

refer	+ed	=	referred
transmit	+er	=	transmitter
begin	+ing	=	beginning
admit	+ance	=	admittance

Practice 3
To practice, add "ed" to the following words.

defer	*deferred*
allot	*allotted*

control _____ *controlled* _____

omit _____ *omitted* _____

remit _____ *remitted* _____

Practice 4

To practice, add "ing" to the following words.

occur _____ *occurring* _____

repel _____ *repelling* _____

extol _____ *extolling* _____

unwrap _____ *unwrapping* _____

acquit _____ *acquitting* _____

Key 3. If a word ends in "e" preceded by a consonant, drop the "e" before adding a suffix that begins with a vowel.

Here are some words to examine that follow the pattern of a suffix that begins with a vowel:

hope	+ing	=	hoping
excuse	+able	=	excusable
cope	+ed	=	coped
scarce	+ity	=	scarcity

Keep the "e" if the suffix begins with a consonant.
Here are some words that follow this pattern.

move	+ment	=	movement
tire	+less	=	tireless
remote	+ness	=	remoteness
strange	+ly	=	strangely

Practice 5

Practice by combining each root word with the suffix given.

judge	+	ment	=	*judgment*
believe	+	able	=	*believable*
compose	+	ing	=	*composing*
delete	+	ing	=	*deleting*
write	+	ing	=	*writing*
relate	+	ing	=	*relating*
replace	+	ment	=	*replacement*
devote	+	ing	=	*devoting*
forgive	+	ness	=	*forgiveness*
encourage	+	ment	=	*encouragement*

Key 4. After a soft "c," write the "e" before the "i" when these two letters appear in sequence, or keep this jingle in mind: "i" before "e" except after "c."

Here are some examples that follow this pattern:

deceive   receive   conceive

The "e" also goes before the "i" if the sound is like an "a" as in *neighbor* and *weigh*.

Practice 6

Practice on these words as you insert either "ie" or "ei" in each blank:

unbel _ie_ vable   r _ei_ gn

fr _ei_ ght   shr _ie_ k

gr _ie_ f   br _ie_ f

rec _ei_ pt   misch _ie_ vous

rel _ie_ ve   n _ie_ ce

Key 5. If a word ends with "y" preceded by a consonant, generally change the "y" to an "i" before adding a suffix other than "ing."

Here are some words that follow this pattern:

worry	+er	=	worrier
worry	+some	=	worrisome
hurry	+s	=	hurries
lazy	+est	=	laziest
company	+s	=	companies

The "y" is kept to preserve the "y" sound in the proper pronunciation of words such as the following:

carry	+ing	=	carrying
worry	+ing	=	worrying
hurry	+ing	=	hurrying

Practice 7

Practice on the following words:

happy	+ness	=	*happiness*
merry	+est	=	*merriest*
vary	+s	=	*varies*
tasty	+er	=	*tastier*
jury	+s	=	*juries*
baby	+ing	=	*babying*
study	+ing	=	*studying*

Spelling List

As you create your personal list of spelling words, you may want to add some of the following words to your list.

absence	category	envelop (verb)	labeling
absorption	ceiling	exaggerate	legitimate
accede	cemetery	exceed	leisure
accessible	changeable	exhaust	license
accommodate	clientele	exhilaration	likable
accumulate	collateral	existence	litigation
achieve	color	extraordinary	loneliness
acoustics	committee	fallacy	loose
acquittal	comparative	familiar	maintenance
advantageous	competitor	flexible	mathematics
affiliated	concede	fluctuation	mediocre
aggressive	connoisseur	forty	minimum
alignment	connotation	gesture	misspelling
all right	conscience	grammar	necessary
aluminum	consensus	gratuity	necessity
analyze	convenient	grievous	negligence
anoint	convertible	haphazard	negotiable
apostrophe	corroborate	hemorrhage	newsstand
apparent	criticism	holiday	nickel
appropriate	definitely	hosiery	noticeable
argument	description	hypocrisy	occurrence
asphalt	desirable	illegible	omission
assistant	despair	immigrant	opponent
asterisk	development	incidentally	oscillate
athletics	dilemma	indelible	pageant
auditor	dilettante	independent	panicky
bachelor	disappear	indispensable	parallel
balloon	disappoint	inimitable	paralyze
bankruptcy	disbursement	inoculate	pastime
believable	discrepancy	insistent	peaceable
benefited	discriminate	intermediary	penicillin
bicycle	dissatisfied	irresistible	permanent
brilliant	dissipate	irritable	perseverance
bulletin	drunkenness	jewelry	persistent
calendar	ecstasy	judgment	personnel
campaign	eligible	judicial	persuade
canceled	embarrassing	khaki	physician
canvass (verb)	endorsement	kindergarten	plagiarism

possesses	questionnaire	sergeant	technique
potato	receive	sheriff	tenant
precede	recommend	stationary (fixed)	tranquilizer
predictable	repetition	stationery (paper)	tranquillizer
preferred	rescind	succeed	truly
privilege	rhythmical	suddenness	tyrannize
procedure	ridiculous	superintendent	unanimous
proceed	sacrilegious	supersede	until
professor	salable	surgeon	vacillate
pronunciation	secretary	surprise	vacuum
psychology	seize	tangible	vicious
pursue	separate	tariff	weird

Tips for Improving Spelling

1. One very common, practical, and logical activity to improve your spelling is to read. Time spent reading is a reinforcement of spelling words, vocabulary, and writing models.

2. Personal spelling lists help you focus on troublesome words. Post the lists on your refrigerator so that you see the list frequently, or perhaps you can make a plan and work on just five words a week. Carry the list of five words on a three-by-five card and look at the words any time, especially during the time you spend waiting for traffic lights to change, buses to come, or classes to begin.

3. As you study your words, be sure to pronounce all the syllables carefully.

4. A computerized dictionary such as a Franklin can be a handy aid to use while writing. Some models contain thousands of words, and the computer can bring the word up instantaneously, so if you can afford the extra purchase, your money might be well spent. Some models allow you to customize your dictionary by adding specialized words that you need for your job.

5. The purchase of a handy paperback dictionary is another very practical option. Most college bookstores have a variety of choices, and your writing instructor could suggest one for you.

6. If you do your writing on the computer, run the spell checker before you submit your final draft to your instructor. Also, use your "find" function for your personal "troublesome word list." "It's," "its," "there," "their," "they're," "your," and "you're" can be searched easily so that you can double-check the spelling for your use of the word.

Appendix E: ESL: Gaining Confidence in Using English

Count Nouns

Count nouns refer to people, places, and things that you can count one by one. These nouns most often refer to concrete objects (something you can see). Their plural forms end in **s** or **es**; however, a few of them have irregular plurals. (See pages 72–73 for irregular plural forms.) Just remember that you can **always** count individually (one by one) the people or objects they refer to. Study the following examples to see how count nouns are used correctly. These are concrete nouns or items you can see.

Concrete Count Nouns (can be seen, touched, or smelled)

Singular	car	The **car** ran the red light.	(correct)
Plural	cars	The **cars** ran the red light.	(correct)
Singular	book	We ordered the **book** online.	(correct)
Plural	books	We ordered the **books** online.	(correct)
Singular	box	We packed the **box** carefully.	(correct)
Plural	boxes	We packed the **boxes** carefully.	(correct)

Although most count nouns refer to concrete things, some common ones refer to abstract or non-concrete things. Abstract or non-concrete nouns identify an idea or something you cannot see exactly with your eyes. You may be able to see some behaviors, but you cannot hold them, smell them, or touch them. The idea may be only in your mind. However, you can still count them one by one. Study the following examples.

Abstract Count Nouns (cannot be seen, touched, or smelled)

Singular	decision	He made his **decision** quickly.	(correct)
Plural	decisions	He made two important **decisions**.	(correct)
Singular	dream	Kim's **dream** was to become a chemist.	(correct)
Plural	dreams	Kim hoped to fulfill her **dreams**.	(correct)

Exercise 1

Determine whether the underlined noun is concrete (can be seen) or abstract (cannot be seen). Circle the C for concrete or A for abstract at the beginning of each sentence.

Example: Ⓒ A   The <u>puppies</u> jumped and rolled in the grass.

  C Ⓐ   She admired her son's <u>courage</u>.

Version A

Ⓒ A **1.** The <u>car</u> was his favorite.

Ⓒ A **2.** Daya was a Hindu <u>priest</u>.

C Ⓐ **3.** Daya's <u>religion</u> was important to her.

(C) A **4.** The cousins went to the basketball <u>game</u> together.

C (A) **5.** Kiko's <u>fear</u> showed when she was speaking in front of a crowd.

Version B

(C) A **1.** Gonzalo studied many hours for the <u>test</u>.

C (A) **2.** The Dalai Lama puts forth the idea of <u>love</u>.

(C) A **3.** Chinese New Year is a time for a dragon <u>parade</u>.

(C) A **4.** Greeks eat rice and spices rolled in a grape <u>leaf</u> called a dolma.

(C) A **5.** The native <u>Indians</u> of Ecuador weave many beautiful rugs.

Noncount Nouns

Noncount nouns refer to things that are wholes. You cannot count them one by one. Sometimes they are concrete and specific, but **there is no plural form with an *s*.** Study the following sentences to see how these nouns are used correctly.

Concrete Noncount Nouns

butter	Do you want **butter** on your pancakes?	(correct)
No plural with *s*	Do you want **butters** on your pancakes?	(incorrect)
sugar	The **sugar** is damp and in a lump.	(correct)
No plural with *s*	The **sugars** are damp and in a lump.	(incorrect)

Although you cannot count the butter, you may still want to express an amount of it. You might want to use one of the indefinite pronouns you have previously studied on page 59. (Remember, though, that when the word comes right in front of the noun, it functions like an adjective, so it describes.)

Do you want **more** butter on your pancakes?

Do you want **some** butter on your pancakes?

We need to buy **more** sugar.

We need to buy **some** sugar.

If you want your meaning to be clearer, you can use a **count** noun to make the meaning more specific. For example, you could say, "Do you want two **pats** of butter on your pancakes?" "We need to buy five **pounds** of sugar."

Abstract Noncount Nouns (cannot be seen, touched, or smelled)

	The **music** from the concert could be heard for miles.	(correct)
No plural with *s*	The **musics** from the concert could be heard for miles.	(incorrect)
	Winning the lottery brought no **happiness** to Nora.	(correct)
No plural with *s*	Winning the lottery brought no **happinesses** to Nora.	(incorrect)
	At ninety-one, she had the **courage** of a fifty-year-old.	(correct)
No plural with *s*	The newspaper recorded the people's **courages.**	(incorrect)

Nouns That Are Either Count or Noncount

Some nouns can refer to things that can be counted one by one and also refer to something that cannot be counted one by one. The meaning needed in the sentence determines which kind of noun you need. Note the following examples.

Count	The **lights** came on throughout the house.	(the individual lamps)
Noncount	We wanted more **light** in the kitchen.	(light in general)
Count	Jay wrote two **papers** for his English class.	(individual essays)
Noncount	Jay uses good-quality **paper** for his assignments.	(paper in general)
Count	The banging **noises** from the dishwasher worry me.	(individual kinds)
Noncount	The **noise** from the traffic woke Geraldo early.	(noise in general)

Exercise 2

Determine whether the underlined noun is a count (C) or noncount (N) noun. Circle the C or N at the beginning of each sentence.

Example: Ⓒ N   The <u>game</u> began just after 10:00 a.m.

        C Ⓝ   She admired her son's <u>courage</u>.

Version A

C Ⓝ   **1.** The hospital patient struggled for <u>survival</u>.

C Ⓝ   **2.** People continue to hope that <u>humanity</u> will learn religious tolerance.

Ⓒ N   **3.** The lawn mower damaged a <u>brick</u> in the fence.

C Ⓝ   **4.** My sister takes <u>calcium</u> every day.

Ⓒ N   **5.** The health <u>magazine</u> recommends yearly mammograms.

Version B

C Ⓝ   **1.** Theresa expressed <u>relief</u> at the end of the test.

C Ⓝ   **2.** We remodeled the house to have more <u>room</u> in the kitchen.

Ⓒ N   **3.** Because of her diabetes, Ingrid could not eat any of the apple <u>pie</u>.

Ⓒ N   **4.** I forgot my <u>appointment</u> at the dentist.

C Ⓝ   **5.** After growing up, my cat did not like <u>milk</u>.

Using Indefinite Articles with Count and Noncount Nouns

A and **an** are indefinite articles. If English is not your native language, you may have had trouble using the correct indefinite articles with count and noncount nouns. To become more fluent in English, you will want to work on using these articles correctly. They do not refer to any specific or clearly identified person, place, or thing. **They are used only with singular count nouns.**

A is used with singular count nouns that begin with a **consonant**.

An is used with singular count nouns that begin with a **vowel**.

When you are trying to choose between **a** or **an**, consider the beginning **sound** of the next word. For example, the word **hour** does not begin with the same sound as the word **house**.

Study these examples:

We waited for **an hour** to get into the movie.	(no particular time)
I looked at **a house** to rent.	(no specified house)
I bought **a book** to read on my trip.	(book not specified)
She ate **a sandwich** for lunch.	(not any kind identified)
He mailed **an invitation** to his sister.	(not any particular invitation)
After the accident, Marcel rented **an automobile.**	(not any type specified)

A and *an* are **not** used with noncount nouns.

We listened to **a music** last night.	(incorrect)
We listened to **music** last night.	(correct)
Rene saw **a snow** for the first time this winter.	(incorrect)
Rene saw **snow** for the first time this winter.	(correct)

Exercise 3

Use **a** or **an** correctly in the sentences below. If the sentence is correct as it is, mark a C in the left margin.

Example: Carlos wanted ___*a*___ motorcycle for his graduation present.

Version A

1. I poured my water into ___*a*___ glass from the cupboard.

C 2. The Arrvizus wanted their new house to be made of _____ brick.

3. To increase her strength, Leta enrolled at ___*a*___ gym.

C 4. My neighbor collects antique bottles made of _____ glass.

5. The elderly gentleman ordered ___*an*___ egg and some toast for his breakfast.

Version B

1. My father made ___*an*___ error in his taxes this year.

2. After Raye worked out for ___*a*___ month, her shoulders were stronger.

C 3. Uraiwan wanted to take a course in _____ geography this semester.

4. We sent ___*a*___ compliment to the chef for his delicious appetizer.

5. The parents had to learn ___*a*___ new method for disciplining their child.

Using the Definite Article "the" Before Singular and Plural Count Nouns

In contrast to indefinite articles, you should use the definite article **the** if a **particular person, place, or thing is specified or pointed out.** This particular meaning can be in the sentence itself or in the context of your paragraph. You can use **the** before both **singular** and **plural count** nouns. Study the following correct examples.

The charro rode the gray <u>horse</u> in the rodeo.   (a particular horse)

Rory used **the** cell phone you loaned him.   (a particular cell phone)

The handyman very quickly washed **the** windows of my house.

(particular handyman;
particular windows)

The computers in our lab are usually dependable.   (particular computers)

Using the Definite Article "the" Before Noncount Nouns

You can use the definite article **the** before **noncount** nouns if there is a particular meaning specified within the sentence or within the context of your paragraph. When no particular meaning is expressed, do not use **the.**

After the race, I was surprised at **the relief** on her face.   (**particular** relief)

I found **relief** from the heat in the shade.

The light from the ball field shines into my house.   (**particular** light)

I do not like **light** coming into my house.

We liked **the music** played by the orchestra last night.   (**particular** music)

I enjoy **music** more than my brother does.

Work through the following exercise to get more practice in using **the** with count and noncount nouns.

Exercise 4

Consider the use of **the** in each sentence below. Write C for correct or I for incorrect in each blank.

Example: _I_ **When we are on vacation, I am happy when he shows the enthusiasm.**

    _C_ **When we are on vacation, I am happy when he shows enthusiasm.**

Version A

_C_ **1.** He experienced failure last Saturday.

_C_ **2.** He was saddened by the failure of his business.

_I_ **3.** He showed the nervousness before his wedding.

_C_ **4.** The nervousness he felt before his wedding soon disappeared.

_C_ **5.** He lacked the courage needed to become a soldier.

_I_ **6.** Becoming a soldier requires the courage.

_____*I*_____ **1.** She does not have the sympathy.

_____*C*_____ **2.** She does not have the sympathy her neighbor needs right now.

_____*C*_____ **3.** In New Orleans, cafés have live jazz every weekend.

_____*I*_____ **4.** In New Orleans, cafés have the live jazz every weekend.

_____*I*_____ **5.** Ursula appreciates the beauty.

_____*C*_____ **6.** Ursula appreciates the beauty of Renaissance art.

Knowing whether to use count or noncount nouns comes fairly naturally to native speakers of English, but if English is not your native language, you will have to have lots of experience talking with fluent speakers and reading as much English as you can. Try to benefit from your mistakes, and, as often as you can, practice using what you have learned. This is also good advice for the next section concerning verbs.

Verbs

English verbs may be troublesome for you if English is not your native language. To help you gain confidence in your fluency, study and then practice using the following verb forms.

Phrasal Verbs

These verbs are two-word verbs that are very common in English, especially in popular usage. They are made up of a verb plus a preposition and have special meaning when used together. Study the following examples:

The mother **checked on** her sleeping child.   (She looked at her closely to see if she was all right.)

The words "checked on" function as a verb. "On" seems like a preposition, but it does not function as a preposition.

Margarita **put off** her education.   (She postponed her education.)

"Put off" functions as a verb, so "off" is not a preposition in this sentence.

Partial List of Common, Two-Word Verbs

ask out	ask a person to go on a date
call off	cancel
call on	ask someone to answer in class
	formal usage—make a formal visit to someone
check on	attend to the needs of someone
cheer up	make somebody feel happy
check out	investigate
	officially take a book out of the library
come across	meet by chance
drop off	leave something or someone at a certain place

figure out	find an answer
fill out	put answers in the blanks of a form, such as an application
find out	get information
give up	quit; do not try anymore
go over	reread carefully
hand in	submit a paper or a document to a person or an office
look over	review or check again
make up	invent (for example, a story)
	complete missed work in school
pass out	distribute (as tests in a class)
	become unconscious
pick out	choose (perhaps an article of clothing in a store)
point out	show or call attention to
put up with	tolerate
run out (of)	use all the supply of something
tear down	destroy, as the confidence of a person
	demolish, as a building
turn down	lessen sound on a stereo or television set
turn off	stop a machine, such as an appliance in a house
	stop a faucet or touch the off switch for a light

Exercise 5

Do you know any other "preposition-like" words that can be used with the verb **turn?**

turn _____, which means _____

turn _____, which means _____

turn _____, which means _____

Now try using some of these verbs in sentences of your own.

Exercise 6

Write three sentences, using any three of the above phrasal verbs. Underline the verb.

Example: I <u>handed in</u> my research paper to the English Department.

1. _____

_____

2. _____

_____

3. _____

_____

Modal Verbs

A modal is a helping verb that has its own meaning. When a modal is used with the main verb, it adds meaning to the main verb. Study the following examples.

The baby **can** walk.	(The baby knows how to walk.)
Zito **might** walk to work.	(We do not know for sure that he is going to walk.)
He **will** walk tomorrow.	(We know this for certain.)
He **should** walk.	(It is advisable for him to walk, perhaps for his health.)

Points to remember about modals

- When you use a modal, do not use an **s** on the main verb
- The modal form does not use an **s** for *he, she,* or *it* (the third person singular)
- Most modals are **not** followed by **to**-plus-a-verb (an infinitive); common exception is "ought." Example: "She **ought** to go."
- Modals function like other helping verbs in questions and in negative sentences. "**Should** he go?" "He **will** not walk tomorrow."
- Modals are **not** immediately followed by **-ing** verb forms. Incorrect: "He must washing his car." Say instead, "He must wash his car."

Partial List of Modals and the Meanings They Add to Main Verbs

can	has the ability; has permission
could	had the ability in the past
have to	expressing obligation or necessity
may	expressing possibility or uncertainty
might	expressing some uncertainty
must	expressing obligation or necessity
should	expressing obligation
would	expressing preference

Work through the following exercise to help you use modal verbs.

Exercise 7

Write a **C** for correct or an **I** for incorrect in the blank before each sentence.

Example: __*I*__ **Rhonda has to making a deposit at her bank.**

__*C*__ **Rhonda has to make a deposit at her bank.**

Version A

__*I*__ **1.** The student can buys her supplies at the discount store.

__*C*__ **2.** We have to go tomorrow morning.

__*I*__ **3.** Sonya must seeing the doctor after all.

__*I*__ **4.** He might jogs around the lake in the morning.

__*C*__ **5.** Walter may study at the library.

Version B

_I_   **1.** After lunch, we could going to the mall to shop.

_C_   **2.** If you prefer, I will enroll immediately.

_I_   **3.** The church bells should to ring at noon.

_I_   **4.** Flavio might mows the lawn next week.

_C_   **5.** Marta may not read the newspaper before breakfast.

Verb Plus *-ing* Verb Form (Gerund)

As you have already learned, an **-ing** verb form (gerund) is a noun that can be either a subject or an object. Certain verbs in English are usually followed by these **-ing** forms. The sentences below show how these commonly used verbs are followed immediately by an **-ing** form of another verb.

> I **advised** *paying* bills on time.
>
> Murti **appreciated** *going* to college.
>
> He **avoided** *rushing* into the new business.
>
> We **considered** *borrowing* money to buy our furniture.
>
> We **discussed** *painting* our house.
>
> Glenda **enjoys** *going* to school.
>
> Elena **finished** *decorating* her cousin's home.
>
> I **keep** *working* on the project even though I am tired.
>
> Chan **quit** *smoking* two years ago.
>
> The agent **suggested** *selling* the house as soon as possible.

These kinds of expressions are so common in English that it would benefit you to practice them and use them whenever you can. The next exercise will help you use these verbs with suitable **-ing** verb forms after them.

Exercise 8

Add an appropriate **-ing** verb form (gerund) to each subject and verb below. Use other words and phrases to make your sentences meaningful and complete.

Example: The instructor discussed _____*revising our essays*_____

Version A

1. The counselor suggested _____*studying harder*_____

2. We will discuss _____*going home early*_____

3. Sharon quit _____*smoking cigarettes*_____

4. Abas kept _____*calling me*_____

5. Mama enjoys _____*having us around*_____

Version B

1. My grandfather advises _____ *taking vitamins each day* _____
2. The customers appreciated _____ *having good service* _____
3. The nurse avoided _____ *coming into my room* _____
4. The builder finished _____ *painting my house* _____
5. The senior citizens will consider _____ *volunteering at the hospital* _____

Note   It is important to remember that the above verbs are **not** followed by an infinitive verb form. It is incorrect to say, "We discussed to go on vacation." Rather say, "We discussed going on vacation."

Verb Followed by to-Plus-a-Verb Form (Infinitive)

Many common verbs are followed by an infinitive—the word **to**-plus-a-verb form. For instance, someone might say, "Jean plans to babysit for us next Saturday." The verb **plan** is one of these common verbs. Study the examples below to see how these verbs work.

Arturo **expects** *to get* a raise next month.

Vaideji **refused** *to go* to Hawaii with me.

The newly married couple **decided** to take a honeymoon later.

Partial List of Verbs That Can Be Followed by an Infinitive		
agree	forget	refuse
appear	need	try
decide	plan	want
expect	promise	

These verbs cannot be followed by an **-ing** verb. For example, you cannot say, "I decided asking for a raise." Rather, say, "I decided to ask for a raise." The next exercise will give you a chance to use these verbs correctly.

Exercise 9

Put a **C** for correct or an **I** for incorrect in each blank below. Use the list above to help you.

Example: __*I*__ **We forgot paying our electric bill.**

Version A

__*I*__ **1.** She promised going to the store tomorrow.

__*C*__ **2.** Ramon refused to lend him any more money.

__*I*__ **3.** Her tax adviser needed having other records.

_____I_____ **4.** The coach promised helping him apply for a college scholarship.

_____C_____ **5.** We tried to drive across town to a special store.

Version B

_____I_____ **1.** I wanted learning to play the piano.

_____I_____ **2.** They expect enrolling in the fitness center.

_____C_____ **3.** The supervisor agreed to hold a meeting with the new employee.

_____I_____ **4.** The cashier forgot putting away the checks.

_____I_____ **5.** The flight attendant refused serving the unruly passenger.

More Help with Prepositions

When using certain common words and expressions, you may have had trouble choosing the correct preposition that native speakers and writers of English expect you to use. You want to be able to choose the correct preposition, but you have to choose the one that is right for the meaning you intend. You may just have to practice and learn as many of these commonly used expressions as you can. Following are some of these common expressions that require prepositions.

agree on (a plan)	We agreed **on** outcomes for the class.
agree to (an offer)	They agreed **to** the salary offer from the company.
angry about (a problem)	We were angry **about** the loss of the money.
angry with (someone)	Mom was angry **with** me for losing my jacket.
capable of	The child was surprisingly capable **of** doing math.
contrast with	This assignment contrasts **with** the previous one.
differ from (some thing)	This computer differs **from** that one.
differ with (a person)	He differed **with** me about the possible result.
impatient with (a person)	I was impatient **with** the sales associate.
responsible for (someone or something)	They are responsible **for** themselves.

In addition to the above expressions, the common prepositions **at, in,** and **on** are sometimes confusing. Consider the following uses for these prepositions:

For a specific place or specific time, use **at.**

Come to my office **at** 50 West State **at** 3:00 p.m.

For a length of time, use **in.**

I went to college **in** the sixties.

Dana's birthday is **in** April.

For names of streets and days of the week or month, use **on.**

The house for sale is **on** 15th Street. We saw it **on** Monday.

On April 22, we want to offer to buy it.

The following exercise will give you practice in using the above prepositions.

Determine if the underlined preposition in each sentence is correct. Put **C** for correct or **I** for incorrect in the blank.

Example: ___*I*___ He agreed <u>to</u> me about the movie.

Version A

___*I*___ 1. We live <u>in</u> 2701 N. 10th Street.

___*I*___ 2. Our boss was angry <u>for</u> us.

___*I*___ 3. I am capable <u>in</u> doing the homework.

___*I*___ 4. My last trip is <u>at</u> Tuesday.

___*C*___ 5. I found my lost purse <u>on</u> June 10, 2003.

Version B

___*I*___ 1. Kiko's birthday is <u>on</u> May.

___*I*___ 2. The voters cannot agree <u>for</u> a plan to raise taxes.

___*C*___ 3. My last test is <u>on</u> Thursday.

___*C*___ 4. I will meet you <u>at</u> the entrance to the shopping center.

___*I*___ 5. We agreed <u>to</u> you about the suggestion.

The material in this appendix may not cover all the problems you are having with English, but perhaps it can help you use English more fluently and confidently.

Appendix F: Using Documented Support

Sometimes when you write a paper, you will want to refer to other writers for additional information to use as support in your paper. You will add credibility to your paper if you include information from people who have spent time studying the subject. This kind of knowledge can be found by searching in books or articles or just by talking to people. To do this, you will need to know how to access information in the library by using the catalog, its databases, and other computer networks. Once you get the information from a source, you will want to analyze it to determine how useful and credible it will be for your paper. If you use an idea or a quotation from any source, you will need to give the author credit.

Finding Reliable Information on the Subject

Your own college library is probably the best place to find information on almost any topic. Once you have your topic and the direction for your paper, then you can find articles that will add support to your subject. For example, your assignment might be to discuss the different ways people can improve their memory. Some of this support might come from observation, but more specific support might come from someone who has studied brain development for years and conducted research that has been published in scholarly magazines. These researchers have gained a reputation for doing research and are considered experts in their field. Another kind of support might come from a journalist who has researched the topic and then objectively presented the information from several credible sources.

When you have chosen your topic, the next step involves going to the library to find one or more articles dealing with memory, such as "Rethinking the Brain" by Michael Specter, an article that appeared in the July 23, 2001, issue of *The New Yorker*. In this article, Specter traces the scientists who have studied the brain in hopes of determining how the mind works. Specter begins the article by giving factual information about Fernando Nottebohm, who has spent years studying the brains of finches, canaries, and chickadees, trying to understand how birds remember songs and how they learn new songs. During his studies, Nottebohm was surprised to find that birds grow new cells in the part of their brain that is responsible for memory. Specter quotes Nottebohm as saying, "Every bird, young or old, was producing thousands of them [cells] each day." Specter then moves to information about Elizabeth Gould, who has continued with research on neurogenesis, the production of new brain cells. One other person Specter mentions is Fred Gage, co-director of the Laboratory of Genetics at the Salk Institute, who is involved in stem-cell science. When the information starts to get this exciting and piques your interest, you will want to find more articles by either Nottebohm, Gould, or Gage, or you might be able to find articles that talk about their findings. The information you find might be documented and used in the paragraphs discussing memory and brain cells. The additional information you find on this subject can be used to support your topic idea.

You might find other information by talking to someone who strongly believes that exercise improves memory, and that person might tell you that since she started doing aerobic exercise three times a week, her ability to think has improved. This information can be included in the same support paragraph, but when you include this information, you might present it by quoting the person who is exercising aerobically. If you do not use a direct quotation but include the information, you will still want to tell the reader the origin of this material.

Avoiding Unreliable or Biased Sources

All sources that you use in your paper must be reliable. They should come from people who have experience with the topic or from magazines or journals that have proved to be reliable in the past. Information that is not based on fact or is written by someone who is not knowledgeable in that field is unreliable. You may read in *The National Enquirer* that a twenty-year-old male was injected with new brain cells that had been grown in a lab using his own bone marrow. This man, who once was determined by tests to have an IQ of 83, now has an IQ of 172. This information should not be used in the paper because the material presented in *The National Enquirer* is not backed up with credible research. Also, you might have a neighbor who tells you that she once heard of a young man who had improved his memory tremendously through a scientific study. Though this might be true, your neighbor is not a credible source because she did not personally know the young man and the information was passed down from an unknown source.

Presenting reliable information also involves using the research findings of knowledgeable people who do not have a self-interest in dispersing the information. This means that the author or authors do not stand to gain fame or money by publishing this information. For example, consider a study to test the effectiveness of using the medication tamoxifen to prevent breast cancer in women who are at increased risk. If the study is published by the manufacturer of tamoxifen, then the manufacturer becomes an "interested" party because the company will make money if the product sells. On the other hand, a study being done by the National Surgical Adjuvant Breast and Bowel Project, funded by the National Cancer Institute, is credible because the information comes from a reputable research institution that will not monetarily profit by conducting the study or by selling the medication. This study includes 16,000 women age 35 and older who live in North America. The high number of participants also makes the study more valid. If you are in doubt about the credibility of a publication, you might talk to your instructor or the reference librarian at your college.

Newspaper articles must present information that is accurate because editors are held liable for any false information printed intentionally. Nevertheless, this does not mean that everything that appears in a newspaper is flawless. A few years ago, a series of newspaper articles was scheduled, investigating nonprofit organizations in a major American city. The first article published condemned the way a particular nonprofit organization trained mentally handicapped adults. The author of the article, however, relied on only one source to obtain information, a citizen who appeared to be interested in the welfare of the handicapped adults. When confronted with this information, the journalist admitted limited reporting, and after further investigation, found that the source was an "interested," therefore biased, party who planned to open a pizza chain hiring these same handicapped adults. Needless to say, the first article in the series was the only one published, and the other nonprofit organizations were not investigated.

Here is another example of unreliable information. A salesperson at a grocery store may tell you that the only type of fish that is good for you is swordfish. This information may be true or the salesperson may be overstocked with swordfish and may want to "unload" a shipment before it gets old. You cannot trust what the salesperson says if his or her motive is to avoid losing money on the swordfish.

When presenting information, you must avoid using anything that is biased or slanted. Now think back to your topic idea about the ways people can improve their memory. In addition to searching in library databases, you do a search on Google.com and find MemoryZine, the Source for Memory Health & Fitness. At this site, you read that "people may grow new brain cells well into old age." This sounds like great support for your paper, but you scroll down to find that the purpose of this site is to sell "breakthrough" products that can improve memory. You need to be aware that this site might be biased because the only author listed is a doctor who is the director of the institute that is selling memory tapes and workbooks online. You need to avoid this site because the material appears to be an advertisement to sell products.

Blending Sources Smoothly into Your Paper

When using ideas and quotations from reliable sources, you must be careful not to string other people's quotations one after the other, either in separate little paragraphs or in one larger paragraph. You still want to include a strong topic sentence to hold the paragraph together and then use your own words to blend the sources together in the paragraph. Using your own words adds coherence to your paragraphs and helps the reader see the relevance of the quotation (example) in your paper. Also, you do not want to end a paragraph with a quotation. The last sentence in your paragraph needs to be a strong concluding sentence of your own.

When writing the paragraph or paper, you may not use any information unless you give the authors credit for their work. This can be done simply by using a few words that lead into the quotation. For instance, you need to give Terrence Sejnowski, who is from the Salk Institute for Biological Studies and who is the lead author of the Howard Hughes Medical Institute report on memory, credit for any information that you take from his article "Exercise Improves Learning and Memory." Look at the following paragraph to see how it might be done.

The paragraph might read:

When people exercise aerobically, not only do their bodies benefit, but their minds also benefit. A direct result of exercise is that people think more clearly and their memory improves. Understanding how this happens is very important. When people exercise, new brain cells are generated. This is explained by Terrence Sejnowski at the Salk Institute for Biological Studies: "Exercise enhances the formation and survival of new nerve cells as well as the connections between nerve cells, which in turn improves long-term memory." This exciting discovery explains why learning and memory continue to improve throughout the lifetime of people who exercise. The connection between memory and the creation of new brain cells is further supported by Nina Wildorf in the June 2001 issue of *Health*. She points out that Fred Gage, also from the Salk Institute, reported finding "new cells in the hippocampus, that part of the brain associated with learning and memory." Exercise means new brain cells, and new brain cells mean better memory; therefore, a person's ability to balance a checkbook or remember an address might well be within that person's own control. Today, when people say that they are going to the gym to get rid of their stress, they are also improving their memory.

Using Lead-ins to Quotations

When using quotations in your papers, lead into them so they flow smoothly into well-developed paragraphs. You can do this several ways.

1. Use a comma to introduce a quotation that is a complete sentence. (Capitalize the first word in the quotation.) Note that after introducing the author's name in full, you will use only his or her last name in additional references.

   In the article "Double Mystery," Laurence Wright states, "At least eleven births out of every thousand are twins."

   Wright further states, "Multiple births are more frequent among older mothers."

   "Multiple births," Wright states, "are more frequent among older mothers."

2. Use a colon to introduce a quotation that has been set off with an introductory sentence, especially if the quotation is introduced formally. (Begin the first word in the quotation with a capital letter.)

   In the article "Double Mystery," Laurence Wright points out the high occurrence of twins: "In the United States today, at least eleven births out of every thousand are twins."

3. Do not use a comma if the quotation is blended into your own sentence. (In this case, do not capitalize the first word in the quotation.)

   She points out that Fred Gage, also from the Salk Institute, reported finding "new cells in the hippocampus, that part of the brain associated with learning and memory."

   According to Enserink, this means that when companies must share materials and cannot agree on matters, they may end up in "high-profile patent infringement lawsuits."

Using Brackets and Ellipses

- Use brackets to insert your own words into a quotation.

  According to Enserink, this means that when companies must share materials and cannot "agree on [legal] matters, they may end up in high-profile patent infringement lawsuits."

- When you leave words out of a direct quotation, you must be careful not to alter the meaning of the citation. Use three dots to indicate that words or phrases have been left out.

  Myrna Armstrong points out that "all of the body art organizations . . . are strong supporters of artist education, and they conduct national and regional hygiene workshops."

- When you leave out not only words and phrases but also a period, you use four dots.

  According to Patricia Cross in *Adults as Learners*, "educators cannot do much about physiological aging. . . . Knowing its cycle, however, they can adapt to it, capitalize on it when desirable, and compensate for it when necessary."

Using Long Quotations

When writing longer papers like research papers, you might use quotations that are over three lines in length. In these cases, you need to single-space and indent those quotations.

> In *The Disciplined Mind*, Howard Gardner talks about designing education for understanding rather than for getting a degree simply to enhance a career. Gardner comments on a recently designed university that he describes as a "franchised profit-making operation":
>
> > It is fair to say that [in this franchised profit-making operation] there is no intellectual life at the university, in any meaningful sense of that term: ideas have value only if they can be put to immediate commercial use. Rather, the university offers students an opportunity to gain desired skills as efficiently as possible.

Once you decide to use a direct quotation or an idea from someone, you need to use the quotations carefully and always give credit to the original source.

Using Formal Citations

When you cite from sources, your teacher may ask you to use a formal citation. You may use either the style of the Modern Language Association, known as MLA format, or you may use the style of the Americal Psychological Association, known as APA. Ask your instructor which style you should use. You may find this information easily on the Internet. Type in the following address:

http://owl.english.purdue.edu/handouts/research

or, using a search engine like Google, type in "MLA documentation" or "APA documentation," and you will find several links to the information you need. These sources will provide current information on using formal citations. If your teacher wants you to include a Works Cited page, these Internet sources will also give you the information you need to do this.

Answers to Odd-Numbered Items in Exercises

Unit 1 Writing Sentences and Paragraphs

Part 1 Writing Skills: Topic Sentences and Paragraphs

Exercise 1 (Page 25)

1. Topic: _City traffic_   Direction: _can be dangerous for pedestrians._

3. Topic: _Staying physically fit_   Direction: _demands self-discipline._

5. Topic: _Good students_   Direction: _often receive encouragement from family members._

7. Topic: _Doing well in college_   Direction: _can be a challenge for many students._

9. Topic: _Soccer_   Direction: _is becoming a popular sport in the United States._

11. Topic: _Going out to eat_   Direction: _can be a cultural experience._

13. Topic: _Owning more than one car_   Direction: _can be expensive._

15. Topic: _Working during a holiday_   Direction: _creates stress for families._

Exercise 2 (Page 27)

1. Buying prescription drugs _can be very expensive. / creates hardships for some senior citizens._

3. Crossword puzzles _provide mental stimulation. / can be difficult for children._

5. Working on my car _requires patience. / is expensive._

7. Country music _often deals with relationships._

9. My sister _gives me good advice. / can be a brat._

11. Swimming _keeps people physically fit. / makes people very hungry._

13. Camping in a tent _can be lots of fun. / can be frustrating._

15. Losing weight fast _can be dangerous. / may be medically necessary._

Exercise 3 (Page 28)

_____F_____ 1. The Britney Spears concert lasted over two hours.

_____TS_____ 3. The background music in the grocery store was annoying.

_____TS_____ 5. Stephanie's room is a disaster.

_____F_____ 7. The 911 call came into the police department at 12:00 noon.

_____F_____ 9. The Iraqi War officially began in March of 2003.

_____B_____ 11. Cultures in America are varied.

_____B_____ 13. The history of evolution spans many years.

_____F_____ 15. Tampa Bay won the Super Bowl in 2003.

_____TS_____ 17. Keeping a diary helped me understand my divorce.

_____F_____ 19. Fifty-one percent of entering college freshmen choose to attend a community college.

Exercise 4 (Page 30)

1. Employees benefit from on-site fitness centers.

3. Christmas in a Mexican home offers many unique foods.

5. Inner-city children have many obstacles to overcome.

7. Spending the day at the beach is often enticing.

9. The beautiful public park offers many inexpensive outdoor activities for city residents.

Exercise 5 (Page 35)
Answers will vary.

Exercise 6 (Page 37)
Answers will vary.

Exercise 7 (Page 38)
Additional support sentences in each paragraph will vary. In each paragraph, the first sentence is the topic sentence, and the last sentence is the concluding sentence.

Exercise 8 (Page 41)

1. __2__ Isaac called his buddy Mario to see if he wanted to go to the car auction.

   __1__ Isaac wanted to go to the car auction with a friend.

3. __3__ Kenita turned in her essay at the beginning of class.

   __1__ Kenita typed her assignment on the computer.

   __2__ Kenita produced a hard copy on her printer.

5. __2__ Sammy and his uncle bought a fruit tree to plant in the backyard.

   __1__ Sammy and his uncle went to the local plant nursery to look at trees.

   __3__ They took the tree home and planted it immediately.

7. __4__ Justin finally bought a new truck.

   __2__ He decided not to have his old car fixed.

   __1__ Justin's old car needed a new transmission.

   __3__ Justin spent two weeks looking for a new vehicle.

9. __4__ Glen came in fourth.

   __2__ Glen prepared by spending hours swimming, biking, and running.

   __3__ Glen arrived early the day of the race.

   __5__ Glen reflected on ways to make his next event even better.

   __1__ Glen decided to participate in a triathlon.

Exercise 9 (Page 44)

1. __TS__ At half-time, the hip-hop dancers entertained the audience.

   __S__ Each member showed off fast-paced jumping movements.

   __U__ My brother still enjoys break dancing.

3. __S__ This fashion trend is reflected in increasing sales of Asian clothes.

   __TS__ Ethnic clothing is becoming increasingly popular in the United States.

   __U__ People enjoy shopping.

5. __S__ Sam wrote a research paper for his pharmacy class.

   __TS__ Sam's pharmacy class required several writing assignments.

   __U__ Sam never missed any of his pharmacy classes.

7. __TS__ In the springtime in Georgia, the vegetation is beautiful.

   __S__ The peach trees are filled with fragrant pink blossoms.

   __U__ The peaches are sweet and juicy.

9. __TS__ Learning to ride a jet ski can be challenging.

    __U__ The neon-blue-striped jet ski goes the fastest.

    __S__ Standing up and making a turn requires excellent balance.

11. __TS__ Swimming is good physical therapy.

    __U__ Many of my neighbors wonder why I swim at 6:00 a.m. every day.

    __S__ Paraplegics increase muscle tone in the swimming pool at Saint Luke's Hospital.

13. __S__ Injured birds are nurtured back to health.

    __TS__ Wildlife centers are dedicated to helping sick and injured animals.

    __U__ Wildlife centers are often privately funded.

15. __U__ Alicia received financial aid while attending college.

    __S__ Alicia, a community-college graduate, earned an A average during her first year at the university.

    __TS__ Community-college graduates perform well at universities.

Exercise 10 (Page 45)

Paragraph 1

People from other countries have different reasons for wanting to come to live in the United States. For example, some might want higher-paying jobs than they can get in their own countries. Some want the freedom to change jobs or professions. Some might want the chance to get more education for themselves and their families. Church groups often sponsor people coming to America. Perhaps one of the most important reasons would be the desire to own and operate a business. Many people wait a long time for the chance to live in the United States. Every year, regardless of the reasons, many more people come to live in America.

Paragraph 3

Teachers who are student-centered create an environment that the students will never forget. Some teachers seem to be rushed and not willing to show their personal sides. Teachers who allow students to introduce themselves and meet others in the class establish an environment where everyone feels worthwhile and respected. Considerate teachers make class expectations clear on assignments and procedures. Teachers take attendance at the beginning of the class period. Instructors who want their students to have the best chance for success call them when the students are ill or absent for several class periods. Teachers who go out of their way to show their concern provide a true learning experience.

Exercise 11 (Page 47)

Paragraph 1

Going to my daughter's soccer game turned out to be a disappointing experience.

Paragraph 3

My favorite birthday present was a trip through the zoo. I was ten years old.

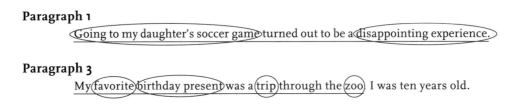

Answers to Odd-Numbered Items in Exercises

Unit 1 Writing Sentences and Paragraphs

Part 4 Parts of Speech

Exercise 1 (Page 64)

1. ~~Without thinking~~, the man spent his entire paycheck ~~in one night.~~

3. Most ~~of Sara's creative ideas~~ occur ~~in the evening~~.

5. ~~After lunch,~~ we went ~~to the lab~~ and worked ~~on our project.~~

7. All ~~of my cousins except Rene~~ decided to go ~~to the park~~.

9. ~~In spite of the snow,~~ they drove their jeep ~~to the airport~~.

11. The ingredients ~~for the cake~~ should be ~~at room temperature.~~

13. I take desserts ~~like chocolate cake~~ to my friend ~~in the retirement center~~.

15. Seven inches ~~of new snow~~ fell ~~on the ski run~~ ~~during the night.~~

17. We floated ~~down the Salt River~~ ~~on an inner tube~~.

19. The message ~~inside the fortune cookie~~ promised good luck ~~for seven years.~~

Exercise 2 (Page 65)

Paragraph 1

Parenting requires major commitments ~~for young couples~~. They must take the responsibility ~~for someone besides themselves~~. Staying ~~at home~~ to care ~~for a new infant~~ twenty-four hours a day demands love and dedication. Parents often spend their money ~~on the child's needs~~ rather than ~~on their own needs~~. They frequently must function ~~on less sleep~~ and be prepared to get up several times each night to feed, change, and comfort a small one. This commitment continues ~~for many years~~.

Exercise 3 (Page 67)

1. There are no <u>seats</u> left ~~for the next basketball game~~.

3. ~~After breakfast,~~ <u>we</u> jogged ~~around the lake~~.

5. Many <u>colleges</u> provide fitness centers and recreational areas ~~for their students~~.

7. The <u>assistants</u> ~~in the geology lab~~ brought their lunches ~~to work~~.

9. ~~During the movie,~~ the <u>father</u> and his <u>children</u> ate popcorn and drank pop.

11. The <u>tomatoes</u>, <u>cucumbers</u>, and <u>lettuce</u> rotted ~~in the refrigerator~~.

You **13.** In spite of the fog, we drove the scenic route around the glacier.

15. In Colorado, the ski resorts at Aspen and Vail provide skiers with many wide, groomed trails.

17. After supper, the band members met for two hours of practice.

You **19.** Please close the door.

Exercise 4 (Page 68)

Paragraph 1

Mr. Socks, Anne's cat, was an ideal visitor at my home. He arrived on a Monday night and immediately found his favorite spot, underneath my bed, inside the box springs. Gradually over the next couple of days, he emerged and walked through the house, inspecting everything. He entertained himself playing with a ping-pong ball and a thick black shoelace. Sometimes he walked to his scratching post and forcefully sharpened his claws, but he never clawed at anything else. After a few days, Mr. Socks napped on top of my bed. One day my dog walked into the room, and Mr. Socks jumped to the floor, rubbed against her fur, and began a friendship. They slept in the same room, drank from the same water dispenser, and ignored each other's food dishes. After a couple of days, Mr. Socks progressed to my lap. I scratched his ears, and he responded with steady purring. This first visit to my house lasted for a short period of time, but it was certainly pleasant and free from stress.

Exercise 5 (Page 73)

1. The automobile mechanics must ___*explain*___ their bills to their customers. (explain, explains)

3. One in ten drivers ___*suffers*___ from fatigue. (suffer, suffers)

5. All links on the website ___*are*___ updated by the students. (are, is)

7. The elementary school teacher ___*rewards*___ students with gold stickers. (reward, rewards)

9. The President of the United States ___*arrives*___ at 6:00 tonight. (arrive, arrives)

11. The ice on the roads ___*makes*___ driving on the highway dangerous. (make, makes)

13. The owner of the Honda Accord often ___*leaves*___ his keys in the car. (leave, leaves)

15. The student fine arts magazine often ___*receives*___ many awards. (receive, receives)

Exercise 6 (Page 74)

sheep enjoys
1. The bighorn sheep enjoy climbing the mountain.

workers   *listen*
3. The worker on the roof listens to the radio.

women   *their*   *dogs walk*

5. The blind woman ~~with her guide dog~~ walks confidently ~~down the street.~~

windows   *are*

7. The stained-glass window ~~in that old chapel~~ is beautiful.

Mice   *live*

9. A mouse lives ~~in the basement~~ ~~of the abandoned building.~~

answers   *surprise*

11. His answer ~~on the math test on fractions~~ surprises me.

churches need

13. The church needs new paint and landscaping.

children remember

15. The child remembers last summer's trip ~~to Alaska.~~

Exercise 7 (Page 75)

provide

1. The trees ~~by Big Lake~~ provides shade ~~for the campground.~~

are

3. Blue herons is abundant ~~on the lakes of northern Colorado.~~

prune

5. My neighbors prunes their rose bushes every February.

sits

7. The well-dressed old man sit ~~on the park bench~~ ~~by the fountain.~~

pitch

9. We often pitches our tent ~~among the Ponderosa pine trees.~~

keep

11. The wild cats ~~at the farm~~ keeps the mouse population ~~under control.~~

cause

13. Speeding drivers causes rollover accidents ~~at intersections.~~

walk

15. The turtles walks freely ~~through Golden Gate Park.~~

Exercise 8 (Page 78)

1. ~~After graduation,~~ most ~~of the students~~ ___*find*___ challenging jobs. (find, finds)

3. All ~~of the tennis players~~ ___*wear*___ comfortable clothes. (wear, wears)

5. ~~After a touchdown~~ somebody ~~in the crowd~~ always ___*yells*___, "Go ~~for two!~~"
(yell, yells)

7. Some ~~of the melons~~ ___*are*___ too expensive ~~for my family.~~ (is, are)

9. Each play ___*makes*___ a difference ~~in the outcome of the game.~~ (make, makes)

11. The gray wolf ___*slides*___ ~~under the electric fence.~~ (slide, slides)

13. More of the fish in the pond ___die___ during the winter. (die, dies)

15. Thousands of bats ___swarm___ from the cave at dusk. (swarm, swarms)

17. According to the coach, there ___is___ something special about this year's team.
(are, is)

19. Few of the children ___like___ school without recess. (like, likes)

Exercise 9 (Page 79)

likes
1. Everybody like time for relaxation and reflection.

close
3. Some of the vendors closes their booths early.

survives
5. Nothing below the dam survive a major flood.

are
7. Children in the pool is supervised by lifeguards.

C　**9.** All of my class projects take hours of hard work.

has
11. Each of the committee members have time for an afternoon meeting.

love
13. Most of my friends loves shopping at the factory outlet stores.

love
15. Without a doubt, most of my dogs loves to go for walks in the evenings.

are
17. All of my friends is going to the museum with their families.

is
19. Any diversion from routine activities are refreshing.

Exercise 10 (Page 80)

Paragraph 1

report
The people in the jury assembly room reports for jury duty in clothing that they

wear　　　　　　　*look*　　　　　　　　　　　　　　*wear*
ordinarily wears to work. Several looks like students or service workers. They wears casual

appear
dresses or sport shirts and jeans. Some in work uniforms appears to be truck drivers or repair

sit
people. A large number of professional men and women sits in more formal suits. One

walks
gentleman apparently does not know the dress code for jurors, and he walk around in shorts

and a bright blue T-shirt. This scene is a good example of the variety of people on juries.

Paragraph 3

Kenting Park is at the southernmost part of Taiwan. <u>It</u> <u>is surrounded</u> by a beach and

are

high cliffs. Luxurious, high-priced <u>hotels</u> <u>is</u> available for those able to afford approximately

are   *look*

$200 a day. When people ~~is~~ tired of playing on the beach, they ~~looks~~ through little shops

for seashells, costume jewelry, hats, and other tourist trinkets. The <u>park</u> north of the beach

has

~~have~~ exotic tropical plants. For example, a 300-year-old bonsai-like <u>tree</u> with old, exposed

illustrates

roots ~~illustrate~~ the coastal park's antiquity. In addition, a small <u>cave</u> with a stalactite forming

brings   *offers*

an imaginative, fossil-like figure ~~bring~~ relief from the sun and ~~offer~~ the passing a peaceful

rest. <u>Kenting Park</u> <u>has</u> many attractions for visitors.

Exercise 11 (Page 83)

Paragraph 1

Tense: _____*Present*_____

David's best friend is Stormy, his pet dog. Every night she goes to bed with him and

stays

~~stayed~~ with him until he gets up the next morning. She sits outside the shower door until

he finishes. She also eats breakfast with him and then sees him off at the front door. After

play   *race*   *bother*

school they ~~played~~ catch or ~~raced~~ through the yard. She always knows when things ~~bothered~~

showers

him, and she gently ~~showered~~ him with "kisses." She becomes his audience when he

practices   *share*

~~practiced~~ his piano or his companion as he builds his Lego structures. They even ~~shared~~ an

afternoon snack of cheese and crackers. Best of all, they are always there for each other.

Paragraph 3

Tense: _____*Present*_____

A large city like San Francisco offers visitors many kinds of exciting activities. If

wants   *has*

someone ~~wanted~~ to attend sporting events, a large city usually ~~have~~ college basketball and

do

football teams as well as professional basketball and football teams. If visitors ~~did~~ not care

fill

for sports, perhaps museums ~~filled~~ the bill. A large city usually has art museums as well as

likes

historical and scientific museums. For the visitor who ~~liked~~ shopping, the large city

provides

~~provided~~ a range of stores from small specialty shops to large department stores. Since San *offers*

Francisco is near the water, it ~~offered~~ fishing, a harbor cruise, surfing, an aquarium, and

give

other waterfront activities. Theaters and nightclubs also ~~gave~~ visitors a chance to experience

do

evening entertainment they ~~did~~ not have at home. A large city usually gives an out-of-town

visitor a wide range of activities for excitement and fun.

Unit 2 Being a Sensitive Writer

Part 1 Interaction of Topic, Purpose, Audience, and Voice

Exercise 1 (Page 94)

Situation 1

Topic:	resignation
Purpose:	notification of resignation with option to return to current employment
Audience:	boss
Voice:	serious, honest, sincere

Situation 3

Topic:	mother-in-law's visit after the baby is born
Purpose:	have the mother-in-law stay with them the second week rather than the first week
Audience:	mother-in-law
Voice:	diplomatic, warm, friendly

Exercise 2 (Page 108)

Paragraph 1

Topic:	employment for childcare workers
Audience:	people who want to work with children
Organizational pattern:	how two things are alike or different (comparison / contrast)

Paragraph 3

Topic:	GED classes and Cuyatino Acosta's education
Audience:	anyone worrying about returning to school
Organizational pattern:	illustration / example

Paragraph 5

Topic:	express appreciation for help in getting into pharmacy school
Audience:	Professor Kalucha
Organizational pattern:	effects / results of an event

Exercise 3 (Page 114)

1. a. *Voice/s:* positive
    b. *Voice/s:* thoughtful and nostalgic
    c. *Voice/s:* negative
    d. *Voice/s:* negative, angry

3. a. *Voice/s:* pleasant, positive
    b. *Voice/s:* negative
    c. *Voice/s:* neutral, factual
    d. *Voice/s:* angry, hostile

5. a. *Voice/s:* irritated, disgruntled
    b. *Voice/s:* positive, warm
    c. *Voice/s:* neutral
    d. *Voice/s:* negative, derogatory

7. a. *Voice/s:* nostalgic, positive
    b. *Voice/s:* complimentary, positive
    c. *Voice/s:* negative, offensive

Exercise 4 (Page 117)

1. *They lived in the old, neglected, run-down section of the city.*
    (negative)

    Their restored home was in the historic section of the city.
    (positive)

3. *The rude concert audience pushed and yelled obscenities.*
    (negative)

    The golden-oldie songs echoed through the park as people recalled college memories.
    (nostalgic)

5. *Sara could hardly wait to greet her old friends at their 20th high school reunion.*
    (happy, excited)

    Sara frowned at her old enemy classmates as she arrived at their 20th high school reunion.
    (negative)

7. *"Old Blue" rusted away in the corner of the car lot.*

(nostalgic)

Please be advised that no cars are allowed overnight in the parking lot.

(polite)

9. *Briana felt that her bedroom was a special place where she could be alone with her thoughts.*

(positive)

As a fifteen-year-old girl, Briana spit fire at anyone who came near her room.

(angry)

Exercise 5 (Page 119)

Answers will vary.

Unit 2   Being a Sensitive Writer

Part 4   Consistent Point of View

Exercise 1 (Page 135)

He
1. ~~Fernando~~ is doing well in chemistry this semester.

We
3. ~~Roger, Stephanie, and I~~ watched the Fourth of July parade, and we enjoyed it.

They
5. ~~The electricians~~ had to rewire the entire building.

He
7. ~~Keshawn~~ played a leading role in the musical production.

It
9. ~~Eating hot dogs at baseball games~~ is an American tradition.

Exercise 2 (Page 137)

I   volunteer
1. ~~Antonio~~ often ~~volunteers~~ at the local food bank.

I
3. ~~The children~~ found a ten-dollar bill on the sidewalk.

I   play
5. ~~Isabella plays~~ trumpet in the band.

I   my
7. Last year, ~~you~~ began the research on ~~your~~ family genealogy.

I
9. ~~Others~~ have procrastinated until the last minute.

Exercise 3 (Page 141)

Paragraph 1

I love to haggle every time I go to a border town in Mexico. First of all, I make out a list

of the items I would like to have. Then I find a market square that has lots of vendors.
I believe that competition
~~Competition~~ allows me to do some comparative scouting and may mean lower-priced items.
I   *I*
~~You~~ should always go dressed in older clothes so that ~~you~~ don't look like the rich American
       I   *I*
tourist. As ~~you~~ enter the store, ~~you~~ should not appear anxious. Next, with a maximum price

in my mind, I casually saunter to the object that I most want. If the vendor's price is way

above my price, I go to the next store. If not, I smile and offer him a price lower than my set
we can
price, and we begin haggling from that point. Usually, ~~a~~ compromise ~~is struck~~, and we both

go away happy.

Purpose: ___to explain shopping in Mexico_____

Audience: ___general reader_____ Voice: ___honest, frank_____

Paragraph 3

The long-time Mexican luminaria tradition warms Christmas Eve in many

neighborhoods in the United States. The tradition of luminarias—paper bags, each one

containing a small candle anchored in a little sand—was imported into the United States
                    their
many years ago as Mexicans brought their simple means to light up ~~your~~ haciendas. To
        people   *their*
participate in the tradition, ~~you~~ line ~~your~~ driveways and sidewalks with many small paper
                  they   *their*
bags, each one holding a flickering candle, anchored in sand. In this way, ~~I~~ turn ~~my~~

neighborhood into an enchanted wonderland. Taking part in this activity provides a way for
neighbors
~~you~~ to celebrate the season together and greet visitors. The luminarias provide a brilliant

transformation from darkness to a magical lighted maze. This primitive version of Christmas
         people
lights has expanded, and now ~~you~~ can buy artificial luminarias, bulbs that are placed in

small plastic bags and lit by electricity. However, the old authentic use of bag, sand, and

them

their

candle is still popular and provides ~~me~~ not only with light but a connection with ~~your~~ past

and a way to bring people together toward a common Christmas goal—harmony and beauty.

Purpose: ___*to explain the tradition of luminarias*___

Audience: ___*general reader*___   Voice: ___*informative, factual, nostalgic*___

Paragraph 5

Changing the oil and the oil filter in an automobile can be a simple task for car owners.

they

By referring to the car manual, ~~I~~ know the correct kind and amount of oil as well as the

They

correct size of oil filter to purchase. ~~You~~ then begin the job by loosening the engine oil cap on

the top of the engine so a little air goes into the oil cavity, making the oil drain more

they   *they*

thoroughly. When ~~I~~ loosen and remove the drain plug at the bottom of the oil pan, ~~I~~ notice

that the used oil will easily drain into a separate container that should be disposed of

according to environmentally safe standards. The owners can now easily remove the used

They

oil filter. ~~You~~ then put a light coat of fresh oil on the new filter's rubber seal and put in the

They

new filter. ~~I~~ then replace the drain plug, remove the oil cap on top of the engine, and put in

They

the fresh oil. ~~You~~ then put the oil cap back on, and the job is done for at least another three

months.

Purpose: ___*to tell how to change an oil filter*___

Audience: ___*car owner*___   Voice: ___*informative, objective*___

Unit 3 Organizing Ideas and Writing Them Clearly

Part 1 The Thesis Sentence

Exercise 1 (Page 154)

1.   ___*b*___   is the most general word or phrase.

   ___*a, c, d*___   are equal to each other.

   ___*e*___   is unrelated or part of another group.

3. ___d___ is the most general word or phrase.

___b, c, e___ are equal to each other.

___a___ is unrelated or part of another group.

5. ___a___ is the most general word or phrase.

___c, d, e___ are equal to each other.

___b___ is unrelated or part of another group.

7. ___c___ is the most general word or phrase.

___b, d, e___ are equal to each other.

___a___ is unrelated or part of another group.

Exercise 2 (Page 156)

1. *Most firefighters are trained to*

(most general idea)

put out fires, administer emergency medical care, handle hazardous materials

(words that are coordinate)

3. *Special Olympics can give physically and mentally challenged people*

(most general idea)

the thrill of competition, a sense of self-worth, pride in reaching a goal

(words that are coordinate)

5. *People in New York City get around by*

(most general idea)

walking, taking taxis, riding on subways

(words that are coordinate)

7. *Having surgery is difficult because it can be*

(most general idea)

expensive, painful, and frightening

(words that are coordinate)

9. *People with diabetes must be concerned with*

(most general idea)

exercise, diet, stress

(words that are coordinate)

Exercise 3 (Page 159)

1. People who love pets are usually caring, patient, and ~~kind~~. *(or caring)*

3. DVDs are preferable to videotapes because they have easy search features, clear resolution, durability, ~~sharp display~~, and compact size. *(or clear resolution)*

5. Many young people gain an education through traveling, ~~attending college~~, volunteering in the community, and going to school. *(or going to school)*

7. Businesses that thrive in America provide ~~quality products~~, excellent service, reasonable prices, and outstanding merchandise. *(or outstanding merchandise)*

9. Acquiring computer skills requires ~~persistence~~, proper equipment, perseverance, clear directions, and time to practice. *(or perseverance)*

Exercise 4 (Page 161)

1. a. *play cards, read stories, do crossword puzzles, sort pictures*

   b. *reading stories, playing cards, doing crossword puzzles, sorting pictures*

   c. *did crossword puzzles, played cards, read stories, sorted pictures*

   d. *to sort pictures, to play cards, to read stories, to do crossword puzzles*

3. a. *visiting cousins, talking to Grandma, hugging favorite aunts, listening to Grandpa*

   b. *talk to Grandma, visit cousins, hug favorite aunts, listen to Grandpa*

   c. *to hug favorite aunts, to visit cousins, to talk to Grandma, to listen to Grandpa*

   d. *listened to Grandpa, visited cousins, talked to Grandma, hugged favorite aunts*

5. a. *formed the bowl, drew the design, fired the vase*

   b. *drawing the design, forming the bowl, firing the vase*

   c. *to fire the vase, to form the bowl, to draw the design*

Exercise 5 (Page 163)

1. Most people celebrate New Year's Eve by eating a special meal, celebrating with
   making
   friends until midnight, and ~~to make~~ future resolutions.

3. For safe driving, one must drive under control, ~~obeying~~ *obey* the speed limit, and

   never ~~to~~ drive under the influence of alcohol.

5. My winter spent in Maine brings pleasant memories of socializing with friends,
   making
   ^extra money, buying my first car, and surviving my first ice storm.

7. I enjoy going to that restaurant because the prices are reasonable, the food is excellent,

the service is good

and ~~good service~~.

9. The gardener mowed the lawns, trimmed the hedges, and ~~he also~~ watered the flowers.

11. Playing the piano provides an opportunity to relax, ~~to~~ entertain friends,

develop

~~developing~~ a talent, and ~~to~~ learn new songs.

13. Making a career change often requires a positive attitude, determination, and ~~to learn~~

new skills.

Exercise 6 (Page 166)

    Answers will vary.

Unit 3 *Organizing Ideas and Writing Them Clearly*

Part 4 Eliminating Fragments, Run-On Sentences, and Comma Splices

Exercise 1 (Page 184)

we

1. Out in the lake, ^ watched the moon rise.

we

3. Then ^ joined the company softball team.

The family also

5. ~~Also~~ ^ toured the Carlsbad Caverns.

Exercise 2 (Page 185)

Paragraph 1

    Large daily newspapers usually present information in the same order each day.

world and national

Section A usually provides an overview of ^ events. ~~World and national events.~~ This section

national or worldwide

may also include local stories with ^ appeal. ~~With national or worldwide appeal.~~ Then,

Section B updates readers on local news. The last page of Section B usually includes general

entire

weather for the nation and more detailed weather forecasts for the ^ state. ~~The entire state.~~

national, international, and local

Another section, business, includes ^ information related to the economy. ~~National,~~

~~international, and local information.~~ Another important section, the sports news, is about

other sporting

athletes, games, and ^ events. ~~Other sporting events.~~ Many newspapers include special

and garden

sections on the weekends, and these sections may specialize in home ^ issues. ~~And garden~~

issue̶s̶. Sometimes sections may be mixed by delivery carriers, or a reader may want to skip

content and implied

or ignore one part, but the order of the sections usually remains the same. C̶o̶n̶t̶e̶n̶t̶ ̶a̶n̶d̶ ̶t̶h̶e̶
                                      ∧
i̶m̶p̶l̶i̶e̶d̶ ̶o̶r̶d̶e̶r̶ ̶o̶f̶ ̶t̶h̶e̶ ̶s̶e̶c̶t̶i̶o̶n̶s̶. Knowing the order can be helpful for readers, and predictability

in this age of constant change is always reassuring.

Exercise 3 (Page 186)

1. *My mother is looking for an apartment to rent.*

Add a subject and an appropriate form of the verb "be."

Looking for an apartment to rent became frustrating.

Make the fragment the subject and add a main verb. (Add other words if needed.)

Looking for an apartment to rent, my mother lost her patience.

Add a sentence (subject and a verb) after the fragment.

3. *We were enjoying a cappuccino after the theater.*

Add a subject and an appropriate form of the verb "be."

Enjoying a cappuccino after the theater ended a lovely evening.

Make the fragment the subject and add a main verb. (Add other words if needed.)

Enjoying a cappuccino after the theater, we discussed the play.

Add a sentence (subject and a verb) after the fragment.

5. *My neighbor is restoring the old furniture.*

Add a subject and an appropriate form of the verb "be."

Restoring the old furniture was her project for the summer.

Make the fragment the subject and add a main verb. (Add other words if needed.)

Restoring the old furniture, my neighbor spent many enjoyable hours.

Add a sentence (subject and a verb) after the fragment.

Exercise 4 (Page 188)

1. *To learn a new skill, the employees attended the conference.*

Link the fragment to a complete sentence.

The employees wanted to learn a new skill.

Add both a subject and a verb before the fragment.

To learn a new skill meant a pay raise.

Make the fragment the subject and add a verb. (Add other words if needed.)

3. *To buy a new camera phone, Jasnia traded in her old phone.*

Link the fragment to a complete sentence.

Jasnia wanted to buy a new camera phone.

Add both a subject and a verb before the fragment.

To buy a new camera phone was expensive.

Make the fragment the subject and add a verb. (Add other words if needed.)

5. *To shop on the Internet, Jason bought a computer.*

Link the fragment to a complete sentence.

Jason learned to shop on the Internet.

Add both a subject and a verb before the fragment.

To shop on the Internet simplified Jason's life.

Make the fragment the subject and add a verb. (Add other words if needed.)

Exercise 5 (Page 190)

1. If Jim finishes his degree, *he will get a good job offer.*

3. After the game was over, *everyone decided to go for pizza.*

5. When the power went off, *everyone stayed inside.*

7. Unless I finish my schoolwork, *I will not be able to go to the play.*

9. Until the lake thaws, *we will be unable to go fishing.*

Exercise 6 (Page 191)

Paragraph 1

With the discovery of penicillin in 1928. ~~Scientists~~ *, scientists* and citizens alike believed that the battle was over and that no one would die from an infection again. ~~The battle over infectious~~ ^*over infectious diseases* ~~diseases.~~ Americans breathed a sigh of relief. However, *they* did not know that other organisms ^ that had survived for thousands of years could not be conquered that easily. These organisms simply produced mutant ~~strains. That~~ *strains that* were resistant to various antibiotics. Today, scientists realize that once again Americans may become ill from *deadly* outbreaks of infections that have ^ no cure. ~~Deadly outbreaks.~~ Because scientists are aware of the serious threats of these mutant ~~strains. Hopefully~~ *strains, hopefully they* will discover new ways of wiping out these infectious diseases soon.

Exercise 7 (Page 193)

1. Humor is important to people's ~~health without~~ humor, they become tired and depressed.
   health. Without

3. Every morning, Trent read the ~~newspaper then~~ he left for work.
   newspaper. Then

5. Kanisha applied for the ~~position she~~ met all the qualifications.
   position. She

7. They look forward to spending the day ~~outdoors it~~ takes them away from stress.
   outdoors. It

9. Toni Morrison won the Nobel Prize in ~~literature the~~ award was $818,000.
   literature. The

Exercise 8 (Page 194)

1. Firefighters spend many hours training for emergencies ∧ they are well prepared.
   , so

3. The hikers walked quietly ∧ they disturbed a rattlesnake.
   , but

5. A broken water pipe stalled traffic ∧ drivers were irate.
   , and

7. Many people went to the coin show ∧ they wanted to sell their collections.
   , for

9. The newest school board member is a paramedic for the fire department ∧ he is involved in community activities.
   , and

Exercise 9 (Page 194)

1. After school, Kayla played soccer ∧ she did her homework later.
   ;

3. The cardiologist has four boys ∧ the youngest three are triplets.
   ;

5. Farmers depend heavily on nature ∧ weather conditions are important to them.
   ;

7. Many older people discover a talent for painting ∧ they produce outstanding pictures.
   ;

9. Chan signed a contract for the job ∧ he promised to start the project immediately.
   ;

Exercise 10 (Page 195)

1. Kristin bought a new digital camera ∧ she had trouble using it.
   ; however,

3. Traffic over the bridge is heavy ∧ thousands of cars cross daily.
   ; in fact,

5. Starting a new job can be exciting ∧ it can also be stressful.
   ; however,

7. Peanuts are high in protein ∧ they taste good.
   ; in addition,

9. Keeping rivers clean should be a priority ∧ children can even get involved.
   ; in fact,

Exercise 11 (Page 196)

                although

1. My cousin and his wife plan to have children ∧ they are not married.

           because

3. I enjoy listening to music ∧ it is relaxing.

              unless

5. Visitors cannot see the special exhibit ∧ they have reservations.

            after

7. Jesus built a pond in his backyard ∧ he bought his new house.

             when

9. The dog knocked over Aunt Harriet's lamp ∧ he ran into the room.

Exercise 12 (Page 198)

           ; consequently,

1. The turtle hibernated for many months, ∧ he emerged famished and began to eat his way

    through the garden.

                        ;

3. When the stone mason finished the wall, he cleaned up the area, ∧ the homeowner was

    happy with the results.

                        ; however,

5. When a tornado touches down, it may destroy everything in its path ∧ the American Red

    Cross assists the victims.

                   because
                    ;

7. Every evening, Toni checks her email messages, ∧ she loves hearing from her friends.

                   because

9. Sara enjoys growing herbs in her garden ∧ she loves to use them in her cooking.

Exercise 13 (Page 197)

Paragraph 1

    The forest service is becoming more sensitive to the needs of physically challenged

people who like the outdoors. Braille camping trails offer a way for the visually impaired to

                remarkable

tramp through America's ∧ forests without fear. ~~America's remarkable forests.~~ Blind hikers can

begin to experience what others take for granted. Braille signs identify the surrounding trees

      as

and plants. ~~As~~ well as mark the trails. These trails are carefully constructed and twist their

               and   *;*

way through wooded valleys. ~~And~~ onto safe hillsides. Some paths are only a quarter of a mile ∧

        so

others stretch for almost a mile. ~~So~~ that hikers can choose a long or short route. Some

                                            and

campgrounds have wheelchair-accessible paths throughout the area, ∧ some even include ramps to lakes where the campers can fish from the bank. Each campground is calm, serene, and accommodating to the physically challenged.

Paragraph 3

Because pizza is so versatile. ~~It~~ , it is no wonder that it is one of America's favorite foods. Pizza is available frozen at the grocery store or piping hot from a variety of pizza restaurants. It can be bought with thin crust ~~or~~ , thick crust, ~~it can be~~ or sandwiched between two crusts. Plain pizza crust can be bought frozen ~~or~~ , already baked in packages much like bread, or mixed at home. Almost every person's individual taste can be satisfied because of the variety of toppings. ~~Toppings~~ spread on the sauce. Pepperoni leads the list of favorites, but jalapeños, anchovies, olives, and sausages are some of the other options, ~~even~~ . Even sausage comes in different types. For a real "like-home" Italian taste. ~~The~~ , the pizza can be topped with garlic bits and a little Parmesan cheese without the sauce. Since pizza can be varied, almost everyone can be satisfied.

Exercise 14 (Page 201)

15.	OK	**10.**	F	**5.**	OK
14.	CS	**9.**	F	**4.**	OK
13.	F	**8.**	OK	**3.**	F
12.	OK	**7.**	CS	**2.**	RO
11.	OK	**6.**	F	**1.**	OK

Unit 4 Writing with More Depth and Variety

Part 1 Writing with Examples

Exercise 1 (Page 217)
Answers will vary.

Exercise 2 (Page 219)
Answers will vary.

Answers to Odd-Numbered Items in Exercises

Exercise 3 (Page 221)

Paragraph 1

Cell phone users often ignore the people that they are around. They are even distracted from paying attention to their own children. At the grocery store, one mother, cradling her phone to her ear, shopped with her two young daughters. She spent the entire thirty minutes talking to whoever was on the other end of her cell phone. ~~Several other people kept staring at her and her daughters.~~ Her main focus was on her conversation, and at one point, without even interrupting her chatting, she glanced at one of her daughters and told her to get off the side of the grocery basket. ~~The girls added four boxes of Froot Loops to the basket.~~ Several minutes later, as she stood in the checkout line, she realized that her daughters were not with her. Alarmed, she quickly glanced around, spotted one daughter, and called to her. Still holding the phone to her ear, she told the little girl she was supposed to stay with her sister and then suddenly realized that the other little girl was still missing. Momentarily distracted from her call, she repeated three times, "Where is your sister?" When the little girl pointed to her sister in another part of the store, the mother motioned with her free hand for her other daughter to come back, and then she continued her phone conversation. Even when the clerk was checking them out, the mother kept her mind on her call. ~~She spent $142 on the groceries.~~ Then she walked her cell phone and her two daughters out the door.

Paragraph 3

Being hospitalized for an illness can cause a person to suffer a financial setback. The extensive bills can mount up. Bo Lewis suffered a severe financial setback when he spent several weeks in the hospital. The seven days in intensive care and four additional weeks in the hospital resulted in astronomical costs. Even though he had insurance, he had to pay a $500 deductible and 20 percent of the bill. Because the hospital bill alone was over $54,000, his responsibilities were $10,700. ~~Also, his wife went on a shopping spree for new summer clothes.~~ On top of this, he had to purchase several hundred dollars' worth of medicine. He also had to purchase medical supplies that were not covered by insurance. Because Bo Lewis was unable to work, he was eligible for disability, but this amount was much less than his regular salary. ~~Before his illness, he smoked only one carton of cigarettes a week, but because of the stress during and after his illness, he smoked two cartons.~~ In just a few weeks, he found himself owing $11,200 in medical expenses. It is scary to think how fast medical bills can accumulate when an extended illness occurs.

Exercise 4 (Page 222)

Answers will vary.

Exercise 5 (Page 224)

Paragraph 1

Early Americans had to rely on their own ingenuity to make life comfortable or even to survive. They turned survival skills into a type of art that was passed down from generation to generation. Some of these art forms, which may no longer be practical in today's society, were a part of living for our great-grandparents. In the West, sturdy houses could be made from adobe brick, but first the brick had to be made from mud and straw. Making clothes was also an art of the past that few people could accomplish today. Even buying material for clothes was a luxury few knew. The process of making a new dress or shirt or pants involved shearing sheep, carding wool, spinning yarn, and weaving cloth. Sometimes the clothing maker dyed the yarn different colors, using natural materials like walnut shells. ~~The women enjoyed growing flowers to make the home look more attractive.~~ Tatting—making lace by hand— became an art form that was used to decorate collars or to bring beauty to something as necessary as pillowcases. ~~People loved to get together in the evenings and have dances.~~ Since there were no refrigerators, families found that making beef jerky was a way to preserve meat and have a year-round supply. And if they wanted to take a bath, they needed soap, but making soap at home, an art almost unheard-of today, was required before that bath could take place. When the supply of candles, the source of night light, became low, there was one solution—making more from melted lard. ~~Sometimes the men and women would work from sunup to sundown so they could take a day off for celebration.~~ Today, we talk of "the good old days" when life was simple, but maybe we should say when families were resourceful and used art in order to survive.

Exercise 6 (Page 226)

Paragraph 1

In order to avoid the high cost of living, many retired couples have become full-time recreational vehicle travelers ("RVers"). After selling or renting their homes, they literally spend all their time traveling. One couple sold their home and bought a fully equipped van. They now pull a boat that provides recreation, and, when the boat is not being used on the water, it provides storage. Another couple sold their home and now spend several months in an Indiana resort area trading a few hours of work for a place to stay and free hookups. When summer comes, they do the same thing at an RV resort in Florida. Another retired couple spend their time working at national and state parks in exchange for a place to live and modest pay. ~~Likewise, a couple who lived in New Mexico now spend all their time moving from one national park to another serving as a host to the RV campground.~~ In this way, these retired people reduce their living costs and are able to live on moderate retirement funds.

Exercise 7 (Page 227)

Paragraph 1   *SIE*

Paragraph 3   *Ext*

Paragraph 5   *Ext*

Exercise 8 (Page 229)
Answers will vary.

Unit 4 *Writing with More Depth and Variety*

Part 4 Sentence Variety—Forming and Punctuating Compound Sentences

Exercise 1 (Page 244)

1. Positive reinforcement motivates people. ~~Paula~~ seldom uses it.   *, yet Paula*

3. Ariana was short on time. ~~Rudolph~~ kept talking.   *, yet*

5. The restaurant cooked healthy food. ~~Their~~ prices were high.   *, but their*

Exercise 2 (Page 245)

               ; nevertheless, they

1. At first, the students were reluctant to do community service. ~~They~~ found it very rewarding.

        ; consequently, she

3. Hope graduated from the community college. ~~She~~ found a good job.

        ; however, they

5. Traditional encyclopedias are losing popularity. ~~They~~ are offered online.

Exercise 3 (Page 246)

       ; they

1. Prison guards have dangerous jobs. ~~They~~ must be alert at all times.

       ; the

3. We enjoyed going to the ocean. ~~The~~ children collected seashells.

       ; she

5. The old dog trembled. ~~She~~ was afraid of thunder and lightning.

Exercise 4 (Page 246)

1. *Savannah admired butterflies, so she had a butterfly tattoo put on her ankle.*

   (coordinate conjunction)

   Savannah admired butterflies; she had a butterfly tattoo put on her ankle.

   (semicolon)

   Savannah admired butterflies; therefore, she had a butterfly tattoo put on her ankle.

   (conjunctive adverb)

3. *Kristen works for a professional baseball team, yet she seldom attends their games.*

   (coordinate conjunction)

   Kristen works for a professional baseball team; she seldom attends their games.

   (semicolon)

   Kristen works for a professional baseball team; nevertheless, she seldom attends their games.

   (conjunctive adverb)

5. *The attorney worked hard on the divorce case, so he won it.*

   (coordinate conjunction)

   The attorney worked hard on the divorce case; he won it.

   (semicolon)

   The attorney worked hard on the divorce case; furthermore, he won it.

   (conjunctive adverb)

7. *Keta and Bede live in Alaska, so they often fish for salmon.*

(coordinate conjunction)

Keta and Bede live in Alaska; they often fish for salmon.

(semicolon)

Keta and Bede live in Alaska; consequently, they often fish for salmon.

(conjunctive adverb)

Exercise 5 (Page 249)

Paragraph 1

Last Saturday, the weather seemed impulsive. One side of the sky was a brilliant blue
, but the
mixed with soft white clouds. ~~The~~ other side was a mass of streaked charcoal gray clouds.

However, right in the middle of the darkest clouds, bright blue patches of sky appeared like
, and the
little lakes in the sky. One minute the air was still. ~~The~~ sun broke through the clouds and

poured sunshine over everything. At these times, the warmth of the sun took over. Then,
; in addition, the
within minutes, the sun retreated. ~~The~~ wind whipped everything around. It twirled leaves
, and then
and twigs in a circle. ~~Then~~ it beat them against tree trunks or whatever came across its path.
, but they
At the same time, the clouds released raindrops everywhere. ~~They~~ only dampened the earth.
, and the
Just moments later, the rain suddenly stopped. ~~The~~ peacefulness of the sun appeared once

more. All day long, the sky played like this.

Paragraph 3

Throughout their adult years, people must adjust to many changes in their lives.
, and often
Technology may require people to retrain for a new job. ~~Often~~ company restructuring causes
; sometimes
change. Sometimes promotion causes change. ~~Sometimes~~ job loss causes changes. Other major

changes occur in people's personal lives, too. For various reasons, some married adults separate
, so they
from their mates. ~~They~~ must take on total responsibility for the household. Many adults must
; however, some
deal with having the last child leave home. ~~Some~~ people must cope with adult children returning
, and other
home. Sometimes they return alone. ~~Other~~ times they return with children. Once in a while, they
, or they
return with a mate. ~~They~~ return with a mate and children. All these situations cause adults to

make shifts in their lifestyles.

Unit 5 Reaching an Audience by Creating Interest

Part 1 Introductory and Concluding Paragraphs

Exercise 1 (Page 260)
Answers will vary.

Exercise 2 (Page 263)
Answers will vary.

Exercise 3 (Page 264)
Answers will vary.

Exercise 4 (Page 266)
Answers will vary.

Exercise 5 (Page 267)
Answers will vary.

Exercise 6 (Page 268)
Answers will vary.

Exercise 7 (Page 271)
Answers will vary.

Exercise 8 (Page 271)

Paragraph 1

Williamsburg, Virginia, offers a time-travel visit to 1775, a year before the American Revolutionary War. The city was restored in the 1930s to its 1775 appearance, so it resembles the town as it was in the 18th century. The governor's palace that housed the royal ruling power exhibits impressive 18th-century guns and swords on the walls and ceiling in organized, decorative patterns. In another historic area near Gentryville and Dale, Indiana, the Lincoln Boyhood National Memorial contains a log cabin that is an approximation of the original log cabin where Lincoln once lived. The area also includes a living historic farm where early 19th-century life is portrayed. Such realistic depictions and information that take people back to earlier times can be obtained by visiting restored historic landmarks. Through these moving re-creations, visitors obtain historical information and gain a feeling for bygone times.

Paragraph 3

"Reading is to the mind, what exercise is to the body," Sir Richard Steele wisely stated.

Steele's quotation draws an analogy between the importance of exercise to tone the body and reading to stimulate the mind. If people do not exercise, they become fat, sluggish, unhealthy, and weak, and this condition is readily visible. When people do not exercise their minds, they become mentally unhealthy and weak, yet this situation is even more dangerous because it is not noticeable. This is especially true for children in their formative years when habits are developing. Reading can make the difference between a strong or a weak mind. Encouraging children to read improves their vocabulary, expands their understanding, and increases their creativity.

Exercise 9 (Page 273)

Answers will vary.

Exercise 10 (Page 277)

Answers will vary.

Exercise 11 (Page 279)

Answers will vary.

Unit 5 Reaching an Audience by Creating Interest

Part 4 Sentence Variety—Using Complex Sentences

Exercise 1 (Page 297)

1. *After Rachel earned a college degree, she became the manager at a retail store.*
   Rachel became the manager at a retail store after she earned a college degree.

3. *Even though fresh Idaho snow covered the high mountaintops, the scouts continued to hike up the trail.*
   The scouts continued to hike up the trail even though fresh Idaho snow covered the high mountaintops.

5. *The manager resigned his position because it created too much stress in his life.*
   Because his job created too much stress in his life, the manager resigned.

Exercise 2 (Page 299)

1. *The children loved the playground that was filled with bright, colorful equipment.*

3. *My brother, who works as a carpenter, built his new home next to the mountain preserve.*

5. *Nick, who is semi-retired, teaches math online.*
   Nick, who teaches math online, is semi-retired.

Exercise 3 (Page 300)

1. *That he even cares about a clean house is surprising to his mother.*

3. *How the house escaped the forest fire seemed to be a miracle.*

5. *How my dog got loose no one seems to know.*

Exercise 4 (Page 301)

1. *I do not understand why he is always late.*

3. *The police officer realized that the elderly man was confused and lost.*

5. *We know that the difficulties can be overcome by hard work.*

Exercise 5 (Page 303)

Paragraph 1

who

People remodel their home. ~~They~~ can save a lot of money by being their own general
                  ^

that

contractor. They do not have to pay someone to subcontract out the various jobs. ~~These jobs~~

If homeowners

require an electrician, plumber, or general carpenter. ~~Homeowners~~ have three of four licensed

, then

and bonded subcontractors bid on a job. ~~Then~~ they can select the most favorable bid. Also, they

that

do not need to hire an expensive architect to create a plan. ~~This kind of plan~~ can run into

who

hundreds of dollars. Instead, homeowners can look into finding a house designer. ~~The designer~~

will simply put their remodeling ideas into a standard blueprint. Sometimes they can also save

money by doing some of the jobs themselves. For example, they might want to install the

because it   *If they*

appliances themselves. ~~It~~ can be done very easily. ~~They might~~ paint the house themselves.

, they

~~They~~ will save the often high cost of a professional subcontractor. Remodeling can be a fun

project, and saving money can make it even more pleasurable.

Paragraph 3

who

Bodybuilding is a sport that demands discipline. Bodybuilders ∧ push themselves until

their muscles won't work anymore. ~~They~~ build muscle mass. Serious athletes must work

until they   *If the*

out at the gym five to seven hours a day. ~~They~~ feel a burning sensation in their muscles. ~~The~~

, they

muscles are sore the next morning. ~~They~~ know they had a good workout. Athletes must also

in which they

have the willpower to adhere to a strict diet. ~~They~~ eat no fatty foods, especially hamburgers

When they   *, they*

and french fries. ~~They~~ need to cut fat. ~~They~~ must stay on an even stricter diet than normal.

When they

They also must get plenty of sleep. ~~They~~ are at a party with their friends and everyone else

, dedicated

wants to stay late. ~~Dedicated~~ athletes will have enough control to go home early. This

dedication, however, will result in a body they can take pride in.

Unit 6 Making Ideas Flow Clearly

Part 1 Coherence

Exercise 1 (Page 318)

Paragraph 1

As part of their job, they

Pharmacy technicians have very responsible jobs. ∧ ~~They~~ must make sure that the drugs

When patients come into the store, technicians

and supplies in the pharmacy are stocked in the right place and in the right order. ~~Technicians~~ ∧

are responsible for typing prescriptions into the computer database and filling prescriptions.

In addition, technicians   *However, they   then*

~~Technicians~~ ∧ are often asked to count out and pour drugs. ~~They~~ must ∧ check with the

pharmacist who verifies that they have the right medications and have put the correct dosage

Also, technicians   be trusted to

into the bottles. ~~Technicians~~ must not ∧ counsel customers or give advice on prescription

that are efficient, capable, and reliable

medications or even over-the-counter drugs. Having technicians ∧ ensures that the

pharmacists and interns are free to do their jobs well.

Paragraph 3

Prepackaged, microwavable dishes are a way of life for people on the go.

For example, prepackaged

~~Prepackaged~~ entrees for babies help working mothers serve nutritional meals to the

                                          soon learn to

small members of the family. Older children can ^ microwave their own dinners. When Mom

                                         then

and Dad are unable to prepare lunch, children can ^ heat up such items as spaghetti and

                                 Also, entrees

meatballs or chicken and rice. ~~Entrees~~ that appeal to the whole family can be stored in the

freezer and popped into the microwave while the cook throws together a quick salad and

sets the table. Chicken and dumplings, vegetable lasagna, or pork back ribs are a few of the

                 of these dishes   *In addition, evening*

many varieties ^ available. ~~Evening~~ snacks can include popcorn in minutes or milk shakes that

                       Therefore, people

defrost in seconds. ~~People~~ with a microwave oven no longer have a reason for skipping a meal.

Exercise 2 (Page 320)

    Answers will vary.

Exercise 3 (Page 321)

Essay 1

    During my morning jog, I stopped and talked to a man who was carefully tending his

garden. When I expressed interest in the luscious garden, he replied, "I got over six

five-gallon buckets of strawberries alone this summer." I was taken by surprise because the

strawberry patch was only about six feet by five feet. His green-bean vines that were growing

along the fence were loaded with long, healthy beans, and I could only wonder how many of

those he had harvested. Seeing his garden made me think of all the benefits that gardening

can bring to anyone who is willing to put in the time and effort. Although having a small

garden can be hard work, it can result in pleasure and savings.

                             , however,   *First, the gardener*

    The benefits of a garden ^ do not come without work. ~~S/he~~ must select a location for the

After the plot of ground is selected, it   *Next, sawdust,*

garden. ~~It~~ needs to be dug out and loosened. ~~Sawdust,~~ ^ peat, and fertilizer mixed and added

                         Just as important, growing

will allow the seeds to grow easily. ~~Growing~~ instructions need to be followed when the seeds

                   Finally, the

are planted. ~~The~~ garden must be watered, weeded, and debugged daily. Watering at the

               sometimes can be difficult, but   *is hard work but*

correct time of day ^ is necessary. Keeping the weeds to a minimum ^ makes the garden

vegetables stronger. A good gardener prepares a good place and watches the plants as if they

were helpless, defenseless creatures.

With a little dirt, water, and sunshine, a
~~A~~ garden can bring many pleasures. The sight of small sprigs reaching up through the
warm   *the enjoyment of*
soil toward the sun gives the *warm* feeling of capturing a small part of nature and *the enjoyment of* getting in touch

with the earth. What greater satisfaction is there for the gardener than to know that s/he has
Usually more   *proudly*
used the elements to produce food? ~~More~~ *Usually more* than enough is produced, and the gardener can *proudly*
delighted
share the crisp flavor of fresh produce with a *delighted* neighbor. In view of the much-publicized use

of insecticides on commercial produce, the gardener can use natural combatants such as
and feel comfortable
ladybugs or praying mantises or ingenuity to preserve the vegetables, *and feel comfortable* knowing the products

from the garden are healthy. A garden can be the source not only of food and pride, but also

of peace of mind.
After the initial work is done, having
~~Having~~ *After the initial work is done, having* a small garden to bring in fresh vegetables provides a savings. Each year
For example, tomatoes
grocery prices slowly creep up on such items as lettuce and tomatoes. ~~Tomatoes~~ *For example, tomatoes* that last
now   *Likewise, lettuce*
year cost 98 cents a pound, *now* cost $1.49. ~~Lettuce~~ *Likewise, lettuce* is sold at 99 cents a pound instead of
These   *increases make*
99 cents a head. ~~The~~ *These* gradual price ~~increase makes~~ *increases make* one wonder if the consumer will ever
The savings are easy to see because a
see the end. ~~A~~ *The savings are easy to see because a* package of tomato or lettuce seeds costs about $1.29 total, and these seeds
Moreover, extra
can provide enough tomatoes and lettuce for an entire summer. ~~Extra~~ *Moreover, extra* vegetables can be
Additional savings occur when surplus
frozen or canned to provide a year-round supply of fresh food. ~~Surplus~~ *Additional savings occur when surplus* vegetables can be
The gardener also saves money by trading   *to prevent*
sold to bring in extra money. ~~Trading~~ *The gardener also saves money by trading* produce with other gardeners ~~prevents~~ *to prevent* buying so
positive
much at the grocery store. Gardens can add much-needed pocket change and give the *positive*

feeling of defeating the inflationary war.

Work, time, and patience
~~One~~ *Work, time, and patience* can transform a tiny seed into baskets of delicious, healthy food. By gardening,
Though a
a person can experience a miracle of nature and can save money at the same time. ~~A~~ *Though a* person

may not be able to get thirty gallons of strawberries in a five-by-six plot of ground, ~~but~~ that
satisfaction and   *hard*
same person may be able to find *satisfaction and* happiness, knowing his/her *hard* work is being rewarded.

Unit 6 Making Ideas Flow Clearly

Part 4 Reviewing Punctuation

Exercise 1 (Page 335)

1. My cousin Jessica can go on vacation with us if she can get off work, save enough money, and find a house sitter.

3. Today's auto mechanics must have computer, management, and interpersonal skills.

5. College counselors help students solve family problems, build self-esteem, and explore career possibilities.

Exercise 2 (Page 336)

Paragraph 1

Grandparents, aunts, uncles, and cousins gathered for the annual picnic at the park. Together they ate the attractive and well-prepared food that smelled delicious, tasted great, and satisfied everyone. Then the older children took turns playing volleyball, tennis, and tetherball. Some of the grandparents spread blankets on the green grass for the little ones to take their bottles, to nap, or just to rest. Sometimes the adults, too, fell asleep. Later they took turns riding on the park's train, looking through the model-train exhibits, and reading about the history of trains. Soon, however, everyone returned to the picnic tables to munch on leftovers and talk about last year's picnic.

Exercise 3 (Page 337)

1. Without thinking, we locked the keys in our car.

3. As soon as we pack the truck, we can head for the mountains.

5. To solve the conflict, the flight attendant seated the passenger by the window.

Exercise 4 (Page 337)

Paragraph 1

People with good credit ratings fear identity theft and spend time every day trying to protect their financial reputation. Usually, they are afraid to throw away anything that contains personal information. For protection, people use cross-cut or confetti shredders to destroy papers with their names, addresses, social security numbers, and any other personal information. In addition, they like to shred unwanted credit card offers that arrive almost daily in the mail. Also, they carefully shred outdated medical records, paid bills, and other personal records no longer needed. In fact, many people spend time every day destroying this information because they do not want anyone to have access to all the personal information needed to open new charge accounts, drain money from their checking account, or apply for large loans in their names. In many cases, people keep in a safe place at home any papers that cannot be destroyed. Though doing these things might become tedious at times, it is a way to make sure that their assets are safe.

Exercise 5 (Page 340)

1. Patches, who is my favorite cat, came to my house as an orphan.

3. Rochester, however, is known for its cool summers.

5. For instance, Steve is an expert plumber.

7. The museum was filled with outstanding exhibits, some more valuable than others.

Exercise 6 (Page 340)

Paragraph 1

The sign reads "No skating, biking, running or loud music." A granite wall progressively emerges from the ground. From one-sixteenth of an inch and one name, the wall grows to one-half inch, then to a foot. Two names appear, then three, five, ten. With no logical mathematical sequence, the names increase on the wall until at midpoint it reaches approximately eight feet tall with hundreds of names tightly embedded one after another. The time depicted by the wall was, of course, the 1960s, and the names represent the soldiers killed or missing in Southeast Asia during the Vietnam War. The visual representation of heartfelt American deaths turns the tourist chatter to silence. Experiencing the Vietnam Veterans Memorial, it seems, makes visitors realize the sacrifices of American youth.

Exercise 7 (Page 342)

None   1. Jesse worked at that restaurant for fifteen years.

3. On November 8, 2003, the nine black lab puppies were born on my cousin's farm near Loveland, Colorado.

None   5. July 4th is a national holiday.

7. What I want to know, Ruby, is how you do your art so well.

Exercise 8 (Page 342)

Paragraph 1

On September 1, 1939, Germany invaded Poland and started World War II. Beginning in 1940, Hitler invaded Belgium, Luxembourg, Denmark, Norway, and France. On April 9, 1940, the Germans seized Denmark and invaded Norway. Just one month later, on May 10, 1940, Germany invaded Belgium. Just a few days later, on May 14, 1940, the Netherlands surrendered. Because England had treaties with France, she made good her commitment, and on September 3, 1940, Great Britain and France declared war on Germany. On May 26, 1940, the Allied Powers began their heroic evacuation at Dunkirk, a seaport in northern France. By 1940, the entire European continent was at war. Then on June 22, 1941, Germany invaded the Soviet Union. On December 7, 1941, Japan attacked Pearl Harbor, bringing the United States into the war. By now, almost all countries in the world were involved in this devastating war.

Exercise 9 (Page 346)

1. I enjoyed reading Leif Enger's novel <u>Peace Like a River</u>.

3. "You need to get your car's oil changed every 3,000 miles," said Phil, "so that the car will last longer."

5. "It's a fact about our dog," said Trudy. "Its nose is a million times more sensitive than ours."

7. <u>The Call of the Wild</u> by Jack London, is a survival story about a perceptive dog.

Exercise 10 (Page 346)

Paragraph 1

My family's trip to the Grand Canyon northwest of Flagstaff, Arizona, was an unforgettable experience. On June 17, 2003, we boarded the steam train in Williams, Arizona, and headed for the canyon. The train moved across the Kaibab Plateau, which was rolling hills covered with scrub cedar. Once there, we got off the train and walked to Bright Angel Lodge, where we bought a lunch that we enjoyed under a tree at the South Rim of the canyon. There we could see the colorful layers of rock, shadows made by clouds, and distant evergreen trees. We were impressed by the vastness of the canyon, and from the canyon's edge, we could see part of Bright Angel Trail. Soon, however, we needed to walk back to the train for the trip back to Williams. Although we were tired, we were inspired by what we had seen.

Paragraph 3

The Epcot Center in Orlando, Florida, authentically portrays the atmosphere of various countries throughout the world. For example, as visitors arrive at the Japanese pavilion, they are welcomed by the large red torii gate similar to the one at the Itsukushima shrine at Hiroshima Bay. At they walk closer to the pavilion, they can hear traditional Japanese folk melodies. At the same time, visitors are drawn to the five-story pagoda's distinct architecture.

Japanese taiko drummers entertain visitors by performing just as they do in their home festival. The pagoda and a Japanese castle are surrounded by a beautiful flower garden with well-tended red and yellow flowers and peaceful ponds filled with koi and water lilies. Inside the castle people can stop at the Japanese tea shop or shop for Japanese clothing porcelain dishes bonsai trees paper fans and many other authentic items. At the pavilions restaurants the smell of Japanese food fills the air and people can purchase full meals or simply get a quick bite at the sushi bar. Visitors to the Epcot Center can then continue to the next exhibits that also feature architecture costumes customs foods and entertainment from around the world.

Exercise 11 (Page 349)

Paragraph 1

During World War II average American citizens experienced many difficulties buying products they wanted or needed. The ability to buy products was restricted by monthly ration stamps for such items as gasoline shoes sugar and meat. Though people had ration stamps meat was especially hard to find because it was put into products like Spam and sent to the soldiers overseas. Even with stamps citizens might not be able to buy the products they wanted. Often the shelves were empty because it seemed as though everything was channeled into America's defense system. For example shoes were difficult to obtain because the shoe producers needed to supply boots for the army. Likewise cloth was difficult to purchase because fabrics were shipped to factories to make uniforms for the Armed Forces. Jim and Alice Basham who owned their own upholstery business said We could not buy goods to upholster furniture because material was shipped to the Armed Forces. They also said that women were unable to buy nylons because the fabric needed to make them went into making parachutes to be used in the war. Imported items like coffee tea sugar and rubber were scarce. The little rubber that the United States could import went into the production of tires for the Armed Forces. For four years no automobiles were made because all American energies were channeled into the production of military vehicles. American citizens who lived through World War II will always remember those hard times.

Paragraph 3

Poetry is an art form that can be enjoyed sometimes because of the meaning sometimes because of the way it is written and other times because of both. Can anyone read Walt

Whitman's Leaves of Grass without saying, "That is nice, really nice." Lines that seem to stick in the mind are often written with a strong message. For instance, the lines from Anne Sexton's poem "The Abortion," "Somebody who should have been born is gone," stay in the mind long after the poem has been read. Whenever the question of abortion arises, these lines are recalled in the mind again and again. Thomas Hood wanted to change labor laws in England. In his poem "The Song of the Shirt," he wrote, "With fingers weary and worn,/With eyelids heavy and red,/A woman sat, in unwomanly rags,/Plying her needle and thread—" John Milton, married but miserable, spent much effort inserting lines about divorce into his poetry in an attempt to change the laws that forbade divorce. Some poets, however, do not moralize but simply present things the way they are. James Dickey, a well-known American poet, wrote of adultery objectively without making any judgment of its wrongness or rightness. On the other hand, Joyce Peseroff expresses her ideas in "The Hardness Scale," a poem in which she seems to be relating a woman's feelings about a man who is not such a perfect man. Diane Wakoski writes of revenge in her poem "You, Letting the Trees Stand as My Betrayer." In this poem, nature will pay back someone who loved her and then left her. The meaning is there in these and many other poems, but the way they are written makes the lines recur over and over in the reader's mind.

Unit 7 Composing with Effective Alternate Patterns

Part 4 Capitalization

Exercise 1 (Page 410)

           L   *M* *P* *R*
~~l~~ast year, ~~mrs.~~ ~~p~~olly ~~r~~eaves, an 87-year-old widow who lived alone, got lucky
                J   *M*
when her son ~~j~~ames called her and told her, "~~m~~om, the family wants to remodel
        S
your home." ~~s~~he has five sons, three daughters, and numerous grandchildren, and
                          S
he told her that all of them wanted to help. ~~s~~he didn't want to put anyone out, but

she knew this would be a blessing. Two of her sons replaced the roof, and the other

sons worked inside fixing the plumbing and repairing the walls. Her daughters
H   *C*
~~h~~elen and ~~c~~arol made new window coverings while the grandchildren painted first
                                     C   *B*
the outside and then the inside of the home. ~~c~~huck and ~~b~~everly worked in her flower
                                                                PJ
garden and even put in a new border. Everyone stayed busy, even her dog ~~pj~~, who

kept everyone company. Several months later, when ~~mrs.~~ [M] ~~reaves~~ [R] looked at her new

home, she simply said, "~~i~~ [I]-thank all of you for your hard work, and ~~i~~ [I]-thank ~~god~~ [G] for my

family." Everyone cheered.

Exercise 2 (Page 412)

Wanting to break the daily routine of living and actually doing something

"different" or "exciting" are all too often unfulfilled wishes. In ~~march~~ [M], some people want

to walk the hiking trails in the ~~south~~ [S] ~~mountain~~ [M] ~~park~~ [P] with a backpack full of ~~doritos~~ [D] and

~~snickers~~ [S] bars. Others want to go to the ~~american~~ [A] ~~automobile~~ [A] ~~association~~ [A] (~~aaa~~) [AAA] to plan a

trip to ~~alaska~~ [A] and capture the wild on ~~kodak~~ [K] film. Some people daydream about flying

to ~~washington~~ [W] to climb ~~mount~~ [M] ~~rainier~~ [R], located in the ~~northwest~~ [N]. Even a summer trip

to the ~~east~~ [E] to remember ~~woodstock~~ [W] seems exciting. When the time comes, though, to

make a "new" choice, breaking the routine and actually doing some of these things

means taking a risk that may be too difficult. In the spring, the ~~sonoran~~ [S] ~~desert~~ [D] may be

in the middle of snake season. ~~alaska~~ [A] may cost too much, even in a ~~chevy~~ [C] van. Climbing

~~mount~~ [M] ~~rainier~~ [R] is reserved for only the few with the skills and courage to make the

effort. Excuses for not breaking the routine all too frequently include "too expensive,"

"too dangerous," or "too busy" on holidays like ~~memorial~~ [M] ~~day~~ [D]. Perhaps after all, people

choose to do what they really want to do, in spite of their yearnings to the contrary.

Exercise 3 (Page 413)

During one recent school year, the fourth grade class at Sunset Elementary

School had an exciting variety of experiences that inspired them to want to learn as

much as possible about the world. In an issue of ~~weekly~~ [W] ~~reader~~ [R], an article about

~~african~~ [A] elephants captured the students' attention. They learned how orphaned baby

elephants are cared for until they are ready to be sent back to the wild. In still

another issue, "~~science~~ [S] for ~~sale~~ [S]" told of scientists discovering in the hills of South

Dakota an almost complete dinosaur, whose bones were eventually auctioned for

more than 8 million dollars to a Chicago museum. These articles certainly inspired

the young readers to think about taking courses in working with wildlife or in

discovering and preserving relics or fossils from the ancient world. Along with

Answers to Odd-Numbered Items in Exercises

reading about animals current and past, the youngsters also heard enthralling

                                                         Z

information about scorpions from a high school student taking ~~z~~oology 112 and
                                          N M

about a summer spent on a ~~new~~ ~~m~~exican "dig" from a community college student
           I   *A*   *T*   *K*

enrolled in ~~i~~ntroduction to ~~a~~rcheology. Later, students read in ~~time for kids~~ (the
             T   *T*

children's version of ~~time~~ magazine) a heart-rending story of ~~t~~ibetan families and
                                         C

their children fleeing ~~c~~hinese rule for more freedom in India. The youngsters from
S   *S*

~~s~~unset ~~s~~chool, reading about these children, talked about how lucky they felt to be
A

~~a~~mericans. They seemed excited about wanting to know as much as possible about

other countries and cultures so they could help make the world a better place.

Exercise 4 (Review) (Page 413)

           L *J*   *E*   *P*   *M*   *I*

    ~~l~~ast ~~j~~une, my family reunion at ~~e~~ncanto ~~p~~ark was relaxing. ~~m~~y family and ~~i~~
    B   *K*   *F* *C*

brought ~~b~~oston baked beans, potato salad, and ~~k~~entucky ~~f~~ried ~~c~~hicken for a stress-
            M

free picnic. ~~m~~y aunts and uncles brought more and more food until we had a spread
                A   *C*

no one could resist. ~~a~~fter we ate, the kids had ~~c~~arnation ice cream for dessert and set
   M   *B*   *A* *M*

up a ~~m~~onopoly game under the shade of a pine tree. ~~b~~efore long, even ~~a~~unt ~~m~~artha
                                          A   *E*

joined the game by serving as the banker. My cousin ~~a~~drian brought his ~~e~~nglish and
M   *I*   *O*   *A*

~~m~~ath books, but ~~i~~ noticed that he never opened either one. ~~o~~n the other hand, ~~a~~unt
M   *T* *K*   *G* *W*   *E*

~~m~~argaret brought out ~~the kitchen god's wife~~, said "excuse me," and began reading.
U   *F*   *U*   *B*

~~u~~ncle ~~f~~red and ~~u~~ncle ~~b~~ob had a lively discussion about the difference between the
V   *W*   *P*   *G* *W*   *G*

~~v~~ietnam ~~w~~ar and the ~~p~~ersian ~~g~~ulf ~~w~~ar when suddenly ~~g~~randpa started telling us
      W   *W*   *S*   *S*   *B*

about ~~w~~orld ~~w~~ar II and his adventures with his good buddy, ~~s~~ergeant ~~s~~holam. ~~b~~efore
                                       H   *K*   *B*

long, he opened his traditional package of ~~h~~ershey ~~k~~isses to share with us. "~~b~~ack
                                           H   *E*

then," he said, "we looked forward to having ~~h~~ershey candy bars. ~~e~~veryone thought
                                                          A *I*

they were a real treat, especially when we handed them out during the war." ~~as i~~
                 I   *I*   *I*

listened to him talk, ~~i~~ kept thinking how proud ~~i~~ was to have him as a grandfather. ~~in~~
                                                         H   *C*

just a few days, my relatives, who had come from as far away as ~~h~~awaii and ~~c~~anada,

would return to their homes, grateful that they knew a little more about each other, but today was ~~saturday~~ *s*, and we would finish the time enjoying each other's company

and perhaps even planning for the family reunion next summer.

Answers to Confusing Words (Appendix A)

Set 1 (Page 423)

a lot
1. Steve often has ~~alot~~ of figs on his tree.

a lot
3. Sonja often caught ~~alot~~ of fish at that lake.

Set 2 (Page 424)

C   **1.** She accepted my apology and walked away with a frown on her face.

C   **3.** She accepted the money greedily.

Set 3 (Page 424)

C   **1.** When people move to a new country, they must adapt to new customs.

adopt
3. They hoped to ~~adapt~~ the little girl.

Set 4 (Page 424)

C   **1.** John advised Butch not to hike the steep mountain.

advised
3. I ~~adviced~~ her to do her household chores early.

Set 5 (Page 424)

affect
1. His action cannot ~~effect~~ us.

C   **3.** His honesty affected everyone around him.

Set 6 (Page 425)

all ready
1. Are you ~~already~~?

C   **3.** When she got to the party, everyone was already there.

Set 7 (Page 425)

altogether
1. Sharon was ~~all together~~ surprised by his comment.

C   **3.** The flowers were planted all together.

Set 8 (Page 426)

1. She divides her time ~~among~~ *between* job and family.

C 3. That item was among the first ones to be considered.

Set 9 (Page 426)

1. ~~Are~~ *Our* children are ready to go to the zoo.

3. The trees ~~our~~ *are* growing faster than we had hoped.

Set 10 (Page 426)

1. The bus driver slammed on the ~~break~~, *brake* and the passengers flew forward.

3. When the car in front of us stopped, I hit the ~~break~~ *brake*.

Set 11 (Page 426)

1. Mrs. Smith needed to ~~by~~ *buy* detergent for her washing machine.

C 3. Mick needs to be at church by 8:30 A.M.

Set 12 (Page 427)

1. The field trip included a visit to the ~~capital~~ *capitol* building.

C 3. When he gets enough capital, he plans to start his own business.

Set 13 (Page 427)

1. This is a wonderful ~~cite~~ *site* for the new building.

3. I was unable to catch any ~~site~~ *sight* of him.

Set 14 (Page 428)

C 1. The course I liked the best was not necessarily the easiest.

3. The ~~coarse~~ *course* he took was a challenge.

Set 15 (Page 428)

C 1. The crowd sighed in relief when she became conscious.

C 3. I didn't want to study, but my conscience reminded me of the importance of making good grades.

Set 16 (Page 428)

have
1. Everyone at the lake should ~~of~~ used sunblock.

C   3. The street leading to the city could have been blocked off.

Set 17 (Page 429)

counsel
1. The ~~council~~ for the defense was an inexperienced attorney.

counsel
3. The father gave ~~council~~ to his son.

Set 18 (Page 429)

C   1. He ate his fourth poppy-seed muffin.

forth
3. From this day ~~fourth,~~ the prime minister will be extremely cautious.

Set 19 (Page 429)

good
1. The flowers smell ~~well~~.

good
3. The apple pie was ~~well~~.

Set 20 (Page 430)

hear
1. Didn't you ~~here~~ the car honking?

hear
3. From our kitchen, we could ~~here~~ birds singing.

Set 21 (Page 430)

hole
1. Be careful; I think there's a ~~whole~~ around here.

whole
3. Tall yellow weeds covered the ~~hole~~ field.

Set 22 (Page 430)

infer
1. What did you ~~imply~~ from the speech?

implied
3. From what he ~~inferred,~~ did you infer the right answer?

Set 23 (Page 430)

it's
1. I believe ~~its~~ going to be a rainy day.

its
3. It's been a long time since ~~it's~~ beginnings.

Set 24 (Page 431)

C   1. The meteorologist knew it was going to rain Wednesday.

knew
3. I ~~new~~ the test would be difficult.

           Answers to Odd-Numbered Items in Exercises

Set 25 (Page 431)

 1. Don't you ~~no~~ *know* not to stick a fork into the toaster?

C 3. I know I shouldn't watch TV when I have homework.

Set 26 (Page 431)

C 1. The young man continued to lie throughout the investigation.

 3. The doctor advised Chad not to ~~lay~~ *lie* in the sun.

Set 27 (Page 432)

 1. Mom didn't want to ~~loose~~ *lose* Amy in the crowd, so she held her hand tightly.

C 3. The knot Bob made was too loose to hold the calf.

Set 28 (Page 432)

 1. My teammate ~~past~~ *passed* the ball to me, and I made a touchdown.

C 3. Mr. Van passed out the test at 8:00.

Set 29 (Page 433)

 1. Pass Julio a ~~peace~~ *piece* of cherry pie.

 3. Roger lost a ~~peace~~ *piece* of my science project, but I passed anyway.

Set 30 (Page 433)

 1. Our ~~principle~~ *principal*, Ms. Jones, is a sensitive woman.

 3. I called her and explained the new club's ~~principals~~ *principles*.

Set 31 (Page 433)

 1. Laura is ~~quiet~~ *quite* a pretty girl.

 3. The Russians were ~~quiet~~ *quite* surprised that they came in second in the gymnastics events.

Set 32 (Page 434)

 1. Beatrice started to ~~rite~~ *write* her essay but was interrupted by another phone call.

 3. I broke my ~~rite~~ *right* hand when I fell.

Set 33 (Page 434)

C 1. We will be through by then.

 3. He has more money ~~then~~ *than* I do.

Set 34 (Page 434)

their
1. They left ~~there~~ book in their car.

C   **3.** The puppy is hiding there in the grass.

Set 35 (Page 435)

C   **1.** Though Juana was tired, she stayed up and baked bread.

C   **3.** The Comets lost the game even though they played their best.

Set 36 (Page 435)

through
1. Sarah climbed ~~threw~~ the tunnel and ran for the slide.

through
3. Ann ran ~~threw~~ the woods, jumping over logs and stones.

Set 37 (Page 435)

two
1. The final score was three to ~~too~~.

too
3. Nicki finished her paper, ~~to~~.

Set 38 (Page 436)

wanders
1. He ~~wonders~~ from one city to another.

C   **3.** I often wonder how my family is doing.

Set 39 (Page 436)

weak
1. Is she too ~~week~~ to go shopping?

week
3. The child gets an allowance every ~~weak~~.

Set 40 (Page 436)

weather
1. The ~~whether~~ is great in Colorado in the summer.

C   **3.** The weather for tomorrow is predicted to be beautiful.

Set 41 (Page 437)

Where
1. ~~Were~~ were you when I needed help?

where
3. Tanya went ~~were~~ the other students were playing volleyball.

Set 42 (Page 437)

Who's
1. ~~Whose~~ at the door, John?

Who's
3. ~~Whose~~ at the other end of the phone?

Set 43 (Page 437)

1. Cecil threw out the food ~~who~~ *that* was spoiled.

C   3. The people that came late to the concert could not get in.

Set 44 (Page 438)

1. The three ~~woman~~ *women* went through nurses' training together.

C   3. The most prestigious award was given to an outstanding woman student.

Set 45 (Page 438)

1. Jesse said that ~~your~~ *you're* not going.

3. I'm sorry, Jane, but ~~your~~ *you're* not going to be able to swim today.

Answers to Spelling (Appendix D)

Practice 1 (Page 444)

star	starred
tag	tagged
drug	drugged
wrap	wrapped
ship	shipped

Practice 3 (Page 444)

defer	deferred
allot	allotted
control	controlled
omit	omitted
remit	remitted

Practice 2 (Page 444)

brag	bragging
swim	swimming
hum	humming
chat	chatting
lug	lugging

Practice 4 (Page 445)

occur	occurring
repel	repelling
extol	extolling
unwrap	unwrapping
acquit	acquitting

Practice 5 (Page 444)

judge	+	ment	=	judgment
believe	+	able	=	believable
compose	+	ing	=	composing
delete	+	ing	=	deleting
write	+	ing	=	writing
relate	+	ing	=	relating

replace	+	ment	=	replacement
devote	+	ing	=	devoting
forgive	+	ness	=	forgiveness
encourage	+	ment	=	encouragement

Practice 6 (Page 446)

unbel _ie_ vable   r _ei_ gn

fr _ei_ ght   shr _ie_ k

gr _ie_ f   br _ie_ f

rec _ei_ pt   misch _ie_ vous

rel _ie_ ve   n _ie_ ce

Practice 7 (Page 446)

happy	+ness	=	happiness
merry	+est	=	merriest
vary	+s	=	varies
tasty	+er	=	tastier
jury	+s	=	juries
baby	+ing	=	babying
study	+ing	=	studying

Answers to ESL: Gaining Confidence in Using English (Appendix E)

Exercise 1 (Page 449)

Version A

(C) A   **1.** The <u>car</u> was his favorite.

C (A)   **3.** Daya's <u>religion</u> was important to her.

C (A)   **5.** Kiko's <u>fear</u> showed when she was speaking in front of a crowd.

Version B

(C) A   **1.** Gonzalo studied many hours for the <u>test</u>.

(C) A   **3.** Chinese New Year is a time for a dragon <u>parade</u>.

(C) A   **5.** The native <u>Indians</u> of Ecuador weave many beautiful rugs.

Exercise 2 (Page 451)

Version A

C (N)   **1.** The hospital patient struggled for <u>survival</u>.

(C) N   **3.** The lawn mower damaged a <u>brick</u> in the fence.

(C) N   **5.** The health <u>magazine</u> recommends yearly mammograms.

Version B

C (N) **1.** Theresa expressed <u>relief</u> at the end of the test.

(C) N **3.** Because of her diabetes, Ingrid could not eat any of the apple <u>pie</u>.

C (N) **5.** After growing up, my cat did not like <u>milk</u>.

Exercise 3 (Page 452)

Version A

1. I poured my water into ___*a*___ glass from the cupboard.

3. To increase her strength, Leta enrolled at ___*a*___ gym.

5. The elderly gentleman ordered ___*an*___ egg and some toast for his breakfast.

Version B

1. My father made ___*an*___ error in his taxes this year.

C **3.** Uraiwan wanted to take a course in _____ geography this semester.

5. The parents had to learn ___*a*___ new method for disciplining their child.

Exercise 4 (Page 453)

Version A

___*C*___ **1.** He experienced failure last Saturday.

___*I*___ **3.** He showed the nervousness before his wedding.

___*C*___ **5.** He lacked the courage needed to become a soldier.

Version B

___*I*___ **1.** She does not have the sympathy.

___*C*___ **3.** In New Orleans, cafés have live jazz every weekend.

___*I*___ **5.** Ursula appreciates the beauty.

Exercise 5 (Page 455)
Answers will vary.

Exercise 6 (Page 455)
Answers will vary.

Exercise 7 (Page 456)

Version A

___*I*___ **1.** The student can buys her supplies at the discount store.

___*I*___ **3.** Sonya must seeing the doctor after all.

___*C*___ **5.** Walter may study at the library.

Version B

_____I_____ **1.** After lunch, we could going to the mall to shop.

_____I_____ **3.** The church bells should to ring at noon.

_____C_____ **5.** Marta may not read the newspaper before breakfast.

Exercise 8 (Page 457)

Version A

1. The counselor suggested _____ _studying harder._

3. Sharon quit _____ _smoking cigarettes._

5. Mama enjoys _____ _having us around._

Version B

1. My grandfather advises _____ _taking vitamins each day._

3. The nurse avoided _____ _coming into my room._

5. The senior citizens will consider _____ _volunteering at the hospital._

Exercise 9 (Page 458)

Version A

_____I_____ **1.** She promised going to the store tomorrow.

_____I_____ **3.** Her tax adviser needed having other records.

_____C_____ **5.** We tried to drive across town to a special store.

Version B

_____I_____ **1.** I wanted learning to play the piano.

_____C_____ **3.** The supervisor agreed to hold a meeting with the new employee.

_____I_____ **5.** The flight attendant refused serving the unruly passenger.

Exercise 10 (Page 460)

Version A

_____I_____ **1.** We live <u>in</u> 2701 N. 10th Street.

_____I_____ **3.** I am capable <u>in</u> doing the homework.

_____C_____ **5.** I found my lost purse <u>on</u> June 10, 2003.

Version B

_____I_____ **1.** Kiko's birthday is <u>on</u> May.

_____C_____ **3.** My last test is <u>on</u> Thursday.

_____I_____ **5.** We agreed <u>to</u> you about the suggestion.

Index

Credits

Unit 1 (page 56). Excerpt from *Martin Luther King* by Rae Bains. © 1985 Troll Associates, Mahwah, NJ 07430. Reprinted by permission.

Unit 1 (page 56). From "Making a World of Difference" in the Spring/Summer 1987 issue of *Experienced Engineer*. © 1987 Peterson's/COG Publishing. Reprinted by permission.

Unit 2 (page 128). From *Plaintext* by Nancy Mairs, © 1986 The Arizona Board of Regents. Reprinted by permission of the University of Arizona Press.

Unit 2 (page 129). Excerpt from "The Casualty" appearing in the March 8, 2004, issue of *The New Yorker*. © 2004 by Dan Baum. Reprinted by permission of the author.

Unit 2 (page 130). Reprinted by permission of Susan P. Halpern, psychotherapist, founder of the New York Cancer Help Program, and author of "The Etiquette of Illness: What to Say When You Can't Find the Words," www.theetiquetteofillness.com.

Unit 2 (page 131). From *Talking from 9 to 5*. © 1994 by Deborah Tannen. Reprinted by permission of HarperCollins Publishers Inc.

Unit 2 (page 132). From *Dear Dad* by Louie Anderson. © 1989 by Louzelle Productions, Inc. Reprinted by permission of the publisher, Viking Penguin, a division of Penguin Books USA Inc.

Unit 3 (page 181). "Building a Better Home" by John K. Terres. © 1987 by the National Wildlife Federation. Reprinted from the April/May 1987 issue of *National Wildlife* magazine.

Unit 4 (page 241). Excerpt from *Kingdom by the Sea* by Paul Theroux. © by Cape Cod Scriveners Co. Reprinted by permission of Houghton Mifflin Co.

Unit 6 (page 332). From "I Don't Like What You're Wearing" by David Updike. © 1999 *Newsweek*.

Unit 7 (page 406). "The Mutt Who Saved Mr. Lambert" by William Thomas, M.D. Reprinted with permission from *Guideposts*. © 1997 by *Guideposts*, Carmel, NY 10512. All rights reserved.

Photo: © Inga Spence/Index Stock Imagery

Instructor's Manual
Writing Paragraphs and Essays

Integrating Reading, Writing, and Grammar Skills

Fifth Edition

Joy Wingersky
Glendale Community College

Jan Boerner
Emerita, Glendale Community College

Diana Holguin-Balogh
Front Range Community College

THOMSON
™
WADSWORTH

Australia Canada Mexico Singapore Spain United Kingdom United States

Contents

Introduction

Teaching writing to basic writers is often a challenge, not necessarily because learning to write is difficult for them, but rather because they have often experienced failure as writers. This failure has left students with the feeling that writing is easy for others but not for themselves. As the instructor, therefore, you can help your students understand that writing is a skill that can be learned. Your students will gain confidence along with their skills if you simplify the process by beginning with one simple concept and adding other skills one at a time. When you give students one task at a time rather than many all at once, you and your students will experience less frustration. For this reason, we have sequenced the writing process into concepts that your students can understand and practice one at a time.

The opening section, "Introduction to Writing," is an overview of the writing process and shows various means of prewriting to generate ideas for writing. The seven units in this text all follow the same arrangement. Each unit shows the student how to do one step of the writing process and gives exercises, including collaborative exercises, for practicing that skill. Each unit includes an article by a professional that can be a model as well as a means for generating ideas for writing assignments. Quotations for additional discussion accompany each article and are followed by a section of model paragraphs and/or essays that demonstrate the skill explained earlier in the same unit. The fourth part of each unit consists of a grammar component (marked with colored edges) that is related to the writing skill taught in the same unit or in previous units. Each unit includes at least two sets of suggested writing assignments that encourage revision but, at the same time, stress the particular concepts taught and illustrated in that unit. Each unit ends with a cumulative exercise, collaborative exercises, and Internet activities that reinforce the materials covered thus far.

The following icons will help you navigate more easily through the text.

 Collaborative Activities   Internet Activities

 Writing Assignments   Quotations

 Cumulative Unit Exercises

We believe that a major goal of an instructor is to help students build confidence by showing them in one-on-one writing conferences what they have done correctly and then what needs to be done next for them to gain greater control of the concept being practiced. The organization of *Writing Paragraphs and Essays* promotes this type of learning. Since the focus of the text is learning one skill at a time, you might consider having students rewrite their assignments until they are "acceptable," without assigning any letter grades. Classroom research has demonstrated that students have a greater chance of succeeding if they do not go on to the next writing assignment until they are ready. "Succeeding" means only that the student has learned those skills that have been practiced. Your students will revise a writing assignment one or more times until they have done it correctly. Therefore, by the time they go on to the next writing assignment, they understand what needs to be done and can apply what they have learned. For example, students rewrite the first writing assignment until they have a topic sentence and until all sentences in the paragraph support the topic sentence. Students must be able to accomplish this before moving on to the next writing concept. Students progressing slowly can easily work collaboratively with other students who have already finished that writing assignment, or they can work individually with you. One-on-one writing conferences, which can be very brief, help you monitor individual student progress.

Because some students will need longer than others to complete an assignment, you might consider self-pacing the classroom. After the first three or four writing assignments, some students are able to work ahead while others are not ready to do so. Self-pacing makes it easy for you to work one-on-one with each student. If you spend half of the class time in an in-class lab/workshop setting, with students either working on computers, writing out the assignments by hand, or bringing in typed drafts of their assignments for you to look at, you can give more individualized instruction. Since few students finish at exactly the same time, you will be free to help students during the process of writing by explaining quite rapidly what needs to be done to accomplish the goal of each assignment. The students can then immediately revise the paper because they understand the revision needed. On the other hand, if the paper is acceptable, students may go on to the next writing assignment, work with someone else, write in journals, or read ahead in the text about the next concept to be studied. Often, you may refer students to a particular section of the text for review or refer them to some of the Internet activities included in this text. Though this workshop approach is very demanding and requires keen concentration from both you and your students, you can feel certain that students understand what is required of them. You also never have to wonder if you are wasting your time writing comments that students might not read or understand.

Being self-paced does not mean that the class has no structure. On the contrary, a self-paced class must be highly structured and organized so the students know everything that must be completed throughout the course. Each student, however, may meet objectives at different times.

One of the most important concepts to get across to students is that effective writing means hard work and revision. However, students who work hard consistently and fairly rapidly should not have to wait for other students to catch up before they can continue with additional assignments. If your course is self-paced, you can allow your students to take their final examination (which should be a writing assignment) as soon as they have completed all assignments. Also, if your department/division policy allows some flexibility, you might consider allowing the students to take the final more than once to receive a grade of "C" or better. (A suggestion for giving finals is included on page 26 in this Instructor's Manual.)

We realize that self-pacing is not desirable for all instructors. Because *Writing Paragraphs and Essays* was written for different classroom formats, it can be used successfully in classes that are not designed around in-class writing workshops. You may assign reading and exercises as homework to be discussed during the next class, or you may assign exercises to be done independently as you wish. If you would like to include a testing component in your class, an A, B, C, and D version of ten tests is included (40): six grammar concepts, one for punctuation review, one for capitalization, and two for writing sections are included in a separate test bank. You might want to have these tests kept in a learning center or testing center so that students may take them whenever they are ready without taking up class time. If you wish to use small-group work, you will find many exercises in *Writing Paragraphs and Essays* that are designed for collaborative activities and others that are adaptable for small group work. (See section on collaborative learning that follows.)

Student Appeal

Many of the examples in the textbook, whether sentences, paragraphs, or essays, include content that will interest a variety of student populations, including various ethnic groups, returning students, and developing students. Also, subject matter includes many job-related topics as well as challenges students may have faced or are facing in their lives today. These include topics such as responsibilities of a pharmacy technician, job choices in childcare, gender and communication in the workplace, and alcohol rehabilitation. In other words, the textbook includes topics that center on real-life experiences so that students can relate to the subject matter.

Internet Activities

The fifth edition of *Writing Paragraphs and Essays* includes exercises that link the text's objectives to the Internet's vast information holdings. Our objective is to create opportunities for students to see how the Internet can provide them with an abundance of learning, researching, and writing opportunities. The Internet activities provided at the end of each unit begin with general information and activities to introduce students to the Internet and build to more specific text-related exercises. As with the design of the text, the Internet activities are introduced gradually to make students comfortable using the Internet to find appropriate writing material for the topics and activities in the text. These activities can be assigned as collaborative projects, individualized lab activities, or homework sessions.

Cumulative Unit Exercises

One of the most engaging features of the text is the step-by-step approach for helping students gain mastery of writing skills. Therefore, cumulative exercises are placed at the end of each unit so students can review the skills they have learned. We want students to see how one unit's application fits with subsequent information and applications to enhance the integration of writing, reading, and grammar skills. Writing is not just memorizing concepts; rather, it is the application that can grow exponentially. We hope these exercises challenge yet build confidence in students as they progress through the text. You might want to consider them as assessments of your students' growing ability. Starting on page 47 of this Instructor's Manual, transparencies are available for the uncorrected cumulative unit exercises.

Collaborative Learning

Current research supports the value of collaborative learning in the classroom; therefore, we have many collaborative activities throughout the text. Collaborative learning increases the students' opportunities to learn and practice skills in situations like those they may encounter in life outside the classroom. To be successful, though, you must plan carefully so that you keep the class organized and on task. You want every activity to be productive for both you and your students. As the class becomes actively involved in group work, it will move away from a teacher-centered classroom to a student-centered classroom where students think and learn through participation in small groups.

If you are experienced at using collaborative techniques, you already know the benefits as well as the responsibilities, but if you are new to this kind of teaching, a list of benefits might be helpful. Collaborative learning

> encourages students to become involved in the learning process and, thereby, take responsibility for their own learning,
>
> helps students utilize ideas and experiences from other students,
>
> creates a need for students to cooperate with each other to achieve success,
>
> prepares students for working as part of a team to solve problems in other classes and in the workplace beyond school,
>
> makes thinking and writing more exciting, and
>
> fosters respect for the ideas and cultures of other people.

The following suggestions are designed to help you plan collaborative activities for your classes:

Consider the number of students in each group, for example, two to five. Decide how the groups will be formed: at random in class by the "count-off method," at random by student choice, or arranged by you ahead of time. Advantages and disadvantages exist for all these methods, but after trying a few collaborative activities, you will arrive at the best arrangements for your class. Part of collaborative learning is modifying procedures based on the particular characteristics of each class.

Decide on the responsibility of each group member: to ask questions, to take notes, to contribute a definite number of ideas, to keep track of time, or to report to the class later for the group, etc. If you decide to have students work in larger groups, you might want to have the students select a group leader whose job is to keep the group on task.

Ahead of time, develop the written materials the students will need and/or the transparencies you want. You might want to model a collaborative exercise by having the class as a whole perform the activity while you assume the role of group leader.

Anticipate how long each activity should take based on the importance of the skills or concepts being learned and practiced. A 20-minute exercise allows ample time for other activities. Decide on the specific outcomes for the activity. For example, each group might develop topic sentences, define words, brainstorm topics, answer specific questions about someone else's essay, or read a model introduction in the text and then collaboratively write a paragraph with the same kind of hook.

At the same time, you must decide if the completed assignment will be written or oral, presented individually or as a group. Finally, decide if you will evaluate each student individually or if the group, as a whole, will receive the same grade. The collaborative activities reflect many of these suggestions.

Part of working collaboratively includes peer review, so we have detailed peer-review activities.

Proficiency Examinations

Writing Paragraphs and Essays provides practice in both "local" and "global" skills required for students to pass proficiency tests in usage, sentence skills, and paragraph and essay writing. It provides exercises that are suitable for individual, small-group, and whole-class practice. An instructor is free to choose whatever will give students the best pretest preparation.

Usage and grammar exercises are integrated into writing sections; however, exercises stressing individual skills can be assigned and discussed as needed. For example, *Writing Paragraphs and Essays* covers the following individual grammar and usage points: subject-verb agreement; consistent verb tense; fragments, run-ons, and comma splices; consistent point of view; a thorough review of punctuation and capitalization; and an ESL section for non-native students. The paragraph exercises (throughout the book) requiring editing for these "local" problems also provide extensive practice for students who need these skills to pass an essay proficiency test. In addition, Appendix A gives simple explanations and exercises in using commonly confused words, such as "their," "there," and "they're," and Appendix D gives spelling tips. Exercises at the sentence-level give practice in using parallel structure.

Writing Paragraphs and Essays provides practice in the skills students need to write and revise an essay for a proficiency test. Students consider purpose, audience, and voice in a writing situation. They generate ideas and examples suitable for the topic chosen. In addition, they organize and think through the relationships of ideas, then draft, revise, and edit both paragraphs and multiparagraph essays. Moreover, the unit on generating and writing topic sentences includes exercises designed to help students discriminate between general (main) and specific (supporting) ideas. Exercises in this unit also help students think through the logical arrangement of ideas within paragraphs. Because variety in sentence structure is one of the major criteria used to evaluate student essays, *Writing Paragraphs and Essays* also includes major sections on sentence combining to achieve sentence variety. Exercises stress more mature simple sentences (with little abstract grammar terminology), compound sentences, and complex sentences.

Furthermore, *Writing Paragraphs and Essays* includes an entire unit on alternate methods of development. If students are required to pass a proficiency test by writing an essay using one of these methods, this section will give them many examples and much practice in these more advanced skills. This unit would be an excellent review for students who already have adequate writing skills but need a simple review of methods of development. *Writing Paragraphs and Essays* covers the following: illustration, comparison-contrast, classification, definition, cause-effect analysis, process, and argument.

Another strength of *Writing Paragraphs and Essays* lies in its many student and professional models that require students to read, answer comprehension questions, and analyze the reading to understand how it incorporates the writing skills being discussed in each unit. The unique sections "Something to Think About, Something to Write About" also encourage students to write in response to thoughtful, well-written essays.

Unit Notes

Introduction to Writing

This section is designed to show students how the writing process works. The students are given strategies for prewriting, writing, and rewriting. Emphasis is placed on the thinking that is an integral part of the writing process. No writing assignments are suggested in this part so that students can simply concentrate on ways to generate ideas and can see how a simple version of the writing process works. The emphasis is on showing students that writing is systematic and can be learned. A collaborative exercise and Internet activities are presented to help students think about the writing process. This is an ideal place for you to model this activity with a simple piece of your own writing, like a memo, letter, or note to a colleague.

Unit 1 Writing Sentences and Paragraphs

Part 1 Writing Skills: Topic Sentences and Paragraphs

The first part of Unit 1 explains and gives examples of the elements in strong paragraphs. First, it shows how to tell a topic sentence from other kinds of sentences and how to develop a topic sentence and support sentences for a paragraph. We use a directed writing assignment first and then discuss the text material on the topic sentence. (We sometimes use the first journal writing assignment [Appendix B] for this first writing assignment.) For example, we have students get out a pencil or pen and a piece of paper. Then we ask them to recall the safest, most secure place they can remember from their childhood or where they went when they got into trouble. Before students begin to write, we answer all questions and explain that they should write only for content, ignoring errors or problems in spelling and punctuation. We then have them concentrate on their special place as we prompt them. We ask the students to begin describing that place on paper as soon as they can visualize it in their minds. We ask them to recall what they saw, what they heard, what they smelled, and who was there. We repeat these sensory-provoking questions as students are asked to look into their memories and then share this place on paper. We stop using these verbal prompts only when all students begin writing.

This exercise can easily be done before studying the topic sentence because most students will have a workable topic sentence. Many will begin by saying, "The safest place I remember as a child was my bedroom" or "my tree house in the backyard." Many of their memories will be of what made this place safe. The prompts we give them to get started help to keep them on the topic. However, if students have not stayed with the idea of a safe place, we help them to see that, during revision, they need to prove "in what way" this place was safe. This freewriting can become the first writing assignment and can provide an opportunity to use a workshop or collaborative approach. For this first writing assignment, we stress only main idea and support. When students are asked to concentrate on too many tasks at one time, they may become frustrated and give up.

How should you give feedback to your students about this first writing assignment? You may want to use a sample student paragraph from another class to show how someone else has done this assignment. One strategy is to show two versions of the same paragraph—one that needs more work and one that has been revised. Before showing the revised version, you might try to get students to make observations about the paragraph to see if they are understanding the concept of main idea and supporting information. Then show the revised draft so they can see the improvements. We never use a current student's paragraph as an example of poor writing.

If you feel comfortable having the class critique class members' papers as a group, you might then show a copy of a current student's paper. First, have the class find several good points about the paragraph. Then have students make suggestions on what could be done to strengthen the paragraph. Do not ever refer to these suggestions as bad points. Though students may be reluctant at first to have their paragraphs critiqued in front of the whole class, they will soon welcome having the other students help them rewrite their paragraph if a nonthreatening atmosphere is maintained. During this activity, we stress revising sentences rather than correcting spelling and punctuation. As students gain enough skills to know what they should be looking for in papers, we have them comment on papers as a class as well as in small groups. After working as a class, students can break into groups to critique each other's papers.

The next section discusses, gives examples of, and includes exercises for achieving unity, logical order, and coherence in paragraphs. Sometimes it is difficult to know when to help basic writers with problems in coherence. Because of the various levels of ability and experience, some students will probably have some sense for coherence and effective writing. Others need patient instruction in the most basic skill needed to connect sentences logically. If a student has many problems in writing, it may be best to concentrate first on basic sentence structure and paragraph unity and not try to teach coherence until later in the term. The best way we have found to help students with basic paragraph writing is to work individually with them on their own paragraphs. Coherence is covered in depth in Unit 6.

The first part of Unit 1 concludes with two collaborative projects: one to help students formulate topic sentences in a group and one to help them evaluate student paragraphs in the text.

Part 2 Something to Think About, Something to Write About

Dr. Coble's article, which discusses childhood memories from the viewpoint of a psychologist, can help students reinforce the value of the past as it provides ideas for writing. The article supports the idea that students' personal experiences are important and are worth writing about. It may also encourage students to share ideas and feelings. You may want to discuss the article in class as a model for writing because it does exemplify topic sentences and support in paragraphs. Writing assignments suggested directly or indirectly by Dr. Coble's discussion are listed at the end of the article.

Following Dr. Coble's article are

1. **quotations** about childhood and
2. **collaborative activities** that lead to a writing assignment.

This is a good time to introduce **journal writing**, which you may or may not want to require. Much current research indicates that this extra writing practice helps students improve. If you decide to require journal writing, some suggestions are in order to give students the opportunity to use journals without adding a burden for you. For example, if you require your students to write for one hour a week, a log can be very useful. We ask students to have a separate notebook for journals. Then they write JE1 (Journal Entry 1) at the top of the first page. In the left margin, they enter the time they start, then write for however long they wish, and then, in the right margin, enter the time when they stop. When they have written for a total of one hour (or however long you might require) they begin on JE2. If you wish to use a one-page log for students' journals, one is provided on page 28 of this Instructor's Manual. This log can be duplicated so that students can attach it to the inside of the front cover of their journals. All you have to do is check the time entered in the log and initial the end of the entry. You may sign the log and/or assign points for each journal entry completed.

We think that reading students' journals makes the students write to please their instructors rather than write what they really think and feel. When the instructor is the audience, students experience inhibitions that defeat the purpose of journal writing of this type. We do not read our students' journals and always let the class know this, so the students get practice and we are not overwhelmed by an undue amount of paperwork. We often use the analogy of learning to drive a car to explain this to our students:

If you want to learn to drive, you can either get instruction or just get in the car and drive. You will probably learn to drive either way; however, you will learn more easily and more rapidly if you receive both instruction and driving practice. We have provided you with a textbook that will help you learn the basics of driving. In return, we ask that you practice driving. The more you practice, the better you will become. Do not wait until the end of the course to practice driving or you will find the driving test difficult to pass. In the same manner, we ask that you practice writing before you try to pass a final essay in this course.

Part 3 Paragraphs for Discussion and Analysis

In this part of Unit 1, student and professional examples illustrate topic sentence and support. Each writing model has questions on both content and form that can be used for class discussion. Most writing models include a vocabulary study. You might want to remind students that these are revised versions of paragraphs. (Answers for this part begin on page 20 of this Instructor's Manual.)

Part 4 Grammar for Effective Writing: Basic Sentence Skills

This part of Unit 1 deals with basic sentence skills. We begin with a brief review of the parts of speech so that students have a reference for these terms. The most common problems include sentence-structure errors, errors in subject-verb agreement, and inconsistent verb tense. Because eliminating sentence-structure errors (fragments, run-on sentences, and comma splices) is so important, we preview them in this section but treat them in depth in the grammar section of Unit 3 when students are better able to understand these types of errors. If you feel these should be covered in depth at this point, you might want to include the grammar section in Unit 3 at this time.

Identifying subjects and verbs is explained simply. We have students identify prepositional phrases first because we find that they often mistake the object of a prepositional phrase for the subject of a sentence. If they can recognize prepositional phrases, they can determine subjects and verbs more easily. Also, when they can identify subjects and verbs, we have them check for subject-verb agreement and consistent verb tense. After students practice on the paragraphs in the text, they can check their own paragraphs and essays for these problems throughout the term. Though we point out other errors and help the students correct these errors, we keep the emphasis at this time on topic sentence, support sentences, and basic sentence skills.

Part 5 Putting It All Together

After teaching Part 4, you will find

1. **a cumulative unit exercise** that reviews the material covered in this unit,

2. **collaborative exercises** leading to a writing assignment,

3. **a final checklist**, and

4. **Internet activities** that reinforce what has been taught or enhance the writing assignments.

Unit 2 Being a Sensitive Writer

Part 1 Writing Skills: Interaction of Topic, Purpose, Audience, and Voice

This part of Unit 2 deals with the interaction of topic, purpose, audience, and voice. In this section, we have added several pages that explain how purpose determines the appropriate organization for each paragraph. We begin with illustration because all paragraphs depend on strong examples and details for development. Once students identify their purpose, they are able to develop a topic sentence.

Once you have covered this material, you might give students a general topic and have them brainstorm as a class to generate information that could be used to write a topic sentence. Then, together as a class or in groups, you might have them write topic sentences for each possible type of organization explained in this section. Have the students verify that each topic sentence has a topic and a direction.

Once students have possible topic sentences, they might then brainstorm in groups or individually to get support information for their next paragraph. Three examples follow (candy, wallets, jobs), but, of course, the topic sentences given are not necessarily the ones that your students will discover in the process. A worksheet that you can duplicate for student use is enclosed in the transparency section of this Instructor's Manual, page 30.

Candy

1. Most children enjoy eating candy. (illustration)
2. Homemade candy is different from store-bought candy. (compare/contrast)
3. Children should not be allowed to eat candy. (persuasion)
4. As a child, I enjoyed making candy with my sister. (narrative)
5. Eating candy can destroy people's teeth. (effects or result of an event)
6. My child went to the dentist because he had many cavities from eating candy. (cause)
7. Candy can be a reward. (definition)
8. Candy comes in different forms. (hard, soft, chewy) (classification)
9. Make caramel apples when you want to entertain children. (2nd person *you*) (process/give directions)
10. Making caramel apples is easy. (3rd person *it*) (process, procedure)

Wallets

1. Men carry important information in their wallets. (illustration)
2. Men's wallets are different from women's wallets. (compare/contrast)
3. Men should carry larger wallets. (persuasion)
4. Losing my wallet was a frightening experience. (narrative)
5. Having my wallet stolen ruined my day. (effects or results of an event)
6. I had to buy a new wallet because my old one was not adequate. (cause)
7. A wallet is more than just a useful object. (symbol of status, wealth) (definition)
8. Men's wallets are made of different types of material. (strong cloth, leather, plastics) (classification)
9. Be thorough when buying a wallet. (2nd person *you*) (process/give directions)
10. Showing a little boy how to buy a wallet is simple. (3rd person *it*) (process, procedure)

Jobs

1. Cleaning houses to fund my college education was a tough job. (illustration)
2. Working at a childcare facility is different from providing child care out of my home. (compare/contrast)
3. Students should not work while attending college. (persuasion)
4. My first day working as a nursing assistant was exciting. (narrative)
5. Getting an education in finance helped me open my own business. (effects or results of an event)
6. Computer growth eliminated my factory job. (cause)
7. A satisfying career is more than making a lot of money. (definition)
8. Employees at a pharmacy are all qualified workers. (pharmacists, interns, and technicians) (classification)
9. Dress appropriately when going for a job interview. (2nd person *you*) (process/give direction)
10. Preparing for an interview is important in doing well. (3rd person *it*) (process, procedure)

You probably want to help students understand that the purpose for writing is not achieved unless it has the appropriate voice to go with it. In this part, students learn to distinguish the elements in a writing situation. The exercises help students gain confidence in their ability to control these elements in their writing. You might consider having each student write a letter in response to an injustice that has been done. You might suggest that they write this letter not in anger, but rather to explain what has happened. We encourage students to write a letter to the editor of the local newspaper or to the president of a company with which they have experienced a problem. If a student's letter is published or if a student receives a response from a company, the student can share the response with the class and let the other students discuss it.

This instruction concludes with one collaborative project that has several options designed to help students practice writing using a particular voice and audience.

Part 2 Something to Think About, Something to Write About

In "Space to Sing," Dean Terasaki argues for the freedom of expression in a time where political correctness dominates. He believes that "Mother Earth," an art piece that became labeled as a racial stereotype, was indeed a labor of love, a tribute to a real person. Terasaki's voice is sincere, pensive, emotional, and at times angry as he talks about this incident that closed the college art show. Some effective language can be seen in several places. In paragraph 6, he says, "I can speak from personal experience that racist stereotypes are a fiction, a lie, a blasphemous, scurrilous oversimplification that deny the humanity and the individuality of those they purport to describe." In paragraph 9, he says, "The solution was not to remove it, denying an innocent voice the space to sing, and forcing the closure of the Student Art Show."

Following Professor Terasaki's letter are

1. **quotations** that deal with prejudice (Students might want to write a short journal entry on a time when they experienced prejudice and then discuss this in groups or as a class.) and
2. **collaborative activities** that encourage discussion as students prepare to do their next writing assignment.

Part 3 Paragraphs and Essays for Discussion and Analysis

This section includes student and professional examples that illustrate the interaction of topic, purpose, audience, and voice. Each writing sample has questions on both content and form that can be used for class discussion. Most writing models include a vocabulary study.

Part 4 Grammar for Effective Writing: Consistent Point of View

The grammar lesson in this unit shows students the importance of maintaining a consistent point of view. Here they learn how point of view affects voice. For example, first person is more personal; third person is more formal and detached. You might have students break into small groups and then collaboratively write paragraphs about purchasing books at the bookstore on the first day of class, using first person (the participant's point of view). The same paragraph can then be changed to third person (an observer's point of view) simply by changing the pronouns. In this way, students will learn to control point of view by learning to control pronouns.

You might want to mention that point of view can also be changed by changing the speaker. For example, if the paragraph were written from the bookstore manager's point of view, third person would probably still be used. The word choice and perspective, however, would be from a different slant.

You might also point out to students that mixing up the point of view unintentionally is a sure sign of lack of experience in writing and is very distracting to the reader. If the students are aware of point of view and have control over it, then when they intentionally want to shift the point of view, it is possible to do so effectively. The better control they have over their language, the more control they have over situations in which language is needed to solve problems.

Part 5 Putting It All Together

After teaching Part 4, you will find

1. **a cumulative unit exercise** that reviews the material covered in Unit 1 but emphasizes voice, audience, purpose, and point of view,
2. **collaborative exercises** leading to a writing assignment,
3. **a final checklist**, and
4. **Internet activities** linked to this instruction.

Unit 3 Organizing Ideas and Writing Them Clearly

Part 1 Writing Skills: The Thesis Sentence

Once again, students are asked to add only one new skill, the thesis sentence. This section of the text covers both a thesis that simply states the topic and direction and one that states topic, direction, and a preview of the main points of the paper. Frequently, students do better when they preview the main points of the paper in the thesis sentence. Another alternative would be to have the students write a thesis that contains only a topic and a direction and then have them include a topic outline with their paper. Because the previewed subpoints are easier for students to understand, we ask them to include these points now, though they will probably do that mentally when they become more experienced writers.

You might want to explain thesis sentences and then put a topic on the board for students to brainstorm as a class. Have them quickly name whatever comes to mind.

Then help the students group these ideas together to form a topic outline that could be used to generate the thesis sentence. After your students do this as a class, have them work in groups, creating thesis sentences that preview the main points of the paper. If you do not want them to preview the main points in the thesis sentence, you might want them to include a topic outline. Possible topics might be summer break, dating, good students, and/or eating. Have the students write on transparencies with felt-tipped pens and then put each group's work on the overhead. A positive critique can help students build confidence in writing thesis sentences. Then, during the next class period, have all students begin a writing assignment that requires a thesis sentence. If you wish, require students to have you approve their thesis sentences before they write the essay. For the remainder of the term, you can allow students to check their thesis sentences with you before continuing with any additional writing assignments.

Because this is the first multiparagraph essay, you will need to show students how each point in the thesis sentence or the topic outline will be used as a topic sentence in the essay.

When the students do their first multiparagraph essay, we ask them to put the thesis sentence by itself, separating it from the support paragraphs of the essay. We find that when our students are asked to limit a thesis to one sentence, then later when they add a hook, transition, and thesis to form the complete introductory paragraph, they are familiar with a concise thesis sentence.

This unit concludes with two collaborative projects, both designed to help students formulate thesis sentences.

Part 2 Something to Think About, Something to Write About

In the article "Drawing the Lines," Professor Liz Hufford humorously talks about the motives people have for getting tattoos. This article has a clear, identifiable thesis sentence and a lively discussion that clearly supports the thesis sentence.

In the article "Your College Years," Dr. Bob Hartman deals with changes that students experience while they are attending college and becoming independent from their parents. Dr. Hartman, a psychologist and minister, has focused on the youth who have gone away to college and are thus in transition from their parents' world to their own new world. Because there may be parents of teenagers in your class, class discussion might also include parents who have watched or are watching their children move away from home. Your class may also include international students who have encountered new values while living in America.

Students also gain value from this article by describing the voice and discussing its appropriateness for the topic. Point out how his article illustrates a clear thesis sentence with fully developed paragraphs that support that thesis sentence. Dr. Hartman does not preview the main points in the thesis sentence, but he does show "in what way" college students experience change.

Following these articles, you have

1. **quotations** that deal with relationships, bonding, and independence and

2. **collaborative activities** that encourage discussion as students prepare to do their next writing assignment.

Part 3 Essays for Discussion and Analysis

These student and professional examples illustrate thesis sentence and support. Each writing sample has questions on both content and form that can be used for class discussion. Most writing models include a vocabulary study.

Part 4 Grammar for Effective Writing: Eliminating Fragments, Run-On Sentences, and Comma Splices

Though sentence-structure errors were briefly introduced in the last part of Unit 1, this unit deals extensively with fragments, run-on sentences, and comma splices. Although this part contains some sentence-level revision exercises, the emphasis in the text is on editing paragraphs rather than isolated sentences. The text groups fragments into four of the most common types of errors students make. If your students' essays show a repetition of the same types of errors, point out the type of errors they are making and have them carefully work though the explanation in the text.

After covering this concept, you might want to place the greatest emphasis on correcting sentence-structure errors in your students' own assignments. This is a good time to include group editing of each other's papers. Since there is more than one way of correcting an error, the students might suggest different ways to their peers.

Part 5 Putting It All Together

After teaching Part 4, you will find

1. **a cumulative unit exercise** that reviews the material covered in Units 1 and 2 but emphasizes thesis sentence and sentence-structure errors,

2. **collaborative exercises** leading to a writing assignment,

3. **a final checklist**, and

4. **Internet activities** linked to this instruction.

Unit 4 Writing with More Depth and Variety

Part 1 Writing Skills: Writing with Examples

The first part of this unit shows development through specific examples. It includes instruction on both short, interrelated examples and extended examples. At this point, students should be able to write a thesis sentence and include support paragraphs. However, they often have a difficult time developing these paragraphs without being redundant. By adding examples, they are clarifying the points being made and are developing their paragraphs more fully.

When students are unable to write using specific examples, you might use the following dialogue. When a student says something like, "The managers at fast-food stores don't seem to care about their employees," you might respond by saying, "How do I know they don't care?" The student might reply, "They are always scheduling me to work when I can't." You then might respond by saying, "I don't understand. Please give me an example." The student might say, "Well, I have classes until 1:00 p.m. on Mondays, Wednesdays, and Fridays, and the managers always schedule me to come in at 12:00 p.m. Sometimes I have to work until 1:00 a.m. when I should have gone home at 8:00 p.m." This would be a more specific example to explain "in what way the managers don't care about their employees." Students can then get a better idea of how to use specific examples.

You might also have the students use specific words instead of general words. For example, when they say "song," have them name specific songs. When they say sports, have them name specific sports and even particular teams. Because some students can apply these ideas more quickly than others, one-on-one revision conferences allow you to work with students at their best pace. (See transparencies on pages 33–34 of this Instructor's Manual for a paragraph without/with specific examples.)

The first part of this unit concludes with one collaborative project designed to help students generate short, interrelated examples.

Part 2 Something to Think About, Something to Write About

In "Refuge for Animals in Distress," Professor Husemoller-Bailor shows how the volunteers and paid staff of a humane society work together to provide care for animals in distress. This essay includes many excellent examples that students should be able to identify. Each paragraph has a clear topic sentence supported by short, interrelated examples. You might want to have the students identify the topic sentences as well as the supporting examples and details.

Following this article are

1. **quotations** that deal with being humane to animals and

2. **collaborative activities** that encourage discussion as students prepare to do their next writing assignment.

Part 3 Paragraphs and Essays for Discussion and Analysis

Student and professional examples illustrate writing with examples. Each writing sample has questions on both content and form that can be used for class discussion. Most writing models include a vocabulary study.

Part 4 Grammar for Effective Writing: Sentence Variety—Forming and Punctuating Compound Sentences

This part of this unit shows various ways of combining simple sentences into compound sentences to achieve more maturity in writing. Though this material is important, you might cover it briefly and then stress having students incorporate compound sentences into their next writing assignment. When covering this material, you also might stress punctuating compound sentences correctly. Again, some students need more help than others in applying these concepts.

Part 5 Putting It All Together

After teaching Part 4, you will find

1. **a cumulative unit exercise** that reviews the material covered in the first three units but emphasizes short interrelated examples or extended examples and compound sentences,

2. **collaborative exercises** leading to a writing assignment,

3. **a final checklist**, and

4. **Internet activities** linked to this instruction.

Unit 5 Reaching an Audience by Creating Interest

Part 1 Writing Skills: Introductory and Concluding Paragraphs

The first part of this unit shows students a simple step-by-step approach to writing introductory paragraphs. It stresses having the students write a thesis first, then a hook, and then a transition from that hook to the thesis sentence, which is the last sentence in the introductory paragraph. The text explains and illustrates six types of hooks. (See transparencies on pages 35–39 of this Instructor's Manual.) You might explain these hooks and then write a thesis sentence on the board. Then have students suggest possible hooks that can be used. After working as a class, you could write a different thesis on the board and have students work collaboratively in groups to create possible introductory paragraphs. Students can work on transparency sheets that can then be put on the overhead. The class can easily see different hooks for the same thesis sentence. Exercises for creating and revising introductions in the text can be used for small-group activities.

After students practice writing introductory paragraphs, they are ready to study concluding paragraphs. The text explains strong conclusions and gives some options for developing conclusions more fully. After you go through these, have students practice writing conclusions based on the introductory paragraphs written previously. (A transparency can be found on page 40 of this Instructor's Manual.)

This section concludes with one collaborative project designed to help students understand as well as compose various types of hooks that can be used in writing introductory paragraphs.

Part 2 Something to Think About, Something to Write About

"Women in Science and Engineering," by Professor Shyrl Emhoff, gives examples of women who are not as well known in their field as their male colleagues even though they have made significant contributions to science and engineering in the past one hundred years. You might have students discuss what the purpose of this article is and how the author gets her point across. The purpose is stated in the thesis, and she gets her point across through detailed examples.

The hook used in the introduction to this article is a statistic and a specific example. The introduction prepares the reader for the kind of information the article includes. Though the thesis sentence does not preview the main points of the paper, it is clearly stated and is the last sentence in the introductory paragraph. This article is both informative and persuasive. In the conclusion, the author comes back to the idea that women's talents have not been recognized, and she uses a quotation that reinforces the main point.

Following this article are

1. **quotations** that deal with personal challenges and
2. **collaborative activities** that encourage discussion as students prepare to do their next writing assignment.

Part 3 Essays for Discussion and Analysis

Student and professional examples illustrate introductions and conclusions. Each writing sample has questions on both content and form that can be used for class discussion. Most writing models include a vocabulary study.

Part 4 Grammar for Effective Writing: Sentence Variety— Using Complex Sentences

This part of this unit expands students' sentence-combining skills. Often students write short, choppy sentences simply to avoid having fragments in their writing. However, once they can recognize what a complete sentence is, they can combine these sentences in different ways to achieve sentence variety. You might put two short sentences on the board and have students combine them in as many ways as possible using the list of subordinators. Punctuation of complex sentences is also stressed. The sentence combining becomes more difficult as the section progresses.

Part 5 Putting It All Together

After teaching Part 4, you will find

1. **a cumulative unit exercise** that reviews the material covered in the first four units but emphasizes introductory and concluding paragraphs and complex sentences,

2. **collaborative exercises** leading to a writing assignment,

3. **a final checklist,** and

4. **Internet activities** linked to this instruction.

This is a good time to review all types of sentence combining and/or revision covered in the text. (A transparency showing sentence combining using compound, complex, and more sophisticated simple sentences is available on page 41 of this Instructor's Manual.)

Unit 6 Making Ideas Flow Clearly

Part 1 Writing Skills: Coherence

At this point, students should be able to handle the concepts of key words, time signals, other transitional words, and pronouns to make ideas flow smoothly. Although you may have already directed the more motivated students to study this section, they could benefit from class discussion of the kinds of transition available to writers.

One strategy is to use sample paragraphs on transparencies. Show the kinds of transition one at a time by underlining the words or phrases on the screen. First, go through the paragraph and show how the **key word** from the topic sentence or a variation of the key word is repeated throughout the paragraph. Then, go through the paragraph and point out one at a time each of the other ways of connecting ideas smoothly. Then you might want to show a paragraph that lacks coherence and have the class add coherence as they work in small groups on transparency sheets.

The first part of this unit concludes with one collaborative project designed to help students evaluate paragraphs for coherence.

Part 2 Something to Think About, Something to Write About

In "Harley a Bad Word to Say," Patrick Haas writes about his motorcycle accident and the kindness he experienced from total strangers, family, and friends. His effective use of time sequence in writing this essay adds coherence. He uses effective transition not only within the paragraphs but between paragraphs. For example, in the third paragraph, he begins with "In the months that followed my accident." You also might want to point out his effective use of sentence variety throughout the article.

Following this article are

1. **quotations** that deal with kindness and gratitude and

2. **collaborative activities** that encourage discussion as students prepare to do their next writing assignment.

Part 3 Essays for Discussion and Analysis

Student and professional examples illustrate coherence. Each writing sample has questions on both content and form that can be used for class discussion. Most writing models include a vocabulary study.

Part 4 Mechanics for Effective Writing: Reviewing Punctuation

Throughout the text, punctuation has been integrated into the writing process. This part, then, simply serves as a review. It includes uses of the comma, quotation marks, and other punctuation needed by basic writers. (See transparency on page 42 of this Instructor's Manual.)

Part 5 Putting It All Together

After teaching Part 4, you will find

1. **a cumulative unit exercise** that reviews the material covered in the first five units but emphasizes coherence and punctuation,
2. **collaborative exercises** leading to a writing assignment,
3. **a final checklist**, and
4. **Internet activities** linked to this instruction.

Using the copy of "Memory Made Manageable" on pages 354–356 of the text, make a copy of the list of sentences, and cut each paragraph into strips, one sentence per strip. Put each set of sentences (paragraph) into a separate envelope to be used in class. (A correct version is available on pages 43–46 of this Instructor's Manual.)

Unit 7 Composing with Effective Alternate Patterns

Part 1 Writing Skills: Patterns of Development

This last unit on writing deals with using alternate patterns of development effectively. The purpose of this section is to show students that no matter what type of pattern is used to develop a topic, all writing has one thing in common—a thesis sentence that restricts and controls the paper. Seven alternate patterns are used and demonstrated. One topic, **homes**, is used to show seven different patterns of development. Illustration (writing with examples) is included first because it has been covered in Unit 4, "Writing with Examples."

An explanation of how to develop the essay, a model essay, and suggested writing assignments are included for each pattern of development. You might decide to use parts of this unit earlier in your course; you might use this part of this unit as a brief explanation of what students will learn in freshman-level composition; or you may choose not to teach it at all.

The first part of this unit concludes with one collaborative project designed to give students experience in identifying the blend of patterns of development used in one essay.

Part 2 Something to Think About, Something to Write About

In his graduation speech, "Did You Do Your Best?", Dr. Reed delivered a motivational speech to the graduating class. He developed his speech by using a blend of patterns. He depends very strongly on **illustration**, including numerous examples throughout the speech. He also uses **comparison/contrast** to show how life for a college graduate twenty-five years ago was both similar to and different from life for a college graduate today. Dr. Reed includes a **definition** in paragraph 10, the definition of motivation. Another pattern Dr. Reed uses is **argumentation** to show that the time in which a person lives doesn't matter, but the importance of doing one's best never changes.

Following this article are

1. **quotations** that deal with success and the future and
2. **collaborative activities** that encourage discussion as students prepare to do their next writing assignment.

Part 3 Paragraphs and Essays for Discussion and Analysis

Student and professional examples illustrate the various methods of development. Each writing sample has questions on both content and form that can be used for class discussion. Most writing models include a vocabulary study.

Part 4 Mechanics for Effective Writing: Capitalization

This part of Unit 7 gives an overview of capitalization rules with paragraph-level editing.

Part 5 Putting It All Together

After teaching Part 4, you will find

1. **a cumulative unit exercise** that reviews the material covered in the first six units but emphasizes methods of development,
2. **collaborative exercises** leading to a writing assignment,
3. **a final checklist**, and
4. **Internet activities** linked to this instruction.

Suggested Writing Assignments

For a sixteen-week semester, the authors suggest eight writing assignments—three paragraphs and five multiparagraph essays—each demanding more of the students. Writing assignments are located in two places in each unit: One group of writing assignments follows each "Something to Think About, Something to Write About" section, and another group of writing assignments follows each grammar component. The first set of writing assignments in each unit includes an article by a professional, quotations, and collaborative activities, including a peer review. The second set of writing assignments in each unit includes collaborative activities, Internet activities, and peer review.

Answers to Questions on Content/Questions on Form

Unit 1

"Summer at Aunt Clara and Uncle Frank's Farm" (page 52)
Content: 1. to help her aunt and uncle because they had no children of their own; 2. the big boar; 3. a camaraderie among family and friends
Form: 1. Things they did every day were progressive, concluding with what they did every evening; 2. all the details of events that occurred from morning to night, including chores and activities; 3. reemphasizes the nostalgic feelings of the memories of the past
"Playhouse under the Orange Tree" (page 53)
Content: 1. spaces between the branches; 2. preened their wings and made small bird noises; 3. father working on car, mother in kitchen, cars going by

Form: 1. first sentence; 2. goes back to the topic sentence
"Concentration Camp" (page 53)
Content: 1. over fifty years ago; 2. a graveyard by night; 3. cold, indifferent, negative/described echoing footsteps, muffled mumbles, and inexplicable, sharp smell
Form: 1. sight, sound, and smell; 2. clear direction: frightful and thoughtful experience; 3. "The major impact this place had on me was that even the most negative thought could not describe the coldness of this place."
"Fort Leonard Wood" (page 54)
Content: 1. foreboding; 2. exploding shells; 3. "the parched sand blowing in the wind"; 4. war and its devastating consequences

Form: 1. the use of vivid descriptions and surprising words; 2. specific details that stay with one idea; 3. a thought that leaves the readers with a penetrating message about war

"Munich" (page 55)

Content: 1. something always going on: "fests," castles, palace, brewery; 2. went shopping at the "Marktplatz"; 3. two or three miles

Form: 1. yes; 2. yes, because it has clear direction

"An Eyewitness Account of the San Francisco Earthquake" (page 55)

Content: 1. absolutely nothing; 2. streets torn apart; walls fallen; steel rails twisted; communication systems disrupted; and water mains burst; 3. 5:15 a.m. on a Wednesday

Form: 1. yes; 2. subject-verb reversal in first sentence; 3. Yes, it sums up vividly the destruction that occurred in thirty seconds.

"Martin Luther King" (page 56)

Content: 1. in the back; 2. gave up their seats to white people; 3. the South

Form: 1. yes; 2. first sentence; 3. specific details

"Making a World of Difference" (page 56)

Content: 1. Peace Corps; 2. spicy rice dish; 3. food

Form: 1. in the second sentence; 2. describes a "cultural hurdle" she had to get through; 3. yes

Unit 2

"The Nursing Home" (page 125)

Content: 1. He loves her and wants to go see her, but he feels uncomfortable when he is there; 2. Alzheimer's; 3. She can't carry on a conversation. She yells; she argues; she uses obscenities.

Form: 1. sad, regretful, loving, and caring; 2. to explain the need to visit her and explain how uncomfortable it is when he gets there; 3. probably himself or someone who knows and loves her

"Subways" (page 126)

Content: 1. New York City; 2. fear of being accosted and threatened by "weirdos" riding the subway; 3. The hair stood up all over her body. Lights went out in each car.

Form: 1. to illustrate the fearful thoughts she had while riding the subway; accomplishes her purpose well; paragraph devoted to hypothetical fears; 2. intense, foreboding; 3. similar feeling that many people have about this kind of experience: "sheer torture for me," "hair stood up all over my body," and "my heart pounded wildly"; 4. people who

have experienced fear in a place where they do not have control over what is happening

"Growing Up Latina" (page 126)

Content: 1. being rejected from a sorority because of her surname and for no other reason; 2. playing the guitar at family gatherings; 3. knowing she was different and giving herself permission to view the world differently

Form: 1. possibly middle-aged; this perspective was more enlightening because, while she was going through the experience, she wasn't able to see the value of her childhood; 2. sincere and open; 3. minorities who might not yet value their cultural environment—able to learn from Eva's experience and develop a new pride in their heritage; those in the majority society—able to gain a new respect and value for differences; 4. to help the author understand herself better; possibly to let go and understand some hidden anger of past years; to let others who had similar experiences gain a new appreciation or understanding of themselves and their backgrounds

"I Am Not a Disease" (page 128)

Content: 1. a disease (multiple sclerosis); 2. a "normal" life span; 3. one who "took to her bed" and one who lived a normal life

Form: 1. comparison/contrast; 2. as an example of the process of adjusting that she has also experienced; 3. Ex. 1—high-backed wheelchair, incontinence, small, quiet husband, retired civil servant, trip to the supermarket, and Ex. 2—illness diagnosed at eighteen, nursing student, married doctor, travels, embroiders, swims

"An American Soldier" (page 129)

Content: 1. thrived; 2. specialist; 3. spent two years training; 4. that he would "win a purple heart"

Form: 1. The military training "gave him the hope of being the man he wanted to be"; 2. 1st sentence; 3. uses two clear examples of decorations

"Etiquette, What to Say When You Can't Find the Words" (page 130)

Content: 1. "correct form of speech and behavior to be used in predictable situations"; 2. "when we are so moved"; 3. to be sure to follow through on our feelings

Form: 1. definition; 2. uses specific examples

"Being a Leader" (page 131)

Content: 1. bossy; 2. "because the high-status boys are expected to give orders and push the low-status boys around"; telling stories, jokes, and information; state their opinions to see if they are challenged

Form: 1. comparison/contrast; 2. She is a woman leader who was referred to as bossy.

"Dear Dad" (page 132)

Content: 1. trumpet; 2. whether his father felt the same about being on stage as he did

Form: 1. regretful and melancholy; 2. how it must have been for his father and how it is for him; 3. himself, his father, or other people who want to come to terms with their childhoods

"Getting Off the Roller Coaster" (page 132)

Content: 1. 20 years; 2. threatened suicide; 3. only black person; 4. stay away from family and friends

Form: 1. general public; 2. to help others and to come to terms with his alcoholism; 3. honest and sincere

Unit 3

"Respect" (page 177)

Content: 1. disrespectfully, angrily; 2. show violence, including murders, street gangs, and mercenaries killing for money; 3. Some families do not set the right examples.

Form: 1. the last sentence in the introductory paragraph; 2. The topic sentence in each paragraph uses one of the points previewed in the thesis sentence; 3. The 1st person point of view would have been limited to one viewpoint whereas the 3rd person point of view is more objective and more authoritative.

"Being a Student" (page 178)

Content: 1. cut down on personal spending for entertainment, clothing, and gifts to friends; 2. buying a house, dealing with husband, making a decision on starting a family, reading books for class, meeting due dates for computer program, doing math, taking tests; 3. tuition, expensive books

Form: 1. last sentence in the introductory paragraph; 2. specific details and examples; 3. her humor

"Golf" (page 179)

Content: 1. blind her so that she cannot see the ball; 2. hole 7: birdied it; hole 9: 10 strokes; 3. nine years old; 4. beginning player; 5. humorously and graphically describes how she felt after bringing so much positive attention to herself only to fail so dismally on the next hole

Form: 1. the conclusion; should reinforce thesis sentence; 2. yes, last sentence in introduction; provides a distinct direction for the essay

"Building a Better Home" (page 181)

Content: 1. the size of the nests; 2. estimated at several tons; 3. when eggs are laid

Form: 1. in the introductory paragraph: "Products of avian ingenuity and tireless labor, nests and nesting places come in bewildering variety of sizes, shapes and styles; each is a marvel of longtime evolution and adaptation of birds in response to the basic need to protect their eggs and young"; 2. yes; 3. yes

Unit 4

"Legacy" (page 235)

Content: 1. school lessons, new knowledge about computers, art, and the determination "never to give up on life"; 2. "great at drawing cars, landscapes, and portraits," interior design, sculpting nails; 3. She was going to have a normal life in spite of her illness.

Form: 1. short, interrelated examples; 2. realistic, honest, and admiring; 3. to honor her sister

"A Surprising Experience" (page 237)

Content: 1. three months; 2. born prematurely; 3. the vision of her wearing an oxygen mask and her body covered with wires and bandages

Form: 1. his first sight of her in the incubator, he and his wife crying, his need to explain the situation to others; 2. shows feeling of pain and concern; instead of anger, shows gratitude for his daughter

"What Have You Done to Help Someone?" (page 238)

Content: 1. diabetes; 2. helped her stay busy, eat well, and made her part of the family; 3. twice a day

Form: 1. took her to a senior center, encouraged her crafts, helped her with her cross-stitch, encouraged her to help another older person; 2. All are short, interrelated examples.

"Responsibility" (page 239)

Content: 1. a rude, screaming tyrant; 2. to be disciplined, to have pride in himself, and to be responsible; 3. knew his nephew had to be responsible to be able to compete in today's job market

Form: 1. first sentence in paragraph; 2. various answers possible; 3. paragraph 2: one short example; paragraph 3: extended example

"Wandering Through Winter" (page 240)

Content: 1. superstitions; 2. scientific basis or valid research; 3. in the Ozarks

Form: 1. the number of short, interrelated examples; 2. short, interrelated examples using animals

"Overheard on a Train Trip Through England" (page 241)

Content: 1. English and American; 2. a comment by an English woman that Americans are "funny"; 3. that in reality it is the English that seem peculiar

Form: 1. that they are uniquely idiosyncratic about the English, and that most Americans would find them amusing; 2. approximately seventeen short, interrelated examples; 3. In actuality, it's the English who are funny.

Unit 5

"Dancer" (page 286)

Content: 1. about five hours; 2. standing ovation by the dance troupe; 3. dance regularly in a professional dance troupe

Form: 1. the hook, a quotation that contrasts with the main idea in the thesis; 2. relates back to the hook and gives the essay a sense of unity

"Qualities I Appreciate about My Dad" (page 287)

Content: 1. his determination to stay with the family, ambition to succeed, natural music ability; 2. graduated from the community college; 3. 11 kids in one car, tie-downs holding the doors closed, the holes in the floor of the car

Form: 1. personal example; 2. "I never met this little boy . . ."; 3. goes back to his father's dream of a better world for his family

"A Good Manager" (page 289)

Content: 1. the Safeway at 19th Avenue and Northern; 2. is a good problem solver, is quick with new technology, knows how to solve any problem with the new scanner, creates good schedules; 3. because he relies on fairness and respect, makes his employees feel as if their jobs are important

Form: 1. questions; yes, because they effectively set up the thesis and the support paragraphs that ultimately answer the questions; 2. reinforces the thesis sentence but could be developed further; yes; 3. no, only example is paragraph 3 about his ability

"The Right Thing To Do" (page 290)

Content: 1. whom his son would live with after his divorce; 2. knowing he had to give up his future life with his son because he wasn't sure he could offer his son as much as his ex-wife could; 3. not being a part of his son's growing up and having his mother disown him

Form: 1. makes the reader empathetic because the voice is not angry, consequently drawing the reader into understanding and possibly relating

to the writer's predicament; 2. presents the final resolutions for the writer, acts as the writer's acceptance of his painful decision

"Living in Another Country" (page 291)

Content: 1. to be with his mother who had a tumor removed from her brain; 2. language, immigrant status, environment; 3. gained legal status, went to school, worked, became used to his new home

Form: 1. personal example; 2. "When I came here, I thought everything was going to be really easy, but living in another country could be very challenging"; 3. reinforces the thesis sentence and goes back to the hook about his mother

Unit 6

"Home: Just How Safe Is It?" (page 328)

Content: 1. keeps the family from recognizing the problem and perpetuates the problem from one family to another; 2. through denial and survival skills such as depersonalization; 3. programs and treatment centers, education

Form: 1. throughout essay, especially paragraph 2; 2. The phrase "sexual abuse" in the topic sentence links to the thesis sentence as well as the preceding paragraph. In paragraph 3, sentence 2 contains the word "emotionally," which links back to the topic sentence. The pronoun "they," used in several sentences, links back to the word "victims." The word "victims" in the concluding sentence links back to the topic sentence. 3. to call attention to the problem of denial by families who experience abusive behavior

"Education" (page 329)

Content: 1. had not achieved enough points to advance to the university; 2. paternal grandmother who lived in Phoenix and his parents' relocation to the United States; 3. almost one year

Form: 1. paragraph 2 (support paragraph 1): school, diploma; paragraph 3 (support paragraph 2): educational goal, draft; paragraph 4 (support paragraph 3): Phoenix, warm climate; 2. "Yet, finishing the educational goal was not the only reason for my coming here"; 3. to help give a chronology of his whole life in Germany and its contrasts with his life in America

"Never Again Homeless" (page 330)

Content: 1. 18 months; 2. in parks, behind buildings, in trees; 3. 17 years old

Form: 1. the comparison between the old woman and herself, detailed conditions leading to her homelessness; 2. reflects on her experiences and reiterates thesis idea in last sentence of essay; 3. by referring to food and hinting at the topic for the next paragraph

"I Don't Like What You're Wearing" (page 332)

Content: 1. the way he dresses; 2. had long hair and wore clothes from the "old-men's store"; 3. racial attitude

Form: 1. clothes; 2. Iverson sneakers, camouflage hat; 3. He brings out the point in the first paragraph and comes back to it in almost every paragraph: 1. "not entirely clear to me"; 3. "the struggle," "surprised to find myself," "it's odd," "struggles with my parents," and "now I recognize." 4. "is less bothered," and "but she was on the front lines of a struggle" 5. "Am I factually," "out of step with the times," "Am I overly sensitive," and "Am I fearful"; 6. "clearly is not," "I don't want to be," and "got some work to do myself" 7. "shouldn't send shivers," and "I was driven from the sport myself, . . . I quit instead." 8. "What does it mean? Why does it bother me?"

Unit 7

"Heroes—'Sung' and 'Unsung'" (page 394)

Content: 1. "their ability to react quickly, calmly, and unselfishly"; 2. floated below the surface of the water and almost drowned; 3. calmly helped other passengers off the plane by holding up obstructing cables and bringing elderly people up on their feet

Form: 1. illustration; 2. the last sentence in the introduction; 3. all extended examples

"The Baptism in Blood and the Beach Party" (page 395)

Content: 1. Vietnam and Persian Gulf; 2. Uncle George and his nephew, the author; 3. Vietnam was a political nightmare, and Persian Gulf was an "armed beach party." One was "impossible to win"; the other was "impossible to lose."

Form: 1. comparison /contrast; 2. alternating; 3. paragraph 3; 4. Uncle George—angry, bitter, profane; author—objective, calm; 5. through the diction and choice of details

"Which One Are You?" (page 398)

Content: 1. perfectionists; 2. "carefree spirits"; non-chalant people who study only when it is convenient, people who do not let school dominate their lives; 3. cheat

Form: 1. how students study for tests; made clear in the introduction; 2. author's observations of students; 3. ending statement shifts to second person and adds a familiar, warm tone

"Wealth" (page 399)

Content: 1. anyone who has a loving family around her/him; 2. "great quantity or store of money or property of value"; 3. memories of beautiful places, relationships with loyal friends, and, most important of all, a loving family

Form: 1. contrast the denotative meaning with the connotative meaning; 2. emphasizes that real wealth is more than money

"Winter" (page 399)

Content: 1. "a period of inactivity and decay"; 2. "time of new activities and growth"; 3. "going to the park on weekends, jogging, playing handball, and trying unsuccessfully to get a tee time"

Form: 1. short, interrelated examples; 2. first and last sentences

"A Run" (page 400)

Content: 1. "a planned motorcycle trip or destination that is meant to be attended by a group of riders"; 2. in any dictionary; 3. because a run specifically has to involve others and is planned

Form: 1. the opening quotation; 2. knowledgeable, informative, informal, humorous; 3. "as stated above"

"Parenting: Singular" (page 401)

Content: 1. drug and alcohol abuse, unwed mothers, and divorce; 2. "a mother and a father and 2.5 children"; 3. "excluded from neighborhood gatherings"; "reminded in storybooks and role playing"; "ashamed to tell their own stories"

Form: 1. helps establish the problem explained in the paper; 2. in the order of importance according to the author; 3. paragraph 2: extended example from a movie; paragraph 3: information from authorities in the field; paragraph 4: personal experience and a statistic; 4. yes, reinforces thesis, provides unity with a reference to causes

"Reducing Fear of a Hospital Stay for a Child" (page 403)

Content: 1. preparing a child for a hospital stay; 2. role-play activities that will happen in the hospital, allow for special toys and people to be present, and give the child informative and accurate details about the hospital stay and the operation; 3. assurance that a child is less anxious and well prepared for the procedure: 4. a favorite stuffed animal or blanket

Form: 1. order in which it would be easiest for the child to understand; 2. third person; 3. realistic details of how little people have done in the past to keep children from being afraid of a hospital stay

Steroids and Bodybuilders (page 405)

Content: 1. to strengthen the body and to improve athletic performance; 2. Lou Ferrigno; 3. acne, baldness, infertility, liver damage, heart disease, strokes, cancer

Form: 1. to outlaw anabolic steroids for athletes and to mandate drug testing; 2. in the introduction; 3.

Steroid use leads to such devastating physical and mental problems that its use should be illegal and testing should be mandated for all competitions.

"The Mutt Who Saved Mr. Lambert" (page 406)

Content: 1. Harvard Medical School; 2. paragraph 5; 3. She did not like the changes; 4. He thought kids, dogs, and cats would be there.

Form: 1. cause/effect (paragraphs 21 to 24), illustration (paragraphs 2, 4, 17, 18, 20, 21, 23), comparison/contrast (paragraphs 5 to 9), definition (paragraph 7); 2. paragraph 11; 3. paragraph 22

Suggested Schedule of Activities

Week 1 Orientation, Writing Sample
Introduction to Writing: Unit 1
Generating Ideas for Writing

Week 2 Topic Sentences, Paragraphs: Unit 1
Twenty-Point Test on Topic Sentences
Writing Workshop, Writing Assignment (WA) 1
Confusing Words: Appendix A
Keeping a Journal: Appendix B
Journal Entry (JE) 1 due

Week 3 Parts of Speech, Subjects, Verbs, and Prepositional Phrases
Subject-Verb Agreement and Consistent Verb Tense: Unit 1
Twenty-Point Test on Subject-Verb Agreement
Twenty-Point Test on Consistent Verb Tense
Writing Workshop, WA2
JE2 due

Week 4 Writing Workshop, Rewrites
Interaction of Topic, Purpose, Audience, and Voice: Unit 2
Reading Student and Professional Examples: Unit 2
JE3 due

Week 5 Consistent Point of View: Unit 2
Twenty-Point Test on Consistent Point of View
Writing Workshop, WA3
JE4 due

Week 6 Thesis Sentence: Unit 3
Twenty-Point Test on Thesis Sentence
Reading Student and Professional Examples: Unit 3
Writing Workshop, WA4
JE5 due

Week 7 Fragments, Run-on Sentences, Comma Splices: Unit 3
Twenty-Point Test on Fragments, Run-On Sentences, and Comma Splices
Writing Workshop, Rewrites
JE6 due

Week 8 Writing with Examples: Unit 4
Reading Student and Professional Examples: Unit 4
Writing Workshop, WA5
JE7 due

Week 9 Sentence Combining, Compound Sentences: Unit 4
Twenty-Point Test on Sentence Combining Using Compound Sentences
Writing Workshop, Rewrites
JE8 due

Week 10 Introductions and Conclusions: Unit 5
Writing Workshop, WA6
JE9 due

Week 11 Reading Student and Professional Examples: Unit 5
Sentence Combining, Complex Sentences: Unit 5
Twenty-Point Test on Sentence Combining Using Complex Sentences
Writing Workshop, Rewrites
JE10 due

Week 12 Coherence: Unit 6
Reading Student and Professional Examples: Unit 6
Writing Workshop, WA7
JE11 due

Week 13 Punctuation Review: Unit 6
Twenty-Point Test on Punctuation
Writing Workshop, Rewrites
Capitalization: Unit 7
JE12 due

Week 14 Writing Workshop, WA8
JE13 due

Week 15 Last day to turn in first draft of any
writing assignment
Practice finals
JE14 due

Week 16 Last day to complete any assignments
Practice finals

Suggested Final Exam Topics

We suggest that a multiparagraph essay similar to writing assignments seven and eight be used as a final exam. We allow our students two to three hours to complete a five-hundred-word essay. If your class is self-paced, students might go to a testing area or a monitored writing center to complete the final exam. As we noted earlier, students could take the final exam as many times as needed until they are ready to succeed in freshman-level writing.

Some suggested topics to be used as finals:

Advantages/disadvantages of living at home while going to school
Violent and/or graphic movies
Reasons humanity does/does not need to worry about the environment
Reasons people watch television
Reasons people spend so much money
Advantages/disadvantages of eating at a restaurant
Advantages/disadvantages of eating at home
Reasons people have parties or reasons people go to parties
Childproofing a house
Moving
Ways to help people after a disaster
Important qualities to teach children before they are grown
Qualities of a good salesperson
If I won the lottery
Ways of coping with frustration
Results of running
Reasons for telling the truth
Advantages/disadvantages of having siblings
Advantages/disadvantages of running for public office
Ways people can prepare for retirement
Ideal environment for a child
Advantages/disadvantages of living in a city/in the country
Advantages/disadvantages of being a foreign student in America
Qualities of a perfect mate
Reasons people participate in sports
Home activities that children enjoy
Favorite weekend activities
Types of adults who attend college
Ways to make life simpler
Reasons conflicts occur between parents and children
How have computers made some people's lives harder?
How has television changed people's lifestyles?
How have personal computers changed people's lives?

Transparencies

Sample Journal Entry

2:40

I was there – escape from the world. I could leave it all bhind – people. As I walked a small opening invited me through. My opening and no one else's. On the other side now not quickly another world opens up to me. I move quickly skipping listening for the creek that gave me directions. I step across, hopping from one stone to another, crossing as it were to another world. Once on the other side it opens up – there is beauty here and noone save the animals. On the ground are small hoof marks. A small rabbit looks at me – not moving – just looking as if to ask wher I have been. There are bushes – many many blackberry bushes – each filled with black ripe berries. I am disturbed by noone. There is no noise – just those of my friends. The sounds of water moving across erase all feelings of humans and it is good. Here noone can tell call to me. No one knows where I an. I reach out and touch the berries plucking them from the bush and my fingers turn a red blue and the juice runs over my fingers.

2:55

Journal Log

Date Submitted for Evaluation	Total Time Spent on Journal Entry	Number of Pages in Journal Entry	Entry #	Grade
			JE1	
			JE2	
			JE3	
			JE4	
			JE5	
			JE6	
			JE7	
			JE8	
			JE9	
			JE10	
			JE11	
			JE12	
			JE13	
			JE14	

Consistent Verb Tense (Unit 1)

(Exercise 11, page 83)

Identify the tense of the verb in the first sentence as either present or past, and then make the remaining sentences match that tense.

Paragraph 2   Tense _____

David's best friend is Stormy, his pet dog. Every night she goes to bed with him and stayed with him until he gets up the next morning. She sits outside the shower door until he finishes. She also eats breakfast with him and then sees him off at the front door. After school they played catch or raced through the yard. She always knows when things bothered him, and she gently showered him with "kisses." She becomes his audience when he practiced his piano or his companion as he builds his Lego structures. They even shared an afternoon snack of cheese and crackers. Best of all, they are always there for each other.

Paragraph 3   Tense _____

The above paragraph would require past tense if Stormy were no longer alive. Edit the above paragraph to reflect this change in time. The first sentence needs to be, "David's best friend was Stormy, his pet dog."

David's best friend was Stormy, his pet dog. Every night she goes to bed with him and stayed with him until he gets up the next morning. She sits outside the shower door until he finishes. She also eats breakfast with him and then sees him off at the front door. After school they played catch or raced through the yard. She always knows when things bothered him, and she gently showered him with "kisses." She becomes his audience when he practiced his piano or his companion as he builds his Lego structures. They even shared an afternoon snack of cheese and crackers. Best of all, they are always there for each other.

Developing Topic Sentences (Unit 2)

(Organization Based on Purpose)

Topic

1. _____

   _____ (illustration)

2. _____

   _____ (compare/contrast)

3. _____

   _____ (persuasion)

4. _____

   _____ (narrative)

5. _____

   _____ (effects or results of an event)

6. _____

   _____ (cause)

7. _____

   _____ (definition)

8. _____

   _____ (classification)

9. _____

   _____ (process/give directions)

10. _____

   _____ (3rd person *it*)(process, procedure)

Generating a Thesis Sentence (Unit 3)

(Exercise 6, pages 166–168)

Topic:

Brainstorm to find direction:

Direction:

Brainstorm with direction:

Groups (topic outline):

1.

2.

3.

4.

Thesis sentence with clear direction:

Thesis sentence with clear direction and previewed subtopics:

Paragraph without Examples (Unit 4)
(Non-text exercise)

A tiny town in northeast Wyoming has a variety of summer activities for people who live in the town and who live on the ranches in the surrounding county. Since the town is too small for a movie theater, other types of pastimes occur frequently during the summer. Some activities are get-togethers for food and entertainment. Other regular events stress historical and patriotic activities and local talents and skills. In addition to these events, the town still finds time for one-of-a-kind activities of local importance. The most prominent bulletin board in the town, the wall next to the front door of the local cafe, is usually full of announcements for coming events.

Paragraph with Examples (Unit 4)

A tiny town in northeast Wyoming has a variety of summer activities for people in the town and on the ranches in the surrounding county. Since the town is too small for a movie theater, other types of pastimes occur frequently during the summer. Some activities are get-togethers for food and entertainment. Two Fridays in June, in the basement of a town government building, the local cafe hosts a barbecue and square dance, with door prizes for both adults and children. Other regular events stress historical and patriotic activities and local talents and skills. Each July fourth, the entire county gathers for a picnic and fireworks, and a county rodeo is usually organized to begin the day after these celebrations. Later in the month, their annual Western Heritage Days celebration takes place to honor the pioneers who settled the area. Dances, food, arts and crafts, and "homemade" skits recreate their old West heritage. In addition to these events, the town still finds time for one-of-a-kind activities of local importance, such as a "traveling bake sale" to raise money to send a town boy to a regional wrestling tournament. The most prominent bulletin board in the town, the wall next to the front door of the local cafe, is usually full of announcements for coming events.

Writing Introductory Paragraphs (Unit 5) (page 259)

Types of hooks

Personal example	Rhetorical question
Quotation	Current event
Fact or statistics	Contrast to the thesis sentence

Personal example (page 259)

On February 19, 2000, life changed for an eighteen-year-old young man. He became very ill from a bacterial infection. His body could not fight the infection. Why? After a week of tests and examinations by several specialists, the diagnosis was made. He had leukemia, a cancer in the bone marrow. I am that young man. When a person finds out that he has cancer, just as I did, his whole world changes. <u>A cancer patient is affected physically, psychologically, and socially by the cancer.</u>

Quotation (page 262)

"I am stupid. I am never going back to school," Micah said when he was in the first grade. With his eyes downcast, he slowly walked to his bedroom, silently crying as he shredded his schoolwork into small pieces. Then both he and his mother cried. This was the first of many times when they would feel the frustration that school presented. Because he reversed his letters and numbers, both he and his papers were at the mercy of teachers who did not understand the situation. The experience of school can be overwhelming for children who have trouble learning. <u>Learning-disabled students in the public education system must deal with academic, social, and emotional problems.</u>

Quotation with personal example (page 262)

"I am stupid. I am never going back to school." These are the words spoken by my learning-disabled child when he was in the first grade. He cried as he slowly walked down the hall, shredding his schoolwork into small pieces. Then we both cried. This was the first of many times when I would feel frustrated because there was nothing I could do to help him. I often felt frustrated when I saw him make low scores on his papers and tests because he reversed his letters and numbers. It was not unusual for him to work a math problem correctly, only to reverse the numbers in the answer. This put him at the mercy of teachers who did not understand the situation. Many other children like him have difficulties that make the experience of school overwhelming. <u>Learning-disabled students in the public educational system must deal with academic, social, and emotional problems.</u>

Fact (page 263)

In the desert regions of Arizona, solar homes date back to the pre-Colombian Indians. These people carefully designed their homes in the recesses of south-facing cliffs to receive the warmth of the winter sun. In the summer, shade was provided by the overhanging cliffs. <u>Today,</u> as then, <u>the desert-region solar home must be carefully designed to use the sun efficiently in the orientation, the exterior, and the interior.</u>

Rhetorical question (page 265)

When people think ahead to the year 2050, many different questions come to mind. Does germ warfare have the potential to destroy the world? Does the medical profession have the knowledge and technology to make gene therapy a natural part of medical care? Will the cloning of humans be successfully accomplished in the next few years? Will terrorist attacks and other violent acts lead to more stringent security precautions in the future? Do people need to have renewed respect for the environment? If the answer to all these questions is yes, then it is only logical that <u>in the next fifty years people will experience major differences in medicine, transportation, lifestyles, and living environments.</u>

Current event (page 266)

An article in this morning's *Arizona Republic* reported the story about migrant workers who contract AIDS while working in the United States and then infect others when they return to Mexico. Jaime Lopez, a twenty-three-year-old migrant worker, spent time in California trying to save money for his future. When he found out he had AIDS, he returned home to the rural area near Guadalajara, Mexico, but never told anyone about his illness, including his girl-friend. After their marriage, he suffered symptoms of AIDS, but he did not seek medical attention because of the stigma this disease carries there. The disease weakened him, and he eventually died; however, it was not until after his death that his wife learned that the illness had been caused by AIDS. It was too late for her and her infant son who was born after her husband's death. Today, both she and the child are HIV positive, but now she keeps the same devastating secret. This unfortunate incident is far from being an isolated case in this rural area where people know little about AIDS. However, the one thing that they do know is that in this area, people who are infected with this disease quickly become outcasts from their neighbors, jobs, and schools.

Contrast to the thesis sentence (page 267)

Since the middle of the 1940s, the female *Cannabis sativa* plant, commonly known as marijuana, has been classified by the United States government as a Schedule 1 drug. This classification recognizes marijuana as a dangerous narcotic, similar in potency to heroin and possessing no redeeming medicinal qualities. <u>Research in the last few years, however, has brought many new discoveries in medicine relating to the possible uses of marijuana to treat many different illnesses, including glaucoma, cancer, asthma, and phantom limb pain suffered by paraplegics and amputees.</u>

Strong Conclusions (Unit 5)

The conclusion should not

repeat the thesis sentence exactly as it appeared in the introduction

repeat the thesis sentence and mechanically repeat the topic sentences

change the tone of the essay

introduce a new idea in the conclusion

The conclusion should

summarize main points made in the paper and creatively restate the ideas in the thesis sentence

end with an obvious closure that leaves the essay with a sense of completeness

Strong conclusions

refer to an example, fact, or statistic mentioned in the introduction

end with a question that leaves the reader thinking about what was said

comment about the future

Sentence Combining: Complex Sentences (Unit 5) (Non-text Examples)

Simple Sentences

The old man enjoyed his garden. He planted many new flowers.

Compound

The old man enjoyed his garden; he planted many new flowers.

The old man enjoyed his garden; as a result, he planted many new flowers.

The old man enjoyed his garden, so he planted many new flowers.

Complex

The old man enjoyed his garden where he planted many new flowers.

Because the old man enjoyed his garden, he planted many new flowers.

The old man enjoyed his garden because he planted many new flowers.

The old man who enjoyed his garden planted many new flowers.

The old man who planted many new flowers enjoyed his garden.

The old man enjoyed his garden that contained many new flowers.

Simple

Enjoying his garden, the old man planted many new flowers.

To enjoy his garden, the old man planted many new flowers.

Enjoying his garden caused the old man to plant many new flowers.

Planting many new flowers helped the old man enjoy his garden.

Punctuation (Unit 6) (page 350)

(Paragraph 3)

Poetry is an art form that can be enjoyed sometimes because of the meaning sometimes because of the way it is written and other times because of both. Can anyone read Walt Whitmans Leaves of Grass without saying That is nice really nice Lines that seem to stick in the mind are often written with a strong message. For instance the lines from Anne Sextons poem Abortion Somebody who should have been born/is gone stay in the mind long after the poem has been read. Whenever the question of abortion arises these lines are recalled in the mind again and again. Thomas Hood wanted to change labor laws in England. In his poem The Song of the Shirt he wrote With fingers weary and worn,/ With eyelids heavy and red,/ A woman sat in unwomanly rags,/ Plying her needle and thread—John Milton, married but miserable, spent much effort inserting lines about divorce into his poetry in an attempt to change the laws that forbade divorce. Some poets however do not moralize but simply present things the way they are James Dickey a well-known American poet wrote of adultery objectively without making any judgment of its wrongness or rightness. On the other hand Joyce Peseroff expresses her ideas in The Hardness Scale a poem in which she seems to be relating a womans feelings about a man who is not such a perfect man. Diane Wakoski writes of revenge in her poem You, Letting the Trees Stand as My Betrayer In this poem nature will pay back someone who loved her and then left her. The meaning is there in these and many other poems but the way they are written makes the lines recur over and over in the readers mind.

Collaborative Exercise (Unit 6) (pages 354–356)

Correct order:

Introduction—2, 7, 1, 4, 6, 5, 3
Support Paragraph #1—6, 1, 3, 4, 7, 11, 8, 5, 9, 2, 10
Support Paragraph #2—8, 3, 5, 1, 6, 7, 9, 10, 2, 4
Support Paragraph #3—3, 2, 4, 9, 5, 6, 7, 10, 1, 8, 11
Conclusion—1, 3, 2, 4

Memory Made Manageable

1   For many people, "89, 71, 30, 24, 18, 2, 14, 29, 65, 10" may not be a difficult string of numerals to repeat. In fact, they probably could learn and repeat two or three similar series of numbers if given enough time to work the numbers into their long-term memory. However, one special person, Shreshevskii, or "S" as psychologist Alexander Luria called him, has a remarkable memory and can repeat up to 70 digits or words that are read about three seconds apart with no other time allowances. Moreover, he can recall the number series backward as easily as forward and recall them even as long as fifteen years later, after having memorized hundreds of other lists. In contrast to "S," most people have to concentrate and put in substantial mental effort to recall unfamiliar information such as formulas, definitions, dates, and facts. With a few techniques, many people can train their minds to use imagery or mental pictures to retain information. Some of these memory tricks are mnemonics, acronyms, and hierarchies.

2   A mnemonic, which means "memory" in Greek, is simply forming mental pictures in a series. This method was developed by ancient Greek scholars and orators as aids to remember long speeches, stories, and dramas. Capitalizing on basic step-by-step mental pictures, they sequentially cued long passages in their minds, and they imagined themselves moving through a familiar series of locations, associating each place with a visual representation of the material. Thus, when calling up the information, the orator would revisit each location mentally and retrieve the stored image. A concrete method of applying this principle is the use of peg words. First, the person must mentally establish a linear foundation such as numbers attached to images. One is a bun; two is a shoe; three is a tree; four is a door. For example, a person has a grocery list of carrots, milk, butter, and peanut butter to recall. To do this, the person can imagine carrots stuck in a bun, milk filling a shoe, a tree dripping with butter, and a door held ajar by a container of peanut butter. This illustration is a simplified example, but the method can still be used with longer more abstract information. When the mnemonic becomes established in people's minds, long series become much easier to recall.

3   Equally effective for memorizing information is the use of acronyms or abbreviations. Many abbreviations exist in the English language. Originating from the military, "radar" stands for "radio detecting and ranging," and "snafu" translates quickly into "situation normal all fouled up." Another common acronym, "REM," denotes the

"rapid eye movement" stage of sleep. An additional way of using letters to form memory cues is creating words to help recall a list of words. For example, "Roy G. Biv" can help a person remember the colors of ultraviolet light, and "fan boys" is a great way to remember coordinating conjunctions. Another version of forming letter cues is by creating sentences to remember information. For example, if students have to remember the psychological stages of classical conditions—acquisition, generalization, distinction, extinction, and spontaneous recovery—they can create the sentence, "Apples going down elevator, stop." By thinking of this "apple elevator" image, the students remember the words for the psychological stages of classical conditions. People soon find that using acronyms can be intriguing as well as worthwhile.

4   Another extremely useful method for remembering information is the implementation of hierarchies. An outline, which is familiar to most people, is an organized hierarchy. Coordinate levels and sublevels for arranging information can greatly simplify the remembering process. Structuring information into general levels, to sub-general, to specific, to sub-specific and on and on sets a framework so that if one can recall the general item, the other information will come more easily. For example, a student may be studying a unit on drugs. Many types may be presented in the textbook, including depressants, alcohol, valium, stimulants, nicotine, cocaine, speed, hallucinogens, marijuana, LSD, and GHB. This list can be organized in such a way so that recall is easier. By finding general categories

such as depressants, stimulants, and hallucinogens, the other words can be placed under those categories, and the remembering of the general words brings up the specific drugs that go into each list. Alcohol and valium are both depressants; nicotine, cocaine, and speed are stimulants; and marijuana, LSD, and GHB are hallucinogens. A textbook might even have headings and sub-headings that can help students organize the drug information or any other information into hierarchies. Once information is streamlined into hierarchies, general cues can bring out the specific sub-lists and topics, enhancing memory.

5   Whatever methods for remembering information are applied, memory techniques are important. At first, students may not wish to take the time to use these devices to imprint the information into long-term memory; however, using a memory trick can be well worth the few minutes needed to develop a process. Mnemonics, acronyms, or hierarchies can become part of people's study technique, and in time these routines will become natural as they store information in such a way that recall will become easier and easier. A good memory is not always a given ability; a good memory is practiced and developed.

Cumulative Exercise (Unit 1) (page 85)

Alzheimer's Disease

(1) Alzheimer's disease, a form of dementia that usually strikes older people, slowly destroys their abilities. (2) At first, victims loses short-term memory and were unable to learn new information. (3) These frustrating signs progress to a more frightening stage where adults with this disease may forget who they are and may also lose their ability to recognize other people, even loved ones like husbands, wives, and children. (4) Before long, it was not unusual for these afflicted people to become confused and misplace items. (5) Also, they often neglects personal hygiene such as brushing their teeth, combing their hair, or even taking a bath. (6) Alzheimer's disease is a sad disease for the victims and their caretakers. (7) Skills they once took for granted, such as paying a bill or balancing a checkbook, are no longer possible. (8) In the last stages of Alzheimer's disease, victims often lose their ability to communicate with others as well as to control bodily functions, so full-time nursing care becomes inevitable. (9) These symptoms progress for many years, but the results are ultimately fatal.

Cumulative Exercise (Unit 2) (page 145)

Overcoming Challenges

Two American teenagers who live in different parts of the country are overcoming major challenges in their lives. Born with no arms below the elbows and no legs below the knees, both of these young men have strong supporting families who made every effort to help them become happy and confident. Having learned at an early age, you set goals for yourself and work hard every day to meet them. Each teenager plays positions on the defensive line for his high school football team and makes valuable contributions to the team. In fact, they both have game balls, given to them during the season for making tackles and recovering fumbles. These young men also make an impression off the playing field. They make above average grades in all their classes and looks forward to going to college. When they have to do the equivalent of a lot of walking, you see them use motorized wheelchairs and cruise around campus from class to class. They seldom need help and do not expect special favors. Perhaps most amazing of all, they always seems to be energetic and upbeat as they face the ventures ahead of them.

Cumulative Exercise (Unit 3) (pages 202–204)

Hummers

1   "Hummers," the world's smallest birds, are amazing creatures because of their movements, appearance, and tame nature.

2   The movements of these small wonders have intrigued people for years. Hummingbirds can hover in the air, fly backward, forward, to the left, to the right, and upside down as they moved through the air with agility and speed, outmaneuvering other birds. Hummingbirds love to bathe or frolic in the rain or in sprinklers where their darting flight can be observed. These jewels or rainbows of color hover in the water droplets, suddenly fly upward or to the side, and then move back into the water as they enjoy an afternoon shower. These unique birds have the ability to zoom through the air at top speed and then stop suddenly to land gracefully, these tiny marvels move about so fast that they are hard to follow, and because of their wing structure, they are able to make a quick getaway by flying upside down. Their bodies gets lift on both the upstroke and the downstroke, making their wings move in what appears to be a figure eight. This gives them the ability to hover and change directions fast. The aerial proficiency of these birds simply captivates you.

3   What delights so many individuals is the fascinating appearance of these astonishing birds. More than three hundred varieties exist, some plain, some with fancy tails, some with colorful crests, some with brilliantly colored throats, but all beautiful to watch. Some hummingbirds are as small as two inches and others as large as eight and a half inches long. Their long, slim bills are often longer than the bird's head

itself. Though their unique bills are generally black, they may also be yellow or red their plumage may include iridescent pinks, violets, blues, and greens. When viewed in the sunlight, the crown and gorget of some hummingbirds simply glow. Their tiny little feet made them look as if they may have no feet at all, but they do, and because their feet are so small, the birds either perch or stay airborne. They do not walk or hop about. Their tail feathers, spread in flight, completes a beautiful creature that fascinates people throughout the world.

4   Perhaps part of the hummingbirds' fascination comes from their tame behavior that makes them seem like pets to some people. They seem to become tame as they eat from feeders that are often just outside people's windows. When they see people moving around, they seem to recognize them and even enjoy being around them. When gardeners work in their yard. These small creatures may perch on a tree limb and "hum" to the people whom they seem to recognize. When feeders become empty, these tiny birds may scold the landlords until they replenish the supply of nectar. Also, it is not unusual for hummingbirds to light on the shoulder of the person who fills the feeders. Some "hummers" may also notice when you come into the backyard and set up sprinklers. These birds, who have wonderful memories, are waiting for a chance to play in the water, knowing that they will not be harmed. Once a hummingbird finds a home, though it may migrate during some seasons of the year, it remembers your friendly backyard and returns year after year. It is no wonder that human friends hang feeders so they can enjoy interacting with these birds who swoop in for a drink or perch on the feeder or a tree branch.

Cumulative Exercise (Unit 4) (pages 251–253)

Investment, Anyone?

1   Investing for one's future takes time, knowing what to judge, and knowledge.

2   Time can be a young investor's best friend. An illustration that clearly points out the concept of time and compound interest involves two people. Gen Frugal at age 22 puts $2,000 per year into an Individual Retirement Account (IRA), a government sponsored tax deferred plan that allows people to deduct and invest up to $2,000 from their taxable income. She invests a total of $16,000 for eight years then she stops. When she retires at age 65, she will have $642,750, assuming Gen reinvests her gains and the investment grew an average of 10 percent a year. Contrast Gen to John Lately. He waits until he is 30 to start investing. He puts $2,000 a year into an IRA until his retirement at age 65. John invests a total of $70,000 over 35 years and accumulates $542,050, assuming the same 10 percent annual growth. He invests $54,000 more than Gen. At age 65, he has made $100,700 less. Gen has used investment time more wisely.

3   Another factor in investing money is judgment. Experienced investors are usually concerned with deciding when to buy, when to sell, and when to hold investments, but this is not always an easy task. Less-experienced investors are probably more concerned with where to invest. Lots of choices exists. Savings in a bank are considered quite safe and generally yield about 3 percent. Money market funds, which are another type of low-risk savings, yields about 6 percent, A conservatively managed mutual fund, which is a type of relatively

safe investment, can yield from 10 percent to 15 percent. A high-risk mutual fund might yield 25 percent on invested money. Of course, anyone wants to get the most return for your invested money, determining how much risk you can handle is crucial in investment selections. Depending on judgments, investors may also lose all or a portion of their investment. Good decisions are extremely important when money is involved.

4   Finally, an investor must be knowledgeable. Reading and research are essential before investing any money. The library is an excellent place to start. Information on mutual funds, money market funds, stocks, and bonds is available in every library. Also, newsletters, such as *Morningstar Investor,* Louis Rukeyser's *Mutual Funds,* Richard F. Band's *Profitable Investing,* or Jack Adamo's *Inside Track,* can be purchased for approximately $100 a year. The business section of most newspapers provided great basic information. A financial expert may have a daily or weekly column in these newspapers to supplement the technical information that appears regularly. Weekly magazines such as *Newsweek, Time,* and *U.S. News and World Report.* Have business sections that deal with specific events as well as trends. Some exclusive magazines that deal only with money investment abound. *Money Magazine, Smart Money, Moneysworth, Your Money, Worth Magazine,* and *Money World* are just a few. Finally, today's investor, whether new or experienced, should have access to the Internet. It provides information similar to that in print. The Internet gives you more direct access to individual mutual fund companies and stock and bond brokers. Whatever someone chooses as sources, a wise investor is a wise reader and researcher.

Cumulative Exercise (Unit 5) (pages 305–308)

Homeward Bound

1   "Mom, Dad, I have a favor to ask. Do you think I could move back home for a little while?" Twenty years ago this question would never have been asked because kids grew up, graduated from high school, and then got married or went off to college, leaving a home empty of offspring. However, today young people are waiting until they are older to get married. They are also taking advantage of community colleges, allowing them to remain at home longer. Many kids move out and become independent, but they no sooner leave than they move back home with one or both parents. Why is this happening so often in our society? Why are more and more young adults returning home to live with their parents for a few months or even for several years? Living at home allows them an opportunity to get back on their feet, save for the future, and lessen their personal obligations.

2   In today's society, young people may find themselves in debt or unable to support themselves on their current income, and one way to deal with this situation is to move home with mom and dad until they can get back on their feet. Perhaps they are working at jobs that pay minimum wage, and they want to go back to college and earn a degree or receive specialized training so they can get a job that pays more money. These young adults find it very difficult to work, go to school, and pay for their independent living, so they move back home where they find inexpensive

rent or, in some cases, no rent at all while they are attending college. Stacy found that moving back home eliminated her rent, and the money she saved was put toward college tuition. Though she continued to work at her $6.10 an hour job, she was able to pay her bills and pay off her credit card, and two years later when she moved out, she was making over twice that as a computer technician. Sometimes adults may have just graduated from college and they are left with a debt such as a student loan. Having shrewd minds, they figure the best way to get this debt out of the way is to return to their childhood home while they recover financially. That is exactly what happened to Brian. *He graduated from college. He moved home for three years until he had paid off not only his college expenses but a three-month tour of Europe that followed his graduation.* Many parents are overjoyed to see their offspring shed themselves of debts and face life with a better future.

3   Many young adults today want to be financially secure, so they return to a nurturing environment before they move out permanently. The personal sacrifices of losing their complete freedom seem to be minute compared to the future rewards. Eric received his paramedic training and was hired as a firefighter/paramedic, but no sooner had this happy news reached his parents than he asked to move back home so he could save most of his paycheck. He paid his parents for room and board and helped out around the house, but before long he bought a condo. Did he move in? No, he rented the condo out for profit and stayed with his parents for several more months until he

could put a hefty down payment on a new home. *He helped out his parents by paying rent. By the time he became financially independent, he owned a big black truck, a condo, and a house, not to mention a big-screen television set and living room furniture.* It isn't just guys who save to purchase the extras they want. Robin moved back in with her parents so that she could save money for the extras she wanted for her wedding. Her parents helped with the expenses for the wedding, but because she was not paying rent, Robin was able to pay for most of the expenses, and she even used her own money to rent an exclusive resort facility for the reception. *She left home. Neither she nor her parents were left with any debts.* These two young people represent the future-mindedness of today's society.

4   Even though some young adults are doing quite well financially, they move back home to ease their personal obligations. Marti had been living on her own for seven years, and she had a high-paying job, but she spent so much time traveling that she found it simpler just to rent the basement from her parents. When she was gone, her parents took care of her dog and watered her plants. This was a perfect arrangement. She still had her freedom, and her parents willingly took on part of their daughter's personal responsibilities. In some cases, complex obligations play a significant role in an adult child's decision to return home. *Todd had been married for nine years. He became the divorced parent of two children, ages five and seven.* He shared custody of his children with his ex-wife, but he found he could have more time with his children if he moved back

in with his parents. Of course, his parents welcomed him and their grandchildren with open arms, at least for a while, and Todd had the perfect baby-sitters who loved his children and were home for them when they got home from school. Sometimes the conveniences are even simpler than this. Adrian moved back with her parents for two months, but when she found how much she enjoyed doing things with her parents, including four-wheeling, and not having to worry about clean clothes or a messy house, she settled in for four years before venturing out on her own again. *None of these young people were suffering hardships. They teamed up with their parents to make life better.*

5   Becoming established in today's society is extremely complex, but families are reaching out to help one another, trying to make life easier. At a time when fast-paced living is the norm, shared households have become more than permissible; they have become acceptable and even desirable. When adult children move back home, they are simply finding workable solutions to existing problems or are seeking a better life for themselves and sometimes for their families. Maybe some day the parents will feel just as comfortable saying to their adult children, "Do you think I could move in for a little while?"

Cumulative Exercise (Unit 6) (pages 351–354)

A Better Tomorrow

1   He is called Doctor Death. In Michigan, he has been tried twice for murder but acquitted both times. He has even become the subject of jokes on late night TV shows. He is Dr. Jack Kevorkian, a physician who helps terminally ill patients take their own lives. He objects to the kind of life some terminally ill patients describe, a lingering, painful life without meaning, without dignity. He has stated that quality of life and the "right to die with dignity" are important for all people. When terminal illness forces patients into circumstances that make not only living but dying with dignity impossible, more and more of these patients, in recent years, have asked for Dr. Kevorkian to arrange assisted suicides. Estimates exist that he has responded to at least a hundred of these requests. Why have these requests occurred? The reality is that a steadily deteriorating quality of life brought inevitably by a terminal illness creates heartbreaking conditions for the patient, the family, and the health care professionals involved with the patient.

2   Some people think death is far in the future and of little concern, but the terminally ill patients consider dying to be a release from hopelessness, pain, and despair. Their lives have no comfort, no joy because daily living has no dignity. In many cases, these patients have lived through many years of gradually diminishing abilities, the patients may face complete paralysis. Once in a while, the person

is fully conscious but cannot swallow food comes through intravenous feeding tubes. In severe instances, a patient may have only head movement and cannot walk or provide self care in any way. In other cases, the patient is in constant pain and may be taking increasingly larger doses of pain killers. After life has turned into darkness. The calls have gone to Dr. Jack Kevorkian.

3   Terminal illness also directly affects the life of family members. Having to see a loved one in pain and despair brings anguish to mothers, fathers, brothers, sisters, and children. _____, you have been in daily contact with the patient, and, _____, you often realize that living has become an intolerable experience. Though they have done all they can to help their family member handle the situation, they are hurt and ultimately in despair as you watch your loved one's life slowly deteriorate. As they accept the reality of the decision, family members may participate in a discussion with Dr. Kevorkian concerning the patient's request for assisted suicide. For example, _____ of Sherry Miller and Marjorie Wantz, Dr. Kevorkian recorded these discussions. (They are on the Internet for anyone to read.) They indicate that the patients and their families did not decide easily or quickly. _____ that everyone understood why Sherry Miller, suffering from multiple sclerosis (MS), wanted Dr. Kevorkian's help. Her brother stated he could not help his sister take her own life but would not interfere in the process. He felt her despair, and he respected her decision. Her father said he would even carry his daughter to the

place chosen by Dr. Kevorkian for the event. _____, Marjorie Wantz and her husband also talked honestly about her situation. _____, she, _____, had no future free of pain or suffering. _____ families confronted their own emotions about their loved one's quality of life and played a role, even if indirectly, in the decision to call Dr. Kevorkian for help.

4   Time after time, health care professionals clearly are aware of the pain and despair patients with terminal, debilitating diseases face. Because they have taken oaths to save lives, to restore the quality of life, they have to balance in their own minds and hearts the integrity of their profession and the patients need for peace. How you handle these emotional situations varies. After many experiences, some simply can block emotion and arrange medication and feeding tubes to prolong life until the patient dies "normally." On May 7 1998 a 91-year-old woman, having suffered a paralyzing stroke, was lying in a nursing home, receiving morphine and other medication to make her final days comfortable, but she was not hooked to feeding tubes or life support. Her doctor and nurses knew she could not live long. Her twin sister spent literally every possible waking hour by her sister's bedside. They were so close that they were described as having separate bodies but one heart. An attending nurse who observed the death said, "This is the way it is supposed to be." She went on to say that there is no reason to hasten the final event. When all hope is gone other professionals undoubtedly have eased the final days of dying patients by convincing

family members not to order intravenous feeding or other life-support systems. However actively helping a person take his or her own life is another situation entirely. Some health care professionals believe you can manage terminal patients in such sophisticated ways now that excruciating pain and suffering no longer have to be a part of the picture. They provide a high level of comfort to quiet the frustration anxieties, and fears of patients themselves and their families. They are convinced that no one like Dr Kevorkian ever has to be involved. When a terminal illness or a debilitating disease progresses, everyone around the patient suffers. Not everybody is fortunate enough to die a simple death, free of suffering and pain. When the suffering is worse than living, when people have exhausted their own strength and that of your families, the natural release from despair is a quick dignified death. Even though families would continue to love and care for the terminally ill, the patients themselves realize there is nothing better in the future for themselves and your families. They no longer want to exist in this way, so they ask for Dr. Jack Kevorkian.

Cumulative Exercise (Unit 7) (pages 415–416)

Children with Confidence

1   When Becky was a little girl, her cat was lying next to the door with its tail under the opening. Becky could not see the cat, and she pulled its tail, making it cry loudly. Instead of stopping her and pointing out that the cat indeed was on the other side of the door hurting, her parents thought it was cute and laughed, but the situation was not funny because the parents lost a great opportunity to teach the child compassion. Many times, the way parents react in these situations determines the type of people their children become. If parents want to raise children who are well adjusted in life, they make time for their children, teach them kindness, and let them find their own way in life.

2   When parents take time for their children, the end result is that the children grow up knowing their parents love them and are proud of them. As infants, babies know that when they cry, their parents will pick them up and comfort them, giving them a sense of security. As these tiny ones grow, they may test their parents and do anything for attention, but if parents just stop what they are doing for five or ten minutes and talk to their children, the unruly children become happy, content kids who return to playing with their toys, satisfied that their parents care about them. Even though parents are often busy trying hard to provide a secure life for their children, scheduling time for each individual child can work miracles. When

Bo was a little boy, he and his mom had plans to go to a movie at 3:00 P.M. As he listened to his mom on the phone, he heard her say, "I can't do that because I already have a three o'clock appointment." As soon as she got off the phone, disappointment showed in his face, and he said, "I thought we were going to the movies." When he heard his mom say, "You are my appointment. You are important, too," the disappointment in his eyes changed to self-worth and importance. At this age, little kids are excited to go on outings or just spend time with their parents; however, as they get older, they still need their parents to listen to their problems or make suggestions about their choices. When parents take advantage of these few early years, they, along with their children, become winners.

3   When parents teach their children to be thoughtful of others, they are nurturing them into becoming outstanding adults. If parents see their children do something that hurts someone else's feelings, they can teach them to say, "I'm sorry." From the time children are small, when someone gives them a gift, parents can teach them to show their appreciation, either with a thank-you note or a phone call. If a friend, a neighbor, or a grandparent needs help, youngsters can learn from their parents the satisfaction of helping without expecting financial rewards. As the kids grow older, they might spend time volunteering in a nursing home or a hospital where they can practice compassion for others. As these children become adults and their grandparents are in the hospital, they will realize the importance of visiting them and making them feel better

even though they might dread seeing their grandparents so helpless. Thoughtfulness is not something that suddenly appears one day; rather, it is a character trait that starts in the early years and continues throughout a child's lifetime.

4   Perhaps most difficult of all, parents who want to watch their children grow into self-sufficient adults let their children make their own decisions and gradually become independent. How parents define self-sufficiency is important. Helping sons and daughters learn to make their own choices does not mean letting children do whatever they want whenever they want. Rather, it means helping them understand the consequences of their actions so they can make intelligent decisions throughout their lifetime. A young child does not have the option of deciding whether or not to wear a seat belt, but that same child might decide if he or she wants to join a Little League ball team or take painting lessons. Sometimes it is difficult for parents to watch their children struggle as they learn to tie their shoes or later budget their money, but letting them try and try again until they are successful helps the children learn that they can "do it themselves." An opposite, perhaps detrimental approach to creating self-sufficiency is using a command: "This is what you are going to do." Wise parents, however, point out the possible outcomes, but they also respect their children's right to make their own decisions. Though parents may want to see their children go to college and become architects, attorneys, or doctors, being supportive of their children's decisions to pursue

their own career choices, such as writing, music, or carpentry, lets their children know that it is all right to pursue their life's dreams. When the time comes for marriage, parents may feel that their child is marrying the wrong person, but they accept the situation and the new family member. A bit later, if that child comes home and says, "I am getting a divorce," the insightful parent will spend time with that adult child and help him/her work through the divorce. Though it is not always easy for parents to understand this concept and support their children in their decisions rather than make the decisions for them, parents who create independent decision making will never be sorry, for they will have confident children who are not afraid to reach for their dreams.

5   Helping a child grow into an understanding, confident, and independent adult is not an easy job. However, if extra time, patience, and effort are invested in nurturing this special person, the emotional satisfaction is like no other in life. No parent is perfect, and no parent makes the right decision all the time, but parents must model what they teach and be willing to admit mistakes and learn patience. A couple of positive words, a few extra minutes, or some insightful advice can make a tremendous difference in a child's future life. Just because Becky's parents missed one opportunity does not mean that they missed others, but parents who take every opportunity to help their children grow into thoughtful adults will never be sorry.